BRIDGING THE GAP
College Reading

Eighth Edition

Brenda D. Smith

Emerita, Georgia State University

PEARSON
Longman

New York   San Francisco   Boston
London   Toronto   Sydney   Tokyo   Singapore   Madrid
Mexico City   Munich   Paris   Cape Town   Hong Kong   Montreal

To

My Mother and Father

Senior Acquisitions Editor:	Melanie Craig
Development Editor:	Susan Moss
Senior Supplements Editor:	Donna Campion
Media Supplements Editor:	Jenna Egan
Marketing Manager:	Tom DeMarco
Production Manager:	Eric Jorgensen
Project Coordination, Text Design, and Electronic Page Makeup:	Pre-Press Co., Inc.
Cover Designer/Manager:	Wendy Ann Fredericks
Cover Illustration/Photo:	Craig C. Sheumaker/ Panoramic Images, Inc.
Photo Researcher:	Shaie Dively, Photosearch, Inc.
Manufacturing Manager:	Mary Fischer
Printer and Binder:	RR Donnelley & Sons Company
Cover Printer:	The Lehigh Press, Inc.

For permission to use copyrighted material, grateful acknowledgment is made to the copyright holders on p. 593, which is hereby made part of this copyright page.

Library of Congress Cataloging-in-Publication Data
Smith, Brenda D., [date]
   Bridging the gap : college reading / Brenda D. Smith.—8th ed.
     p. cm.
   Includes bibliographical references and index.
   ISBN 0-321-27351-6
   1. Reading (Higher education) 2. Study skills. I. Title.
LB2395.3.S64 2004
428.4'071'1—dc22   2004057331

Visit us at www.ablongman.com/smith

ISBN 0-321-41675-9 (student edition)
ISBN 0-321-41676-7 (instructor's annotated edition)

2345678910—DOC—080706

Brief Contents

Detailed Contents

2   Vocabulary   53

5 Patterns of Organization   217

6 Organizing Textbook Information   279

8 Point of View   399

10 Graphic Illustrations   489

11 Rate Flexibility   525

12   Test Taking   555

Preface

Even before I wrote the first word of the first edition of *Bridging the Gap*, the title was somehow in my mind. In many ways, the title describes my reasons for writing the book. I initially wanted students to have a textbook that would fill in the gaps between successful high school reading and what is needed for the more independent and challenging task of college reading and learning.

Little did I know that the title would become even more relevant as reading theory has evolved. Not only are we bridging the demands of the two institutional settings, but we are also bridging concept development by creating schemata for college content courses with academic readings. We are forming strong learning links by bridging new knowledge with prior knowledge. In accordance with evolving reading theory, this new eighth edition emphasizes the importance of three deliberate, but not totally new, bridges that are necessary for successful reading and learning: (1) connecting the text and your own personal experiences, (2) connecting the new text and other written material, and (3) connecting with bigger issues, events and societal concerns. Needless to say, I still like the title and remain committed to helping students actively learn and consequently succeed in the academic courses required for graduation.

New to the Eighth Edition

To take a broader and more inclusive view of abilities, Chapter 1 includes practical information on Howard Gardner's theory of *multiple intelligences*. Students can discover their innate strengths by looking at eight different ways to be smart and respond to an associated self-inventory on the text's Web site. In the vocabulary chapter (Chapter 2), coverage of **mnemonics, synonyms, antonyms,** and **homonyms** has been made more explicit; and **additional practice passages—including a short essay—**have been included in connection with the context clues discussion. The chapter on strategic reading and study (Chapter 3) delineates the value of making **text-to-self, text-to-text,** and **text-to-world connections**; and throughout the text, enriched **Establish a Purpose for Reading** preview activities before the longer reading selections encourage students to do just that while activating schemata.

The separate chapters on main idea (Chapter 4) and patterns of organization (Chapter 5) have been amplified with additional practice opportunities in finding **stated and unstated main idea in longer passages** and identifying **mixed patterns in longer passages,** respectively. In addition, Chapter 4 now contains Evan Hunter's **powerful short story,** "On the Sidewalk, Bleeding" linked to a new **Concept Prep in Literature.** A **new inventory on reading fitness** is included in the chapter on organizing textbook information

(Chapter 6), along with a **life stress inventory** to promote connections with the "Nutrition and Stress" selection.

Instructors and students will find **increased attention to thinking while reading** in the eighth edition. **Comments and inferential questions modeling the comprehension strategies of good readers** are strategically placed in the margins alongside the longer reading selections. To promote deeper understanding of an author's implied meaning, the inference chapter (Chapter 7) has been strengthened by new instruction on **euphemisms, hyperbole, appropriate and inappropriate inferences,** and **implied meaning in humor.** Chapter 7 also has **new instruction on figurative language and implied meaning in poetry** and two entertaining new **short stories.** Emphasis on **reading between the lines** continues in the point of view chapter (Chapter 8), which includes two new editorial cartoons and a compelling new **essay exploring points of view,** "Leaving Islam and Living Islam," by a self-described political prisoner and victim of Islamic forces.

The critical thinking chapter (Chapter 9) includes a new **essay on cell phone usage and its possible link to brain damage;** and **seven new color figures from a variety of current texts**—including a table, a map, a chart, a bar graph, a cumulative bar graph, a line graph, and a flow chart—have been added to serve as the basis of new exercises in the graphic illustrations chapter (Chapter 10). The rate flexibility chapter (Chapter 11) includes one new timed reading; and the test-taking chapter (Chapter 12) **is left until the end for flexibility but meant to be used much sooner.** Skip to it prior to your first big reading comprehension test.

Approximately one-third of the shorter practice passages in the text are new, along with eleven new longer reading selections. Many of these readings, such "International Terrorism" and "Slave Redemption in Sudan," address serious international concerns and will challenge students to think critically about global issues.

The intent of this edition, as with previous editions, is to personally involve readers, to build and enrich the knowledge networks for academic reading, to stimulate engaging class discussion, and to foster independent learning and thinking. I hope students enjoy learning from this colorful new edition.

Content and Organization

The eighth edition continues the tradition of previous editions by using actual college textbook material for teaching and practice. Designed for an upper-level course in college reading, each chapter introduces a new skill, provides short practice exercises to teach the skill, and then offers practice through longer textbook selections.

Presentation of skills in the text moves from the general to the specific. Initial chapters discuss active learning (Chapter 1), vocabulary (Chapter 2), study strategies (Chapter 3), main idea (Chapter 4), and patterns of organization (Chapter 5), while later chapters teach inference (Chapter 7), point of view (Chapter 8), critical thinking (Chapter 9), graphic illustrations (Chapter 10), rate flexibility (Chapter 11), and test-taking skills (Chapter 12). The reading and study skills discussions in the first portion of the book stress the need to construct the main idea of a passage and to select significant supporting details. Exercises encourage "engaged thinking" before reading, while reading, and after reading. Four different methods of organizing textbook information for later study are explained.

Special Features of the Eighth Edition

■ In **Concept Prep**, a popular feature carried over from the seventh edition, key concepts in a variety of academic disciplines are matched with the subjects in many of the longer reading selections. These selected concepts, reflecting common knowledge that lies at the core of each academic area, are also an important part of the shared cultural heritage of educated thinkers.

The purpose of this innovative feature is to develop schema and prior knowledge for students' later academic success. For example, the first Concept Prep for Psychology discusses people and ideas at the heart of every introductory psychology course, including Sigmund Freud's and Carl Jung's theories, Ivan Pavlov's discovery of and experiments with classical conditioning, and B. F. Skinner's behaviorism.

■ **Establish a Purpose for Reading** preview activities have been enriched to connect text-to-self by recalling prior knowledge and experiences, to encourage predictions, and to state a purpose.

■ Twenty new **Contemporary Focus** articles paired with the longer textbook readings are included to activate schemata, enrich content knowledge, connect text-to-text, and to promote group discussion. Each article is drawn from a popular source, such as a magazine or newspaper, to demonstrate the textbook reading's relevance to the "real world."

■ **Write About the Selection** questions encourage text-to-self and text-to-world connections by asking students to make a personal link to the text book selection or to link to the larger global issues.

■ **Contemporary Link** questions promote text-to-text and critical thinking by demonstrating the relevance of the introductory articles to the textbook selections that they accompany. A list of textbook readings, along with their accompanying **Contemporary Focus** features, follows the Preface.

■ **Vocabulary Booster** activities focus on linking and learning words through word parts or word families. These lessons, which introduce more than 200 words, have been transposed from the Appendix to the ends of chapters by popular demand. The lessons can be assigned weekly, and student progress can be measured using the assessment quizzes in the Instructor's Manual. In addition, this edition includes more than 160 vocabulary words in context after the longer reading selections

■ **Eleven new longer reading selections** are included. Of these, three are short stories; six are essays or pieces of narrative nonfiction; and 16 derive from a variety of college texts, for a total of 25 longer readings.

- **More than three dozen new photos** have been carefully chosen to amplify the exposition.

- Improved **Search the Net** activities after the longer textbook reading selections encourage students to amplify textbook study through Internet research. Because electronic reading skills are now essential for college students, the first Search the Net activity in Chapter 1 begins with a general explanation of how to plan and conduct an effective Internet search. Subsequent activities encourage students to find suggestions on the text's Web site (http://www.ablongman.com/smith) to connect Internet exploration with the textbook topics in each longer reading selection.

- **Making Sense of Figurative Language and Idioms** (Appendix) presents updated idiomatic expressions that will be of particular value to ESL students seeking practice opportunities with English similes, metaphors, and idioms.

- A **Progress Chart** is located on the inside back cover so students can record their progress in understanding the longer reading selections.

- Chapter-by-chapter **Reader's Journal** activities now appear on the text's Web site. With these reflective activities, students can learn about themselves, consider their strengths and weaknesses, and monitor their progress. After these activities are completed, they can either be e-mailed to the instructor or printed out and handed in.

Continuing Features

Other classroom-tested features of the book include the following:

- Actual **textbook selections** are used for practice exercises.

- **Many academic disciplines** are represented throughout, including psychology, history, communications, economics, business, allied health, sociology, criminal justice, computer science, and literature—including essay, short story, poetry, and narrative nonfiction forms.

- **Vocabulary is presented in context;** and vocabulary exercises follow each of the longer textbook reading selections. In addition to the end-of-chapter **Vocabulary Booster** lessons, a broad range of **vocabulary development** topics and corresponding exercises is presented in Chapter 2.

- **Reader's Tip** boxes give easy-to-access advice for readers, condensing strategies for improving reading into practical hints for quick reference.

- Each longer textbook selection has both **explicit and inferential questions.** Multiple-choice items are labeled as *main idea, inference,* or *detail questions.*

- Some selections include essay questions that elicit an organized **written response.**

- Although skills build and overlap, **each chapter can be taught as a separate unit** to fit individual class or student needs.

- **Pages are perforated** so that students can tear out and hand in assignments.

- Discussion and practice **exercises on barriers to critical thinking**—including cultural conditioning, self-deception, and oversimplification—appear throughout the book.
- Practice is offered in **identifying fallacies** in critical thinking and in **evaluating arguments**.

The Teaching and Learning Package

For Instructors

Each component of the teaching and learning package has been crafted to ensure that the course is a rewarding experience for both instructors and students.

The **Annotated Instructor's Edition** (0-321-27362-1) is an exact replica of the student edition but includes all answers printed directly on the fill-in lines provided in the text.

The **Instructor's Manual** (0-321-27654-X) contains overhead transparency masters and additional vocabulary and comprehension questions for each reading selection. The true-false, vocabulary, and comprehension quizzes can be used as prereading quizzes to stimulate interest or as evaluation quizzes after reading. Vocabulary-in-context exercises are also included to reinforce the words in the longer textbook selections. In addition, a true-false quiz is provided for each of the new Concept Prep sections. To receive an examination copy of the Instructor's Manual, please contact your Longman sales representative. You may also request an examination copy by calling 1-800-552-2499, or by sending your request via e-mail to exam@ablongman.com.

The **Test Bank** (0-321-27655-8) includes additional reading selections, chapter tests and vocabulary tests. To receive an examination copy of the Test Bank, please contact your Longman sales representative. You may also request an examination copy by calling 1-800-552-2499, or by e-mailing your request to exam@ablongman.com.

Electronic Test Bank for Reading (CD-ROM: 0-321-08179-X). This electronic test bank offers more than 3,000 questions in all areas of reading, including vocabulary, main idea, supporting details, patterns of organization, language, critical thinking, analytical reasoning, inference, point of view, visual aids, and textbook reading. With this easy-to-use CD-ROM, instructors simply choose questions from the electronic test bank, then print out the completed test for distribution.

Teaching Online: Internet Research, Conversation, and Composition, Second Edition. (0-321-01957-1) Ideal for instructors who have never surfed the Net, this easy-to-follow guide offers basic definitions, numerous examples, and step-by-step information about finding and using Internet sources. Free to adopters.

The Longman Guide to Classroom Management (0-321-09246-5) is the first in a series of monographs for developmental educators. Written by Joannis Flatley of St. Philip's College, it focuses on issues of classroom etiquette, providing guidance on dealing with unruly, unengaged, disruptive, or uncooperative students.

The Longman Instructor Planner (0-321-09247-3) is an all-in-one resource for instructors. It includes monthly and weekly planning sheets, to-do lists, student contact forms, attendance rosters, a gradebook, an address/phone book, and a mini almanac. It is free upon request.

For a wealth of additional materials, including online chapter summaries, quizzes, and Internet activities, be sure to visit the *Bridging the Gap* **Companion Website** at http://www.ablongman.com/smith.

For Students

My Skills Lab 2.0 (www.ablongman/myskillslab). MySkillsLab is the only online resource students need to develop their reading and writing skills. Free when packaged with this text, this site houses all media tools for developmental English (reading, writing, and study skills) in one place: The newly revised Reading Roadtrip 4.0, Longman Vocabulary Website, Longman Study Skills Website, Research Navigator, Avoiding Plagiarism, Exercise Zone, and Longman Writer's Warehouse. Each of the 16 modules in Reading Roadtrip corresponds to a reading or study skill (for example, finding the main idea, understanding patterns of organization, thinking critically). The newly updated 4.0 includes even more practice exercises and mastery tests.

The Dictionary Deal. Two dictionaries can be shrinkwrapped with *Bridging the Gap* at a nominal fee. *The New American Webster Handy College Dictionary* is a paperback reference text with more than 100,000 entries. *Merriam Webster's Collegiate Dictionary*, tenth edition, is a hardback reference with a citation file of more than 14.5 million examples of English words drawn from actual use. For more information on how to shrinkwrap a dictionary with your text, please contact your Longman sales representative.

Penguin Quality Paperback Titles. A series of Penguin paperbacks is available at a significant discount when shrinkwrapped with any Longman Basic Skills title. Some titles available are Toni Morrison's *Beloved*, Julia Alvarez's *How the Garcia Girls Lost Their Accents*, Mark Twain's *Huckleberry Finn, Narrative of the Life of Frederick Douglass*, Harriet Beecher Stowe's *Uncle Tom's Cabin*, Dr. Martin Luther King, Jr.'s *Why We Can't Wait*, and plays by Shakespeare, Miller, and Albee. For a complete list of titles or more information, please contact your Longman sales consultant.

The Longman Textbook Reader. This supplement, for use in developmental reading courses, offers five complete chapters from Addison-Wesley/Longman textbooks: computer science, biology, psychology, communications, and business. Each chapter includes additional comprehension quizzes, critical thinking questions, and group activities. Available FREE with the adoption of this Longman text. For information on how to bundle *The Longman Textbook Reader* with your text, please contact your Longman sales representative. Available in two formats: with answers and without answers.

Newsweek **Alliance**. Instructors may choose to shrinkwrap a 12-week subscription to *Newsweek* with any Longman text. The price of the subscription is 59 cents per issue (a total of $7.08 for the subscription). Available with the subscription is a free"" "Interactive Guide to *Newsweek*"—a workbook for students who are using the text. In addition, Newsweek provides a wide variety of instructor supplements free to teachers, including maps, Skills Builders, and weekly quizzes. For more information on the Newsweek program, please contact your Longman sales representative.

Research Navigator Guide for English, by H. Eric Branscomb & Linda R. Barr (Student/ 0-321-20277-5). Designed to teach students how to conduct high-quality online research and to document it properly, Research Navigator guides provide discipline-specific academic resources; in addition to helpful tips on the writing process, online research, and finding and citing valid sources. Free when packaged with any Longman text, Research Navigator guides include an access code to Research Navigator™—providing access to thousands of academic journals and periodicals, the NY Times Search by Subject Archive, Link Library, Library Guides, and more.

Ten Practices of Highly Successful Students. (0-205-30769-8) This popular supplement helps students learn crucial study skills, offering concise tips for a successful career in college. Topics include time management, test-taking, reading critically, stress, and motivation.

Thinking Through the Test, by D. J. Henry. This special workbook, prepared specially for students in Florida, offers ample skill and practice exercises to help student prep for the Florida State Exit Exam. To shrinkwrap this workbook free with your textbook, please contact your Longman sales representative. Available in six versions: Combined reading and writing workbook with answers, combined reading and writing workbook without answers, reading workbook with answers, reading workbook without answers, writing workbook with answers, and writing workbook without answers. Also available: Two laminated grids (one for reading, one for writing) that can serve as handy references for students preparing for the Florida State Exit Exam.

The Longman Reader's Journal, by Kathleen T. McWhorter. (0-321-08843-3) This reader's journal offers students a space to record their questions about, reactions to, and summaries of materials they've read. Also included is a personal vocabulary log, as well as ample space for free writing. For an examination copy, contact your Longman sales consultant.

The Longman Reader's Portfolio and Student Planner. (0-321-29610-9) This unique portfolio and student planner supplement provides students with a space to think, plan, and present their work, as well as a calendar to schedule their semester and keep key instructor information. The portfolio includes a learning style questionnaire, personal reading log, vocabulary log, textbook reading response sheet, literature reading response sheet, a progress chart, and much more.

For Texas Adopters

The Longman THEA Study Guide, by Jeannette Harris (Student/0-321-20271-6). Created specifically for students in Texas, this study guide includes straightforward explanations and numerous practice exercises to help students prepare for the reading and writing sections of THEA Test.

For New York/CUNY Adopters

Preparing for the CUNY-ACT Reading and Writing Test, edited by Patricia Licklider (Student/0-321-19608-2). This booklet, prepared by reading and writing faculty from across the CUNY system, is designed to help students prepare for the CUNY-ACT exit test. It includes test-taking tips, reading passages, typical exam questions, and sample writing prompts to help students become familiar with each portion of the test.

Acknowledgments

I would like to thank my new Basic Skills Editor, Susan Kunchandy, for her enthusiasm and drive in getting this new eighth edition into production. From the outset, she sent me many new textbooks from which to choose the new passages and longer reading selections. I also greatly appreciate the insight and diligence of Susan Moss, my developmental editor. Sue worked very hard to add quality and ensure that we were able to meet an early publication date. I am greatly indebted to her for her brain-power.

My researcher, Lisa Moore, has done a great job in helping locate interesting Contemporary Focus articles. She has been prompt and incredibly responsive, sometimes on a short notice. Jackie Stahlecker of St. Philip's College served as technical reviewer. This book has benefited from the excellent contributions of all these individuals.

Again, I feel extremely privileged to have received advice from so many learned colleagues in the college reading profession. I am particularly grateful to Helen Carr of San Antonio College and Melinda Schomaker of Georgia Perimeter College. This book is strengthened by their insightful, sincere, and constructive comments. I would also like to thank these knowledgeable and concerned instructors:

Dena Beeghly, West Chester University
Helen R. Carr, San Antonio College
Dianne Cates, Central Piedmont Community College
Barbara J. Grossman, Essex County College
Barbara McLay, University of South Florida
Erin M. Pushman, Limestone College

Brenda D. Smith

An Overview of *Bridging the Gap*

The eighth edition of *Bridging the Gap* features paired readings at the end of most chapters, in many cases followed by a Concept Prep for a particular academic discipline. Each reading selection begins with a Contemporary Focus article drawn from a popular source, such as a newspaper or magazine, that introduces the subject and promotes learning by connecting the academic selection to current issues. The Concept Prep feature continues to highlight academic knowledge expected of educated thinkers.

Discipline/Genre of Reading Selection	Textbook or Academic Selection	Accompanying Contemporary Focus Article	Accompanying Concept Prep
Chapter 1 Active Learning			
Computer Science	Security and Privacy for Computers and the Internet	Police in India to Monitor Cybercafes	Computer Science
Psychology	Critical-Period Hypothesis	Lions, Tigers, Wild Animals; Not Pets	Psychology
Chapter 3 Strategic Reading and Study			
History	Tejanos at the Alamo	TV: Remembering the Alamo From a Tejano Perspective	History
Sociology	Unity in Diversity	Mixed Signals on Body Language	Anthropology
Chapter 4 Main Idea			
Psychology	Monkey Love	Centers Strive to Break the Cycle of Violence	Psychology
Short Story	On the Sidewalk, Bleeding	Former L.A. Gang Member	Literature
Criminal Justice	International Terrorism	U.S. Coast Guard's Efforts to Protect Ports	—
Chapter 5 Patterns of Organization			
Economics	Slave Redemption in Sudan	Enslaved at An Early Age	Economics
History	Women in History	Trusted Policy Advisor	Art History
Business	Why Is Papa John's Rolling in the Dough?	Low-Carb Pizza Options	Business

Discipline/Genre of Reading Selection	Textbook or Academic Selection	Accompanying Contemporary Focus Article	Accompanying Concept Prep
Chapter 6 Organizing Textbook Information			
Communications	Influences of Magazines Communications and Language	Media-Promoted Morals Cloud Judgment	
Allied Health	Nutrition, Health, and Stress	Signs of Stress	Health
Chapter 7 Inference			
Short Story	Ah Bah's Money	High-Stakes Palaces of Gambling	Philosophy and Literature
Short Story	Witches' Loaves	O. Henry's Storytelling	
Narrative Nonfiction	Learning to Read: Malcolm X	Remembering a Civil Rights Hero	Political Science
Chapter 8 Point of View			
Essay	Elderly Parents	Orphans-to-Be?	
Essay	Leaving Islam and Living Islam	Bridging the Gap Between Muslims and the West	
Chapter 9 Critical Thinking			
Essay	The Importance of Being Beautiful	Physical Beauty Involves More than Good Looks	
Essay	Study Links Cell Phones to Brain Damage	Cell Phones and Cancer: No Clear Connection	
Chapter 10 Graphic Illustrations			
Allied Health	Alcohol and Nutrition	Message in a Bottle	Nutrition
Chapter 11 Rate Flexibility			
Allied Health	Passive Smoking		
Sociology	Heredity or Environment? The Case of Identical Twins		
History	Margaret Sanger: Birth Control Pioneer		

Active Learning

- What is active learning?
- How does the brain "pay attention"?
- Can you do two things at once?
- What are multiple intelligences?
- How can you improve your concentration?
- What are common internal and external distractors and cures?
- Why is your syllabus important?

Chicago Interior by J. Theodore Johnson, ca. 1934. Oil on canvas, 28 1/8 x 34" (71.2 x 86.4 cm). Smithsonian American Art Museum, Washington, DC, USA. Photo: Smithsonian American Art Museum, Washington, DC/Art Resource, NY.

What Is Active Learning?

Active learning is not just a single task; it is a *project with multiple components*. You, your instructor, your textbook, and your classmates are all parts of the project. Learn to use all four effectively and you are on the road to success.

As a starting point, active learning requires concentration and attention to details beyond academics. You must manage yourself, manage the assignment or learning task, and manage others who can contribute to or detract from your success. In this chapter, we discuss many factors that contribute to your ability to become an effective active learner. First, however, let's consider what psychologists have to say about focusing your attention, thinking, and learning. Understanding these cognitive aspects is a part of managing yourself.

What Is Cognitive Psychology?

Cognitive psychology is the body of knowledge that describes how the mind works, or at least how experts think the mind works. Fortunately or unfortunately, the activity of the brain when concentrating, reading, and remembering cannot be observed directly. These cognitive processes are invisible, as are thinking and problem solving.

Because so little is actually known about thinking, the ideas of cognitive psychologists are frequently described as *models*, or comparisons of something else we understand. For more than thirty years, for example, the central processing unit of a computer has been a popular model for describing how the brain processes information. The human brain is more complex than a computer, but the analogy provides a comparison that can help us understand.

How Does the Brain Screen Messages?

Cognitive psychologists use the word **attention** to describe a student's uninterrupted mental focus. Thinking and learning, they say, begin with attention. During every minute of the day, the brain is bombarded with millions of sensory messages. How does the brain decide which messages to pay attention to and which to overlook? At this moment, are you thinking about the temperature of the room, outdoor noises, or what you are reading? With all this information available to you at the same time, how can your brain choose what's most important?

The brain relies on a dual command center to screen out one message and attend to another. According to a researcher at UCLA, receptor cells send millions of messages per minute to your brain.[1] Your reticular activating system (RAS)—a network of cells at the top of the spinal cord that runs to the brain—tells the cortex of the brain—the wrinkled outer layer that handles sensory processing, motor control, and memory storage—not to bother with most of the sensory input. Your RAS knows that most sensory inputs do not need attention. For example, you are probably not aware at this moment of your back pressing against your chair or your clothes pulling on your body. Your RAS has decided not to clutter your brain with such irrelevant information and to alert the cortex only when there is an extreme problem, like your foot going to sleep because you have been sitting on it.

The cortex can also make attention decisions and tells your RAS to hold some messages while you concentrate on others. How well are your RAS and cortex cooperating in blocking out distractions so you can concentrate on learning?

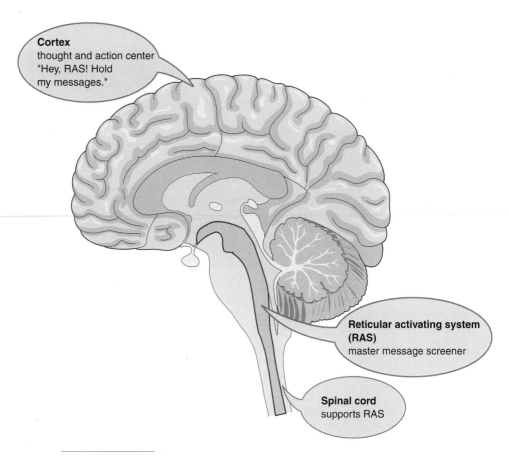

Cortex
thought and action center
"Hey, RAS! Hold my messages."

Reticular activating system (RAS)
master message screener

Spinal cord
supports RAS

---

[1]H. W. Magoun, *The Waking Brain*, 2nd ed. (Springfield, IL: Charles C. Thomas, 1963).

Is Divided Attention Effective?

Is it possible to do two things at once, such as watching television and doing homework? Is it safe to drive and talk on a cell phone? In a 2002 study, researchers Rodriguez, Valdes-Sosa, and Freiwald found that dividing your attention usually has a cost.[2] You are more likely to perform one or both tasks less efficiently than if you were to concentrate on a single task. This corroborated, or made more certain, the earlier findings of two other scientists who tested the effectiveness of divided attention.[3] These researchers asked participants questions as they watched two televised sports events with one superimposed over the other. When participants were instructed to watch only one of the games, they successfully screened out the other and answered questions accurately. When asked to attend to both games simultaneously, however, the participants made eight times more mistakes than when focusing on only one game. Thus, this research seems to confirm the old adage "You can't do two things at once and do them well."

Dividing your attention can have a cost. Researchers have found that the auto accident rate among people who drive while talking on the phone (including those using headsets) is four times that of drivers who do not use the phone as they drive.[4]
David Young-Wolff/Stone/Getty Images

---

[2]V. Rodriguez, M. Valdes-Sosa, and W. Freiwald, "Dividing Attention Between Form and Motion During Transparent Surface Perception, *Cognitive Brain Research* 13 (2002): 187–93.
[3]D. A. Redelmeier and R. J. Tibshiramni, "Association between Cellular-Telephone Calls and Motor Vehicle Collisions," *New England Journal of Medicine* 336 (1997): 453–58.
[4]U. Neisser and R. Becklen, "Selective Looking: Attending to Visually Significant Events," *Cognitive Psychology* 7 (1975): 480–94.

Can Tasks Become Automatic?

Can you walk and chew gum at the same time? Does every simple activity require your undivided attention? Many tasks—walking, tying shoelaces, and driving a car, for example—begin under controlled processing, which means that they are deliberate and require concentrated mental effort to learn. After much practice, however, such tasks become automatic. Driving a car, for example, is a learned behavior that researchers would say becomes an automatic process after thousands of hours of experience. You can probably drive and listen to the radio at the same time, but it may not be a good idea to drive and talk on a cell phone. Similarly, a skilled athlete can dribble a basketball automatically while also attending to strategy and position. Attention is actually not divided because it can shift away from tasks that have become automatic.

Automatic Aspects of Reading

The idea of doing certain things automatically is especially significant in reading. As a first-grade reader, you had to concentrate on recognizing letters, words, and sentences, as well as trying to construct meaning. After years of practice and overlearning, much of the recognition aspect of reading has become automatic. You no longer stop laboriously to decode each word or each letter. For example, when you look at the word *child*, you automatically think the meaning. Thus, you can focus your mental resources on understanding the *message* in which the word appears, rather than on understanding the word itself.

College reading can be frustrating because it is not as automatic as everyday reading. College textbooks often contain many unfamiliar words and complex concepts that the brain cannot automatically process. Your attention to a book's message can be interrupted by the need to attend to unknown words, creating the dilemma of trying to do two things at once—trying to figure out word meaning as well as trying to understand the message. After the break, you can regain your concentration, and little harm is done if such breaks are infrequent. However, frequent interruptions in the automatic aspect of reading can undermine your ability to concentrate on the message. Thus, mastering the jargon or vocabulary of a new course early on can improve your concentration.

Cognitive Styles

Do you learn easily by reading or do you prefer a demonstration or a diagram? Do you like to work with details or do you prefer broad generalizations? Many psychologists believe that people develop a preference for a particular style or manner of learning at an early age and that these preferences affect concentration and learning. Cognitive style theorists focus on strengths and assert that there is no right or wrong way. These researchers believe that instruction is best when it matches the learner's particular preference.

Although knowing your preferences may not affect how your classes are taught, such knowledge can improve your attitude about yourself as a learner and your ability to focus by enabling you to build on your strengths.

Cognitive Style Preferences. One popular inventory that can be used to determine individual cognitive style preferences is the Myers-Briggs Type Indicator (MBTI). Based on psychologist Carl Jung's theory of personality types, it measures personality traits in four categories. The results are used as indicators for learning styles, teaching styles, management styles, career planning, team building, organizational development, and even marriage counseling. The inventory must be administered by a licensed specialist and is frequently given to entering college freshmen. The following descriptions of the four MBTI categories give an idea of the kinds of issues its proponents consider significant:

1. *Extroverted—introverted:* Extroverts prefer to talk with others and learn through experience, whereas introverts prefer to think alone about ideas.
2. *Sensing—intuitive:* Sensing types prefer working with concrete details and tend to be patient, practical, and realistic. Intuitive types like abstractions and are creative, impatient, and theory oriented.
3. *Thinking—feeling:* Thinking types tend to base decisions on objective criteria and logical principles. Feeling types are subjective and consider the impact of the decision on other people.
4. *Judging—perceiving:* Judging types are time oriented and structured, whereas perceivers are spontaneous and flexible.

Another test that uses the same type indicators as the MBTI is the Keirsey Temperament Sorter II. You can take this seventy-item personality inventory online and receive an extensive printout. However, experts do not consider it to have passed the same rigorous standards for validation and reliability as the MBTI. The Keirsey Web site (http://www.keirsey.com) provides background information about the test. It begins with a brief questionnaire and then has a link to the longer Keirsey Temperament Sorter II.

Right- Versus Left-Brain Dominance. Another popular cognitive style theory is concerned with right- or left-brain dominance. Proponents of this theory believe that left-brain dominant people are analytical and logical and excel in verbal skills. Right-brain people, on the other hand, are intuitive, creative, and emotional, and tend to think in symbols. Albert Einstein, for example, said that he rarely thought in words but that his concepts appeared in symbols and images.

If you are "turned off" by an assignment, try to translate it into activities and ideas that are more compatible with your learning preferences. For example, if you prefer right-brain activities, use maps, charts, and drawings to help you concentrate while studying. Acknowledge your strengths and use them to enhance your concentration.

Multiple Intelligences: There Is More Than One Way to Be Smart

Has our culture put too much emphasis on verbal and logical thinking? How did we start thinking of intelligence as a single score? Let's take a closer look at the way this all evolved.

In early twentieth-century France, the government enacted universal elementary education and wanted to identify public school children who might need extra help to be successful. In response, French psychologist Alfred Binet and his collaborator Theodore Simon invented an IQ (intelligence quotient) test—an intelligence test—that quickly caught on. Adapted for use in the United States by professors at Stanford University, it was renamed the Stanford-Binet Intelligence Scale. During World War I, its popularity increased as the test was given to more than a million U. S. military recruits. Although criticized for measuring only *schoolhouse giftedness*, it nevertheless remained the standard for assessing abilities for many years.

However, in 1983, Harvard professor Howard Gardner changed the way many people think about being smart. Taking a much broader, more inclusive view of abilities, he developed a **theory of multiple intelligences.** According to this theory, there are eight different ways to be intelligent, and some people develop certain ways of being intelligent to a greater extent than they do others.

The following list describes Gardner's eight ways to be smart, with possible career choices for each. In which area do you excel?

1. **Word smart.** *Linguistic* thinkers like reading, writing, and speaking. They become journalists, teachers, executives, and comedians.

2. **Picture smart.** *Spatial* thinkers like pictures, charts, and maps. They become architects, artists, and surgeons.

3. **Logical smart.** *Logical-mathematical* thinkers like to reason, sequence, and think in terms of cause and effect. They become scientists, accountants, bankers, and computer programmers.

4. **Body smart.** *Bodily-kinesthetic* thinkers like to control body movements and handle objects skillfully. They become athletes, dancers, craftspeople, mechanics, and surgeons.

5. **People smart.** *Interpersonal* thinkers who work well with people can perceive the moods, intentions, and desires of others. They become networkers, negotiators, social service professionals, and teachers.

6. **Self smart.** *Intrapersonal* thinkers are introspective and meditative or can be self-disciplined, goal directed independents who understand the inner self. They become counselors, theologians, and self-employed businesspeople.

7. **Music smart.** *Musical* thinkers with a "good ear" can sing and play in tune, keep time, and listen with discernment. They become musical audio engineers, symphony conductors, music educators, and musicians.

8. **Nature smart.** *Naturalistic* thinkers have expertise in flora and fauna, have "green thumbs," a knack for gardening, and an affinity for animals. They become landscapers, landscape architects, and veterinarians.

How does the multiple intelligences theory provide another way to look at strengths and weaknesses in learning? See for yourself. You may excel in several of these eight intelligences. Match Gardner's eight listed intelligences

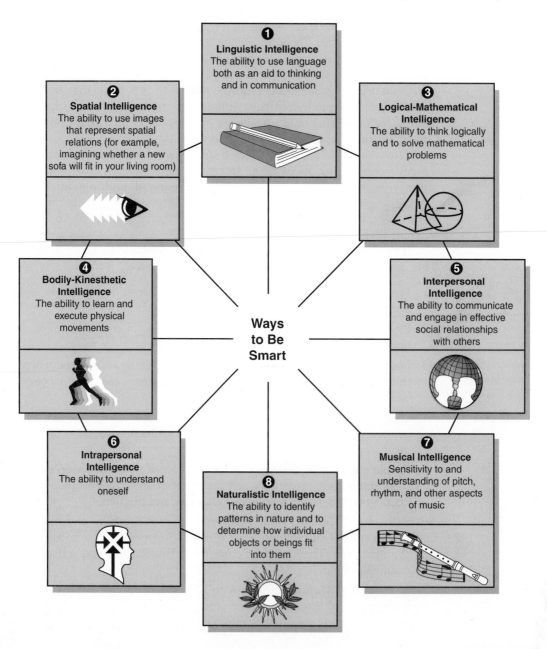

with the numbers listed below and honestly rank yourself from 1 to 10 on each (with 10 being the highest agreement):

1. _6_   2. _5_   3. _5_   4. _2_
5. _3_   6. _4_   7. _7_   8. _4_

For a more scientific evaluation of your strengths, go to http://www.mitest.com/o7inte~1.htm and respond to a quick-scoring Multiple Intelligence Test (which includes only seven intelligences). Use the Web site to find out what your score means and to get suggestions for learning and studying strategies to match your strongest intelligences.

What If I'm Not a Verbal or Logical Learner? Most college teaching is geared toward linguistic and logical-mathematical smarts. If those are not your strengths, how can you compensate? First, and most importantly, recognize the dilemma and be happy with your strengths, knowing that you have areas of high intelligence. Next, devise a few tricks to make the most of your strengths.

- For picture smarts, create diagrams and maps for study. Watch films on the subject.
- For music smarts, use rhymes and rhythms as memory devices, or *mnemonics*, to enhance memory.
- For people smarts, network and study with classmates.
- For body smarts, seek hands-on experiences to complement your tactile sensitivity.
- For self smarts, reflect for self-understanding to enrich and guide your life.
- For nature smarts, relate learning to environmental issues.

In summary, cognitive psychologists offer many ways of looking at attention and learning by encouraging us to recognize our strengths and weaknesses. Use your strengths and be proud of them.

What Is Concentration?

Regardless of your intelligences and the way you learn, knowing how to concentrate is critical to college success. Concentration is a skill that is developed through self-discipline and practice. It is a **habit** that requires time and effort to develop for consistent success. Athletes have it, surgeons have it, and successful college students must have it. *Concentration is essential for active learning.*

Concentration can be defined as the process of *paying attention*—that is, focusing full attention on the task at hand. Someone once said that the mark of a genius is the ability to concentrate completely on one thing at a time. This is easy if the task is fun and exciting, but it becomes more difficult when you are required to read something that is not very interesting to you. In such cases, you may find yourself looking from word to word and spacing out.

Poor Concentration: Causes and Cures

The type of intense concentration that forces the RAS and cortex to close out the rest of the world is the state we would all like to achieve each time we sit down with a textbook. Most of the time, however, lots of thoughts compete for attention.

Students frequently ask, *How can I keep my mind on what I'm doing?* or they say, *I finished the assignment, but I don't understand a thing I read.* The best way to increase concentration is not by using some simple mental trick to fool the brain; rather, it involves a series of practical short- and long-range planning strategies targeted at reducing external and internal distractions.

External Distractions

External distractions are the temptations of the physical world that divert your attention away from your work. They are the people in the room, the noise in the background, the time of day, or your place for studying. To control these external distractions, you must create an environment that says, "Now this is the place and the time for me to get my work done."

Create a Place for Studying. Start by establishing your own private study cubicle; it may be in the library, on the dining room table, or in your bedroom. Wherever your study place is, choose a straight chair and face the wall. Get rid of gadgets, magazines, and other temptations that trigger the mind to think of *play*. Stay away from your bed because it triggers *sleep*. Spread out your papers, books, and other symbols of studying, and create an atmosphere in which the visual stimuli signal *work*. Be consistent by trying to study in the same place at the same time.

Use a Pocket Calendar, Assignment Book, or Personal Digital Assistant. At the beginning of the quarter or semester, record dates for tests, term papers, and special projects on some kind of planner, like a calendar or personal digital assistant (PDA). Use your planner to organize all course assignments. The mere sight of your planner will remind you of the need for both short- and long-term planning. Assigned tests, papers, and projects will be due whether you are ready or not. Your first job is to devise a plan for being ready.

Schedule Weekly Activities. Successful people do not let their time slip away; they manage time, rather than letting time manage them. Plan realistically and then follow your plan.

Use the weekly activity chart shown here. First, write your fixed activities—including class hours, work time, mealtime, and bedtime. Next, estimate how much time you plan to spend on studying and how much on recreation. Plug those estimates into the chart. For studying, indicate the specific subject and exact place involved.

Weekly Activity Chart

Time	Monday	Tuesday	Wednesday	Thursday	Friday	Saturday	Sunday
7:00–8:00							
8:00–9:00							
9:00–10:00							
10:00–11:00							
11:00–12:00							
12:00–1:00							
1:00–2:00							
2:00–3:00							
3:00–4:00							
4:00–5:00							
5:00–6:00							
6:00–7:00							
7:00–8:00							
8:00–9:00							
9:00–10:00							
10:00–11:00							
11:00–12:00							

Make a fresh chart at the beginning of each week because responsibilities and assignments vary. Learn to estimate the time you usually need for typical assignments. Always include time for a regular review of lecture notes.

Examinations require special planning. Many students do not realize how much time it takes to study for a major exam. Spread your studying out over several days, and avoid last-minute cramming sessions late at night. Plan additional time for special projects and term papers to avoid deadline crises.

Take Short Breaks. Even though it is not necessary to write this on the chart, remember that you need short breaks. Few students can study uninterrupted for two hours without becoming fatigued and losing concentration. In fact, research shows that studying in chunks rather than long spans is most efficient.[5] Try the *50:10 ratio*—study hard for fifty minutes, take a ten-minute break, and then promptly go back to the books for another fifty minutes.

Internal Distractions

Internal distractions are the concerns that come repeatedly into your mind as you try to keep your attention focused on an assignment. You have to run errands, do laundry, make telephone calls, and pay bills. How do you stop worrying about getting an inspection sticker for the car or about picking up tickets for Saturday's ball game when you need to be concentrating completely on your class assignment?

Make a List. To gain control over mental disruptions, make a list of what is on your mind and keeping you from concentrating on your studies. Jot down on paper your mental distractions, and then analyze each to determine if immediate action is possible. If you decide you can do something right away, get up and do it. Make that phone call, write that e-mail, or finish that chore. Maybe it will take a few minutes or maybe half an hour, but the investment will have been worthwhile if the quality of your study time—your concentration power—has improved. Taking action is the first step in getting something off your mind.

For a big problem that you can't tackle immediately, ask yourself, "Is it worth the amount of brain time I'm dedicating to it?" Take a few minutes to think and make notes on possible solutions. Jotting down necessary future action and forming a plan of attack will help relieve the worry and clear your mind for studying.

Right now, list five things that are on your mind that you need to remember to do. Alan Lakein, a pioneer specialist in time management, calls this a **to-do list.** In his book, *How to Get Control of Your Time and Your Life,* Lakein claims that successful business executives start each day with such a list.[6] Rank the activities on your list in order of priority, and then do the most important things first. Some people even make a list before they go to sleep at night.

---

[5]H. P. Bahrick, L. E. Bahrick, A. S. Bahrick, and P. E. Bahrick, "Maintenance of Foreign Language Vocabulary and the Spacing Effect," *Psychological Science 4*, no. 5 (September 1993): 316–21.
[6]A. Lakein, *How to Get Control of Your Time and Your Life* (New York: Signet, 1974).

To-Do List	Sample
1.	1. Get hair cut
2.	2. Do my book report
3.	3. Buy stamps
4.	4. Call power co.
5.	5. Pay phone bill

Increase Your Self-Confidence. Saying "I'll never pass this course" or "I can't get in the mood to study" is the first step to failure. Concentration requires self-confidence. Getting a college degree is not a short-term goal. Your enrollment indicates that you have made a commitment to a long-term goal. Ask yourself, "Who do I want to be in five years?" In the following space, describe how you view yourself, both professionally and personally, five years from now:

Five years from now, I hope to be *a Proffesional Docter to own my new house and business and to have enough Money in the bank, to cover all My needs*

Sometimes, identifying the traits you admire in others can give you insight into your own values and desires. Think about the traits you respect in others and your own definition of success. Answer the two questions that follow, and consider how your responses mirror your own aspirations and goals:

Who is the person that you admire the most? *My Mom*

Why do you admire this person? *because My Mom has gone through a lot of struggles and she still as been able to accomplished all her goals*

Improve Your Self-Concept. Have faith in yourself and in your ability to be what you want to be. How many people do you know who have passed the particular course that is worrying you? Are they smarter than you? Probably not. Can you do as well as they did? Turn your negative feeling into a positive attitude. What are some of your positive traits? Are you a hard worker, an honest person, a loyal friend? Take a few minutes to pat yourself on the back. Think about your good points, and in the following spaces, list five positive traits that you believe you possess:

Positive Traits

1. Good Personalities
2. helpfull
3. Positive thinker
4. Abitious
5. hard worker

What have you already accomplished? Did you participate in athletics in high school, win any contests, or master any difficult skills? Recall your previous achievements, and in the following spaces, list three accomplishments that you view with pride:

Accomplishments

1. Graduate from highschool
2. Get My own apartment and pay all bills
3. Pass all My college classes

Reduce Anxiety. Have you ever heard people say, "I work better under pressure?" This statement contains a degree of truth. A small amount of tension can help you direct your full attention on an immediate task. For example, concentrated study for an exam is usually more intense two nights before, rather than two weeks before, the test.

Yet too much anxiety can cause nervous tension and discomfort, which interfere with the ability to concentrate. Students operating under excessive tension sometimes "freeze up" mentally and experience nervous physical reactions. The causes of high anxiety can range from fear of failure to lack of organization and preparation; the problem is not easily solved. Some people like to go for a run or a brisk walk when they feel overly stressed. Sustained physical activity can change the blood chemistry and improve mood, increasing the odds of focusing successfully on what needs to be done.

Another immediate, short-term fix for tension is muscle relaxation exercises and visualization. For example, if you are reading a particularly difficult section in a chemistry book and are becoming frustrated to the point that you can no longer concentrate, stop your reading and take several deep breaths. Use your imagination to visualize a peaceful setting in which you are calm and relaxed. Imagine yourself rocking back and forth in a hammock or lying on a beach listening to the surf; then focus on this image as you breathe deeply to help relax your muscles and regain control. Take several deep breaths, and allow your body to release the tension so you can resume reading and concentrate on your work. Try that right now.

As a long-term solution to tension, nothing works better than success. Just as failure fuels tension, success tends to weaken it. Each successful experience helps to diminish feelings of inadequacy. Early success in a course—passing the first exam, for instance—can make a big psychological difference and replace anxiety with confidence.

Spark an Interest. Make a conscious effort to stimulate your curiosity before reading, even if in a contrived manner. Make yourself want to learn something. First look over the assigned reading for words or phrases that attract your attention, glance at the pictures, check the number of pages, and then ask yourself the following questions: "What do I already know about this topic?" and "What do I want to learn about it?"

With practice, this method of thinking before reading can create a spark of enthusiasm that will make the actual reading more purposeful and make concentration more direct and intense. We will cover this in greater depth in Chapter 3.

Set a Time Goal. An additional trick to spark your enthusiasm is to set a time goal. Study time is not infinite; and short-term goals create a self-imposed pressure to pay attention, speed up, and get the job done. After looking over the material, predict the amount of time you will need to finish it. Estimate a reasonable completion time, and then push yourself to meet the goal. The purpose of a time goal is not to "speed read" the assignment but to be realistic about the amount of time to spend on a task and to learn how to estimate future study time. The Reader's Tip summarizes how you can raise your level of concentration while studying.

READER'S TIP

Improving Concentration

◆ Create an environment that says, "Study."

◆ Use a calendar, assignment book, or PDA for short- and long-term planning.

◆ Keep a daily to-do list.

◆ Take short breaks.

◆ Visualize yourself as a successful graduate.

◆ Reduce anxiety by passing the first test.

◆ Spark an interest.

◆ Set time goals for completing daily assignments.

Successful Academic Behaviors

Good concentration geared toward college success involves more than the ability to comprehend reading assignments. College success demands concentrated study, self-discipline, and the demonstration of learning. If the "focused athlete" can be successful, so can the "focused student." Begin to evaluate and eliminate behaviors that waste your time and divert you from your goals. Direct your energy toward activities that will enhance your chances for success. Adopt the following behaviors of successful students.

Attend Class. At the beginning of the course, college professors distribute an outline of what they plan to cover during each class period. Although they may not always check class attendance, the organization of the daily course work assumes perfect attendance. College professors *expect* students to attend class; and they usually do not repeat lecture notes or give makeup lessons for those who are absent, although some post lecture notes on a course Web site. Be responsible and set yourself up for success by coming to class. You paid for it!

Be on Time. Professors usually present an overview of the day's work at the beginning of each class, as well as answer questions and clarify assignments. Arriving late puts you at an immediate disadvantage. You are likely to miss important "class business" information. In addition, tardy students distract both the professor and other students. Put on a watch and get yourself moving.

Be Aware of Essential Class Sessions. Every class session is important, but the last class before a major test is the most critical of all. Usually, students will ask questions about the exam that will stimulate your thinking. In reviewing, answering questions, and rushing to finish uncovered material, the professor will often drop important clues to exam items. Unless you are critically ill, take tests on time because makeups are usually more difficult. In addition, be in class when the exams are returned to hear the professor's description of an excellent answer.

Read Assignments Before Class. Activate your knowledge on the subject before class by reading homework assignments. Look at the illustrations and read the captions. Jot down several questions that you would like to ask the professor about the reading. Then the lecture and class discussion can enhance your newly created knowledge network.

Review Lecture Notes Before Class. Always, always, always review your lecture notes before the next class period, preferably within twenty-four hours after the class. Review with a classmate during a break or on the phone. Fill in gaps and make notations to ask questions to resolve confusion.

Consider Using a Tape Recorder. If you are having difficulty concentrating or are a strong audio or linguistic learner, with the professor's permission, tape-record the lecture. Take notes as you record, and you can later review your notes while listening to the recording.

Predict the Exam Questions. Never go to an exam without first predicting test items. Turn chapter titles, subheadings, and boldface print into questions, and then brainstorm the answers. Outline possible answers on paper. Preparation boosts self-confidence.

Pass the First Test. Stress interferes with concentration. Do yourself a favor and overstudy for the first exam. Passing the first exam will help you avoid a lot of tension while studying for the second one.

Learn from Other Student Papers. Talking about an excellent paper is one thing, but actually reading one is another. In each discipline, we need models of excellence. Find an "A" paper to read. Don't be shy. Ask the "A" students (who should be proud and flattered to share their brilliance) or ask the professor. Don't miss this important step in becoming a successful student.

Network with Other Students. You are not in this alone; you have lots of potential buddies who can offer support. Collect the names, phone numbers, and e-mail addresses of two classmates who are willing to help you if you do not understand the homework, miss a day of class, or need help on an assignment. Be prepared to help your classmates in return for their support.

Classmate _____ Phone _____ E-mail _____

Classmate _____ Phone _____ E-mail _____

Form a Study Group. Research involving college students has shown that study groups can be very effective. Studying with others is not cheating; it is making a wise use of available resources. Many professors assist networking efforts by posting the class roll with e-mail addresses. A junior on the dean's list explained, "I e-mail my study buddy when I have a problem. One time I asked about an English paper because I couldn't think of my thesis. She asked what it was about. I told her and she wrote back, 'That's your thesis.' I just couldn't see it as clearly as she did." Use the Internet to create an academic support group to lighten your workload and boost your grades. Manage e-mail efficiently, as indicated in the Reader's Tip.

Collaborate. When participating in group learning activities, set expectations for group study so that each member contributes, and try to keep the studying on target. As a group activity, ask several classmates to join you in discovering

READER'S TIP

Managing E-mail Efficiently

◆ Always fill in an appropriate subject header to guide your reader.

◆ Don't recycle the same subject header over and over. Unless it is important to see the thread of e-mail exchanges, write a new one to get your reader's attention.

◆ Keep your message short and to the point. People are busy.

◆ Use correct grammar, spelling, and punctuation. Your message represents you.

◆ Use consecutive uppercase letters sparingly. They YELL, which is called flaming.

◆ In formal messages, avoid emoticons—combinations of keyboard characters that represent emotions, such as smileys :-).

◆ Use an autoreply if you are away for a week or longer.

◆ If appropriate, save time by using the same message for several individual replies.

◆ Don't feel you have to reply to everything.

◆ If pressed for time, save your message as "new" and reply later.

◆ Delete unwanted advertisements without reading them after reporting them as spam.

◆ Do not reply to an entire group when an individual reply is more appropriate.

◆ Know your group before sending humor.

◆ If you are unsure about a group member, seek permission before forwarding a message. If sending humor, cut and paste as a new message rather than forwarding with many group member names.

◆ When sending a single message to many people, mail the message to yourself and list other recipients as blind copies (bcc) to protect their e-mail address privacy.

◆ Monitor how much time you spend on e-mail.

some campus resources by answering the questions in Exercise 1.1. First, brainstorm with the group to record answers that are known to be true. Next, divide responsibilities among group members to seek information to answer unknown items. Finally, reconvene the group in person or on the Internet to share responses.

| Exercise 1.1 | **Campus Facts** |

Form a collaborative study group to answer the following questions.

1. Where are the academic advisors located? _____

_____

2. Where is the learning lab, and what kind of help is offered? _____

_____

3. When does the college offer free study skills workshops? _____

_____

4. Are classrooms wired with modem ports? _____

_____

5. Where can you use a computer and check your e-mail? _____

_____

6. Where do you get an identification number for the Internet? _____

_____

7. Where is your professor's office, and what are his or her phone number and e-mail address? _____

_____

8. What kind of financial aid is available, and where can you find this information? _____

_____

9. What services does the dean's office offer to students? _____

_____

10. How late is the library open on weekends? _____

_____

11. What free services does the counseling center offer? _____

_____

Use the Syllabus. A syllabus is a general outline of the goals, objectives, and assignments for the entire course. Typically, a syllabus includes examination dates, course requirements, and an explanation of the grading system. Most professors distribute and explain the syllabus on the first day of class.

    Ask questions to help you understand the "rules and regulations" in the syllabus. Keep it handy as a ready reference, and use it as a plan for learning. Three-hole-punch it for your binder or staple it to your lecture notes; tape a second copy to your wall or door. Devise your own daily calendar for completing weekly reading and writing assignments.

    The following is a syllabus for Psychology 101. Study the course syllabus and answer the questions that follow.

INTRODUCTION TO PSYCHOLOGY

Class: 9:00–10:00 a.m. daily   Dr. Julie Wakefield
10-week quarter   Office: 718 Park Place
Office hours: 10:00–12:00 daily   Telephone: 404-651-3361
                                        E-mail: JuWake@ABC.edu

Required Texts
Psychology: An Introduction, by Josh R. Gerow
Paperback: Select one book from the attached list for
a report.

Course Content
The purpose of Psychology 101 is to overview the general
areas of study in the field of psychology. An understanding
of psychology gives valuable insights into your choices
and behaviors and those of others. The course will also
give you a foundation for later psychology courses.

Methods of Teaching
Thematic lectures will follow the topics listed in the
textbook assignments. You are expected to read and master
the factual material in the text as well as take careful
notes in class. Tests will cover both class lectures and
textbook readings.

Research Participation
All students are required to participate in one psychological experiment. Details and dates are listed on a separate
handout.

Grading
Grades will be determined in the following manner:
Tests (4 tests at 15% each)   60%
Final exam   25%
Written report   10%
Research participation   5%

Tests
Tests will consist of both multiple-choice and identification items as well as two essay questions.

Important Dates
Test 1: 1/13
Test 2: 1/29
Test 3: 2/10
Test 4: 2/24
Written report: 3/5
Final exam: 3/16

Written Report
Your written report should answer one of three designated questions and reflect your reading of a book from the list. Each book is approximately 200 pages long. Your report should be at least eight typed pages. More information to follow.

Assignments
Week 1: Ch. 1 (pp. 1-37), Ch. 2 (pp. 41-75)
Week 2: Ch. 3 (pp. 79-116)
    TEST 1: Chapters 1-3
Week 3: Ch. 4 (pp. 121-162), Ch. 5 (pp. 165-181)
Week 4: Ch. 5 (pp. 184-207), Ch. 6 (pp. 211-246)
    TEST 2: Chapters 4-6
Week 5: Ch. 7 (pp. 253-288), Ch. 8 (pp. 293-339)
Week 6: Ch. 9 (pp. 345-393)
    TEST 3: Chapters 7-9
Week 7: Ch. 10 (pp. 339-441), Ch. 11 (pp. 447-471)
Week 8: Ch. 11 (pp. 476-491), Ch. 12 (pp. 497-533)
    TEST 4: Chapters 10-12
Week 9: Ch. 13 (pp. 539-577), Ch. 14 (pp. 581-598)
    WRITTEN REPORT
Week 10: Ch. 14 (pp. 602-618), Ch. 15 (pp. 621-658)
    FINAL EXAM: Chapters 1-15

Exercise 1.2

Review the Syllabus

Refer to the syllabus to answer the following items with *T* (true) or *F* (false).

_____ 1. Pop quizzes count for 5 percent of the final grade.
_____ 2. The written report is due more than a week before the final exam.
_____ 3. The professor is not in her office on Thursdays.
_____ 4. Each of the four tests covers two weeks of work.
_____ 5. Two books are required for the course.

| Exercise 1.3 | **Review Your Own Course Syllabus** |

Examine your syllabus for this college reading course and answer the following questions.

1. How many weeks are in your quarter or semester?

   15 weeks

2. When is your next test, and how much does it count?

   feb 7

3. Will your next major exam have a multiple-choice or essay format?

   yes

4. What is the professor's policy about absences?

   students are expected to attend all
   scheduled classes

5. Which test or assignment constitutes the largest portion of your final grade?

   _____

   Explain. _____

   _____

6. Do you have questions that have not been answered on your syllabus? Name two issues that you would like the professor to clarify.

   I dont have any questions
   G issues that I have with
   the syllabus

   _____

   _____

Summary Points

● What is active learning?

Active learning is your own intellectual involvement with the teacher, the textbook, and fellow learners in the process of aggressively accumulating, interpreting, assimilating, and retaining new information.

● **How does the brain "pay attention"?**

Research indicates that the brain has two cooperating systems, the RAS and the cortex, that allow it to selectively attend to certain inputs and to block out others.

● **Can you do two things at once?**

The ability to do several tasks at once depends on the amount of cognitive resources required for each.

● **What are multiple intelligences?**

Gardner's theory of multiple intelligences changed the way many people view intelligence. According to his theory, there are eight types of abilities or intelligences for problem solving and understanding complex materials.

● **What are common internal and external distractors?**

External distractions are physical temptations that divert your attention. Internal distractions are mental wanderings that vie for your attention.

● **How can you improve your concentration?**

Concentration requires self-confidence, self-discipline, persistence, and focus. You can manipulate your study area to remove external distractions. You can learn to control internal distractions by organizing your daily activities, planning for academic success, and striving to meet your goals for the completion of assignments.

● **What academic behaviors can lead to college success?**

Adopt successful academic behaviors, including networking with other students and collaborating on assignments, to focus your energy and enhance your chances for success. Use your syllabus as a guide for learning.

● **Why is your syllabus important?**

Your syllabus is the learning guide designed by the instructor to document the goals and requirements of the course.

CONTEMPORARY FOCUS

New technology brings a sequence of challenges. First, it is "Please use it," and later it's "Let's not abuse it." With a World Wide Web, how can police apprehend abusers without threatening the freedom of all?

POLICE IN INDIA TO MONITOR CYBERCAFES

By Ramola Talwar Badam

Associated Press, January 18, 2004, International News

Relatively few Indians can afford home PCs, so millions go online in the nation's jammed Internet cafes, enjoying their low cost and anonymity. But police in Bombay are planning to monitor cybercafes, a move some are decrying as excessive regulation that could create a dangerous precedent.

Increasingly fearful that terrorists and other criminals are taking advantage of cybercafes, Bombay police want to require customers to show photo identification and give their home addresses. Cafe owners would have to retain such records for up to a year and show them to police on request.

The requirements initially cover Bombay's 3,000 cybercafes, used by an estimated 1.5 million, but Internet users fear that other cities will follow suit for the 200,000 cybercafes across the country.

Very few countries regulate Internet cafes, certainly among democracies like India. Among nations that have them, China was the most strident, closing down thousands in 2002 in what it called a safety crackdown.

Bombay police are convinced their proposed measures will make "wrongdoers" think twice before misusing Internet cafes.

"Terror organizations are known to use chat rooms and keep in touch by e-mail. This is a worry for the whole world, not just for Bombay," said Ramesh Mohite, assistant police inspector with the CyberCell unit. "Once cybercafes are regulated, these people may stop going there."

Collaborate

Collaborate on responses to the following questions:

■ If terrorists willfully used a Bombay cybercafe as the location from which to insert crippling computer viruses, why would the culprits be difficult to apprehend?

■ How do experts track computer hackers in the United States?

■ Why would honest customers be reluctant to show identification at a cybercafe?

Skill Development: Active Learning

Before reading the following selection, take a few minutes to analyze your active learning potential and answer the following questions.

1. **Physical Environment**   Where are you and what time is it? _____

_____

What are your external distractions? _____

_____

2. **Internal Distractions**   What is popping into your mind and interfering with your concentration? _____

3. **Spark Interest**   Glance at the selection and predict what it will cover. What do you already know about this topic? What about the selection will be of interest to you? _____

4. **Set Time Goals**   How long will it take you to read the selection? _____ minutes. To answer the questions? _____ minutes.

Increase Word Knowledge

What do you know about these words?

prying	caper	sinister	advent	miscreants
ply	defacing	unscrupulous	fraudulently	neophyte

Your instructor may give a true-false vocabulary review before or after reading.

Time Goal

Record your starting time for reading. _____:_____

SECURITY AND PRIVACY FOR COMPUTERS AND THE INTERNET

From H. L. Capron, *Computers: Tools for an Information Age*, 6th ed.

There was a time when security and privacy issues related to computers were easily managed: You simply locked the computer room door. Those centralized days are, of course, long gone. Now, in theory, anyone can hook

up to any computer from any location. In light of data communications
access, the first issue is security. The vast files of computer-stored information must be kept secure—safe from destruction, accidental damage, theft,
and even espionage.

A second issue is privacy. Private data—salaries, medical information, Social
Security numbers, bank balances, and much more—must be kept from prying
eyes. The problems are many, and the solutions are complex. The escalating
expansion of the Internet has only heightened the existing problems and
added new problems of its own.

Computer Crime

It was 5 o'clock in the morning, and 14-year-old Randy Miller was startled to
see a man climbing in his bedroom window. "FBI," the man announced, "and
that computer is mine." So ended the computer caper in San Diego where
23 teenagers, ages 13 to 17, had used their home computers to invade computer
systems as far away as Massachusetts. The teenagers were hackers, people who
attempt to gain access to computer systems illegally, usually from a personal
computer, via a data communications network.

The term *hacker* used to mean a person with significant computer expertise, but the term has taken on the more sinister meaning with the advent of
computer miscreants. In this case the hackers did not use the system to steal
money or property. But they did create fictitious accounts and destroyed or
changed some data files. The FBI's entry through the bedroom window was
calculated: The agents figured that, given even a moment's warning, the
teenagers were clever enough to alert each other via computer.

This story—except for the names—is true. Hackers ply their craft for a
variety of reasons but most often to show off for their peers or to harass people they do not like. A favorite trick, for example, is to turn a rival's telephone into a pay phone, so that when his or her parents try to dial a number
an operator interrupts to say, "Please deposit 25 cents." A hacker may have
more sinister motives, such as getting computer services without paying for
them or getting information to sell.

You will probably not be surprised to learn that hackers have invaded
Web sites. These vandals show up with what amounts to a digital spray can,
defacing sites with taunting boasts, graffiti, and their own private jokes.
Although the victims feel violated, the perpetrators view their activities
as mere pranks. In reality, such activity is antisocial and can result in
great expense.

Of all targets that hackers might choose, one would expect the venerable
New York Times to be far down the list. But, no, the *Times*'s Web site was seriously invaded. Hackers plastered messages across the screen, forcing the *Times*
to shut down the site entirely.

The *Times* was not chosen randomly, however. The hackers, it seems, were
displeased with articles in the newspaper about fellow hacker Kevin Mitnick,
who had been convicted on a series of computer-related theft and forgery

charges. (When arrested, he was in possession of over 10,000 credit card numbers taken from a customer database of an Internet service provider site.) The messages placed on the *Times*'s site demanded his release. Mitnick, however, remains in prison.

Hackers and Other Miscreants

Hacking has long been thought the domain of teenagers with time on their hands. The pattern is changing, however. A recent government survey showed that the computer systems of over half of the largest U.S. corporations had been invaded, but not by teenagers. Most intruders were competitors attempting to steal proprietary information. Even more astounding, federal investigators told a U.S. Senate hearing that the U.S. Department of Defense computers are attacked more than 200,000 times per year. Most worrisome is the emerging computer attack abilities of other nations, which, in a worst-case scenario, could seriously degrade the nation's ability to deploy and sustain military forces.

Hackers ply their craft by surprisingly low-tech means. Using what is called social engineering, a tongue-in-cheek term for con artist actions, hackers simply persuade unsuspecting people to give away their passwords over the phone. Recognizing the problem, employers are educating their employees to be alert to such scams.

Hackers are only a small fraction of the security problems. The most serious losses are caused by electronic pickpockets who are usually a good deal older and not so harmless. Consider these examples:

■ A brokerage clerk sat at his terminal in Denver and, with a few taps of the keys, transformed, 1,700 shares of his own stock, worth $1.50 per share, to the same number of shares in another company worth 10 times that much.

■ A Seattle bank employee used her electronic fund transfer code to move certain bank funds to an account held by her boyfriend as a "joke"; both the money and the boyfriend disappeared.

■ A keyboard operator in Oakland, California, changed some delivery addresses to divert several thousand dollars' worth of department store goods into the hands of accomplices.

■ A ticket clerk at the Arizona Veteran's Memorial Coliseum issued full-price basketball tickets for admission and then used her computer to record the sales as half-price tickets and pocketed the difference.

These stories point out that computer crime is not always the flashy, front-page news about geniuses getting away with millions of dollars. These people were ordinary employees in ordinary businesses—committing computer crimes. In fact, computer crime is often just white-collar crime with a new medium. Every time an employee is trained on the computer at work, he or she also gains knowledge that—potentially—could be used to harm the company.

Alleged to be one of the world's leading computer fraudsters, Maksym Vysochansky, age 25 and from Ukraine, was arrested in Bangkok. According to U.S. officials, he is thought to have been involved in computer crimes worth up to one billion dollars.
STR/AFP/Getty Images

The Changing Face of Computer Crime

Computer crime once fell into a few simple categories, such as theft of software or destruction of data. The dramatically increased access to networks has changed the focus to damage that can be done by unscrupulous people with online access. The most frequently reported computer crimes fall into these categories:

- *Credit-card fraud.* Customer numbers are floating all over public and private networks, in varying states of protection. Some are captured and used fraudulently.

- *Data communications fraud.* This category covers a broad spectrum, including piggybacking on someone else's network, the use of an office network for personal purposes, and computer-directed diversion of funds.

- *Unauthorized access to computer files.* This general snooping category covers everything from accessing confidential employee records to the theft of trade secrets and product pricing structures.

- *Unlawful copying of copyrighted software.* Whether the casual sharing of copyrighted software among friends or assembly-line copying by organized crime, unlawful copying incurs major losses for software vendors.

Keeping a Secret

Employers wish that computer passwords were better-kept secrets. Here are
some hints on password use.

- Do not name your password after your child or car or pet, an important date,
  or your phone number. Passwords that are easy to remember are also easy to
  crack. If a hacker can find out personal details about a victim, he or she can
  deduce a password from this information about 40 percent of the time.

- Make passwords as random as possible. Include both letters and numbers.
  The more characters the better. Embed at least one nonalphabetic charac-
  ter, and consider mixing uppercase and lowercase letters. Example:
  GO*tOp6.

- Keep your password in your head or in a safe. Astonishingly, an occasional
  thoughtless user will scribble the password on paper and stick it on the
  computer monitor where anyone can see it.

- Change your password often, at least once a month. In some installations,
  passwords are changed so seldom that they become known to many people, thus defeating the purpose.

- Do not fall for hacker phone scams—"social engineering"—to obtain your
  password. Typical ruses are callers posing as a neophyte employee ("Gosh,
  I'm so confused, could you talk me through it?"); a system expert ("We're
  checking a problem in the network that seems to be coming from your
  workstation. Could you please verify your password?"); a telephone company employee ("There seems to be a problem on your phone line"); or
  even an angry top manager ("This is outrageous! How do I get into these
  files anyway?").

Most people are naturally inclined to be helpful. Do not be inappropriately
helpful. Keep in mind that you will be—at the very least—embarrassed if you
are the source of information to a hacker who damages your company.

White-Hat Hackers

Faced with threats on every side, most network-laced companies have chosen
a proactive stance. Rather than waiting for the hackers and snoops and thieves
to show up, they hire professionals to beat them to it. Called *white-hat hackers*
or tiger teams, or sometimes "intrusion testers" or "hackers for hire," these
highly trained technical people are paid to try to break into a computer
system before anyone else does.

Using the same kind of finesse and tricks a hacker might, white-hat hackers
exploit the system weaknesses. Once such chinks are revealed, they can be
protected. The hacker's first approach, typically, is to access the company's
system from the Internet. The quality of security varies from company to
company. Sometimes security is fairly tight; other times, as one hacker put it,
"It's a cake-walk."

145   Sometimes companies will hire one company to establish security and then hire white-hat hackers to try to defeat it. The company may not even alert its own employees to the hacker activities, preferring to see whether the intrusions are detected and, if so, how employees react.

Time Goals

Record your finishing time: _____:_____

Calculate your total reading time: _____

Rate your concentration as high _____ medium _____ or low _____.

Recall what you have read, and review what you have learned.

Your instructor may choose to give a true-false comprehension review.

Write about the Selection

Evaluate your own computer and Internet security and privacy issues. How are you vulnerable to hackers? List and explain four ways hackers could get information about you and cause harm.

Response Suggestion: Blend the text ideas with your own thoughts, and form a list of four possible situations that could cause you harm. Explain and give examples of each.

Contemporary Link

With technology, business is becoming increasingly globalized. For example, reservation calls to Delta Airlines are now being answered by operators in India. Although you may feel far removed from the cybercafe problems of Bombay, in reality you are only one click away. What rules of identification do you think should be imposed on cybercafes in India? Why? Since you can be affected, should you have a voice? Should there be international rules for cybercafes?

Check Your Comprehension

After reading the selection, answer the following questions with *a, b, c,* or *d.* In order to help you analyze your strengths and weaknesses, the question types are indicated.

Main Idea   _____ 1. The best statement of the main idea is

a. security and privacy of computers and the Internet can be maintained by following a few simple rules of prevention.

b. millions of dollars are lost each year because of computer crimes by hackers and other miscreants.

c. computer crime is a growing and serious threat to the security and privacy of computers and the Internet.

d. in the future, computers and the Internet will be protected by white-hat hackers who defeat intrusions.

Detail   _____ 2. According to the passage, the FBI entered by the bedroom window of Randy Miller's house primarily because

a. they feared a personal attack if entering through the front door.

b. the teenagers were gathered in the bedroom.

c. they suspected that the computers at the U.S. Department of Defense had been invaded.

d. they wanted to secure the evidence before Miller could alert the other teenagers on his computer.

Detail   _____ 3. According to the passage, changes in the pattern of hacking show a progressive movement from

a. espionage to graffiti.

b. teen pranks to corporate theft and espionage.

c. stealing proprietary information to turning a rival's phone into a pay phone.

d. electronically pickpocketing money from companies to spray painting Web sites.

Detail   _____ 4. In a social engineering scam, a password is obtained by

a. asking.

b. electronically entering the system.

c. figuring it out from family records.

d. reading it off a note on a computer.

Detail   _____ 5. The term white-collar crime refers to

a. vandalism by teenagers.

b. theft by workers with office jobs.

c. spying for defense secrets by foreign agents.

d. defacing Web sites with private jokes.

Inference   _____ 6. The author implies that the motive for the hacker attack on the *New York Times* was

a. greed.

b. a teenage prank.

c. revenge.

d. to support Mitnick's imprisonment.

Inference   _____ 7. The author implies all the following about credit cards except that

a. some companies do not have sufficient protection of credit-card information.

    b. credit-card numbers are housed in many places on the Internet.

    c. money can be made from credit-card fraud.

    d. copyright theft is the first largest crime on the Internet, and credit-card theft is the second.

Detail   _____ 8. According to the author's advice on keeping your password secure, you should

    a. mix alphabetic and nonalphabetic characters.

    b. change it no more than once a year.

    c. use your phone number or family names.

    d. write your password down and keep it in the office.

Detail   _____ 9. White-hat hackers are hired by companies to

    a. invade the computer security of a rival company.

    b. find ways to infiltrate the computer security of the company that hired them.

    c. locate and prosecute rival computer hackers.

    d. train technical people to become computer hackers.

Inference   _____ 10. The underlying reason for the author to present the four different examples of electronic pickpocketing is to

    a. show four different ways ordinary people can commit computer crimes.

    b. compare and contrast adult and teenage hackers.

    c. show that people who commit computer crimes are usually detected and exposed.

    d. calculate the revenue that companies lose through computer theft by employees.

Answer the following with *T* (true) or *F* (false).

Inference   _____ 11. The author would be more likely to compare the old key to the computer room to your current password than to your computer's speed and power.

Inference   _____ 12. The author implies that teenage hackers are not serious threats on the Internet and should not be prosecuted.

Inference   _____ 13. The reader can conclude that companies always alert employees when white-hat hackers are hired.

Inference   _____ 14. The reader can conclude that computer hacking that crosses state lines is a federal offense.

Inference   _____ 15. The author implies that security and privacy issues will lead to a gradual decline of Internet popularity.

Build Your Vocabulary

According to the way the italicized word was used in the selection, select *a, b, c,* or *d* for the word or phrase that gives the best definition. The number in parentheses indicates the line of the passage in which the word is located.

_____ 1. "kept from *prying* eyes" (9)
   a. dishonest
   b. curious
   c. disapproving
   d. illegal

_____ 2. "ended the computer *caper*" (15)
   a. illegal escapade
   b. arrest
   c. investigation
   d. trail

_____ 3. "more *sinister* meaning" (21)
   a. humorous
   b. significant
   c. relevant
   d. evil

_____ 4. "with the *advent*" (21)
   a. coming
   b. violation
   c. assault
   d. domination

_____ 5. "computer *miscreants*" (22)
   a. mistakes
   b. investigators
   c. villains
   d. coming

_____ 6. "*ply* their craft" (27)
   a. learn
   b. perform
   c. share
   d. desire

_____ 7. "*defacing* sites" (36)
   a. canceling
   b. locating
   c. monitoring
   d. disfiguring

_____ 8. "by *unscrupulous* people" (90)
   a. unethical
   b. ignorant
   c. knowledgeable
   d. unknowing

_____ 9. "used *fraudulently*" (94)
   a. frequently
   b. occasionally
   c. mysteriously
   d. deceitfully

_____ 10. "as a *neophyte* employee" (122)
   a. sneaky
   b. beginner
   c. disloyal
   d. careless

Skill Development

Record your time for answering the questions: _____:_____

Calculate your total time for reading and answering the questions:

_____

What changes would you make to enhance your concentration on the new selection? _____

_____

Search **the Net**

To challenge your computer skills, research skills, and critical thinking skills, most of the reading selections in this book will be accompanied by an Internet exercise. You will use the Internet, also known as the World Wide Web (WWW) or the Web, to research a question and find information at different Web sites. You can conduct your own search or use sites suggested on this textbook's companion Web site, http://www.ablongman.com/smith/. You will then blend the new information with your own thoughts to produce a written response. These Internet exercises can be done individually or as group activities. To help you get started, read the following suggestions for successful Internet searches.

Secrets of a Successful Search

Searching for information on the Internet can be both rewarding and frustrating. The key to avoiding frustration, or at least minimizing it, is organization. Organization requires a plan, an ongoing search strategy, and good record keeping. A successful Internet search consists of the following five steps:

1. Make a plan.

2. Search and search again.

3. Read selectively.

4. Record as you go.

5. Consider the source.

1. Make a Plan

Locating information on the Web requires the use of a search engine such as Google, Yahoo, AltaVista, Excite, Infoseek, Dogpile, or Lycos. Once you have selected a search engine, enter a search term or phrase, which may consist of one or more words, a phrase, or a name. The search engine will comb the Internet for sites that contain your term or phrase, count them, and display the best ten to twenty-five sites (called "hits") on your computer screen. A successful search depends on the wording of your chosen terms and the way you enter them.

For serious research, experts recommend using a notebook to organize your search strategy. Begin by writing down your general research topic and related questions. Next, jot down all the key terms you can think of that relate to your topic, and create additional questions if necessary. At this beginning point, prior knowledge of the topic is extremely helpful. If your knowledge of the topic is limited, however, you can familiarize yourself with related terminology, names, and events by performing a quick search to select and read a few sites on the topic.

Sample Search Notebook Page

Research topic	Computer crimes
Research questions	How are computers used to commit crimes? How can someone prevent being the victim of a computer crime?
What I already know	Hacker—someone who attempts to gain access to computer systems illegally White-hat hacker—computer expert hired to find weaknesses in computer systems Data communications fraud—piggybacking on someone else's network; use of an office network for personal purposes; computer-directed diversion of funds Social engineering—hacker phone scams

Search Terms	**Notes and Web sites**
■ *Computer crimes*	New government agency (http://www.cybercrime.gov/) International organization that fights Internet crimes (http://www.web-police.org/) Database of fraudulent Internet activities (http://www.ScamWatch.com/) Internet law-enforcement site (http://www.intergov.org/)
■ *Data communications fraud*	Provides information about preventing telecommunications fraud (http://www.tariffpatrol.com/index.cfm?ID=9)
■ *Preventing Internet crimes*	Department of Justice information on preventing Internet crimes against children (http://www.ojp.usdoj.gov/ovc/publications/bulletins/internet_2_2001/welcome.html)
■ *Internet privacy*	Guide to online privacy resources (http://epic.org/privacy/privacy_resources_faq.html) Provides legal information about internet privacy issues (http://www.netatty.com/privacy/privacy.html) Instant analysis of the privacy of one's Internet connection (http://www.Privacy.net/analyze/)
■ *Encryption*	Center for Internet Security Expertise (http://www.cert.org/) UC Davis Computer Security Laboratory (http://seclab.cs.ucdavis.edu/) Information on electronic privacy issues (http://www.epic.org/crypto/)
Research topic	Maternal instincts of birds
Research questions	What are some unusual maternal instincts of birds? How do these instincts aid in the survival of the species?

What I already know	Birds and other animals have some unusual instincts such as imprinting. Imprinting is the process where attachments are formed by young birds on the first social objects they encounter. Konrad Lorenz led the research on imprinting using goslings.
Search Terms	**Notes and Web sites**
■ *Bird behavior*	Poor results—sites are related to pet bird behaviors
■ *Maternal instincts*	Only found instincts on cows, pigs, and sheep
■ *Bird instincts*	Host-parasite conflict (http://birding.miningco.com/library/weekly/aa060797.htm)
■ *Maternal instincts of birds*	Killdeer mother feigns broken wing (http://www.birdwatching.com/stories/killdeer.html) Personal report (http://www.newton.dep.anl.gov/natbltn/400-499/nb482.htm) Very brief description (http://www.baylink.org/wpc/killdeer.html)

Decide on a few key words that you believe will help you locate the information you want, and use them as search terms. Using a two-column format in your notebook, list each search term on the left side of the paper and allow room on the right side for writing the locations of Web sites and comments about the site. For example, if your research topic is computer crimes and prevention, your list of search terms may include computer hackers, Internet security, social engineering, and computer scams. A sample search notebook page is illustrated above.

Check with your college library on how to gain access to online databases containing online journals, collections, and other resources that can provide a wealth of information. Some of the most commonly used databases are listed in the Reader's Tip.

2. Search and Search Again

One of the most important tasks in conducting a successful search is to enter search terms that will produce the information that you want. Search terms that are too *wide* may bring thousands of hits. Some researchers suggest beginning with a *broad* search (a single term) and then narrowing the search, whereas others suggest beginning with a *narrow* search (multiple terms) and broadening it later. Both methods are acceptable, and you can experiment to discover which method works best for you. Be flexible in trying new terms and different combinations. In the previous example, searching for *prosecution, computer,* or *crimes* alone will bring a multitude of hits. Narrowing your search by typing in *prosecution for computer crimes* should produce sites more attuned to your research. Entering too many terms, however, may result in no hits or

> ### READER'S TIP
>
> ## Popular College Databases
>
> ◆ Galileo
>
> ◆ Periodical abstracts
>
> ◆ Newspaper abstracts
>
> ◆ LexisNexis Academic Universe
>
> ◆ MLA Bibliography
>
> ◆ ABI Inform
>
> ◆ PsycFIRST
>
> ◆ Social Science abstracts
>
> ◆ ERIC
>
> ◆ Medline

only limited information. Searches also provide additional terms to pursue. More search suggestions are offered in the Reader's Tip.

> ### READER'S TIP
>
> ## Manipulating the Search
>
> In our sample case, by entering *computer crimes* in the search term box, you will receive all sites that contain either *computer, crimes,* or *computer crimes.* Placing quotation marks around a phrase or the term—that is, *"computer crimes"*—will pull up only those sites containing the full term. Another way to find suitable sites is to add an AND, +, OR, or NOT in the phrase.

At some point, you may need to find the home page of a particular company—for example, Harley-Davidson. If your search does not produce the home page of the company, try to guess or work out the company's Uniform Resource Locator (URL). Remember that a simple URL is composed of four or five parts. The first part is usually *http://. Http* is a protocol or mechanism used by browsers to communicate with Web sites. The second part is *www* for the World Wide Web. The third part is usually the name or abbreviation of a company, product, or institution. The fourth part is the site's designation or

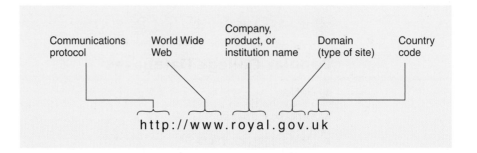

type, such as http://www.cnn.com for the CNN News Corporation and http://www.whitehouse.gov for the White House.

The three-letter designation at the end of the URL, sometimes called the *domain*, depends on the type of site. For example, *gov* is for government, *org* is for organization, *com* is for commercial site, and *edu* is for education. Some URLs have a fifth part; they end in a two-letter code to signify a country. For example, *uk* means *United Kingdom* in the Web site for the British monarchy, http://www.royal.gov.uk (see the diagram above).

3. Read Selectively

The amount of information on the Internet can be overwhelming. Rarely, however, is it desirable or practical to read all the available information on a subject. Read selectively to narrow the scope of your research. After entering a search term and receiving a list of possible sites, scan the list of hits to look for key words relating to your search needs. The sites that contain the most information are usually listed first. Some search engines, such as Excite and Infoseek, will place a percentage value next to the site link indicating the like-lihood that the information being sought is located at that site. In addition, a summary of the site may also be included.

After selecting a Web site or link that appears to have the information you need, study the table of contents or outline and move around the site to deter-mine its layout or structure. Check secondary links that look promising. Skim definitions, statements, quotes, and other text while asking yourself, "Is this the information I am looking for?" Web pages follow some uniform patterns, but styles vary because there are no requirements for a standard format. Most Web sites, however, contain a title, subtitles, links, a table of contents, and an outline or introductory paragraph.

4. Record As You Go

As you discover sites, make sure to record them in your notebook. Once you have searched a term, check it off on your term list and note the results of the search next to the term. This will help you avoid searching for the same term a second time. Include the site location (the URL), particularly if you would like to return to the site or include it as a reference. If you are trying to locate a specific URL, such as a Web site listed in this textbook, do not be surprised if the URL has changed. Unfortunately, site locations often change without notice, thus making mastery of the steps in the search process even more important.

There are three ways of noting the site: (1) by recording the URL in your notebook next to the term, (2) by printing out the site material, since the URL is usually listed at the top of the printout, or (3) by **bookmarking** or saving the site so you can return to it at a later date. If you are using a computer in a location that you may not again have access to, save your bookmarks on a disk.

5. Consider the Source

Information on the Internet, although abundant, may not necessarily be accurate. In 1998, a U.S. congressman saw an obituary for a prominent entertainer posted on the Web and announced the death to Congress. As it turned out, the obituary had been posted by accident, and the entertainer, comedian Bob Hope, was quite alive and hitting golf balls at the time.

Unfortunately, much of the information posted on the Web can be misleading, unfounded, or based on personal opinions and beliefs rather than facts. One of the best ways to avoid collecting poor data on the Internet is to use good judgment. In the case of the congressman, he could have avoided embarrassment by confirming the information.

When reviewing information from a Web site, ask yourself, "What person, company, or agency is providing the information?" and "Is this a reliable source?" Reliable information usually comes from reliable sources. Information gathered from sites such as news stations, libraries, city newspapers, and government databases is probably more reliable than that from obscure sites with no obvious signs of credibility. Finally, when you are doing a research paper, do not rely entirely on Internet sources. Use books, journals, and other reliable print sources as well.

Search the Net

Use a search engine such as Google, Yahoo, AltaVista, Excite, Infoseek, Dogpile, or Lycos to find information on recent computer viruses. List three different viruses, explain how each was spread, and describe the damage caused by each. For suggested Web sites and other research activities, go to http://www.ablongman.com/smith/.

Concept Prep

for Computer Science

Why learn concepts in different academic areas?

Your success in college reading will be measured by your ultimate success in the academic courses that you will take, such as psychology, history, sociology, and biology. The goal of this text is to prepare you to apply your skills in the courses required for your graduation so you will make good grades without struggling. In reality, both your skills and your knowledge interact to help you achieve that success.

As you will learn in Chapter 3, prior knowledge, or what you already know in a subject area, is a significant factor in your academic performance. Thus, in order to enhance your background knowledge and boost your success, key academic subject concepts are presented at the end of most of the longer reading selections in this textbook. Study these concepts and arm yourself with valuable knowledge for the courses ahead. The following concepts provide background in computer science.

What is the Internet?

The **Internet** is a collection of about 25,000 computer networks, owned by no one with no central headquarters. It is used globally for communication.

Who invented the Internet?

The Internet grew out of the **Cold War** of the 1950s, a period of icy relationships between the United States and communist countries. During this time, people feared a nuclear attack by the Soviet Union. The U.S. Department of Defense wanted to create a safe way to communicate in case a bomb wiped out all computing capabilities. The RAND Corporation worked with the government to design a message system that would rely on many computers scattered in different places around the world. No single computer would be in charge. Thus, if one computer failed, the others could carry messages by alternative routes. This system, established in 1969, was used by defense contractors and university researchers as well as the military. It was twenty-five years before the general public even knew it existed.

Tim Berners-Lee speaks at the Internet Caucus Speakers Series and explains the importance of keeping the Web universal as the technology moves forward.
AFP/Corbis

In 1990, **Tim Berners-Lee**, a Swiss physicist, thought his research would be easier if he could link quickly to his colleagues' computers around the world in links that he saw as a spider web. The home site he created is thus considered the birthplace of the World Wide Web. Lee was a key figure in popularizing the Internet.

What were the new business opportunities associated with computers and the Internet?

- **Steven Jobs** founded Apple Computer and popularized the personal computer (PC), making low-cost computing available to the general public.

- **Bill Gates** and his friend Paul Allen dropped out of college in 1975 to work on writing software (computer instructions) for a company in Albuquerque, New Mexico. They kept the rights to their work and formed their own company, called **Microsoft.** Later Gates and Allen secured an opportunity to write an operating system for IBM, a large computer manufacturer. The operating system, MS-DOS, launched their rise to fame and fortune.

- **Silicon Valley** is a high-tech, affluent region near San Francisco where the electronics computer industry is centered. The name refers to the element **silicon,** which is used in manufacturing computers.

- The **Ethernet** is a popular local area network that uses high-speed network cables.

- **Spamming** is mass advertising on the Internet through e-mail.

- Dot-com entrepreneurs **are investors who take big risks to start Internet businesses.**

Source: Adapted from H. L. Capron, *Computers: Tools for an Information Age,* 6th ed.

REVIEW QUESTIONS

After studying the material above, answer the following questions:

1. What is the Internet? *is a collection of about 25*

2. Why did the Internet start? _____

3. What did Tim Berners-Lee do for the Internet? _____

4. What did Steven Jobs do? _____

5. What did Bill Gates do? _____

6. What is Silicon Valley? _____

Your instructor may choose to give a true-false review of these computer science concepts.

CONTEMPORARY FOCUS

After centuries of breeding, dogs and cats were domesticated into household pets. Wild animals, however, are another story. Unfortunately some people think that the instinctive behaviors of wild animals can be reprogrammed with a lot of tender love and care. Only when the animals attack do owners discover that instincts prevail.

LIONS, TIGERS WILD ANIMALS; NOT PETS

By Joe Bauman

Deseret Morning News (Salt Lake City, Utah), November 3, 2003

The tiger that attacked Roy Horn was not trying to protect him, as one report suggested; it was intent on killing him.

That's the assessment of Barrie K. Gilbert, one of Utah's most renowned animal behaviorists. He says the attack underscores the lesson that humans should not have close contact with certain large carnivores like tigers, lions and mountain lions. In fact, private ownership of these animals should be outlawed, he says.

According to news reports, on Oct. 3 Horn was attacked by a 600-pound white tiger named Montecore while performing before a sold-out audience of 1,500. The tiger lunged at the famed illusionist and dragged him offstage. An audience member said Horn looked like a rag doll.

Wild animals have instincts that have served them for thousands of generations. This internal programming to attack or hunt cannot be erased by making a pet of a cub and caring for it for several years.

Big carnivores are not the same as domestic animals or pets that have lived with humans since ancient times.

Some of the most dangerous wild animals are deer and elk. Someone may find an orphan fawn and raise it but still end up seriously injured.

"Imprinting with deer and elk and cattle is not a good idea with males, because they treat you as a competitor," Gilbert noted. If the creature accepts you as one of its kind, it means "you have to be part of how they socialize—which is often by fighting."

During the mating season a deer may attack its competitors. "The biggest killer of zookeepers in Europe, I'm told, is male deer," Gilbert said.

If zookeepers get into the deer pen at the wrong time, "that deer is dangerous and ends up stabbing people with antlers," he added.

When Horn was attacked, Montecore grabbed his neck with what is known as a "killing bite," Gilbert said.

"That's a particularly harsh bite that clamps. . . . That's not play behavior."

The conical teeth will chomp down hard on the neck of prey, separating the spine. The cat holds on until the prey dies. Horn was rescued yet still suffered massive injuries.

"That cat really clamped down," Gilbert added. "This is not how a cat will carry one of its kittens off to safety."

Collaborate

Collaborate on responses to the following questions:

■ What is an instinct?

■ Would you feel safe in the front row of the audience with white tigers on stage?

■ Why are deer the biggest killers of European zookeepers?

Skill Development: Active Learning

Before reading the following selection, take a few minutes to analyze your active learning potential and answer the following questions.

1. **Physical Environment**   Where are you and what time is it? _____

   _____

   What are your external distractions? _____

   _____

2. **Internal Distractions**   What is popping into your mind and interfering with your concentration? _____

3. **Spark Interest**   Glance at the selection and predict what it will cover. What do you already know about the topic? What about the selection will be of interest to you? _____

4. **Set Time Goals**   How long will it take you to read the selection?

   _____ minutes. To answer the questions? _____ minutes.

Increase Word Knowledge

What do you know about these words?

hypothesis	incubator	genetic	instinctive	sustain
restrained	inseminate	disrupted	irreversible	coax

Your instructor may give a true-false vocabulary review before or after reading.

Time Goal

Record your starting time for reading. _____:_____

CRITICAL-PERIOD HYPOTHESIS
From James V. McConnell, *Understanding Human Behavior*

There is some evidence that the best time for a child to learn a given skill is at the time the child's body is just mature enough to allow mastery of the behavior in question. This belief is often called the *critical-period hypothesis*—that is, the belief that an organism must have certain experi-
5   ences at a *particular time* in its developmental sequence if it is to reach its mature state.

There are many studies from animal literature supporting the critical-period hypothesis. For instance, German scientist Konrad Lorenz discovered many years ago that birds, such as ducks and geese, will follow the first moving
10   object they see after they are hatched. Usually the first thing they see is their mother, of course, who has been sitting on the eggs when they are hatched. However, Lorenz showed that if he took goose eggs away from the mother and hatched them in an incubator, the fresh-hatched *goslings* would follow him around instead.
15   After the goslings had waddled along behind Lorenz for a few hours, they acted as if they thought he was their mother and that they were humans, not geese. When Lorenz returned the goslings to their real mother, they ignored her. Whenever Lorenz appeared, however, they became very excited and flocked to him for protection and affection. It was as if the visual image of the
20   first object they saw moving had become so strongly *imprinted* on their con-sciousness that, forever after, that object was "mother."

During the past 20 years or so, scientists have spent a great deal of time studying *imprinting* as it now is called. The effect occurs in many but not in all types of birds, and it also seems to occur in mammals such as sheep and seals.
25   Whether it occurs in humans is a matter for debate. Imprinting is very strong in ducks and geese, however, and they have most often been the subjects for study.

The urge to imprint typically reaches its strongest peak 16 to 24 hours after the baby goose is hatched. During this period, the baby bird has an innate ten-dency to follow anything that moves, and will chase after its mother (if she is

Lorenz swims with the goslings who have imprinted on him.
Nina Leen/Time Life Pictures/Getty Images

30 around), or a human, a bouncing football or a brightly painted tin can that the experimenter dangles in front of the gosling. The more the baby bird struggles to follow after this moving object, the more strongly the young animal becomes imprinted to the object. Once the goose has been imprinted, this very special form of learning cannot easily be reversed. For example, the geese
35 that first followed Lorenz could not readily be trained to follow their mother instead; indeed, when these geese were grown and sexually mature, they showed no romantic interest in other geese. Instead, they attempted to court and mate with humans.

If a goose is hatched in a dark incubator and is not allowed to see the world
40 until two or three days later, imprinting often does not occur. At first it was thought that the "critical period" had passed and hence the bird could never become imprinted to anything. Now we know differently. The innate urge to follow moving objects does appear to reach a peak in geese 24 hours after they are hatched, but it does not decline thereafter. Rather, a second innate
45 urge—that of fearing and avoiding new objects—begins to develop, and within 48 hours after hatching typically overwhelms the prior tendency the bird had to follow after anything that moves. To use a human term, the goose's *attitude* toward strange things is controlled by its genetic blueprint—at first it is attracted to, then it becomes afraid of, new objects in its environment. As we
50 will see in a moment, these conflicting "attitudes" may explain much of the data on "critical periods" in both animals and humans.

How might these two apparently conflicting
behavioral tendencies help a baby goose survive
in its usual or natural environment?

In other experiments, baby chickens have been hatched and raised in the dark for the first several days of their lives. Chicks have an innate tendency to peck at small objects soon after they are hatched—an instinctive behavior
55 pattern that helps them get food as soon as they are born. In the dark, of course, they cannot see grain lying on the ground and hence do not peck (they must be hand-fed in the dark during this period of time). Once brought into the light, these chicks do begin to peck, but they do so clumsily and ineffectively, as if their "critical period" for learning the pecking skill had
60 passed. Birds such as robins and blue jays learn to fly at about the time their wings are mature enough to sustain flight (their parents often push them from the nest as a means of encouraging them to take off on their own). If these young birds are restrained and not allowed to fly until much later, their flight patterns are often clumsy and they do not usually gain the necessary
65 skills to become good fliers.

The "Maternal Instinct" in Rats

Suppose we take a baby female rat from its mother at the moment of its birth and raise the rat pup "by bottle" until it is sexually mature. Since it has never seen other rats during its entire life (its eyes do not open until several days after birth), any sexual or maternal behavior that it shows will presumably be due to the natural unfolding of its genetic blueprint—and not due to learning or imitation. Now, suppose we inseminate this hand-raised female rat artificially—to make certain that she continues to have no contact with other rats. Will she build a nest for her babies before they are born, following the usual pattern of female rats, and will she clean and take care of them during and after the birth itself?

The answer to that question is yes—*if.* If, when the young female rat was growing up, there were objects such as sticks and sawdust and string and small blocks of wood in her cage, and which she played with. Then, when inseminated, the pregnant rat will use these "toys" to build a nest. If the rat grows up in a bare cage, she won't build a nest *even though we give her the materials to do so once she is impregnated.* If this same rat is forced to wear a stiff rubber collar around her neck when she is growing up—so that she cannot clean her sex organs, as rats normally do—she will not usually lick her newborn babies clean *even though we take off the rubber collar a day or so before she gives birth.* The genetic blueprint always operates best within a particular environmental setting. If an organism's early environment is abnormal or particularly unusual, later "innate" behavior patterns may be disrupted.

Overcoming the "Critical Period"

All of these examples may appear to support the "critical-period" hypothesis—that there is one time in an organism's life when it is best suited to learn a particular skill. These studies might also seem to violate the general rule that an organism can "catch up" if its development has been delayed. However, the truth is more complicated (as always) than it might seem from the experiments we have cited so far.

Baby geese will normally not imprint if we restrict their visual experiences for the first 48 hours of their lives—their fear of strange objects is by then too great. However, if we give the geese tranquilizing drugs to help overcome their fear, they can be imprinted a week or more after hatching. Once imprinting has taken place, it may seem to be irreversible. But we can occasionally get a bird imprinted on a human to accept a goose as its mother, if we coax it enough and give it massive rewards for approaching or following its natural mother. Chicks raised in darkness become clumsy eaters—but what do you think would happen if we gave them special training in how to peck, rather than simply leaving the matter to chance? Birds restrained in the nest too long apparently learn other ways of getting along and soon come to fear heights; what do you think would happen if we gave these birds tranquilizers and rewarded each tiny approximation to flapping their wings properly?

There is not much scientific evidence that human infants have the same types of "critical periods" that birds and rats do. By being born without strong innate behavior patterns (such as imprinting), we seem to be better able to adjust and survive in the wide variety of social environments human babies are born into. Like many other organisms, however, children do appear to have an inborn tendency to imitate the behavior of other organisms around them. A young rat will learn to press a lever in a Skinner box much faster if it is first allowed to watch an adult rat get food by pressing the lever. This learning is even quicker if the adult rat happens to be the young animal's mother. Different species of birds have characteristic songs or calls. A European thrush, for example, has a song pattern fairly similar to a thrush in the United States, but both sound quite different from blue jays. There are *local dialects* among songbirds, however, and these are learned through imitation. If a baby thrush is isolated from its parents and exposed to blue jay calls when it is very young, the thrush will sound a little like a blue jay but a lot like other thrushes when it grows up. And parrots, of course, pick up very human-sounding speech patterns if they are raised with humans rather than with other parrots.

Time Goals

Record your finishing time: _____:_____ Calculate your total reading time: _____

Rate your concentration as high _____ medium _____ or low_____.

Recall what you have read, and review what you have learned.

Your instructor may choose to give you a true-false comprehension review.

Write about the Selection

Provide proof that a critical period exists during which an organism must have certain experiences to reach its normal mature state.

Response Suggestion: Review the selection and number the experiments that provide proof of the hypothesis. Define the hypothesis and describe three to five supporting examples from the text.

Contemporary Link

Using the studies on the critical period for the development of instinctive behaviors in chicks, rats, and birds, explain why you think there should or should not be laws forbidding the ownership of large animals. If Horn owned the tiger since birth, why do you think Montecore attacked?

Check Your Comprehension

Main Idea

After reading the selection, answer the following questions with *a, b, c,* or *d.*

_____ 1. The best statement of the main idea of this selection is
  a. studies show that goslings can be imprinted on humans.
  b. a particular few days of an animal's life can be a crucial time for developing long-lasting "natural" behavior.

    c. imprinting seems to occur in mammals but is very strong in ducks and geese.

    d. the "crucial period" of imprinting is important but can be overcome with drugs.

Detail

_____ 2. The critical-period hypothesis is the belief that
    a. there is a "prime time" to develop certain skills.
    b. most learning occurs during the first few days of life.
    c. fear can inhibit early learning.
    d. the "maternal instinct" is not innate but is learned.

Detail

_____ 3. In Lorenz's studies, after the goslings imprinted on him, they would do all of the following except
    a. follow him around.
    b. flock to him for protection.
    c. return to their real mother for affection.
    d. become excited when Lorenz appeared.

Detail

_____ 4. The author points out that in Lorenz's studies, the early imprinting of geese with humans
    a. was easily reversed with training.
    b. caused the geese to be poor mothers.
    c. later produced sexually abnormal behavior in the geese.
    d. made it difficult for the goslings to learn to feed themselves.

Inference

_____ 5. The author suggests that by 48 hours, the innate urge to imprint in geese is
    a. decreased significantly.
    b. increased.
    c. overwhelmed by the avoidance urge.
    d. none of the above.

Inference

_____ 6. In a small gosling's natural environment, the purpose of the avoidance urge that develops within 48 hours of hatching might primarily be to help it
    a. learn only the behavior of its species.
    b. follow only one mother.
    c. escape its genetic blueprint.
    d. stay away from predators.

Inference

_____ 7. The author suggests that there is a critical period for developing all the following except
    a. the desire to eat.
    b. pecking.
    c. flying.
    d. cleaning the young.

Inference _____ 8. The studies with rats suggest that nest-building and cleaning behaviors are
    a. totally innate behaviors.
    b. totally learned behaviors.
    c. a combination of innate and learned behaviors.
    d. neither innate nor learned behaviors.

Detail _____ 9. Abnormal imprinting during the critical period can later be overcome by using all of the following except
    a. tranquilizing drugs.
    b. natural tendencies.
    c. special training.
    d. massive reward.

Inference _____ 10. Because humans do not seem to have strong innate behavior patterns, the author suggests that humans
    a. are better able to adapt to changing environments.
    b. have more difficulty learning early motor skills.
    c. find adjustment to change more difficult than animals.
    d. need more mothering than animals.

Answer the following with *T* (true) or *F* (false).

Detail _____ 11. The author states that whether imprinting occurs in humans is a matter of debate.

Inference _____ 12. The author implies that a goose can be imprinted on a painted tin can.

Inference _____ 13. In the author's opinion, studies show that organisms can catch up adequately without special training when skill development has been delayed past the critical period.

Inference _____ 14. If an abandoned bird egg is hatched and raised solely by a human, the author suggests that the bird will be abnormal.

Inference _____ 15. The author suggests that the urge to imitate is innate in both humans and animals.

Build Your Vocabulary

According to the way the italicized word was used in the selection, select *a, b, c,* or *d* for the word or phrase that gives the best definition. The number in parentheses indicates the line of the passage in which the word is located.

_____ 1. "The critical-period
hypothesis" (3)
a. association
b. tentative assumption
c. law
d. dilemma

_____ 2. "in an _incubator_" (13)
a. cage
b. electric enlarger
c. nest
d. artificial hatching
apparatus

_____ 3. "its _genetic_ blueprint"
(48)
a. sexual
b. emotional
c. hereditary
d. earned

_____ 4. "an _instinctive_ behavior
pattern" (54)
a. desirable
b. innate
c. early
d. newly acquired

_____ 5. "to _sustain_ flight" (61)
a. support
b. imitate
c. begin
d. imagine

_____ 6. "birds are _restrained_" (63)
a. pressured
b. pushed
c. held back
d. attacked

_____ 7. "suppose we _inseminate_" (71)
a. imprison
b. artificially impregnate
c. injure
d. frighten

_____ 8. "may be _disrupted_" (87)
a. thrown into disorder
b. repeated
c. lost
d. destroyed

_____ 9. "seem to be _irreversible_"(98)
a. temporary
b. changeable
c. frequent
d. permanent

_____ 10. "_coax_ it enough" (100)
a. encourage fondly
b. punish
c. feed
d. drill

Time Goals

Record your time for answering the questions: _____:_____

Calculate your total time for reading and answering the questions: _____

What changes would you make to enhance your concentration on the
new selection?

Search the Net

Use a search engine such as Google, AltaVista, Excite, Infoseek, Dogpile, or
Lycos to find autobiographical information on Konrad Lorenz. Describe the
experiences that led to his interest in imprinting. For suggested Web sites and
other research activities, go to http://www.ablongman.com/smith/.

Concept Prep

for Psychology

What does psychology cover?

Psychology is the scientific study of behavior and the mind. Behavior is observed, studied, and measured with the ultimate objective of explaining why people act and think as they do. Special areas that you will study in psychology include the following:

Biological psychology: How do your genes, brain, and hormones affect your behavior?

Behavioral psychology: What stimulus in the environment triggers your response?

Cognitive psychology: How do you think and remember?

Humanistic psychology: Can you be anything you want to be? Do you control your destiny?

Life span psychology: How do thoughts, desires, and actions differ in infancy, childhood, adolescence, adulthood, and old age?

Cross-cultural psychology: How do cultural differences affect your behavior and sense of self?

Why is Freud so important?

Sigmund Freud was a physician in Vienna, Austria, who formulated a theory of personality and a form of psychotherapy called **psychoanalysis**. Freud emerged as a leader in modern psychology and wrote twenty-four books popularizing his theories. After Freud's death in 1939, psychologists questioned many of his ideas and criticized him because of his focus on sexual desires. Still, Freud has contributed many ideas to our culture and words to our vocabulary.

Freud's theories evolved from observing and treating patients who suffered ailments without any visible physical basis but who responded favorably to hypnosis. He believed in treating their problems by tracing difficulties back to childhood experiences. Freud also believed in **dream interpretation,** a process in which the unconscious mind provides clues to psychological problems.

Freud's basic theories suggest that people are driven from early childhood by three principal unconscious

Sigmund Freud theorized that mundane behavior has underlying psychological causes.
akg-images

forces: the **id** (an animal instinct and desire for pleasure), the **ego** (the sense of self that fights the id for reasonable compromises), and the **superego** (the social feeling of right and wrong and community values). Other terms that Freud established include **pleasure principle,** which refers to an instinctive need to satisfy the id regardless of the consequences; **libido,** which refers to sexual drive; and **egotism,** which refers to a sense of self-importance and conceit.

Other words we use today emerge from Freud's five stages of personality development: *oral, anal, phallic, latency*, and *genital*. An **oral personality** is fixated in the first stage of sucking and is satisfied by the pleasures of the mouth—for example, talking, smoking, eating, and chewing gum excessively. An **anal personality** is associated with the childhood period that involves bowel control and toilet training and as an adult is excessively focused on details and orderliness. Another term Freud popularized is **Oedipus complex,** which suggests that a young boy has a sexual desire for his mother. Finally, Freud was the originator of the **Freudian slip,** which is a misspoken word—such as *sex* for *six*—that reveals unconscious thoughts.

Who was Carl Jung?

Carl Jung was a Swiss psychologist who classified people as **introverts** (shy) or **extroverts** (outgoing). Jung was one of the original followers of Freud but later broke with him. Adding to Freud's theory of repressed personal experiences, Jung believed that we also inherit the memories and symbols of ancestors in an **inherited collective unconscious**. He believed this was exhibited in an inborn fear of snakes or spiders. Jung also developed theories about concrete and abstract learning stages. Many of his theories are used as a basis for the Myers-Briggs Type Indicator.

REVIEW QUESTIONS

After studying the material, answer the following questions:

1. Using visual images on concept cards to improve memory of vocabulary words suggests what area of psychology? _____

2. Desiring a rocky road ice cream cone after passing a Baskin-Robbins store suggests what area of psychology? _____

3. Mapping physical activity in different areas of the brain as people read or listen to music suggests what area of psychology? _____

4. Attending a motivational seminar to become salesperson of the year suggests what area of psychology? _____

5. What is psychoanalysis? _____
_____

6. What are the goals of the id, ego, and superego? _____
_____

7. How does Freud relate dreams to reality? _____
_____

8. Why did some psychologists break with Freud? _____
_____

9. How do the theories of Jung and Freud differ? _____
_____

10. What is Jung's inherited collective unconscious? _____
_____

Your instructor may choose to give a true-false review of these psychology concepts.

Vocabulary

- How do you remember new words?
- What are context clues?
- Why learn prefixes, roots, and suffixes?
- What will you find in a dictionary?
- What is a glossary?
- What is a thesaurus?
- What are analogies?
- What are acronyms?
- How are transitional words used?

© 2005 by Pearson Education, Inc.

Freedom Quilt (detail) by Jessie B. Telfair, Parrott, Georgia, 1983. Cotton with muslin backing and pencil inscription, 73 x 75". Collection American Folk Art Museum. Gift of Judith Alexander in loving memory of her sister, Rebecca Alexander, 2004.9.1. Photo: Gavin Ashworth.

53

Remembering New Words

Have you ever made lists of unknown words that you wanted to remember? Did you dutifully write down the word, a colon, and a definition, and promise to review the list at night before going to bed? Did it work? Probably not! Memorization can be an effective cramming strategy, but it does not seem to produce long-term results. Recording only the word and definition does not establish the associations necessary for long-term memory.

Think smart and use clever memory techniques to expand your vocabulary. With these tricks, or **mnemonic devices**, you visualize and organize units into new relationships. You can also use rhymes to tie words together. For example, to remember the word *mnemonics*, think of Nem-on-ic as in remembering by putting a name on it. To remember that *suppression* means to force out bad thoughts, visualize SUPerman PRESSing evil thoughts out of someone's head. A noted speaker, John Berthoud, usually begins a speech by explaining how to pronounce and remember his last name, which is French. He tells audiences to think, "Not one bear, but two" or to think, "You are naked, and I am bare, too." The following suggestions can help you associate and organize.

Associate Words in Phrases. Never record a word in isolation. Think of the word and record it in a phrase that suggests its meaning. The phrase may be part of the sentence in which you first encountered the word, or it may be a vivid creation of your own imagination. Such a phrase provides a setting for the word and enriches the links to your long-term memory.

For example, the word *caravel* means a small sailing ship. Record the word in a phrase that creates a memorable setting, like "a caravan of gliding caravels on the horizon of the sea."

Associate Words with Rhymes or Sounds. Link the sound of a new word with a rhyming word or phrase. The brain appreciates connections and patterns. For example, the word *hoard*, which means to accumulate or stockpile, can be linked with *stored* as in "He stored his hoard of Halloween candy in the closet."

Associate Words with Images. Expand the phrase chosen for learning the word into a vivid mental image. Create a situation or an episode for the word. Further, enrich your memory link by drawing a picture of your mental image.

For example, the word *candid* means frank and truthful. Imagine a friend asking your opinion on an unattractive outfit. A suggestive phrase for learning the word might be "My candid reply might have hurt her feelings."

Associate Words in Families. Words, like people, have families that share the same names. In the case of words, the names are called *prefixes*, *roots*, and *suffixes*. A basic knowledge of word parts can help you unlock the meaning to thousands of associated family members.

The prefix *ambi-* means both, as in the word *ambivert*, which means being both introverted and extroverted. Although this word is seldom used, a useful association transfer occurs when the knowledge of *ambi-* is applied to new family members like *ambidextrous*, *ambiguous*, and *ambivalence*.

Seek Reinforcement. Look and listen for your new words. As suggested previously, you will probably discover that they are used more frequently than you ever thought. Notice them, welcome them, and congratulate yourself on your newfound wisdom.

Create Concept Cards. Many students use index cards for recording information on new words. As illustrated below, you write the word in a phrase on the front of the card, along with a notation of where the word was encountered. On the back of the card, write an appropriate definition, use the word in a new sentence, and draw an image illustrating the word. Review the cards to reinforce the words and quiz yourself.

Front   Back

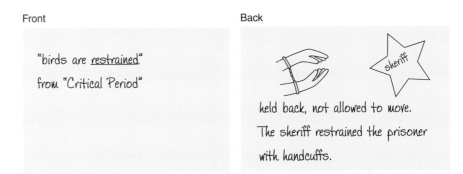

"birds are <u>restrained</u>"
from "Critical Period"

held back, not allowed to move.
The sheriff restrained the prisoner
with handcuffs.

The concept card is elevated to a new level in *Vocabulary Cartoons,* a series of inventive books by a father-son team in which humor is skillfully combined with the techniques of association.[1] The idea for the books came from the son's inability to remember the definition of *aloof.* His father asked him for a rhyming word, and they envisioned the family cat being "so aloof that she hid on the roof." To illustrate, the father drew a cartoon with an accompanying word link and playful sentence; and his son never forgot the definition. The rhyme, the image, and the humor all became mnemonics for learning. When the authors tested the power of their cartoons on 500 Florida students, they found that students who had been given definitions and cartoons learned 72 percent more words than those who had been given definitions only.

Try adding rhymes and sound associations to your own concept cards. Notice in the illustration on page 56 how cleverly the authors use sound and images to form memory links for the words *irascible* and *curtail.*

---

[1]S. Burchers, M. Burchers, and B. Burchers, *Vocabulary Cartoons I* and *Vocabulary Cartoons II* (Punta Gorda, FL: New Monic Books, 1997 and 2000).

IRASCIBLE
(i RAS uh bul)
easily angered, irritable
Link: **WRESTLE BULLS**

*"When he became IRASCIBLE, the Masked Marvel
would WRESTLE BULLS."*

CURTAIL
(ker TALE)
to truncate or abridge; to lessen,
usually by cutting away from
Link: **CAT TAIL**

*"Rex readies himself to CURTAIL
the CAT'S TAIL."*

Courtesy of New Monic Books, publisher of Vocabulary Cartoons SAT Word Power.

| **Exercise 2.1** | **Creating Mnemonics to Associate Meaning** |

Pair up with a classmate to create your own mnemonics for the following words. For each item, use rhyme and imagery to create a word link, a playful sentence, and a cartoon.

1. *scrutinize:* to look very carefully; to examine
2. *dormant:* asleep or inactive
3. *entreat:* to ask earnestly; to implore, plead, beg
4. Make up a mnemonic to help people remember your name.

Share your creations, and ask your instructor to show you what the authors created for the three words.

Using Context Clues

What strategies can you use to figure out the meaning of a new word? While associations strengthen memory for words that you understand, using **context clues** is the most common method of unlocking the meaning of unknown words. The *context* of a word refers to the sentence or paragraph in which it appears. Readers use several types of context clues. In some cases, words are defined directly in the sentences in which they appear; in other instances, the sentence offers clues or hints that enable the reader to arrive indirectly at the meaning of the word. The following are examples of how each type of clue can be used to figure out word meanings in textbooks.

Definition or Synonym

Complex material, particularly scientific material, has a heavy load of specialized vocabulary. Fortunately, new words are often directly defined as they are introduced in the text. Often, **synonyms**—words with the same meaning as the unknown word—are given. Do you know the meaning of *erythrocytes* and *oxyhemoglobin?* Read the following textbook sentence in which these two words appear, and then select the correct definition for each word.

EXAMPLE   When oxygen diffuses into the blood in external respiration, most of it enters the red blood cells, or erythrocytes, and unites with the hemoglobin in these cells, forming a compound called oxyhemoglobin.

Willis H. Johnson et al., *Essentials of Biology*

_____ *Erythrocytes* means
   a. diffused oxygen.
   b. red blood cells.
   c. the respiration process.

_____   Oxyhemoglobin means
a. hemoglobin without oxygen.
b. dominant oxygen cells.
c. a combination of oxygen and hemoglobin.

EXPLANATION The answers are _b_ and _c_. Notice that the first word, _erythrocytes_, is used as a synonym. Sometimes a signal word for a synonym is _or_. Other signal words that will help you discover meaning through the use of definition are _is, that is, in other words, for example,_ and _as defined as_. The second word, _oxyhemoglobin_, is part of the explanation of the sentence.

Elaborating Details

Terms are not always directly defined in the text. Instead, an author may give descriptive details that illustrate meaning. In political science texts, for example, you may come across the term _confederation_. Keep reading and see if you can figure out the meaning from the hints in the following paragraph.

EXAMPLE   There is a third form of governmental structure, a _confederation._ The United States began as such, under the Articles of Confederation. In a confederation, the national government is weak and most or all the power is in the hands of its components, for example, the individual states. Today, confederations are rare except in international organizations such as the United Nations.

Robert Lineberry, _Government in America_

_____   A _confederation_ is a governmental structure with
a. strong federal power.
b. weak federal power.
c. weak state power.
d. equal federal and state power.

EXPLANATION The answer is _b_ and can be figured out from the details in the third sentence.

Examples

At other times, examples will be given to clarify meaning. In psychology courses, for example, you will frequently encounter a complicated word describing something you have often thought about but not named. Read the following paragraph to find out what _psychokinesis_ means.

EXAMPLE   Another psychic phenomenon is psychokinesis, the ability to affect physical events without physical intervention. You can test your powers of psychokinesis by trying to influence the fall of dice from a mechanical shaker. Are you able to have the dice come up a certain number with a greater frequency than would occur by chance?

Douglas W. Matheson, *Introductory Psychology: The Modern View*

_____ *Psychokinesis* means
    a. extrasensory perception.
    b. an influence on happenings without physical tampering.
    c. physical intervention affecting physical change.

EXPLANATION The answer is *b*. Here the word is first directly defined in a complicated manner and then the definition is clarified by a simple example.

Comparison

In certain cases, complex concepts are best understood when compared with something else. Economics texts, for example, include many concepts that are difficult to understand. The use of a familiar term in a comparison can help the reader relate to a new idea. Can you explain a *trade deficit*? The following comparison will help.

EXAMPLE When the United States imports more than it exports, we have a *trade deficit* rather than a trade balance or surplus. Similarly, a store manager who buys more than she sells will create a financial deficit for the company.

_____ A *trade deficit* means that a nation
    a. sells more than it buys.
    b. buys more than it sells.
    c. sells what it buys.

EXPLANATION The answer is *b*. The comparison explains the definition by creating a more understandable situation.

Contrast

In other cases, a contrast is made to help you read between the lines and infer word meaning. Can you explain what *transsexuals* are and how they differ from *homosexuals*? The following paragraph gives you some clues.

EXAMPLE *Transsexuals* are people (usually males) who feel that they were born into the wrong body. They are not homosexuals in the usual sense. Most homosexuals are satisfied with their anatomy and think of themselves as appropriately male or female; they simply prefer members of their own sex. Transsexuals, in contrast, think of themselves as members of the opposite sex (often from early childhood) and may be so desperately unhappy with their physical appearance that they request hormonal and surgical treatment to change their genitals and secondary sex characteristics.

Rita Atkinson et al., Introduction to Psychology

_____   A *transsexual* is a person who thinks of himself or herself as a
   a. homosexual.
   b. heterosexual.
   c. member of the opposite sex.
   d. person without sex drive.

EXPLANATION The answer is *c*. By contrasting homosexuals and transsexuals, the reader is better able to infer the difference between the two. Signal words that indicate contrast are *but*, *yet*, *however*, and *in contrast*.

Antonyms

Finally, the context clue may be an **antonym**, or a word that means the opposite of the unknown word. Antonyms are signaled by words and phrases such as *however, but, yet, in contrast*, or *on the other hand*. Using the following context, is *nonconfrontational* behavior violent?

EXAMPLE Some passive belief systems call for *nonconfrontational* behavior; yet others call for rebellion.

Adapted from Daniel G. Bates and Elliot M. Franklin, Cultural Anthropology, 3rd ed.

_____   A *nonconfrontational* behavior is
   a. violent.
   b. rebellious.
   c. not openly rebellious.
   d. sympathetic.

EXPLANATION The signal word *yet* suggests that *nonconfrontational* is the opposite of violent and rebellious, so *c* is correct. The word *passive* is also a clue to the meaning.

Limitations of Context Clues

Although the clues in the sentence in which an unknown word appears are certainly helpful in deriving the meaning of the word, these clues will not always give a complete and accurate definition. To understand totally the meaning of a word, take some time after completing your reading to look up the word in a glossary or dictionary. Context clues operate just as the name suggests; they are hints and not necessarily complete definitions.

Exercise 2.2

The Power of Context Clues

How can context clues assist you in clarifying or unlocking the meaning of unknown words? For each of the following vocabulary items, make two responses. First, without reading the sentence containing the unknown word, select *a*, *b*, *c*, or *d* for the definition that you feel best fits each italicized word. Then read the material in which the word is used in context and answer again. Compare your answers. Did reading the word in context help? Were you initially uncertain of any word but then able to figure out the meaning after reading it in a sentence?

 1. *usurped*
   a. shortened
   b. acknowledged
   c. aggravated
   d. seized

    Henry, to the end of his life, thought of himself as a pious and orthodox Catholic who had restored the independent authority of the Church of England *usurped* centuries before by the Bishop of Rome.

   Shepard B. Clough et al., *A History of the Western World*

 2. *assimilationist*
   a. one who adopts the habits of a larger cultural group
   b. a machinist
   c. a typist
   d. one who files correspondence

   When members of a minority group wish to give up what is distinctive about them and become just like the majority, they take an *assimilationist* position. An example is the Urban League.

   Reece McGee et al., *Sociology: An Introduction*

 3. *dyad*
   a. star
   b. two-member group
   c. opposing factor
   d. leader

   George Simmel was one of the first sociologists to suggest that the number of members in a group radically transforms its properties. He began with an analysis of what happens when a *dyad*, a two-member group, becomes a triad, a three-member group.

   Ibid.

4. *hyperthermophiles*
   a. animals
   b. heat lovers
   c. birds
   d. winter plants

 Another group of archaea, the *hyperthermophiles*, thrive in very hot waters; some even live near deep-ocean vents where temperatures are above 100°C, the boiling point of water at sea level.

Neil Campbell et al., *Biology: Concepts & Connections,* 3rd ed.

 5. *expropriated*
   a. took from its owners
   b. industrialized
   c. approximated
   d. increased in size

_____ Under a decree of September 1952, the government *expropriated* several hundred thousand acres from large landholders and redistributed this land among the peasants.

Jesse H. Wheeler, Jr., et al., *Regional Geography of the World*

_____ 6. *adherents*
   a. children
   b. followers
   c. instigators
   d. detractors

_____ One of the fundamental features of Hinduism has been the division of its *adherents* into the most elaborate caste system ever known.

Ibid.

 7. *stimulus*
   a. writing implement
   b. distinguishing mark
   c. something that incites action
   d. result

_____ While we are sleeping, for example, we are hardly aware of what is happening around us, but we are aware to some degree. Any loud noise or other abrupt *stimulus* will almost certainly awaken us.

Gardner Lindzey et al., *Psychology*

 8. *debilitating*
   a. weakening
   b. reinforcing
   c. exciting
   d. enjoyable

_A_   However, anyone who has passed through several time zones while flying east or west knows how difficult it can be to change from one sleep schedule to another. This "jet lag" can be so _debilitating_ that many corporations will not allow their executives to enter negotiations for at least two days after such a trip.

Ibid.

_C_ 9. _autocratic_
   a. automatic
   b. democratic
   c. self-starting
   d. dictatorial

_C_   Autocratic leadership can be extremely effective if the people wielding it have enough power to enforce their decisions and if their followers know that they have it. It is especially useful in military situations where speed of decision is critical. Among its disadvantages are the lack of objectivity and the disregard for opinions of subordinates.

David J. Rachman and Michael Mescon, _Business Today_

_D_ 10. _ice page_
   a. Web page that wiggles to center itself
   b. Web page anchored to the right of the screen
   c. Web page anchored to the left of the screen
   d. Web page that flows to fit any size screen

_C_   Ice, jello, and liquid are related terms describing three approaches to controlling content placement on a Web page. An ice page is one in which the primary content has a fixed width and is "frozen" to the left margin.

H. L. Capron, _Computers: Tools for an Information Age,_ 6th ed.

**Exercise
2.3**

Context Clues in Academic Reading

Use the context clues of the sentence to write the meaning of each of the following italicized words.

1. Andrew was a thin old man despite his toughness, and soon he was in danger. Fortunately, friends formed a cordon and managed to _extricate_ him through a rear door.

John Garraty, _The American Nation_

Extricate means ___take him out, sneak him out___

2. But they were unfamiliar with the *regenerative* powers of the starfish. The central disk merely grows new arms, and a single arm can form a new animal.

Robert Wallace, Biology: The World of Life

Regenerative means _____.

3. To our delight, the *planarians* that had eaten educated victims learned much faster than did the worms that had consumed their untrained brethren.

Ibid.

Planarians are _____.

4. Belle Starr, the *moniker* of one Myra Belle Shirley, was immortalized as "the bandit queen," as pure in heart as Jesse James was socially conscious.

John Garraty, The American Nation

Moniker means _____.

5. Calamity Jane (Martha Cannary), later said to have been Wild Bill's *paramour,* wrote her own romantic autobiography in order to support a drinking problem.

Ibid.

A *paramour* is a ___wife_____.

Exercise 2.4   **Context Clues in Short Passages**

Use context clues of each passage that follows to write the meaning of the italicized words.

Passage A

The February carnival in Andalusia (southern Spain) is probably the oldest surviving pagan festival in Europe. The Latin Carnival is a period of madcap and *licentious* celebration with a moral "time out." It precedes the *deprivations* or sacrifices of Lent. Without being direct, the joyous *revelers subversively mock* the high and mighty in a comic political commentary.

Adapted from Daniel G. Bates and Elliot M. Franklin, Cultural Anthropology, 3rd ed.

1. licentious _____

2. deprivations ___Sacrifices_____

3. revelers _____

4. subversively _____

5. mock _____

Passage B

Traditionally, a board of directors sets corporate policy, provides an independent *perspective*, elects officers, and lets them do their job. But the Internet is *spawning* a new breed of board member. Today's e-commerce start-ups are headed by younger, less-experienced executives, who know little about corporate governance. To *compensate* for its *deficiency*, entrepreneurs rely on board members to help build the e-business from the ground up. Most provide the company with much sought after e-commerce expertise and sit on multiple dot-com boards. Asked if they are worried about revealing too much to competitors, most reply that if you don't give, you don't get back. Put differently, if you remain *insular* in the e-world, you'll get eaten alive.

Michael Mescon et al., Business Today, 10th ed.

1. perspective _____Opinion_____

2. spawning _____To Produce,_____

3. compensate _____make up_____

4. deficiency _____weakness_____

5. insular _____isolated for other ideas_____

Exercise 2.5

Context Clues in a Short Essay

Use the context clues in the sentences to write the meaning of each italicized word appearing below the selection.

E. B.'s View from the Cow Pasture: He's Been Sleeping in My Bed
By E. B. Harris from Warrenton, North Carolina

E.B. Harris, a well-known North Carolina auctioneer of farm equipment, raises cattle and goats on his farm.
The Carolina Cattle Connection, *June 2003*

The other day I ran into a friend of mine who dates all the way back to my childhood. Her name is Brenda Davis Smith. Brenda's family and my family go back a long way. Brenda's daddy was sheriff of Warren County for many years.

Brenda had two brothers, Ashley and John Hugh. Ashley was the same age as me, and John Hugh was two years younger. Every Sunday afternoon after church they were at my house or I was at theirs, or we were in the woods playing. As a matter of fact, Ashley, John Hugh, and I are blood brothers. When we were about ten years old we did that cowboy and Indian trick. We got a little blood from each other by cutting with a dull knife from each one and rolling it in the cut of the next one. Back in those days, no one had heard of all the blood diseases that are going on now.

This incident I am going to tell you about with Brenda dates back to about 1969. At that time I was doing some custom disking about a mile from the Davis home in the community of Marmaduke for a man named Clifford Robertson. It was early to midspring and Clifford was fixing to put in some milo and had hired me to disk the land. That day I went on up there and finished his job. I was then planning to go to Warrenton to do some work for Hal Connell on the Bar C farm. Mr. Connell was a Charolais breeder and was going to put in some summer grazing.

After I finished the work at Clifford's I really did not feel that well. By the time I reached the Davis home, it was probably about 10:30 to 11:00 a.m. and I was really feeling bad. It was getting so warm I pulled the tractor into the Davis yard and cut it off.

Rachel, their mom, wasn't there, but I made myself at home because Rachel had always called me one of her boys. The house was unlocked so I went in, lay down in the hallway where it was cool, and went to sleep. Rachel came in about 1:30 to 2:00 p.m. and woke me up. She asked if I was all right, and I told her that I really did not feel that well. She wanted to know if she could get me anything, and I told her no thank you. She then told me to lay in Brenda's bed until I felt better.

I got up out of the hall and lay down in Brenda's bed. Brenda was away at college. By around 3:00 p.m. I was feeling even worse. Rachel called my mama, and mama and daddy came and got me and carried me to the doctor's office.

I was running a high fever and they immediately put me in the hospital. About three days later and after a bunch of tests, I thought I was feeling better. I had started to turn yellow and they found out I had hepatitis. Mama came over and told me that I was going to be put in quarantine with no visitors for a week.

They immediately started calling all the folks that I had had close contact with to come and get vaccinated against hepatitis. Brenda had come home the next day after I had been at their house, so she was one of the ones who came to get a shot. Brenda told the nurse she had been in close contact with me. The nurse filling out the paperwork asked what kind of contact she had had with me.

Now Brenda is one of those people who say exactly what is on their mind. Brenda told her that I had been sleeping in her bed. You can imagine how that sounded. The rumor got started that Brenda and I had something going, which was the furthest thing from the truth. Brenda had to come back and clarify her statement.

I guess you have to be careful about what you say and who you say it to because the right thing can be taken the wrong way.

From *The Carolina Cattle Connection*, June 2003

1. go back a long way _Now each other For a long time_

2. blood brothers _real brothers Pact with fingers_

3. blood diseases _____

4. custom disking _____

5. fixing to put in _____

6. early to midspring _____

7. milo _____

8. Charolais breeder _____

9. hepatitis _____

10. in quarantine _____

Multiple Meanings of a Word

Even when word meaning seems clear, many words—particularly short ones—can be confusing because they have more than one meaning. The word *bank*, for example, can be used as a noun to refer to a financial institution, the ground rising from a river, or a mass of clouds. As a verb, *bank* can mean to laterally incline an airplane, to accumulate, or to drive a billiard ball into a cushion. Thus, the meaning of the word depends on the sentence and paragraph in which the word is used. Be alert to context clues that indicate an unfamiliar use of a seemingly familiar word.

Exercise 2.5

Multiple Meanings

The boldface words in the following sentences have multiple meanings. Write the definition of each boldface word as it is used in the sentence.

1. The **dates** were rolled in powdered sugar, packaged by Dromedary, and shipped for holiday treats. _____

2. As a team player for IBM, she demonstrated **industry** and intelligence in accomplishing the goals. _____

3. After being **canned** by the dot-com company, she looked for a new job marketing Verizon products. _____

4. A chicken bone can **lodge** in a pet's throat and cause a medical emergency. ___STUCK_____

5. The insect did not **light** long enough to be caught. _____

6. Exercise, rather than shopping, can be a positive and inexpensive **outlet** for stress. _____

Understanding the Structure of Words

What is the longest word in the English language and what does it mean? Maxwell Nurnberg and Morris Rosenblum, in *How to Build a Better Vocabulary* (Prentice-Hall, 1989), say that at one time the longest word in *Webster's New International Dictionary* was

pneumonoultramicroscopicsilicovolcanokoniosis

Look at the word again and notice the smaller and more familiar word parts. Do you know enough of the smaller parts to figure out the meaning of the word? Nurnberg and Rosenblum unlock the meaning as follows:

pneumono:	pertaining to the lungs, as in *pneumon*ia
ultra:	beyond, as in *ultra*violet rays
micro:	small, as in microscope
scopic:	from the root of Greek verb *skopein*, to view or look at
silico:	from the element silicon, found in quartz, flint, and sand
volcano:	the meaning of this is obvious
koni:	the principal root, from a Greek word for dust
osis:	a suffix indicating illness, as trichinosis

Now putting the parts together again, we deduce that *pneumonoultramicroscopicsilicovolcanokoniosis* is a disease of the lungs caused by extremely small particles of volcanic ash and dust.

This dramatic example demonstrates how an extremely long and technical word can become more manageable by breaking it into smaller parts. The same is true for many of the smaller words that we use every day. A knowledge of word parts will help you unlock the meaning of literally thousands of words. One vocabulary expert identified a list of thirty prefixes, roots, and suffixes and claims that knowing these 30 word parts will help unlock the meaning of 14,000 words.

Like people, words have families and, in some cases, an abundance of close relations. Clusters, or what might be called *word families*, are composed of words with the same base or **root**. For example, *bio* is a root meaning life. If you know that *biology* means the study of life, it becomes easy to figure out the definition of a word like *biochemistry*. Word parts form new words as follows:

prefix + root   root + suffix   prefix + root + suffix

Prefixes and suffixes are added to root words to change the meaning. A **prefix** is added to the beginning of a word and a **suffix** is added to the end. For example, the prefix *il* means not. When added to the word *legal*, the resulting word, *illegal*, becomes the opposite of the original. Suffixes can change the meaning or change the way the word can be used in a sentence. The suffix *cide* means to kill. When added to *frater*, which means brother, the resulting word, *fratricide*, means to kill one's brother. Adding *ity* or *ize* to *frater* changes both the meaning and the way the word can be used grammatically in a sentence.

EXAMPLE   To demonstrate how prefixes, roots, and suffixes overlap and make families, start with the root *gamy*, meaning marriage, and ask some questions.

1. What is the state of having only one wife called? _____
   (*mono* means one)

2. What is a man who has two wives called? _____
   (*bi-* means two and *ist* means one who)

3. What is a man who has many wives called? _____
   (*poly-* means many)

4. What is a woman who has many husbands called? _____
   (*andro-* means man)

5. What is someone who hates marriage called? _____
   (*miso-* means hater of)

EXPLANATION The answers are (1) monogamy, (2) bigamist, (3) polyga-
mist, (4) polyandrist, and (5) misogamist. Notice that in several of the- *gamy*
examples, the letters change slightly to accommodate language sounds. Such
variations of a letter or two are typical when you work with word parts. Often
you have to drop or add letters to maintain the rhythm of the language, but
the meaning of the word part remains the same regardless of the change in
spelling. For example, the prefix *con* means with or together, as in *conduct*.
This same prefix is used with variations in many other words:

    cooperate   *collection*   *correlate*   *communicate*   *connect*

Thus, *con-*, *co-*, *col-*, *cor-*, and *com-* are all forms of the prefix that means
with or together.

Exercise 2.6

Word Families

Create your own word families from the word parts that are supplied. For
each of the following definitions, supply a prefix, root, or suffix to make the
appropriate word.

Prefix: *bi-* **means** two

1. able to speak two languages: bi __lingual__
2. having two feet, like humans: bi _____
3. representing two political parties: bi _____
4. occurring at two-year intervals: bi _____
5. having two lenses on one glass: bi __focals__
6. cut into two parts: bi _____
7. mathematics expression with two terms: bi _____
8. instrument with two eyes: bi _____

9. tooth with two points: bi _____

10. coming twice a year: bi_____

Root: *-vert-* means to turn

1. to change one's beliefs: _Con_vert

2. to go back to old ways again: _Con___ vert

3. a car with a removable top: _Con_ vert _ible_

4. to change the direction of a stream: _Con___ vert

5. activities intended to undermine or destroy: _____vers_____

6. an outgoing, gregarious person: _____vert

7. a quiet, introspective, shy person _____vert

8. conditions that are turned against you; misfortune _____vers_____

9. one who deviates from normal behavior, especially sexual: _____vert

10. one who is sometimes introspective and sometimes gregarious: _____vert

Suffix: *-ism* means doctrine, condition, or characteristic

1. addiction to alcoholic drink: _alcoholic_ism

2. a brave and courageous manner of acting: _braver_ism

3. prejudice against a particular gender or sex: _prejud_ism

4. doctrine concerned only with fact and reality: _____ism

5. system using terror to intimidate: _Terror_ism

6. writing someone's words as your own: _____ism

7. driving out an evil spirit: _Spirit_ism

8. purification to join the church: _____ism

9. informal style of speech using slang: _argual_ism

10. being obsessive or fanatical about something: _____ism

| Exercise 2.7 | **Prefixes, Roots, and Suffixes** |

Using the prefix, root, or suffix provided, write the words that best fit the following definitions:

1. *con* means with
   infectious or catching: con_tuminate_

2. *sub* means under
   under the conscious level of the mind: sub_____

3. *post* means after
   to delay or set back: post_*pone*___

4. *vita* means life
   a pill to provide essential nutrients: vita_*mins*___

5. *pel* means drive or push
   to push out of school: ____*es*____pel

6. *thermo* means heat
   device for regulating furnace heat: thermo_*stat*___

7. *ven* means come
   a meeting for people to come together: ____*con*____ ven_*tional*_

8. *rupt* means break or burst
   a volcanic explosion: ____*e*____rupt_*ed*____

9. *meter* means measure
   instrument to measure heat: ___*Thermo*_meter

10. *naut* means voyager
    voyager in the sea: _____naut

Using a Dictionary

Do you have an excellent collegiate dictionary, such as *Merriam-Webster's Collegiate Dictionary?* Every college student needs two dictionaries: a small one for class and a large one to keep at home. In class, you may use a small paperback dictionary for quick spelling or word-meaning checks. The paperback is easy to carry but does not provide the depth of information needed for college study that is found in the larger collegiate editions.

Several online dictionaries offer easy and free access for limited use but require a yearly subscription fee for premium services. At http://www. Merriam-Webster.com/, for example, you can type your word into the Search window and receive the definition, word origin, pronunciation, and links to Top 10 Search Results (the word in use) for free. The site also provides an encyclopedia link, "Word of the Day" services, word games, an online thesaurus, a dictionary for kids, and an online store for purchases. Another easy-to-use free site, http://www.dictionary.com, includes definitions, foreign dictionaries, translations into foreign languages, a thesaurus, games, a word of the day, and a bookstore. Try these sites and see how they compare with your collegiate dictionary. In evaluating the sites, consider that good dictionaries not only contain the definitions of words but also provide the following additional information for each word.

Guide Words. The two words at the top of each dictionary page are the first and last entries on the page. They help guide your search for a particular entry by indicating what is covered on that page.

In the sample that follows, *flagrante delicto* is the first entry on the page of the dictionary on which *flamingo* appears, and *flappy* is the last entry. Note that the pronunciation of the word *flamingo* is followed by part of speech *(n)*, plural spellings, and the origin of the word.

flagrante delicto ● flappy

fla·min·go \flə-'miŋ-(,)gō\ *n, pl* **-gos** *also* **-goes** [obs. Sp *flamengo* (now *flamenco*), lit., Fleming, German (conventionally thought of as ruddy-complexioned)] (1565) : any of several large aquatic birds (family Phoenicopteridae) with long legs and neck, webbed feet, a broad lamellate bill resembling that of a duck but abruptly bent downward, and usu. rosy-white plumage with scarlet wing coverts and black wing quills

flamingo

\ə\ abut \ᵊ\ kitten, F table \ər\ **further** \a\ ash \ā\ ace \ä\ mop, mar
\aú\ **out** \ch\ **chin** \e\ bet \ē\ **easy** \g\ go \i\ hit \ī\ **ice** \j\ **job**
\ŋ\ **sing** \ō\ go \ò\ **law** \òi\ **boy** \th\ **thin** \th̲\ **the** \ü\ **loot** \ú\ **foot**
\y\ **yet** \zh\ **vision** \à, k̲, ⁿ, œ, œ̄, ᴜ, ᴜ̄, ᵞ\ *see* Guide to Pronunciation

By permission. From Merriam-Webster's Collegiate® Dictionary, Tenth Edition; © 2001 by Merriam-Webster, Incorporated.

Pronunciation. The boldface main entry divides the word into sounds, using a dot between each syllable. After the entry, letters and symbols show the pronunciation. A diacritical mark (′) at the end of a syllable indicates stress on that syllable. A heavy mark means major stress; a lighter one indicates minor stress.

As shown in the illustration above, a key explaining the symbols and letters appears at the bottom of the dictionary page. For example, a word like *ragweed* (rag′-wēd) would be pronounced with a short *a* as in *ash* and a long *e* as in *easy*.

The *a* in *flamingo* sounds like the *a* in *abut*, and the final *o* has a long sound as in *go*. The stress is on the first syllable.

Part of Speech. The part of speech is indicated in an abbreviation for each meaning of a word. A single word, for example, may be a noun with one definition and a verb with another. The noun *flamingo* can be used as only one part of speech, but *sideline* can be both a noun and a verb (see the following entry).

¹**side·line** \-,līn\ *n* (1862) **1** : a line at right angles to a goal line or end line and marking a side of a court or field of play for athletic games **2 a** : a line of goods sold in addition to one's principal line **b** : a business or activity pursued in addition to one's regular occupation **3 a** : the space immediately outside the lines along either side of an athletic field or court **b** : a sphere of little or no participation or activity — usu. used in pl.
²**sideline** *vt* (1943) : to put out of action : put on the sidelines

By permission. From Merriam-Webster's Collegiate® Dictionary, Tenth Edition; © 2001 by Merriam-Webster, Incorporated.

Spellings. Spellings are given for the plural of the word and for special forms. This is particularly useful in determining whether letters are added or dropped to form the new words. The plural of *flamingo* can be spelled correctly in two different ways. Both *flamingos* and *flamingoes* are acceptable.

Origin. For many entries, the foreign word and language from which the word was derived will appear after the pronunciation. For example, *L* stands for a Latin origin and G for Greek. A key for the many dictionary abbreviations usually appears at the beginning of the book.

The word *flamingo* has a rich history. It is Portuguese *(Pg)* and comes from the Spanish *(fr Sp)* word *flamenco*. It is derived ultimately from the Old Provençal *(fr OProv) flamenc*, from *flama* for *flame*, which comes from the Latin *(fr L)* word *flamma*.

Multiple Meanings. A single word can have many shades of meaning or several completely different meanings. The various meanings are numbered.

The word *flamingo* on the facing page has only one meaning. The word *sideline*, however, has several, as shown in the previous entry.

A sideline can be a business, a product, or a designated area. In addition, it can mean to move something out of the action. To select the appropriate meaning, consider the context or the way the word is used in the sentence. For example, consider the intended meaning in "As a sideline to being a full-time student, I also play in a band on the weekends."

| Exercise 2.8 | **Using the Dictionary** |

Answer the following questions, using the page from *Merriam-Webster's Collegiate Dictionary* reproduced on page 74, with *T* (true) or *F* (false):

1. *Leicester* is a county in England, a breed of sheep, and a cheese.
2. A Hawaiian *lei* is a necklace of flowers.
3. The word *lemming* is derived from the Greek word *lemmus*, which means to drown.
4. The word *leisurely* can be used as both an adverb and an adjective.
5. A *lemon* tree has both fruit and flowers.
6. The plural of *leman* is *lemen*.
7. One of the origins of *lemur* is the Latin word *lemures*, meaning ghosts.
8. The word *lemures* can be correctly pronounced in two different ways.
9. When the words *lend* and *lease* are used together to mean a transfer of goods, no hyphen is required.
10. The plural for *lemma* can be either *lemmas* or *lemmata*.

664 legitimate • lenient

1 a : lawfully begotten; *specif* : born in wedlock **b** : having full filial rights and obligations by birth ⟨a ~ child⟩ **2** : being exactly as purposed : neither spurious nor false ⟨~ grievance⟩ ⟨a ~ practitioner⟩ **3 a** : accordant with law or with established legal forms and requirements ⟨a ~ government⟩ **b** : ruling by or based on the strict principle of hereditary right ⟨a ~ king⟩ **4** : conforming to recognized principles or accepted rules and standards ⟨~ advertising expenditure⟩ ⟨~ inference⟩ **5** : relating to plays acted by professional actors but not including revues, burlesque, or some forms of musical comedy ⟨the ~ theater⟩ ***syn*** see LAWFUL — **le·git·i·mate·ly** *adv*

[2]**le·git·i·mate** \-ˌmāt\ *vt* **-mat·ed; -mat·ing** (1531) : to make legitimate: **a** (1) : to give legal status or authorization to (2) : to show or affirm to be justified **b** : to put (a bastard) in the state of a legitimate child before the law by legal means — **le·git·i·ma·tion** \-ˌji-tə-ˈmā-shən\ *n* — **le·git·i·mat·or** \-ˈji-tə-ˌmā-tər\ *n*

le·git·i·ma·tize \li-ˈji-tə-mə-ˌtīz\ *vt* **-tized; -tiz·ing** (1791) : LEGITIMATE

le·git·i·mise *Brit var of* LEGITIMIZE

le·git·i·mism \li-ˈji-tə-ˌmi-zəm\ *n, often cap* (1877) : adherence to the principles of political legitimacy or to a person claiming legitimacy — **le·git·i·mist** \-mist\ *n, often cap* — **legitimist** *adj*

le·git·i·mize \-ˌmīz\ *vt* **-mized; -miz·ing** (1848) : LEGITIMATE — **le·git·i·mi·za·tion** \-ˌji-tə-mə-ˈzā-shən\ *n* — **le·git·i·miz·er** \-ˈji-tə-ˌmī-zər\ *n*

leg·man \ˈleg-ˌman *also* ˈlāg-\ *n* (1923) **1** : a reporter assigned usu. to gather information **2** : an assistant who performs various subordinate tasks (as gathering information or running errands)

leg–of–mut·ton *or* **leg–o'–mut·ton** \ˌle-gə(v)-ˈmə-tᵊn *also* ˌlāg-\ *adj* (1840) : having the approximately triangular shape or outline of a leg of mutton ⟨~ sleeve⟩ ⟨~ sail⟩

leg out *vt* (1965) : to make (as a base hit) by fast running

leg–pull \ˈleg-ˌpu̇l *also* ˈlāg-\ *n* [fr. the phrase *to pull one's leg*] (1915) : a humorous deception or hoax

leg·room \-ˌrüm, -ˌru̇m\ *n* (1926) : space in which to extend the legs while seated

le·gume \ˈle-ˌgyüm, li-ˈgyüm\ *n* [F *légume*, fr. L *legumin-, legumen* leguminous plant, fr. *legere* to gather — more at LEGEND] (1676) **1 a** : the fruit or seed of leguminous plants (as peas or beans) used for food **b** : a vegetable used for food **2** : any of a large family (Leguminosae syn. Fabaceae) of dicotyledonous herbs, shrubs, and trees having fruits that are legumes (sense 3) or loments, bearing nodules on the roots that contain nitrogen-fixing bacteria, and including important food and forage plants (as peas, beans, or clovers) **3** : a dry dehiscent one-celled fruit developed from a simple superior ovary and usu. dehiscing into two valves with the seeds attached to the ventral suture : POD

le·gu·mi·nous \li-ˈgyü-mə-nəs, le-\ *adj* (15c) **1** : of, relating to, or consisting of plants that are legumes **2** : resembling a legume

leg up *n* (1837) **1** : a helping hand : BOOST **2** : HEAD START

leg warmer *n* (1974) : a usu. knitted covering for the leg

leg·work \ˈleg-ˌwərk *also* ˈlāg-\ *n* (1891) : active physical work (as in gathering information) that forms the basis of more creative or mentally exacting work (as writing a book)

le·hua \lā-ˈhü-ə\ *n* [Hawaiian] (1888) : a common very showy chiefly Polynesian tree (*Metrosideros collinus*) of the myrtle family having bright red flowers and a hard wood; *also* : its flower

[1]**lei** \ˈlā, ˈlā-ˌē\ *n* [Hawaiian] (1843) : a wreath or necklace usu. of flowers or leaves

[2]**lei** \ˈlā\ *pl of* LEU

Leices·ter \ˈles-tər\ *n* [*Leicester*, county in England] (1798) **1** : an individual of either of two English breeds of white-faced long-wool sheep raised esp. for mutton **2** : a hard usu. orange-colored cheese similar to cheddar

leish·man·ia \lēsh-ˈma-nē-ə\ *n* [NL, fr. Sir W. B. *Leishman* †1926 Brit. medical officer] (1914) : any of a genus (*Leishmania*) of flagellate protozoans that are parasitic in the tissues of vertebrates; *broadly* : an organism resembling the leishmanias that is included in the family (Trypanosomatidae) to which they belong — **leish·man·ial** \-nē-əl\ *adj*

leish·man·i·a·sis \ˌlēsh-mə-ˈnī-ə-səs\ *n* [NL] (1912) : infection with or disease caused by leishmanias

leis·ter \ˈlēs-tər\ *n* [of Scand origin; akin to ON *ljóstr* leister] (ca. 1534) : a spear armed with three or more barbed prongs for catching fish

lei·sure \ˈlē-zhər, ˈle-, ˈlā-\ *n* [ME *leiser*, fr. MF *leisir*, fr. *leisir* to be permitted, fr. L *licēre*] (14c) **1** : freedom provided by the cessation of activities; *esp* : time free from work or duties **2** : EASE, LEISURELINESS — **leisure** *adj* — **at leisure** *or* **at one's leisure** : in one's leisure time : at one's convenience ⟨read the book *at her leisure*⟩

lei·sured \-zhərd\ *adj* (1631) : having leisure : LEISURELY

[1]**lei·sure·ly** \-zhər-lē\ *adv* (15c) : without haste : DELIBERATELY

[2]**leisurely** *adj* (1604) : characterized by leisure : UNHURRIED — **lei·sure·li·ness** *n*

leisure suit *n* (1975) : a suit consisting of a shirt jacket and matching trousers for informal wear

leit·mo·tiv *or* **leit·mo·tif** \ˈlīt-mō-ˌtēf\ *n* [G *Leitmotiv*, fr. *leiten* to lead + *Motiv* motive] (ca. 1876) **1** : an associated melodic phrase or figure that accompanies the reappearance of an idea, person, or situation esp. in a Wagnerian music drama **2** : a dominant recurring theme

[1]**lek** \ˈlek\ *n* [Sw, short for *lekställe* mating ground, fr. *lek* mating, sport + *ställe* place] (1871) : an assembly area where animals (as the prairie chicken) carry on display and courtship behavior

[2]**lek** *n, pl* **leks** *or* **le·ke** \ˈle-kə\ *also* **lek** *or* **le·ku** \ˈle-(ˌ)kü\ [Alb] (1927) — see MONEY table

lek·var \ˈlek-ˌvär\ *n* [Hung *lekvár* jam] (ca. 1958) : a prune butter used as a pastry filling

le·man \ˈle-mən, ˈlē-\ *n* [ME *lefman, leman*, fr. *lef* lief] (13c) *archaic* : SWEETHEART, LOVER; *esp* : MISTRESS

[1]**lem·ma** \ˈle-mə\ *n, pl* **lemmas** *or* **lem·ma·ta** \-mə-tə\ [L, fr. Gk *lēmma* thing taken, assumption, fr. *lambanein* to take — more at LATCH] (1570) **1** : an auxiliary proposition used in the demonstration of another proposition **2** : the argument or theme of a composition prefixed as a title or introduction; *also* : the heading or theme of a comment or note on a text **3** : a glossed word or phrase

[2]**lemma** *n* [Gk, husk, fr. *lepein* to peel — more at LEPER] (1906) : the lower of the two bracts enclosing the flower in the spikelet of grasses

lem·ming \ˈle-miŋ\ *n* [Norw] (1713) : any of various small short-tailed furry-footed rodents (as genera *Lemmus* and *Dicrostonyx*) of circumpolar distribution that are notable for the recurrent mass migrations of a European form (*L. lemmus*) which often continue into the sea where vast numbers are drowned — **lem·ming·like** \-ˌlīk\ *adj*

lem·nis·cate \lem-ˈnis-kət\ *n* [NL *lemniscata*, fr. fem. of L *lemniscatus* with hanging ribbons, fr. *lemniscus*] (ca. 1781) : a figure-eight shaped curve whose equation in polar coordinates is $\rho^2=a^2 \cos 2\theta$ or $\rho^2=a^2 \sin 2\theta$

lem·nis·cus \lem-ˈnis-kəs\ *n, pl* **-nis·ci** \-ˈnis-ˌkī, -ˌkē; -ˈni-ˌsī\ [NL, fr. L, ribbon, fr. Gk *lēmniskos*] (ca. 1905) : a band of fibers and esp. nerve fibers — **lem·nis·cal** \-kəl\ *adj*

[1]**lem·on** \ˈle-mən\ *n* [ME *lymon*, fr. MF *limon*, fr. ML *limon-, limo*, fr. Ar *laymūn*] (15c) **1 a** : an acid fruit that is botanically a many-seeded pale yellow oblong berry and is produced by a small thorny tree (*Citrus limon*) **b** : a tree that bears lemons **2** : one (as an automobile) that is unsatisfactory or defective — **lem·ony** \ˈle-mə-nē\ *adj*

lemon 1: branch with fruit and flowers

[2]**lemon** *adj* (1598) **1** : of the color lemon yellow **2 a** : containing lemon **b** : having the flavor or scent of lemon

lem·on·ade \ˌle-mə-ˈnād\ *n* (1604) : a beverage of sweetened lemon juice mixed with water

lemon balm *n* (ca. 1888) : a bushy perennial Old World mint (*Melissa officinalis*) often cultivated for its fragrant lemon-flavored leaves

lem·on·grass \ˈle-mən-ˌgras\ *n* (1801) : a grass (*Cymbopogon citratus*) of robust habit that grows in tropical regions, is used as an herb, and is the source of an essential oil with an odor of lemon or verbena

lemon law *n* (1982) : a law offering car buyers relief (as by repair, replacement, or refund) for defects detected during a specified period after purchase

lemon shark *n* (1942) : a medium-sized requiem shark (*Negaprion brevirostris*) of the warm Atlantic that is yellowish brown to gray above with yellow or greenish sides

lemon sole *n* (1876) : any of several flatfishes and esp. flounders: as **a** : a bottom-dwelling flounder (*Microstomus kitt*) of the northeastern Atlantic that is an important food fish **b** : WINTER FLOUNDER

lemon yellow *n* (1807) : a brilliant greenish yellow color

lem·pi·ra \lem-ˈpir-ə\ *n* [AmerSp, fr. *Lempira*, 16th cent. Indian chief] (ca. 1934) — see MONEY table

le·mur \ˈlē-mər\ *n* [NL, fr. L *lemures*, pl., ghosts] (1795) : any of various arboreal chiefly nocturnal mammals that were formerly widespread but are now largely confined to Madagascar, are related to the monkeys but are usu. regarded as constituting a distinct superfamily (Lemuroidea), and usu. have a muzzle like a fox, large eyes, very soft woolly fur, and a long furry tail

lemur

le·mu·res \ˈle-mə-ˌrās, ˈlem-yə-ˌrēz\ *n pl* [L] (1555) : spirits of the unburied dead exorcised from homes in early Roman religious rites

lend \ˈlend\ *vb* **lent** \ˈlent\; **lend·ing** [ME *lenen, lenden*, fr. OE *lǣnan*, fr. *lǣn* loan — more at LOAN] *vt* (bef. 12c) **1 a** : to give for temporary use on condition that the same or its equivalent be returned **b** : to let out (money) for temporary use on condition of repayment with interest **2 a** : to give the assistance or support of : AFFORD, FURNISH ⟨a dispassionate and scholarly manner which ~s great force to his criticisms —*Times Lit. Supp.*⟩ **b** : to adapt or apply (oneself) readily : ACCOMMODATE ⟨a topic that ~s itself admirably to class discussion⟩ ~ *vi* : to make a loan ***usage*** see LOAN — **lend·able** \ˈlen-də-bəl\ *adj* — **lend·er** *n*

lending library *n* (1708) : a library from which materials are lent; *esp* : RENTAL LIBRARY

lend–lease \ˈlend-ˈlēs\ *n* [U.S. *Lend-Lease* Act (1941)] (1941) : the transfer of goods and services to an ally to aid in a common cause with payment made by a return of the original items or their use in the cause or by a similar transfer of other goods and services — **lend–lease** *vt*

length \ˈleŋ(k)th, ˈlen(t)th\ *n, pl* **lengths** \ˈleŋ(k)ths, ˈlen(t)ths, ˈleŋ(k)s\ [ME *lengthe*, fr. OE *lengthu*, fr. *lang* long] (bef. 12c) **1 a** : the longer or longest dimension of an object **b** : a measured distance or dimension ⟨10 feet in ~⟩ — see METRIC SYSTEM table, WEIGHT table **c** : the quality or state of being long **2 a** : duration or extent in time **b** : relative duration or stress of a sound **3 a** : distance or extent in space **b** : the length of something taken as a unit of measure ⟨his horse led by a ~⟩ **4** : the degree to which something (as a course of action or a line of thought) is carried — often used in pl. ⟨went to great ~s to learn the truth⟩ **5 a** : a long expanse or stretch **b** : a piece constituting or usable as part of a whole or of a connected series : SECTION ⟨a ~ of pipe⟩ **6** : a vertical dimension of an article of clothing — **at length 1** : FULLY, COMPREHENSIVELY **2** : at last : FINALLY

length·en \ˈleŋ(k)-thən, ˈlen(t)-\ *vb* **length·ened; length·en·ing** \ˈleŋ(k)th-niŋ, ˈlen(t)th-; ˈleŋ(k)-thə-, ˈlen(t)-\ *vt* (14c) : to make longer ~ *vi* : to grow longer ***syn*** see EXTEND — **length·en·er** \ˈleŋ(k)th-nər, ˈlen(t)th-; ˈleŋ(k)-thə-, ˈlen(t)-\ *n*

length·ways \ˈleŋ(k)th-ˌwāz, ˈlen(t)th-\ *adv* (1599) : LENGTHWISE

length·wise \-ˌwīz\ *adv* (ca. 1580) : in the direction of the length : LONGITUDINALLY — **lengthwise** *adj*

lengthy \ˈleŋ(k)-thē, ˈlen(t)-\ *adj* **length·i·er; -est** (1689) **1** : protracted excessively : OVERLONG **2** : EXTENDED, LONG — **length·i·ly** \-thə-lē\ *adv* — **length·i·ness** \-thē-nəs\ *n*

le·nience \ˈlē-nyən(t)s, -nē-ən(t)s\ *n* (1796) : LENIENCY

le·nien·cy \ˈlē-nē-ən(t)-sē, -nyən(t)-sē\ *n, pl* **-cies** (1780) **1** : the quality or state of being lenient **2** : a lenient disposition or practice ***syn*** see MERCY

le·nient \ˈlē-nē-ənt, -nyənt\ *adj* [L *lenient-, leniens*, prp. of *lenire* to soften, soothe, fr. *lenis* soft, mild; prob. akin to Lith *lėnas* tranquil — more

Word Origins

The study of word origins is called **etymology**. Not only is it fascinating to trace a word back to its earliest recorded appearance, but your knowledge of the word's origin can strengthen your memory for the word. For example, the word *narcissistic* means egotistically in love with yourself. Its origin is a Greek myth in which a beautiful youth named Narcissus falls in love with his own reflection; he is punished for his vanity by being turned into a flower. Thus, the myth creates an intriguing image that can enhance your memory link for the word.

The amount of information on word origins varies with the type of dictionary. Because of its size, a small paperback dictionary such as the *American Heritage Dictionary* usually contains very little information on word origins, whereas a textbook-size edition of *Merriam-Webster's Collegiate Dictionary* offers more. For the most information on word origins, visit the reference room in your college library, and use an unabridged dictionary such as *Webster's Third New International Dictionary*, the *Random House Dictionary of the English Language*, or the *American Heritage Dictionary of the English Language*.

Exercise 2.9

Word Origins

Read the following dictionary entries and answer the questions about the words and their origins.

> ¹**bribe** \'brib\ *n* [ME, something stolen, fr. MF, bread given to a beggar] (15c) **1** : money or favor given or promised in order to influence the judgment or conduct of a person in a position of trust **2** : something that serves to induce or influence
> ²**bribe** *vb* **bribed; brib·ing** *vt* (1528) : to induce or influence by or as if by bribery ~ *vi* : to practice bribery — **brib·able** \'bri-bə-bəl\ *adj* —

By permission. From Merriam-Webster's Collegiate® Dictionary, Tenth Edition; © 2001 by Merriam-Webster, Incorporated.

1. *Bribe* means ___Something stolen___.

2. Explain the origin: ___Frensh___

> ¹**scape·goat** \'skāp-ˌgōt\ *n* [¹*scape*; intended as trans. of Heb *'azāzēl* (prob. name of a demon), as if *'ēz 'ōzēl* goat that departs—Lev 16:8 (AV)] (1530) **1** : a goat upon whose head are symbolically placed the sins of the people after which he is sent into the wilderness in the biblical ceremony for Yom Kippur **2 a** : one that bears the blame for others **b** : one that is the object of irrational hostility
> ²**scapegoat** *vt* (1943) : to make a scapegoat of — **scape·goat·ism** \-ˌgō-ˌti-zəm\ *n*

3. *Scapegoat* means ___Name of a demon___.

4. Explain the origin: ___Frensh___

> **mar·a·thon** \'mar-ə-ˌthän\ *n, often attrib* [*Marathon*, Greece, site of a victory of Greeks over Persians in 490 B.C., the news of which was carried to Athens by a long-distance runner] (1896) **1** : a long-distance race: **a** : a footrace run on an open course usu. of 26 miles 385 yards (42.2 kilometers) **b** : a race other than a footrace marked esp. by great length **2 a** : an endurance contest **b** : something (as an event, activity, or session) characterized by great length or concentrated effort

By permission. From Merriam-Webster's Collegiate® Dictionary, Tenth Edition; © 2001 by Merriam-Webster, Incorporated.

√

5. *Marathon* means _A Long Distance race_ .

6. Explain the origin: _Greek word_

---

om·buds·man \\'äm-‚bùdz-mən, 'ȯm-, -bədz-, -‚man; äm-'bùdz-, ȯm-\\ *n*,
pl **-men** \\-mən\\ [Sw, lit., representative, fr. ON *umbothsmathr*, fr. *um-
both* commission + *mathr* man] (1959) **1** : a government official (as in
Sweden or New Zealand) appointed to receive and investigate complaints made by individuals against abuses or capricious acts of public
officials **2** : one that investigates reported complaints (as from students or consumers), reports findings, and helps to achieve equitable
settlements — **om·buds·man·ship** \\-‚ship\\ *n*

*By permission. From Merriam-Webster's Collegiate® Dictionary, Tenth Edition; © 2001 by
Merriam-Webster, Incorporated.*

7. *Ombudsman* means _One that investigates complaints_

8. Explain the origin: _Frensh word_

---

van·dal \\'van-dᵊl\\ *n* [L *Vandalii* (pl.), of Gmc origin] (1555) **1** *cap* : a
member of a Germanic people who lived in the area south of the Baltic
between the Vistula and the Oder, overran Gaul, Spain, and northern
Africa in the 4th and 5th centuries A.D., and in 455 sacked Rome **2**
: one who willfully or ignorantly destroys, damages, or defaces property belonging to another or to the public — **vandal** *adj, often cap* —

*By permission. From Merriam-Webster's Collegiate® Dictionary, Tenth Edition; © 2001 by Merriam-
Webster, Incorporated.*

9. *Vandal* means _One who willfull or ignorantly destroys_

10. Explain the origin: _____ .

Using a Glossary

Each college subject seems to have a language, or jargon, of its own. For example, words like *sociocultural* or *socioeconomic* crop up in sociology. In truth,
these words are somewhat unique to the subject-matter area—they are
invented words. The best definitions of such words can usually be found in the
textbook itself rather than in a dictionary. The definitions may be displayed in
the *margins* of a page, or more frequently, in a glossary of terms at the end of
the book or each chapter. The glossary defines the words as they are used in
the textbook. At the end of most textbooks is an index, which helps you find
pages on which topics are discussed. In some large texts, the glossary and
index are combined.

Consider the following examples from the glossary of a psychology textbook. These terms are part of the jargon of psychology and would probably
not be found in the dictionary.

latent learning   Hidden learning that is not demonstrated in performance
until that performance is reinforced.

learning set   An acquired strategy for learning or problem solving; learning to learn.

Exercise 2.10	**Using Your Glossary**

Turn to the glossary at the end of this book for help in defining the following terms. Write a definition for each in your own words.

1. schema: _A Skeketch or knowledge about a subject_
2. bias: _An opinion on a subject_
3. context clues: _Hints that help you figure out the definition of a word_
4. metacognition: _Knowledge of how to read_
5. inference: _Subtle suggestion expressed with out direct statment_

Using a Thesaurus

A thesaurus is a writer's tool. It is not a dictionary, and it does not include all words. The first thesaurus was compiled in 1852 by Dr. Peter Mark Roget, an English physician, who collected lists of synonyms as a hobby. The book, called *Roget's Thesaurus*, focuses mainly on suggested synonyms for commonly used words, but it also includes antonyms. Since its publication, the book has been updated many times and has been imitated by others, as well.

Use a thesaurus to add variety to your writing and avoid repetitious wording. For example, if you find yourself repeating the word *guilt* in a research paper, consult a thesaurus for substitutes. *Roget's 21st Century Thesaurus* suggests synonyms such as *delinquency, fault, misconduct, shame,* and *transgression.*

> **guilt** [*n*] *blame; bad conscience over responsibility*
> answerability, blameworthiness, contrition, crime, criminality, culpability, delinquency, dereliction, disgrace, dishonor, error, failing, fault, indiscretion, infamy, iniquity, lapse, liability, malefaction, malfeasance, malpractice, misbehavior, misconduct, misstep, offense, onus, peccability, penitence, regret, remorse, responsibility, self-condemnation, self-reproach, shame, sin, sinfulness, slip, solecism, stigma, transgression, wickedness, wrong; SEE CONCEPTS *101,532, 645,690*

Reprinted by permission. Roget's 21st Century Thesaurus. Published by Dell Publishing, a Division of Random House. Copyright 1992, 1993, 1999 by the Philip Lief Group, Inc.

At the end of the entry, inclusion of the words SEE CONCEPTS (printed in capitals and followed by numbers) indicates that you can find additional synonyms under these numbers at the end of the book.

Most word-processing programs have an electronic thesaurus. Usually, it is located near the spelling checker or in the Tools pull-down menu. Use your cursor to highlight (select) the word for which you want alternatives, and then click on the thesaurus. Consider the context of your sentence in choosing from the array of words that appear. Be aware, though, that a thesaurus in book form will offer more choices than the one offered by your word-processing program.

Exercise 2.11

Using a Thesaurus

Use the entries below for *edge* in *Roget's 21st Century Thesaurus* to select an alternative word that fits the meaning of *edge* in the following sentences:

1. On the tenth hole, the least experienced golfer took the *edge* with a long putt. _border,_

2. The new software company is on the *edge* of bankruptcy. _border_

3. Disruptive children can reach the *edge* of a parent's patience. _defeat_

4. The decorator wanted to *edge* the blue fabric with a yellow one. _Outline_

5. The baseball player's face was shaded by the *edge* of his hat. _Sharpen_

edge [*n1*] *border, outline*
bend, berm, bound, boundary, brim, brink, butt, circumference, contour, corner, crook, crust, curb, end, extremity, frame, fringe, frontier, hem, hook, ledge, limb, limit, line, lip, margin, molding, mouth, outskirt, peak, perimeter, periphery, point, portal, rim, ring, shore, side, skirt, split, strand, term, threshold, tip, trimming, turn, verge; SEE CONCEPTS *484,513*
edge [*n2*] *advantage*
allowance, ascendancy, bulge, dominance, draw, handicap, head start, lead, odds, start, superiority, upper hand*, vantage; SEE CONCEPT *712*
edge [*v1*] *border, trim*
bind, bound, decorate, fringe, hem, margin, outline, rim, shape, skirt, surround, verge; SEE CONCEPTS *751,758*
edge [*v2*] *defeat narrowly*
creep, ease, inch, infiltrate, nose out*, sidle, slip by, slip past, squeeze by*, squeeze past*, steal, worm*; SEE CONCEPT *95*
edge [*v3*] *sharpen*
file, grind, hone, polish, sharpen, strop, whet; SEE CONCEPTS *137,250*

Reprinted by permission. Roget's 21st Century Thesaurus. Published by Dell Publishing, a Division of Random House. Copyright 1992, 1993, 1999 by the Philip Lief Group, Inc.

Using Analogies

Analogies are comparisons that measure not only your word knowledge but also your ability to see relationships. They can be difficult, frustrating, and challenging. Use logical thinking and problem-solving skills first to pinpoint the initial relationship and then to establish a similar relationship with two other words.

READER'S TIP

Categories of Analogy Relationships

◆ **Synonyms:** Similar in meaning
  Find is to *locate* as *hope* is to *wish.*

◆ **Antonyms:** Opposite in meaning
  Accept is to *reject* as rude is to *polite.*

◆ **Function, use, or purpose:** Identifies what something does; watch for the object (noun) and then the action (verb)
  Pool is to *swim* as *blanket* is to *warm.*

◆ **Classification:** Identifies the larger group association
  Sandal is to *shoe* as *sourdough* is to *bread.*

◆ **Characteristics and descriptions:** Shows qualities or traits
  Nocturnal is to *raccoon* as humid is to *rainforest.*

◆ **Degree:** Shows variations of intensity
  Fear is to *terror* as *dislike* is to *hate.*

◆ **Part to whole:** Shows the larger group
  Page is to *book* as *caboose* is to *train.*

◆ **Cause and effect:** Shows the reason (cause) and result (effect)
  Study is to *graduation* as *caffeine* is to *insomnia.*

**Exercise
2.12**

Identifying Analogies

Study the analogies that follow to establish the relationship of the first two words. Record that relationship, using the categories outlined in the Reader's Tip. Then choose the word that duplicates that relationship to finish the analogy.

1. *Trash* is to *refuse* as *soil* is to ___Dirt___.

   Relationship ___B___
   a. earthworms
   b. dirt
   c. minerals
   d. growing

2. *Burdened* is to *overwhelmed* as *tired* is to _____.

   Relationship ___B___
   a. sleepy
   b. exhausted
   c. energetic
   d. rested

3. *Cappuccino* is to *coffee* as *jazz* is to ___Dance___

   Relationship ___D___
   a. singer
   b. opera
   c. rock
   d. music

4. *Excited* is to *dull* as *fancy* is to ___ugly___.

   Relationship _____
   a. rich
   b. fortunate
   c. plain
   d. colorful

5. *Fork* is to *eat* as *television* is to ___watch___.

   Relationship ___C___
   a. video
   b. actor
   c. entertain
   d. produce

6. *Sleeve* is *shirt* to as *lens* is to ___glasses___

   Relationship ___C___
   a. book
   b. motor
   c. movement
   d. camera

7. *Smart* is to *genius* as *rigid* is to ___stire___.

   Relationship ___A___
   a. steel
   b. comedy
   c. angle
   d. focus

8. *Recklessness* is to *accident* as *laziness* is to ___Failure___

   Relationship ___C___
   a. work
   b. money
   c. failure
   d. ability

Easily Confused Words

Pairs or groups of words may cause confusion because they sound exactly alike, or almost alike, but are spelled and used differently. *Stationary* and *stationery* are examples of such words. You ride a stationary bike to work out and you write a business letter on your office stationery. For a memory link, associate the *e* in *letter* with the *e* in *stationery*. Students frequently confuse *your* and *you're: your* shows possession, and *you're* is a contraction for *you are.* To differentiate confusing words, create associations to aid memory. **Homonyms**, words with different meanings that are spelled and sound alike, are not as confusing. They tend to be simple words such as *bear* in "bear the burden" or "kill the bear."

Exercise 2.13

Distinguishing Confusing Words

Study the following easily confused words, and then circle the one that is correct in each sentence.

> **accept:** receive
> **except:** all but

1. When children reach adolescence, they begin to **(accept,** except) the values of their peers. _Accept_

> **to:** a preposition
> **too:** additionally
> **two:** the number

2. Entrapment is used as an excuse from criminal liability in **(to,** too, two) many undercover drug cases. _To_

> **thorough:** careful
> **threw:** tossed
> **through:** by means of

3. A **(thorough,** threw, through) investigation can help reveal whether the murder was premeditated. _Thorough_

> **consul:** foreign representative
> **council:** elected officials
> **counsel:** a lawyer appointed to give advice on legal matters; also a verb: give advice

4. The court will appoint (consul, council, **counsel)** for an armed robbery defendant who has no money to pay for a lawyer. _Counsel_   ✓

> **site:** place
> **cite:** quote
> **sight:** vision

5. Attorneys need to (**site, cite, sight**) references from previous trials to support their interpretation of the law. _____sight_____

Recognizing Acronyms

An **acronym** is an abbreviation that is pronounced as a word. Acronyms can thus be considered invented words that are often thoughtfully contrived to simplify a lengthy name and gain quick recognition for an organization or agency. For example, *UNICEF* is the abbreviation for the United Nations International Children's Emergency Fund. The arrangement of consonants and vowels formed by the first letter of each word in the title creates an invented term that we can easily pronounce and quickly recognize. When names are created for new organizations, clever organizers thoughtfully consider the choice and sequence of words in order to engineer a catchy acronym. In some cases, acronyms have become so ingrained in our language that the abbreviations have become accepted as words with lowercase letters. An example of this is the word *radar*, which is a combination of the initial letters of the phrase *radio detecting and ranging*.

Exercise 2.14

Recognizing Acronyms

The following letters are abbreviations. Write an *A* beside those that are pronounced as words and thus are considered acronyms.

A _____ 1. CNN
A _____ 2. NAFTA
_____ 3. MP3
A _____ 4. NASA
_____ 5. IRS
_____ 6. DVD
A _____ 7. UNESCO
A _____ 8. OSHA
_____ 9. MCI
A _____ 10. NASDAQ

Recognizing Transitional Words

Transitional words are connecting words that signal the direction of the writer's thought. They are single words or short phrases that lead the reader to anticipate a continuation or a change in thought. For example, the phrase *in addition* signals a continuation, whereas *but* or *however* signals a change.

READER'S TIP

Signals for Transition

◆ **For addition:** in addition, furthermore, moreover

◆ **For examples:** for example, for instance, to illustrate, such as

◆ **For time:** first, second, finally, last, afterward

◆ **For comparison:** similarly, likewise, in the same manner

◆ **For contrast:** however, but, nevertheless, whereas, on the contrary, conversely, in contrast

◆ **For cause and effect:** thus, consequently, therefore, as a result, furthermore, similarly, consequently, however, for example

**Exercise
2.15**

Anticipating Transitions

Read to understand the direction of the author's thought, and then choose a signal word from the boxed list to complete the following sentences.

furthermore   similarly   consequently   however   for example

1. The Internet is a valuable research tool; *however*, it can be frustrating.

2. Ragweed causes allergies; _____, mildew and dust mites stimulate allergic reactions.

3. The chemist walked to class yesterday in the rain and *consequently* has a cold today.

4. Papers are due at the beginning of the period, and *however*, they should be put on my desk when you first enter the classroom.

5. Runners train for many different events. *For example*, the Boston Marathon attracts thousands of athletes.

Summary Points

● How do you remember new words?

To remember new words, use mnemonic devices to associate words in phrases, in families, and in images. Use concept cards to record a new word's definition with a phrase and an image that suggest the meaning.

● What are context clues?

The context clues in a sentence or paragraph can help unlock the meaning of unknown words. These can be definitions or synonyms, details, examples, and comparisons, contrasts, or antonyms.

● Why learn prefixes, roots, and suffixes?

A knowledge of prefixes, roots, and suffixes can reveal smaller and more familiar word parts in unknown words.

● What will you find in a dictionary?

A collegiate dictionary contains definitions, word origins, pronunciations, and spellings.

● What is a glossary?

A glossary defines words that are unique to a subject matter area.

● What is a thesaurus?

A thesaurus is a reference book that contains synonyms for frequently used words to add variety to writing.

● What are analogies?

Analogies are comparisons that fall into different categories of relationships.

● What are acronyms?

Acronyms are abbreviations that are pronounced as words.

● How are transitional words used?

Transitional words are used to connect words that signal the writer's thought.

Search the Net

Use a search engine such as Google, AltaVista, Excite, Infoseek, Dogpile, Yahoo, or Lycos to find exercises on analogies. Select, print, and bring to class five sample analogies that your classmates would enjoy solving. For suggested Web sites and other research activities, go to http://www.ablongman.com/smith/.

Vocabulary Booster:

Over, Under, Around, and Through

This is the first of ten end-of-chapter vocabulary lessons in this textbook designed to expand your vocabulary. Each lesson links words through shared prefixes, roots, and suffixes. The words are organized into different clusters or families to enhance memory, to organize your learning, and to emphasize that most new words are made up of familiar old parts. Strengthen your vocabulary by identifying your old friends in the new words. Then apply your knowledge of word parts to unlock and remember the meanings of the new words. You will learn more than 200 words through this easy word family approach.

Your instructor may choose to use these as weekly lessons by introducing the words at the beginning of the week, assigning review items for practice, and quizzing your knowledge of the words at the end of the week. All lessons follow the same format, except for slight variations in the lesson on doctors and the one on foreign terms. Following is the first one.

Study the following prefixes, words, and sentences.

Prefixes

sur-: over, above, more
amb-, *ambi-*: around, about, both

sub-: under, beneath
dia-: through

Words with *sur-*: over, above, or more

The fugitive *surrendered* himself to the police when he could no longer avoid capture.

■ *surcharge:* an additional charge, tax, or cost

The *surcharge* on an item such as cigarettes or alcohol is sometimes called a "sin tax" because these items are considered by some to be vices rather than necessities.

■ *surface:* uppermost or outermost area; top layer

When the deep-sea diver reached the *surface*, he saw that he had drifted far from his boat.

■ *surfeit:* overindulgence in eating or drinking, an excessive amount

Thanksgiving dinner usually means a *surfeit* of foods far beyond the usual amount served for an everyday meal.

■ *surmise:* to guess, to infer without certain evidence

At the point that Cindy and Gary were thirty minutes late to the ball game, I *surmised* that they probably were not coming.

- *surveillance:* a watch kept over someone or something

  The United States flies *surveillance* missions all over the world to collect information vital to our security.

- *surplus:* an amount greater than needed

  The government had collected more taxes than needed, so the *surplus* was returned to the taxpayers.

Words with *sub-:* under, beneath

Jorge's *subconscious* belief that he wasn't a good athlete probably contributed to his poor performance during basketball tryouts.

- *subsequent:* occurring later, following

  Ill health is usually *subsequent* to long periods of ignoring good nutrition and getting little sleep.

- *subservient:* excessively submissive

  Victorian husbands expected their wives to be *subservient*.

- *subsidiary:* subordinate or secondary

  The food products corporation decided to sell its *subsidiary* clothing company and remain focused on foods.

- *substantiate:* to establish by proof

  A witness was able to *substantiate* Linda's story that the auto accident was not her fault.

- *subvert:* to overthrow something, such as a government; to cause the ruin of

  Castro's regime in Cuba came into power by *subverting* Batista's presidency.

- *subsistence:* a means of supporting life

  Her small *subsistence* check from the government was all the octogenarian had for living expenses after her husband died.

Words with *ambi-:* around, about, both

The horse's gait was kept to an *amble* as the jockey slowly walked him into the winner's circle.

- ***ambiance*** or ***ambience:*** the mood or atmosphere of a place or situation

  The day spa's low lighting, comfortable furnishings, and quiet music produced an *ambience* of soothing relaxation.

- *ambidextrous:* able to use both hands equally well; unusually skillful

    Being *ambidextrous* allows Keisha to write for long periods of time by switching hands when one gets tired.

- *ambiguous:* having two or more possible meanings

    Rosa was *ambiguous* when she said she fell on the skiing trip. We expected to see a cast on her leg, not a new boyfriend on her arm.

- *ambivalent:* fluctuating between two choices; having opposing feelings

    Jealousy and tremendous familial pride were the two *ambivalent* feelings Juan was experiencing over his brother's acceptance at a prestigious school.

- *ambulatory:* capable of walking

    Doctors didn't think Nora would be *ambulatory* again after the accident damaged her spinal cord.

- *ambition*: strong desire for fame or power

    His *ambition* to climb the corporate ladder drove Jim to work long hours to accomplish his goal.

Words with *dia-:* through

If you know the *diameter* of a circle, it is easy to find the circumference.

- *diagnosis:* a determination of the cause of medical symptoms; analysis of the cause of a situation

    The doctor's *diagnosis* of strep throat was proved correct when the lab report came back.

- *dialogue:* conversation between two or more persons

    The three actors practiced the scenes in which they had a humorous *dialogue* together.

- *diametrical:* pertaining to a diameter; at opposite extremes

    Susan was pro-life and *diametrically* opposed to any pro-choice legislation in Congress.

- *diatribe:* a bitter, abusive criticism

    After listening to a *diatribe* from her possessive boyfriend because she spent time with her girlfriends, Angelina decided to end the unhealthy relationship.

- *dialect:* a distinct variety of a language that differs from the standard

    Parts of rural England have *dialects* that differ from the English spoken in London.

- *diagonal:* an oblique or slanting line connecting opposite corners or angles

    Rather than being laid square, the floor tiles were laid on the *diagonal* for an additional decorative effect.

Review

Part I

Choose the best word from the box to complete the sentences below.

ambience	~~ambulatory~~	diagnosis	dialect	diametric	subsequent
	subsidiaries	surface	surfeit	surveillance	

1. Even though the patient was *ambulatory,* the hospital required her to leave the facility in a wheelchair.

2. *Sub* _____ to receiving his college degree, Jose secured job interviews with four companies he had been unable to interview with before.

3. The literary *dialect* of Shakespeare's time differs from the ordinary language in word order and vocabulary.

4. The *ambience* created by the candlelight, flowers, and violins made the restaurant dinner especially romantic.

5. Jordan's speedy *diagnosis* of the computer problem in the office got everyone back online quickly and prevented a significant delay in the work schedule.

6. For many people, freckles show up on the *surface* of the skin after exposure to the sun.

7. Many large companies are diversified and own *subsidiaries* that are secondary to their main areas of business.

8. The sick feeling I had when I woke up this morning was a result of the *surfeit* of food and drink at the party the night before.

9. Feelings of love and hate are at *diametric* ends of the spectrum.

10. The murder suspect was under *surveillance* by police who were hoping to catch him with new evidence.

Part II

Choose the best synonym from the boxed list for each of the words below.

confirm	conversation	corrupt	excess	(presume)	skillful
	stroll	subordinate	tirade	vague	

11. surmise *presume*

12. ambidextrous *skillful*

13. surplus *excess*

14. dialogue *conversation*

15. subvert *corrupt*

16. substantiate *confirm*

17. amble *stroll*

18. diatribe *tirade*

19. ambiguous *vague*

20. subservient *subordinate*

Your instructor may choose to give you a multiple-choice review.

Strategic Reading and Study

- What is strategic reading?
- What is a study strategy?
- What are the three stages of reading?
- What are the strategies for previewing?
- Why should you activate your schema?
- What is metacognition?
- What are the strategies for integrating knowledge during reading?
- Why recall or self-test what you have read?

Study or The Schoolgirl by Jean Puy, ca. 1933-1934. Oil on canvas, 61 x 72 cm. Musée d'Art Moderne de la Ville de Paris, Paris, France. © 2006 Artist Rights Society (ARS) New York/ADAGP, Paris. Photo: Bridgeman-Giraudon/Art Resource, NY.

What Is Strategic Reading?

In college you can expect a demanding course load and, most likely, a greater volume of difficult material than you have been assigned in the past. How can you meet the challenge and become a more effective reader? The answer is to have an arsenal of techniques, or strategies, to help you navigate through the required reading in your courses. For example, mastering the decoding or sounding out of words is one strategy. It is an initial and essential one, but college readers must go far beyond this level into the realm of associating and remembering.

Reading strategically means using specific techniques for understanding, studying, and learning. Research studies find that students who systematically learn such techniques score higher on reading comprehension tests. These strategies—previewing, questioning, connecting, recalling, determining the main idea, recognizing significant supporting details, drawing inferences, and others—will be presented throughout the various chapters in this text. Keep in mind, though, that for greatest success, you must do more than understand the strategies. You must also know when, why, and how to use them.

Four Types of Readers.   Just as not all types of reading are the same, not all readers are the same. To understand how readers differ, read the following description of the four levels of reading and learning:[1]

- *Tacit learners/readers.* These readers lack awareness of how they think when reading.

- *Aware learners/readers.* These readers realize when meaning has broken down or confusion has set in but may not have sufficient strategies for fixing the problem.

- *Strategic learners/readers.* These readers use the thinking and comprehension strategies described in this text to enhance understanding and acquire knowledge. They are able to monitor and repair meaning when it is disrupted.

- *Reflective learners/readers.* These readers are strategic about their thinking and apply strategies flexibly depending on their goals or purposes for reading. In addition, they "reflect on their thinking and ponder and revise their future use of strategies."[2]

Which type describes your reading now? With this textbook, you are on your way to becoming a strategic and reflective learner and reader! The dynamic process of reading and learning can be broken into manageable pieces. Master the parts and see how they contribute to the whole. We begin by breaking reading into three stages and explaining strategies to use for each.

---

[1]S. Harvey and A. Goudvis, *Strategies That Work* (Portland, ME: Stenhouse Publishers, 2000), p. 17.
[2]D. Perkins, *Smart Schools: Better Thinking and Learning for Every Child* (New York: Free Press, 1992).

What Are the Stages of Reading?

In 1946, after years of working with college students at Ohio State University, Francis P. Robinson developed a textbook study system designed to help students efficiently read and learn from textbooks and effectively recall information for exams. The system was called SQ3R, with the letters standing for the following five steps: <u>S</u>urvey, <u>Q</u>uestion, <u>R</u>ead, <u>R</u>ecite, and <u>R</u>eview.

Numerous variations have been developed since SQ3R was introduced. One researcher, Norman Stahl, analyzed 65 textbook reading/learning systems and concluded that they have more similarities than differences.[3] The common elements in the systems include a previewing stage, a reading stage, and a final self-testing stage.

In the *previewing* stage that occurs before reading, students make predictions, ask questions, activate schema (past knowledge), and establish a purpose for reading. In the *knowledge integration* stage that occurs during reading, students make predictions, picture images, answer questions, continually relate

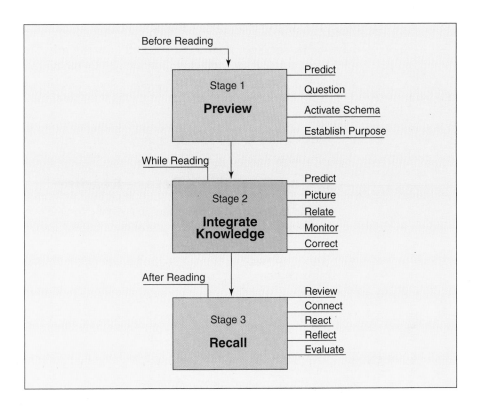

---

[3]N. A. Stahl, "Historical Analysis of Textbook Study Systems" (Ph.D. dissertation, University of Pittsburgh, 1983).

and integrate old and new knowledge, monitor understanding to clarify confusing points, and use correction strategies. The *recall* stage that occurs after reading involves reviewing to self-test and improve recall, making connections to blend new information with existing knowledge networks, and reacting and reflecting to evaluate and accept or reject ideas.

Stage 1: Strategies for Previewing

Previewing is a method of personally connecting with the material before you start to read. When you preview, you look over the material, predict what the material is probably about, ask yourself what you already know about the topic, decide what you will probably know after you read, and make a plan for reading. See the Reader's Tip for useful questions to ask before reading.

To preview, look over the material, think, and ask questions. The focus is, "What do I already know, what do I need to know, and how do I go about finding it out?"

Signposts for Asking Preview Questions

Like public speakers, textbook authors follow the rule, "Tell them what you are going to tell them, tell them, and then tell them what you told them." Typically, a chapter begins with a brief overview of the topic, an outline, or

READER'S TIP

Asking Questions Before Reading

◆ **What is the topic of the material?** What does the title suggest? What do the subheadings, italics, and summaries suggest?

◆ **What do I already know?** What do I already know about this topic or a related topic? Is this new topic a small part of a larger idea or issue that I have thought about before?

◆ **What is my purpose for reading?** What will I need to know when I finish?

◆ **How is the material organized?** What is the general outline or framework of the material? Is the author listing reasons, explaining a process, or comparing a trend?

◆ **What will be my plan of attack?** What parts of the textbook seem most important? Do I need to read everything with equal care? Can I skim some parts? Can I skip some sections completely?

questions. The ideas are then developed in clearly marked sections. Concluding statements at the end summarize the important points. Although this pattern does not apply in every case, use it when available as a guide in determining what to read when previewing textbook material.

Previewing can be a hit-or-miss activity because of differences in writing styles, so no one set of rules will work for all materials. Consider the following signposts when previewing.

Title. A title attracts attention, suggests content, and is the first and most obvious clue. Think about the title and turn it into a question. For an article entitled "Acupuncture," ask "What is acupuncture?" For other questions, use the "five-*W* technique" of journalists to find out *who, what, when, where,* and *why*.

Introductory Material. To get an overview of an entire book, refer to the table of contents and preface. Sophisticated students use the table of contents as a study guide, turning the chapter headings into possible exam items. Many textbook chapters open with an outline, preview questions, or an interesting anecdote that sets the stage for learning. Italicized inserts, decorative symbols, and colored type are also used to highlight key concepts. The first paragraph frequently sets expectations.

Subheadings. Subheadings are titles for sections within chapters. The subheadings, usually appearing in **boldface print** or *italics*, outline the main points of the author's message and thus give the reader an overview of the organization and the content. Turn these subheadings into questions to answer as you read.

Italics, Boldface Print, and Numbers. Italics and boldface print are used to highlight words that merit special attention. These are usually new words or key words that you should be prepared to define and remember. For example, an explanation of sterilization in a biology text might emphasize the words *vasectomy* and *tubal ligation* in italics or boldface print. Numbers can also be used to signal a list of important details. The biology book might emphasize the two forms of sterilization with enumeration: (1) vasectomy and (2) tubal ligation.

Visual Aids. Photographs with their captions, charts, graphs, and maps emphasize important points and sometimes condense text. Reviewing visuals provides clues to what will be significant.

Concluding Summary. Many textbooks include a summary at the end of each chapter to highlight the important points within the material. The summary can serve not only as a review to follow reading but also as an introduction for overviewing the chapter prior to reading.

| Exercise 3.1 | **Previewing This Textbook for the Big Picture** |

To get an overview of the scope of this textbook and its sequence of topics, look over the table of contents and preface. Think about how the different chapter topics fit into the goals of college reading. Glance at the chapters to get a sense of the overall organization, and then answer the following questions.

1. Who is the author? Is the author an instructor? _____
   _____

2. What seems to be the purpose of the numbered reading selections?
   _____

3. List six different college disciplines that are represented in the numbered reading selections. _____
   _____

4. What seems to be the purpose of the Contemporary Focus selections?
   _____

5. Does the text have any study aids such as an index, a glossary, or summaries?
   _____

6. Which reading selection do you think will be the most interesting?
   _____

7. How does this textbook include Internet activities? What additional information is provided on the Web site? _____
   _____

| Exercise 3.2 | **Previewing This Chapter** |

To get an overview of this chapter, first look at the table of contents at the beginning of the book, and then read the list of questions at the beginning of the chapter. Flip to the chapter summary points and read them. Use your previewing to answer the following questions.

1. What is strategic reading? using specifec Techniques For understanding, studying and learning

2. What is a schema? A Skeleton or network of knowledge about a subject

3. What is metacognition? knowledge of how to read as well as the ability to regulate and and direct the process

4. What is the purpose of a recall diagram? _To help students_ _efficiently read and learn from textbooks_ _and effectively recall information_

5. Which reading selection do you think will be most interesting? _The stages of reading_

6. What are the five thinking strategies used by good readers? _Survey, Question, Read, Recite, Review_

Use your answers to these questions to help establish a purpose or a learning strategy goal for reading the chapter. Why is this chapter important, and what do you hope to gain from reading it?

Preview to Activate Schemata

What do you bring to the printed page? As a reader, you are thinking and interacting before, during, and after reading. Your previewing of material first helps you predict the topic. Then, as a further part of the prereading stage, you need to activate your schema for what you perceive the topic to be.

A **schema** (plural, *schemata*) is like a computer file in your brain that holds all you know on a subject. Each time you learn something new, you pull out the computer file on that subject, add the new information, and return the file to storage. The depth of the schema or the amount of information contained in the file varies according to previous experience. For example, a scientist would have a larger, more detailed file for DNA than would most freshman biology students.

The richness of your background determines the amount you can activate. In general, the more schemata you are able to activate, the more meaningful your reading will be. In fact, most experts agree that the single best predictor of your reading comprehension is what you already know. In other words, the rich get richer. Why is that good for you?

Once you have struggled with and learned about a subject, the next time you meet the subject, reading/learning will be easier. You will have greatly expanded your schema for the subject. Does this help explain why some say that the freshman year is the hardest? Some students who barely make C's in introductory courses end up making A's and B's in their junior and senior years. They profited from previous hard work to establish the frameworks of knowledge in building schemata. Comfort yourself during the early struggles by saying, "The smart get smarter, and I'm getting smart!"

Stage 2: Strategies for Integrating Knowledge While Reading

What are you thinking about when you read? Do you visualize? Do you make comparisons? If you don't understand, do you *notice* that you don't understand?

EXAMPLE   Read the following passage to answer the question, "What are echinoderms?" Are your thoughts similar to the inserted thoughts of the reader?

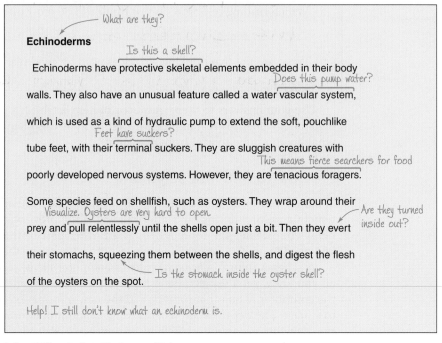

Robert Wallace, Biology: The Science of Life

Were you able to follow the reader's inserted thoughts? Do you know what an echinoderm is? Can you guess? If you had known before reading that starfish are echinoderms, the passage would have been more entertaining and less challenging. If you have opened an oyster, you know the tenacity needed to open its shell. Reread the passage with this knowledge, and visualize the gruesome drama. Later in this chapter, be ready to pull out your now enlarged schema on echinoderms and network knowledge on a new passage.

Integrating Ideas: How Do Good Readers Think?

Understanding and remembering complex material requires as much thinking as reading. As illustrated in the previous passage, the good reader is always predicting, visualizing, and drawing comparisons to assimilate new knowledge. Beth Davey, a reading researcher, broke these thoughts down into five manageable and teachable strategies. The Reader's Tip lists the five thinking strategies of good readers.[4] Study them and visualize how you use each.

---

[4]B. Davey, "Think Aloud—Modeling for Cognitive Processes of Reading Comprehension," *Journal of Reading* 27 (October 1983): 44–47.

READER'S TIP

Using Thinking Strategies While Reading

◆ **Make predictions.** Develop hypotheses.
"From the title, I predict that this section will give another example of a critical time for rats to learn a behavior."
"In this next part, I think we'll find out why the ancient Greeks used mnemonic devices."
"I think this is a description of an acupuncture treatment."

◆ **Describe the picture you're forming in your head from the information.** Develop images during reading.
"I have a picture of this scene in my mind. My pet is lying on the table with acupuncture needles sticking out of its fur."

◆ **Share an analogy.** Link prior knowledge with new information in text. We call this the *"like-a" step.*
"This is like my remembering, 'In 1492 Columbus sailed the ocean blue.'"

◆ **Monitor your ongoing comprehension.** Clarify confusing points.
"This is confusing."
"This just doesn't make sense. How can redwoods and cypress trees both be part of the same family?"
"This is different from what I had expected."

◆ **Correct gaps in comprehension.** Use fix-up correction strategies.
"I'd better reread."
"Maybe I'll read ahead to see if it gets clearer."
"I'd better change my picture of the story."
"This is a new word to me. I'd better check the context to figure it out."

The first three thinking strategies used by good readers are perhaps the easiest to understand and the quickest to develop. From short stories as a young reader, you quickly learned to predict actions and outcomes. You would see the characters and scenes in your head. Such visualizing increased your level of involvement and enjoyment. You compared the character's reactions and adventures to your own.

When ideas get more complicated and reading becomes more difficult, however, the last two thinking strategies become essential elements in the pursuit of meaning. College textbooks are tough, requiring constant use of the monitoring strategy and frequent use of the correction strategy.

The final strategies involve a higher level of thinking than just picturing an oyster or a starfish. They reflect a deeper understanding of the process of getting meaning, and they require a reader who both understands the thinking process and controls that process. This ability to know and control is called *metacognition* (knowing about knowing).[5]

Metacognition

When you look at the following words, what is your reaction?

feeet   thankz   supplyyied

Your reaction is probably, "The words don't look right. They are misspelled." The reason you realize the errors so quickly is that you have a global understanding of the manner in which letters can and cannot occur in the English language. You instantly recognize the errors through an immediate scan of your knowledge of words and the rules of ordering letters. Through your efficient recognition and correction, you have used information that goes beyond knowing about each of the three individual words. You have demonstrated a metacognitive awareness and understanding of spelling in the English language.[6]

The term **metacognition** is a coined word. *Cognition* refers to knowledge or skills that you possess. The Greek prefix *meta-*suggests an abstract level of understanding, as if viewed from the outside. Thus, *metacognition* not only means having the knowledge but also refers to your own awareness and understanding of the thinking processes involved and your ability to regulate and direct these processes. If you know how to read, you are operating on a cognitive level. To operate on a metacognitive level, you must know the processes involved in reading—predicting, visualizing, relating new knowledge to old, clarifying points to monitor comprehension, and using correction strategies and be able to regulate them.

The Strategies of Metacognition

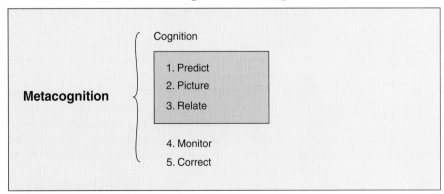

[5]A. L. Brown, "The Development of Memory: Knowing, Knowing about Knowing, and Knowing How to Know," in H. W. Reese, ed., *Advances in Child Development and Behavior*, vol. 10 (New York: Academic Press, 1975), pp. 104–146.

[6]The author is grateful to Professor Jane Thielemann, University of Houston (Downtown), for inspiring this paragraph.

Let's take a real-life example. If you are reading a biology assignment and failing to understand it, you must first recognize that you are not comprehending. Next you must identify what and why you don't understand. Maybe you don't have enough background knowledge, your focus is overshadowed by details, you are relying on misconceptions that are not valid, or your attention is waning. Once you figure out the reason for your confusion, you can attempt a correction strategy. If your strategy does not work, try another and remain confident that you will succeed. The point of metacognition is to understand how to get meaning, to know when you don't have it, and to know what to do about straightening things out.

Here is another example: Do you know when you are really studying? In other words, what is the difference between really studying and simply going through the motions of studying? Sometimes you can study intensely for an hour and accomplish a phenomenal amount. At other times, you can put in twice the time with books and notes but learn practically nothing. Do you know the difference and do you know what to do about it?

Keep Your Eye on the Ball. Some students know the difference, whereas others do not. If you occasionally find yourself in the "going through the motions" frame of mind, think of your attention lapse not as lack of ability but as a wake-up call to reanalyze the task in front of you. Ask yourself, "What is my goal today? What can I do to focus more successfully on what needs to be done?" Picture yourself as an athlete who must keep an eye on the ball to win the game. Be your own coach by telling yourself that you can correct your problems and be more productive.

The Reader's Tip describes how you can improve your reading using metacognition.

READER'S TIP

Developing a Metacognitive Sense for Reading

With instruction and practice, you can improve your reading performance.

◆ **Know about reading.** Are you aware of the many strategies you use to comprehend? These include knowledge about words, main ideas, supporting details, and implied ideas. Also, think about the organization of the text and where meaning can be found.

◆ **Know how to monitor.** Monitor as an ongoing process throughout your reading. Use predicting and questioning to corroborate or discard ideas. Continually clarify and self-test to reinforce learning and pinpoint gaps in comprehension.

◆ **Know how to correct confusion.** Reread to reprocess a complex idea. Unravel a confusing writing style on a sentence level. Read ahead for ideas that unfold slowly. Consult a dictionary or other sources to fill in background knowledge you lack.

Gain Insight Through Think-Alouds. Experts say that the best way for instructors to teach comprehension strategies is not by just telling students what to do, but by showing them what to do.[7] Students seem to get the message best *when instructors demonstrate how they themselves actually think while reading.* How can that be done? Some instructors read a short passage aloud and verbalize internal thinking, similar to the thoughts inserted in the previous passage on echinoderms. Such modeling activities are called think-alouds. They will be inserted throughout this book to heighten your awareness of how good readers think.

EXAMPLE   Apply both your cognitive and metacognitive knowledge to answer the following test item. Interact with the material, monitor, and predict the ending phrase before reading the options. The inserted handwriting simulates a think-aloud by modeling the thinking of a good reader.

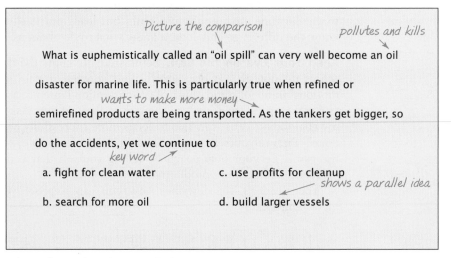

Picture the comparison

pollutes and kills

What is euphemistically called an "oil spill" can very well become an oil

disaster for marine life. This is particularly true when refined or

wants to make more money

semirefined products are being transported. As the tankers get bigger, so

do the accidents, yet we continue to

key word

a. fight for clean water   c. use profits for cleanup

                                   shows a parallel idea

b. search for more oil   d. build larger vessels

Robert Wallace, Biology: The Science of Life

EXPLANATION   Because you were an engaged thinker, you probably predicted the correct answer *d*, even before reading the four options.

In this test item as well as in the passage at the top of page 101, the inserted comments may be confusing to read because involvement differs and many thoughts occur on the subconscious level rather than on the conscious level. Stopping to consciously analyze these reactions may seem artificial and disruptive. It is important, however, to be aware of how you are incorporating the five thinking strategies into your reading.

The passage at the top of the next page illustrates the use of these thinking strategies with longer textbook material. Modeled thoughts of the reader are again inserted for a simulated think-aloud. Again, keep in mind that each reader reacts differently to material, depending on background and individual differences.

Exercise 3.3 will heighten your awareness of the process of interacting analytically with a piece of writing.

[7]S. Harvey and A. Goudvis, *Strategies That Work* (Portland, ME: Stenhouse Publishers, 2000) p. 13.

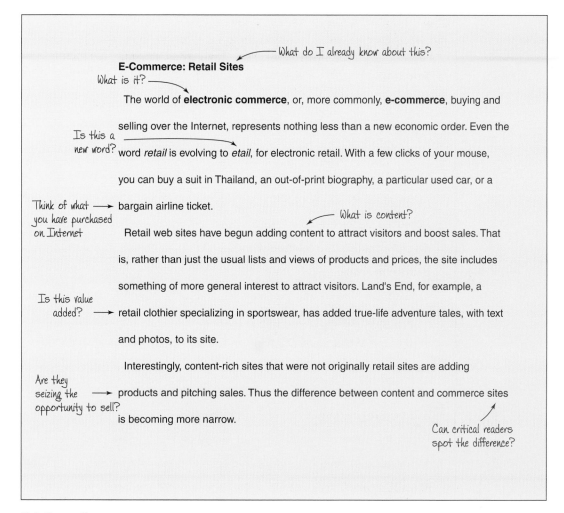

The annotated passage reads:

What do I already know about this?

E-Commerce: Retail Sites

What is it?

The world of **electronic commerce**, or, more commonly, **e-commerce**, buying and

Is this a new word? selling over the Internet, represents nothing less than a new economic order. Even the

word *retail* is evolving to *etail*, for electronic retail. With a few clicks of your mouse,

you can buy a suit in Thailand, an out-of-print biography, a particular used car, or a

Think of what you have purchased on Internet bargain airline ticket.

What is content?

Retail web sites have begun adding content to attract visitors and boost sales. That

is, rather than just the usual lists and views of products and prices, the site includes

Is this value added? something of more general interest to attract visitors. Land's End, for example, a

retail clothier specializing in sportswear, has added true-life adventure tales, with text

and photos, to its site.

Interestingly, content-rich sites that were not originally retail sites are adding

Are they seizing the opportunity to sell? products and pitching sales. Thus the difference between content and commerce sites

is becoming more narrow.

Can critical readers spot the difference?

H. L. Capron, Computers

Exercise 3.3	**Integrating Knowledge While Reading**

For the following passage, demonstrate with written notes the way you use the five thinking strategies as you read. The passage is double-spaced so you can insert your thoughts and reactions between the lines. Begin by looking at the title and pulling out your recently enhanced computer file. Make a conscious effort to implement all the following strategies as you read:

1. Predict (develop hypotheses).

2. Picture (develop images during reading).

3. Relate (link prior knowledge with new ideas).

4. Monitor your ongoing comprehension (clarify confusing points).

5. Correct gaps in comprehension (use correction strategies).

Sea Stars

Let's take a look at one class of echinoderms—the sea stars. Sea stars (starfish) are well known for their voracious appetite when it comes to gourmet foods, such as oysters and clams. Obviously, they are the sworn enemy of oystermen. But these same oystermen may have inadvertently helped the spread of the sea stars. At one time, when they caught a starfish, they chopped it apart and vengefully kicked the pieces overboard. But they were unfamiliar with the regenerative powers of the starfish. The central disk merely grows new arms, and a single arm can form a new animal.

Stars are slow-moving predators, so their prey, obviously, are even slower-moving or immobile. Their ability to open an oyster shell is a testimony to their persistence. When a sea star finds an oyster or clam, the prey clamps its shell together tightly, a tactic that discourages most would-be predators, but not the starfish. It bends its body over the oyster and attaches its tube feet to the shell, and then begins to pull. Tiring is no problem since it uses tube feet in relays. Finally, the oyster can no longer hold itself shut, and it opens gradually—only a tiny bit, but it is enough. The star then protrudes its stomach out through its mouth. The soft stomach slips into the slightly opened shell, surrounds the oyster, and digests it in its own shell.

Robert Wallace, *Biology: The Science of Life*

At first glance, you recognized the echinoderm as an old friend and activated your newly acquired schema. The description of the starfish lends itself to a vivid visualization. Were some of your predictions corroborated as you read the passage? Did you find yourself monitoring to reconcile new facts with old ideas? Did you need to use a correction strategy? Did you guess about the regenerative powers? Has your computer file been expanded?

Stage 3: Strategies for Recalling

To recall, you tell yourself what you have learned, relate it to what you already know, react, and evaluate. Actually, you do all this before and during reading, but a deliberate recall is necessary when you finish reading to assimilate knowledge and improve learning. Call it a short conversation with yourself to debrief and digest. You need to be sure you know the content, make connections, and update your schemata or computer files.

Recalling Through Writing

Answering multiple-choice questions after reading requires one type of mental processing, but writing about the reading requires another type of processing. Experts define writing as a "mode of learning," which means that writing is a process that helps students blend, reconcile, and gain personal ownership of new knowledge. When you write about a subject, you not only discover how much you know and don't know, but you begin to unfold meaningful personal connections.

A humorous adage about the power of writing says, "How do I know what I think until I see what I say?" Writing can be hard work, but it helps you clarify and crystallize what you have learned. You discover your own thinking as you write. Use the power of this valuable tool to take your recall to a higher level. For the longer chapter reading selections in this text, both multiple-choice and writing questions are offered to help you learn.

How to Recall

Recall can be broken down into three manageable steps: self-testing, making connections, and reacting.

Self-Test. First, test yourself to be sure you understand the content. To have confidence in your opinions, make sure that you clearly understand the facts. You can do this simply by taking a few minutes after reading to recap what you have learned. Do it either in your head or on paper. For practice, use a recall diagram as a learning tool to visualize the main points. On a straight line across the top of a piece of paper, briefly state the topic, or what the passage seems to be mainly about. Indent underneath the topic and state the supporting details that seem to be most significant.

Make Connections. In the next step of recall, create bridges between what is new to you and what you already know. Ask yourself, "What do I already know that relates to this information?" Your answer will be unique because you are connecting the material to your own knowledge networks. Returning to the recall diagram you started in the previous step, draw a dotted line—your thought line—and write down a related idea, issue, or concern. Connect the text with your personal life experiences, with other things you have read, and with larger global issues. Researchers Harvey and Goudvis categorize these connections in the following way:[8]

- **Text-to-self:** Readers connect with their own personal experiences and background knowledge.
- **Text-to-text:** Readers connect new text with other written material.
- **Text-to-world:** Readers connect to bigger issues, events, or societal concerns.

How can you translate this theory into practice? Certainly, you can easily relate new reading to yourself. Relating to other written material may seem

---

[8]S. Harvey and A. Goudvis, *Strategies That Work* (Portland, ME: Stenhouse Publishers, 2000), p. 21.

> ## READER'S TIP
>
> ## Recalling After Reading
>
> ◆ **Pinpoint the topic.** Get focused on the subject. Use the title and the subheading to help you recognize and narrow down the topic.
>
> ◆ **Select the most important points.** Poor readers want to remember everything, thinking all facts have equal importance. Good readers pull out the important issues and identify significant supporting information.
>
> ◆ **Relate the information.** Facts are difficult to learn in isolation. In history, events should not be seen as isolated happenings but rather as results of previous occurrences. Network your new knowledge to enhance memory. Relate new knowledge to yourself, to other written material, and to global issues.
>
> ◆ **React.** Form opinions and evaluate the material and the author. Decide what you wish to accept and what you will reject. Blend old and new knowledge, and write about what you have read.

difficult initially but will be less challenging if you make everyday reading a part of your life. To help you with these connections, the longer reading selections in this text are preceded by a Contemporary Focus feature. These excerpts from recent publications introduce the selection; and later you are asked to answer a question that connects the two. Finally, your ability to make societal or global connections depends on your own interests and knowledge. Your awareness of these kinds of connections will encourage you to dig deeper to relate meaning.

React and Reflect. The final step in recalling is to react to the material. Formulate an opinion about the author and evaluate the message. Returning to your recall diagram, do you agree or disagree with the facts, opinions, and conclusions? How do you feel about the topic? Is this information significant to you? Did the author do a good job? Is this quality work? Your answers will be unique, and there are no right or wrong responses. You are thinking, and you are in control. In all three steps in recalling, you are strengthening your ties to new material. You must link it to own it.

EXAMPLE   ### Autopsies

Today, many dead people receive some form of autopsy or postmortem examination. At least two main reasons for this are (1) the desire of the family to know the exact cause of death, and (2) the fact that increased medical knowledge results. Because of the important moral and legal restrictions on human experimentation, much of our knowledge of pathology comes from autopsies. This fact prompts many people to donate their bodies to medical schools and/or donate certain organs for possible transplantation.

John Cunningham, *Human Biology*, 2nd ed.

EXPLANATION Remember that the recall diagram is a temporary and artificial format. The diagram below graphically demonstrates a process that you will learn to do in your head. Using the diagram will help you learn to organize and visualize your reading.

(Topic)	Why autopsies are done
(Significant details— examples, facts, or phrases)	To know exact cause of death
	To increase medical knowledge
	— thus donations
(Relate)	Do I want medical students studying my body?
(React)	I would donate my organs but not my body to medical school.

Exercise 3.4

Using Recall Diagrams

After reading each of the following passages, stop to recall what the passage contained. Use recall diagrams to record what the passage seems to be mainly about. List significant supporting details, identify a related idea, issue, or concern to which you feel the information is connected, and react.

Passage A: The Depression and Its Victims

The Depression affected the families of the jobless in many ways. It caused a dramatic drop in the birthrate, from 27.7 per thousand population in 1920 to 18.4 per thousand in the early 1930s, the lowest in American history. Sometimes it strengthened family ties. Some unemployed men spent more time with their children and helped their wives with cooking and housework. Others, however, became impatient when their children demanded attention, refused to help around the house, sulked, or took to drink. The influence of wives in families struck by unemployment tended to increase, and in this respect women suffered less psychologically from the depression. They were usually too busy trying to make ends meet to become apathetic.

Children often caused strains in families. Parental authority declined when there was less money available to supply children's needs. Some youngsters became angry when their allowance was cut or when told they could not have something they particularly wanted. Some adolescents found part-time jobs to help out. Others refused to go to school.

John Garraty and Mark Carnes, *The American Nation*, 10th ed.

(Topic) _Depression affected the families of the Jobless in many ways_

(Significant details) _Dramatic drop in birthrate_
Strenghtend Family ties
Children often cause strains in familys

(Relate)

(React)

Passage B: Kangaroos

Kangaroos and Australia are synonymous for most people, and the abundance of the large kangaroos has gone up since the British colonized Australia. The increase in kangaroo populations has occurred in spite of intensive shooting programs, since kangaroos are considered pests by ranchers and are harvested for meat and hides. The reason seems to be that ranchers have improved the habitat for the large kangaroos in three ways. First, in making water available for their sheep and cattle, the ranchers have also made it available for the kangaroos, removing the impact of water shortage for kangaroos in arid environments. Second, ranchers have cleared timber and produced grasslands for livestock. Kangaroos feed on grass, and so their food supply has been increased as well as the water supply. Third, ranchers have removed a major predator, the dingo. The dingo is a doglike predator, the largest carnivore in Australia. Because dingoes eat sheep, ranchers have built some 9,660 kilometers of fence in southern and eastern Australia to prevent dingoes from moving into sheep country. Intensive poisoning and shooting of dingoes in sheep country, coupled with the dingo fence that prevents recolonization, has produced a classic experiment in predator control.

Charles Krebs, *The Message of Ecology*

(Topic)

(Significant details)

(Relate)

(React)

Summary Points

● What is strategic reading?

Strategic reading is knowing and using techniques for understanding, studying, and learning.

● What is a study strategy?

All study systems include a previewing stage to ask questions and establish a purpose for reading, a reading stage to answer questions and integrate knowledge, and a final stage of self-testing and reviewing to improve recall.

● What are the three stages of reading?

Reading is an active rather than a passive process. Good readers preview before reading, integrate knowledge while reading, and recall after reading.

● What are the strategies for previewing?

Previewing is a way to assess your needs before you start to read by deciding what the material is about, what needs to be done, and how to go about doing it.

● Why should you activate your schema?

If you brainstorm to make a connection with your reading topic before you begin to read, the information will be more meaningful and memorable.

● What is metacognition?

Good readers control and direct their thinking strategies as they read. They know about knowing.

● What are the strategies for integrating knowledge during reading?

Students make predictions, picture images, answer questions, continually relate and integrate old and new knowledge, monitor understanding to clarify confusing points, and use correction strategies.

● Why recall or self-test what you have read?

Recalling what you have read immediately after reading forces you to select the most important points, to relate the supporting details, to integrate new information into existing networks of knowledge, and to react.

CONTEMPORARY FOCUS

To some observers, a source of national embarrassment is that over the course of history, certain groups have been excluded from the initial telling. As societal perceptions change and the predecessors of these slighted groups attain positions of importance and influence, long-overlooked stories are researched and told.

TELEVISION: REMEMBERING THE ALAMO FROM A TEJANO PERSPECTIVE

Suzanne C. Ryan

Boston Globe, February 1, 2004

As a young Chicano growing up in segregated San Antonio in the 1960s, Joseph Tovares remembers piling into a school bus for a field trip to the Alamo.

At the mission, he and his Mexican-American classmates were lectured about the bravery of white Americans such as David Crockett, who sacrificed his life defending about 200 settlers from an advancing Mexican army during the Texas Revolution of the 1830s.

"It was unbearable to be told about the courageous white defenders who died at the hands of this horde of Mexicans," Tovares said recently.

Especially, he said, since the Tejanos—the Mexican nationals who settled the Texas frontier and fought for independence from Spain and later Mexico "were never credited with defending the Alamo alongside the Anglos."

Now Tovares, a descendent of Tejanos and the PBS filmmaker who produced the 2001 "American Experience" film "Zoot Suit Riots," has a chance to set the record straight about a battle that's still part of Anglo-Texan heritage.

WGBH will broadcast on "American Experience" the documentary "Remember the Alamo," which chronicles the six-decade struggle of Tejanos as they fought the policies of Spain, Mexico, and eventually, the United States.

The film focuses on Jose Antonio Navarro, the influential leader of the Tejanos who served as mayor of San Antonio and was instrumental in luring thousands of American families to Texas with the promise of cheap land and the right to own slaves. Navarro, a wealthy landowner, didn't anticipate that those settlers would one day turn on him.

Tovares became interested in the Alamo's history after completing some genealogical research a few years ago. "I had ancestors who came over from Northern Mexico in the late 1700s. My great-great-great-grandmother was 13 at the time of the battle of the Alamo. My family said she watched the battle unfold from a nearby rooftop."

From his perspective, Tovares said his research has answered lots of personal questions. "I used to walk down Navarro Street every day on my way to high school," he said. "I had no idea who he was."

ate

Collaborate on responses to the following questions:

- What other groups tend to be overlooked in history books?
- Why were the Tejanos left out of the original history of the Alamo?
- How does the filmmaking of Tovares show that history is still being written?

Skill Development: Preview

Preview the next selection to predict its purpose and organization and to formulate your learning plan.

Activate Schema

What happened at the Alamo?

Why were the Mexicans and Americans fighting?

Establish a Purpose for Reading

Who are Tejanos, and what do you expect to learn from this selection?

After recalling what you already know about Texas history, read the selection with the intention of discovering the important contributions and rewards of the Tejanos. As you read, think about who decides who our national heroes are and why.

Increase Word Knowledge

What do you know about these words?

| resolve | contingent | lavishly | hacienda | prominent |
| couriers | posterity | renounce | contempt | malice |

Your instructor may give a true-false vocabulary review before reading.

Integrate Knowledge While Reading

Questions have been inserted in the margins to stimulate your thinking while reading. Remember to

Predict   Picture   Relate   Monitor   Correct

→

TEJANOS AT THE ALAMO

From J. K. Martin et al, *America and Its Peoples*, vol. 1, 5th ed.

General Antonio López de Santa Anna, backed by some 2400 Mexican
troops, put the Alamo under siege on February 23, 1836. On that day Santa
Anna ordered the hoisting of a red flag, meaning "no quarter," or no mercy

→ toward potential prisoners of war. This only hardened the resolve of the
5 Alamo's small contingent of defenders, including the legendary Jim Bowie,

→ Davy Crockett, and William Barret Travis. Also inside the Alamo were men

→ like Juan Seguin and Gregorio Esparza. They represented a handful of Tejano

→ defenders. As native residents of Texas (named the province of Tejas in 1691
by the conquering Spanish), they despised Santa Anna for having so recently
10 overthrown the Mexican Constitution of 1824 in favor of dictatorship.

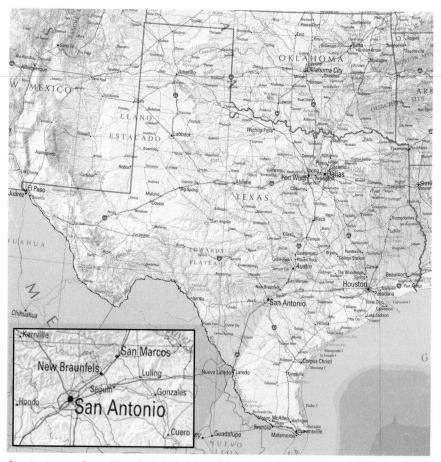

San Antonio is located in the southeastern part of Texas.
*Portion of National Atlas of the United States of America, General Reference Map. U.S. Geological Survey,
2001. University of Texas Map Collection.*

San Antonio was a center of the Tejano population of Texas. Juan Seguin's father, Don Erasmo, was a wealthy local rancher who in earlier years had encouraged the opening of the Mexican province of Coahuila y Tejas to non-natives from the United States. Most of the Americans settled far to the east
15 ▸ of San Antonio, but those who traveled to the Tejano settlements knew Don Erasmo as a generous host who entertained lavishly at his *hacienda*, "Casa Blanca." His son Juan was also locally prominent and had helped immeasurably in driving Mexican troops under General Martin Perfecto de Cós, Santa Anna's brother-in-law, out of San Antonio in 1835. His reward was a commis-
20 ▸ sion as a captain of Texas cavalry.

Much less is known about Gregorio Esparza. He lived with his wife and four children in San Antonio when Juan Seguin recruited him for his cavalry company. When Santa Anna's advance troops appeared on February 23, Esparza quickly gathered up his family and rushed for protection behind the
25 thick walls of the old Spanish mission known locally as the Alamo.

The Alamo defenders were in an all but impossible position, especially with Santa Anna tightening his siege lines every day. Inside the Alamo, the defenders looked to Jim Bowie for leadership, but he was seriously ill with pneumonia. So they accepted orders from William Barret Travis. With 1000 troops, Travis had
30 argued, the Alamo would never fall. His numbers, however, were hardly more than 150. As a result, Travis regularly sent out couriers with urgent messages for relief. His words were direct. He would never "surrender or retreat." He would "die like a soldier who never forgets what is due to his own honor and that of his country." For those at the Alamo, the alternatives were now "Victory or death."
35 Late in February Travis, who would gain only 32 troops as reinforcements, prepared yet another appeal, this time addressed to Sam Houston, commander-in-chief of the Texas army. Time was running out, Travis wrote. "If they overpower us," he explained, "we hope posterity and our country will do our memory justice. Give me help, oh my country!" Travis handed
40 the message to Juan Seguin, who borrowed Jim Bowie's horse and rode off with his aide, Antonio Cruz, under the cover of a driving rainstorm. They eventually found Houston, far to the east, but there was nothing anyone could do now to save those defenders still with Travis.

Early on the morning of March 6, 1836, the Alamo fell to 1800 attacking
45 ▸ Mexican soldiers. The fighting was so brutal that 600 of Santa Anna's troops lay dead or wounded before the last of the 183 defenders faced mutilation from countless musket balls, bayonet thrusts, or summary executions after the battle. Gregorio Esparza was torn to shreds as the Mexicans reached the church inside the courtyard. Only women, children, Colonel Travis's slave Joe, and one
50 Tejano, who claimed that he was a prisoner, survived. Later that day Mrs. Esparza got permission to bury her husband with Christian rites. Santa Anna issued orders to have the bodies of all other defenders heaped into piles and set on fire.

During the next several weeks Santa Anna's troops pushed steadily eastward with the goal of destroying another Texas army being hastily assembled by Sam
55 Houston. The Seguins, father and son, played key parts in providing resistance. Don Erasmo worked furiously to collect needed food supplies, and Juan led troops in harassing and delaying the Mexican column, all of which aided in the

Margin annotations:
- Why...ld settlers?
- Visualize Texas map
- Recent trouble?
- He joined the military.
- He also joined the military.
- Was Alamo sitting duck?
- Was leadership a defeat factor?
- Is it 2400 vs. 150?
- Why not all leave?
- Bet they felt bad.
- Did he see defeat?
- Why not? Was it too late?
- Amazing number. Calculate ratio.
- Killing prisoners?
- Visualize the horror.
- Why did Santa Anna let her?
- Visualize fire.
- Tejanos continued support.

The painting *Chili Queens at the Alamo* by Julian Onderdonk portrays nineteenth-century life in the Military Plaza outside the mission.
Chili Queens at the Alamo by Julian Onderdonk, date unknown. Oil on canvas, 12 x 16". Courtesy of the Witte Museum, San Antonio, Texas.

staging of Houston's stunning victory over Santa Anna at the Battle of San Jacinto on April 21, 1836—the day the Republic of Texas secured its independence.

60   As the Texas Revolution gained momentum in late 1835 and early 1836, Tejanos had to choose which side to support. Some hoped that uniting with the Americans would force Santa Anna to renounce his dictatorship in favor of the liberal 1824 constitution. Few Tejanos actually favored independence because they knew that Americans held them in contempt. This caused men

65   like Gregorio Esparza's brother to join Santa Anna's army and fight against the Alamo defenders. He suspected that heavy-handed rule under the Mexican dictator could not be worse and might well be better than living under culturally and racially intolerant Americans.

Juan Seguin received an honorable military discharge before serving as

70   mayor of San Antonio until 1842, when Anglo rumormongers accused him of supporting an attempted military invasion from Mexico. To save himself, Seguin had to flee across the border. Eventually he returned to his native Texas and quietly lived out his days far removed from the public limelight. No doubt Seguin wondered whether he had made the right decision by not

75   joining the side of Santa Anna, especially as he experienced the racial and cultural malice directed at Mexican Americans as the United States surged forward toward the Pacific. Although his thoughts are not known, it is fortunate that his story and those of other Tejano resisters have not been forgotten. Surely they too deserve remembrance as heroes of the Alamo and the

80   Texas Revolution.

Margin notes:
How long was fighting?

Wanted old Mexico back

What other war was brother vs. brother?

Why lie to disgrace him?

Unfairly treating hero?

What would you have done?

Set record straight!

Recall

Stop to self-test, relate, and react.

Your instructor may choose to give you a true-false comprehension review.

Write About the Selection

To better understand the conflict, make a timeline of the events surrounding the fall of the Alamo and the independence of Texas. List the contributions of Tejanos within your timeline.

    Response Suggestion: List events in chronological order and insert contributions. Begin with 1691.

Contemporary Link

How do political power and influence affect how history is written in the first place and, later, how and if history is reinterpreted and revised?

Check Your Comprehension

After reading the selection, answer the following questions with *a*, *b*, *c*, or *d*. To help you analyze your strengths and weaknesses, the question types are indicated.

Main Idea   _____ 1. Which is the best statement of the main idea of this selection?
- a. Because of cultural and racial intolerance, Tejanos regret supporting the Americans against Santa Anna.
- b. Houston could not have defeated Santa Anna without the help of the Tejanos.
- c. The defenders lost the battle of the Alamo because Houston did not send reinforcements.
- d. Along with other Alamo defenders, the Tejano resisters also deserve remembrance as heroes of the Alamo and the Texas Revolution.

Detail   _____ 2. With the hoisting of the red flag, Santa Anna wanted to alert the defenders inside the Alamo that
- a. they would all be killed.
- b. they would be treated fairly if they surrendered.
- c. the defenders were outnumbered and should give up.
- d. the Alamo was surrounded and no reinforcements would arrive.

Detail   _____ 3. According to the author, the primary reason Tejanos supported the Americans was
- a. they wanted a Republic of Texas.
- b. Santa Anna had been cruel and taken their land.
- c. they hated Santa Anna for establishing a dictatorship.
- d. they feared revenge from the Americans if they did not cooperate.

Detail _____ 4. All the following are true about Don Erasmo except
   a. he was the father of Juan Seguin.
   b. he welcomed Americans into the province of Tejas.
   c. he fought to drive Mexican troops out of San Antonio in 1835.
   d. he entertained Americans at "Casa Blanca."

Inference _____ 5. The author suggests that William Barret Travis was the leader of the defenders of the Alamo because
   a. Travis has once commanded 1000 troops.
   b. Travis would never surrender or retreat.
   c. defenders preferred Travis to Bowie.
   d. Jim Bowie was sick.

Inference _____ 6. By writing "we hope posterity and our country will do our memory justice," Travis
   a. motivates the troops in the Alamo.
   b. lets Houston know that they are hopeful of winning.
   c. indicates that he knows they will all die without reinforcements.
   d. refuses to understand the possible consequences.

Inference _____ 7. The author suggests that when Juan Sequin and Antonio Cruz found Houston,
   a. no reinforcement troops were available.
   b. it was too late to send troops to the Alamo.
   c. Houston doubted the truthfulness of the reports.
   d. a rainstorm prevented the rapid movement of rescue troops.

Inference _____ 8. Based on the selection, the reader can conclude that
   a. women and children were executed.
   b. the bodies of Jim Bowie, Davy Crockett, and William Barret Travis were burned in a fire.
   c. Colonel Travis's slave Joe joined the Mexican army.
   d. Gregorio Esparza pretended to be a prisoner.

Inference _____ 9. The Mexican soldiers who attacked the Alamo outnumbered the defenders of the Alamo by almost
   a. 2 to 1.
   b. 3 to 1.
   c. 5 to 1.
   d. 10 to 1.

Inference _____ 10. The author suggests that
   a. at the time the Alamo fell, Houston's army to the east was fully assembled and ready for Santa Anna's attack.
   b. the delaying of Santa Anna's army gave Houston time to prepare for victory.

c. Houston doubted the truthfulness of the reports.

d. Houston attacked Santa Anna's from the west and secured independence.

Answer the following with *T* (true), *F* (false), or *CT* (can't tell).

_____ 11. The province of Tejas was first Mexico and then Texas.

Inference

_____ 12. The reader can conclude that Gregorio Esparza and his brother were both killed in the fierce Battle of the Alamo.

Inference

_____ 13. Juan Seguin successfully fought against the Mexican army one year before the Battle of the Alamo.

Inference

_____ 14. The reader can conclude that Santa Anna executed wounded troops at the fall of the Alamo.

Inference

_____ 15. The author suggests that Juan Sequin fled because he lacked the administrative skills necessary to serve as mayor of San Antonio.

Inference

Build Your Vocabulary

According to the way the italicized word was used in the selection, select *a*, *b*, *c*, or *d* for the word or phrase that gives the best definition. The number in parentheses indicates the line of the passage in which the word is located.

_____ 1. "hardened the *resolve*" (4)
a. faces
b. uncertainty
c. determination
d. luck

_____ 2. "small *contingent* of defenders" (5)
a. group
b. legacy
c. miracle
d. stronghold

_____ 3. "entertained *lavishly*" (16)
a. frequently
b. knowingly
c. politically
d. sumptuously

_____ 4. "his *hacienda*, 'Casa Blanca'" (16)
a. office
b. outpost
c. estate
d. river cottage

_____ 5. "locally *prominent*" (17)
a. born
b. educated
c. aggressive
d. important

_____ 6. "sent out *couriers*" (31)
a. leaders
b. messengers
c. scouts
d. traders

_____ 7. "we hope *posterity*" (38)
    a. present citizens
    b. the media
    c. God
    d. future generations

_____ 8. "*renounce* his dictatorship" (62)
    a. fulfill
    b. reject
    c. renew
    d. hold

_____ 9. "held them in *contempt*" (64)
    a. awe
    b. bondage
    c. scorn
    d. suspicion

_____ 10. "racial and cultural *malice*" (76)
    a. revolution
    b. feeling
    c. murder
    d. hatred

Search the Net

Use a search engine such as Google, AltaVista, Excite, Infoseek, Dogpile, Yahoo, or Lycos to find information on other Tejano heroes. Select one and describe his or her contributions. For suggested Web sites and other research activities, go to http://www.ablongman.com/smith/.

What events led up to World War II?

After Germany was defeated in World War I, supposedly the "war to end all wars," the **Allies** (United States, Britain, France, and Russia) expected Germany to pay for the war they helped start. The Allies also changed the world map by taking away much of the German empire. The German people were stunned at their defeat, angry over the demands of the victors, and eventually unable to meet their debt payments. **Adolf Hitler**, a skillful and charismatic leader, seized this opportunity and tapped into the country's anger. He promised to restore national pride, and consequently many Germans were drawn to him. He became the leader of the **Nazi** party, created the **swastika** as its symbol, and eventually became dictator of Germany.

Hitler strengthened the military, forged an alliance with Japan and Italy, and attacked and conquered much of continental Europe. When Britain, under the leadership of Prime Minister **Winston Churchill**, refused to bargain with Germany, Hitler ordered the **Luftwaffe**, the German air force, to destroy Britain from the air. The air raids, known as the **blitz**, failed in their purpose when the Royal Air Force (RAF) won the Battle of Britain. Hitler then attacked Russia.

What was the U.S. role in the war?

The United States, under **Franklin D. Roosevelt**, remained neutral. **Isolationists** opposed foreign involvement. That changed, however, on December 7, 1941, at 7:02 A.M., when the Japanese bombed **Pearl Harbor**, an American naval base in Hawaii. America declared war on that day. **General Douglas MacArthur** was put in charge of all army troops in the Pacific, and **General Dwight D. Eisenhower** led the Allied soldiers in Europe.

What was D-Day?

Allied forces planned the liberation of Europe, and on June 6, 1944—on what came to be known as **D-Day**—thousands of brave soldiers secretly left England and stormed the beaches of Normandy, France. After two weeks of desperate fighting, the troops moved inland and liberated Paris by August. The Allied armies drove toward **Berlin**, the capital of Germany, and on April 30, Hitler committed suicide to avoid capture. The Germans surrendered one week later, and the European part of the war was over. Hitler, with his

Prime Minister Winston Churchill, President Franklin Roosevelt, and Soviet leader Joseph Stalin pose for pictures at the Yalta Conference in 1945.
Keystone/Hulton | Archive/Getty Images

anti-Semitic hatred, had killed more than 6 million innocent Jews. Many were taken by trains to concentration camps for extermination in gas chambers. This horrible carnage was called the **Holocaust**.

How did the war with Japan end?

The American forces in the Pacific were moving from island to island against fierce Japanese resistance. Victories were won with great loss of life. Harry Truman had become president and was told of the **Manhattan Project**, a top-secret plan to develop an atomic bomb. On August 6, 1945, the **Enola Gay** flew over **Hiroshima, Japan**, and dropped an atomic bomb that obliterated the city. Three days later, a second bomb was dropped over **Nagasaki**. Within a few days, the Japanese asked for peace, and a month later they officially surrendered to General MacArthur aboard the battleship **U.S.S. *Missouri*** in Tokyo Bay. World War II had come to an end.

REVIEW QUESTIONS

After studying the material, answer the following questions:

1. How did the end of World War I affect the beginning of World War II? _____
   _____

   _____

2. Why were the Germans drawn to Hitler's message? _____

   _____

3. Who were Germany's allies in World War II? _____

   _____

4. Why did the Luftwaffe strike England? _____

   _____

5. Who were the isolationists? _____

   _____

6. What prompted the United States to enter the war? _____

   _____

7. What was the Holocaust? _____

   _____

8. What was D-Day? _____

   _____

9. What ended the war in Europe? _____

   _____

10. What ended the war in Japan? _____

   _____

   _____

Your instructor may choose to give a true-false review of these history concepts.

CONTEMPORARY FOCUS

Customs and culture vary from country to country. What may seem acceptable to us may be offensive to others. Although the following suggestions are intended for business travelers, the advice given is relevant to anyone.

MIXED SIGNALS ON BODY LANGUAGE

By David Atkinson

Business Traveler, January 1, 2004

According to social anthropologist Edward T. Hall, 60 percent of all human communication is nonverbal. Our gestures, therefore, are as integral to doing business as a good presentation or smart attire.

Next time you're globetrotting on business, beware that your nonverbal communication can take on vastly different nuances between cultures. What can be construed as giving someone a thumbs-up in one country is tantamount to giving them the finger in another. Brush up on your body language with our guide.

BANGLADESH Bursting to go to the toilet? Hold it. It is considered very rude to excuse yourself from the table to use the bathroom.

BULGARIA Bulgarians nod the head up and down to mean no, not yes. To say yes, a Bulgarian nods the head back and forth.

CHINA In Eastern culture, silence really can be golden. So don't panic if long periods of silence form part of your meeting with Chinese clients. It simply means they are considering your proposal carefully.

EGYPT As across the Arab world the left hand is considered unclean, use your right to accept business cards and to greet someone. Use only your right hand for eating.

FIJI To show respect to your Fijian hosts when addressing them, stand with your arms folded behind your back.

FRANCE The French don't like strong handshakes, preferring a short, light grip or air kissing. If your French colleague is seen to be playing an imaginary flute, however, it means he thinks you are not being truthful.

GERMANY When Germans meet across a large conference table and it is awkward to reach over and shake hands, they will instead rap their knuckles lightly on the table by way of a greeting.

HONG KONG When trying to attract someone's attention, don't use your index finger with palm extended upward. This is how the Cantonese call their dogs.

INDIA Beware of whistling in public—it is the height of rudeness here.

JORDAN No matter how hungry you are, it is customary to refuse seconds from your host twice before finally accepting the third invitation.

MEXICO Mexicans are very tactile and often perform a handshake whereby, after pressing together the palms, they will slide their hands upward to grasp each other's thumbs.

PAKISTAN The overt display of a closed fist is an incitement to war.

RUSSIA The Russians are highly tactile meet and greeters, with bear hugs and kisses direct on the lips commonplace. Don't take this habit to nearby Uzbekistan, however. They'd probably shoot you.

SAUDI ARABIA If a Saudi man takes another's hand on the street, it's a sign of mutual respect.

Collaborate

Collaborate on responses to the following questions:

- When business is conducted in the United States, how is silence regarded?
- How would you react if a same-gender Russian businessperson kissed you on the mouth?
- Besides its soup-eating custom, why is Japan a "minefield for Western businesspeople"?

Skill Development: Preview

Preview the next selection to predict its purpose and organization and to formulate your learning plan.

Activate Schema

Is it wrong for primitive tribal people to wear no clothes?

Does social status exist in primitive cultures?

Would you eat insects if doing so meant survival?

Establish a Purpose for Reading

The phrase "unity in diversity" is a paradox. What does the author mean by this, and what do you expect to learn from this selection?

As you read, notice the author's use of examples to help you fully absorb the concepts of cultural universals, adaptation, relativity, ethnocentrism, norms, and values. Read with the intention of discovering that there are behavior patterns and institutions essential to all known societies, despite wide cultural variations in their expression.

Increase Word Knowledge

What do you know about these words?

curb	naïveté	adornments	articulate	bizarre
smirk	abstained	postpartum	agile	consign

Your instructor may give a true-false vocabulary review before or after reading.

Integrate Knowledge While Reading

Questions have been inserted in the margins to stimulate your thinking while reading. Remember to

Predict	Picture	Relate	Monitor	Correct

Does this title make sense or are these words opposites?

UNITY IN DIVERSITY

From Donald Light, Jr., and Suzanne Keller, *Sociology*, 5th ed.

What is more basic, more "natural" than love between a man and woman? Eskimo men offer their wives to guests and friends as a gesture of hospitality; both husband and wife feel extremely offended if the guest declines. The Banaro of New Guinea believe it would be disastrous for a woman to con-
5 ceive her first child by her husband and not by one of her father's close friends, as is their custom.

The real father is a close friend of the bride's father. . . . Nevertheless the first-born child inherits the name and possessions of the husband. An American would deem such a custom immoral, but the Banaro tribesmen
10 would be equally shocked to discover that the first-born child of an American couple is the offspring of the husband.

The Yanomamö of Northern Brazil, whom anthropologist Napoleon A. Chagnon named "the fierce people," encourage what we would consider extreme disrespect. Small boys are applauded for striking their mothers and
What would your parents do if you slapped either of them in the face?
15 fathers in the face. Yanomamö parents would laugh at our efforts to curb aggression in children, much as they laughed at Chagnon's naïveté when he first came to live with them.

The variations among cultures are startling, yet all peoples have customs and beliefs about marriage, the bearing and raising of children, sex, and

In a traditional Indian wedding ceremony the bride and groom pray at the altar.
Omni Photo Communications Inc. /Index Stock Imagery, Inc.

20   hospitality—to name just a few of the universals anthropologists have discovered in their cross-cultural explorations. But the *details* of cultures do
indeed vary: in this country, not so many years ago, when a girl was serious
about a boy and he about her, she wore his fraternity pin over her heart; in
the Fiji Islands, girls put hibiscus flowers behind their ears when they are in
25   love. The specific gestures are different but the impulse to symbolize feelings, to dress courtship in ceremonies, is the same. How do we explain this
unity in diversity?

Cultural Universals

Cultural universals are all of the behavior patterns and institutions that have
been found in all known cultures. Anthropologist George Peter Murdock
30   identified over sixty cultural universals, including a system of social status,
marriage, body adornments, dancing, myths and legends, cooking, incest
taboos, inheritance rules, puberty customs, and religious rituals.

Why would incest have to be a taboo for a surviving culture? →

The universals of culture may derive from the fact that all societies must
perform the same essential functions if they are to survive—including organi-
35   zation, motivation, communication, protection, the socialization of new members, and the replacement of those who die. In meeting these prerequisites for
group life, people inevitably design similar—though not identical—patterns
for living. As Clyde Kluckhohn wrote, "All cultures constitute somewhat distinct answers to essentially the same questions posed by human biology and
40   by the generalities of the human situation."

The way in which a people articulates cultural universals depends in large
part on their physical and social environment—that is, on the climate in which
they live, the materials they have at hand, and the peoples with whom they
establish contact. For example, the wheel has long been considered one of
45   humankind's greatest inventions, and anthropologists were baffled for a long
time by the fact that the great civilizations of South America never discovered
it. Then researchers uncovered a number of toys with wheels. Apparently the
Aztecs and their neighbors did know about wheels; they simply didn't find

What is your mental picture? →

them useful in their mountainous environment.

Adaptation, Relativity, and Ethnocentrism

50   Taken out of context, almost any custom will seem bizarre, perhaps cruel, or
just plain ridiculous. To understand why the Yanomamö encourage aggressive
behavior in their sons, for example, you have to try to see things through their
eyes. The Yanomamö live in a state of chronic warfare; they spend much of their
time planning for and defending against raids with neighboring tribes. If
55   Yanomamö parents did not encourage aggression in a boy, he would be ill
equipped for life in their society. Socializing boys to be aggressive is adaptive for
the Yanomamö because it enhances their capacity for survival. "In general, cul-

ture is . . . adaptive because it often provides people with a means of adjusting to the physiological needs of their own bodies, to their physical-geographical environment and to their social environments as well."

In many tropical societies, there are strong taboos against a mother having sexual intercourse with a man until her child is at least two years old. As a Hausa woman explains,

> A mother should not go to her husband while she has a child who is suck-ing . . . if she only sleeps with her husband and does not become pregnant, it will not hurt her child, it will not spoil her milk. But if another child enters in, her milk will make the first one ill. (Smith, in Whiting 1969, p. 518)

Undoubtedly, people would smirk at a woman who nursed a two-year-old child in our society and abstained from having sex with her husband. Why do Hausa women behave in a way that seems so overprotective and overindul-gent to us? In tropical climates protein is scarce. If a mother were to nurse more than one child at a time, or if she were to wean a child before it reached the age of two, the youngster would be prone to *kwashiorkor*, an often fatal disease resulting from protein deficiency. Thus, long postpartum sex taboos are adaptive. In a tropical environment a postpartum sex taboo and a long period of breast-feeding solve a serious problem.

No custom is good or bad, right or wrong in itself; each one must be exam-ined in light of the culture as a whole and evaluated in terms of how it works in the context of the entire culture. Anthropologists and sociologists call this *cultural relativity*. Although this way of thinking about culture may seem self-evident today, it is a lesson that anthropologists and the missionaries who often preceded them to remote areas learned the hard way, by observing the effects their best intentions had on peoples whose way of life was quite differ-ent from their own. In an article on the pitfalls of trying to "uplift" peoples whose ways seem backward and inefficient, Don Adams quotes an old Orien-tal story:

> Once upon a time there was a great flood, and involved in this flood were two creatures, a monkey and a fish. The monkey, being agile and experi-enced, was lucky enough to scramble up a tree and escape the raging waters. As he looked down from his safe perch, he saw the poor fish strug-gling against the swift current. With the very best intentions, he reached down and lifted the fish from the water. The result was inevitable. (1960, p. 22)

Ethnocentrism is the tendency to see one's own way of life, including behav-iors, beliefs, values, and norms as the only right way of living. Robin Fox points out that "any human group is ever ready to consign another recognizably different human group to the other side of the boundary. It is not enough to possess culture to be fully human, you have to possess *our* culture."

Why did missionaries want to clothe islanders?

What is the difference between adaptation and relativity?

Values and Norms

100 The Tangu, who live in a remote part of New Guinea, play a game called *taketak*, which in many ways resembles bowling. The game is played with a top that has been fashioned from a dried fruit and with two groups of coconut stakes that are driven into the ground (more or less like bowling pins). The players divide into two teams. Members of the first team take
105 turns throwing the top into the batch of stakes; every stake the top hits is removed. Then the second team steps to the line and tosses the top into their batch of stakes. The object of the game, surprisingly, is not to knock over as many stakes as possible. Rather, the game continues until both teams have removed the *same* number of stakes. Winning is completely
110 irrelevant.

What will be covered in this next part?

In a sense games are practice for "real life"; they reflect the values of the culture in which they are played. *Values* are the criteria people use in assessing their daily lives, arranging their priorities, measuring their pleasures and pains, choosing between alternative courses of action. The Tangu value equivalence:
115 the idea of one individual or group winning and another losing bothers them, for they believe winning generates ill-will. In fact, when Europeans brought soccer to the Tangu, they altered the rules so that the object of the game was for two teams to score the same number of goals. Sometimes their soccer games went on for days! American games, in contrast, are highly competitive;
120 there are *always* winners and losers. Many rule books include provisions for overtime and "sudden death" to prevent ties, which leave Americans dissatisfied. World Series, Superbowls, championships in basketball and hockey, Olympic Gold Medals are front-page news in this country. In the words of the late football coach Vince Lombardi, "Winning isn't everything, it's the only
125 thing."

How do you know appropriate dress for a place of worship? Are rules written on the door?

Norms, the rules that guide behavior in everyday situations, are derived from values, but norms and values can conflict. You may recall a news item that appeared in American newspapers in December 1972, describing the discovery of survivors of a plane crash 12,000 feet in the Andes. The crash
130 had occurred on October 13; sixteen of the passengers (a rugby team and their supporters) managed to survive for sixty-nine days in near-zero temperatures. The story made headlines because, to stay alive, the survivors had eaten parts of their dead companions. Officials, speaking for the group, stressed how valiantly the survivors had tried to save the lives of the injured
135 people and how they had held religious services regularly. The survivors' explanations are quite interesting, for they reveal how important it is to people to justify their actions, to resolve conflicts in norms and values (here, the positive value of survival vs. the taboo against cannibalism). Some of the survivors compared their action to a heart transplant, using parts of a dead per-
140 son's body to save another person's life. Others equated their act with the sacrament of communion. In the words of one religious survivor, "If we would have died, it would have been suicide, which is condemned by the Roman Catholic faith."

Recall

Stop to self-test, relate, and react. Use the subheadings in the recall diagram shown here to guide your thinking. For each subheading, jot down a key idea that you feel is important to remember.

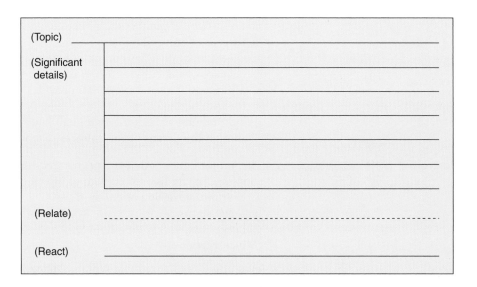

Your instructor may choose to give you a true-false comprehension review.

Write About the Selection

Define the following terms and describe two examples for each that are not mentioned in the selection:

cultural   universals   adaptation   relativity

ethnocentrism   norms   values

Response Suggestion: Define the cultural concepts in your own words and relate examples from contemporary society.

Contemporary Link

From a cultural relativity perspective, discuss how certain gestures can be acceptable in one culture but unacceptable in another.

Check Your Comprehension

After reading the selection, answer the following questions with *a*, *b*, *c*, or *d*. To help you analyze your strengths and weaknesses, the question types are indicated.

Main Idea _____ 1. The best statement of the main idea of this selection is
    a. the variety of practices and customs in society show few threads of cultural unity.
    b. the unusual variations in societies gain acceptability because of the cultural universals in all known societies.
    c. a variety of cultural universals provides adaptive choices for specific societies.
    d. cultural universals are found in all known societies, even though the details of the cultures may vary widely.

Inference _____ 2. The author believes that the primary cultural universal addressed in the Eskimo custom of offering wives to guests is
    a. bearing and raising of children.
    b. social status.
    c. hospitality.
    d. incest taboos.

Detail _____ 3. The custom of striking practiced by the Yanomamö serves the adaptive function of
    a. developing fierce warriors.
    b. binding parent and child closer together.
    c. developing physical respect for parents.
    d. encouraging early independence from parental care.

Detail _____ 4. *Cultural universals* might be defined as
    a. each culture in the universe.
    b. similar basic living patterns.
    c. the ability for cultures to live together in harmony.
    d. the differences among cultures.

Inference _____ 5. The author implies that cultural universals exist because of
    a. a social desire to be more alike.
    b. the differences in cultural behavior patterns.
    c. the competition among societies.
    d. the needs of survival in group life.

Inference _____ 6. The author suggests that the wheel was not a part of the ancient Aztec civilization because the Aztecs
    a. did not find wheels useful in their mountainous environment.
    b. were not intelligent enough to invent wheels.

c. were baffled by inventions.

d. did not have the materials for development.

Inference _____ 7. The underlying reason for the postpartum sexual taboo of the Hausa is

a. sexual.

b. nutritional.

c. moral.

d. religious.

Inference _____ 8. The term *cultural relativity* explains why a custom can be considered

a. right or wrong regardless of culture.

b. right or wrong according to the number of people practicing it.

c. right in one culture and wrong in another.

d. wrong if in conflict with cultural universals.

Inference _____ 9. The author relates Don Adams's oriental story to show that missionaries working in other cultures

a. should be sent back home.

b. can do more harm than good.

c. purposefully harm the culture to seek selfish ends.

d. usually do not have a genuine concern for the people.

Inference _____ 10. The tendency of ethnocentrism would lead most Americans to view the Eskimo practice of wife sharing as

a. right.

b. wrong.

c. right for Eskimos but wrong for most Americans.

d. a custom about which an outsider should have no opinion.

Answer the following questions with *T* (true) or *F* (false):

Inference _____ 11. An American's acceptance of the Banaro tribal custom of fathering the firstborn is an example of an understanding by cultural relativity.

Inference _____ 12. The author feels that the need to symbolize feelings in courtship is a cultural universal.

Inference _____ 13. The author feels that culture is not affected by climate.

Detail _____ 14. The author states that all societies must have a form of organization if they are to survive.

Inference _____ 15. The author implies that the rugby team that crashed in the Andes could have survived without eating human flesh.

Build Your Vocabulary

According to the way the italicized word was used in the selection, select *a*, *b*, *c*, or *d* for the word or phrase that gives the best definition. The number in parentheses indicates the line of the passage in which the word is located.

_____ 1. "efforts to *curb* aggression" (15)
   a. stabilize
   b. release
   c. promote
   d. restrain

_____ 2. "To *symbolize* feelings" (25)
   a. represent
   b. hide
   c. ignore
   d. simplify

_____ 3. "body *adornments*" (31)
   a. ailments
   b. treatments
   c. scars
   d. decorations

_____ 4. "*articulates* cultural universals" (41)
   a. remembers
   b. designs
   c. expresses clearly
   d. substitutes

_____ 5. "will seem *bizarre*" (50)
   a. phony
   b. unjust
   c. grotesque
   d. unnecessary

_____ 6. "*smirk* at a woman" (69)
   a. refuse to tolerate
   b. smile conceitedly
   c. lash out
   d. acknowledge approvingly

_____ 7. "*abstained* from having sex" (70)
   a. matured
   b. regained
   c. refrained
   d. reluctantly returned

_____ 8. "long *postpartum* sex taboos" (75)
   a. after childbirth
   b. awaited
   c. subcultural
   d. complicated

_____ 9. "being *agile* and experienced" (89)
   a. eager
   b. nimble
   c. young
   d. knowledgeable

_____ 10. "ready to *consign*" (97)
   a. assign
   b. remove
   c. reorganize
   d. overlook

Search the Net

Use a search engine such as Google, AltaVista, Excite, Infoseek, Dogpile, Yahoo, or Lycos to find information on Latin American business and cultural etiquette, and highlight sensitive differences. Pretend your company wishes to expand into Latin America, and write a memo to the company president summarizing your research. For suggested Web sites and other research activities, go to http://www.ablongman.com/smith/.

Concept Prep

for Anthropology

Although the "Unity in Diversity" selection is from a sociology textbook, the passage deals with concepts in anthropology. Thus, this section will also explore anthropology.

What is anthropology?

Anthropology is the study of humankind. It focuses on the origins and development of humans and their diverse cultures. By seeking to understand, respect, and applaud human diversity, anthropology might be considered the first multicultural course on college campuses. Special areas that you can study in anthropology include the following:

- **Physical anthropology:** How did humans evolve? What does genetic and fossil evidence reveal about our place in the animal kingdom?

- **Cultural anthropology:** What was the purpose of primitive customs and behaviors and what do they reveal about contemporary social problems?

- **Archaeology:** What can we reconstruct about extinct societies and their cultures from artifacts such as ancient bones, pieces of pottery, and excavated ruins?

Who are famous anthropologists?

- In search of our human origins, **Louis and Mary Leakey** sifted through the dirt of **Olduvai Gorge** in Tanzania, East Africa, for more than 25 years. Finally, in 1959 they unearthed a humanlike upper jaw with teeth and a skull. This discovery of a hominid 1.75 million years old revealed that the first humans originated in Africa.

- Cultural anthropology was popularized by **Margaret Mead** with the publication of her book *Coming of Age in Samoa*, published in 1928. Mead observed children moving into adolescence and described the transition as happy. She argued that the stress of adolescence is cultural, but others later disagreed. Mead also studied male and female roles in different societies and argued that gender roles are cultural rather than inborn.

Who were our early ancestors?

- **Lucy,** one of the greatest archaeological treasures, is the nickname for the most complete human skeleton of

Husband and wife Louis and Mary Leakey study fossilized skull fragments that might belong to the "missing link" between ape and man.
Bettmann/CORBIS

early ancestors ever found. Lucy is more than 3 million years old and was unearthed in Ethiopia.

- The **Cro-Magnons** were the earliest form of modern humans, who lived about 35,000 years ago. Their cave paintings in Europe are the first known human art.

- The earliest societies were **hunting and gathering societies.** People roamed widely to hunt wild animals and fish and to gather fruits and nuts. Usually, this **nomadic** wandering was seasonal and calculated to create the best opportunities for finding available food. Not until 10,000 years ago did humans begin to domesticate plants and animals and thus remain in one area.

REVIEW QUESTIONS

After studying the material, answer the following questions:

1. Digging in New Mexico for prehistoric artifacts suggests what area of anthropology? _____

2. Living with tribal people in the Amazon to study their ways suggests what area of anthropology?

3. Analyzing DNA to link Asian and African people suggests what area of anthropology? _____

4. What did Mary and Louis Leakey discover? _____

5. Why was the Leakey discovery especially significant? _____

6. What did Margaret Mead investigate in Samoa? _____

7. Why was Mead's work especially significant? _____

8. Why is Lucy significant? _____

9. What was the artistic contribution of Cro-Magnons? _____

10. What phenomenon usually ends hunting and gathering societies? _____

Your instructor may choose to give a true-false review of these anthropology concepts.

Vocabulary Booster

The Good, the Bad, and the Ugly

Prefixes

bene-: well, good   *eu-:* good
mal-: bad, evil   *kakos- (caco-):* harsh, bad, ugly

Words with *bene-:* well, good

During the *benediction,* the minister blessed the infant and called for all family members to be positive influences in the child's life.

- **benefaction:** a charitable donation

The anonymous *benefaction* came just in time to prevent the foreclosure on the school for the deaf.

- **beneficial:** producing a benefit; helpful

The week away from work proved *beneficial* to Miguel, and he returned refreshed and cheerful.

- **beneficiary:** a person or group who receives advantages; one named to receive funds or property in a will

The lawyer's call telling Rosa she was named as a *beneficiary* in a will came as a complete surprise to her.

- **benefit:** something that causes improvement or an advantage; a public event to raise money for a charitable cause

As a prospective new father, Charles was relieved when he became eligible for medical *benefits* at work.

- **benevolent:** expressing goodwill or kindness; charitable; set up to do charitable works

The *Benevolent* Women's Society set a priority of addressing the needs of the elderly in the community.

- **benefactor:** person who gives a benefit

The wealthy *benefactor* achieved great satisfaction from donating money to the charity.

Words with *eu-:* good

The *eulogy* delivered at the funeral was full of praise, befitting the benevolent character of the deceased.

- *euphony:* a pleasant sounding combination of words

    The poem had a lilting rhythm and a harmonious *euphony* that fell like music on the ears.

- *euphoria:* a feeling of well-being, confidence, or happiness

    After winning the State Salsa Championship, Jose and his dancing partner experienced a *euphoria* that lasted for days.

- *euphemism:* a substitution of a milder word or expression for a more blunt or offensive one

    Barry expressed his condolences to the widow at the funeral by using the *euphemism* "passed away" rather than expressing sorrow that her loved one had committed suicide.

- *euthanasia:* putting to death painlessly or allowing to die; mercy killing

    Dr. Jack Kevorkian is well known as an advocate of *euthanasia* for patients who are terminally ill and request his services.

- *eureka:* an exclamation of triumph at a discovery, meaning, "I have found it!"

    Archimedes exclaimed, "*Eureka!*" when he discovered a test for the purity of gold.

Words with *mal-:* bad, evil

    After being confronted, Marie realized the pain she had caused Janice by continuing to *malign* her in public about a previous boyfriend.

- *maladroit:* lacking resourcefulness; awkward; not skillful in using the hands or body

    Because of his *maladroit* sawing and hammering, Jules wasn't going to sign up for the furniture-making class.

- *malady:* a sickness or disorder of the body; an unhealthy condition

    Some of the volunteers working in the impoverished country had come down with an unidentified *malady*.

- *malaise:* general weakness or discomfort usually before the onset of a disease

    Emily canceled her long-anticipated trip due to her general feelings of *malaise* for the past several days.

- *malapropism:* an amusing misuse of words that produces an inappropriate meaning

    After asking the waiter to bring the soap du jour, John was embarrassed to have made such a *malapropism*.

- *malcontent:* someone unsatisfied with current conditions

    Numerous *malcontents* were protesting outside the school about the hiring of the famous professor.

■ *malevolent:* wishing evil or harm to others; injurious

Georgia had *malevolent* feelings toward the girls on the newly selected cheerleading squad and wished one of them would break a leg.

■ *malfeasance:* misconduct or wrongdoing, especially by a public official

Some voters feel that Bill Clinton committed the greatest *malfeasance* in office of any elected official—lying to the American people; others feel he committed a crime—lying under oath.

■ *malfunction:* fail to function properly

Although it worked well at the store, the computer *malfunctioned* when we got it home and set it up.

Words with *kakos- (caco-):* harsh, bad, ugly

■ *cacophony:* a harsh, jarring sound; a discordant and meaningless mixture of sound

The toddler's attempt to play an improvised drum set of pots, pans, and spoons created such a *cacophony* that her father required earplugs.

■ *cacography:* bad handwriting; poor spelling

His sister's beautiful calligraphy was in stark contrast to Mark's messy *cacography*.

Review

Part I

Indicate whether the underlined word in each of the following sentences is used correctly (C) or incorrectly (I).

___C___ 1. The unexplained *cacophony* of shrieks, banging, and irritating musical sounds that frequently woke the Williamsons in the early morning made them think their house was haunted.

___C___ 2. Marguerite's prescription proved *beneficial*, and she was over her symptoms of bronchitis in a few days.

___I___ 3. *"Eureka!"* shrieked Marielle as she lost her ring down the sink drain.

___C___ 4. The *beneficiary* of a will is entrusted with the duties of carrying out the wishes of the deceased and receives nothing for performing these duties.

___C___ 5. The new play was an experimental performance that was made possible by a patron of the arts, a *benefactor* who funded the production.

_____I_____ 6. The new car that Manuel received as a graduation present gave him such a feeling of *eulogy* that he didn't even feel bad when his girlfriend broke up with him.

_____I_____ 7. Jeanette's *malaise* had given her so much energy she just wanted to stay out dancing all night.

_____C_____ 8. The harsh criticisms of the drill instructor were *euphonious* to the ears of the overworked recruits.

_____C_____ 9. Film buffs know Clint Eastwood's character in *The Good, the Bad, and the Ugly* as a man of few words; those few words, however, weren't wasted on *euphemisms*—he just said it like it was.

_____I_____ 10. Benito learned how *maladroit* he was after the audition for the new *Survivor* show revealed his lack of skill and resourcefulness in the wild.

Part II

Choose the best synonym from the boxed list for the words below.

> ailment ~~blessing~~ ~~clumsy~~ discord elation ~~misconduct~~
> ~~gift~~ libel ~~mercy killing~~ ~~complainer~~

11. euphoria _blessing_   16. maladroit _clumsy_

12. cacophony _____   17. benediction _____

13. malign _____   18. benefaction _Gift_

14. euthanasia _Mercy killing_   19. malcontent _Complainer_

15. malfeasance _MISconduct_   20. malady _____

Your instructor may choose to give you a multiple-choice review.

Main Idea

- What is the difference between a topic and a main idea?
- What are the strategies for finding stated and unstated main ideas?
- What are the functions of major and minor supporting details?
- What is a summary?

The Circus by George Bellows, 1912. Oil on canvas, 33 7/8 by 44". Addison Gallery of Art. Gift of Elizabeth Paine Metcalf, 1947.8.

What Is a Topic?

In this chapter we will discuss and practice what many experts believe is the most important reading skill and the key to comprehension: recognizing the main idea of a paragraph, passage, or selection. As you read—and regardless of what you are reading, whether it is a chapter from your history text or an article in the Sunday paper—it is important to answer the question, "What's the point?" However, before attempting to discover the central point of a piece of writing, you must have a good sense of its topic.

A **topic** is like the title of a book or song. It is a word, name, or phrase that labels the subject but does not reveal the specific contents of the passage. Take a moment and flip back to the Table of Contents of this text. As you can see, the title of each chapter reflects its general topic. What's more, boldface heads within a chapter reflect subordinate topics, or subtopics. Similarly, individual passages beneath those heads have their own topics.

Think of the topic of a passage as a big umbrella under which specific ideas or details can be grouped. For example, consider the words *carrots, lettuce, onion,* and *potatoes*. What general term would pull together and unify these items?

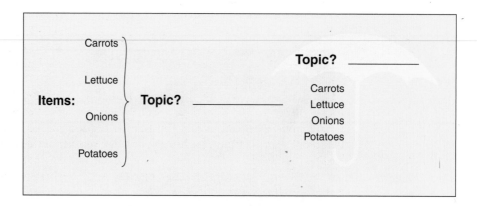

Topic: _____

Exercise 4.1

Identifying Topics

Each of the following lists includes four specific items or ideas that could relate to a single topic. At the top of each list, write a general topic that could form an umbrella under which the specific ideas can be grouped.

1. *Clothing*	2. *Computer*	3. *Democracies*	4. *Islands*	5. *Caffeine*
shirt	mouse	democracy	Bermuda	coffee
pants	keyboard	autocracy	Cuba	tea
jacket	hard drive	oligarchy	Haiti	cola
sweater	screen	monarchy	Tahiti	chocolate

JJ

What Is a Main Idea?

Using the topic as an initial indicator, the **main idea** of a passage becomes more focused and is the central message that the author is trying to convey about the material. It is a sentence that condenses thoughts and details into a general, all-inclusive statement of the author's point.

Reading specialists use various terms when referring to the main idea. In classroom discussions, a variety of words are used to help students understand its meaning. How many of these have you heard?

Main point

Central focus

Gist

Controlling idea

Central thought

Thesis

The last word on the list, *thesis*, is a familiar word in English composition classes. You have probably had practice in stating a thesis sentence for English essays, but you may not have had as much practice in stating the main idea of a reading selection. Can you see the similarity between a thesis and a main idea statement?

How important is it to be able to find and comprehend the main idea? Experts say that it is *crucial to your comprehension of any text*. In fact, if all reading comprehension techniques were combined and reduced to one essential question, that question might be, "What is the main idea the author is trying to get across to the reader?" Whether you read a single paragraph, a chapter, or an entire book, your most important single task is to understand the main idea of what you read.

What Are Supporting Details?

Details are statements that support, develop, and explain a main idea. Specific details can include reasons, incidents, facts, examples, steps, and definitions.

There are important differences between *major details*, which are critical to the support of the main idea and your understanding of a passage, and *minor details*, which amplify the major details. One way to distinguish the two is to pay attention to signal words, which are words that link thoughts and help you anticipate the kind of detail that is coming next. Key signal words for major supporting details are *one, first, another, furthermore, also*, and *finally*. Key signal words for minor details are *for example, to be specific, that is*, and *this means*. We will deepen our discussion of major and minor details later in this chapter.

Distinguishing Topics, Main Ideas, and Details: A Closer Look

We have seen that a topic is a general category, and that a main idea is the author's central message about the topic. Let's explore the difference between them—and the importance of supporting details—a little more closely.

As we saw in Exercise 4.1, *caffeine* is a general term or topic that unifies the items *coffee, tea, cola*, and *chocolate*. If those items were used as details in a paragraph, the main idea could not be expressed by simply saying "caffeine." The word *caffeine* would answer the question, "What is the passage about?" However, only your evaluation of the supporting details in the paragraph would answer the question, "What is the author's main idea?"

Think of some of the very different paragraphs about caffeine that a writer could devise using the same four details as support. If you were that writer, what would be the main idea or thesis—using the four items as details—of your paragraph?

Topic: Caffeine

Main idea or thesis: _____

EXAMPLE Read the following examples of different main ideas that could be developed in a paragraph about the topic of caffeine. Explanations appear in italicized type.

1. Consumption of caffeine is not good for your health. (*Details would enumerate health hazards associated with each item.*)

2. Americans annually consume astonishing amounts of caffeine. (*Details would describe amounts of each consumed annually.*)

3. Caffeine makes money as the Starbucks star rises. (*Details would show the profits and expansion of the coffee giant.*)

4. Reduce caffeine consumption with the decaffeinated version of popular caffeine-containing beverages. (*Details would promote the decaffeinated version of each item.*)

EXAMPLE Following are examples of a topic, main idea, and supporting detail.

Topic ——————→ **Early Cognitive Development**

Main Idea ——————→ { Cognitive psychologists sometimes study young children to observe the very beginnings of cognitive activity. For example, when children first begin to utter

Detail ——————→ words and sentences, they overgeneralize what they know and make language more consistent than it actually is.

Christopher Peterson, *Introduction to Psychology*

EXPLANATION The topic pulls your attention to a general area, and the main idea provides the focus. The detail offers elaboration and support.

**Exercise
4.2**

Differentiating Topic, Main Idea, and Supporting Details

This exercise is designed to check your ability to differentiate statements of the main idea from the topic and supporting details. Compare the items within each group, and indicate whether each one is a statement of the main idea *(MI)*, a topic *(T)*, or a specific supporting detail *(SD)*.

Group 1

___MI___ a. For poor farm families, life on the plains meant a sod house or a dugout carved out of the hillside for protection from the winds.

___SD___ b. One door and usually no more than a single window provided light and air.

___T___ c. Sod Houses on the Plains

James W. Davidson et al., Nation of Nations

Group 2

___SD___ a. She was the daughter of English poet Lord Byron and of a mother who was a gifted mathematician.

___T___ b. Babbage and the Programming Countess

___MI___ c. Ada, the Countess of Lovelace, helped develop the instructions for doing computer programming computations on Babbage's analytical engine.

___SD___ d. In addition, she published a series of notes that eventually led others to accomplish what Babbage himself had been unable to do.

Adapted from H. L. Capron, Computers: Tools for an Information Age, 6th ed.

Group 3

___MI___ a. Fabiola Garcia worked at a 7-Eleven evenings and swing shifts, learning all aspects of the business as part of the screening and training process for prospective 7-Eleven franchise owners.

___T___ b. Evaluating a Franchising Opportunity

___SD___ c. One of the best ways to evaluate a prospective franchisor is to spend a few months working for someone who already owns a franchise you're interested in.

___SD___ d. Fabiola also worked at headquarters to learn the franchisor's paperwork procedures.

Adapted from Michael Mescon et al., Business Today, 10th ed.

Group 4

___ a. Mexican American Political Gains

___SD___ b. During the 1960s, four Mexican Americans—Senator Joseph Montoya of New Mexico and Representatives Eligio de la

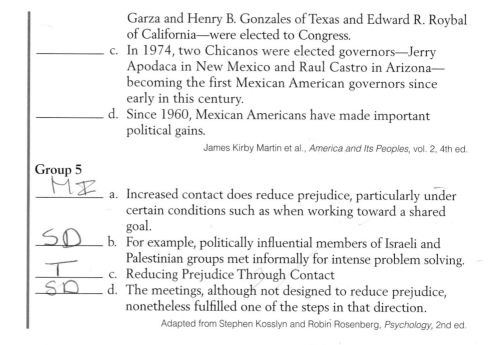

Garza and Henry B. Gonzales of Texas and Edward R. Roybal of California—were elected to Congress.

_____ c. In 1974, two Chicanos were elected governors—Jerry Apodaca in New Mexico and Raul Castro in Arizona—becoming the first Mexican American governors since early in this century.

_____ d. Since 1960, Mexican Americans have made important political gains.

James Kirby Martin et al., *America and Its Peoples*, vol. 2, 4th ed.

Group 5

_____MI____ a. Increased contact does reduce prejudice, particularly under certain conditions such as when working toward a shared goal.

_____SD____ b. For example, politically influential members of Israeli and Palestinian groups met informally for intense problem solving.

_____T_____ c. Reducing Prejudice Through Contact

_____SD____ d. The meetings, although not designed to reduce prejudice, nonetheless fulfilled one of the steps in that direction.

Adapted from Stephen Kosslyn and Robin Rosenberg, *Psychology*, 2nd ed.

Importance of Prior Knowledge in Constructing the Main Idea

How exactly do you figure out the main idea of a paragraph or passage? Research has been done investigating the processes readers use to construct main ideas. One researcher, Peter Afflerbach, asked graduate students and university professors to "think aloud" as they read passages on both familiar and unfamiliar topics.[1] These expert readers spoke their thoughts to the researcher before, during, and after reading. From these investigations, Afflerbach concluded that expert readers use different strategies for familiar and unfamiliar materials.

Here is the important finding: This research showed that *already knowing something about the topic is the key* to easy reading. When readers are familiar with the subject, constructing the main idea is effortless and, in many cases, automatic. These readers quickly assimilate the unfolding text into already well-developed knowledge networks. They seem to organize text into chunks for comprehension and later retrieval. These "informed" readers do not have to struggle with an information overload. Again, this shows that the rich get richer, and the initial struggle to build knowledge has many benefits.

---

[1]P. Afflerbach, "How Are Main Idea Statements Constructed? Watch the Experts!," *Journal of Reading* 30 (1987): 512–518; and "The Influence of Prior Knowledge on Expert Readers' Main Idea Construction Strategies," *Reading Research Quarterly* 25 (1990): 31–46.

By contrast, expert readers with little prior knowledge of the subject are absorbed in trying to make meaning out of unfamiliar words and confusing sentences. Because they are struggling to recognize ideas, few mental resources remain for constructing a main idea. These "uninformed" experts are reluctant to guess at a main idea and to predict a topic. Instead, they prefer to read all the information before trying to make sense of it. Constructing the main idea is a difficult and deliberate task for these expert but uninformed readers. Even a proven expert reader in history, for example, might struggle to read chemistry until enough knowledge is built for main idea construction to be automatic.

Main Idea Strategies

The following strategies for getting the main idea were reported by Afflerbach's expert readers. Can you see the differences in the thinking processes of the informed and uninformed experts?

"Informed" Expert Readers

Strategy 1: The informed expert readers skimmed the passage before reading and took a guess at the main idea. Then they read for corroboration.

Strategy 2: The informed experts automatically paused while reading to summarize or reduce information. They frequently stopped at natural breaks in the material to let ideas fall into place.

"Uninformed" Expert Readers

Strategy 1: Expert readers who did not know about the subject were unwilling to take a guess at the main idea. Instead, they read the material, decided on a topic, and then looked back to pull together a main idea statement.

Strategy 2: The uninformed experts read the material and they reviewed it to find key terms and concepts. They tried to bring the key terms and concepts together into a main idea statement.

Strategy 3: The uninformed experts read the material and then proposed a main idea statement. They double-checked the passage to clarify or revise the main idea statement.

What differences do you see in these approaches? Since introductory college textbooks address many topics that are new and unfamiliar, freshmen readers will frequently need to use the strategies of uninformed expert readers to comprehend the main ideas of their college texts. Until you build up your reserves of prior knowledge gathered from the college courses you take, constructing main ideas for course textbooks is likely to be a *conscious effort* rather than an automatic phenomenon.

Using Main Idea Strategies with Sentences

Before identifying main ideas in paragraphs, practice with a simple list of sentences. Read the sentences in the following group. They are related to a single subject, with one sentence expressing a main idea and two other sentences expressing detailed support. Circle the number of the sentence that best expresses the main idea, and write the general topic for the group.

EXAMPLE

1. The 1960 debate between John Kennedy and Richard Nixon boosted Kennedy's campaign and elevated the role of television in national politics.

2. Televised presidential debates are a major feature of presidential elections.

3. Ronald Reagan's performance in 1980 and 1984 debates confirmed the public view of him as decent, warm, and dignified.

Topic: _____

Adapted from James MacGregor Burns et al., *Government by the People*, 20th ed.

EXPLANATION The second sentence best expresses the main idea, declaring the importance of televised presidential debates. The other two sentences are details offering specific facts in support of the topic, which is the importance of televised presidential debates.

Exercise 4.3

Discovering Topics and Main Ideas in Sentence Groups

Circle the number of the sentence that best expresses the general main idea, and write the general topic.

Group 1

1. At any one point in time, 20 percent of the land's surface is undergoing a drought.

2. Water availability and quality are rapidly becoming one of the most important political and international issues facing us.

3. Some environmentalists are predicting that cities built in naturally arid regions of the world, such as Los Angeles and San Diego, are really heading for trouble.

4. Topic: water availability

Carl Rischer and Thomas Easton, *Focus on Human Biology*, 2nd ed.

Group 2

1. Instead of saying, "I'm stupid and I'll never get through this class," say, "I didn't do so well on this last test, but I'm going to do better. I'm doing it in another class."

2. View your mistakes as opportunities to know yourself better or as growth experiences that will teach you to do things differently next time.

3. There are many things you can do in your day-to-day life that, when practiced regularly and added to other actions, can have significant impact on the way you feel about yourself.

4. Topic: _____ Learn From Your Mistakes _____

Adapted from Rebecca Donatelle, *Access to Health*, 8th ed.

Group 3

1. Although blinded as a newborn when given too much oxygen in an incubator, at age 12, Stevie Wonder began a performing and recording career that included such hits as "My Cherie Amour" and "Signed, Sealed, Delivered."

2. Blind people sometimes achieve greatness through the medium of sound, perhaps because they adapt and compensate for the loss by enhancing their skills in another area.

3. At age 12, Andrea Bocelli lost his sight in a soccer mishap, but today at 40, after a career as a lawyer, he has taken the music world by storm with his magnificent, classically trained voice.

4. Topic: _____ Blind People _____

Adapted from John Santrock, *Psychology*, 7th ed.

Group 4

1. After authorities gained control in the Sao Paulo prison riot of 1992, police ordered inmates to strip and began shooting them until 111 prisoners were dead.

2. A series of riots ripped through 21 Sao Paulo state prisons in February 2001, and prisoners armed with knives, guns, and clubs took more than 1,000 hostages.

3. According to the Human Rights Watch/Americas, the Brazilian prisons system is a time bomb and the bomb is exploding on a regular basis in the form of prison riots.

4. Topic: _____ Human Rights _____

Adapted from Steven Barkan and George Bryjak, *Fundamentals of Criminal Justice*

Group 5

1. On a global scale, the countries of the Middle East and North Africa are not major players in the world's tourism industry.

2. Deteriorating security conditions in Algeria and Egypt, where civil war and religious fundamentalist terrorism have occasionally targeted tourists, have slowed tourist growth in the entire region.

3. Turkey ranks highest in the region but stands in nineteenth place internationally, as measured in tourist arrivals, and in thirteenth place in terms of money earned from tourism.

4. Topic: ___world's tourism industry___

Adapted from David Clawson and Merrill Johnson, *World Regional Geography*, 8th ed.

Questioning for the Main Idea

To determine the main idea of a paragraph, article, or book, follow the three basic steps shown in the box below, and ask the questions posed in the Reader's Tip on page 146. The order of the three steps may vary depending on your prior knowledge of the material. If you are familiar with the material, you might find that constructing the main idea is automatic and you can select significant supporting details afterward. If you are unfamiliar with the material, as may often be the case in your textbook reading, you would need to identify the details through key terms and concepts first, and from them you would form a topic and a main idea statement.

Routes to the Main Idea

For Familiar Material
Determine topic ► ► ► Identify key terms ► ► ► Find main idea

For Unfamiliar Material
Identify key terms ► ► ► Determine topic ► ► ► Find main idea

---

Stated Main Ideas

Like paragraphs, photographs also suggest main ideas. Artists compose and select to communicate a message. Look at the picture shown on the next page and then answer the questions that follow.

Association of American Publishers

What is the general topic of the picture? _____

What details seem important? _____

What is the main idea the artist is trying to convey about the topic?

_____

_____

The topic of the picture is reading. The details show the famous baseball player Sammy Sosa sitting on the edge of the field reading a book. The stands are empty so we can assume that this is a practice. With the bat at his side, the champ is probably taking a break from hitting homeruns. He has escaped to a quiet place for a few minutes of pleasurable reading, but the camera has caught him. The main idea, "Get caught reading," is written at the bottom of the picture. The message is that we should copy this noted athlete and escape to enjoy a good book.

> ## READER'S TIP
>
> ## Finding the Main Idea
>
> ◆ **Determine the topic.** Who or what is this reading about? Find a general word or phrase that names the subject. The topic should be broad enough to include all the ideas, yet restrictive enough to focus on the direction of the details. For example, the topic of an article might be correctly identified as Politics, Federal Politics, or Corruption in Federal Politics, but the last might be the most descriptive of the actual contents.
>
> ◆ **Identify key terms.** What are the major supporting details? Look at the details that seem to be significant to see if they point in a particular direction. What aspect of the topic do they address? What seems to be the common message? Details such as kickbacks to senators, overspending on congressional junkets, and lying to the voters could support the idea of corruption in federal politics.
>
> ◆ **Find the main idea.** What is the message the author is trying to convey about the topic? The statement of the main idea should be
>
> A complete sentence
>
> Broad enough to include the important details
>
> Focused enough to describe the author's slant
>
> The author's main idea about corruption in federal politics might be that voters need to ask for an investigation of seemingly corrupt practices by federal politicians.

Topic Sentence. As in the photo, an author's main point can be directly stated in the material. When the main idea is stated in a sentence, the statement is called a **topic sentence** or **thesis statement**. Such a general statement is helpful to the reader because it provides an overview of the material.

Read the following examples and answer the questions for determining the main idea using the three-question technique.

EXAMPLE

Managers can regain control over their time in several ways. One is by meeting whenever possible in someone else's office, so that they can leave as soon as their business is finished. Another is to start meetings on time without waiting for late-comers. The idea is to let late-comers adjust their schedules rather than everyone else adjusting theirs. A third is to set aside a block of time to work on an important project without interruption. This may require ignoring the telephone, being protected by an aggressive secretary, or hiding out. Whatever it takes is worth it.

Joseph Reitz and Linda Jewell, *Managing*

1. Who or what is this passage about? _____

2. What are the major details? _____

_____

3. What is the main idea the author is trying to convey about the topic?

_____

EXPLANATION The passage is about managers controlling their time. The major details are *meet in another office, start meetings on time,* and *block out time to work.* The main idea, stated in the beginning as a topic sentence, is that managers can do things to control their time.

EXAMPLE New high-speed machines also brought danger to the workplace. If a worker succumbed to boredom, fatigue, or simple miscalculation, disaster could strike. Each year of the late nineteenth century some 35,000 wage earners were killed by industrial accidents. In Pittsburgh iron and steel mills alone, in one year 195 men died from hot metal explosions, asphyxiation, and falls, some into pits of molten metal. Men and women working in textile mills were poisoned by the thick dust and fibers in the air; similar toxic atmospheres injured those working in anything from twine-making plants to embroidery factories. Railways, with their heavy equipment and unaccustomed speed, were especially dangerous. In Philadelphia over half the railroad workers who died between 1886 and 1890 were killed by accidents. For injury or death, workers and their families could expect no payment from employers, since the idea of worker's compensation was unknown.

James W. Davidson et al., *Nation of Nations*

1. Who or what is this passage about? _____

2. What are the major details? _____

_____

3. What is the main idea the author is trying to convey about the topic?

_____

EXPLANATION The passage is about injuries from machines. The major details are 35,000 killed, 195 died from explosions and other accidents in iron and steel mills, poisoned dust killed workers in textile mills, and half of the rail workers who died were killed in accidents. The main idea is that new high-speed machines brought danger to the workplace.

Frequency of Stated Main Idea. Research shows that students find passages easier to comprehend when the main idea is directly stated within the passage. How often do stated main ideas appear in college textbooks? Should the reader expect to find that most paragraphs have stated main ideas?

For psychology texts, the answer seems to be about half and half. One research study found that stated main ideas appeared in *only 58 percent* of the sampled paragraphs in introductory psychology textbooks.[2] In one of the books, the main idea was directly stated in 81 percent of the sampled paragraphs, and the researchers noted that the text was particularly easy to read.

Given these findings, we should recognize the importance of being skilled in locating and, especially, in constructing main ideas. In pulling ideas together to construct a main idea, you will be looking at the big picture and not be bound to the text in search of any single suggestive sentence.

Location of Stated Main Ideas. Should college readers wish for all passages in all textbooks to begin with stated main ideas? Indeed, research indicates that when the main idea is stated at the beginning of the passage, the text tends to be comprehended more easily. In their research, however, Smith and Chase found only 33 percent of the stated main ideas to be positioned as the first sentence of the paragraph.

Main idea statements can be positioned at the beginning, in the middle, or at the end of a paragraph. Both the beginning and concluding sentences of a passage can be combined for a main idea statement.

Exercise 4.4

Locating Main Ideas

The following diagrams and the examples after them demonstrate the different possible positions for stated main ideas within paragraphs. Make notations as you read the examples, and then insert the main ideas and supporting details into the blank spaces provided beside the geometric diagrams.

1. **An introductory statement of the main idea is given at the beginning of the paragraph.**

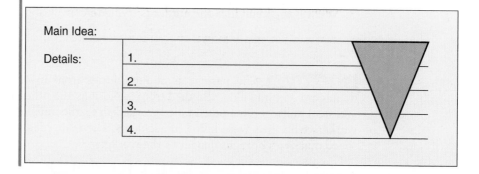

Main Idea:

Details: 1.

2.

3.

4.

---

[2]B. Smith and N. Chase, "The Frequency and Placement of Main Idea Topic Sentences in College Psychology Textbooks," *Journal of College Reading and Learning* 24 (1991): 46–54.

EXAMPLE

Under hypnosis, people may recall things that they are unable to remember spontaneously. Some police departments employ hypnotists to probe for information that crime victims do not realize they have. In 1976, twenty-six young children were kidnapped from a school bus near Chowchilla, California. The driver of the bus caught a quick glimpse of the license plate of the van in which he and the children were driven away. However, he remembered only the first two digits. Under hypnosis, he recalled the other numbers and the van was traced to its owners.

David Dempsey and Philip Zimbardo, Psychology and You

2. A concluding statement of the main idea appears at the end of the paragraph.

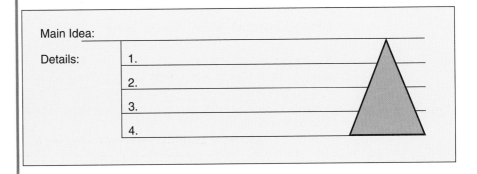

Main Idea: _____

Details:
1. _____
2. _____
3. _____
4. _____

EXAMPLE

Research is not a once-and-for-all-times job. Even sophisticated companies often waste the value of their research. One of the most common errors is not providing a basis for comparisons. A company may research its market, find a need for a new advertising campaign, conduct the campaign, and then neglect to research the results. Another may simply feel the need for a new campaign, conduct it, and research the results. Neither is getting the full benefit of the research. When you fail to research either the results or your position *prior* to the campaign, you cannot know the effects of the campaign. For good evaluation you must have both before and after data.

Edward Fox and Edward Wheatley, Modern Marketing

3. Details are placed at the beginning to arouse interest, followed by a statement of the main idea in the middle of the paragraph.

Details:
1. _____
2. _____

Main Idea: _____

Details:
3. _____
4. _____

EXAMPLE

After losing $1 billion in Euro-Disney's first year of operation, the company realized that Paris was not Anaheim or Orlando. French employees were insulted by the Disney dress code, and European customers were not accustomed to standing in line for rides or eating fast food standing up. Disney had to adjust and customize its market mix after learning that international customers are not all alike. The company ditched its controversial dress code, authorized wine with meals, lowered admission prices, hired a French investor relations firm, and changed the name to Disneyland Paris to lure the French tourist.

Adapted from Michael Mescon et al, *Business Today*, 8th ed.

4. Both the introductory and concluding sentences state the main idea.

Main Idea: _____

Details:
1. _____
2. _____
3. _____
4. _____

Main Idea: _____

EXAMPLE

You cannot avoid conflict but you can learn to face it with a four step conflict resolution plan. Before you bring up the issue that's upsetting you, know what you want to achieve. Have a positive outcome in mind. Then listen to what the other side says, but go beyond that to try to understand as well. Express empathy for their position. It may not be easy, but try to see the big picture. Place the conflict in context. Finally, if at all possible, end your discussion on a positive note. Set the stage for further discussion by keeping those lines of communication open. Use these four strategies for handling tensions constructively and enjoy stronger social bonds.

Adapted from Rebecca Donatelle, *Access to Health*, 8th ed.

5. Details combine to make a point but the main idea is not directly stated.

Unstated Main Idea: _____

Details:
1. _____
2. _____
3. _____
4. _____

| **EXAMPLE** | This creature's career could produce but one result, and it speedily followed. Boy after boy managed to get on the river. The minister's son became an engineer. The doctor's sons became "mud clerks"; the wholesale liquor dealer's son became a bar-keeper on a boat; four sons of the chief merchant, and two sons of the county judge, became pilots. Pilot was the grandest position of all. The pilot, even in those days of trivial wages, had a princely salary—from a hundred and fifty to two hundred and fifty dollars a month, and no board to pay. Two months of his wages would pay a preacher's salary for a year. Now some of us were left disconsolate. We could not get on the river—at least our parents would not let us. |

Mark Twain, Life on the Mississippi

EXPLANATION Although not directly stated, the main idea is that young boys in the area have a strong desire to leave home and get a job on the prestigious Mississippi River.

Exercise 4.5

Questioning for Stated Main Ideas

Read the following passages and use the three-question system to determine the author's main idea. For each passage in this exercise, the answer to the third question will be stated somewhere within the paragraph.

Passage A

The single largest contributor to American immigration is Mexico. Today, one out of five immigrants living in the United States is Mexican born. Immigration has been propelled by the rapid growth of Mexico's population, which tripled in the past fifty years, as well as by the wages paid in the United States, which are six times higher than those in Mexico.

James Kirby Martin, America and Its People, vol. 2, 5th ed.

1. Who or what is this about? _Immigrants fro Mex_

2. What are the major details? _immigration has been Propelled by the rapid growth of Mexicos Population_

3. What is the main idea the author is trying to convey about the topic? _American immigration is Mexico._

4. Underline the main idea.

Passage B

Time is especially linked to status considerations, and the importance of being on time varies with the status of the individual you are visiting. If the person is extremely important, you had better be there on time or even early just in case he or she is able to see you before schedule. As the person's status decreases, so does the importance of being on time. Junior executives, for example, must be on time for conferences with senior executives, but it is even more important to be on time for the company president or the CEO. Senior executives, however, may be late for conferences with their juniors but not for conferences with the president. Within any hierarchy, similar unwritten rules are followed with respect to time. This is not to imply that these "rules" are just or fair; they simply exist.

Joseph DeVito, *Interpersonal Communication*, 6th ed.

1. Who or what is this about? _Being On time_

2. What are the major details? _The importance of being on time varies with the status of the individual you are visiting_

3. What is the main idea the author is trying to convey about the topic? _As the Persons status decreases, so does the importance of being on time._

4. Underline the main idea.

Passage C

Courting behavior in birds is also believed to be instinctive. In one experiment Daniel Lehrman of Rutgers University found that when a male blond ring dove was isolated from females, it soon began to bow and coo to a stuffed model of a female—a model that it had previously ignored. When the model was replaced by a rolled-up cloth, he began to court the cloth; and when this was removed the sex-crazed dove directed his attention to a corner of the cage, where it could at least focus its gaze. It seems that the threshold for release of the behavior pattern became increasingly lower as time went by without the sight of a live female dove. It is almost as though some specific "energy" for performing courting behavior were building up within the male ring dove.

Robert Wallace, *Biology: The World of Life*

1. Who or what is this about? _Courting behavior in birds_

2. What are the major details? _Daniel Lehrman of Rutgers University found that when a male blond ring dove was isolated from females, it soon began to bow and coo to a stuffed model of a female_

3. What is the main idea the author is trying to convey about the topic? _Courting behavior in birds is also believed to be instinctive._

4. Underline the main idea.

Passage D

To retrieve a fact from a library of stored information, you need a way to gain access to it. In recognition tests, retrieval cues (such as photographs) provide reminders of information (classmates' names) we could not otherwise recall. Retrieval cues also guide us where to look. If you want to know what the pyramid on the back of a dollar bill signifies, you might look in *Collier's Encyclopedia* under "dollar," "currency," or "money." But your efforts would be futile. To get the information you want, you would have to look under "Great Seal of the United States." Like information stored in encyclopedias, memories are inaccessible unless we have cues for retrieving them. The more and better learned the retrieval cues, the more accessible the memory.

David G. Myers. *Psychology*

1. Who or what is this about? _Retriving information from library_

2. What are the major details? _To retrive a fact from a library of stored information, you need a way to gain access to it_

3. What is the main idea the author is trying to convey about the topic? _The more and better learned the retrieval cues, the more accessible the memory_

4. Underline the main idea.

Passage E

Most of the Plains Indians believed that land could be utilized, but never owned. The idea of owning land was as absurd as owning the air people breathed. To some, the sacredness of the land made farming against their religion. Chief Somohalla of the Wanapaun explained why his people refused to farm. "You ask me to plow the ground! Shall I take a knife and tear my mother's bosom?. . . You ask me to cut grass and make hay and sell it, and be rich like white men! But how dare I cut off my mother's hair?"

James Kirby Martin et al., *America and Its Peoples,* 4th ed.

1. Who or what is this about? _Farming_

2. What are the major details? _The sacredness of the land made farming against their religion._

3. What is the main idea the author is trying to convey about the topic? _Most of the Plains indians believed that land could be utilized, but never owned_

4. Underline the main idea.

Passage F

A crab lives at the bottom of its ocean of water and looks upward at jellyfish drifting above it. Similarly, we live at the bottom of our ocean of air and look upward at balloons drifting above us. A balloon is suspended in air and a jellyfish is suspended in water for the same reason: each is buoyed upward by a displaced weight of fluid equal to its own weight. In one case the displaced fluid is air, and in the other case it is water. In water, immersed objects are buoyed upward because the pressure acting up against the bottom of the object exceeds the pressure acting down against the top. Likewise, air pressure acting up against an object immersed in air is greater than the pressure above pushing down. The buoyancy in both cases is numerically equal to the weight of fluid displaced. **Archimedes' principle** holds for air just as it does for water: An object surrounded by air is buoyed up by a force equal to the weight of the air displaced.

Paul Hewitt, *Conceptual Physics*, 8th ed.

1. Who or what is this about? _Archimedes Principle_
2. What are the major details? _Air Pressure acting up against an object immersed in air is greater than the Pressure above, pushing down_
3. What is the main idea the author is trying to convey about the topic? _An object surrounded by air is buoyed up by a force equal to the weight of the air displace_
4. Underline the main idea.

What Are Major and Minor Details?

Textbooks are packed full of details, but fortunately all details are not of equal importance. Major details tend to support, explain, and describe main ideas—they are essential. Minor details, by contrast, tend to support, explain, and describe the major details. Ask the following questions to determine which details are major in importance and which are not:

1. Which details logically develop the main idea?
2. Which details help you understand the main idea?
3. Which details make you think the main idea you have chosen is correct?

Key signal words, like those listed in the Reader's Tip, form transitional links among ideas and can sometimes help you distinguish between major and minor details.

READER'S TIP

Signals for Significance

◆ Key words for major details:

| one | first | another | furthermore | also | finally |

◆ Key words for minor details:

| for example | to be specific | that is | this means |

EXAMPLE
Selena was the undisputed queen of Tejano, the music of the Texas-Mexico border. Her music epitomized the complexity of the border culture. Tejano music originated in the nineteenth century, when European immigrants introduced the accordion to the Texas-Mexico border. A fast-paced blend of Latin pop, German polka, and country rhythms, Tejano music combined the oompah music of Europeans with Mexican ballads known as *cumbias* and *rancheras*. Unlike many earlier Latina personalities, like Rita Hayworth and Raquel Welch, who gained their fame only after changing their names and projecting an exotic and sexy image, Selena never abandoned her Mexican American identity. Selena, who was 23 years old when she was slain, nevertheless achieved extraordinary popularity.

Adapted from James Kirby Martin et al., *America and Its Peoples*, vol. 2, 5th ed.

1. The topic of the passage is
   a. Selena Was Slain.
   b. Tejano Music.
   c. Queen of Tejano Music.
   d. Mexican Ballads.
2. Indicate whether each of the following details is major or minor in support of the author's topic:
   a. Selena was true to her Mexican American identity.
   b. Raquel Welch changed her name.
   c. Selena was popular when she was slain at 23.
3. Underline the sentence that best states the main idea of this passage.

EXPLANATION For the first response, the topic of the passage is *c*. Both *b* and *d* are too broad and *a* is an unfortunate detail. For the second item, *a* is a major detail because her music is Tejano, *b* is a minor detail not directly related to Selena, and c is a major detail because she is no longer living. The first sentence states the main idea.

Exercise 4.6

Identifying Topics, Stated Main Ideas, and Details in Passages

Read the following passages and apply the three-question system. Select the letter of the author's topic, identify major and minor details, and underline the main idea. For each passage in this exercise, the answer to the third question will be stated somewhere within the paragraph.

Passage A

Experts agree that the crux of Brazil's disastrous prison situation is rooted in overcrowding. Many prisons have two to five times the number of inmates they were designed to hold. A Human Rights Watch/Americas inspection team discovered that single-person cells contained eight to ten prisoners, with some inmates tied to windows to reduce demand for floor space. While some slept in hammocks suspended from the ceiling, others were forced to lie on top of hole-in-the-floor toilets.

Adapted from Steven Barkan and George Bryjak, *Fundamentals of Criminal Justice*

1. The topic of the passage is
   a. Human Rights Watch in Brazil.
   b. Brazil's Prisons Overcrowded.
   c. More Inspections Needed in Brazil.
   d. Sleeping in Hammocks in Brazil.

2. Indicate whether each of the following details is major or minor in support of the author's topic:

   Minor a. Many prisons have two to five times capacity.

   Major b. A Human Rights Watch team inspected prisons in Brazil.

   minor c. Single-person cells contained eight to ten prisoners.

3. Underline the sentence that best states the main idea of this passage.

Passage B

The term *vegetarian* means different things to different people. Strict vegetarians, or *vegans*, avoid all foods of animal origins, including dairy products and eggs. Far more common are *lacto-vegetarians*, who eat dairy products but avoid flesh foods. Their diets can be low in cholesterol, but only if they consume skim milk and other low- or nonfat products. **Ovo-vegetarians** add eggs to their diet, while *lacto-ovo-vegetarians* eat both dairy products and eggs. *Pesco-vegetarians* eat fish, dairy products, and eggs. Some people in the semivegetarian category prefer to call themselves "non-red meat eaters."

Rebecca J. Donatelle, *Health: The Basics,* 4th ed.

1. The topic of the passage is
   a. Vegetarians Without Dairy Products.
   b. Becoming a Vegetarian.
   c. Different Vegetarian Categories.
   d. Health Issues for Vegetarians.

2. Indicate whether each of the following details is major or minor in support of the author's topic:

   minor a. Pesco-vegetarians eat fish.

   Major b. Lacto-vegetarians can have low cholesterol if they consume skim milk.

   minor c. Ovo-vegetarians add eggs to their diet.

3. Underline the sentence that best states the main idea of this passage.

Passage C

Building and equipping the pyramids focused and transformed Egypt's material and human resources. Artisans had to be trained, engineering and transportation problems solved, quarrying and stone-working techniques perfected, and laborers recruited. In the Old Kingdom, whose population has been estimated at perhaps 1.5 million, more than 70,000 workers at a time were employed in building the great temple-tombs. No smaller work force could have built such a massive structure as the Great Pyramid of Khufu.

Mark Kishlansky et al., *Civilization in the West,* 4th ed.

1. The topic of the passage is
   a. Training Laborers for the Pyramids.
   b. Resources Needed for Building Pyramids.
   c. Pyramid Building Problems.
   d. The Pyramids.

2. Indicate whether each of the following details is major or minor in support of the author's topic:

   Major   a. The Old Kingdom had an estimated population of 1.5 million.

   Major   b. More than 70,000 workers at a time were employed in building the great temple-tombs.

   minor   c. Artisans had to be trained.

3. Underline the sentence that best states the main idea of this passage.

Passage D

If you're upset or tired, you're at risk for an emotion-charged confrontation. If you ambush someone with an angry attack, don't expect her or him to be in a productive frame of mind. Instead, give yourself time to cool off before you try to resolve a conflict. In the case of the group project, you could call a meeting for later in the week. By that time, you could gain control of your feelings and think things through. Of course, sometimes issues need to be discussed on the spot; you may not have the luxury to wait. But whenever it's practical, make sure your conflict partner is ready to receive you and your message. Select a mutually acceptable time and place to discuss a conflict.

Adapted from Steven A. Beebe, Susan J. Beebe, and Diana K. Ivy, *Communication*

A

1. The topic of the passage is
   a. Planning for Conflict Resolution.
   b. Confrontation.
   c. Being Productive.
   d. Solving Problems.

2. Indicate whether each of the following details is major or minor in support of the author's topic:

   Minor   a. Give yourself time to cool off before you try to resolve a conflict.

   Major   b. If you are upset, you are at risk for a confrontation.

Minor   c. Call a meeting a week later for a group project.

3. Underline the sentence that best states the main idea of this passage.

Passage E

In a Utah case, the defendant fell asleep in his car on the shoulder of the highway. Police stopped, smelled alcohol on his breath, and arrested him for driving while intoxicated. His conviction was reversed by the Utah Supreme Court because the defendant was not in physical control of the vehicle at the time, as required by the law. In freeing the defendant, the Supreme Court judged that the legal definition of sufficiency was not established in this case because the act observed by the police was not *sufficient* to confirm the existence of a guilty mind. In other words, the case against him failed because he was not violating the law at the time of the arrest and because it was also possible that he could have driven while sober, then pulled over, drank, and fell asleep.

Adapted from Jay S. Albanese, *Criminal Justice, Brief Edition*

1. The topic of the passage is
   a. Driving Drunk.
   b. The Utah Supreme Court.
   c. Sleeping Behind the Wheel.
   d. Establishing Sufficiency for Drunken Driving.

2. Indicate whether each of the following details is major or minor in support of the author's topic:

   Major   a. Police arrested the defendant for driving while intoxicated.

   Minor   b. The defendant was not violating a law at the time of the arrest.

   Minor   c. The case was tried in Utah.

3. Underline the sentence that best states the main idea of this passage.

Unstated Main Ideas

Unfortunately, even if details are obvious you cannot always depend on the author to provide a direct statement of a stated main idea. To add drama and suspense to a description or narrative, the main idea may be hinted at or implied rather than directly stated Main ideas are often unstated in other media as well, such as movies and photographs.

Look at the details in the photo on page 159 to decide what message the photographer is trying to communicate. Determine the topic of the picture, propose a main idea using your prior knowledge, and then list some of the significant details that support this point.

Scott Olson/Getty Images

What is the topic? _____

_____

What are the significant supporting details? _____

_____

What is the point the photograph is trying to convey about the topic? _____

_____

The topic of the photograph is a disaster. The roof of the house has been torn off, and one side of the house has collapsed. Yet many of the contents remain seemingly unharmed. The overhead light fixture, television, and pictures on the wall seem undisturbed. The bookcase has fallen with the pink living room wall, but the books remain on the shelf. Such a pattern of destruction, without water damage or a broken ceiling, suggests a tornado. The couple surveying the damage are probably the owners. They look with sadness at what is left of their home and belongings. The main idea the photographer is trying to convey is that this couple has suffered an overwhelming loss from the tragic touchdown of a violent tornado. This main idea is suggested by the details but not directly stated in the picture.

Determining Unstated Main Ideas in Sentences

Before identifying unstated main ideas in paragraphs, practice with a simple list of sentences. First, read the related sentences in the following group. Next, create a sentence that states a general main idea for the three related thoughts.

EXAMPLE

1. A landmark 1990 study found that 30 percent of Americans under 35 had read a newspaper the day before—a much lower percentage than their parents.

2. Attempts to win a younger audience have included *USA Today*'s color and glitz, originally aimed at younger readers.

3. By 2000, daily newspaper circulation was down to 52.8 million from a 62.8 million high in 1988.

John Vivian, The Media of Mass Communication

Main idea: _____

EXPLANATION   The first sentence states that young readership is low. The second states an attempt to lure young readers, and the third states that circulation has declined by 10 million. The general main idea that reflects these sentences is that daily newspapers are not winning young readers, and circulation is down.

Exercise 4.7

Determining Unstated Main Ideas

Read the following related sentences and state the main idea:

Group 1

1. For over 200 years, *Encyclopedia Britannica* was considered the ultimate reference source.

2. *Britannica* looked the other way as competitors took advantage of new technologies and produced cheaper encyclopedias on CD-ROM.

3. *Britannica*'s sales slumped as consumers snapped up *Encarta* for $50 to $70 or enjoyed the free version installed on new computers.

Michael Mescon et al., *Business Today*, 10th ed.

Main idea: _____

_____

Group 2

1. The middle class seldom uses the double negative ("I can't get no satisfaction"), whereas the working class often does.

2. The middle class rarely drops the letter "g" in present participles ("doin'" for "doing," "singin'" for "singing"), perhaps because they are conscious of being correct.

3. The middle class also tend to say "lay" instead of "lie," as in "Let's lay on the beach," without suggesting a desire for sex.

Alex Thio, *Sociology*, 5th ed.

Main idea: _____

_____

Group 3

1. The AIDS virus (HIV), which seemed to arise abruptly in the early 1980s, and the new varieties of flu virus that frequently appear, are not the only examples of newly dangerous viruses.

2. A deadly virus called the Ebola virus menaces central African nations periodically, and many biologists fear its emergence as a global threat.

3. In 2003, a deadly new disease called SARS (severe acute respiratory syndrome) appeared in China and soon spread throughout the world.

Neil Campbell et al., *Essential Biology*

Main idea: _____

_____

Group 4

1. President George Washington converted the paper thoughts outlined in the Constitution into an enduring, practical governing process, setting precedents that balance self-government and leadership.

2. Thomas Jefferson, a skilled organizer and a resourceful party leader and chief executive, adapted the presidency to the new realities of his day with territorial expansions and sponsorship of the Lewis and Clark expedition westward.

3. President Lincoln is remembered for saving the Union and is revered as the nation's foremost symbol of democracy and tenacious leadership in the nation's ultimate crisis.

James MacGregor Burns, *Government by the People*, 20th ed.

Main idea: _____

_____

Group 5

1. Sales prospects are much more inclined to buy from people who make them feel good and with whom they have developed a personal bond, so begin by building a rapport.

2. Ask questions to find out the prospect's real needs, and describe the product or service accordingly to focus on the buyer's benefits.

3. Go for the final close and remember to ask for the order and stop talking so the customer can make the purchase.

Michael Mescon et al., *Business Today*, 8th ed.

Main idea: _____

_____

Questioning for the Unstated Main Idea

The difference between questioning for a stated main idea and questioning for an unstated main idea is subtle. As you approach a passage with an implied or unstated main idea, begin by asking, "What is this about?" Reading carefully to identify key terms and major supporting details, draw a conclusion about the topic. Once you have determined the general topic of the paragraph, then ask yourself, "What do all or most of the key terms or major details suggest?" It is now up to you to figure out the author's point. Think as you read. Create an umbrella statement that brings these concepts together into a main idea statement.

EXAMPLE   Michael Harner proposes an ecological interpretation of Aztec sacrifice and cannibalism. He holds that human sacrifice was a response to certain diet deficiencies in the population. In the Aztec environment, wild game was getting scarce, and the population was growing. Although the maize-beans combination of food that was the basis of the diet was usually adequate, these crops were subject to seasonal failure. Famine was frequent in the absence of edible domesticated animals. To meet essential protein requirements, cannibalism was the only solution. Although only the upper classes were allowed to consume human flesh, a commoner who distinguished himself in a war could also have the privilege of giving a cannibalistic feast. Thus, although it was the upper strata who benefited most from ritual cannibalism, members of the commoner class could also benefit. Furthermore, as Harner explains, the social mobility and cannibalistic privileges available to the commoners through warfare provided a strong motivation for the "aggressive war machine" that was such a prominent feature of the Aztec state.

Serena Nanda, *Cultural Anthropology*, 4th ed.

1. Who or what is this about? _____

_____

2. What are the major details? _____

_____

_____

3. What is the main idea the author is trying to convey about the topic?

_____

EXPLANATION The passage is about Aztec sacrifice and cannibalism. The major details are: diet deficiencies occurred, animals were not available, and members of the upper class and commoners who were war heroes could eat human flesh. The main idea is that Aztec sacrifice and cannibalism met protein needs of the diet and motivated warriors to achieve.

**Exercise
4.8**

Identifying Unstated Main Ideas in Passages

Read the following passages and apply the three-question system. Select the letter of the author's topic, identify major and minor details, and choose the letter of the sentence that best states the main idea.

Passage A

Until recently, the U.S. census, which is taken every ten years, offered only the following categories: Caucasian, Negro, Indian, and Oriental. After years of complaints from the public the list was expanded. In the year of 2000 census, everyone had to declare that they were or were not "Spanish/Hispanic/Latino." They had to mark "one or more races" that they "considered themselves to be." Finally, if these didn't do it, you could check a box called "Some Other Race" and then write whatever you wanted. For example, Tiger Woods, one of the top golfers of all time, calls himself Cablinasian. Woods invented this term as a boy to try to explain to himself just who he was—a combination of Caucasian, Black, Indian, and Asian. Woods wants to embrace both sides of his family.

Adapted from James M. Henslin, *Sociology*, 5th ed.

____ 1. The topic of the passage is
   a. Tiger Woods Speaks Out.
   b. The U.S. Census.
   c. Identify Your Race.
   d. The Emerging Multiracial Identity.

2. Indicate whether each of the following details is major or minor in support of the author's topic:

Major a. Tiger Woods is one of the top golfers of all time.

Major b. Tiger Woods wants to embrace both sides of his family.

minor c. Until recently, the U.S. census offered only four racial categories.

_B_ 3. The sentence that best states the main idea of this passage is
   a. Citizens complained about the four categories of the previous census.
   b. The 2000 census took a new approach and allowed citizens to identify themselves as being of more than one race.
   c. Tiger Woods considers himself a combination of Caucasian, Black, Indian, and Asian.
   d. Information from the 2000 census will be more useful than data gathered from the previous census.

Passage B

The rate of incarceration in prison increased from 27 per 100,000 women in 1985 to 57 per 100,000 in 1998. Men still outnumber women in the inmate population by a factor of about 14 to 1, but the gap is narrowing—from 17 to 1 a decade ago. Women constituted only 4 percent of the total prison and jail population in the United States in 1980 but more than 6 percent in 1998.

Adapted from Jay S. Albanese, Criminal Justice, Brief Edition

_A_ 1. The topic of the passage is
   a. Men Versus Women in Jail.
   b. Incarceration in America.
   c. The Increasing Number of Women in Jail.
   d. Overcrowded Prisons.

2. Indicate whether each of the following details is major or minor in support of the author's topic:

minor a. The rate of incarceration of women in prison in 1985 was 27 per 100,000.

minor b. The rate of incarceration of women in prison in 1998 was 57 per 100,000.

major c. A decade ago men outnumbered women 17 to 1.

_B_ 3. Which sentence best states the main idea of this passage?
   a. Men continue to outnumber women in the prison and jail population.
   b. The rate of incarceration is increasing for both men and women.

   c. In the last decade, the rate of women incarcerated has
    doubled.

   d. The role of women in society has changed in the last decade.

Passage C

Each year in the United States approximately 50,000 miscarriages are attributed to smoking during pregnancy. On average, babies born to mothers who smoke weigh less than those born to nonsmokers, and low birth weight is correlated with many developmental problems. Pregnant women who stop smoking in the first three or four months of their pregnancies give birth to higher-birth-weight babies than do women who smoke throughout their pregnancies. Infant mortality rates are also higher among babies born to smokers.

Rebecca J. Donatelle, Health: The Basics, 4th ed.

 1. The topic of the passage is
  a. Infant Mortality.
  b. Smoking.
  c. Smoking and Pregnancy.
  d. Smoking and Miscarriages.

 2. Indicate whether each of the following details is major or minor in support of the author's topic:

   a. Low birth weight is correlated with many developmental problems.

   b. Infant mortality rates are also higher among babies born to smokers.

  _____ c. Babies born to mothers who smoke weigh less than those born to nonsmokers.

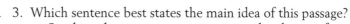

 3. Which sentence best states the main idea of this passage?
  a. Smoking during pregnancy increases the chance of miscarriages, low-weight babies, and infant mortality.
  b. Smoking during pregnancy causes many miscarriages.
  c. Ceasing smoking during pregnancy can increase infant birth weight.
  d. Smoking is a major contributor to infant mortality.

Passage D

The young reporter with the slow Missouri drawl stamped the cold of the high Nevada desert out of his feet as he entered the offices of the Virginia City *Territorial Enterprise*. It was early in 1863. The newspaper's editor, Joseph T. Goodman, looked puzzled at seeing his Carson City correspondent in the home office, but Samuel Clemens came right to the point: "Joe, I want to sign my articles. I want to be identified to a wider audience." The editor, already impressed with his colleague of six months, readily agreed. Then came the question of a pen name, since few aspiring writers of the time used their legal names. Clemens had something in mind: "I want to sign them 'Mark Twain,'" he declared. "It is an old river term, a leadsman's call, signifying two fathoms—twelve feet. It has a richness about it; it was always a pleasant sound for a pilot to hear on a dark night; it meant safe water."

Roderick Nash and Gregory Graves, From These Beginnings, vol. 2, 6th ed..

1. The topic of the passage is
   a. Becoming a Reporter
   b. How Mark Twain Got His Name
   c. Safe Water on the River
   d. Working for the Virginia City *Territorial Enterprise*

2. Indicate whether each of the following details is major or minor in support of the author's topic:
   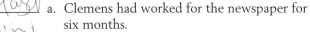 a. Clemens had worked for the newspaper for six months.
   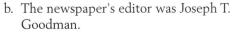 b. The newspaper's editor was Joseph T. Goodman.
   _____ c. Clemens wanted to sign his articles to be known to a wider audience.

C

3. Which sentence best states the main idea of this passage?
   a. Samuel Clemens worked as a young reporter for the Virginia City *Territorial Enterprise.*
   b. The newspaper's editor, Joseph T. Goodman, was impressed with the young reporter, Samuel Clemens.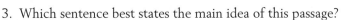
   c. "Mark Twain" is a river term that means two fathoms—twelve feet.
   d. The young reporter, Samuel Clemens, decided to take the pen name "Mark Twain."

Passage E

Credit card companies entice students to apply for cards and take on debt with free T-shirts, music CDs, and promises of an easy way to pay for spring break vacations. Many students, however, can't even keep up with the minimum payment. In fact, it is estimated that in one year 150,000 people younger than 25 will declare personal bankruptcy. That means for 150,000 young people, their first significant financial event as an adult will be to declare themselves a failure. And for each one who goes into bankruptcy, there are dozens just behind them, struggling with credit cards bills. In one 4-month period, for instance, a Texas A&M freshman piled up $2,500 of charges on two Visa cards and four retail credit cards. The student couldn't afford to pay the $25 minimum a month on all the cards, so she accumulated $150 in late fees and over-credit-limit fees.

Adapted from Michael Mescon et al., Business Today, 8th ed.

1. The topic of the passage is
   a. The Credit-Card Industry.
   b. Paying Off Debt.

JJ

c. Bankruptcy Options.

d. Danger of Credit Cards for College Students.

2. Indicate whether each of the following details is major or minor in support of the author's topic:

Minor a. Credit-card companies give away music CDs.

Major b. Young people are declaring bankruptcy over credit cards.

Minor c. A Texas A&M freshman cannot pay her minimum payments.

_C_ 3. Which sentence best states the main idea of this passage?

a. Credit-card companies engage in illegal activities to hook students on debt.

b. It should be illegal for credit-card companies to enroll college students who have no means of payment.

c. Credit-card companies entice college students into debt that can be financially disastrous.

d. Bankruptcy is an easy option for college students with overwhelming credit-card debt.

Exercise 4.9

Writing Unstated Main Ideas

Read the following passages and use the three-question system to determine the author's main idea. Pull the ideas together to state the main ideas in your own words.

Passage A

According to the U.S. Department of the Census, the demographic shift in the population will be "profound" in the next 50 years. By 2050, Hispanics will make up 24.5 percent of the population, up from 10.2 percent in 1996. The annual growth rate of the Hispanic population is expected to be 2 percent through the year 2030. To put this growth in perspective, consider the fact that even at the height of the baby boom explosion in the late 1940s and early 1950s, the country's annual population increase never reached 2 percent. Demographers, it seems, are alerting us to the enormous importance of such change. Says Gregory Spencer, Director of the Census Bureau's Population Projections Branch, "The world is not going to be the same in thirty years as it is now."

Ronald Ebert and Ricky Griffin, *Business Essentials*, 2nd ed.

1. Who or what is this about? _____

2. What are the major details? _____

_____

_____

3. What is the main idea the author is trying to convey about the topic?

_____

_____

Passage B

Prior to the time of Jan Baptiste van Helmont, a Belgian physician of the 17th century, it was commonly accepted that plants derived their matter from materials in the soil. (Probably, many people who haven't studied photosynthesis would go along with this today.) We aren't sure why, but van Helmont decided to test the idea. He carefully stripped a young willow sapling of all surrounding soil, weighed it, and planted it in a tub of soil that had also been carefully weighed. After five years of diligent watering (with rain water), van Helmont removed the greatly enlarged willow and again stripped away the soil and weighed it. The young tree had gained 164 pounds. Upon weighing the soil, van Helmont was amazed to learn that it had lost only 2 ounces.

Robert Wallace et al., *Biology: The Science of Life*, 3rd ed.

1. Who or what is this about? _____

2. What are the major details? _____

_____

3. What is the main idea the author is trying to convey about the topic?

_____

_____

Passage C

The Aswan High Dam, built in Egypt with Russian support, was supposed to provide hydroelectric power and to increase Egypt's food supply by controlling the unpredictable Nile River. The project meant that great art treasures were flooded as submerged land was drained for cultivation. However, only one-tenth of an acre of land was made available for each person added to Egypt's population during the period of construction. One result of the dam was that the Nile no longer flooded the delta farmlands annually. These annual floods served to restore the farmland fertility with deposited silt. This no longer the case, the quality of the farmland decreased. The dam also cut off the nutrients that had been washed to the Mediterranean Sea as a result of the annual floodings. Because of this, or the change in the salinity of the sea that the dam produced, the sardine catch dropped from 18,000 tons per year to 500 tons per year. The stable lake created by the dam allowed aquatic snails to flourish. The snails serve as an intermediate host to a blood fluke that bores into humans causing the dreaded disease, schistosomiasis. The construction of the dam had important political implications at the time.

Robert Wallace, *Biology: The World of Life*

1. Who or what is this about? _____

2. What are the major details? _____

_____

_____

3. What is the main idea the author is trying to convey about the topic?

_____

_____

Passage D

If using sunscreen, apply it at least 30–45 minutes before exposure, then reapply it periodically, especially after you swim or sweat. It is especially important to protect children. One or more severe sunburns with blisters in childhood or adolescence can double the risk of the skin cancer melanoma later in life. Additional protection can be provided by a wide-brimmed hat to protect your head and face, and opaque clothing to cover those body areas you wish to protect. Any fabric or material you can see through, including some beach umbrellas, does not give full protection. You should stay out of the sun between 10 A.M. and 2 P.M. when the rays are strongest.

Curtis O. Byer and Louis W. Shainberg, *Living Well: Health in Your Hands*, 2nd ed.

1. Who or what is this about? _____

2. What are the major details? _____

_____

_____

3. What is the main idea the author is trying to convey about the topic?

_____

_____

Passage E

In 1979 when University of Minnesota psychologist Thomas Bouchard read a newspaper account of the reuniting of 39-year-old twins who had been separated from infancy, he seized the opportunity and flew them to Minneapolis for extensive tests. Bouchard was looking for differences. What "the Jim twins," Jim Lewis and Jim Springer, presented were amazing similarities. Both had married women named Linda, divorced, and married women named Betty. One had a son James Alan, the other a son James Allan. Both had dogs named Toy, chain-smoked Salems, served as sheriff's deputies, drove Chevrolets, chewed their fingernails to the nub, enjoyed stock car racing, had basement workshops, and had built circular white benches around trees in their yards. They also had similar medical histories: Both gained 10 pounds at about the same time and then lost it; both suffered what they mistakenly believed were heart attacks, and both began having late-afternoon headaches at age 18.

Identical twins Oskar Stohr and Jack Yufe presented equally striking similarities. One was raised by his grandmother in Germany as a Catholic and a Nazi, while the other was raised by his father in the Caribbean as a Jew. Nevertheless, they share traits and habits galore. They like spicy foods and sweet liqueurs, have a habit of falling asleep in front of the television, flush the toilet before using it, store rubber bands on their wrists, and dip buttered toast in their coffee. Stohr is domineering toward women and yells at his wife, as did Yufe before he was separated.

David G. Myers, *Psychology*

1. Who or what is this about? _____

2. What are the major details? _____

   _____

   _____

3. What is the main idea the author is trying to convey about the topic?

   _____

   _____

Interpreting the Main Idea of Longer Selections

Understanding the main idea of longer selections requires a little more thinking than does finding the main idea of a single paragraph. Since longer selections such as articles or chapters contain more material, tying the ideas together can be a challenge. Each paragraph of a longer selection usually represents a new aspect of a supporting detail. In addition, several major ideas may contribute to developing the overall main idea. Your job is to group the many pieces together under one central theme.

For longer selections, add an extra step between the two questions "What is the topic?" and "What is the main idea the author is trying to convey?" The step involves organizing the material into manageable subunits and then relating those to the whole. Ask the following two additional questions: "Under what subsections can these ideas be grouped?" and "How do these subsections contribute to the whole?"

Use the suggestions in the Reader's Tip to determine the main idea of longer selections. The techniques are similar to those used in previewing and skimming, two skills that also focus on the overall central theme.

READER'S TIP

Getting the Main Idea of Longer Selections

◆ **Think about the significance of the title.** What does the title suggest about the topic?

◆ **Read the first paragraph or two for a statement of the topic or thesis.** What does the selection seem to be about?

◆ **Read the subheadings** and, if necessary, glance at the first sentences of some of the paragraphs. Based on these clues, what does the article seem to be about?

◆ **Look for clues that indicate how the material is organized.** Is the purpose to define a term, to prove an opinion or explain a concept, to describe a situation, or to persuade the reader toward a particular point of view? Is the material organized into a list of examples, a time order or sequence, a comparison or contrast, or a cause-and-effect relationship?

◆ **As you read, organize the paragraphs into subsections.** Give each subsection a title. These become your significant supporting details.

◆ **Determine how the overall organization and subsections relate to the whole.** Answer the question, "What is the main idea the author is trying to convey in this selection?"

Exercise 4.10

Getting the Main Idea of a Longer Selection

Read the following passage and use the strategies in the Reader's Tip to determine the author's main idea.

The Benefits of a Good Night's Sleep

College students are well known for "all nighters," during which they stay up through the night to study for an exam or to finish—or even to start—a paper due in the morning. Lack of sleep is nothing to brag or laugh about. Sleep is vital to your life and can help you function at optimal levels both physically and mentally.

On the physical side, sleep helps regulate your metabolism and your body's state of equilibrium. On the mental side, it helps restore your ability to be optimistic and to have a high level of energy and self-confidence. To keep your body in balance, more sleep is needed when you are under stress, experiencing emotional fatigue, or undertaking an intense intellectual activity such as learning.

During sleep, most people experience periods of what is called rapid eye movement (REM). These movements can be observed beneath closed eyelids. In REM sleep, the body is quiet but the mind is active, even hyperactive. Some researchers believe that REM sleep helps you form permanent memories; others believe that this period of active brain waves serves to rid your brain of overstimulation and useless information acquired during the day. REM sleep is the time not only for dreams but also for acceleration of the heart rate and blood flow to the brain.

During non-REM sleep, in contrast, the body may be active—some people sleepwalk during this period—but the mind is not. In spite of this activity, non-REM sleep is the time when the body does its repair and maintenance work, including cell regeneration.

Although much still needs to be learned about sleep and its functions, few would disagree that sleep plays a role in the maintenance of good mental health.

B. E. Pruitt and Jane J. Stein, *Decisions for Healthy Living*

1. What does the title suggest about the topic? _____

2. What sentence in the first paragraph suggests the main idea? _____

   _____

3. What subtitles would you give the second, third, and fourth paragraphs?

   _____

4. What is the main idea of the selection? _____

   _____

Summary Writing: A Main Idea Skill

A **summary** is a series of brief, concise statements in your own words of the main idea and the significant supporting details. The first sentence should state the main idea or thesis; and subsequent sentences should incorporate the significant details. Minor details and material irrelevant to the learner's purpose should be omitted. The summary should be in paragraph form and should always be shorter than the material being summarized.

Why Summarize?

Summaries can be used for textbook study and are particularly useful in anticipating answers for essay exam questions. For writing research papers, summarizing is an essential skill. Using your own words to put the essence of an article into concise sentences requires a thorough understanding of the material. As one researcher noted, "Since so much summarizing is necessary for writing papers, students should have the skill before starting work on research papers. How much plagiarism is the result of inadequate summarizing skills?"[3]

Writing a research paper may mean that you will have to read as many as 30 articles and four books over a period of a month or two. After each reading, you want to take enough notes so you can write your paper without returning to the library for another look at the original reference. Since you will be using so

---

[3]K. Taylor, "Can College Students Summarize?" *Journal of Reading* 26 (March 1983): 540–544.

many different references, do your note taking carefully. The complete sentences of a summary are more explicit than underscored text or the highlighted topic-phrase format of an outline. Your summary should demonstrate a synthesis of the information. The Reader's Tip outlines how to write an effective summary.

READER'S TIP

How to Summarize

◆ **Keep in mind the purpose of your summary.** Your projected needs will determine which details are important and how many should be included.

◆ **Decide on the main idea the author is trying to convey.** Make this main idea the first sentence in your summary.

◆ **Decide on the major ideas and details that support the author's point.** Mark the key terms and phrases. Include in your summary the major ideas and as many of the significant supporting details as your purpose demands.

◆ **Do not include irrelevant or repeated information in your summary.**

◆ **Use appropriate transitional words and phrases to show relationships between points.**

◆ **Use paragraph form.**

◆ **Do not add your personal opinion** as part of the summary.

EXAMPLE Read the following excerpt on political authority as if you were researching for a term paper and writing a summary on a note card. Mark key terms that you would include in your summary. Before reading the example provided, anticipate what you would include in your own summary.

Types of Authority

Where is the source of the state's authority? Weber described three possible sources of the right to command, which produce what he called traditional authority, charismatic authority, and legal authority.

Traditional Authority

In many societies, people have obeyed those in power because, in essence, "that is the way it has always been." Thus, kings, queens, feudal lords, and tribal chiefs did not need written rules in order to govern. Their authority was based on tradition, on long-standing customs, and it was handed down from parent to child, maintaining traditional authority from one generation to the next. Often, traditional authority has been justified by religious tradition. For example, medieval European kings were said to rule by divine right, and Japanese emperors were considered the embodiment of heaven.

Charismatic Authority

People may also submit to authority, not because of tradition, but because of the extraordinary attraction of an individual. Napoleon, Gandhi, Mao Tse-tung, and Ayatollah Khomeini all illustrate authority that derives its legitimacy from *charisma*—an exceptional personal quality popularly attributed to certain individuals. Their followers perceive charismatic leaders as persons of destiny endowed with remarkable vision, the power of a savior, or God's grace. Charismatic authority is inherently unstable. It cannot be transferred to another person.

Legal Authority

The political systems of industrial states are based largely on a third type of authority: legal authority, which Weber also called *rational authority*. These systems derive legitimacy from a set of explicit rules and procedures that spell out the ruler's rights and duties. Typically, the rules and procedures are put in writing. The people grant their obedience to "the law." It specifies procedures by which certain individuals hold offices of power, such as governor or president or prime minister. But the authority is vested in those offices, not in the individuals who temporarily hold the offices. Thus, a political system based on legal authority is often called a "government of laws, not of men." Individuals come and go, as American presidents have come and gone, but the office, "the presidency," remains. If individual officeholders overstep their authority, they may be forced out of office and replaced.

Alex Thio, *Sociology*, 3rd ed.

1. To begin your summary, what is the main point? _____

_____

2. What are the major areas of support? _____

_____

3. Should you include an example for each area? _____

_____

Begin your summary with the main point, which is that Weber describes the three sources of authority as traditional, charismatic, and legal. Then define each of the three sources, but do not include examples.

Read the following summary and notice how closely it fits your own ideas.

Political Authority

Weber describes the three command sources as traditional, charismatic, and legal authority. Traditional authority is not written but based on long-standing custom such as the power of queens or tribal chiefs. Charismatic authority is based on the charm and vision of a leader such as Gandhi. Legal authority, such as that of American presidents, comes from written laws and is vested in the office rather than the person.

Exercise 4.11

Summarizing Passages

Read the following passages, and mark the key terms and phrases. Begin your summary with a statement of the main point, and add the appropriate supporting details. Use your markings to help you write the summary. Be brief, but include the essential elements.

Passage A: Prosecutors

The task of prosecutors is to represent the community in bringing charges against an accused person. The job of the prosecutor is constrained by political factors, caseloads, and relationships with other actors in the adjudication process.

First, most prosecutors are elected (although some are appointed by the governor), so it is in their interests to make "popular" prosecution decisions—and in some cases these may run counter to the ideals of justice. For example, prosecution "to the full extent of the law" of a college student caught possessing a small amount of marijuana may be unwarranted, but failure to prosecute may be used by political opponents as evidence that the prosecutor is "soft on crime."

A second constraint is caseload pressures, which often force prosecutors to make decisions based on expediency rather than justice. A prosecutor in a jurisdiction where many serious crimes occur may have to choose which to prosecute to the full extent of the law and which ones to plea-bargain.

Third, prosecutors must maintain good relationships with the other participants in the adjudication process: police, judges, juries, defense attorneys, victims, and witnesses. Cases typically are brought to prosecutors by the police, and police officers usually serve as witnesses.

Jay S. Albanese, *Criminal Justice*

Use your marked text to write a summary.

Passage B: Suicide Among College Students

Compared to nonstudents of the same age, the suicide rate among college students is somewhat higher. Why is this so? For one thing, among the younger college students who commit suicide (ages 18–22), a common thread is the inability to separate themselves from their family and to solve problems on their own. College presents many of these younger students with the challenge of having to be independent in many ways while remaining dependent on family in other ways, such as financially and emotionally.

Several other characteristics of the college experience may relate to suicide. A great emphasis is put on attaining high grades, and the significance of grades may be blown out of proportion. A student may come to perceive grades as a measurement of his or her total worth as a person, rather than just one of many ways a person can be evaluated. If a student is unable to achieve expected grades, there may be a total loss of self-esteem and loss of hope for any success in life.

In the college setting, where self-esteem can be tenuous, the end of a relationship can also be devastating. A student who has recently lost a close friend or lover can become so deeply depressed that suicide becomes an attractive alternative. The problem can be compounded when depression interferes with coursework and grades slip.

Curtis O. Byer and Louis W. Shainberg, *Living Well: Health in Your Hands*, 2nd ed.

Use your marked text to write a summary.

Passage C: Alcohol Advertising and College Students

The alcohol industry knows a receptive market when it sees it. Each year, college students spend a reported $5.5 billion ($446 per student) on alcohol, consuming some 4 billion cans' worth of alcohol and accounting for 10 percent of total beer sales. For brewers, student drinking spells not just current sales, but future profits as well, because most people develop loyalty to a specific beer between the ages of 18 and 24. To secure this lucrative market, brewers and other alcohol producers spend millions of dollars each year promoting their products to college students. One conservative estimate places annual expenditures for college marketing between $15 million and $20 million. According to one survey, alcohol advertising of local specials in many college newspapers has increased by more than half over the past decade, stymieing college and community efforts to reduce binge drinking.

Rebecca J. Donatelle, *Health: The Basics*, 4th ed.

Use your marked text to write a summary.

Summary Points

- **What is the difference between a topic and a main idea?**

  The topic of a passage is the general term that forms an umbrella for the specific ideas presented, whereas the main idea is the message the author is trying to convey about the topic.

- **What are the strategies for finding stated and unstated main ideas?**

  In some passages the main idea is stated in a sentence, and in others it is unstated. For both, ask "Who or what is this about?" to establish the topic. Then look for the key supporting details that seem to suggest a common message. Finally, focus on the message of the topic by asking "What is the main idea the author is trying to convey about the topic?"

- **What are the functions of major and minor supporting details?**

  Major details support, develop, and explain the main idea, whereas minor details develop the major details..

- **What is a summary?**

  Summaries condense material and include the main ideas and major details.

CONTEMPORARY FOCUS

Are you born with an instinct to be a good parent or do you learn it from positive role models? By the same token, what are the consequences of childhood abuse? Can negative role models teach children to become adult abusers or silent victims of abuse?

CENTERS STRIVE TO BREAK THE CYCLE OF VIOLENCE

By Lee Arnold

From *The Herald-Dispatch*, Huntington, February 25, 2004

There is no easy solution for plotting an escape from a lifetime of violence.

Devona Lewis is on the upswing in her second attempt to escape the abuse she has known since she was a child.

On July 4, she checked into Safe Harbor Domestic Violence Shelter in Ashland, Ky., for the second time. The day before, a man beat her in front of her 9-year-old son until she was unconscious. Her 12-year-old daughter helped her make the call to the shelter. It is her second stay at Safe Harbor.

She was there once before attempting to escape another abusive relationship with another man.

The 37-year-old Lewis has had a life filled with explosive relationships that began with her family as a child. To her, violence was the norm.

The abusive cycle is difficult to escape for many of the women, due to poor preparation for the workforce and total financial dependence on their abusers, Gibson said. Shelters offer direct counseling, court advocacy and provide leads to housing and employment opportunities, she said.

Children of battered women are 15 times more likely to be battered as adults than those whose mothers did not experience violence, according to statistics released to the U.S. Judiciary Committee during a hearing on domestic violence recently.

A study performed by the St. Bartholomew's Hospital in London of 1,200 battered women revealed that 381 of them had a history of violence against them as children.

The same can be said for the men who commit the abuse.

Statistics provided by the West Virginia Coalition Against Domestic Violence indicate that slightly more than 50 percent of the men who frequently batter their wives were victims of abuse as children. Branches reported that more than 60 percent of the abusers of the women who were assisted in the 2002 fiscal year had a history of abuse.

To break the repetitive cycle and establish independence is an extremely difficult thing to do.

Collaborate

Collaborate on responses to the following questions:

- Why do people think that being a good parent is an instinctive behavior?
- What do children want from a parent?
- Why do some people resort to violence in relationships?

Preview

Preview the next selection to predict its purpose and organization and to formulate your learning plan.

Activate Schema

Do parents who were abused as children later abuse their own children?

As a child, what did you use as a "security blanket"?

Establish a Purpose for Reading

What does monkey love have to do with human behavior? In this selection, discover how scientists explain the importance of contact comfort and trust in an infant-mother relationship. Notice how the Harlows came to understand the psychological needs of an infant monkey and the effect that deprivation of those needs can have on the whole pattern of psychological development. As you read, predict what the implications of the Harlows' animal research might be for our understanding of human development.

Increase Word Knowledge

What do you know about these words?

surrogate	functional	anatomy	tentatively	novel
desensitized	ingenious	deprived	persisted	deficient

Your instructor may give a true-false vocabulary review before or after reading.

Integrate Knowledge While Reading

Questions have been inserted in the margins to stimulate your thinking while reading. Remember to

    Predict   Picture   Relate   Monitor   Correct

MONKEY LOVE

From James V. McConnell, *Understanding Human Behavior*

The scientist who has conducted the best long-term laboratory experiments on love is surely Harry Harlow, a psychologist at the University of Wisconsin. Professor Harlow did not set out to study love—it happened by accident.

Like many other psychologists, he was at first primarily interested in how organisms learn. Rather than working with rats, Harlow chose to work with monkeys.

Since he needed a place to house and raise the monkeys, he built the Primate Laboratory at the University of Wisconsin. Then he began to study the effects of brain lesions on monkey learning. But he soon found that young animals reacted somewhat differently to brain damage than did older monkeys, so he and his wife Margaret devised a breeding program and tried various ways of raising monkeys in the laboratory. They rapidly discovered that monkey infants raised by their mothers often caught diseases from their parents, so the Harlows began taking the infants away from their mothers at birth and tried raising them by hand. The baby monkeys had been given cheesecloth diapers to serve as baby blankets. Almost from the start, it became obvious to the Harlows that their little animals developed such strong attachments to the blankets that, in the Harlows' own terms, it was often hard to tell where the diaper ended and the baby began. Not only this, but if the Harlows removed the "security" blanket in order to clean it, the infant monkey often became greatly disturbed—just as if its own mother had deserted it.

Did you have a "security blanket" as a child?

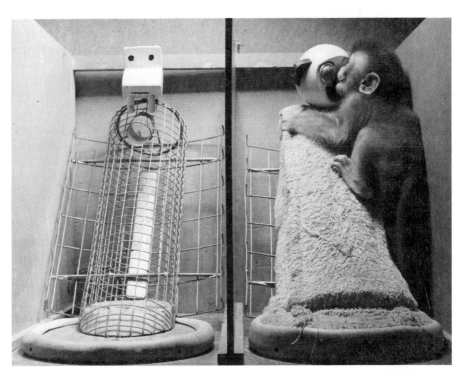

Although the baby monkey receives milk from Harlow's wire mother, it spends most of its time with the terry-cloth version and clings to the terry-cloth mother when frightened.
Harlow Primate Library, University of Wisconsin

The Surrogate Mother

What the baby monkeys obviously needed was an artificial or *surrogate* mother—something they could cling to as tightly as they typically clung to their own mother's chest. The Harlows sketched out many different designs, but none really appealed to them. Then, in 1957, while enjoying a champagne flight high over the city of Detroit, Harry Harlow glanced out of the airplane window and "saw" an image of an artificial monkey mother. It was a hollow wire cylinder, wrapped with a terry-cloth bath towel, with a silly wooden head at the top. The tiny monkey could cling to this "model mother" as closely as to its real mother's body hair. This surrogate mother could be provided with a functional breast simply by placing a milk bottle so that the nipple stuck through the cloth at an appropriate place on the surrogate's anatomy. The cloth mother could be heated or cooled; it could be rocked mechanically or made to stand still; and, most important, it could be removed at will.

While still sipping his champagne, Harlow mentally outlined much of the research that kept him, his wife, and their associates occupied for many years to come. And without realizing it, Harlow had shifted from studying monkey learning to monkey love.

Infant-Mother Love

The chimpanzee or monkey infant is much more developed at birth than the human infant, and apes develop or mature much faster than we do. Almost from the moment it is born, the monkey infant can move around and hold tightly to its mother. During the first few days of its life the infant will approach and cling to almost any large, warm, and soft object in its environment, particularly if that object also gives it milk. After a week or so, however, the monkey infant begins to avoid newcomers and focuses its attentions on "mother"—real or surrogate.

During the first two weeks of its life warmth is perhaps the most important psychological thing that a monkey mother has to give to its baby. The Harlows discovered this fact by offering infant monkeys a choice of two types of mother-substitutes—one wrapped in terry cloth and one that was made of bare wire. If the two artificial mothers were both the same temperature, the little monkeys always preferred the cloth mother. However, if the wire model was heated, while the cloth model was cool, for the first two weeks after birth the baby primates picked the warm wire mother-substitutes as their favorites. Thereafter they switched and spent most of their time on the more comfortable cloth mother.

Why is cloth preferable to bare wire? Something that the Harlows called *contact comfort* seems to be the answer, and a most powerful influence it is. Infant monkeys (and chimps too) spend much of their time rubbing against their mothers' skins, putting themselves in as close contact with the parent as they can. Whenever the young animal is frightened, disturbed, or annoyed, it typically rushes to its mother and rubs itself against her body. Wire doesn't

How do toddlers explore and seek security?

© 2005 by Pearson Education, Inc.

"rub" as well as does soft cloth. Prolonged "contact comfort" with a surrogate cloth mother appears to instill confidence in baby monkeys and is much more rewarding to them than is either warmth or milk. Infant monkeys also prefer a "rocking" surrogate to one that is stationary.

According to the Harlows, the basic quality of an infant's love for its mother is *trust*. If the infant is put into an unfamiliar playroom without its mother, the infant ignores the toys no matter how interesting they might be. It *screeches* in terror and curls up into a furry little ball. If its cloth mother is now introduced into the playroom, the infant rushes to the surrogate and clings to it for dear life. After a few minutes of contact comfort, it apparently begins to feel more secure. It then climbs down from the mother-substitute and begins tentatively to explore the toys, but often rushes back for a deep embrace as if to reassure itself that its mother is still there and that all is well. Bit by bit its fears of the novel environment are "desensitized" and it spends more and more time playing with the toys and less and less time clinging to its "mother."

Good Mothers and Bad

The Harlows found that, once a baby monkey has come to accept its mother (real or surrogate), the mother can do almost no wrong. In one of their studies, the Harlows tried to create "monster mothers" whose behavior would be so abnormal that the infants would desert the mothers. Their purpose was to determine whether maternal rejection might cause abnormal behavior patterns in the infant monkeys similar to those responses found in human babies whose mothers ignore or punish their children severely. The problem was—how can you get a terry-cloth mother to reject or punish its baby? Their solutions were ingenious—but most of them failed in their main purpose. Four types of "monster mothers" were tried, but none of them was apparently "evil" enough to impart fear or loathing to the infant monkeys. One such "monster" occasionally blasted its babies with compressed air; a second shook so violently that the baby often fell off; a third contained a catapult that frequently flung the infant away from it. The most evil-appearing of all had a set of metal spikes buried beneath the terry cloth; from time to time the spikes would poke through the cloth making it impossible for the infant to cling to the surrogate.

The baby monkeys brought up on the "monster mothers" did show a brief period of emotional disturbance when the "wicked" temperament of the surrogates first showed up. The infants would cry for a time when displaced from their mothers, but as soon as the surrogates returned to normal, the infant would return to the surrogate and continue clinging, as if all were forgiven. As the Harlows tell the story, the only prolonged distress created by the experiment seemed to be that felt by the experimenters!

There was, however, one type of surrogate that uniformly "turned off" the infant monkeys. S. J. Suomi, working with the Harlows, built a terry-cloth mother with ice water in its veins. Newborn monkeys would attach themselves to this "cool momma" for a brief period of time, but then retreated to a corner of the cage and rejected her forever.

Do abused children return to cruel mothers?

From their many brilliant studies, the Harlows conclude that the love of an infant for its mother is *primarily a response to certain stimuli the mother offers*. Warmth is the most important stimulus for the first two weeks of
110 the monkey's life, then contact comfort becomes paramount. Contact comfort is determined by the softness and "rub-ability" of the surface of the mother's body—terry cloth is better than are satin and silk, but all such materials are more effective in creating love and trust than bare metal is. Food and mild "shaking" or "rocking" are important too, but less so than
115 warmth and contact comfort. These needs—and the rather primitive responses the infant makes in order to obtain their satisfaction—are programmed into the monkey's genetic blueprint. The growing infant's requirement for social and intellectual stimulation becomes critical only later in a monkey's life. And yet, if the baby primate is deprived of contact
120 with other young of its own species, its whole pattern of development can be profoundly disturbed.

Mother-Infant Love

The Harlows were eventually able to find ways of getting female isolates pregnant, usually by confining them in a small cage for long periods of time with a patient and highly experienced normal male. At times, however, the Harlows
125 were forced to help matters along by strapping the female to a piece of apparatus. When these isolated females gave birth to their first monkey baby, they turned out to be the "monster mothers" the Harlows had tried to create with mechanical surrogates. Having had no contact with other animals as they grew up, they simply did not know what to do with the furry little strangers that
130 suddenly appeared on the scene. These motherless mothers at first totally ignored their children, although if the infant persisted, the mothers occasionally gave in and provided the baby with some of the contact and comfort it demanded.

Surprisingly enough, once these mothers learned how to handle a baby,
135 they did reasonably well. Then, when they were again impregnated and gave birth to a second infant, they took care of this next baby fairly adequately.

Maternal affection was totally lacking in a few of the motherless monkeys, however. To them the newborn monkey was little more than an object to be abused the way a human child might abuse a doll or a toy train. These moth-
140 erless mothers stepped on their babies, crushed the infant's face into the floor of the cage, and once or twice chewed off their baby's feet and fingers before they could be stopped. The most terrible mother of all popped her infant's head into her mouth and crunched it like a potato chip.

We tend to think of most mothers—no matter what their species—as
145 having some kind of almost divine "maternal instinct" that makes them love their children and take care of them no matter what the cost or circumstance. While it is true that most females have built into their genetic blueprint the tendency to be interested in (and to care for) their offspring, this inborn tendency is always expressed in a given environment. The "maternal

Is mothering an instinctive or learned behavior?

150   instinct" is strongly influenced by the mother's past experiences. Humans seem to have weaker instincts of all kinds than do other animals—since our behavior patterns are more affected by learning than by our genes, we have greater flexibility in what we do and become. But we pay a sometimes severe price for this freedom from genetic control.

155   Normal monkey and chimpanzee mothers seldom appear to inflict real physical harm on their children; human mothers and fathers often do. Serapio R. Zalba, writing in a journal called *Trans-action*, estimated in 1971 that in the United States alone, perhaps 250,000 children suffer physical abuse by their parents each year. Of these "battered babies," almost 40,000

160   may be very badly injured. The number of young boys and girls killed by their parents annually is not known, but Zalba suggests that the figure may run into the thousands. Parents have locked their children in tiny cages, raised them in dark closets, burned them, boiled them, slashed them with knives, shot them, and broken almost every bone in their bodies. How can

165   we reconcile these facts with the much-discussed maternal and paternal "instincts"?

    The research by the Harlows on the "motherless mothers" perhaps gives us a clue. Mother monkeys who were themselves socially deprived or isolated when young seemed singularly lacking in affection for their infants.

170   Zalba states that most of the abusive human parents that were studied turned out to have been abused and neglected *themselves* as children. Like the isolated monkeys who seemed unable to control their aggressive impulses when put in contact with normal animals, the abusive parents seem to be greatly deficient in what psychologists call "impulse control."

175   Most of these parents also were described as being socially isolated, as having troubles adjusting to marriage, often deeply in debt, and as being unable to build up warm and loving relationships with other people—including their own children. Since they did not learn how to love from their own parents, these mothers and fathers simply did not acquire the social skills neces-

180   sary for bringing up their own infants in a healthy fashion. (2,192 words)

> How can the cycle of abuse be broken?

Recall

Stop to self-test, relate, and react.

Your instructor may choose to give you a true-false comprehension review.

Write About the Selection

Explain and give examples of findings from the Harlows' experiments that you believe are applicable to human infants.

    Response Suggestion: Describe the experimental finding and use examples to relate it to the psychological needs of human infants.

Contemporary Link

What are some of the many factors that draw people into a generational cycle of abuse? Why is this cycle so difficult to break? What suggestions would you have for breaking this cycle for both the victims and the abusers?

Summarize

Using this selection as a source, summarize on index cards the information that you might want to include in a research paper entitled "Animal Rights: Do Scientists Go Too Far?"

Skill Development: Find the Main Idea

Answer the following with *T* (true) or *F* (false):

_____ 1. The main point of the first four paragraphs is that the Harlows' shift to studying monkey love occurred by accident.

_____ 2. In the second section titled "Infant-Mother Love," the main point is that an infant monkey needs the "contact comfort" of the mother to give it a feeling of security while interacting with the environment.

_____ 3. In the beginning of the section titled "Good Mothers and Bad," the main point is that baby monkeys will reject monster mothers.

_____ 4. In the beginning of the section titled "Mother-Infant Love," the main point is that the maternal instinct is not influenced by the mother's past experiences.

Check Your Comprehension

After reading the selection, answer the following questions with *a, b, c,* or *d.* To help you analyze your strengths and weaknesses, the question types are marked.

Main Idea

1. Who or what is the topic? _____

_____

What is the main idea the author is trying to convey about the topic?

_____

_____

Inference _____ 2. When Harry Harlow originally started his experiments with monkeys, his purpose was to study
    a. love.
    b. breeding.
    c. learning.
    d. disease.

Inference _____ 3. The reason that the author mentions Harry Harlow's revelations on the airplane is to show
    a. that he had extrasensory perception.
    b. that he liked to travel.
    c. that he was always thinking of his work.
    d. in what an unexpected way brilliant work often starts.

Detail _____ 4. In their experiments, the Harlows used all the following in designing his surrogate mothers except
    a. a terry-cloth bath towel.
    b. real body hair.
    c. a rocking movement.
    d. temperature controls.

Detail _____ 5. The Harlows manipulated their experiments to show the early significance of warmth by
    a. heating wire.
    b. changing from satin to terry cloth.
    c. equalizing temperature.
    d. creating "monster mothers."

Inference _____ 6. The Harlows found that for contact comfort, the cloth mother was preferable to the wire mother for all the following reasons except
    a. the cloth mother instilled confidence.
    b. the wire mother didn't "rub" as well.
    c. the wire mother was stationary.
    d. with the cloth mother, the infant felt a greater sense of security when upset.

Detail _____ 7. The Harlows' studies show that when abused by its mother, the infant will
    a. leave the mother.
    b. seek a new mother.
    c. return to the mother.
    d. fight with the mother.

Detail _____ 8. The Harlows' studies show that for an infant to love its mother, in the first two weeks the most important element is
    a. milk.
    b. warmth.
    c. contact comfort.
    d. love expressed by the mother.

Inference   _____ 9. The Harlows' studies with motherless monkeys show that the techniques of mothering are
    a. instinctive.
    b. learned.
    c. inborn.
    d. natural.

Inference   _____ 10. The Harlows feel that child abuse is caused by all the following problems except
    a. parents who were abused as children.
    b. socially isolated parents.
    c. parents who cannot control their impulses.
    d. parents who are instinctively evil.

Answer the following with *T* (true) or *F* (false):

Inference   _____ 11. The author feels that love in infant monkeys has a great deal of similarity to love in human children.

Inference   _____ 12. The author implies that isolated monkeys have difficulty engaging in normal peer relationships.

Detail   _____ 13. After learning how to handle the first baby, many motherless mothers became better parents with the second infant.

Inference   _____ 14. Zalba's studies support many of the findings of the Harlow studies.

Detail   _____ 15. Harlow had initially planned to perform drug experiments on the monkeys.

Build Your Vocabulary

According to the way the italicized word was used in the selection, indicate *a, b, c,* or *d* for the word or phrase that gives the best definition. The number in parentheses indicates the line number of the passage in which the word is located.

_____ 1. "*surrogate* mother" (23)
    a. mean
    b. thoughtless
    c. loving
    d. substitute

_____ 2. "a *functional* breast" (32)
    a. mechanical
    b. operational
    c. wholesome
    d. imitation

_____ 3. "on the surrogate's *anatomy*" (33)
    a. body
    b. head
    c. offspring
    d. personality

_____ 4. "begins *tentatively* to explore" (75)
   a. rapidly
   b. hesitantly
   c. aggressively
   d. readily

_____ 5. "fears of the *novel* environment" (77)
   a. hostile
   b. literary
   c. dangerous
   d. new

_____ 6. "fears . . . are '*desensitized*'" (77)
   a. made less sensitive
   b. made more sensitive
   c. electrified
   d. communicated

_____ 7. "solutions were *ingenious*" (86)
   a. incorrect
   b. noble
   c. clever
   d. honest

_____ 8. "*deprived* of contact" (119)
   a. encouraged
   b. denied
   c. assured
   d. ordered into

_____ 9. "if the infant *persisted*" (131)
   a. stopped
   b. continued
   c. fought
   d. relaxed

_____ 10. "to be greatly *deficient*" (174)
   a. lacking
   b. supplied
   c. overwhelmed
   d. secretive

Search the Net

Use a search engine such as Google, AltaVista, Excite, Infoseek, Dogpile, Yahoo, or Lycos to find information on the signs of child abuse. List five indicators that a child may be suffering from abuse or neglect. For suggested Web sites and other research activities, go to http://www.ablongman.com/smith/.

for Psychology

What is classical conditioning?

Classical conditioning is the learning that takes place when a subject is taught, or conditioned, to make a new response to a neutral stimulus. This is illustrated by the research of **Ivan Pavlov**, a Russian scientist in the late nineteenth century. Pavlov was studying the basic processes of digestion, focusing on salivation in dogs. Because salivation is a **reflex**, it is an unlearned, automatic response in dogs. When presented with food, dogs will automatically salivate. As his research progressed, Pavlov noticed that the dogs would salivate at the sight of the assistant who delivered the food. At this point, Pavlov decided to investigate learning.

Pavlov reasoned that no learning was involved in the dog's automatic salivation (the **unconditioned response**) when presented with food (the **unconditioned stimulus**). He wondered, however, if he could teach the dogs to salivate at the sound of a bell. To investigate this, Pavlov decided to pair the sound of a bell with the presentation of the food—sound first, food second. The bell alone was a **neutral stimulus** that had never before caused salivation. After a number of **trials** (presenting sound and food together), the dogs became conditioned to associate the sound of the bell with the food. The dogs soon would salivate at the sound, even when the food was withheld. Learning had taken place; Pavlov had taught the dogs to react to a neutral stimulus. Once learning or conditioning had taken place, the sound became a **conditioned stimulus** and the salivation became a **conditioned response**. To take this experiment a step further, if the sound is consistently presented without food, the salivation response will gradually weaken until the dogs completely stop salivating at the sound of the bell **(extinction)**. Pavlov's work on animals and learning laid the groundwork for the American behaviorists of the twentieth century.

What is behaviorism?

At the beginning of the twentieth century, many American psychologists disagreed with Freud's psychoanalytical approach (see page 51). They wanted to measure behavior in the laboratory and explain personality in terms of learning theories and observable behaviors.

Two pigeons seek food in a box developed by psychologist B.F. Skinner as part of his operant conditioning research.
Bettmann/CORBIS

B. F. Skinner was a leader in this new movement. He borrowed from Pavlov's work and conducted research on operant conditioning.

Skinner posed questions such as, What are your beliefs about rewards and punishments? Do consequences affect your behaviors? Are you a reflection of your positive and negative experiences? Skinner believed that consequences shape behavior and that your personality is merely a reflection of your many learned behaviors.

Skinner demonstrated **operant conditioning** (behaviors used to operate something) by putting a rat inside a small box that came to be known as a **"Skinner box."** The rat explored the box until eventually it found that it could make food appear by pressing a lever. The rat enjoyed the food and dramatically increased the lever pressings. The food was a **positive reinforcer** for the lever pressing. In other words, the food reinforced the behavior and increased it. To stop the lever-pressing behavior **(extinction)**, the rat was given a shock each time the lever was touched. The shock was a **negative reinforcer**. Rewards are positive reinforcers, and punishments are negative reinforcers.

Behavior modification, a type of **behavior therapy**, uses the principles of classical and operant conditioning to increase desired behaviors and decrease problem behaviors. You can use these principles to train a pet, stop a smoking habit, or overcome a fear of flying. Does the desire to make a good grade (reward) affect your studying behavior? Skinner would say yes.

REVIEW QUESTIONS

After studying the material, answer the following questions:

1. Who was Ivan Pavlov? _____

   _____

2. What is a reflex? _____

   _____

3. What is a neutral stimulus? _____

   _____

4. Why is the response to the food called unconditioned? _____

   _____

5. What is a conditioned stimulus? _____

   _____

6. What is extinction? _____

   _____

7. How did B. F. Skinner differ from Freud? _____

   _____

8. How does operant conditioning differ from classical conditioning? ____

   _____

9. What is the role of a positive reinforcer? _____

   _____

10. In behavior modification, what makes you want to change behaviors? ____

   _____

Your instructor may choose to give a true-false review of these psychology concepts.

CONTEMPORARY FOCUS

What motivates urban youth to join violent street gangs? Do they think they are bullet proof and invincible? Can members ever break free, or are they forever brothers, warriors, and criminals?

FORMER LOS ANGELES GANG MEMBER

By Yashekia Smalls

Ball State University, Muncie, Indiana, February 18, 1994

© 2003 Daily News via U-WIRE

A former Los Angeles gang member is now a nationally renowned social activist. Award-winning poet Luis Rodriguez, according to the poet's Web site, became an active street gang member in an East Lost Angeles barrio at age 11. Between the ages of 13 and 18, he was arrested several times for stealing, rioting and attempted murder, among other crimes, the site said.

Rodriguez, however, eventually broke free from his violent lifestyle and became a Chicano poet, producing a memoir, short stories and three collections of poetry: "Poems Across the Pavement," "The Concrete River" and "Trochemoche." His novel, "Music of the Mill," will be published this fall.

When Rodriguez's son later joined a gang, the poet also wrote about his fight to help his son in his bestseller "Always Running: La Vida Loca," according to the site.

"Rodriguez's immigrant background gives him the point of view of a large minority of Americans," English professor Tom Koontz of Ball State University said. "At the same time, he participates in the great American history and mythic tale of migration, struggle and, for some, success."

Collaborate

Collaborate on responses to the following questions:

- Why do gangs want 11-year-old kids?
- What is a social activist, and what might Rodriguez be doing in this regard?
- What do you know about gang activity in your area of the country?

Preview

Preview the next selection to predict its purpose and organization and to formulate your learning plan.

Activate Schema

What is the proper ethical behavior if you encounter a seriously injured person?

Why do teens join street gangs?

What kind of violence is prevalent among urban street gangs?

Establish a Purpose for Reading

Why is someone on the sidewalk, bleeding? In this story, read about the fatal consequences of an act of gang violence with the intention of discovering the author's unstated message about gang culture in our society. As you read, be aware of the author's use of symbolism, and note the way the rainy setting and the reactions of other characters contribute to the story's mood and the main character's realizations.

Increase Word Knowledge

What do you know about these words?

excruciating	clutching	rumble	neon	lurched
soothing	relentless	foraging	loathing	hysterically

Your instructor may give a true-false vocabulary review before or after reading.

Integrate Knowledge While Reading

Questions have been inserted in the margins to stimulate your thinking while reading. Remember to

Predict   Picture   Relate   Monitor   Correct

ON THE SIDEWALK, BLEEDING
By Evan Hunter

The boy lay on the sidewalk bleeding in the rain. He was sixteen years old, and he wore a bright purple silk jacket, and the lettering across the back of the jacket read THE ROYALS. The boy's name was Andy and the name was delicately scripted in black thread on the front of the jacket, just over the heart. ANDY.

5   He had been stabbed ten minutes ago. The knife entered just below his rib cage and had been drawn across his body violently, tearing a wide gap in his flesh. He lay on the sidewalk with the March rain drilling his jacket and drilling his body and washing away the blood that poured from his open wound. He had known excruciating pain when the knife had torn across his

> Why would the author choose the name *Royal?*

10 body, and then sudden comparative relief when the blade was pulled away. He had heard the voice saying, "That's for you Royal!" and then the sound of footsteps hurrying into the rain, and then he had fallen to the sidewalk, clutching his stomach, trying to stop the flow of blood.

15   He tried to yell for help, but he had no voice. He did not know why his voice had deserted him, or why the rain had become so steadily fierce, or why there was an open hole in his body from which his life ran redly, steadily. It was 11:13 p.m. but he did not know the time.

There was another thing he did not know.

20   He did not know he was dying. He lay on the sidewalk, bleeding, and he thought only: *That was a fierce rumble. They got me good that time*, but he did not know he was dying. He would have been frightened had he known. In his ignorance he lay bleeding and wishing he could cry out for help, but there was no voice in his throat. There was only the bubbling of blood from between his lips whenever he opened his mouth to speak. He lay in his pain, waiting, wait-
25   ing for someone to find him.

He could hear the sound of automobile tires hushed on the rain-swept streets, far away at the other end of the long alley. He lay with his face pressed to the sidewalk, and he could see the splash of neon far away at the other end of the alley, tinting the pavement red and green, slickly brilliant in the rain.

30   He wondered if Laura would be angry.

He had left the jump to get a package of cigarettes. He had told her he would be back in a few minutes, and then he had gone downstairs and found the candy store closed. He knew that Alfredo's on the next block would be open until at least two, and he had started through the alley, and that was
35   when he had been ambushed.

On a California street, Filipino teen gang members confront another teen.
Michael Newman, PhotoEdit Inc.

He could hear the faint sound of music now, coming from a long, long way off. He wondered if Laura was dancing, wondered if she had missed him yet. Maybe she thought he wasn't coming back. Maybe she thought he'd cut out for good. Maybe she had already left the jump and gone home. He thought of
40   her face, the brown eyes and the jet-black hair, and thinking of her he forgot his pain a little, forgot that blood was rushing from his body.

Someday he would marry Laura. Someday he would marry her, and they would have a lot of kids, and then they would get out of the neighborhood. They would move to a clean project in the Bronx, or maybe they would move
45   to Staten Island. When they were married, when they had kids . . .

He heard footsteps at the other end of the alley, and he lifted his cheek from the sidewalk and looked into the darkness and tried to cry out, but again there was only a soft hissing bubble of blood on his mouth.

The man came down the alley. He had not seen Andy yet. He walked, and
50   then stopped to lean against the brick of the building, and then walked again. He saw Andy then and came toward him, and he stood over him for a long time, the minutes ticking, ticking, watching him and not speaking.

Then he said, "What's a matter, buddy?"

Andy could not speak, and he could barely move. He lifted his face slightly
55   and looked up at the man, and in the rain-swept alley he smelled the sickening odor of alcohol and realized the man was drunk. He did not know he was dying, and so he felt only mild disappointment that the man who found him was drunk

The man was smiling.

"Did you fall down, buddy?" he asked. "You mus' be as drunk as I am." He
60   grinned, seemed to remember why he had entered the alley in the first place, and said, "Don' go way. I'll be ri' back."

The man lurched away. Andy heard his footsteps, and then the sound of the man colliding with a garbage can, and some mild swearing, and then the sound of the man urinating, lost in the steady wash of the rain. He waited for
65   the man to come back.

It was 11:39.

When the man returned, he squatted alongside Andy. He studied him with drunken dignity.

"You gonna catch cold there," he said. "What's the matter? You like layin' in
70   the wet?"

Andy could not answer. The man tried to focus his eyes on Andy's face. The rain spattered around them.

"You like a drink?"

Andy shook his head.

75   "I gotta bottle. Here," the man said. He pulled a pint bottle from his inside jacket pocket. He uncapped it and extended it to Andy. Andy tried to move, but pain wrenched him back flat against the sidewalk.

"Take it," the man said. He kept watching Andy. "Take it." When Andy did not move, he said, "Nev' mind, I'll have one m'self." He tilted the bottle to his
80   lips, and then wiped the back of his hand across his mouth. "You too young to be drinkin' anyway. Should be 'shamed of yourself, drunk and layin' in a alley, all wet. Shame on you. I gotta good mind to call a cop."

How was the drunk compassionate?

Andy nodded. Yes, he tried to say. Yes, call a cop. Please. Call one.

"Oh, you don' like that, huh?" the drunk said. "You don' wanna cop to fin'
you all drunk an' wet in an alley, huh: Okay, buddy. This time you get off
easy." He got to his feet. "This time you lucky," he said again. He waved
broadly at Andy, and then almost lost his footing. "S'long, buddy," he said.

Wait, Andy thought. *Wait, please, I'm bleeding.*

"S'long," the drunk said again, "I see you aroun'," and then he staggered off
up the alley.

Andy lay and thought: *Laura, Laura. Are you dancing?*

The couple came into the alley suddenly. They ran into the alley
together, running from the rain, the boy holding the girl's elbow, the girl
spreading a newspaper over her head to protect her hair. Andy lay crum-
pled on the pavement and he watched them run into the alley laughing,
and then duck into the doorway not ten feet from him.

"Man, what rain!" the boy said. "You could drown out there."

"I have to get home," the girl said. "It's late, Freddie. I have to get home."

"We got time," Freddie said. "Your people won't raise a fuss if you're a little
late. Not with this kind of weather."

"It's dark," the girl said, and she giggled.

"Yeah," the boy answered, his voice very low.

"Freddie? . . .

"Um?"

"You're . . . standing very close to me."

"Um."

There was a long silence. Then the girl said, "Oh," only that single word,
and Andy knew she had been kissed, and he suddenly hungered for Laura's
mouth. It was then that he wondered if he would ever kiss Laura again. It was
then that he wondered if he was dying.

No, he thought, *I can't be dying, not from a little street rumble, not from just
being cut. Guys get cut all the time in rumbles. I can't be dying. No, that's stupid.
That don't make any sense at all.*

"You shouldn't," the girl said.

"Why not?"

"I don't know."

"Do you like it?"

"Yes."

"So?"

"I don't know."

"I love you, Angela," the boy said.

"I love you, too, Freddie," the girl said, and Andy listened and thought: *I love
you, Laura. Laura, I think maybe I'm dying. Laura, this is stupid but I think
maybe I'm dying. Laura, I think I'm dying.*

He tried to speak. He tried to move. He tried to crawl toward the doorway
where he could see two figures embrace. He tried to make a noise, a sound, and
a grunt came from his lips, and then he tried again, and another grunt came, a
low animal grunt of pain.

"What was that?" the girl said, suddenly alarmed, breaking away from the boy.

"I don't know," he answered.

130   "Go look, Freddie."

"No. Wait."

Andy moved his lips again. Again the sound came from him.

"Freddie!"

"What?"

135   "I'm scared."

"I'll go see," the boy said.

He stepped into the alley. He walked over to where Andy lay on the ground. He stood over him, watching him.

"You all right?" he asked.

140   "What is it?" Angela said from the doorway.

"Somebody's hurt," Freddie said.

"Let's get out of here," Angela said.

"No. Wait a minute." He knelt down beside Andy. "You cut?" he asked.

Andy nodded. The boy kept looking at him. He saw the lettering on the

145   jacket then. THE ROYALS. He turned to Angela.

"He's a Royal," he said.

"Let's . . . what . . . what . . . do you want to do, Freddie?"

"I don't know. I don't know. I don't want to get mixed up in this. He's a Royal. We help him, and the Guardians'll be down on our necks. I don't want

150   to get mixed up in this, Angela."

"Is he . . . is he hurt bad?"

"Yeah, it looks that way."

"What shall we do?"

"I don't know."

155   "We can't leave him here in the rain," Angela hesitated. "Can we?"

"If we get a cop, the Guardians'll find out who," Freddie said. "I don't know, Angela. I don't know."

Angela hesitated a long time before answering. Then she said, "I want to go home, Freddie. My people will begin to worry."

160   "Yeah," Freddie said. He looked at Andy again. "You all right?" he asked. Andy lifted his face from the sidewalk, and his eyes said: *Please, please help me*, and maybe Freddie read what his eyes were saying, and maybe he didn't.

Behind him, Angela said, "Freddie, let's get out of here! Please!" There was urgency in her voice, urgency bordering on the edge of panic. Freddie stood

165   up. He looked at Andy again, and then mumbled, "I'm sorry." He took Angela's arm and together they ran towards the neon splash at the other end of the alley.

> What would you have done at this point? What is ethical?

Why, they're afraid of the Guardians, Andy thought in amazement. *But why should they be? I wasn't afraid of the Guardians. I never turkeyed out of a rumble*

170   *with the Guardians. I got heart. But I'm bleeding.*

The rain was soothing somehow. It was a cold rain, but his body was hot all over, and the rain helped cool him. He had always liked rain. He could remember sitting in Laura's house one time, the rain running down the windows, and just looking out over the street, watching the people running from

175   the rain. That was when he'd first joined the Royals.

He could remember how happy he was when the Royals had taken him. The Royals and the Guardians, two of the biggest. He was a Royal. There had been meaning to the title.

Now, in the alley, with the cold rain washing his hot body, he wondered
180   about the meaning. If he died, he was Andy. He was not a Royal. He was simply Andy, and he was dead. And he wondered suddenly if the Guardians who had ambushed him and knifed him had ever once realized he was Andy. Had they known that he was Andy or had they simply known that he was a Royal wearing a purple silk jacket? Had they stabbed *him*, Andy, or had they only
185   stabbed the jacket and the title and what good was the title if you were dying?

I'm Andy, he screamed wordlessly, *For Christ's sake, I'm Andy.*

An old lady stopped at the other end of the alley. The garbage cans were stacked there, beating noisily in the rain. The old lady carried an umbrella with broken ribs, carried it with all the dignity of a queen. She stepped into the mouth
190   of the alley, shopping bag over one arm. She lifted the lids of the garbage cans delicately, and she did not hear Andy grunt because she was a little deaf and because the rain was beating a steady relentless tattoo on the cans. She had been searching and foraging for the better part of the night. She collected her string and her newspapers, and an old hat with a feather on it from one of the garbage cans, and
195   a broken footstool from another of the cans. And then delicately she replaced the lids and lifted her umbrella high and walked out of the alley mouth with a queenly dignity. She had worked quickly and soundlessly, and now she was gone.

The alley looked very long now. He could see people passing at the other end of it, and he wondered who the people were, and he wondered if he
200   would ever get to know them, wondered who it was of the Guardians who had stabbed him, who had plunged the knife into his body.

"That's for you, Royal!" the voice had said, and then the footsteps, his arms being released by the others, the fall to the pavement. "That's for you, Royal!" Even in his pain, even as he collapsed, there had been some sort of pride in
205   knowing he was a Royal. Now there was no pride at all. With the rain beginning to chill him, with the blood pouring steadily between his fingers, he knew only a sort of dizziness. He could only think: *I want to be Andy.*

It was not very much to ask of the world.

He watched the world passing at the other end of the alley. The world didn't
210   know he was Andy. The world didn't know he was alive. He wanted to say, "Hey, I'm alive! Hey, look at me! I'm alive! Don't you know I'm alive? Don't you know I exist?"

He felt weak and very tired. He felt alone, and wet and feverish and chilled, and he knew he was going to die now, and the knowledge made him suddenly
215   sad. He was not frightened. For some reason, he was not frightened. He was filled with an overwhelming sadness that his life would be over at sixteen. He felt all at once as if he had never done anything, never seen anything, never been anywhere. There were so many things to do, and he wondered why he'd never thought of them before, wondered why the rumbles and the jumps and
220   the purple jackets had always seemed so important to him before, and now they seemed like such small things in a world he was missing, a world that was rushing past at the other end of the alley.

I don't want to die, he thought. *I haven't lived yet.*

It seemed very important to him that he take off the purple jacket. He was

Does Andy deserve to die? How is his life wasted?

225   very close to dying, and when they found him, he did not want them to say, "Oh, it's a Royal." With great effort, he rolled over onto his back. He felt the pain tearing at his stomach when he moved, a pain he did not think was possible. But he wanted to take off the jacket. If he never did another thing, he wanted to take off the jacket. The jacket had only one meaning now, and that

230   was a very simple meaning.

What is the author's view of gang culture?

If he had not been wearing the jacket, he wouldn't have been stabbed. The knife had not been plunged in hatred of Andy. The knife hated only the purple jacket. The jacket was a stupid meaningless thing that was robbing him of his life. He wanted the jacket off his back. With an enormous loathing, he wanted the

235   jacket off his back.

He lay struggling with the shiny wet material. His arms were heavy, pain ripped fire across his body whenever he moved. But he squirmed and fought and twisted until one arm was free and then the other, and then he rolled away from the jacket and lay quite still, breathing heavily, listening to the sound of his

240   breathing and the sounds of the rain and thinking: *Rain is sweet, I'm Andy.*

She found him in the doorway a minute past midnight. She left the dance to look for him, and when she found him, she knelt beside him and said, "Andy, it's me, Laura."

He did not answer her. She backed away from him, tears springing into her

245   eyes, and then she ran from the alley hysterically and did not stop running until she found a cop.

And now, standing with the cop, she looked down at him, and the cop rose and said, "He's dead," and all the crying was out of her now. She stood in the rain and said nothing, dead boy on the pavement, looking at the pur-

250   ple jacket that rested a foot away from his body.

The cop picked up the jacket and turned it over in his hands.

"A Royal, huh?" he said.

The rain seemed to beat more steadily now, more fiercely.

What happens next?

She looked at the cop and, very quietly, she said, "His name is Andy."

255   The cop slung the jacket over his arm. He took out his black pad, and he flipped it open to a blank page.

"A Royal," he said.

Then he began writing.

(3,040 words)

Recall

Stop to self-test, relate, and react.

Your instructor may choose to give you a true-false comprehension review.

Write About the Selection

How do Andy's thoughts of his own life evolve from the beginning to the end of the story?

    Response Suggestion. Use the italicized thoughts to trace Andy's emotional journey.

Contemporary Link

If you had survived being a member of a street gang, what would you do to persuade your children never to join such a gang?

Skill Development: Find the Main Idea

Answer the following with *T* (true) or *F* (false):

_____ 1. One of the central themes of this story is that Andy initially thought the jacket gave him identity, but he learned instead that it robbed him of his identity.

_____ 2. The main point of the story is that Andy could have lived if others had helped him.

_____ 3. The fact that the murder happened in March is a major detail.

Check Your Comprehension

After reading the selection, answer the first item in your own words and answer the subsequent questions with *a, b, c,* or *d*. To help you analyze your strengths and weaknesses, the question types are indicated.

1. Who or what is the topic? _____

Main Idea   What is the main idea the author is trying to convey about the topic?

_____

Detail   _____ 2. All of the following are true about Andy's jacket except
   a. it was purple.
   b. *The Royals* was written on the back.
   c. *Andy* was written on the left side of the front.
   d. it was torn in the back from the stab wounds.

Inference   _____ 3. The reader can assume that the primary reason Andy was stabbed was because
   a. he was threatening a member of the Guardian gang.
   b. he was wearing a jacket that said *The Royals*.
   c. he witnessed Guardians engaged in illegal activity in the alley.
   d. he was dating a girlfriend of the Guardians.

Inference   _____ 4. The reader can conclude that the drunk
   a. thought he was helping Andy.
   b. was afraid and did not want to help Andy.
   c. understood that Andy was dying.
   d. saw the blood and left.

Inference   _____ 5. The reader can conclude that Angela and Freddie
   a. would not have called the police if Andy did not have the jacket.
   b. recognized Andy from the dance.
   c. feared retribution from the Guardians.
   d. contacted Laura so that she could find Andy.

Inference _____ 6. The reader can conclude all the following about the old lady except
    a. she never heard Andy.
    b. she was salvaging from trash like the homeless.
    c. the author felt she carried herself with dignity despite her actions.
    d. she saw trouble and wanted no involvement.

Detail _____ 7. The author suggests that the person who could most accurately be called a coward in the story is
    a. the drunk.
    b. the old lady.
    c. Freddie.
    d. Laura.

Inference _____ 8. The author suggests that Andy took off the jacket because
    a. he did not want Laura to find him wearing the jacket.
    b. he wanted other members of the Royals to be proud of him.
    c. he wanted to reclaim his personal identity.
    d. as a sign of honor, he wanted to avoid implicating gang members in his death.

Detail _____ 9. The author suggests all the following about the cop except
    a. he recognized Andy as a person.
    b. he recorded the death as a meaningless gang killing.
    c. he was familiar with the activities of the gangs.
    d. his thinking was changed by Laura's attitude.

Inference _____ 10. The author suggests that Andy's anger at his death was directed primarily toward
    a. the Guardians.
    b. the Royals.
    c. himself.
    d. Angela and Freddie.

Answer the following with *T* (true), *F* (false), or *CT* (can't tell):

Inference _____ 11. The jacket was first a symbol of inclusion for Andy and then it became a symbol of meaningless death.

Inference _____ 12. According to the story, the time that elapsed from the stabbing until Andy was found by Laura was 58 minutes.

Detail _____ 13. Andy cut through the alley because it was the shortest way to the candy store.

Inference _____ 14. The author suggests that there are other gangs in the area besides the Guardians and the Royals.

Inference _____ 15. As Andy got closer to death, he thought more about his wasted life and less about Laura.

Build Your Vocabulary

According to the way the italicized word was used in the selection, select *a, b, c,* or *d* for the word or phrase that gives the best definition. The number in parentheses indicates the line of the passage in which the word is located.

_____ 1. "*scripted* in black thread" (4)
- a. painted
- b. carved
- c. blocked
- d. handwritten

_____ 2. "known *excruciating* pain" (9)
- a. immediate
- b. humiliating
- c. agonizing
- d. tantalizing

_____ 3. "*clutching* his stomach" (12)
- a. tightly holding
- b. scratching
- c. tearing
- d. skinning

_____ 4. "fierce *rumble*" (20)
- a. knife
- b. gang member
- c. gang fight
- d. gang order

_____ 5. "man *lurched* away" (62)
- a. sneaked
- b. staggered
- c. ran
- d. excused himself

_____ 6. "rain was *soothing*" (171)
- a. cold
- b. endless
- c. calming
- d. irritating

_____ 7. "steady *relentless* tattoo" (192)
- a. noisy
- b. ugly
- c. rhythmical
- d. persistent

_____ 8. "*foraging* for the better part" (193)
- a. singing
- b. looking for food
- c. speaking aloud
- d. hiding

_____ 9. "enormous *loathing*" (234)
- a. hatred
- b. eagerness
- c. strain
- d. energy

_____ 10. "ran from the alley *hysterically*" (245)
- a. quickly
- b. fearfully
- c. sadly
- d. frantically

Search the Net

Use a search engine such as Google, AltaVista, Excite, Infoseek, Dogpile, Yahoo, or Lycos to find information on urban street gangs. Choose a major U.S. city and describe its gang problems. For suggested Web sites and other research activities, go to http://www.ablongman.com/smith/.

Concept Prep

for Literature

What is literature?

Literature, the art form of language, is invented from the author's imagination. The purpose is to entertain an audience, to explore the human condition, and to reveal universal truths through shared experiences. As a reader, you are allowed inside the minds of characters, and you feel what they feel. You learn about life as the characters live it or as the poet entices you to feel it. After reading, you are enriched, not just entertained. Literature includes four categories, or **genres**: essays, fiction, poetry, and drama. Although the four genres differ in intent, they share many of the same elements.

What are literary elements?

Plot. The **plot** describes the action in a story, play, or epic poem. It is a sequence of incidents or events linked in a manner that suggests their causes.

Incidents in the story build progressively to reveal conflict to the reader. The **conflict** is a struggle or a clash of ideas, desires, or actions. Conflicts can exist between the main character and another character, a group, external forces, or within the character.

As the plot moves forward, the **suspense** builds. You are concerned about the character's well-being. The conflict intensifies to a peak, or **climax**, which comes near the end of the story and is the turning point, for better or worse. The **denouement** is the outcome of conflicts. Then the action falls and leads to a **resolution**, which answers any remaining questions and explains the outcome.

Characters. In literature you are told what characters think and feel. Thus you are better able to understand the complexities of human nature. By the shared experience of "living through" significant events with the character, you learn compassion for others.

Characters should be consistent in behavior, and they should grow and change according to their experiences in the story. You learn what kind of person the character is by what the character does and says, and by what others say about the character.

Point of View. The **point of view** in literature is not defined as bias or opinion as it is in Chapter 8. Rather, it describes who tells the story. It can be in *first person*, as

Awarded the Nobel Prize for Literature in 1993, author Toni Morrison also won a Pulitzer Prize for her bestselling novel Beloved, *which was later made into a movie.*
Evan Agostini/Getty Images

the *I* in a diary; *second person*, using the word *you*; or most commonly, *third person*, in which the author is the omniscient or all-knowing observer revealing what all characters think and do.

Tone. The **tone** is the writer's attitude toward the subject or the audience. When people speak, we recognize their tone of voice. In stories, however, we must rely on the author's choice of words to convey attitudes. Word clues may suggest that the author is being humorous. Cutting remarks, on the other hand, may suggest *sarcasm*, which is an expression of disapproval designed to cause pain. The author's emotional and intellectual attitude toward the subject also describes the **mood**, or overall feeling of the work.

Setting. All stories exist in a time and place. Details must be consistent with the setting or else they distract your attention. The **setting** is the backdrop for the story and the playground for the characters.

Figures of Speech and Symbolism. Literary writing appeals to the five senses and, unlike scientific or academic writing, uses images to convey a figurative or symbolic meaning rather than an exact literal meaning. Consider the noun *hunger*. Other than simply wanting a hamburger, a student may hunger for the reassuring touch of a friend's hand. *Metaphors* and *similes* are the most common, and they both suggest a comparison of unlike things. For more on figurative language, see Chapter 7.

The imagery or **symbolism** in a story can be an object, action, person, place, or idea that carries a condensed and recognizable meaning. For example, an opened window might represent an opportunity for a new life.

Theme. The **theme** is the main idea or the heart and soul of the work. The theme is central insight into life or universal truth. This message is never preached but is revealed to your emotions, senses, and imagination through powerful, shared experiences. Too often readers want to oversimplify and reduce the theme to a one-sentence moral such as "Honesty is the best policy" or "Crime does not pay." To deduce the theme, ask yourself, "What has the main character learned during the story?" or "What insight into life does the story reveal?"

REVIEW QUESTIONS

After studying the material, answer the following questions:

1. What is literature? _____

    _____

2. What is plot? _____

    _____

3. What is the climax of "On the Sidewalk, Bleeding"? _____

    _____

4. What is the resolution? _____

    _____

5. How do you learn about the characters in "On the Sidewalk, Bleeding"? _____

    _____

    _____

6. What is the most common point of view in a story? _____

7. How does the definition of *point of view* differ in literature and in the phrase, "What is your point of view on cloning?" _____

    _____

8. What do you feel is the author's attitude toward the subject in "On the Sidewalk, Bleeding"?

    _____

    _____

9. What is the overriding symbol in "On the Sidewalk, Bleeding"? _____

    _____

10. What is the theme of a story? _____

    _____

Your instructor may choose to give a true-false review of these literary concepts.

CONTEMPORARY FOCUS

After the horrors of September 11, 2001, airline security has increased significantly. Is it possible, however, to apply the same level of security to large cargo ships entering U.S. ports from all over the world?

U. S. COAST GUARD'S EFFORTS TO PROTECT PORTS

By Randall Richard

Associated Press, International News, New Orleans, February 8, 2004

© 2004 Daily News via U-Wire

With 361 ports to protect, 95,000 miles (152,855 kilometers) of navigable waterways to defend and 20,000 oceangoing vessels to keep an eye on, the Coast Guard is focusing on what it considers the United States' 11,700 most likely maritime targets of a terrorist attack.

It is to the water, not to the skies, that America needs to be looking if it hopes to thwart the most devastating terrorist attacks, many maritime experts say.

"An airplane is fine if you want to take down the twin towers," says Dennis Bryant, a former Coast Guard lawyer who is now senior counsel with Holland and Knight, a major maritime law firm. "But if you want to bring a nuclear device into this country, you're going to have a hard time doing it by plane."

As every schoolchild in Halifax, Nova Scotia, learns, it doesn't take a nuclear device to create a maritime disaster of World Trade Center proportions.

On December 6, 1917, two ships, one of them carrying 2,500 tons of volatile chemicals bound for the Allied war effort in Europe, collided in Halifax harbor. The blast leveled 1,630 homes and killed nearly 2,000 of the city's 50,000 residents.

Modern explosives in a major port city could do far worse.

Collaborate

Collaborate on responses to the following questions:

- Which U. S. ports could be prime targets for terrorists?
- What should the Coast Guard do to prevent terrorism?
- How would you conduct security to protect passengers on a cruise ship?

Preview

Preview the next selection to predict its purpose and organization and to formulate your learning plan.

Activate Schema

Why are recent acts of terrorism almost exclusively conducted by radical Muslims?

What is a Jihad?

Establish a Purpose for Learning

Do you ever worry about being the victim of a terrorist attack? Since September 11, 2001 and, more recently, because of repeated incidents in Europe and the Middle East, many Americans in large cities are concerned about the international threat of terrorism. In the following selection, learn what investigators have discovered about terrorists' mission-specific and sleeper cells, terrorist wealth, and reconnaissance operations. As you read, ask yourself why terrorism is so difficult to eradicate.

Increase Word Knowledge

What do you know about these words?

intimidate	executing	anomalies	formidable	lucrative
infidel	preempted	surrogates	stealth	sustain

Your instructor may give a true-false vocabulary review before or after reading.

Integrate Knowledge While Reading

Questions have been inserted in the margins to stimulate your thinking while reading. Remember to

Predict	Picture	Relate	Monitor	Correct

INTERNATIONAL TERRORISM

From Charles Swanson, Neil Chamelin, and Leonard Territo,
Criminal Investigation, 8th ed.

The tragic events of September 11, 2001, were clearly the most horrendous and devastating terrorist acts ever to occur on U.S. soil. Few people would argue that 9/11 forever changed the lives of all Americans, not only in terms of coping with the loss experienced that day but also in terms of living with the possibility of future terrorists threats.

5   The world and the United States are not strangers to terrorism. The first U.S. plane hijacking occurred in 1961, when Puerto Rican Antuilo Ortiz, armed with a gun, diverted a National Airlines flight to Cuba, where he was

The south tower of the New York World Trade Center collapses as smoke billows from the 110-story buildings after the terrorist attack on September 11, 2001.
AP/Wide World Photos

given asylum. A rebel faction in Guatemala assassinated the U.S. Ambassador John Mein by gunfire in 1968 after forcing his car from the road. Black September terrorists struck in Munich at the Olympics in 1972. In 1979, the Italian Prime Minister was kidnapped and killed by Red Brigade members; the U.S. Embassy in Tehran was seized by Iranian radicals; and Mecca's Grand Mosque was taken over by 200 Islamic terrorists who took hundreds of pilgrims hostage, an incident that resulted in 250 people killed and 600 wounded.

What was the
purpose of 9/11?

Even a partial accounting of terrorist activities over the past two decades indicates a continuing pattern of such violence worldwide. Acts of international terrorism are intended to intimidate a civilian population, influence the policy of a government, or affect the conduct of a government.

Mission-Specific Cells

Mission-specific cells are put together for the purpose of executing a specific mission. Information is often tightly compartmentalized to prevent the mission from being "blown" if one or more people are arrested. Individuals may know what skills they need to develop or keep sharp but not how their activities fit in the overall plan. That level of detail may be revealed only at the last moment.

The attacks on September 11, 2001, are a prime example of the operation of mission-specific cells. From the analysis of those attacks and the surrounding circumstances, a profile of the terrorists and their activities was developed.

The Terrorists

The terrorists ranged in age from early twenties to the mid-thirties and were from Middle Eastern countries. Their command of the English language was limited. They came in groups of three to four to open accounts at branch banks located in areas where there was a high Muslim population. Usually there was only one spokesman for the group, who wanted to deal with only one person and was somewhat reluctant to deal with a woman. Sixteen of the 9/11 terrorists entered this country legally under business, tourist, or student visas; at least six of the hijackers attended flight schools abroad or attempted to get flight training in the United States. For the most part, they lived quiet lives, and at least one attacker used his family as a cover. The hijackers traveled across the country.

Terrorists' Bank Accounts

Who sends the
cash?

With cash or its equivalent, attackers opened 24 domestic bank accounts in four different banks, averaging $3,000 to $5,000 per account. The identification used to open the accounts were visas issued through Saudi Arabia or the United Arab Emirates; none of the terrorists had a Social Security number. The addresses used for the accounts were often temporary (for example, a mailbox) and changed frequently. Some of the terrorists used the same address and telephone number for their account records. No savings accounts were opened, nor were safety deposit boxes acquired. All accounts had debit cards.

Terrorists' Transactions

The accounts were funded primarily by cash and overseas wire transfers and were kept below $10,000 to avoid federal banking reporting requirements. Account transactions did not reflect normal living expenses, such as rent, utilities, and insurance, nor was there any consistency with the timing of deposits and withdrawals. The terrorists made numerous balance inquiries, often exceeding their balances when making debit card withdrawals. The number of debit card transactions was much higher than the number of checks issued.

The profiles of other terrorists operating in this country may or may not match this profile. Officers and investigators should look for anomalies in otherwise unremarkable data. Stated differently, they have to pick out the fish that really differs from the school in which it swims.

Sleeper Cells

Sleeper cells are individuals or small groups who are in place in target or other countries. Potential terrorists or sympathizers who have been recruited are ordered to lead "everyday lives" and not bring attention to themselves. Classically, they may be in place for years before they are activated. Sleepers may also perform limited services for the group with which they are allied, including servicing as couriers, providing financing, maintaining a safe house, providing transportation, and engaging in reconnaissance tasks.

Externally, international terrorists are a formidable challenge because of the heretofore relaxed U.S. policies on obtaining visas and the presence of numerous lucrative and relatively "soft" American targets abroad, where access is less problematic for terrorists. The foreign threats are classified into three categories: (1) the radical international Jihad movement, largely consisting of Sunni Islamic extremists, such as those in Al-Qaeda, (2) formal terrorist groups, including Hamas and Hezbollah, and (3) state-sponsored terrorism, primarily by Iran, Iraq, Sudan, and Libya.

Radical Muslims regard the United States as an infidel because it is not governed according to their beliefs. In their view, the United States has provided support for other infidel regimes, particularly Saudi Arabia, Egypt, Israel, and the United Arab Emirates. Al-Qaeda opposed U.S. involvement in the Gulf War in 1991 and feels that Americans have violated its holy lands by their presence and are plundering the riches of Arabic countries. Moreover, Al-Qaeda is further aggrieved by the United States' arrest, conviction, and imprisonment of its members, and those of allied groups, for terrorist and criminal activities.

What does Al-Qaeda want? →

Al-Qaeda and its allies are the greatest international terrorist threat to the United States because they have the money, equipment, training, and patience needed to carry out their murderous attacks. Regardless of who is leading these terrorist groups, the United States can expect the following:

1. Future attacks on Americans at home and abroad are highly probable.
2. Everyone in the United States is considered a combatant; it is "open season" on American children, women, and men.
3. Targets will be selected on the basis of their economic and symbolic significance; there may be few attacks, but they will produce high casualties.
4. Softer, high-casualty-producing targets will be preferred.

5. The United States has preempted some terrorist strikes, but the opposing force continues to have the capability to launch sophisticated, multiple
95 operations simultaneously with little or no warning.

6. To avoid detection and blame, the attackers will attempt to develop surrogates to conduct their operations.

Be Alert for Reconnaissance Operations

The execution of an attack is predated by reconnaissance, often involving multiple efforts, although not necessarily by the same person. While some of
100 these efforts may be carried out in stealth at night, many of them will occur during normal business hours. Operatives may rent rooms that give them a view of the target and may recruit insiders who provide them with drawings or copies of plans. They may also take legitimate jobs that allow them to have access to sites (for example, driving a delivery truck).

105 In a small town, alert police noticed an Arabic man, who was unknown to them, taking photographs of chemical tankers on a siding of a railroad track. He may have been an engineer or an employee of the railroad. He may also have been an operative or the dupe of an operative (for example, a local photographer recruited by a legitimate-appearing businessman who said he had "insur-
110 ance claims to be settled and needed some shots taken" of a specific siding). In Colorado in 2002, sensitive information about roads at Hoover dam was stolen, along with an engineer's identification badge. Is the dam being targeted? By whom? At the time of this writing these matters are under investigation.

Confronting terrorism is not an occasional or seasonal venture; it is an
115 ongoing responsibility. With the help of allies, the United States has the capacity to significantly disrupt terrorist groups and their finances and operations. Information systems must be improved and the products shared; genuine teamwork across numerous agencies will ensure progress. The United States must have the political will to be decisively and continuously engaged, and
120 the public must help sustain the effort and provide information. The greatest untapped resource in the fight against terrorism is local public safety officers: they are an army of eyes and ears on the nation's streets.

> Would you turn in a suspect?

Recall

Stop to self-test, relate, and react.

Your instructor may choose to give you a true-false comprehension review.

Write About the Selection

Explain why it is so difficult to eradicate terrorism

Response Suggestion: Describe how terrorists operate using secrecy within their own organizations while taking advantage of the openness of American society.

Contemporary Link

Why are ports more difficult than airlines to police? How might the terrorist cells work to launch an attack on a port?

Skill Development: Find the Main Idea

Answer the following with *T* (true) or *F* (false):

_____ 1. The main idea of the last paragraph is that terrorism should be primarily fought by local public safety officers.

_____ 2. A major detail in the passage is that the United States Embassy in Tehran was seized by Iranian radicals

_____ 3. A minor detail is that the bank accounts for terrorists averaged between $3,000 and $5,000.

Check Your Comprehension

After reading the selection, answer the following questions with *a, b, c,* or *d.* To help you analyze your strengths and weaknesses, the question types are indicated.

Main Idea _____ 1. Which is the best statement of the main idea of this selection?
a. The tragic events of 9/11 were not the first terrorist acts committed against the United States.
b. The United States continues to be under attack from organized terrorists and must remain alert to possible terrorist activities.
c. Foreign governments finance terrorists and enable them to commit violent acts against the United States.
d. Radical Muslims are using terrorism to fight a holy war to regain the riches of Arabic countries.

Inference _____ 2. In 1979, the author suggests that terrorist incidents took place in
a. Italy, Tehran, and Mecca.
b. Munich, Tehran, and Mecca.
c. Guatemala, Munich, and Mecca.
d. Mecca, Tehran, and Cuba.

Detail _____ 3. According to the passage, in mission-specific cells, individual terrorists know
a. what skills they need to develop.
b. the overall plan.
c. the purpose of other members to the mission.
d. how their own skills fit into the overall plan.

Detail   _____   4. A profile of the 9/11 terrorists suggests all of the following
were true except
a. they knew three or four other members of the mission.
b. they were equal to or less than 35 years of age.
c. they spoke a little English.
d. Their bank accounts were opened with female bankers.

Detail   _____   5. According to the typical profile of the 9/11 terrorists, the
bank accounts were
a. more than $10,000.
b. used to pay rent and utilities.
c. sometimes overdrawn.
d. sent to home addresses.

Inference   _____   6. In the analogy, "they have to pick out the fish that really differs
from the school in which it swims," the author suggests that
a. investigators must look for small differences among
similarities.
b. terrorists seek the cover offered by allies in order to survive.
c. prevention is too late when the terrorist joins the other fish.
d. among the fish, the terrorist will be the easiest to spot.

Inference   _____   7. The author suggests that a "soft" American target abroad is
a. highly secure.
b. not well guarded.
c. expensive real estate.
d. highly populated.

Detail   _____   8. According to the passage, the United States is targeted by
radical Muslims because
a. the United States has a large Muslim population.
b. the United Nations opposed the war in Iraq.
c. the United States fought in the Gulf War.
d. Al-Qaeda was responsible for 9/11.

Detail   _____   9. According to the author, the United States can expect all the
following from terrorist groups except
a. a push to negotiate grievances for the peace and prosperity of Arab countries.
b. several strikes at the same time.
c. attacks from substitutes for Muslim extremists.
d. high-casualty attacks that include children.

Inference   _____   10. The "dupe of an operative" might be all the following except
a. unknowingly hired to document information for terrorists.
b. paid to get an illegal identification badge.
c. hired to watch a target and formulate a terrorist attack plan.
d. hired for a legitimate job such as truck driving and paid
unknowingly by terrorists.

Answer the following with *T* (true), *F* (false), or *CT* (can't tell):

Detail _____ 11. Puerto Rican Antuilo Ortiz hijacked a United States plane to seek freedom in Cuba.

Inference _____ 12. The author suggests that a "blown" mission is a failed mission.

Detail _____ 13. The 9/11 terrorists used visas and Social Security numbers.

Inference _____ 14. The difference between mission-specific and sleeper cells is that one has a job and one has no function for the organization.

Inference _____ 15. The author suggests that local public safety officers are overburdened in the fight against terrorism.

Build Your Vocabulary

According to the way the italicized word was used in the selection, select *a*, *b*, *c*, or *d* for the word or phrase that gives the best definition. The number in parentheses indicates the line of the passage in which the word is located.

_____ 1. "intended to *intimidate*" (19)
   a. confuse
   b. kill
   c. fool
   d. frighten

_____ 2. "*executing* a specific mission" (21)
   a. conducting
   b. beginning
   c. eliminating
   d. infiltrating

_____ 3. "look for *anomalies*" (57)
   a. irregularities
   b. fugitives
   c. theories
   d. fish

_____ 4. "*formidable* challenge" (67)
   a. disappearing
   b. constant
   c. unforgettable
   d. frightening

_____ 5. "*lucrative* and relatively 'soft'" (69)
   a. hidden
   b. profitable
   c. diplomatic
   d. unguarded

_____ 6. "regard the U.S. as an *infidel*"(75)
   a. democracy
   b. nonbeliever
   c. distraction
   d. super power

_____ 7. "*preempted* some terrorist strikes" (93)
   a. intercepted
   b. overlooked
   c. spied on
   d. disregarded

_____ 8. "develop *surrogates*" (96)
   a. plans
   b. strategies
   c. substitutes
   d. finances

_____ 9. "*stealth* at night" (100)
   a. secret cover
   b. late hours
   c. early hours
   d. groups

_____ 10. "*sustain* the effort" (120)
   a. fight
   b. advertise
   c. avoid
   d. keep it going

Search the Net

Use a search engine such as Google, AltaVista, Excite, Infoseek, Dogpile, Yahoo, or Lycos to find information on recent terrorist attacks. Describe the attack and the goals of the terrorists. For suggested Web sites and other research activities, go to http://www.ablongman.com/smith/.

Vocabulary Booster

Who's Who in Medicine?

Suffixes

-ist, -ician: one who   *-ologist:* one who studies

- *dermatologist:* skin doctor (*derma:* skin)

  Dermatologists remove skin cancers.

- *internist:* medical doctor for internal organs (*internus:* inside)

  The *internist* will administer a series of tests to determine the cause of Ben's mysterious pain.

- *intern:* a medical school graduate serving an apprenticeship at a hospital

  The *interns* work under the close supervision of doctors on the staff.

- *gynecologist:* doctor for reproductive systems of women (*gyne:* women)

  The *gynecologist* recommended a Pap smear to check for cervical cancer.

- *obstetrician:* doctor who delivers babies (*obstetrix:* midwife)

  Many *obstetricians* are also gynecologists.

- *pediatrician:* doctor for children (*paidos:* children)

  Pediatricians use antibiotics to treat sore throats and earaches.

- *ophthalmologist* or *oculist:* doctor who performs eye surgery

  The *ophthalmologist* performed cataract surgery on the woman.

- *optometrist:* specialist for measuring vision

  An *optometrist* tests eyesight and fits glasses and contact lenses.

- *optician:* specialist who makes visual correction lenses for eyeglasses and contact lenses

  Opticians usually work behind the scene, often at an optometrist's office.

- *orthopedist:* doctor who corrects abnormalities in bones and joints (*orthos:* straight or correct)

  The *orthopedist* set up his practice near a ski area.

- *orthodontist:* dentist for straightening teeth

  Her braces had to be adjusted every six weeks by the *orthodontist*.

- *cardiologist:* heart doctor (*cardio:* heart)

  Cardiologists treat patients who have had heart attacks.

- *psychiatrist:* doctor for treating mental disorders (*psycho:* mind)

  The *psychiatrist* prescribed drugs for the treatment of depression.

- ***psychologist:*** counselor for treating mental disorders

  The *psychologist* administered tests to determine the cause of the child's behavior.

- ***neurologist:*** doctor for disorders of the brain, spinal cord, and nervous system (*neuron:* nerve)

  Neurologists are searching for new treatments for patients who have suffered spinal cord injuries.

- ***oncologist:*** doctor for treating cancer and tumors (*onkos:* mass)

  The *oncologist* recommended various methods for dealing with the cancerous tumor.

- ***urologist:*** doctor specializing in the urinary tract (*ouro:* urine)

  The urologist was treating several patients for impotence.

- ***podiatrist:*** specialist in the care and treatment of the foot (*pod:* foot)

  The *podiatrist* knew the best way to deal with blisters, corns, and bunions.

- ***anesthesiologist:*** doctor who administers anesthesia to patients undergoing surgery (*anesthesia:* insensibility)

  Usually a patient will meet the *anesthesiologist* just before surgery.

- ***hematologist:*** doctor who studies the blood and blood-forming organs (*hemat:* blood)

  A hematoma is treated by a *hematologist.*

- ***radiologist:*** doctor using radiant energy for diagnostic and therapeutic purposes (*radio:* radiant waves)

  After the removal of a cancerous tumor, further treatment by a *radiologist* is usually recommended.

Review

Part I

Indicate whether the following sentences are true (T) or false (F):

___F___ 1. A hematologist puts patients to sleep for operations.

___T___ 2. Dermatologists treat acne.

___T___ 3. An internist investigates stomach pain.

___F___ 4. An optometrist can fit eyeglasses.

___F___ 5. A pediatrician operates primarily on the feet.

___F___ 6. A psychologist is a medical doctor.

___F___ 7. An obstetrician treats cancer.

False 8. *Optometrists* and *oculists* are two terms for doctors who do eye surgery.

False 9. An anesthesiologist attends to a patient in the days after an operation.

False 10. Neurologists treat patients who have a family history of breast cancer.

Part II

Choose the doctor from the boxed list that best fits the job description.

> gynecologist   radiologist   intern   optician   cardiologist
>
> orthodontist   urologist   orthopedist   psychiatrist   oncologist

11. Treats mental disorders with drugs _Psychiatrist_

12. Medical student still in training _Intern_

13. Doctor for women's reproductive systems _Gynecologist_

14. Sets broken arms and legs _Orthopedist_

15. Makes the lenses for eyeglasses _Optician_

16. Straightens teeth _Orthodontist_

17. Operates on the urinary tract _Urologist_

18. Specialist for treating cancer _Oncologist_

19. Performs surgery on the heart _Cardiologist_

20. Uses radiation to diagnose and treat cancer _Radiologist_

Your instructor may choose to give a multiple-choice review.

Patterns of Organization

- How do transitional words signal organizational patterns?
- What organizational patterns are used in textbooks?
- Why are several organizational patterns sometimes combined to develop a main idea?

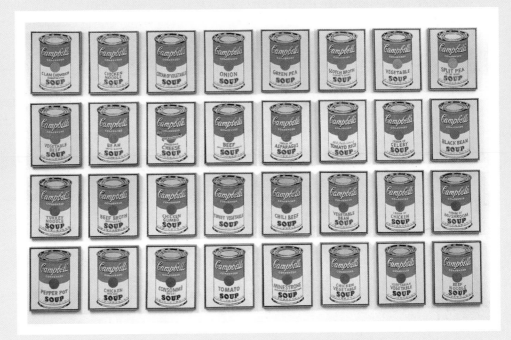

Campbell's Soup Cans *by Andy Warhol, 1962. Synthetic polymer paint on 32 canvases, each 20 x 16". The Museum of Modern Art, New York, NY, USA. Gift of Irving Blum; Nelson A. Rockefeller Bequest, gift of Mr. and Mrs. William A.M. Burden, Abby Aldrich Rockefeller Fund, gift of Nina and Gordon Bunshaft in honor of Henry Moore, Lillie P. Bliss Bequest, Philip Johnson Fund, Frances Keech Bequest, gift of Mrs. Bliss Parkinson, and Florence B. Wesley Bequest (all by exchange). (476.1996.a-ff). ©2004 Andy Warhol Foundation /ARS, NY/™ Licensed by Campbell's Soup Co. All rights reserved. Photo: ©The Museum of Modern Art/Licensed by SCALA/Art Resource, NY..*

Textbook Organization

The **pattern of organization** in a textbook is the presentation plan, format, or structure for the message. Why is it important to identify organizational patterns in textbooks and other pieces of writing? Basically, such patterns are important because they serve as the book's blueprints, showing the reader how the book was built, just as an outline probably helped the author write the book. They signal how facts and ideas are presented. The number of details in a textbook can be overwhelming. Identifying the pattern of organization of a section or chapter can help you master the complexities of the material. If you know the pattern of organization, you can predict the format of upcoming information.

Although key transitional words can signal a particular pattern, the most important clue to the pattern is the main idea itself because it usually dictates the organizational pattern. Your aim as a reader is to identify the main idea, be alert to the signal words, anticipate the overall pattern of organization, and place the major supporting details into the outline or pattern used by the author.

What Do Transitional Words Do?

Small words can carry a big load. A single word can signal the level of importance, connection, and direction of thought. For example, if a friend begins a sentence by saying "I owe you $100," would you prefer that the next word be *and* or that it be *but*? The word *and* signals addition and would give you high hopes for the return of your money. However, the word *but* signals a change of thought which, in this case, would be in a negative direction. If the next word were *first*, you would anticipate a sequence of events before repayment. If it were *consequently*, you would hope the positive result would be your $100.

Such words are **transitional words**—sometimes called *signal words*—that connect parts of sentences or whole sentences and lead you to anticipate either a continuation of or a change in thought. Transitions show the relationships of ideas within sentences, between sentences, and between paragraphs. Writers use transitions to keep their readers' comprehension on track and to guide them through the logic of the message. To avoid repetition, authors choose from a variety of signal words to indicate the transition of thought. These signal words or transitions can be categorized as shown in the following examples and in the Reader's Tip on page 220.

Words That Signal Addition

in addition   moreover   furthermore   and   also   another

EXAMPLE   José was given a raise after six months at his job. *In addition*, he became eligible for health insurance benefits.

After causing a disturbance in the movie theater, Brian and his friends were asked to leave. *Furthermore*, they were barred from attending that theater ever again.

Words That Signal Examples or Illustrations

for example   for instance   to illustrate   such as   including

EXAMPLE

Traffic seems to be getting heavier. *For instance*, last year it took only 20 minutes to get to school, and now it takes 30.

Some experts believe that a fetus in the womb can be affected by sounds *such as* classical music or the mother's voice.

Words That Signal Time or Sequence

first   second   finally   last   afterward   after   during

while   before   then   previously   until   now   next

EXAMPLE

Apply sunscreen while walking on the beach and before swimming in the surf. *Afterward*, reapply the sunscreen even if it is waterproof.

To build a good financial foundation, *first* pay yourself in the form of savings, and *then* pay your bills.

Words That Signal Comparison

similarly   likewise   in the same manner   like   as   just as   as well

EXAMPLE

If you treat someone with kindness, he or she will probably treat you in kind. *Likewise*, if you treat someone with disrespect, you will probably be disrespected.

Portland is a port city in Oregon; *similarly*, it is a seaport in Maine.

Words That Signal Contrast

however	but	nevertheless	whereas
on the contrary	conversely	yet	in contrast
even though	on the other hand	although	instead

EXAMPLE

Using a knife to cut a bagel can be dangerous to the fingers. *On the other hand*, using a bagel holder keeps fingers safe from the falling blade.

Today many families eat dinner separately and on the run, *whereas* in the past the family dinner hour was a time for bonding and an opportunity to instill values or share dreams.

Words That Signal Cause and Effect

thus	consequently	therefore	as a result	because
accordingly	since	so	because of	

EXAMPLE   *Because of* his work to end apartheid in South Africa, Nelson Mandela spent 27 years in prison. Upon his release, Mandela treated his oppressors with respect and worked to unite the country. *Consequently*, he shared a Nobel Peace Prize with then-president de Klerk.

There has been a severe shortage of rainfall this year. *Therefore*, we have instituted a ban on outdoor watering.

READER'S TIP

Signal Words for Transition

◆ **Addition:** in addition • furthermore • moreover

◆ **Examples:** for example • for instance • to illustrate • such as

◆ **Time:** first • second • finally • last • afterward

◆ **Comparison:** similarly • likewise • in the same manner

◆ **Contrast:** however • but • nevertheless • whereas • on the contrary • conversely • in contrast

◆ **Cause and Effect:** thus • consequently • therefore • as a result

Exercise 5.1

Signal Words

Choose a signal word from the boxed lists to complete the sentences that follow.

however	~~for example~~	in addition	~~consequently~~
	~~in the meantime~~		

1. Forget the boring tourist narrative and turn walking around a city into a hip audio tour experience with Soundwalk CDs. In New York, _however_, you can pop in a 50-minute audio CD to explore Chinatown, the meat-packing district, or Wall Street.

2. The United States has an ever-increasing demand for oil. _Consequently_, we are researching alternative sources of energy, such as solar energy, to reduce our dependence on oil.

JJ

3. _In the meantime_ to alternative energy research, we may begin drilling for oil on a small portion of our public lands to lessen our dependence on foreign sources of oil.

4. Drilling on public lands, _for example_, is not popular with environmentalists who believe the drilling cannot be done without spoiling the land.

5. _In addition_, we can strive to be more fuel efficient to help reduce our demand for energy.

~~therefore~~   on the contrary   ~~for instance~~   ~~in the same manner~~
furthermore

6. One way to conserve energy is to drive a fuel-efficient car. _On the contrary_ some hybrid cars that run on both gas and electricity are currently available. _On the contrary_, these cars get up to 68 miles per gallon.

7. The ancient Chinese practice of acupuncture is based on a belief that chi, a life force, flows along meridians throughout the body. _For instance_, Feng Shui practitioners believe that the same chi flows throughout the earth, and that by harnessing the chi of our surroundings, we can improve the flow of energy in our bodies.

8. Coretta Scott King felt strongly that her husband's legacy should be celebrated nationally. _Therefore_, she worked successfully with others to have Martin Luther King, Jr.'s birthday recognized as a federal holiday beginning in 1983.

9. The U.S. Postal Service works to raise social awareness of important issues. _Therefore_, the USPS has issued commemorative stamps for causes that include diabetes awareness, breast cancer awareness, and hospice care.

10. The popular Harry Potter books are not only for children. _In the same manner_, many adults enjoy reading about Harry's magical adventures at Hogwarts.

furthermore   for example   nevertheless   finally   in contrast

✓✓

11. African American music in twentieth-century America evolved from ragtime, to jazz, to rhythm and blues, to soul, and _____finally_____, to rap.

12. Gloria Estefan and the Miami Sound Machine's recording of "Conga" was on Billboard's pop, Latin, soul, and dance charts at the same time. _____Nevertheless_____, it was the only song in history to have this distinction.

13. Mardi Gras as celebrated in New Orleans is similar to Carnaval as celebrated throughout Latin America. Carnaval lasts for five days; _____In contrast_____, Mardi Gras lasts only one day.

14. Internet car sales, rather than hurting auto dealerships, have actually helped them. _____For example_____ most customers conduct research on the Net but still visit a dealer to actually buy automobiles. A well-informed consumer who is ready to purchase makes the salesperson's job easier.

| moreover | but | simultaneously | as a result | similarly |

15. The concert tickets were outrageously priced. _____but_____, this was a once-in-a-lifetime opportunity, and other luxuries would have to be sacrificed to compensate for the expense.

16. Is chocolate a food or a drug? Chocolate contains antioxidants and minerals like many foods, _____but_____ it also contains a neurotransmitter naturally found in the brain that, like many drugs, makes us feel good.

17. The 2000 U.S. Census shows a dramatic increase in the Hispanic population in the South. This influx was due to a recession in California occurring _____Moreover_____ with a robust economy in the South during the 1990s.

18. Vicente Fox, the president of Mexico, has vowed to improve his country's economy with foreign investment and jobs programs. _____Simultaneously_____ he has pledged to work toward an open border between Mexico and the United States, where workers would be able to cross the border freely.

19. Musicians protested the swapping of their songs on the Napster Web site without royalties being paid. _Likewise_ , journalists have protested their past works being electronically reproduced without royalty payments.

20. Gamblers with an illusion of control delude themselves into thinking that they can control outcomes in games of chance. _As a result,_ they lose substantial sums at casinos, racetracks, lotteries, and Internet gaming sites.

Patterns of Organization in Textbooks

As transitional words signal connections and relationships of ideas within and among sentences, they also help signal the overall organizational pattern of the message. When you write, you have a pattern for organizing your thoughts that enables you to present your ideas with logic. That organizational pattern is probably dictated by the main idea of your message. Before beginning to write, you must ask, "If this is what I want to say, what is the best logical pattern to organize my message?"

The next exercise contains examples of the patterns of organization you will encounter in textbooks. Some are used much more frequently than others, and some occur more frequently in particular disciplines. For example, history textbooks often use the patterns of time order and cause and effect. Management textbooks frequently use the simple-listing pattern, whereas psychology textbooks make heavy use of the definition-and-example pattern. The Reader's Tip following the exercise (see page 231) lists each type of pattern of organization along with some signal words.

Exercise 5.2

Patterns of Organization

Notice the outline that accompanies each pattern of organization described in the following paragaraphs. After reading each example, enter the key points into the blank outline display to show that you understand the pattern.

Simple Listing

With **simple listing,** items are randomly listed in a series of supporting facts or details. These supporting elements are of equal value, and the order in which they are presented is of no importance. Changing the order of the items does not change the meaning of the paragraph.

Signal words, often used as transitional words to link ideas in a paragraph with a pattern of simple listing, include _in addition, also, another, several, for example, a number of._

Work-Related Stress

Work-related stress has increased significantly in the last few years. People are spending more hours at work and bringing more work home with them. Job security has decreased in almost every industry. Pay, for many, has failed to keep up with the cost of living. Women are subject to exceptionally high stress levels as they try to live up to all the expectations placed on them. Finally, many people feel that they are trapped in jobs they hate but can't escape.

Curtis O. Byer and Louis W. Shainberg, *Living Well: Health in Your Hands,* 2nd ed.

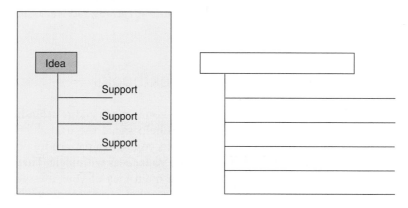

Definition

Frequently in a textbook, an entire paragraph is devoted to defining a complex term or idea. With **definition,** the concept is defined initially and then expanded with examples and restatements. In a textbook, a defined term is usually signaled by *italic* or **bold** type.

Ultrasound

Ultrasound is a relatively new technique that uses sound waves to produce an image that enables a physician to detect structural abnormalities. Useful pictures can be obtained as early as seven weeks into pregnancy. Ultrasound is frequently used in conjunction with other techniques such as amniocentesis and fetoscopy.

John Dacey and John Travers, *Human Development,* 2nd ed.

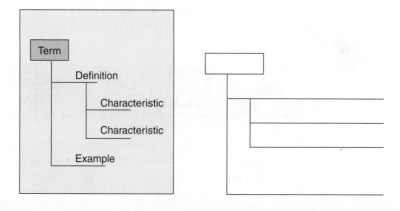

Description

Description is like listing; the characteristics that make up a description are no more than a definition or a simple list of details.

EXAMPLE

Caribbean

Caribbean America today is a land crowded with so many people that, as a region (encompassing the Greater and Lesser Antilles), it is the most densely populated part of the Americas. It is also a place of grinding poverty and, in all too many localities, unrelenting misery with little chance for escape.

H. J. De Blij and Peter O. Muller, *Geography: Realms, Regions, and Concepts*, 7th ed.

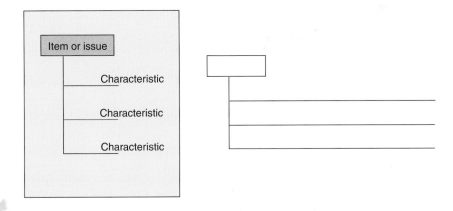

Time Order, Sequence, or Narration

Items are listed in the order in which they occurred or in a specifically planned order in which they must develop. In this case, the **time order** is important, and changing it would change the meaning. Narrative writing, which tells a story, is an example of writing in which time order is important.

Signal words that are often used for time order, sequence, or narration include *first, second, third, after, before, when, until, at last, next, later.* Actual time periods, such as days or years, also signal sequence and time.

EXAMPLE

Mormon Movement

The idea of the Mormon Church began when a young Joseph Smith, Jr., went into the New York woods in 1820 and was told by God that the true church of God would be reestablished. In 1823, another revelation led him to find buried golden plates and translate the *Book of Mormon*. Smith attracted thousands of followers and in the 1830s moved from Ohio to Missouri to Illinois to seek religious freedom for his group. In 1844 Smith was shot by an angry mob. After his death, a new leader, Brigham Young, led the Mormons to the Great Salt Lake.

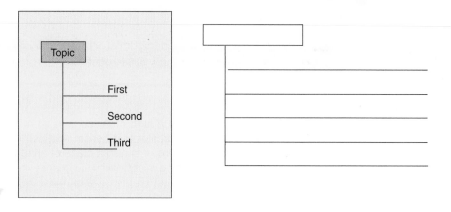

Contrast

With **contrast,** items are presented according to differences between or among them. Signal words that are often used for contrast include *different, in contrast, on the other hand, but, however, bigger than.*

Oranges

An orange grown in Florida usually has a thin and tightly fitting skin, and it is also heavy with juice. Californians say that if you want to eat a Florida orange you have to get into a bathtub first. On the other hand, California oranges are light in weight and have thick skins that break easily and come off in hunks.

John McPhee, Oranges

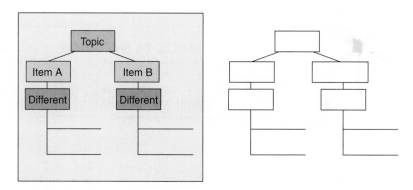

Comparison

With **comparison,** items are presented according to similarities between or among them. Signal words that are often used for comparison include *similar, in the same way, parallels.*

Jazz Greats

Jazz greats Louis Armstrong and Billie Holiday overcame similar obstacles in their struggling early years. Both were raised in the slums by working mothers, and both learned the discipline needed for success through hard work. As a teen, Armstrong hauled coal from 7 a.m. to 5 p.m. for 75 cents a day and then practiced on his trumpet after work. Similarly, after school, Holiday scrubbed the white stone steps of neighbors' houses to earn an average of 90 cents a day, and then she came home to practice her singing.

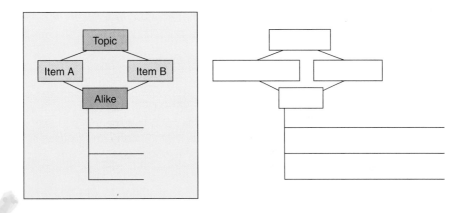

Comparison-Contrast

Some passages combine comparison and contrast into a single paragraph. This combination is called a **comparison-contrast** pattern and is demonstrated in the following examples.

EXAMPLE

Hispanic Americans

The primary groups in the rising new minority are Mexican Americans and Cuban Americans. Mexican Americans are heavily concentrated in the Southwest, whereas Cuban Americans are concentrated in Florida, particularly in the Miami area. Together the groups are called Hispanic Americans or Latinos. Although their histories are different, they share several similarities. They both speak the Spanish language and most of them, at least 85 percent, are Roman Catholic.

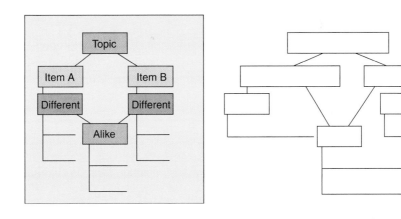

Cause and Effect

With **cause and effect,** an element is shown as producing another element. One is the *cause* or the "happening" that stimulated the particular result or *effect*. A paragraph may describe one cause or many causes, as well as one or many results. Signal words that are often used for cause and effect include *for this reason, consequently, on that account, hence, because*.

EXAMPLE   **Winter Camp at Valley Forge**

General George Washington's Continental army set up camp on the frozen grounds of Valley Forge in December 1777 and experienced dire consequences. The winter was particularly cold that year, and the soldiers lacked straw and blankets. Many froze in their beds. Food was scarce, and soldiers died of malnutrition. Because of the misery and disease in the camp, many soldiers deserted the army and went home.

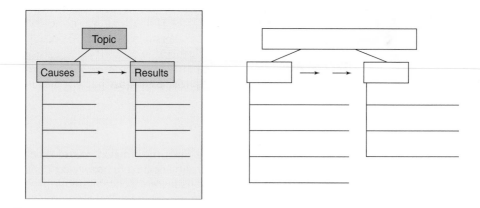

Classification

To simplify a complex topic, authors frequently begin introductory paragraphs by stating that the information that follows is divided into a certain number of groups or categories. The divisions are then named and the parts are explained. Signal words often used for **classification** include *two divisions, three groups, four elements, five classes, six levels, seven categories,* and so on.

EXAMPLE   **Predation**

Predation, the interaction in which one species kills and eats another, involves two groups. The predator, or consumer, must be alert and skillful to locate and capture the prey. The consumable group, or prey, constantly must adapt its behavior to defend against being eaten.

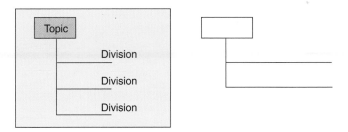

Addition

The addition pattern is used to provide more information to something that has already been explained. Signal words are *furthermore, again, also, further, moreover, besides, likewise.*

EXAMPLE

Entrepreneur Quincy Jones

Not only is Quincy Jones the talented producer who helped drive Michael Jackson's "Beat It" to a number one hit and "Thriller" to the best-selling album of all time, he is also the founder of *VIBE* magazine and the co-owner of *SPIN* magazine. Furthermore, Jones, who has been awarded 26 Grammys and a Grammy Legend, is chairman and CEO of the Quincy Jones Media Group.

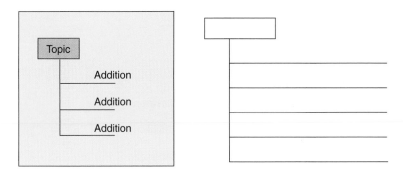

Summary

A **summary**, which usually comes at the end of an article or chapter, condenses the main idea or thesis into a short and simple concluding statement with a few major supporting details. Signal words are *in conclusion, briefly, to sum up, in short, in a nutshell.*

EXAMPLE

WWII Total War

In conclusion, World War II was more of a total war than any previous war in history. Some 70 nations took part in the war, and fighting took place on the continents of Europe, Asia, and Africa. Entire societies participated, either as soldiers, war workers, or victims of occupation and mass murder.

James Kirby Martin et al, *America and Its People* (adapted)

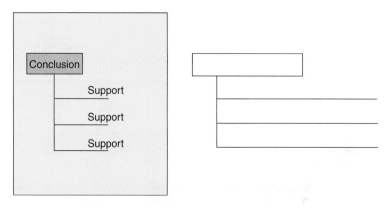

Location or Spatial Order

Location or **spatial order** identifies the whereabouts of a place or object. Signal words are *north, east, south, west, next to, near, below, above, close by, within, without, adjacent to, beside, around, to the right or left side, opposite.*

EXAMPLE   **Egypt**

The Republic of Egypt is located in the northeastern corner of Africa. The northern border of Egypt is the Mediterranean Sea. Libya is the country to the west, and the Sudan lies to the south. Across the Suez Canal and to the east lies Israel.

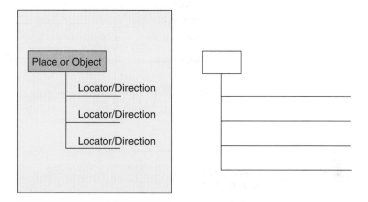

Generalization and Example

In the **generalization-and-example** pattern, a general statement or conclusion is supported with specific examples. Signal words include *to restate that, that is, for example, to illustrate, for instance.*

EXAMPLE   **Smoking**

To restate it in simple terms, smoking kills. The American Cancer Society estimates that tobacco smoking is the cause of 30 percent of all deaths from cancer. Lung cancer is the leading cause of death from cancer in the United States, with 85 percent to 90 percent of these cases being from smoking. Save your life by not smoking.

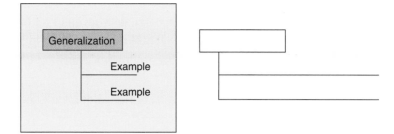

READER'S TIP

Patterns of Organization and Signal Words

◆ **Addition:** furthermore • again • also • further • moreover • besides
 • likewise
 (provides more information)

◆ **Cause and Effect:** because • for this reason • consequently
 • hence • as a result • thus • due to • therefore
 (shows one element as producing or causing a result or effect)

◆ **Classification:** groups • categories • elements • classes • parts
 (divides items into groups or categories)

◆ **Comparison:** in a similar way • similar • parallels • likewise
 • in a like manner
 (lists similarities among items)

◆ **Contrast:** on the other hand • bigger than • but • however
 • conversely • on the contrary • although • nevertheless
 (lists differences among items)

◆ **Definition:** can be defined • means • for example • like
 (initially defines a concept and expands with examples and
 restatements)

◆ **Description:** is • as • like • could be described
 (lists characteristics or details)

◆ **Generalization and Example:** to restate • that is • for example
 • to illustrate • for instance
 (explains with examples to illustrate)

◆ **Location or Spatial Order:** next to • near • below • above
 • close by • within • without • adjacent to • beside • around
 • to the right or left side • opposite
 (identifies the whereabouts of objects)

(continued)

- ◆ **Simple Listing:** also • another • several • for example
  (randomly lists items in a series)

- ◆ **Summary:** in conclusion • briefly • to sum up • in short • in a nutshell
  (condenses major points)

- ◆ **Time Order, Sequence, or Narration:** first • second • finally • after
  • before • next • later • now • at last • until • thereupon • while
  • during
  (lists events in order of occurrence)

**Exercise
5.3**

Identifying Paragraph Patterns

Each of the following items presents the first two sentences of a paragraph stating the main idea and a major supporting detail. Select the letter that indicates the pattern of organization that you would predict for each.

 1. Jim Vicary coined the term *subliminal advertising*, claiming that inserting messages like "Eat popcorn" and "Drink Coca-Cola" into movies would increase consumption. According to Vicary, the messages, flashed too fast for the human eye but registered in the brain, would prompt a rush to the snack bar.
   a. summary
   b. classification
   c. definition
   d. comparison-contrast

2. Now an integral part of the recruiting strategy, companies of all sizes are finding that e-cruiting, job recruiting over the Internet, has many benefits. To begin, the Internet is a fast, convenient, and inexpensive way to find prospective job candidates.
   a. description
   b. simple listing
   c. time order
   d. classification

3. Most prisons are designed to have three levels of custody: maximum, medium, and minimum. Maximum security prisons usually have a 25-foot wall surrounding the entire facility to prevent the escape of dangerous felons.
   a. classification
   b. cause and effect
   c. definition
   d. comparison

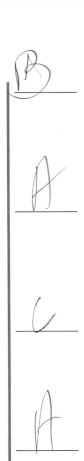

4. As a result of the Great Depression, Hollywood flourished. Cheap tickets, free time, and the lure of fantasy brought 60 million to 80 million Americans to the movies each week.
   a. comparison-contrast
   b. simple listing
   c. cause and effect
   d. description

5. Queens ruled England in the second half of the sixteenth century. In 1553, Mary I took the throne. She was followed in 1558 by Elizabeth I, who ruled for the next 45 years.
   a. summary
   b. contrast
   c. classification
   d. time order

6. The great white shark is a 6- to 7-meter predator. This most dangerous of all sharks gets extra power and speed from its warm muscles.
   a. description
   b. addition
   c. location or spatial order
   d. generalization and example

7. Although both artists lived in Spain, Pablo Picasso and Salvador Dali had styles that differed dramatically. Picasso depicted his subjects in abstract terms, whereas Dali painted the stark reality of the image.
   a. description
   b. comparison-contrast
   c. time order
   d. simple listing

8. Michelangelo depicted the creation of Eve in a panel that is almost in the center of the Sistine Chapel ceiling. The Creation of Adam, a larger and more famous panel, is located adjacent to it and toward the back of the chapel.
   a. simple listing
   b. time order
   c. location or spatial order
   d. definition

9. In short, the Internet can be a source of dangerous misinformation. Anyone can develop a Web site and fill it with distortions of the truth and inflammatory accusations.
   a. classification
   b. summary
   c. definition
   d. time order

_____ D _____ 10. In case of a sprained ankle, you should first apply ice to
constrict the blood vessels and stop internal bleeding. Next,
elevate your foot above the level of your heart to further
control bleeding by making the blood run downhill.
  a. summary
  b. classification
  c. generalization and example
  d. sequence

Exercise 5.4

Patterns of Organization and Main Idea

Read the following passages, and use the three-question system you learned in
Chapter 4 to determine the author's main idea. In addition, indicate the dominant pattern of organization used by the author. Select from the following list:

| simple listing | definition | description | time order |
| comparison-contrast | | cause and effect | |

Passage A

Let us follow the story of how rabbits were introduced into Australia. European
rabbits reached Australia with the first European settlers in 1788, and repeated
introductions followed. By the early 1800s rabbits were being kept in every large
settlement and had been liberated many times. All the early rabbit introductions
either died out or remained localized. No one knows why.

On Christmas Day, 1859, the brig H.M.S. *Lightning* arrived at Melbourne with
about a dozen wild European rabbits bound for an estate in western Victoria. Within
three years rabbits had started to spread, after a bush fire destroyed the fences
enclosing one colony. From a slow spread at first the colonization picked up speed
during the 1870s, and by 1900 the European rabbit had spread 1,000 miles to the
north and west, changing the entire economy of nature in southeastern Australia.

Charles Krebs, *The Message of Ecology*

1. Who or what is this about? _____ rabbits _____

2. What are the major details? _____ European rabbits
reached Australia with the
first European settlers
in 1768 _____

3. What is the overall pattern of organization? _____ Time order _____

4. What is the main idea the author is trying to convey about the topic?
_____ how rabbits were introduce
to australia _____

Passage B

Sloppy people can't bear to part with anything. They give loving attention to every detail. When sloppy people say they're going to tackle the surface of a desk, they really mean it. Not a paper will go unturned; not a rubber band will go unboxed.

Neat people are bums and clods at heart. They have cavalier attitudes toward possessions, including family heirlooms. Everything is just another dust-catcher to them. If anything collects dust, it's got to go and that's that.

Suzanne Britt, *Neat People vs. Sloppy People*

1. Who or what is this about? Sloppy and neat people

2. What are the major details? Sloppy people cant bear to part with anything Neat people are bums and clods at heart

3. What is the overall pattern of organization? Comparison and contrast

4. What is the main idea the author is trying to convey about the topic? Comparison between neat and sloppy people.

Passage C

The disadvantage faced by children who attempt morning schoolwork on an empty stomach appears to be at least partly due to hypoglycemia. The average child up to the age of ten or so needs to eat every four to six hours to maintain a blood glucose concentration high enough to support the activity of the brain and nervous system. A child's brain is as big as an adult's, and the brain is the body's chief glucose consumer. A child's liver is considerably smaller, and the liver is the organ responsible for storing glucose (as glycogen) and for releasing it into the blood as needed. The liver can't store more than about four hours' worth of glycogen; hence the need to eat fairly often. Teachers aware of the late-morning slump in their classrooms wisely request that a midmorning snack be provided; it improves classroom performance all the way to lunchtime. But for the child who hasn't had breakfast, the morning may be lost altogether.

Eva May Nunnelley Hamilton et al., *Nutrition*, 5th ed.

1. Who or what is this about? disadvantage faced by children who attempt morning schooleg

2. What are the major details? _____

_____

3. What is the overall pattern of organization? Description

4. What is the main idea the author is trying to convey about the topic?

_____

_____

Passage D

Money motivates employees only if it is tied directly to performance. The most common method of establishing this link is the use of *incentive programs*—special pay programs designed to motivate high performance. A sales bonus is a typical incentive. Employees receive *bonuses*—special payments above their salaries—when they sell a certain number or certain dollar amount of goods for a year. Employees who fail to reach this goal earn no bonuses. *Merit salary systems* link raises to performance levels in nonsales jobs. For example, many baseball players have contract clauses that pay them bonuses for hitting over .300, making the All-Star team, or being named Most Valuable Player. Executives commonly receive *stock options* as incentives. If a CEO's managerial talent leads to higher profits and stock prices, the CEO can buy the stock at a price lower than the market value for which, in theory, he or she is largely responsible. A newer incentive plan is called *pay for performance* or *variable pay*. In essence, middle managers are rewarded for especially productive output.

Ronald Ebert and Ricky Griffin, *Business*, 7th ed.

1. Who or what is this about? _____

2. What are the major details? _____

_____

3. What is the overall pattern of organization? _____

4. What is the main idea the author is trying to convey about the topic?

_____

Passage E

Over the past few years, psychologists and psychiatrists have discovered that although everyone is affected to a greater or lesser extent, some people suffer from seasonal affective disorder, or SAD—a form of depression that strikes during the short, dark, cold days of late autumn and winter. Every year, people with SAD who live in relatively cool regions of the world fall into a lethargic emotional state that resembles hibernation. They become listless, drowsy, and withdrawn. They also sleep more, eat more, crave pasta and other carbohydrates, gain weight, lose interest in sex, and falter in their work and social relationships. Consistent with the hypothesis that SAD is related to climate, surveys show that both SAD sufferers and people in general report feeling worse during the winter months and that the prevalence of SAD increases with a region's distance north of the equator. SAD is far more common, for example, in Alaska and New Hampshire than in Maryland and Florida.

Saul Kassin, *Psychology*, 4th ed.

1. Who or what is this about? _____

2. What are the major details? _____

_____

3. What is the overall pattern of organization? _____

4. What is the main idea the author is trying to convey about the topic?

_____

_____

Mixed Organizational Patterns

Suppose you were writing an orientation article describing support services available at your own college. You could present the resources in a **simple listing** pattern, or you could discuss them in the **sequence** or **time order** in which a freshman is likely to need them or in terms of the most convenient geographic locations to students. Within your article, you might use a **description** or **definition** pattern to identify a relatively unknown service on campus, with **examples** of how it has helped others. You could demonstrate **cause and effect** with facts and statistics on how using services has helped students. You might also choose to **compare and contrast** a special service with that at another college.

You could supply **additional** information by presenting the qualifications of professional staff providing the services. To wrap things up, you could create an overall **summary** about the support services. Thus, one long article might have an overall **simple listing** pattern of organization yet contain individual paragraphs that follow other patterns.

Exercise 5 | **Identifying Combined Organizational Patterns in a Longer Passage**

Read the following textbook excerpt and answer the questions that follow. Note how organizational patterns may be combined to help you understand the main idea of a slightly longer piece of writing. Signal words are in bold type, and think-alouds about the various patterns appear in the margin alongside the passage.

What pattern does the title suggest?

Are these two definitions?

What is this pattern?

What pattern is signaled?

Why Do People Eat Dirt?

Geophagia, the eating of earth, **is defined as** a special form of "pica," or the "habitual consumption of items not commonly considered to be food, or the compulsive consumption of otherwise normal food items." There is a preference for certain kinds of earth or clay, and clay is often baked before consumption, or formed into tablets, or mixed with other substances such as honey.

Geophagia presents a fascinating puzzle that occurs in **several areas** of the world. It has been documented in Native American groups of South America, in the Mediterranean region, among women and children in India, among pregnant African American women and children, and in some African cultures.

Many medical experts feel **the reason** people eat dirt is **because** there is something wrong with them. Some ailments implicated in geophagia are colon perforation, fecal impaction, severe tooth abrasion, and especially, anemia.

According to this view, anemic persons consume earth as an unconscious way of increasing iron levels. **Therefore**, geophagia can be "cured" through iron therapy. Other experts argue the arrow of **causation** points in the opposite direction: Clay consumption reduces the body's ability to absorb iron, so it **causes** anemia, but the data are inconclusive. **Thus**, while an association between geophagia and anemia seems often (but not always) to exist, the direction of **causation** is undetermined.

Some medical anthropologists propose that geophagia may have **several** positive adaptive values. Eating clay, they say, may function as a supplement to dietary minerals. Clay from markets in Ghana, for example, have been found to contain phosphorus, potassium, calcium, magnesium, copper, zinc, manganese, and iron. **Another** adaptive role of geophagia is in traditional antidiarrheal preparations. Many clays of Africa have similar compositions to that of Kaopectate, a Western commercial antidiarrheal medicine. A **third** hypothesis is that consumption of clay along with plant materials that contain certain toxins (poisons) serves as a detoxicant. Nausea or indigestion from eating such foods is thus avoided. This hypothesis receives support from the common practice of clay eating during famines. This would help people digest leaves, bark, and other uncommonly eaten and hard-to-digest foods. **In addition**, laboratory rats react to exposure to chemical toxins or new flavors by eating clay.

Barbara Miller, Cultural Anthropology, 2nd (adapted)

What is this pattern?

1. Who or what is this about? _____

2. What overall pattern is suggested by the title? _____

3. What is the pattern of organization in the first paragraph? _____

_____

4. What is the pattern of organization in the second paragraph? _____

5. What is the pattern of organization in the third paragraph? _____

6. What is the pattern of organization in the fourth paragraph? _____

7. What is the main idea the author is trying to convey about the topic? _____

_____

_____

Summary Points

● What are transitional words?

Transitional or signal words connect parts of sentences and lead you to anticipate a continuation or a change in thoughts. They guide you through the logic of the message by showing the relationships of ideas within sentences, between sentences, and between paragraphs.

● What is an organizational pattern, and how many types of patterns can be used in textbooks?

An organizational pattern is the presentation plan, format, or structure of a message. It is a way to present ideas with logic. There are at least 13 possible configurations or patterns for logically presenting details.

● Why are several organizational patterns sometimes combined to develop a main idea?

To fully present and explore the message, one long article may have a general overall pattern of organization yet contain individual paragraphs that follow other patterns.

CONTEMPORARY FOCUS

Human rights violations occur throughout the world. Slavery, unfortunately, is not just a disgrace of the past. How can those of us who enjoy freedom work to liberate those around the world who are less fortunate?

ENSLAVED AT AN EARLY AGE

The Economist, U. S. Edition, February 21, 2004, Books and Art

Francis Bok's childhood ended when he was seven. He was uprooted from a happy life on his family farm in southern Sudan when an Arab militia descended on the nearby village, slaughtering men while harvesting children and women as slaves. The young Francis spent the following ten years tending the livestock of his master. He was continually beaten and generally despised, his life reduced to misery, loneliness and constant fear. He was 17 when he escaped.

Mr. Bok, now aged 23 and living in the United States, has become an activist on behalf of the millions of people believed to live in slavery around the world, but particularly in Sudan. He has testified before the Senate Foreign Relations Committee and spoke out against Sudan's slavery at the United Nations.

Mende Nazer comes from the Nuba Mountains. Her people are Muslims, but they are black, unlike the Muslims from the north. She was a lively and smart child, with dreams of being a doctor. She describes a simple life made of laughter and storytelling around the fire, but also of the customs of excruciating female circumcisions and child brides.

When she first came to Khartoum, the capital, she saw strange trees with fruits made of bright lights lining the streets, and there were so many cars she thought they were reproducing, like cattle. She was 12 and about to be sold as a house slave, after being kidnapped during a raid on her village. She became a frightened and lonely shadow of herself.

In her late teens, she was shipped to her owner's sister and her diplomat husband in London, and continued her life as a slave. Helped by a fellow Sudanese, she escaped. Slowly, Miss Nazer has learned freedom—as well as English and how to cope with such challenges as negotiating her way through London's buses.

Miss Nazer and Mr. Bok are free today, but thousands are still enslaved. To western readers, the slave trade may seem from another age, but their tales of uprooting, brutality and despair remind us that it exists today.

Collaborate

Collaborate on responses to the following questions:

■ How can international pressure control such kidnappings and enslavement?

■ What aspects of slavery seem to be political?

■ What can Bok and Nazer hope to achieve for the "voiceless"?

Preview

Preview the next selection to predict its purpose and organization and to formulate your learning plan.

Activate Schema

Where is Sudan, and what countries are adjacent to it?

Why would the government of Sudan allow slaves to be captured?

Establish a Purpose for Reading

Why has the slave trade flourished for centuries in Sudan? What do humanitarian efforts to redeem slaves have to do with the economic concepts of supply and demand? What do you expect to learn from this selection? After recalling what you already know about slavery and what you may already know about Sudan, read the selection to explain the reasons why the slave redemption program in the largest African nation has not worked as envisioned.

Increase Word Knowledge

What do you know about these words?

adherents	alleviate	suppressed	inception	unilateral
vicious circle	maritime	vein	incentive	enticing

Your instructor may give a true-false vocabulary review before or after reading.

Integrate Knowledge While Reading

Questions have been inserted in the margin to stimulate your thinking while reading. Remember to

Predict   Picture   Relate   Monitor   Correct

SLAVE REDEMPTION IN SUDAN

From Roger LeRoy Miller, Daniel K. Benjamin, and Douglass C. North, *The Economics of Public Issues*, 12th ed.

Where is Sudan on a map? → Sudan is Africa's largest nation. Located immediately south of Egypt, it encompasses nearly one million square miles and is home to 35 million people. It is also home to poverty, disease, civil war—and the emergence of modern-day slavery. The slave trade, in turn, has given rise to a new humanitarian

5 movement, whose adherents seek to alleviate Sudan's misery by buying freedom for its slaves. Well-intentioned though they are, these humanitarian efforts
may be making things worse.

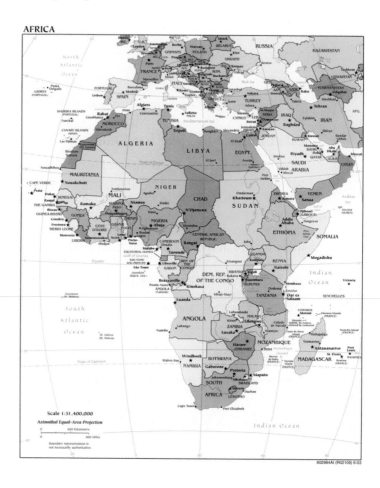

Sudan, located in the northeastern part of Africa, has been embroiled in
a civil war since 1983, resulting in more than 2 million deaths and the
displacement of more than 4 million people.
CIA

Slavery is a centuries-old practice in Sudan, one that colonial British rulers
finally managed to halt during World War I. The Sudanese gained indepen-
10 dence in 1956 but, despite ensuing periods of civil war, the slave trade initially
remained a piece of history. This changed in 1989, when the National Islamic
Front (NIF) took control of the government. The NIF quickly began arming
the Muslim Baggara tribe in the northern part of the country to fight against
the rebellious Christian tribes of the south. The Baggara previously had made
15 a regular practice of enslaving members of the southern Dinka tribe, and once
armed by the NIF the Baggara resumed the slave raids the British had sup-

© 2005 by Pearson Education, Inc.

Chart the differences among NIF, Baggara, and Dinka.)

pressed. This activity was further aided by the government, which supplied horses to the Baggara and permitted slave markets to open in the cities controlled by the NIF. Perhaps as many as 20,000 Dinkas, mostly women and
20   children, were enslaved and taken north, selling for as little as $15 each. The slaves were branded with the names of their owners and put to work as cooks, maids, field hands, and concubines.

    Within a few years, word of the revived slave trade began filtering out of Sudan. In response, a variety of humanitarian groups from other nations began
25   buying slaves in large batches and setting them free. The process is called "slave redemption," and its purpose—one hopes—is to reduce the number of people who are enslaved.

    Raising money for slave redemption has become big business, spreading rapidly among public schools and evangelical churches. A middle school in
30   Oregon, for example, raised $2500 to be used for slave redemption. Even more impressive was an elementary school class in Colorado. After the children's efforts caught the media's eye, the class raised more than $50,000 for slave redemption.

    The largest of the humanitarian groups involved in slave redemption is
35   Christian Solidarity International (CSI). This group says it has freed almost 8000 slaves since 1995, most at prices of about $50 each. In 1999 alone, for example, CSI purchased the freedom of nearly 3000 slaves. Several other groups also purchased the freedom of several hundred slaves that year, sometimes at prices of up to $100 each.

40   Per capita income in Sudan is about $500 per year, which makes slave prices of $50 to $100 apiece quite attractive to the Baggara slave raiders. This

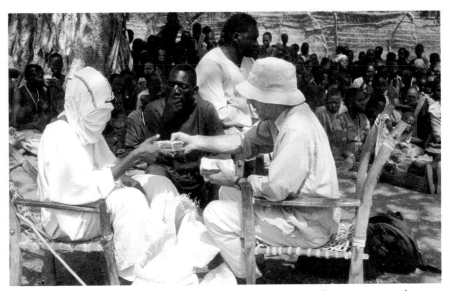

In a slave trade in Sudan, John Eibner hands over money to a slave retriever to buy freedom for the slaves.
Getty Images

is particularly true when the redeemers are buying in the south, where the targeted Dinkas live, and prices in the north, the traditional market for slaves, are as low as $15 apiece. In fact, says one individual who used to be active in
45   slave redemption, "We've made slave redemption more profitable than narcotics." What are the consequences of such profitability?

How does redeemer demand affect supply?

There have been two sets of responses. First, on the demand side, the higher prices for slaves make it more costly for owners in the north to hold slaves. So rather than own slaves, some of them have offered their slaves to the
50   redeemers. This, of course, is exactly the effect the slave redemption movement has desired. But there is also a supply response: When the market value of slaves rises due to an increase in demand (the demand of the slave redeemers), we expect an increase in the quantity supplied. That is, we expect the raiders who produce slaves by capturing them to engage in more of that
55   activity. This is exactly what has happened in Sudan.

Slave redemption began in earnest in 1995 and, according to local authorities, the number of slave raids has grown each year since. Moreover, the size of a typical raiding party has grown from roughly 400 attackers to more than 2500. Why the growth? Slaves used to be traded in relatively small batches,
60   but the redeemers prefer to buy in large lots—1000 or more at a time. Collecting and assembling the number of slaves required to satisfy the redemption buyers thus requires considerably more manpower. Hence, the slave trade is gradually being transformed from a cottage industry into a large-scale business enterprise. Overall, it is estimated that the number of slaves cap-
65   tured in raids each year has risen steadily since the inception of slave redemption. Initially, it is likely that the impact of slave redemption was chiefly on the demand side: that is, the first slaves redeemed were almost surely "freed from slavery" in the sense that we would normally use the terminology. But once the stock of slave holdings in the north had adjusted
70   downward in response to the newly elevated equilibrium price, there was only one place for the slave traders to get the slaves demanded by the redemption buyers. This was from the raiders who were now taking slaves for

How are redeemers paying for a lie?

one purpose only—sale to the redeemers. Thus, once the stock of slaves in the north is adjusted to its lower equilibrium level, *all* of the slaves subse-
75   quently "freed" by the redeemers are in fact individuals who never would have been enslaved had the redeemers not first made a market for them. In addition, because large numbers of new slaves now spend some time in captivity awaiting redemption, it is even possible that the total number of people in slavery at any point in time is actually *higher* because of the well-
80   intentioned efforts of the slave redeemers.

As unpleasant as such reasoning is, it agrees with the opinions of people who observe the slave trade firsthand. As a local humanitarian worker says, "Giving money to the slave traders only encourages the trade. It is wrong and must stop. Where does the money go? It goes to the raiders to buy more guns,
85   raid more villages. . . . It is a vicious circle." In a similar vein, the chief of one village that has been targeted by the slave raiders says, "Redemption is not the solution. It means you are encouraging the raiders."

In addition to encouraging the capture of new slaves, redemption also reduces any incentive for owners to set free their less productive slaves. Prior to 1995, about 10 percent of all slaves, chiefly older women and young children, were allowed to escape or even told to go home, because the costs of feeding, clothing, and housing them exceeded their value to their owners. Now slaves who have been freed on their own are instead held in captivity until a trader can be found to haul them south for sale to the redeemers.

The final effect of redemption has been to create a trade in fictitious slaves—individuals who are paid to pose as slaves for the purposes of redemption, and who are then given a cut of the redemption price after they are "freed." Although redemption groups obviously try to avoid participating in such deals, observers familiar with the trade consider them a regular part of the redemption business.

> Would you donate money for slave redemption?

Is there another way to combat slavery in Sudan? On the demand side, the U.S. government has long refused to negotiate with terrorists or pay ransom to kidnappers, simply because it believes that such tactics encourage terrorism and kidnapping. It recognizes that paying a ransom increases the profits of kidnapping, thus enticing more individuals into the trade.

On the supply side, the British were originally successful in ending the slave trade in Sudan and elsewhere in their empire by dispatching soldiers to kill or disarm slave raiders, and by sending warships to close off maritime slave-trading routes. Sudan, of course, is an independent sovereign nation today; both the United Nations and the British electorate would likely oppose unilateral military action by the British government against Sudanese slave raiders. Yet even the people who used to be subject to British colonial rule have mixed feelings. When asked to compare the colonial British policies to the redeemers' policies of today, a schoolmaster in the affected area remarked, "If the colonial government were standing for election, I would vote for them." So too might the victims of the slave trade in Sudan. (1,400 words)

> How can the slave trade be stopped?

Recall

Stop to self-test, relate, and react.

Your instructor may choose to give you a true-false comprehension review.

Write About the Selection

What are the demand and supply sides of the slavery redemption program? Describe the intended and the actual results of each.

Response Suggestion: Define both sides and list the intended and actual results of each.

Contemporary Link

Given the existing problems and human suffering with slave redemption, what other solutions would you suggest to end the slavery in Sudan?

Skill Development: Identify Organizational Patterns

Fill in the organizational diagram below to reflect the cause-and-effect pattern of the selection.

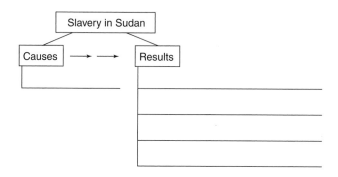

Check Your Comprehension

After reading the selection, answer the following questions with *a*, *b*, *c*, or *d*. To help you analyze your strengths and weaknesses, the question types are indicated.

Main Idea

_____ 1. Which is the best statement of the main idea?
   a. Humanitarian efforts in Sudan have captured worldwide attention.
   b. The government and the humanitarians have united to free slaves from Sudan.
   c. The slave redemption program in Sudan has increased rather than decreased the number of slaves captured.
   d. The new government has brought independence to most of the people of Sudan.

Detail

_____ 2. The slave trade in Sudan reemerged in 1989 because
   a. the British never got rid of the slave trade.
   b. the Muslim government failed in its attempt to stop the slave trade.
   c. the NIF lost in a civil war against the Muslim Baggara tribe.
   d. The Muslim government allowed and even encouraged the enslavement of members of rebellious Christian tribes.

Detail _____ 3. Slave redemption is a process of
  a. capturing slaves.
  b. selling victims into slavery.
  c. buying the freedom of slaves.
  d. the government allowing slavery.

Detail _____ 4. The resumption of the slave trade in 1989 was aided by all of
  the following except
  a. the NIF.
  b. the Baggara tribe.
  c. Muslims in Sudan.
  d. Christian tribes.

Inference _____ 5. From an economic perspective, the author implies that
  humanitarian efforts would have worked to reduce
  slavery if
  a. the demand were met and the supply was not
    increased.
  b. both supply and demand increased.
  c. only the supply increased.
  d. supply grew greater than demand.

Inference _____ 6. The author implies that a "cottage industry" is
  a. a small business.
  b. a large-scale business enterprise.
  c. a corporation.
  d. a government program.

Detail _____ 7. The desire of redeemers to purchase slaves in large lots
  created all the following except
  a. a dramatic increase in the number of attackers.
  b. fictitious slaves.
  c. the voluntary release of slaves whose costs for owners
    exceeded their value.
  d. a greater effort to increase supply.

Detail _____ 8. A fictitious slave is a
  a. recaptured slave who is sold twice.
  b. person who is paid to pretend to be a slave.
  c. person who, by false accounting, is sold but the person
    does not physically exist.
  d. kidnapped slave.

Detail _____ 9. The British ended slavery in Sudan by
  a. paying ransoms.
  b. kidnapping slave raiders.
  c. attacking slave raiders.
  d. voting in elections.

Inference   _____ 10. The reader can conclude that
                                                   a. the Sudanese government will join with the United
Nations to use force against the slave raiders.
                                                   b. the humanitarian groups are beginning to support mili-
tary force rather than redemption as a means of ridding
Sudan of slavery.
                                                   c. the success of the humanitarian group in raising money
for slave redemption has also led to the failure in ridding
the Sudan of slavery.
                                                   d. the United Nations and the British will use force to cut
the maritime slave-trading routes.

Answer the following with T (true) or F (false).

Detail   _____ 11. Prior to World War II, the Baggara tribe conducted slave raids
against the Dinka tribe.

Inference   _____ 12. The primary purpose of initially reviving the slave trade was
to profit from slave redemption.

Detail   _____ 13. As soon as the Sudanese gained independence in 1956, the
slave trade resumed.

Inference   _____ 14. The author feels that organizations such as Christian Solidarity International have intensified the slave problem.

Inference   _____ 15. In the final quotation, the author suggests that some people
in Sudan feel that the British were better rulers than the
Sudanese.

Build Your Vocabulary

According to the way the italicized word was used in the selection, select *a,
b, c,* or *d* for the word or phrase that gives the best definition. The number
in parentheses indicates the line of the passage in which the word is
located.

_____ 1. "*adherents* seek" (5)
      a. followers
      b. founders
      c. opponents
      d. demonstrators

_____ 2. "*alleviate* Sudan's misery" (5)
      a. assault
      b. relieve
      c. confront
      d. recognize

_____ 3. "British had *suppressed*" (16)
      a. curtailed
      b. started
      c. disliked
      d. disowned

_____ 4. "*inception* of slave redemption" (65)
      a. violation
      b. reduction
      c. justification
      d. beginning

_____ 5. "It is a *vicious circle*" (85)
   a. unethical act
   b. crime against humanity
   c. solution that creates a problem
   d. religious challenge

_____ 6. "In a similar *vein*" (85)
   a. line of thought
   b. community
   c. strategy
   d. phase

_____ 7. "*incentive* for owners" (89)
   a. allowance
   b. reluctance
   c. financial motivation
   d. power

_____ 8. "*enticing* more individuals" (106)
   a. surrendering
   b. attracting
   c. surrounding
   d. demanding

_____ 9. "*maritime* slave-trading routes" (109)
   a. popular
   b. sea
   c. successful
   d. temporary

_____ 10. "*unilateral* military action" (112)
   a. one-sided
   b. two-sided
   c. immediate
   d. united

Search the Net

Use a search engine such as Google, AltaVista, Excite, Infoseek, Dogpile, Yahoo, or Lycos to find information on modern-day slavery. Give an overview of the extent of the problem. List and explain five situations of modern-day slavery. For suggested Web sites and other research activities, go to http://www.ablongman.com/smith/.

Concept Prep

for Economics

What is economics?

Economics involves analyzing different aspects of the demands of the marketplace and the supply or scarcity of available products and services. Economists study inflation, minimum wages, unemployment, taxation, and the many factors that affect our economic well-being. One such factor is the stock market.

What is a stock?

A **stock** is a share of the ownership in a company. Corporations sell shares to raise money, and a large company may have millions of shareholders. If a private company desires to go public (sell stock) and meets the qualifications of the stock exchange, the price of a share of stock is set for the **initial public offering (IPO)**. The company then sells shares to get money for reinvestment or for the owners to get some of their investment money out. The shares are traded on one of the exchanges of the stock market.

Usually shares are purchased in lots of 100, but you can buy any amount you wish. You pay a fee to a licensed **broker** for completing the purchase. Many investors buy with online discount brokers and pay a fee of approximately $30 for each purchase and each sale. No longer do you get certificates for your stocks; instead, the documentation for your purchase is held by the brokerage firm in **"Street Name"** (in the broker's name).

The price of a stock should reflect the value of the company, including its **earnings** (profits) and **assets** (holdings that have a monetary value). All too often, however, the price of a stock represents what people are willing to pay for it. Thus a stock can be overvalued because of wild expectations, as happened with Internet stocks, or a stock can be undervalued because of temporary problems with earnings or sales.

You can realize the financial rewards from stocks in two ways. The first is through annual **dividends,** which are shares of the profits based on the number of stocks owned. The second and greatest reward, however, will come if the company flourishes and your shares appreciate. After a few years, you might triple your money and sell 100 shares of a $25 stock for $75 each and make a nice profit. On the other hand, there are no guarantees with stocks. The price of the stocks may decline and you may lose money. You will hope

Traders buy and sell stocks on the floor of the New York Stock Exchange in lower Manhattan.
Chris Hondros/Getty Images

for a **bull market,** a rising trend in stock prices, rather than a **bear market,** which is a declining price trend.

What are stock exchanges?

Stock exchanges are organizations formed to sell the stocks of their members.

● The **New York Stock Exchange (NYSE),** with its trading floor located on **Wall Street** in New York City, is the oldest exchange. Known as the **"Big Board,"** it is also the largest exchange and sells many of the **blue chip stocks** issued by large, established companies such as Coca-Cola and General Electric. These blue chips are well known, widely held by investors, and unlikely to go bankrupt. The name comes from poker, where the blue chips have the highest value.

- The **American Stock Exchange (AMEX)** is also located in New York. Its minimum requirements for membership are less stringent. As firms grow, they often transfer from the AMEX to the NYSE.

- The **National Association of Securities Dealers Automated Quotation (NASDAQ)** system has no trading floor but is an electronic network for trading stocks. Many high-tech and dot-com stocks, such as Microsoft, Oracle, and Cisco, are traded on the NASDAQ.

What are stock indexes?

- The **Dow-Jones average** (the **Dow**) is an index or sum of the market prices for 30 of the largest industrial firms listed on the NYSE. If the many blue chips indexed by the Dow are increasing in value, the Dow is up.

- The **Standard & Poor's Composite Index (the S & P)** gives a broader view of the strength of the market. It is a sum of the market prices for 500 stocks, which includes 400 industries, 40 utilities, 40 financial institutions, and 20 transportation companies.

REVIEW QUESTIONS

After studying the material, answer the following questions:

1. Why would a company go public and sell stock? _____

   _____

2. What is an IPO? _____

   _____

3. What is the discount broker's commission on a stock purchase? _____

   _____

4. Who keeps the stock if it is in "Street Name"? _____

   _____

5. Is the greater potential for gain in a stock dividend or in stock appreciation? _____

   _____

6. If you are forced to sell, is it usually better to sell a stock in a bear or a bull market? _____

   _____

7. What are blue chip companies? _____

   _____

8. Which stock exchange is the oldest and most established? _____

   _____

9. Which stock exchange is on an electronic network with no trading floor? _____

   _____

10. Which of the indexes mentioned summarizes more stocks? _____

    _____

Your instructor may choose to give a true-false review of these economics concepts.

CONTEMPORARY FOCUS

Dr. Condoleezza Rice is the first woman to occupy the key post of national security adviser. As a trusted member of President George W. Bush's team, she led the tricky negotiations with Russia over missile defense. While growing up, Rice recalls that parental expectations were always high. In an interview she said, "My parents had me absolutely convinced that, well, you may not be able to have a hamburger at Woolworth's but you can be president of the United States." She is also a pianist, ice skater, and sports fan.

TRUSTED POLICY ADVISOR

By Steve Kettmann

Salon.com, March 20, 2000

In a recent phone interview, Rice recalled her rise to political renown. She was born in Birmingham, Ala., in 1954, and since both parents were teachers, education was a major theme of her youth. So was faith. Her father, John Rice, was an ordained Presbyterian minister, as well as dean of Stillman College in Tuscaloosa, and later vice chancellor of the University of Denver. He was also a Republican who influenced the political thinking of his daughter, who calls herself an "all-over-the-map Republican." Rice considers herself "very conservative" on foreign policy but "almost shockingly libertarian" or "moderate" on some issues.

A gifted student who skipped two grades, Rice enrolled at the University of Denver when she was 15, and graduated when she was 19. She gave up on a career as a pianist midway through, and eventually wound up falling under the spell of Josef Korbel, a former Czech diplomat best known for being the father of Madeleine Albright. Rice sometimes dined at the Korbel home, along with the future secretary of state—but emerged with views much more in line with Korbel's than Albright's.

Rice mixes confidence and a light touch, as she made clear in a recent interview. Recalling the time she met Russia's acting president, Vladimir Putin, at a reception (when Putin

National Security Advisor Condoleeza Rice testifies on the Bush Administration's anti-terror policy before the 9/11 Commission in 2004.
Alex Wong/Getty Images

was working for the mayor of St. Petersburg), Rice insisted he would not remember her. Right. No doubt he meets smart, charming, Russian-speaking Americans with names like Condoleezza all the time. (The name, by the way, came from her mother, like Rice a pianist, who made a variation on the musical direction *con dolcezza*, or "with sweetness.")

Her mentor at Stanford, Coit Blacker, said Rice possesses "a kind of intellectual agility mixed with velvet-glove forcefulness."

Collaborate

Collaborate on responses to the following questions:

- What is the job of the national security advisor?
- Who is Madeleine Albright?
- What other president did Condoleezza Rice work for, and what was her job?

Preview

Preview the next selection to predict its purpose and organization and to formulate your learning plan.

Activate Schema

Who was Sojourner Truth?

Why did the Civil War throw women into many leadership roles?

Establish a Purpose for Reading

Although history books tend to be mostly about the accomplishments of men, over time, women also have made contributions and pursued political and other professions. Who were some of the early women leaders? After recalling what you already know about women in history, read the selection to explain the contributions of individuals and groups toward changing the image of women.

Increase Word Knowledge

What do you know about these words?

restrictive	detriment	defiant	communal	hecklers
pursue	hygiene	incessant	convalescent	naive

Your instructor may give a true-false vocabulary review before or after reading.

Integrate Knowledge While Reading

Questions have been inserted in the margin to stimulate your thinking while reading. Remember to

Predict   Picture   Relate   Monitor   Correct

WOMEN IN HISTORY
From Leonard Pitt, *We Americans*

Three Radical Women

Amelia Bloomer (1818–1894) published the first newspaper issued expressly for women. She called it *The Lily*. Her fame, however, rests chiefly in dress reform. For six or eight years she wore an outfit composed of a knee-length skirt over full pants gathered at the ankle, which were soon known every-

5 where as "bloomers." Wherever she went, this style created great excitement and brought her enormous audiences—including hecklers. She was trying to make the serious point that women's fashions, often designed by men to suit their own tastes, were too restrictive, often to the detriment of the health of those who wore them. Still, some of her contemporaries thought she did the

10 feminist movement as much harm as good.

Very few feminists hoped to destroy marriage as such. Most of them had husbands and lived conventional, if hectic, lives. And many of the husbands supported their cause. Yet the feminists did challenge certain marital customs. When Lucy Stone married Henry Blackwell, she insisted on being called "Mrs.

15 Stone," a defiant gesture that brought her a lifetime of ridicule. Both she and her husband signed a marriage contract, vowing "to recognize the wife as an independent, rational being." They agreed to break any law which brought the husband "an injurious and unnatural superiority." But few of the radical feminists indulged in "free love" or joined communal marriage experiments. The

20 movement was intended mainly to help women gain control over their own property and earnings and gain better legal guardianship over their children. Voting also interested them, but women's suffrage did not become a central issue until later in the century.

Many black women were part of the movement, including the legendary

25 Sojourner Truth (1797–1883). Born a slave in New York and forced to marry a man approved by her owner, Sojourner Truth was freed when the state abolished slavery. After participating in religious revivals, she became an active abolitionist and feminist. In 1851 she saved the day at a women's rights convention in Ohio, silencing hecklers and replying to a man who had belittled

30 the weakness of women:

Why would Bloomer have hurt the movement?

Why was voting a later issue?

Former slave Isabella
Van Wagener became
the abolitionist
Sojourner Truth.
*MPI/Hulton | Archive/Getty
Images*

The man over there says women need to be helped into carriages and
lifted over ditches, and to have the best place everywhere. Nobody ever
helps me into carriages or over puddles, or gives me the best place—and
ain't I a woman? . . . Look at my arm! I have ploughed and planted and
35 gathered into barns, and no man could head me—and ain't I a woman? I
could work as much and eat as much as a man—when I could get it—and
bear the lash as well! And ain't I a woman? I have borne thirteen children,
and seen most of 'em sold into slavery, and when I cried out my mother's
grief, none but Jesus heard me—and ain't I a woman?

What makes this
speech powerful?
Read it aloud.

Changing the Image and the Reality

40 The accomplishments of a few women who dared pursue professional careers
had somewhat altered the image of the submissive and brainless child-woman.
Maria Mitchell of Nantucket, whose father was an astronomer, discovered
a comet at the age of twenty-eight. She became the first woman professor of

astronomy in the U.S. (at Vassar in 1865). Mitchell was also the first woman elected to the American Academy of Arts and Sciences and a founder of the

45   Association for the Advancement of Women. Elizabeth Blackwell applied to twenty-nine medical schools before she was accepted. She attended all classes, even anatomy class, despite the sneers of some male students. As a physician, she went on to make important contributions in sanitation and hygiene.

Why would there be sneers in anatomy? →

By about 1860 women had effected notable improvements in their status.
50   Organized feminists had eliminated some of the worst legal disadvantages in fifteen states. The Civil War altered the role—and the image—of women even more drastically than the feminist movement did. As men went off to fight, women flocked into government clerical jobs. And they were accepted in teaching jobs as never before. Tens of thousands of women ran farms and busi-
55   nesses while the men were gone. Anna Howard Shaw, whose mother ran a pioneer farm, recalled:

How did the Civil War force an image change? →

> It was an incessant struggle to keep our land, to pay our taxes, and to live.
> Calico was selling at fifty cents a yard. Coffee was one dollar a pound.
> There were no men left to grind our corn, to get in our crops, or to care
60   > for our livestock; and all around us we saw our struggle reflected in the
> lives of our neighbors.

Women took part in crucial relief efforts. The Sanitary Commission, the Union's volunteer nursing program and a forerunner of the Red Cross, owed much of its success to women. They raised millions of dollars for medicine,
65   bandages, food, hospitals, relief camps, and convalescent homes.

North and South, black and white, many women served as nurses, some as spies and even as soldiers. Dorothea Dix, already famous as a reformer of pris-ons and insane asylums, became head of the Union army nurse corps. Clara Barton and "Mother" Bickerdyke saved thousands of lives by working close
70   behind the front lines at Antietam, Chancellorsville, and Fredericksburg. Har-riet Tubman led a party up the Combahee River to rescue 756 slaves. Late in life she was recognized for her heroic act by being granted a government pen-sion of twenty dollars per month.

Southern white women suffered more from the disruptions of the Civil War
75   than did their northern sisters. The proportion of men who went to war or were killed in battle was greater in the South. This made many women self-sufficient during the war. Still, there was hardly a whisper of feminism in the South.

The Civil War also brought women into the political limelight. Anna Dickson skyrocketed to fame as a Republican speaker, climaxing her career
80   with an address to the House of Representatives on abolition. Stanton and Anthony formed the National Woman's Loyal League to press for a consti-tutional amendment banning slavery. With Anthony's genius for organiza-tion, the League in one year collected 400,000 signatures in favor of the Thirteenth Amendment.

85

Once abolition was finally assured in 1865, most feminists felt certain that suffrage would follow quickly. They believed that women had earned the vote by their patriotic wartime efforts. Besides, it appeared certain that black men would soon be allowed to vote. And once black men had the ballot in hand,

> Why was suffrage slow to come?

90 ▸ how could anyone justify keeping it from white women—or black women? Any feminist who had predicted in 1865 that women would have to wait another fifty-five years for suffrage would have been called politically naive. (1,102 words)

Recall

Stop to self-test, relate, and react.

Your instructor may choose to give you a true-false comprehension review.

Write About the Selection

Have we been taught to believe that dynamic women are the exception rather than the rule in history? Is this idea confirmed when we see stories of women in box inserts and footnotes in history textbooks? How did the actions of many early women "somewhat alter the image of the submissive and brainless child-woman"? Is that image still being altered?

Response Suggestion: List dynamic women and discuss how each has changed stereotypical thinking.

Contemporary Link

How does Condoleezza Rice continue to change the image and the reality for women? What characteristics do you admire about her? How would you compare her to the three radical women in the selection?

Skill Development: Identify Organizational Patterns

Fill in the organizational diagram to reflect the simple-listing pattern of the first part of the selection.

Check Your Comprehension

After reading the selection, answer the following questions with *a, b, c,* or *d*. To help you analyze your strengths and weaknesses, the question types are indicated.

Main Idea   _____   1. What is the best statement of the main point of this selection?
a. Women made impressive gains because of their work during the Civil War.
b. Many women made early contributions toward changing the stereotypical image of the female role.
c. Bloomer, Stone, and Truth changed a radical image into a reality.
d. Women were slow to get the right to vote despite their efforts.

Detail   _____   2. In originating "bloomers," Amelia Bloomer's greatest concern was
a. fashion.
b. principle.
c. expense.
d. good taste.

Inference   _____   3. The major purpose of Sojourner Truth's quoted speech was to
a. prove that women are stronger than men.
b. reprimand men for social courtesy.
c. dramatize the strengths of women.
d. praise childbearing as a womanly virtue.

Detail   _____   4. Lucy Stone's major motive in retaining the name "Mrs. Stone" after marriage was to
a. condone "free love" without marriage.
b. de-emphasize the responsibilities of marriage.
c. purchase property in her own name.
d. be recognized as an independent person equal to her husband.

Detail   _____   5. The article explicitly states that women worked during the Civil War in all the following except
a. farms and businesses.
b. the military.
c. government clerical jobs.
d. the Red Cross.

Inference   _____   6. The author implies that the eventual assumption of responsible roles by large numbers of women was primarily due to
a. the feminist movement.
b. the determination and accomplishments of female professionals.

c. a desire to give women a chance.

d. economic necessity.

Inference _____ 7. The author believes that the Civil War showed southern women to be

a. as capable but less vocal than northern women.

b. more capable than their northern sisters.

c. capable workers and eager feminists.

d. less able to assume responsible roles than northern women.

Inference _____ 8. The author's main purpose in mentioning the accomplishments of Maria Mitchell is to point out that

a. she discovered a comet.

b. her professional achievements in astronomy were exceptional and thus somewhat improved the image of women.

c. she was the first woman professor of astronomy in the United States.

d. she was a founder of the Association for the Advancement of Women.

Detail _____ 9. The article states or implies that all the following women worked to abolish slavery except

a. Anna Howard Shaw.

b. Harriet Tubman.

c. Anna Dickson.

d. Stanton and Anthony.

Inference _____ 10. In the author's opinion, the long wait by women after the Civil War for suffrage

a. was predictable in 1865.

b. would not have been expected in 1865.

c. was due to the vote of black men.

d. was justified.

Answer the following with *T* (true) or *F* (false).

Detail _____ 11. Women were granted the right to vote in 1920.

Detail _____ 12. Sojourner Truth had been a southern slave.

Inference _____ 13. The author implies that feminist leaders were more concerned with their own right to vote than with the abolition of slavery.

Detail _____ 14. From the very beginning, the right to vote was the focal point of the women's movement.

Detail _____ 15. Sojourner Truth had thirteen children.

Build Your Vocabulary

According to the way the italicized word was used in the selection, indicate *a*, *b*, *c*, or *d* for the word or phrase that gives the best definition. The number in parentheses indicates the line of the passage in which the word is located.

_____ 1. "were too *restrictive*" (8)
   a. showy
   b. expensive
   c. complicated
   d. confining

_____ 2. "to the *detriment of*" (8)
   a. harm
   b. anger
   c. apology
   d. objection

_____ 3. "a *defiant* gesture" (15)
   a. unlucky
   b. resistive
   c. admirable
   d. ignorant

_____ 4. "*communal* marriage experiments" (19)
   a. permanent
   b. living together in groups
   c. illegal
   d. uncommon

_____ 5. "silencing *hecklers*" (29)
   a. soldiers
   b. rioters
   c. disciples
   d. verbal harassers

_____ 6. "*pursue* professional careers" (39)
   a. strive for
   b. abandon
   c. acknowledge
   d. indicate

_____ 7. "sanitation and *hygiene*" (48)
   a. garbage disposal
   b. biology
   c. health care
   d. mental disorders

_____ 8. "an *incessant* struggle" (57)
   a. earlier
   b. final
   c. novel
   d. unceasing

_____ 9. "*convalescent* homes" (65)
   a. sanitary
   b. government
   c. reclaimed
   d. recuperating

_____ 10. "called politically *naive*" (92)
   a. unsophisticated
   b. well informed
   c. dishonest
   d. unfortunate

Search the Net

Use a search engine such as Google, AltaVista, Excite, Infoseek, Dogpile, Yahoo, or Lycos to find information on Rosa Parks. Explain her pivotal role in the civil rights movement. For suggested Web sites and other research activities, go to http://www.ablongman.com/smith/.

Concept Prep

for Art History

Why study art history?

Just as written history is a verbal record of the events and personalities of the past, fine art is a visual interpretation of reality and a reflection of past taste and values. Art tells us about people and their culture as illustrated in the earliest primitive cave drawings depicting animals and hunters or in the elaborately decorated tombs in the Egyptian pyramids built for the ascension of pharaohs into heaven. Through art, we can glimpse a likeness of Elizabeth I, feel the power of a ship battle at sea, or view the majesty of the American frontier. Artists link us to the past through beauty, creativity, and emotion.

When we say "the arts," what do we mean?

The **arts** and the **fine arts** refer to creative works in painting, sculpture, literature, architecture, drama, music, opera, dance, and film. A work that is exceptionally well crafted is said to aspire to the level of fine art.

Museums, a word derived from Greek to mean places presided over by the Muses, display fine arts in paintings and sculpture. Some of the greatest museums in the world are the **Louvre** in Paris, the **Prado** in Madrid, and the **Metropolitan Museum of Art** in New York.

Ram's Head, White Hollyhock-Hills (Ram's Head and White Hollyhock, New Mexico) by Georgia O'Keeffe, 1935. Oil on canvas, 20 x 36" (76.2 x 91.44 cm). Brooklyn Museum of Art. Bequest of Edith and Milton Lowenthal, 1992.11.28. © 2006 The Georgia O'Keeffe Foundation/Artist Rights Society (ARS), New York.

Who are considered some of the greatest artists?

- One of the most extraordinary artists was **Leonardo da Vinci** (1452–1519). He was considered a **Renaissance man** because of his genius, insatiable curiosity, and wide interests in art, engineering, anatomy, and aeronautics. He painted the **Mona Lisa,** the world's most famous painting. This woman with the mysterious smile whose eyes seem to follow you is displayed in the Louvre behind several layers of bulletproof glass.

- **Michelangelo** (1475–1564) was a sculptor, painter, architect, and poet. Before he was 30 years old, he created the famous marble statue of **David,** which portrays the biblical king in his youth. Michelangelo was commissioned by the Pope to paint the ceiling of the **Sistine Chapel** in the Vatican in Rome. For four years, the artist worked on his back in the chapel to complete **The Creation of Adam,** which contains more than 400 individual figures.

- The founder and leading artist of the **impressionists** was **Claude Monet** (1840–1926). Critics said the feathery brushstrokes and play of light in his works conveyed the "impression" of a particular moment. Monet advocated getting out of the studio and painting outdoors facing the subject. He painted many scenes of the gardens and water lily ponds surrounding his home in **Giverny** near Paris.

- **Van Gogh** (1853–1890) borrowed from the impressionists but achieved another dimension in the swirling brushstrokes of his work to convey his unique vision. His sunflower paintings and *Starry Night* are among his most famous works, now popularized in mass reproductions, but in his lifetime Van Gogh sold only one painting. He suffered from depression and spent his last years in a mental institution. In an argument with another artist, he cut off his own ear, which he later sent to a prostitute.

- **Pablo Picasso** (1881–1973) is one of the most influential of all modern artists. Because traditional skills in painting were so easy for him, he looked for new modes of expression. He was the originator of cubism, an abstract style of painting that displays several perspectives of an object simultaneously. One of his most acclaimed paintings is *Guernica,* a haunting visual protest against the savagery of war.

- By the twentieth century, female artists were becoming more prominent. **Mary Cassatt** (1861–1914), an impressionist, holds a unique place in American art. She was one of the first women artists to succeed professionally. Cassatt began her work in Pennsylvania but later settled in Paris. Domestic scenes became her theme, and she portrayed women and children in intimate relationships.

- **Frida Kahlo** (1907–1954), a Mexican artist, is sometimes called the "portrait genie." She dramatized her life story in self-portraits, interweaving them with symbolism, myth, and surrealistic elements. Kahlo was studying to be a physician when a serious car accident hospitalized her. She took up painting and did not return to medicine. Her colorful creations reflect the endurance of life and the traditions of Mexico.

- **Georgia O'Keeffe** (1887–1986) was one of the first American artists to experiment with abstract form. She interpreted nature into beautiful geometric shapes. O'Keeffe combined the appearance of sculpture and photography in her paintings of flowers, sun-bleached animal bones, clouds, and surreal desert scenes. Her clear, bright colors reflect her love of the Southwest and her American independence.

REVIEW QUESTIONS

After studying the material, answer the following questions:

1. What do works included in "the arts" have in common? _____

2. Where is the Louvre? _____

3. What is a Renaissance man? _____

4. What is unusually engaging about Mona Lisa's face? _____

_____

5. What story is painted on the ceiling of the Sistine Chapel? _____

6. How did the impressionists get the name? _____

_____

7. What scenes did Monet paint at Giverny? _____

8. Which painter advocated painting outdoors? _____

9. How did Van Gogh disfigure himself? _____

10. Why did Picasso turn to cubism? _____

Your instructor may choose to give a true-false review of these art history concepts.

CONTEMPORARY FOCUS

Making changes to accommodate trendy diets and health crazes can affect profits for fast-food companies. Money could be lost or profits could increase and previous business retained. How much should companies alter old favorites to meet new demands?

LOW-CARB PIZZA OPTIONS

By John Keenan

Omaha World Herald, Nebraska, February 23, 2004

The carbohydrate-loaded pizza crust is an Atkins no-no, prompting some pizzeria owners to rethink their menus and offer low-carb dough or thin-crust pizzas. And some dieters are eating their pies a little differently, forgetting the crust and just eating the toppings.

This isn't the first time pizza has come up against a popular diet, said Joe Straughan, executive director of the National Association of Pizzeria Operators.

"Six or seven years ago, we had probably close to the same sort of a public cry about saturated fats," Straughan said. "A lot of pizzerias probably still have low-fat pizzas on the menu, but the interest on the part of the public didn't sustain."

Still, pizzerias nationwide are moving to accommodate customers who want low-carb versions.

"One of them has pizza in a bucket, if you can imagine that," Straughan said.

Vistar, the largest food-service distributor for pizzeria operators, has rushed into the marketplace with low-carb alternatives to pizza ingredients, Straughan said. The industry's most popular trade publication offers a low-carb crust recipe.

"Whether or not the customers really want pizza in a bucket or how far they want to go in avoiding the carbs is yet to be seen," said Straughan. "Most of us like the crunch. Under the toppings, we want that crunch."

Collaborate

Collaborate on responses to the following questions:

- Is pizza a healthy food?
- What toppings would you order for a pizza in a bucket?
- Why are consumers no longer as concerned with fats?

Preview

Preview the next selection to predict its purpose and organization and to formulate your learning plan.

Activate Schema

Do you prefer pizzas from Domino's, Pizza Hut, or Papa John's?

If your dream could become a reality, what small business would you start?

Establish a Purpose for Reading

Downsizing, outsourcing, women's increasing presence in the workforce, and the spread of Internet technology are contributing to the continuing American entrepreneurial spirit. The advantages and rewards of small business ownership are great, but so are the risks. What do you expect to learn from this selection about Papa John's and small businesses? After recalling what you already know about start-up businesses, read the selection to learn what defines a small business, why people open them, and why Papa John's is successful.

Increase Word Knowledge

What do you know about these words?

void	successive	droves	dominant	titans
novice	debut	vaulted	stagnant	heritage

Your instructor may give a true-false vocabulary review before or after reading.

Integrate Knowledge While Reading

Questions have been inserted in the margin to stimulate your thinking while reading. Remember to

Predict   Picture   Relate   Monitor   Correct

WHY IS PAPA JOHN'S ROLLING IN THE DOUGH?
Courtland Bovee, John Thill, Barbara Schatzman, *Business in Action*

As a high school student working at a local pizza pub, John Schnatter liked everything about the pizza business. "I liked making the dough; I liked kneading the dough; I liked putting the sauce on; I liked putting the toppings on; I liked running the oven," recalls Schnatter. Obsessed with perfect pizza

Why are bubbles bad?

5 topping and bubble-free melted cheese, Schnatter knew that something was missing from national pizza chains: superior-quality traditional pizza delivered to the customer's door. And his dream was to one day open a pizza restaurant that would fill that void.

Schnatter worked his way through college making pizzas, honing the tech-
10 niques and tastes that would someday become Papa John's trademark. Shortly after graduating from Ball State University with a business degree, he faced his

first business challenge. His father's tavern was $64,000 in debt and failing. So Schnatter sold his car, used the money to purchase $1,600 of used restaurant equipment, knocked out a broom closet in the back of his father's tavern, and
15   began selling pizzas to the tavern's customers. Soon the pizza became the tavern's main attraction and helped turn the failing business around. In 1985 Schnatter officially opened the first Papa John's restaurant. Then he set about opening as many stores and the market would bear.

But Schnatter needed a recipe for success. With Little Caesar's promoting
20   deep discounts and Domino's emphasizing fast delivery, Papa John's needed a fresh approach to compete successfully with the big chains. If you were John Schnatter, how would you grow a small pizza operation into one that could compete with national players? Would you franchise your concept? Would you remain a private enterprise or go public? Would you expand overseas?
25   Where would you focus your efforts?

Understanding the World of Small Business

Many small businesses start out like Papa Johns: with an entrepreneur, an idea, and a drive to succeed. In fact, the United States was originally founded by people involved in small business—the family farmer, the shopkeeper, the craftsperson. Successive waves of immigrants carried on the tradition, launch-
30   ing restaurants and laundries, providing repair and delivery services, and opening newsstands and bakeries.

The 1990s were a golden decade of entrepreneurship in the United States. Entrepreneurs launched small companies in droves to fill new consumer

| What companies succeeded? | → | needs. Many took advantage of Internet technologies to gain a competitive |

35   edge. Some succeeded; others failed. But the resurgence of small businesses helped turn the U.S. economy into the growth engine for the world.

Today, over 5.8 million small companies exist in the United States. But defining what constitutes a small business is surprisingly tricky, because *small* is a relative term.
40   One reliable source of information for small businesses is the Small Business Administration (SBA). This government agency serves as a resource and advocate for small firms, providing them with financial assistance, training, and a variety of helpful programs. The SBA defines a **small business** as a firm that (a) is independently owned and operated, (b) is not dominant in its field,
45   (c) is relatively small in terms of annual sales, and (d) has fewer than 500 employees. The SBA reports that 80 percent of all U.S. companies have annual sales of less than $1 million and that about 60 percent of the nation's employers have fewer than five workers.

Factors Contributing to the Increase in the Number of Small Businesses

Three factors are contributing to the increase in the number of small busi-
50   nesses today: technological advances, an increase in the number of women and minority business owners, and corporate downsizing and outsourcing.

Technology and the Internet

Do Internet companies have low start-up costs?

55 The Internet, together with e-commerce, has spawned thousands of new business ventures. ShippingSupply.com is one such firm. Karen Young, a collector of knickknacks, founded this small business when she was looking for affordable packing and shipping materials for her mail-order items. On a whim, Young decided to market bubble wrap, plastic foam, and shipping tubes she purchased direct from manufacturers to eBay sellers. Today, ShippingSupply.com has eight full-time employees, occupies 7,000 feet of warehouse space, and has over 35,500 customers in its database.

Rise in Number of Women and Minority Small-Business Owners

60 The number of women-owned small businesses has also increased sharply over the past three decades—from 5 percent to over 39 percent of all small businesses. These businesses now employ more than 18.5 million people and ring up more than $3.1 trillion in annual sales. Women are starting small businesses for a number of reasons. Some choose to run their own

65 companies so they can enjoy a more flexible work arrangement; others start their own businesses because of barriers to corporate advancement, known as the glass ceiling. Josie Natori is a perfect example of such a scenario. By her late twenties, Natori was earning six figures as the first female vice president of investment banking at Merrill Lynch. But Natori knew that

70 her chances of further advancement were slim in the male-dominated financial world. So she started her own lingerie line. Today, Natori is the owner of a multi-million-dollar fashion empire that sells elegant lingerie and evening wear.

John Schnattner, founder and President of the Papa John's Pizza chain, makes a surprise check at one of his 1,049 outlets.
Taro Yamasaki/Time Life Pictures/Getty Images

Downsizing and Outsourcing

Contrary to popular wisdom, business start-ups soar when the economy sours.
During hard times, many companies downsize or lay off talented employees,
who then have little to lose by pursuing self-employment. In fact, several
well-known companies were started during recessions. Tech titans William
Hewlitt and David Packard joined forces in Silicon Valley in 1938 during the
Great Depression. Bill Gates started Microsoft during the 1975 recession. And
the founders of Sun Microsystems, Compaq Computer, Adobe Systems, Silicon Graphics, and Locus Development started their companies in 1982—in
the midst of a recession and high unemployment.

To make up for layoffs of permanent staff, some companies **outsource** or
subcontract special projects and secondary business functions to experts outside the organization. Others turn to outsourcing as a way to permanently
eliminate entire company departments. Regardless of the reason, the increased
use of outsourcing provides opportunities for smaller businesses to serve the
needs of larger enterprises.

> Is this a cause and effect relationship?

Behind the Scenes: Papa John's Piping Hot Performance

John Schnatter did a remarkable job of expanding from a single pizza store
he started in his father's tavern. Three years after Schnatter opened his first
Papa John's, he expanded outside of the Louisville, Kentucky area. He was no
novice. He knew the grass roots of the pizza business, he had an intuitive
grasp on what customers wanted, and he knew how to make pizzas taste a
little bit better than the competition. Moreover, he had the qualities of an
entrepreneur: driven, intense, willing to make things happen, visionary, and
very competitive.

John Schnatter used franchising to grow the business. Today about 75 percent of Papa John's are franchised; the rest are company owned. He was
encouraged by Kentucky Fried Chicken, Long John Silvers, Chi Chi's, and
other Kentucky-born restaurants that had successfully taken their franchised
restaurants national. Schnatter thought, "What the heck, maybe I could do it
too." But to keep growth under control, Papa John's didn't just move into an
area and open up 200 stores. Schnatter grew the stores one at a time—spending up to six months to a year assessing an area's potential.

It wasn't long before Papa John's began grabbing business from such
giants as Pizza Hut, Little Caesar's, and delivery king Dominos. Then in
1999 Papa John's made its European debut by acquiring Perfect Pizza Holdings, a 205-unit delivery and carryout pizza chain in the United Kingdom.
The acquisition gave Papa John's instant access to proven sites that would
have been difficult to obtain. Besides the real estate, Perfect Pizza had a
good management team that Schnatter could fold into his organization.

Today, Papa John's has vaulted past Little Caesar's to become the nation's
third-largest pizza chain. The company now boasts over 2,700 stores in

47 states and 9 international markets. Annual sales have mushroomed to
about $1.7 billion. In spite of its tremendous growth, Schnatter insists on
maintaining the highest quality standards. He does so by keeping things

₁₁₅

simple. About 95 percent of the restaurants are takeout only. The menu is
simple—just two types of pizza, thin crust or regular—no exotic toppings,
no salads, no sandwiches, and no buffalo wings. Owners are trained to
remake pies that rate less than 8 on the company's 10-point scale. If
the cheese shows a single air bubble or the crust is not golden brown, out
the offender goes. Schnatter's attention to product quality has earned the
company awards. Papa John's was twice voted number one in customer
satisfaction among all fast-food restaurants in the American Consumer Satisfaction Index.

₁₂₀

₁₂₅

> Does lack of diversity lower costs? →

To keep things in order, Schnatter visits four to five stores a week, often
unannounced. He also trains managers how to forecast product demand. Stores
project demand one to two weeks in advance. They factor in anything from
forthcoming promotions to community events to the next big high school
football game. If a big game is on TV, Schnatter wants to make sure the store
owners are ready for the surge in deliveries.

₁₃₀

Still, like many companies today, Papa John's faces new challenges. It's
becoming increasingly difficult to grow the company's share of the pie.
Although Americans consume pizza at a rate of 350 slices a second, the
pizza industry is stagnant and highly competitive. Growth usually comes at
the expense of a competitor's existing business. Moreover, to keep profitability in line, Schnatter has scaled back company expansion plans and
even closed some unprofitable outlets. But Schnatter is determined to
succeed. And if one strength rises above the others in Schnatter's path to
success, it's his ability to recruit and retain the right people. "There's nothing special about John Schnatter except the people around me," Schnatter
says. "They make me look better" and they make Papa John's what it is—
committed to its heritage of making superior-quality, traditional pizza.
(1,634 words)

₁₃₅

₁₄₀

Recall

Stop to self-test, relate, and react.

Your instructor may choose to give you a true-false comprehension review.

Write About the Selection

What factors contribute to people opening small businesses? Why did John
Schnatter open his pizza business?

Response Suggestion: Discuss and explain the cause-and-effect relationship of at least five factors that prompt people to take risks and start something new.

Contemporary Link

Entrepreneurs in the fast-food business must be sensitive to changing public demands. Large fast-food chains frequently try out new products. You can probably think of several products that have succeeded and some that have failed. If sales in the pizza business are stagnant, perhaps new items should be considered. If you were opening a pizza store, what additional menu items would you add to expand sales and why? What trends or public needs would you seek to meet?

Skill Development: Identify Organizational Patterns

Answer the following with *T* (true) or *F* (false).

_____ 1. The first and last sections are examples with anecdotal information about a real business.

_____ 2. The section, *Understanding the World of Small Business*, defines a small business.

_____ 3. The organizational pattern of the section *Factors Contributing to the Increase in the Number of Small Businesses* is a simple listing.

_____ 4. The organizational pattern of the section *Downsizing and Outsourcing* is comparison-contrast.

Check Your Comprehension

After reading the selection, answer the following questions with *a, b, c,* or *d.* To help you analyze your strengths and weaknesses, the question types are indicated.

Main Idea _____ 1. Which is the best statement of the main idea of this selection?
   a. Through hard work, Papa John's has expanded globally and become the third-largest pizza company in the world.
   b. The golden decade for entrepreneurship has peaked but is not over as proved by Papa John's Pizza.
   c. Current factors are contributing to a rise in the number of small businesses, and Papa John's Pizza is a glowing example of one such entrepreneurial success.
   d. The highly competitive pizza business requires more than good tomato sauce to turn dough into dollars.

Detail   _____ 2. When John Schnatter started his pizza business, he had all the following except
    a. years of experience making pizza dough.
    b. a college degree in business.
    c. training in running the pizza ovens.
    d. restaurant equipment from his father's business.

Inference   _____ 3. The author implies that John Schnatter
    a. pulled his father's business out of a $64,000 debt.
    b. closed his father's tavern to open his pizza parlor.
    c. was financed in the pizza business by his father.
    d. continued to use the formula of liquor sales with pizza.

Detail   _____ 4. As defined by the Small Business Administration, a small business is all the following except
    a. has fewer than 500 employees.
    b. independently operated.
    c. owned by stock holders.
    d. not dominant in its field.

Inference   _____ 5. The author suggests that Karen Young's ShippingSupply.com business is
    a. primarily a retail store that customers enter to buy supplies.
    b. a prime candidate for franchising.
    c. a mail-order knickknack venture.
    d. a firm that conducts business over the Internet with supplies shipped from a warehouse.

Inference   _____ 6. The author implies that a glass ceiling is
    a. a barrier to high-level corporate advancement.
    b. a more flexible work arrangement.
    c. an entry into investment banking.
    d. a barrier to male-dominated entry positions.

Detail   _____ 7. Downsizing in a company means to
    a. fire incompetent workers.
    b. lay off valued employees.
    c. freeze hiring until profits improve.
    d. subcontract for special projects.

Inference   _____ 8. An example of an American company outsourcing would be
    a. selling products in India.
    b. hiring experienced European workers for an American company.
    c. contracting for payroll accounting to be done by a company in Ireland.
    d. buying coffee beans from Latin America and processing them in the United States.

Detail _____ 9. The author suggests that Schnatter's success can be attributed to all the following except
a. hiring good people.
b. adding a variety of items to the menu.
c. insisting on high-quality standards for pizzas.
d. personally visiting stores to keep things in order.

Inference _____ 10. The reader can conclude that of the company's 2,700 stores,
a. most are owned by Schnatter.
b. all but 340 stores are now franchised.
c. the company owns about 675 of them.
d. Perfect Pizza Holdings franchised 2,400 stores.

Answer the following with *T* (true), *F* (false), or *CT* (can't tell).

Detail _____ 11. During a recession and times of high unemployment, few
new businesses are started.

Detail _____ 12. According to the Small Business Administration, over half of
the small American businesses hire fewer than five workers.

Inference _____ 13. Schnatter bought Perfect Pizza in the United Kingdom
because it was poorly managed.

Inference _____ 14. The author suggests that Papa John's plans to expand into
salads and sandwiches.

Inference _____ 15. The author suggests that the pizza industry is rapidly increasing its customer base and adding new patrons who have
never tried pizza.

Build Your Vocabulary

According to the way the italicized word was used in the selection, select *a, b, c,* or *d* for the word or phrase that gives the best definition. The number in parentheses indicates the line of the passage in which the word is located.

_____ 1. "would fill that *void*" (8)
a. goal
b. empty space
c. union
d. demand

_____ 2. "*Successive* waves of
immigrants" (29)
a. one after another
b. eager
c. unsteady
d. overwhelming

_____ 3. "launched small companies
in *droves*" (33)
a. efforts
b. desperation
c. reactions
d. large numbers

_____ 4. "not *dominant* in its field" (44)
a. growing
b. foremost
c. secure
d. competitive

_____ 5. "Tech *titans*" (77)
   a. enthusiasts
   b. explorers
   c. giants
   d. hobbiests

_____ 6. "was no *novice*" (91)
   a. beginner
   b. pushover
   c. coward
   d. follower

_____ 7. "its European *debut*" (107)
   a. achievement
   b. marketing ploy
   c. market entry
   d. diversity

_____ 8. "has *vaulted* past
   Little Caesar's" (112)
   a. sneaked
   b. crawled
   c. leaped
   d. slowly moved

_____ 9. "pizza industry is *stagnant*"
   (135)
   a. nervous
   b. cutthroat
   c. small
   d. not growing

_____ 10. "committed to its *heritage*"
   (143)
   a. logo
   b. brand
   c. management
   d. tradition

Search the Net

Use a search engine such as Google, AltaVista, Excite, Infoseek, Dogpile, Yahoo, or Lycos to find information on the nutritional value of your favorite slice of pizza, as well as two other frequently consumed fast-food items. List the calories, carbohydrates, fats, and proteins for each. For suggested Web sites and other research activities, go to http://www.ablongman.com/smith/.

Concept Prep

for Business

What is a CD?

When you put money into a **CD (certificate of deposit)** through a bank, you are essentially loaning the bank money for a fixed interest rate and for a designated period, called the **maturity**. The CD matures for one month or up to five years, and the interest rate is higher for the more mature CDs. Banks then lend out the money at a higher rate for people to buy cars or houses. With a CD, the return of your **principal** (original money) is guaranteed. You do not have to worry about losing your money.

What is a bond?

A **bond** is a loan to a government or a corporation. For example, many cities sell **municipal bonds** to finance infrastructure improvements or schools. When you buy bonds, you are lending the city money, and the taxpayers will pay you interest. The interest rate on bonds is usually higher than that on CDs, but the risk is greater. You have a promise that you will be paid back at **maturity** (a specified period), and you hope the city will be able to fulfill this promise. If you buy a **U.S. Treasury Bill** or a **savings bond,** you are lending money to the federal government, which uses the money to pay down the national debt. Because U.S. Treasury bills are backed by the federal government, they are safer investments than are municipal bonds.

What is a mutual fund?

A **mutual fund** is a company that pools the investment money of many individuals and purchases a **portfolio** (array of holdings) of stocks, bonds, and other securities. Each investor then shares accordingly in the profits or losses. Investors also pay a fee for professionals to manage the portfolio, which includes bookkeeping, researching, buying, and selling. All fees for management come out of profits before they are shared.

An advantage of mutual funds is that they offer instant **diversification.** With a $1,000 purchase, you can have a part ownership in many different stocks and bonds. Also, if you do not have the expertise to research individual

John H. Johnson, publisher of Ebony magazine, and his daughter, Linda Johnson Rice, company president, run the fifty-year-old publishing business.
AP/Wide World Photos

stocks, you can rely on the judgment of the professional money managers. Different mutual funds specialize in different areas such as large companies, small companies, or even IPOs. You would want to find one that matches your investment interests and also has a positive track record of growth.

What is a capital gain?

A capital gain is a profit on the sale of a property or a security. A **short-term capital gain** is a profit made on a property or security owned for less than one year. This profit is taxed as ordinary income and may be as high as 40 percent for people in upper tax brackets. A **long-term capital gain,** on the other hand, is a profit on a property or security owned for over a year. On this, investors are taxed at a maximum of 20 percent.

REVIEW QUESTIONS

After studying the material, answer the following questions:

1. Are CD rates better for a month or a year? _____
   _____

2. What does the bank do with your CD money? _____
   _____

3. What is your principal? _____
   _____

4. What is a municipal bond? _____
   _____

5. What are the advantages of a mutual fund? _____
   _____

6. Is tax greater on a short- or long-term capital gain? _____
   _____

7. How long must you hold a property before selling to achieve a long-term capital gain? _____
   _____

8. What is a portfolio? _____
   _____

9. For the safest choice, should you pick bonds, CDs, or a mutual fund? _____
   _____

10. What does diversification mean? _____
    _____

Your instructor may choose to give a true-false review of these business concepts.

Vocabulary Booster

What's In, What's Out? What's Hot, What's Not?

Prefixes	Root
en-, em-: in	*e-, ec-, ef-, ex-:* out
non-: not	*calor:* heat

Words with *en-, em-:* in

Jackson was able to *employ* several of his friends as tech reps for his Internet software company.

■ *encapsulate:* to place in a capsule; to condense or summarize

Drug manufacturers *encapsulate* some medications so that they are easier to swallow.

■ *enclave:* any small, distinct area or group within a larger one

Before the Berlin Wall came down, West Berlin was a democratic *enclave* surrounded by communist East Germany.

■ *enmesh:* to catch in a net; entangle

Animal rights groups are against the use of nets in tuna fishing because dolphins become *enmeshed* in the nets and die.

■ *ensemble:* all parts of a thing considered only as the whole, not separately, such as an entire costume or a group of musicians, singers, dancers, or actors.

The cast of NBC's sitcom *Friends* was an *ensemble* of six actors.

■ *embed:* to fix or place firmly in a surrounding mass; to insert, as a clause in a sentence

The senator knew that to get her controversial proposal passed by Congress she had to *embed* it in a more popular bill.

■ *embroiled:* to be involved in conflict or confusion

The twins were *embroiled* in a wrestling match when their father finally had to separate them.

■ *embellish:* to beautify with ornamental or elaborate details

The speechwriter's goal was to enhance but not overly *embellish* the governor's speeches.

■ *enroll*: to register or become a member of a group

Jenny needed to *enroll* in the Psychology 101 class before it became filled.

Words with *e-, ec-, ef-, ex-*: out

It's best to renew your driver's license before it *expires* to avoid having to take the driving test again.

- *eclipse:* any obscuring of light (darkening) especially of planets; to surpass by comparison

To protect your eyes during a solar *eclipse*, wear sunglasses and look at the sun only through a pinhole in a piece of paper.

- *emaciate:* to make abnormally thin; a gradual wasting away

Tanica had lost so much weight on her fad diet that she looked *emaciated*.

- *eccentric:* peculiar or odd; not having the same center

The neighbor on the corner is an *eccentric* man who wears pajamas to the grocery store.

- *effervescent:* bubbling; lively or enthusiastic

The bottled spring water was so *effervescent* that they let it set awhile so the bubbles of gas could escape.

- *exalt:* raise or elevate in rank or character; praise highly

In his opening remarks, the club president *exalted* the literary talent and accomplishments of the guest speaker.

- *exaggerate:* to stretch the limits of the truth or overstate

John always *exaggerates* the size of the fish he claims he almost caught.

Words with *non-*: not

Military personnel such as surgeons or chaplains who are not fighters are considered *noncombatants*.

- *nonchalant:* coolly indifferent, unconcerned, unexcited

Tonia's *nonchalant* way of accepting dates makes it seem as though she just has nothing better to do.

- *nondescript:* undistinguished or dull, a person or thing of no specific type or kind; not easy to describe

Since the dorm rooms were extremely *nondescript*, students used imagination and money to decorate their space to reflect their own personalities.

- *nonpartisan:* an objective person; not controlled by any established political party

It is almost a necessity to have *nonpartisan* politics when the government is split evenly between two parties.

- **nonplussed:** completely puzzled, totally perplexed so as to become unable to continue

  The stand-up comedian was inexperienced and became totally *nonplussed* by the hecklers in the audience.

- **nonconformist:** someone who refuses to act in accordance with established customs

  A *nonformist* would not be a good candidate for a private school where uniforms are worn.

Words with *calor-*: heat

When capitalized, the word C*alorie* refers to a kilocalorie (1,000 small calories) and is used to measure the amount of energy produced by food when oxidized in the body.

- **calorie:** a specific unit of heat (cal.) in physics; a unit expressing the energy value of food (Cal.) in nutrition

  Judy always tries to eat low-*calorie* meals including salads, fish, lots of vegetables, and few desserts to maintain a healthy weight.

- **caloric:** of or pertaining to calories or heat; high in calories

  Eating highly *caloric* meals makes it necessary to exercise more often just to maintain your current weight.

- **scald:** to burn with hot liquid or steam; to bring to a temperature just short of the boiling point

  Some recipes require the cook to *scald* milk before adding it to the other ingredients.

- **caldera:** a basinlike depression or collapsed area caused by the explosion of the center of a volcano

  The scientists were injured by hot lava when they got too close to the edge of the *caldera* of a still active volcano.

- **cauldron:** a large kettle for boiling

  Shakespeare's *Macbeth* includes a scene with witches stirring their boiling mixture in a *cauldron*.

Review

Part I

Indicate whether the following sentences are true (*T*) or false (*F*).

_____ 1. An encapsulated version of a book is a shortened or condensed version.

_____ 2. Nonplussed is a mathematical term for omitting addition.

_____ 3. Starvation causes the body to become emaciated.

_____ 4. A person with an effervescent personality would probably be dull and uninteresting.

_____ 5. Embroiled describes a healthy way to have meats cooked.

_____ 6. A red BMW convertible would most likely be considered a nondescript vehicle.

_____ 7. Caldera is the lava that spills from a volcano.

_____ 8. An ensemble can be a group of people or things.

_____ 9. A Kilocalorie is equivalent to one hundred small calories.

_____ 10. A person who does not like parties or celebrations is known as a nonpartisan.

Part II

Choose the best antonym from the boxed list for the words below.

criticize	compliant	chill	dislodge	fatten	interested
minimized	undecorated	untangled	usual		

11. eccentric _____

12. embellished _____

13. exalt _____

14. exaggerated _____

15. emaciate _____

16. enmeshed _____

17. embed _____

18. nonchalant _____

19. scald _____

20. nonconformist _____

Your instructor may choose to give a multiple-choice review.

Organizing Textbook Information

- What is study reading?
- What is annotating?
- What is the Cornell Method of note taking?
- What is outlining?
- What is mapping?

Development II *by M. C. Escher, 1939. Woodcut in brown, grey-green and black, printed from 3 blocks. M. C. Escher's "Development II" © 2004 The M. C. Escher Company - Baarn - Holland. All rights reserved.*

The Demands of College Study

If you are like most students, you have already confronted new challenges in college. Your courses may cover a great deal of information more rapidly than you are used to; and the study techniques you used in high school may not be as effective in college. In a sense, college textbook assignments are like the Olympics of reading. Can you train like an athlete to meet the challenge?

Exercise 6.1

Discovering Your Fitness as a Reader

Take the following inventory to see how you already measure up. Check *yes* or *no* for your response.

What Kind of Reader Are You?

1. Do you mark your text while reading?   Yes_____ No_____
2. Do you make marginal notes while reading?   Yes_____ No_____
3. Do you take notes on paper while reading?   Yes_____ No_____
4. Do you differentiate between details and main ideas? Yes_____ No_____
5. Do you stop to summarize while reading?   Yes_____ No_____
6. Do you have a purpose behind note taking?   Yes_____ No_____
7. Do you review your textbook notes?   Yes_____ No_____
8. Do you review class lecture notes within 24 hours?   Yes_____ No_____
9. Do you link old and new information to remember it? Yes_____ No_____
10. Do you use maps or charts to condense notes for study? Yes_____ No_____

If all your answers were yes, you are well on your way to becoming an Olympic champ in the college arena! If some of your answers were no, you will want to start training now.

Your first assignment in most college courses will be to read Chapter 1 of the assigned textbook. At that time, you will immediately discover that a textbook chapter contains an amazing amount of information. Your instructor will continue to assign the remaining chapters in rapid succession. Don't panic! Your task is to select the information that you need to remember, learn it, and organize it for future study for a midterm or final exam that is weeks or months away.

In a study of the demands on students in introductory college history courses during a ten-week period,[1] three professors analyzed the actual reading demands of classes they observed and found that students were asked to

---

[1]J. G. Carson, N. D. Chase, S. U. Gibson, and M. F. Hargrove, "Literacy Demands of the Undergraduate Curriculum," *Reading, Research, and Instruction* 31 (1992): 25–30.

read an average of 825 pages in each class. The average length of weekly assignments was more than 80 pages, but the amount varied both with the professor and the topic. In one class, students had to read 287 pages in only ten days.

Students were expected to be able to see relationships between parts and wholes, to place people and events into a historical context, and to retain facts. Professors spent 85 percent of class time lecturing and 6 percent of the time giving tests, which often amounted to 100 percent of the final grade. In short, the demands were high and students were expected to work independently to organize textbook material efficiently and effectively to prepare for that crucial 6 percent of test-taking time

The task is difficult, but you have seen many others succeed—and even earn A's. Train for the challenge by using the skills of a successful learner. Consciously build knowledge networks—your foundation for thought interaction—and organize your materials for learning.

Building Knowledge Networks

The old notion of studying and learning is that studying is an information-gathering activity. Knowledge is the "product" you can acquire by transferring information from the text to your memory. According to this view, good learners locate important information, review it, and then transfer the information to long-term memory. The problem with this model is that review does not always guarantee recall, and rehearsal is not always enough to ensure that information is encoded into long-term memory.

Experts now know that studying and learning is more than review, rehearsal, and memorization; it requires making meaningful connections. Cognitive psychologists focus on schemata, or prior knowledge, and the learner's own goals. To understand and remember, you must link new information to already existing schemata, creating networks of knowledge. As your personal knowledge expands, you create new networks. As the learner, you—not your professor—decide how much effort you need to expend, and you adjust your studying according to your answers to questions such as "How much do I need to know?" "Will the test be multiple-choice or essay?" and "Do I want to remember this forever?" In this way, you make judgments and select the material to remember and integrate into knowledge networks.

Methods of Organizing Textbook Information

In this chapter, we discuss four methods of organizing textbook information for future study: (1) annotating, (2) note taking, (3) outlining, and (4) mapping. Why four? In a review of more than 500 research studies on organizing textbook information, two college developmental reading professors concluded that "no one study strategy is appropriate for all students in all study situations."[2] On the basis of these findings, they established guidelines encouraging students to develop a repertoire of skills in study reading. They felt that students need to know, for example, that underlining takes less time than note taking but that note taking or outlining can result in better test scores.

Your selection of a study-reading strategy for organizing textbook material will vary according to the announced testing demands, the nature of the material, the amount of time you have to devote to study, and your preference for a particular strategy. Being familiar with all four strategies affords a repertoire of choices.

The following comments on organizing textbook and lecture materials come from college freshmen taking an introductory course in American history. These students were enrolled in a Learning Strategies for History course that focused on how to be a successful student. Their comments probably address some of your experiences in trying to rapidly organize large amounts of textbook material.

From a student who earned an A:

Organization of my class notes is very important. The notes can be very easy to refer to if they are organized. This enables me to go back and fill in information, and it also helps me to understand the cycle of events that is taking place. I generally try to outline my notes by creating sections. Sections help me to understand the main idea or add a description of a singular activity. I usually go back and number the sections to make them easy for reference.

Taking notes can be very difficult sometimes. In class, if my mind strays just a few times, I can easily lose track of where my notes were going. Then again, when I am reading my textbook, I may read without even realizing what I just read. The difference in class and the textbook is that I can go back and reread the text.

It is very easy to overdo the notes that I take from the text. Originally, I tended to take too much information from the book, but now, as I read more, I can better grasp the main idea. Underlining also makes a big difference. When I underline, I can go back and reread the book.

From another student who earned an A:

I think that the best way to do it is to completely read the assignment and then go back over it to clear up any confusion. I would also recommend going over your lecture notes before starting your reading assignment, which is something I didn't do this past week. I also try to key in on words like "two significant changes" or "major factors." Sometimes you may go three or four pages without seeing anything like that. My question is, "What do you do then?" I think that you should write down the point or points that were repeated the most or stressed the most.

---

[2]D. Caverly and V. Orlando, *Textbook Strategies in Teaching Reading and Study Strategies at the College Level* (Newark, NJ: International Reading Association, 1991), pp. 86–165.

From a student who earned a B:

Taking notes is no longer something that you can just do and expect to have good and complete notes. I have learned that taking notes is a process of learning within itself.

From a student who earned a C:

In starting college, I have made a few changes in how I take notes. For instance, I am leaving a lot more space in taking notes. I find that they are easier to read when they are spread out. I have also been using a highlighter and marking topics and definitions and people's names. I make checks near notes that will definitely be on a test so I can go over them.

When I am reading, I have begun to do a lot of underlining in the book, which I would never do before because my school would not take back books if they were marked. I have also started to note important parts with a little star and confusing parts with a question mark.

All these students were successful in the history class, although the final grades varied. Each student's reflection offers sincere and sound advice. Regardless of the way you organize material—by annotating, note taking, outlining, or mapping—your goal should be to make meaning by making connections.

Annotating

Which of the following would seem to indicate the most effective use of the textbook as a learning tool?

1. A text without a single mark—not even the owner's name has spoiled the sacred pages
2. A text ablaze with color—almost every line is adorned with a red, blue, yellow, and/or green colored marker
3. A text with a scattered variety of markings—highlighting, underlines, numbers, and stars are interspersed with circles, arrows, and short, written notes

Naturally, option three is the best. The rationale for the first is probably for a better book resale value, but usually used books resell for the same price whether they are marked or unmarked. The reason for the second is probably procrastination in decision making. Students who highlight everything—the "yellow book disease"—rely on coming back later to figure out what is *really* important. Although selective highlighting in a light color such as yellow is a helpful strategy, highlighting everything is inefficient. The variety of markings in the third strategy enables you to pinpoint ideas for later study.

Why Annotate?

The textbook is a learning tool and should be used as such; it should not be preserved as a treasure. A college professor requires a particular text because it contains information vital to your understanding of the course material. The text places a vast body of knowledge in your hands, much more material than the professor could possibly give in class. It is your job to cull through this information, make some sense out of it, and select the important points that need to be remembered.

Annotating is a method of highlighting main ideas, major supporting details, and key terms. The word *annotate* means to add marks. By using a system of symbols and notations rather than just colored stripes, you mark the text after the first reading so that a complete rereading will not be necessary. The markings indicate pertinent points to review for an exam. If your time is short, however, highlighting with a colored marker is better than not making any marks at all. The Reader's Tip offers an example of annotation.

Marking in the textbook itself is frequently faster than summarizing, outlining, or note taking. In addition, since your choices and reactions are all in one place, you can view them at a glance for later study rather than referring to separate notebooks. Your textbook becomes a workbook.

Students who annotate, however, will probably want to make a list of key terms and ideas on their own paper to have a reduced form of the information for review and self-testing.

READER'S TIP

How to Annotate

Develop a system of notations. Use circles, stars, numbers, and whatever else helps you put the material visually into perspective. *Anything that makes sense to you is a correct notation.* Here is an example of one student's marking system:

Main idea	( )
Supporting material	————
Major trend or possible essay exam question	*
Important smaller point to know for multiple-choice item	✓
Word that you must be able to define	⬯
Section of material to reread for review	{ }
Numbering of important details under a major issue	(1), (2), (3)
Didn't understand and must seek advice	?
Notes in the margin	Ex., Def., Topic
Questions in the margin	Why signif.?
Indicating relationships	⌒
Related issue or idea	← R

When to Annotate

Plan to annotate after a unit of thought has been presented and you can view the information as a whole. This may mean marking after a single paragraph or after three pages; your marking will vary with the material.

When you are first reading, every sentence seems of major importance as each new idea unfolds, and you may be tempted to annotate too much. Resist this tendency, as overmarking wastes both reading time and review time. Instead, be patient and read through a passage or section until the end, at which point the author's complete thought will have been fully developed; and the major points will emerge from a background of lesser details. With all the facts at your fingertips and in your consciousness, you can decide what you want to remember. At the end of the course, your textbook should have that worn but well-organized look.

EXAMPLE The following passage is taken from a biology textbook. Notice how the annotations have been used to highlight main ideas and significant supporting details. This same passage will be used throughout this chapter to demonstrate each of the four methods of organizing textbook material.

Circulatory Systems

When we examine the systems by which blood reaches all the cells of an animal, we find two general types, known as open and closed circulatory systems.

Def. I

Open Circulatory Systems

The essential feature of the (**open circulatory system**) is that the blood moves through a body cavity—such as the abdominal cavity—and bathes the cells directly. The open circulatory system is particularly characteristic of insects and other arthropods, although it is also found in some other organisms.

In most insects the blood does not take a major part in oxygen transport. Oxygen enters the animal's body through a separate network of branching tubes that open to the atmosphere on the outside of the animal. (This type of respiratory system will be discussed in more detail in the next chapter.) Blood in an open circulatory system moves somewhat more slowly than in the average closed system. The slower system is adequate for insects because it does not have to supply the cells with oxygen.

Def. II

~~Closed Circulatory Systems~~

In a (**closed circulatory system**,) the <u>blood flows</u> through a well-defined

system of <u>vessels with many branches.</u> In the majority of closed systems the

blood is responsible for oxygen transport. To supply all the body cells with

sufficient oxygen, the blood must <u>move quickly through</u> the blood vessels. A

closed circulatory system must therefore have an efficient <u>pumping</u> mechanism,

or heart, to set the blood in motion and keep it moving briskly through the

body.

Ex. 4

<u>All vertebrates</u> possess closed circulatory systems. Simple closed systems are

also found in some invertebrates, including annelid worms. A good example of

such a simple closed circulatory system can be seen in the <u>earthworm.</u>

Ex. R ——→ regeneration?

Exercise 6.2

Annotating

Using a variety of markings, annotate the following selection as if you were preparing for a quiz on the material. Remember, do not underscore as you read, but wait until you finish a paragraph or a section and then mark the important points.

Stress Management

Each of us has our own optimum stress level, which is influenced by heredity and other factors. Some people thrive at stress levels that would quickly lead others to the state of exhaustion. How can we tell if we are stressed beyond our optimum level? Sometimes it is obvious; but, more often we fail to associate the symptoms we experience with their cause. Different people respond to stress differently. For example, one person might gorge him- or herself with food while another might lose his or her appetite. One person might have trouble falling asleep at night while another person might sleep most of the time.

General Guidelines for Stress Management

Adopt a new way of looking at life. Stress management begins with adopting the philosophy that you, as an individual, are basically responsible for your own emotional and physical well-being. You can no longer allow other people to determine whether or not you are happy. You have little control over the behavior of anyone but yourself, and your emotional well-being is too important to trust to anyone but yourself. Your goal should be to develop such positive emotional wellness that nobody can ruin your day.

A positive outlook on life. This is absolutely essential to successful stress management. Your perception of events, not the events themselves, is what causes stress. Almost any life situation can be perceived as either stressful or nonstressful, depending on your interpretation. A negative view of life guarantees a high stress level. People who habitually view life negatively can recondition themselves to be more positive. One way is by applying a thought-stopping technique: Whenever you catch yourself thinking negatively, force yourself to think about the positive aspects of your situation. Eventually you will just automatically begin to see life more positively.

A regular exercise program. Exercise is an excellent tension reliever. In addition to the physical benefits, exercise is also good for the mind. Participating in at least three aerobic exercise sessions a week for at least 20 minutes each can greatly reduce stress. Daily stretching exercises provide relaxation and improve flexibility and posture. Participate in leisure activities that keep you physically active.

Be reasonably organized. Disorganization, sloppiness, chaos, and procrastination may seem very relaxed, but they are stressful. Set short-term, intermediate-term, and long-term goals for yourself. Every morning list the things you want and need to accomplish that day.

Learn to say no. Some people accept too many responsibilities. If you spread yourself too thin, not only will you be highly stressed, but important things will be done poorly or not at all. Know your limits and be assertive. If you don't have time to do something or simply don't want to do it, don't. Practice saying no effectively. Try, "I'm flattered that you've asked me, but given my commitments at this time, I won't be able to. . . ."

Learn to enjoy the process. Our culture is extremely goal oriented. Many of the things we are directed toward achieving a goal, with no thought or expectation of enjoying the process. You may go to college for a degree, but you should enjoy the process of obtaining that degree. You may go to work for a paycheck, but you should enjoy your work. Happiness can seldom be achieved when pursued as a goal. It is usually a by-product of other activities. In whatever you do, focus on and enjoy the activity itself, rather than on how well you perform the activity or what the activity will bring you.

Don't be a perfectionist. Perfectionists set impossible goals for themselves, because perfection is unattainable. Learn to tolerate and forgive both yourself and others. Intolerance of your own imperfections leads to stress and low self-esteem. Intolerance of others leads to anger, blame, and poor relationships, all of which increase stress.

Look for the humor in life. Humor can be an effective part of stress management. Humor results in both psychological and physical changes. Its psychological effects include relief from anxiety, stress, and tension, an escape from reality, and a means of tolerating difficult life situations. Physically, laughter increases muscle activity, breathing rate, heart rate, and release of brain chemicals such as catecholamines and endorphins.

Practice altruism. **Altruism** is unselfishness, placing the well-being of others ahead of one's own. Altruism is one of the best roads to happiness, emotional health, and stress management. As soon as you start feeling concern for the needs of others, you immediately feel less stressed over the frustration of your own needs. Invariably, the most selfish people are the most highly stressed as they focus their attention on the complete fulfillment of their own needs, which can never happen.

Let go of the past. Everyone can list things in the past that he or she might have done differently. Other than learning through experience and trying not to make the same mistakes again, there is nothing to be gained by worrying about what you did or didn't do in the past. To focus on the past is nonproductive, stressful, and robs the present of its joy and vitality.

Eat a proper diet. How you eat affects your emotions and your ability to cope. When your diet is good you feel better and deal better with difficult situations. Try eating more carefully for two weeks and feel the difference it makes.

There is no unique stress-reduction diet, despite many claims to the contrary. The same diet that helps prevent heart disease, cancer, obesity, and diabetes (low in sugar, salt, fat, and total calories; adequate in vitamins, minerals, and protein) will also reduce stress.

Get adequate sleep. Sleep is essential for successfully managing stress and maintaining your health. People have varying sleep requirements, but most people function best with seven to eight hours of sleep per day. Some people simply don't allot enough time to sleep, while others find that stress makes it difficult for them to sleep.

Avoid alcohol and other drugs. The use of alcohol and other drugs in an effort to reduce stress levels actually contributes to stress in several ways. In the first place, it does *not* reduce the stress from a regularly occurring stressor such as an unpleasant job or relationship problems. Further, as alcohol and other drugs wear off, the rebound effect makes the user feel very uncomfortable and more stressed than before.

Don't overlook the possibility that excess caffeine intake is contributing to your stress. Caffeine is a powerful stimulant that, by itself, produces many of the physiological manifestations of stress. Plus, its effect of increased "nervous" energy contributes to more stressful, rushed behavior patterns. Remember that not only coffee and tea but chocolate and many soft drinks contain caffeine.

Checkpoint

1. Why might two people in the same situation experience very different stress levels?

2. What is meant by "learn to enjoy the process"?

3. In what ways can being other-centered help reduce stress?

Curtis O. Boyer and Louis W. Shainberg, *Living Well*

Review your annotations. Have you sufficiently highlighted the main idea and the significant supporting details?

Note Taking

Many students prefer **note taking,** or jotting down on their own paper brief sentence summaries of important textbook information. With this method, margin space to the left of the summaries can be used to identify topics. Thus, important topics and their explanations are side-by-side on notepaper for later study. To reduce notes for review and trigger thoughts for self-testing, highlight key terms with a yellow marker. The Reader's Tip summarizes one note-taking method.

READER'S TIP

How to Take Notes

One of the most popular systems of note taking is called the Cornell Method. The steps are as follows:

1. Draw a line down your paper two and one-half inches from the left side to create a two-and-one-half-inch margin for noting key words and a six-inch area on the right for sentence summaries.

2. After you have finished reading a section, tell yourself what you have read, and jot down sentence summaries in the six-inch area on the right side of your paper. Use your own words, and make sure you have included the main ideas and significant supporting details. Be brief, but use complete sentences.

3. Review your summary sentences and underline key words. Write these key words in the column on the left side of your paper. These words can be used to stimulate your memory of the material for later study.

Why Take Textbook Notes?

Students who prefer note taking say that working with a pencil and paper while reading keeps them involved with the material and thus improves concentration. This method takes longer than annotating, but after annotating the text, you may at times feel an additional need—based on later testing demands, time, and the complexity of the material—to organize the information further into notes.

You can use the Cornell Method to take notes on classroom lectures. The chart shown on the following page, developed by Norman Stahl and James King, explains the procedure and gives a visual display of the results.

The example on page 291 applies the Cornell Method of note taking to the biology passage on the circulatory system that you have already read (see pages 285–286). Although the creators of this method recommend the writing of sentence summaries, you may find that writing short phrases can sometimes be as or more efficient and still adequately communicate the message for later study.

Taking Class Notes: The Cornell Method	
← 2¹/₂ INCHES →	← 6 INCHES →
REDUCE IDEAS TO CONCISE JOTTINGS AND SUMMARIES AS CUES FOR RECITING.	RECORD THE LECTURE AS FULLY AND AS MEANINGFULLY AS POSSIBLE.
Cornell Method	This sheet demonstrates the Cornell Method of taking classroom notes. It is recommended by experts from the Learning Center at Cornell University.
Line drawn down paper	You should draw a line down your notepage about 2¹/₂ inches from the left side. On the right side of the line simply record your classroom notes as you usually do. Be sure that you write legibly.
After the lecture	After the lecture you should read the notes, fill in materials that you missed, make your writing legible, and underline any important materials. Ask another classmate for help if you missed something during the lecture.
Use the recall column for key phrases	The recall column on the left will help you when you study for your tests. Jot down any important words or key phrases in the recall column. This activity forces you to rethink and summarize your notes. The key words should stick in your mind.
Five Rs	The Five Rs will help you take better notes based on the Cornell Method.
Record	1. Record any information given during the lecture which you believe will be important.
Reduce	2. When you reduce your information you are summarizing and listing key words/phrases in the recall column.
Recite	3. Cover the notes you took for your class. Test yourself on the words in the recall section. This is what we mean by recite.
Reflect	4. You should reflect on the information you received during the lecture. Determine how your ideas fit in with the information.
Review	5. If you review your notes you will remember a great deal more when you take your midterm.
Binder & paper	Remember it is a good idea to keep your notes in a standard-sized binder. Also you should use only full-sized binder paper. You will be able to add mimeographed materials easily to your binder.
Hints	Abbreviations and symbols should be used when possible. Abbrev. & sym. give you time when used automatically.

Circulatory System	
Two types Open and closed	There are two types, the open and the closed, by which blood reaches the cells of an animal.
Open	In the open system, found mostly in insects and other arthropods, blood moves through the body and bathes the cells directly. The blood moves slower
Bathes cells	than in the closed system, and oxygen
Oxygen from outside	is supplied from the outside air through tubes.
Closed Blood vessels Blood carries oxygen Heart pumps	In the closed system, blood flows through a system of vessels, oxygen is carried by the blood so it must move quickly, and the heart serves as a pumping mechanism. All vertebrates, as well as earthworms, have closed systems.

Exercise 6.3

Note Taking

In college courses, you will usually take notes on lengthy chapters or entire books. For practice with note taking here, use the passage, "Stress Management," which you have already annotated (pages 286–288). Prepare a two-column sheet, and take notes using the Cornell Method.

Outlining

Outlining enables you to organize and highlight major points and subordinates items of lesser importance. In a glance, the indentations, Roman numerals, numbers, and letters quickly show how one idea relates to another and how all aspects relate to the whole. The layout of the outline is simply a graphic display of main ideas and significant supporting details.

The following example is a picture-perfect version of the basic outline form. In practice your "working outline" would probably not be as detailed or as regular as this. Use the tools of the outline format, *especially the indentations and numbers,* to devise your own system for organizing information.

I. First main idea
   A. Supporting idea
      1. Detail
      2. Detail
      3. Detail
         a. Minor detail
         b. Minor detail
   B. Supporting idea
      1. Detail
      2. Detail
   C. Supporting idea
II. Second main idea
   A. Supporting idea
   B. Supporting idea

Why Outline?

Students who outline usually drop the preciseness of picture-perfect outlines but still make good use of the numbers, letters, indentations, and mixture of topics and phrases from the system to take notes and show levels of importance. A quick look to the far left of an outline indicates the topic with subordinate ideas indented underneath. The letters, numbers, and indentations form a visual display of the significance of the parts that make up the whole. Good outliners use plenty of paper so the levels of importance are evident at a glance.

Another use of the outline is to organize notes from class lectures. During class, most professors try to add to the material in the textbook and put it into perspective for students. Since the notes taken in class represent a large percentage of the material you need to know to pass the course, they are extremely important.

How to Outline

While listening to a class lecture, you must almost instantly receive, synthesize, and select material and, at the same time, record something on paper for future reference. The difficulty of the task demands order and decision making. Do not be so eager to copy down every detail that you miss the big picture. One of the most efficient methods of taking lecture notes is to use a modified outline form—a version that adds stars, circles, and underlines to emphasize further the levels of importance.

Professors say that they can walk around a classroom and look at the notes students have taken from the text or from a lecture and tell how well each student has understood the lesson. The errors most frequently observed fall into the following categories. The Reader's Tip provides more details about how to outline.

1. Poor organization

2. Failure to show importance

3. Writing too much

4. Writing too little

READER'S TIP

Guidelines for Successful Outlining

The most important thing to remember when outlining is to ask yourself, *"What is my purpose?"* You don't need to include everything, and you don't need a picture-perfect version for study notes. Include only what you believe you will need to remember later, and use a numbering system and indentations to show how one item relates to another. There are several other important guidelines to remember:

♦ **Get a general overview before you start.**

How many main topics do there seem to be?

♦ **Use phrases rather than sentences.**

Can you state it in a few short words?

♦ **Put it in your own words.**

If you cannot paraphrase it, do you really understand it?

♦ **Be selective.**

Are you highlighting or completely rewriting?

♦ **After outlining, indicate key terms with a yellow marker.**

Highlighting makes them highly visible for later review and self-testing.

EXAMPLE   Notice how numbers, letters, and indentations are used in the following outline to show levels of importance.

Circulatory System

I. Open circulatory system
   A. Blood moves through the body and bathes cells directly
   B. Examples—insects and other arthropods
   C. Oxygen supplied from outside air through tubes
   D. Slower blood movement since not supplying cells with oxygen
II. Closed circulatory system
   A. Blood flows through system of vessels
   B. Oxygen carried by blood so it must move quickly
   C. Heart serves as pumping mechanism
   D. Example—all vertebrates
   E. Example—earthworms

Exercise 6.4

Outlining

Outline the key ideas in the following selection as if you were planning to use your notes to study for a quiz. You may want to annotate before you outline.

Reacting to Stress with Defense Mechanisms

Stress may occasionally promote positive outcomes. Motivated to overcome stress and the situations that produce it, we may learn new and adaptive responses. It is also clear, however, that stress involves a very unpleasant emotional component. **Anxiety** is a general feeling of tension or apprehension that often accompanies a perceived threat to one's well-being. It is this unpleasant emotional component that often prompts us to learn new responses to rid ourselves of stress.

There are a number of techniques, essentially self-deception, that we may employ to keep from feeling the unpleasantness associated with stress. These techniques, or tricks we play on ourselves, are not adaptive in the sense of helping us to get rid of anxiety by getting rid of the source of stress. Rather, they are mechanisms that we can and do use to defend ourselves against the *feelings* of stress. They are called **defense mechanisms.** Freud believed defense mechanisms to be the work of the unconscious mind. He claimed that they are ploys that our unconscious mind uses to protect us (our *self* or *ego*) from stress and anxiety. Many psychologists take issue with Freud's interpretation of defense mechanisms and consider defense mechanisms in more general terms than did Freud, but few will deny that defense mechanisms exist. It *is* true that they are generally ineffective if consciously or purposively employed. The list of defense mechanisms is a long one. Here, we'll review some of the more common defense mechanisms, providing an example of each, to give you an idea of how they might serve as a reaction to stress.

Repression. The notion of **repression** came up earlier in our discussion of memory. In a way, it is the most basic of all the defense mechanisms. It is sometimes referred to as *motivated forgetting,* which gives us a good idea of what is involved. Repression is a matter of conveniently forgetting about some stressful, anxiety-producing event, conflict, or frustration. Paul had a teacher in high school he did not get along with at all. After spending an entire semester trying his best to do whatever was asked, Paul failed the course. The following summer, while walking with his girlfriend, Paul encountered this teacher. When he tried to introduce his girlfriend, Paul could not remember his teacher's name. He had repressed it. As a long-term reaction to stress, repressing the names of people we don't like or that we associate with unpleasant, stressful experiences is certainly not a very adaptive reaction. But at least it can protect us from dwelling on such unpleasantness.

Denial. **Denial** is a very basic mechanism of defense against stress. In denial, a person simply refuses to acknowledge the realities of a stressful situation. When a physician first tells a patient that he or she has a terminal illness, a common reaction is denial; the patient refuses to believe that there is anything seriously wrong.

Other less stressful events than serious illness sometimes evoke denial. Many smokers are intelligent individuals who are well aware of the data and the statistics that can readily convince them that they are slowly (or rapidly) killing themselves by continuing to smoke. But they deny the evidence. Somehow they are able to convince themselves that they aren't going to die from smoking; that's something that happens to other people, and besides, they *could* stop whenever they wanted.

Rationalization. **Rationalization** amounts to making excuses for our behaviors when facing the real reasons for our behaviors would be stressful. The real reason Kevin failed his psychology midterm is that he didn't study for it and has missed a number of classes. Kevin hates to admit, even to himself, that he could have been so stupid as to flunk that exam because of his own actions. As a result, he rationalizes: "It wasn't really *my* fault. I had a lousy instructor. We used a rotten text. The tests were grossly unfair. I've been fighting the darn flu all semester. And Marjorie had that big party the night before the exam." Now Susan, on the other hand, really did want to go to Marjorie's party, but she decided that she wouldn't go unless somebody asked her. As it happens, no one did. In short order, Susan rationalized that she "didn't want to go to that dumb party anyway"; she needed to "stay home and study."

Compensation. We might best think of **compensation** in the context of personal frustration. This defense mechanism is a matter of overemphasizing some positive trait or ability to counterbalance a shortcoming in some other trait or ability. If some particular goal-directed behavior becomes blocked, a person may compensate by putting extra effort and attention into some other aspect of behavior. For example, Karen, a seventh grader, wants to be popular. She's a reasonably bright and pleasant teenager, but isn't—in the judgment of her classmates—very pretty. Karen *may* compensate for her lack of good looks by studying very hard to be a good student, or by memorizing jokes and funny stories, or by becoming a good musician. Compensation is not just an attempt to be a well-rounded individual. It is a matter of expending *extra* energy and resources in one direction to offset short-comings in other directions.

Fantasy. **Fantasy** is one of the more common defense mechanisms used by college students. It is often quite useful. Particularly after a hard day when stress levels are high, isn't it pleasant to sit in a comfortable chair, kick off your shoes, lie back, close your eyes, and daydream, perhaps about graduation day, picturing yourself walking across the stage to pick up your diploma—with honors?

When things are not going well for us, we may retreat into a world of fantasy where everything always goes well. Remember that to engage from time to time in fantasizing is a normal and acceptable response to stress. You should not get worried if you fantasize occasionally. On the other hand, you should realize that there are some potential dangers here. You need to be able to keep separate those activities that are real and those that occur in your fantasies. And you should realize that fantasy in itself will not solve whatever problem is causing you stress. Fantasizing about academic successes may help you feel better for a while, but it is not likely to make you a better student.

Projection. **Projection** is a matter of seeing in others those very traits and motives that cause us stress when we see them in ourselves. Under pressure to do well on an exam, Mark may want to cheat, but his conscience won't let him. Because of projection, he may think he sees cheating going on all around him.

Projection is a mechanism that is often used in conjunction with hostility and aggression. When people begin to feel uncomfortable about their own levels of hostility, they often project their aggressiveness onto others, coming to believe that others are "out to do me harm," and "I'm only defending myself."

Regression. To employ **regression** is to return to earlier, even childish, levels of behavior that were once productive or reinforced. Curiously enough, we often find regression in children. Imagine a four-year-old who until very recently was an only child. Now Mommy has returned from the hospital with a new baby sister. The four-year-old is no longer "the center of the universe," as her new little sister now gets parental attention. The four-year-old reverts to earlier behaviors and starts wetting the bed, screaming for a bottle of her own, and crawling on all fours in an attempt to get attention. She is regressing.

Many defense mechanisms can be seen on the golf course, including regression. After Doug knocks three golf balls into the lake, he throws a temper tantrum, stamps his feet, and tosses his three-iron in the lake. His childish regressive behavior won't help his score, but it may act as a release from the tension of his stress at the moment.

Displacement. The defense mechanism of **displacement** is usually discussed in the context of aggression. Your goal-directed behavior becomes blocked or thwarted. You are frustrated, under stress, and somewhat aggressive. You cannot vent your aggression directly at the source of the frustration, so you displace it to a safer outlet. Dorothy expects to get promoted at work, but someone else gets the new job she wanted. Her goal-directed behavior has been frustrated. She's upset and angry at her boss, but feels (perhaps correctly) that blowing her top at her boss will do more harm than good. She's still frustrated, so she displaces her hostility toward her husband, children, and/or the family cat.

Displacement doesn't have to involve hostility and aggression. A young couple discovers that having children is not going to be as easy as they thought. They want children badly, but there's an infertility problem that is causing considerable stress. Their motivation for love, sharing, and caring may be displaced toward a pet, nephews and nieces, or some neighborhood children—at least until their own goals can be realized with children of their own.

The list of defense mechanisms provided above is not an exhaustive one. These are among the most common, and this list gives you an idea of what defense mechanisms are like.

Josh Gerow, *Psychology: An Introduction,* 2nd ed.

Exercise 6.5

Outlining

For additional practice, outline the selection on "Stress Management" beginning on page 286. Use your annotations and notes to help.

Mapping

Mapping is a visual system of condensing material to show relationships and importance. A map is a diagram of the major points, with their significant subpoints, that support a topic. The purpose of mapping as an organizing strategy is to improve memory by grouping material in a highly visual way.

Why Map?

Proponents of popular learning style theories (see the discussion of multiple intelligences in Chapter 1) would say that mapping offers a visual organization that appeals to learners with a preference for spatial representation, as opposed to the linear mode offered by outlining and note taking. A map provides a quick reference to overviewing an article or a chapter and can be used to reduce notes for later study. The Reader's Tip shows the steps in mapping.

READER'S TIP

How to Map

Use the following steps for mapping:

- ◆ **Draw a circle or a box** in the middle of a page, and in it write the subject or topic of the material.

- ◆ **Determine the main ideas** that support the subject, and write them on lines radiating from the central circle or box.

- ◆ **Determine the significant details,** and write them on lines attached to each main idea. The number of details you include will depend on the material and your purpose.

Maps are not restricted to any one pattern but can be formed in a variety of creative shapes, as the diagrams on the next page illustrate.

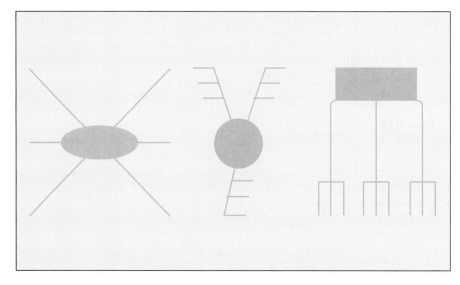

The following map highlights the biology passage on the circulatory system (see pages 285–286). Notice how the visual display emphasizes the groups of ideas supporting the topic.

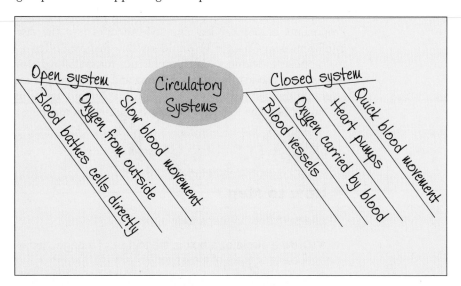

Exercise 6.6	**Mapping**

Return to Exercise 6.4 and design a map for the selection entitled "Reacting to Stress with Defense Mechanisms," which you previously outlined. Use your outline to help you design the map. Experiment with several different shapes for your map patterns on notebook or unlined paper. For additional practice, design a map for the selection in Exercise 6.2.

Summary Points

● What is study reading?

Study reading is textbook reading. It is reading to learn and involves establishing knowledge networks. Students must select which textbook information to remember and organize it to facilitate further study.

● What is annotating?

Annotating is a method of using symbols and notations to highlight main ideas, significant supporting details, and key terms.

● What is the Cornell Method of note taking?

The Cornell Method is a system of note taking that includes writing summary sentences and marginal notes.

● What is outlining?

Outlining is a method that follows a specified sequence of main ideas and significant supporting details.

● What is mapping?

Mapping is a visual system of condensing material to show relationships and importance.

CONTEMPORARY FOCUS

With such great power to capture our attention and influence thinking, does mass media—that is, newspapers, magazines, television, radio, movies, the Internet—conduct business in a responsible manner? How has our perception of "what's acceptable" changed over the years? Have we become slaves to the quest for profitability? Is this new tolerance for acceptability changing our values and cultural norms?

MEDIA-PROMOTED MORALS CLOUD JUDGMENT

By Jessica Smith

The Sentry, via University Wire Crowder College, Neosho, Mo., February 3, 2004

College students go to class, study for exams and generally enjoy the freedom that we have after leaving the parental nest. However, that freedom can be abused and moral relativism is leading many to do exactly that.

Moral relativism is a way of thinking in which right and wrong don't exist. A moral relativist thinks that anyone who does something morally wrong isn't a criminal. They are just doing what they feel like doing, and that is freedom of expression protected by the Constitution. This applies as much to a pedophile as it does to an ordinary person. How does it apply to college students?

College students are often criticized for "living for the moment" and often feel compelled to live up to that stereotype of heavy drinking, casual sex, and flying in the face of the moral values they were raised on.

Even though it is ultimately up to students how they conduct themselves, the outside world has a tremendous effect on what influences them. Magazines, TV, music and the Internet have created an explosion that is bombarding us with images and lyrics of partying, drinking and casual sex.

Unfortunately, those who were not raised with good morals are likely to believe the lifestyle portrayed is acceptable when, in fact, it's likely to destroy them from within. This is exactly what moral relativism does. Take these examples.

Television routinely markets garbage because it's profitable. MTV's Spring Break coverage is pretty much the same flood of images of young college students drinking with abandon, wet T-shirt contests and general hedonism. The "Girls Gone Wild" videos further push the envelope by showing likely drunk girls flashing their breasts for video cameras.

One side effect of this explosion of garbage is that fewer people take responsibility for their own actions anymore. However, we can fight back if we remember the values that our country was founded upon. Values like honesty, morality, and self-discipline are hallmarks every American citizen should follow.

Collaborate

Collaborate on responses to the following questions:

- Was this written by a student? How do you know?
- How would you explain moral relativism? Give an example.
- What media stereotyping of college students do you find objectionable?

Preview

Preview the next selection to predict its purpose and organization and to formulate your learning plan.

Activate Schema

Which print or electronic magazines do you read regularly?

Why do you think people participate in blogging and Web sites like Friendster?

Establish a Purpose for Reading

What impact have magazines had on our culture? What do you expect to learn from this selection? After recalling what you already know about the history and evolution of magazines, read the selection to find out how we are influenced by magazines. What early innovations made magazines such a popular medium?

Increase Word Knowledge

What do you know about these words?

means	vie	aficionados	haunting	indelible
universal	diminutive	scoffers	novel	disdained

Your instructor may give a true-false vocabulary review before or after reading.

Integrate Knowledge While Reading

Questions have been inserted in the margin to stimulate your thinking while reading. Remember to

Predict	Picture	Relate	Monitor	Correct

Skill Development: Note Taking

Annotate this selection and then make a study outline for the key ideas as if you were planning to use your notes to study for a quiz.

INFLUENCE OF MAGAZINES

From John Vivian, *The Media of Mass Communication*

The first successful magazines in the United States, in the 1820s, were much less expensive than books. People of ordinary means could afford them. Unlike newspapers, which were oriented to their cities of publication, early magazines created national audiences. This contributed to a sense of nationhood at a time when an American culture, distinctive from its European heritage, had not yet emerged. The American people had their magazines in common. The *Saturday Evening Post*, founded in 1821, carried fiction by Edgar Allan Poe, Nathaniel Hawthorne and Harriet Beecher Stowe to readers who could not afford books. Their short stories and serialized novels flowed from the American experience and helped Americans establish a national identity.

> What is a national identity?

With the Postal Act of 1879, Congress recognized the role of magazines in creating a national culture and promoting literacy—in effect, binding the nation. The law allowed a discount on mailing rates for magazines, a penny a pound. Magazines were being subsidized, which reduced distribution costs and sparked dramatic circulation growth. New magazines cropped up as a result.

National Advertising Medium

Advertisers used magazines through the 1800s to build national markets for their products, which was an important factor in transforming the United States from an agricultural and cottage industry economy into a modern economy. This too contributed to a sense of nationhood.

Massive Magazine Audience

The American people have a tremendous appetite for magazines. According to magazine industry studies, almost 90 percent of U.S. adults read an average 10 issues a month. Although magazines are affordable for most people, the household income of the typical reader is 5 percent more than the national average. In general, the more education and higher income a person has, the greater the person's magazine consumption.

> How many do I read?

The massiveness of the audience makes the magazine an exceptionally competitive medium. About 12,000 magazines vie for readers in the United States, ranging from general interest publications such as *Reader's Digest* to such specialized publications as *Chili Pepper*, for people interested in hot foods, and *Spur*, for racehorse aficionados. In recent years 500 to 600 new magazines have been launched annually, although only one in five survives into its third year. Even among major magazines, a huge following at the moment is no guarantee of survival. Of the 23 U.S. magazines with a circulation of more than 1 million in 1946, 10 no longer exist. Magazine publishing is a risky business.

Magazines as Media Innovators

Magazines have led other media with significant innovations in journalism, photojournalism, circulation, and niche marketing

Margaret Bourke-White's Photojournalism

The oversized *Life* magazine created by Henry Luce was the perfect forum for the work of Margaret Bourke-White. The giant pages, 13½ inches high

40 and opening to 21-inch spreads, gave such impact to photos that they seemed to jump off the page at readers. Bourke-White was there at the beginning, shooting the immense Fort Peck Dam in Montana for *Life*'s first cover in 1936. Over her career, Bourke-White shot 284 assignments for *Life*, many of them enduring images from World War II. These included Holo-

45 caust victims in a Nazi concentration camp, great military movements, and the leaders of the time in both triumph and defeat. She was among the first great photojournalists.

Bourke-White's photojournalism went beyond the news and emotions of any given day to penetrate the core of great social problems. In collaboration with

Did her stories change their lives?

50 writer Erskine Caldwell, to whom she was later married, Bourke-White created a photo documentary on the tragic lives of sharecroppers in the American South. Later, in South Africa, she went underground to photograph gold miners who were known only by numbers. Her haunting photos from the Midwest drought of the 1930s created indelible images in the minds of a genera-

55 tion. These were socially significant projects that moved people and changed public policy.

DeWitt and Lila Wallace's Mass Circulation

Reader's Digest is usually considered to have the largest circulation of any U.S. magazine. Dewitt and Lila Wallace had an idea but hardly any money. The idea was a pocket-sized magazine that condensed informational, inspiring and

60 entertaining nonfiction from other publications—a digest. With borrowed money the Wallaces brought out their first issue of *Reader's Digest* in 1922.

The rest, as they say, is history. In 1947 the *Digest* became the first magazine to exceed a circulation of 9 million. Except for the Sunday newspaper supplement

Why has it been so popular?

Parade, Reader's Digest has been the nation's largest-circulation magazine most of 65 the time since then. In 1999 *Reader's Digest* circulation was 12.6 million—not counting an additional 12.2 million overseas in 18 languages.

The magazine has remained true to the Wallaces' successful formula. DeWitt and Lila Wallace, children of poor Presbyterian clergy, wanted "constructive articles," each with universal appeal. The thrust was upbeat but

70 not Pollyanna. Digested as they were, the articles could be quickly read. America loved it.

For its first 33 years, *Reader's Digest* was wholly reader supported. It carried no advertising. Rising postal rates forced a change in 1955. There was scoffing

American photographer and journalist Margaret Bourke-White focuses a
camera on New York City from a perch on an eagle head at the top of the
Chrysler building in 1935.
Oscar Graubner/Time Life/Getty Images

75 about whether advertisers would go for "postage-stamp-sized ads" in *Reader's
Digest* with its diminutive pages, but the scoffers were wrong. Today, advertisers—except for cigarette manufacturers—pay more than $100,000 a page for
a color advertisement. Consistent with the Wallaces' standards, cigarette
advertisements are not accepted and never have been.

Hale's Women's Magazine

80 The first U.S. magazine edited to interest only a portion of the mass audience,
but otherwise to be of general interest, was *Ladies' Magazine*, which later
became *Godey' Lady's Book*. Sara Josepha Hale helped start the magazine in
1828 to uplift and glorify womanhood. Its advice on fashion, morals, taste,

sewing and cooking developed a following, which peaked with a circulation of 150,000 in 1860.

85　During her tenure Hale defined women's issues and in indirect ways contributed importantly to women's liberation. She campaigned vigorously for educational opportunities for women. When Matthew Vassar was setting up a women's college, she persuaded him to include women on the faculty—a novel idea for the time. Unlike other magazine editors of the time, she dis-

90　dained reprinting articles from other publications. Hence, *Ladies' Magazine* created opportunities for new writers, particularly women, and enriched the nation's literary output.

The tradition is maintained today in seven competing magazines known as the Seven Sisters because of their female following: *Better Homes & Gardens,*

95　*Family Circle, Good Housekeeping, Ladies' Home Journal, McCall's, Redbook* and *Woman's Day.*

Johnson's *Ebony*

From John Pavlik and Shawn McIntosh, *Converging Media*

One entrepreneur who decided to do something to serve the media needs of African Americans in the mid-1900s was John H. Johnson, then a young African American whose hometown high school in Arkansas City,

100　Arkansas, was "whites only." As a result, John's family moved to Chicago, where Johnson got his formal high school education. His mother funded his business undertaking by pawning her household furniture and giving her son $500 to start *Ebony* magazine. *Ebony* has become one of the leading magazines targeting the interests of African Americans, with a circulation of more

105　than 1.5 million. Johnson has become one of the leading cross media owners in the United States, with a book publishing company, a nationally syndicated television program, and two radio stations.

> What other magazines target African American readers?

Skill Development

Stop to self-test, relate, and react. Review your study outline.

Your instructor may choose to give you a true-false comprehension review.

Write About the Selection

How did magazines help create a national identity for a young United States, and how did the later innovations continue to strengthen that common bond?

Response Suggestion: List ways in which magazines subtly drew a large national audience toward common concerns and pleasures. Explain how later innovations continued to build unity by targeting causes and audiences.

Contemporary Link

Given the influence of magazine in forging a national identity and uplifting the spirits, what positive and negative effects on society do you see emerging from contemporary print, broadcast, and electronic media? What trends do you see? Are the media changing the way we think?

Check Your Comprehension

After reading the selection, answer the following questions with *a, b, c,* or *d.*

Main Idea

_____ 1. Which is the best statement of the main idea of this selection?
a. Magazines increased in American popularity because they were much less expensive than books.
b. Magazines created a medium for mass advertising before the advent of television.
c. Magazines enriched the nation's literary output by providing a vehicle for gifted American fiction writers to reach the public.
d. Magazines created national audiences, a sense of nationhood, and innovations in mass communication.

Detail

_____ 2. The success of magazines in the 1800s can be attributed to the following except
a. they were affordable.
b. they were oriented toward their cities of publication.
c. they included quality fiction from books readers could not afford to buy.
d. they created a national audience with a common bond.

Inference

_____ 3. The Postal Act of 1879 subsidized magazine mailings, which means that
a. the postal rate for magazines was less than its true cost and thus was supported by tax money.
b. the laws for magazines and newspapers were the same.
c. cheaper mailing rates were available if the content of the magazine were approved by the government.
d. both letters and magazines could be delivered for a penny a pound.

Inference   _____   4. The phrase "an agricultural and cottage industry economy" refers to
   a. farms with tenet farmers working the land while living in cottages on the property.
   b. family farms and small, locally owned businesses.
   c. a barter economy in which goods were traded rather than sold.
   d. farmers supplying the goods for urban economies.

Detail   _____   5. According to magazine industry studies, the typical adult magazine reader
   a. reads fewer than 10 issues a month.
   b. has a household income 5 percent more than the national average.
   c. shows no change in magazine consumption in accordance with education.
   d. reads fewer as magazines as income increases.

Detail   _____   6. According to the passage, if 500 new magazines were launched this year, the predicted number to survive into the third year would be
   a. 10.   c. 50.
   b. 23.   d. 100.

Inference   _____   7. The author suggests that Bourke-White's photo-journalism was socially significant and changed public policy because
   a. her pictures opened to 21-inch spreads.
   b. she showed the immenseness of the Fort Peck Dam for *Life*'s first cover.
   c. she shot the news and emotions of World War II and Nazi concentration camps.
   d. she showed the suffering at the core of the social problems of southern sharecroppers, South African gold miners, and victims of the Midwestern drought.

Inference   _____   8. With the *Reader's Digest*, DeWitt and Lila Wallace wanted all the following except
   a. previously published nonfiction.
   b. inspiring articles.
   c. quality fiction.
   d. condensed nonfiction.

Inference   _____   9. The author suggests that Sara Josepha Hale
   a. created a magazine to voice social reform for women.
   b. was the first woman to work on a national magazine.
   c. initially tried to appeal to the household interests of both men and women.
   d. indirectly promoted woman's liberation while focusing primarily on fashion, morals, taste, sewing, and cooking.

Inference   _____ 10. The author suggests all the following about John H. Johnson except
          a. he was born in a time of overt racial prejudice.
          b. his family wanted him to get a good education.
          c. his mother was against his starting a risky magazine venture.
          d. his family hoped for greater opportunities in Chicago.

Answer the following with *T* (true), *F* (false), or *CT* (can't tell):

Inference   _____ 11. The reader can conclude that Congress appreciated the national propaganda value of magazines.

Inference   _____ 12. The serialized novels in early magazines were broken into small readable segments for the monthly publication.

Inference   _____ 13. The reader can conclude that *Reader's Digest* would probably not accept liquor advertisements.

Inference   _____ 14. The phrase "but not too Pollyanna," in referring to *Reader's Digest* articles, means not too feminine to attract male readers.

Inference   _____ 15. The reader can conclude that niche marketing refers to appealing to a specific population or interest group.

Build Your Vocabulary

According to the way the italicized word was used in the selection, select *a, b, c,* or *d* for the word or phrase that gives the best definition. The number in parentheses indicates the line of the passage in which the word is located.

_____ 1. "People of ordinary *means*" (2)
    a. ability
    b. intelligence
    c. talent
    d. income

_____ 2. "*vie* for readers" (27)
    a. line up
    b. compete
    c. publish
    d. circulate

_____ 3. "racehorse *aficionados*" (30)
    a. owners
    b. devotees
    c. jockeys
    d. gamblers

_____ 4. "*haunting* photos" (53)
    a. unforgettable
    b. unrealistic
    c. elegant
    d. happy

5. "created *indelible* images" (54)
   a. delicate
   b. large
   c. artistic
   d. permanent

8. "*scoffers* were wrong" (75)
   a. staff members
   b. mocking disbelievers
   c. subscribers
   d. mail carriers

6. "*universal* appeal" (69)
   a. limited
   b. sophisticated
   c. widespread
   d. cultured

9. "*novel* idea" (89)
   a. new
   b. unpopular
   c. controversial
   d. thoughtful

7. "*diminutive* pages" (75)
   a. very small
   b. divided
   c. congested
   d. over priced

10. "*disdained* reprinting" (89)
   a. prohibited
   b. looked down on
   c. promoted
   d. incorporated

Search the Net

Use a search engine such as Google, AltaVista, Excite, Infoseek, Dogpile, Yahoo, or Lycos to find the classic cover photographs for *Life* magazine. Notice Margaret Bourke-White's Fort Peck Dam cover. Select, print, and share your three favorite covers with classmates. For suggested Web sites and other research activities, go to http://www.ablongman.com/smith/.

Concept Prep

for Communications and Language

What is communications?

Little wonder, given the importance of mass communication in our daily lives, that **communications** is one of the fastest growing departments in many colleges. The courses that focus on technologically based means of communicating examine the role of mass media in educating the public and influencing cultural, social, and economic change. Popular courses include mass media, journalism, film, and video. Other communications courses, the ones you are more likely to take as introductory courses, focus on interpersonal and intrapersonal communications. The courses are usually interactive and stress group and team performance by learning leadership and responsible group membership skills.

What are the important elements of communications?

- Public speakers and others in leadership roles usually have **charisma**, a magnetically charming personality and an extraordinary power to inspire loyalty and enthusiasm in others. Leaders such as John F. Kennedy and Martin Luther King, Jr., are described as charismatic.

- **Ethics** is another significant aspect of sound leadership, team performance, and business. Ethical decision making and behavior are aimed at distinguishing between right and wrong and acting in a manner that is morally correct and virtuous.

- When speaking formally, use fresh and concise language. Avoid using **clichés** such as "Don't let the cat out of the bag" and "Let's get down to brass tacks." These hackneyed, overused expressions create images that were probably humorous when first used but are now considered tiresome. If interpreted **literally,** exactly word for word, the phrases do not make sense. The words are intentionally designed to take on a new descriptive or **figurative** meaning. In the previous phrases, the "cat in the bag" is a secret, and the "brass tacks" are the real issues. Such phrases are also called **idioms,** and they are es-

American civil rights activist Dr. Martin Luther King, Jr., addresses a large crowd gathered at the Lincoln Memorial for the March on Washington.
Hulton | Archive/Getty Images

pecially confusing to people who speak English as a second language.

- Use appropriate **diction** for your audience. Diction refers to your choice of words. It can also refer to the quality of your pronunciation. Use clear and effective words, and enunciate them correctly.

- If you don't want snickers in the audience, avoid **double entendres**—expressions that have a double meaning. The second meaning is usually a mischievous and sexual interpretation of an innocent expression, such as "The athletes were hanging out in the locker room."

- More snickers may come if you make a **malapropism,** a humorous confusion of two words that sound alike. Saying "a blue tarpon was spread over the building under repair" will have your audience envisioning a huge blue fish covering the structure rather than a large plastic tarp.
- Give credit when you use the words or ideas of another person. To steal the thoughts of others as your own is **plagiarism.** Acknowledging credit to others does not detract from your work but enhances your status as a researcher.
- If you are duplicating published materials for distribution to a group, obtain **copyright** permission so that you are not acting illegally. A copyright is a legal protection granted to an author or publishing company to prevent others from pirating a body of work. To obtain reprint permission, you will probably need to pay a fee.

- When receiving constructive criticism, don't be a **prima donna.** The word is derived from Latin and refers to the "first lady" in an opera. The connotation, however, is that the person is overly sensitive and difficult to work with. If you become a prima donna, you may suddenly discover that you are a **persona non grata,** a person who is no longer acceptable or in favor.
- Strive for excellence, and perhaps you will graduate with honors or **cum laude.** Colleges differ on the grade point averages required for different designations of distinction and high honor. At some institutions, a cumulative grade point average of 3.500–3.699 is required for **cum laude,** a 3.700–3.899 for **magna cum laude,** and a 3.900–4.000 for **summa cum laude.** Some students, however, are satisfied to graduate with a "Thank the Lordy."

REVIEW QUESTIONS

After studying the material, answer the following questions:

1. What areas are usually included in a communications department? _____

2. What is ethical behavior? _____

3. What is a cliché? _____

4. What is good diction? _____

5. What is a double entendre? _____

6. What is a malapropism? _____

7. What is plagiarism? _____

8. What is a prima donna? _____

9. What is a *persona non grata*? _____

10. What is summa cum laude? _____

Your instructor may choose to give a true-false review of these communications and language concepts.

CONTEMPORARY FOCUS

The demands of college can certainly be stressful. With assignments, exams, work schedules, roommates, and personal responsibilities, life can become hectic, and your body and mind may be absorbing the trauma. Do you have any of the following signs of stress that might be warning you to take better care of yourself?

SIGNS OF STRESS

By Edward M. Eveld

Kansas City Star, March 7, 2004

Stress is sending you signals. Are you paying attention? Stress experts say you should ask these questions:

1. Are you in pain? Headache and back pain are often stress symptoms. Take stock of muscle stiffness in the neck and jaw. Do you have to consciously drop your jaw to relax it?

2. How does your skin look? Stress has real physical effects, including skin eruptions.

3. Are you snapping at everyone? Stress makes you irritable.

4. Have your eating habits changed? Some people eat more when they are stressed. Some eat less.

5. How's your digestion? Stress can wreak havoc on your food processing system. Are you having more heartburn, bowel problems, stomachache? Stress can aggravate ulcers.

6. Does your mind race? The inability to focus can be a stress sign. So is indecisiveness. Or are you fixated on one thing? Some stressed people can't move off dead center.

7. Are you finding that things aren't funny? Losing the ability to laugh is one of the first casualties of stress.

8. Are you tossing and turning at night?

9. Are you over-consuming? Some people numb themselves with high-fat food, alcohol, a buying binge. Take a look at excessive behaviors.

10. Have you picked up new nervous habits, or have old ones intensified? Notice your cuticle picking, nail biting, hair twisting, and finger rapping.

Collaborate

Collaborate on responses to the following questions:

- What is your typical sleep schedule? Does it create or reduce stress?
- Do cluttered surroundings make you feel unsettled and add to stress?
- How can laughing be relaxing?

Skill Development: Preview

Preview the next selection to predict its purpose and organization and to formulate your learning plan.

Activate Schema

What causes stress for you, and what is your response to it?

What do you think of the low-carbohydrate diet craze that has swept the nation?

Establish a Purpose for Reading

Do you have bad habits that sabotage your energy? What can you do to attain a higher level of performance? After recalling what you already know about keeping your body healthy, read this selection to explain the scientific impact of nutrition, exercise, and stress on the body.

Increase Word Knowledge

What do you know about these words?

attribute	crankiness	optimal	judiciously	mimic
aroused	prone	precursor	salient	euphoria

Your instructor may give a true-false vocabulary review before or after reading.

Integrate Knowledge While Reading

Questions have been inserted in the margin to stimulate your thinking while reading. Remember to

Predict	Picture	Relate	Monitor	Correct

Skill Development: Note Taking

Use an informal outline to take notes for later study.

NUTRITION, HEALTH, AND STRESS
From Barbara Brehm, *Stress Management*

Nutrition and Stress: Running on Empty

Good nutrition and eating habits contribute significantly to good health and stress resistance. They are especially important during high-stress times, but these may be the times when we are least likely to eat well! The cupboard is bare, we have no time to plan a shopping list and no money to go shopping, so we skip meals or grab whatever fast food is closest at hand. Sometimes we depend on a dining hall whose schedule doesn't match our own, or whose ideas of good nutrition and fine cuisine are limited to meat, potatoes, and overcooked vegetables with lots of butter. Dessert is usually the high point of every meal.

5

What should
I eat?

On many public beaches in southern California, volleyball enthusiasts enjoy the sport with their feet in the soft sand.
Arthur Tilley/Stone/Getty Images: Creative Collection

Food and Energy: The Role of Blood Sugar

Everyone has experienced the fatigue and irritability that can result from being hungry. While many of the body's systems can make energy from fat, the central nervous system, including the brain, relies primarily on blood sugar, or glucose, for fuel. When blood sugar falls, these symptoms of fatigue result. Parents and people who work with children have observed the hungry-cranky connection on many occasions. As adults, we tend to attribute our moods to external events and ignore our internal physiology, but hunger can cause crankiness in us just the same.

10

15

After you consume a meal, your blood glucose level rises as sugar enters the bloodstream from the digestive tract. A rising blood sugar level signals the pancreas to release **insulin.** Insulin is a hormone that allows sugar to enter the
20   cells and be used for energy. As the glucose gradually leaves the bloodstream, blood glucose levels begin to decrease.

Some people have more trouble regulating blood sugar than others and are prone to **hypoglycemia,** or low blood sugar, especially if they forget to eat or when they participate in physical activity. Symptoms of hypoglycemia include
25   hunger, shakiness, nervousness, dizziness, nausea, and disorientation.

The following are recommendations for keeping your blood sugar at a healthful level without peaks and dips.

| Do I have hypoglycemia? |

Eat Regularly

Your body likes a regular schedule. Skipping meals means guaranteed hypoglycemia in people prone to this condition. Set up times for meals and snacks
30   that are convenient for your schedule and stick to this routine as much as possible. This may mean planning ahead and carrying snacks with you if you are at work or out running errands. Many people, including those with hypoglycemia, find that eating five or six small meals or snacks each day helps them feel more energetic than three large meals.

Include Protein Foods at Every Meal

35   Carbohydrate foods eaten without foods containing much protein are digested and enter the bloodstream quickly and are thus likely to challenge blood sugar regulatory processes in people prone to hypoglycemia. Protein slows digestion and allows blood sugar to rise more gradually. Protein servings may be small: a slice or two of meat or cheese; a half-cup of cottage cheese,
40   yogurt, or tuna salad; small servings of fish or shellfish; a dish made with lentils or other legumes; or soy products like tofu.

Avoid Sugar Overload

| Do sweets work as snacks? |

When you eat a large amount of carbohydrates, blood sugar rises quickly. A high blood sugar level calls forth a high insulin response, which in some people causes a sort of rebound effect: glucose enters the cells, and the blood
45   sugar level drops quickly, causing hypoglycemia. While you may feel energized for a short period of time after too much sugar, you may eventually begin to feel tired, irritable, and hungry.

Drink Plenty of Fluids

Many people fail to maintain optimal levels of hydration. The next time you feel tired, try drinking a glass of water. Dehydration causes fatigue and irritability.
50   Thirst is not an adequate indicator of dehydration; you become dehydrated before you get thirsty. Nutritionists advise drinking at least eight cups of fluid each day, more with physical activity or hot weather. Caffeinated and alcoholic

beverages don't count. Not only do they increase your stress, but they also dehydrate you and thus increase your fluid needs. Your urine will be pale if you
55 are adequately hydrated; dark-colored urine is a sign of dehydration.

Limit Caffeine

Caffeine is a **sympathomimetic** substance, which means its effects mimic those of the sympathetic nervous system and thus cause the fight-or-flight response. If you add caffeine to an already aroused sympathetic nervous system, the results can be stressful and produce high levels of anxiety, irritability,
60 headache, and stress-related illness. Most caffeine drinks, including coffee, tea, and cola soft drinks, can also cause stomachaches and nausea, which often get worse under stress.

One or two caffeinated beverages consumed judiciously at appropriate times during the day appear to do no harm for most people. Indeed, a little
65 caffeine can increase alertness. The problem with caffeine is that people are likely to overindulge in it when they are stressed. When summoning the energy necessary to get through the day feels like trying to squeeze water from a rock, they reach for a shot of caffeine. Caffeine cannot substitute for a good night's sleep, however. When you are truly fatigued, caffeine does not
70 help you concentrate; it simply leaves you wired, too jittery to sleep, and too tired to do anything productive.

> Why do people consume too much caffeine?

Eating in Response to Stress: Feeding the Hungry Heart

Few people look on eating and food only in terms of hunger and nutrition. Every culture in the world has evolved rituals around food and eating. Feasting and fasting carry layers of religious, cultural, and emotional overtones. As
75 children, we learn to associate food with security, comfort, love, reward, punishment, anger, restraint. It's no wonder that we eat for many reasons other than hunger: because we're lonely, angry, sad, happy, nervous, or depressed. Unlike alcohol, which we can give up if we are prone to a drinking problem, we must learn to live with food. If eating is the only way we take the time to
80 nurture ourselves, we eat more than we are really hungry for. In extreme cases, an inability to control eating can develop into an eating disorder, known as **compulsive overeating,** that often gets worse under stress.

> Why do we celebrate with food?

Food and Mood: The Role of Neurotransmitters

Most people feel relaxed and lazy after a big feast. For this reason many cultures have incorporated a siesta after the large midday meal, and professors who
85 teach a class right after lunch or dinner rarely turn out the lights for a slide show. Why do we feel tired? Certainly our blood sugar should be adequate after eating all that food. Changes in brain biochemistry may be the reason. The food we eat supplies the precursor molecules for manufacturing neurotransmitters

that influence our emotions and mood. Some researchers believe that by select-
90   ing the right kinds of food we can encourage states of relaxation or alertness.

Big meals, especially those with a lot of fat, take a long time to digest, and
with a full stomach we feel like relaxing rather than working. On the other
hand, smaller meals low in fat take less time and energy to digest and leave us
feeling more energetic and alert.

95   Meals that are composed primarily of carbohydrates encourage production
of the neurotransmitter *serotonin*, which makes us feel drowsy and relaxed.
High-carbohydrate meals are a prescription for relaxation and may be the reason some people overeat: it makes them feel good. A small, high-carbohydrate
snack before bedtime can encourage sleep. Many people find that eating car-
100 bohydrates helps them feel less stressed and more relaxed. Some people find
that a meal or snack with carbohydrate but little protein, especially in the
middle of the day, leaves them feeling tired.

Meals that include a small serving of protein foods, with or without carbohydrates, encourage alertness by favoring production of neurotransmitters
105 such as *dopamine* and *norepinephrine*. A small lunch that includes protein
foods is best for students who need to stay alert for a 1:00 class.

What would be
a great lunch
for me?

Physical Activity and Stress Resistance

Participation in regular physical activity is one of the most effective ways to
increase your stress resistance. Countless studies comparing people with high
and low levels of stress resistance have found exercise to be one of the most
110 salient discriminators between these two groups. An important note is that
the amount and intensity of exercise required to produce stress management
benefits need not be overwhelming. While many athletes enjoy extended periods of intense activity, other people find stress relief with a brisk walk, an hour
of gardening, or a game of volleyball on the beach.

Exercise High: Endorphins, Hormones, and Neurotransmitters

115 In addition to canceling the negative effects of stress, exercise may induce some
positive biochemical changes. Many exercisers report feelings of euphoria and
states of consciousness similar to those described by people using drugs such as
heroin. Such accounts have led to use of the term *runner's high*, since these
descriptions first came primarily from long-distance runners. These reports have
120 intrigued both exercise scientists and the lay public and have suggested the possibility that certain types of exercise, particularly vigorous exercise of long duration, may cause biochemical changes that mimic drug-induced euphoria.

As scientists have come to understand something of brain biochemistry,
some interesting hypotheses have emerged. The most publicized of these has
125 focused on a group of chemical messengers found in the central nervous system
(brain and spinal cord) called opioids, since they are similar in structure and
function to the drugs that come from the poppy flower: opium, morphine, and

heroin. **Beta-endorphins** belong to this group. They not only inhibit pain but also seem to have other roles in the brain as well, such as aiding in memory and learning and registering emotions. It is difficult for scientists to measure opioid concentrations in the central nervous system of humans, but animal research has suggested that endogenous (produced by the body) opioid concentrations increase with level of exercise: more exercise, more opioids.

130

Rhythmic Exercise: Relaxed Brain Waves

| What will be my exercise regimen? |

Rhythmic exercises such as walking, running, rowing, and swimming increase **alpha-wave** activity in the brain. The electrical activity of the brain can be monitored in the laboratory using an instrument called an **electroencephalograph (EEG)**. Alpha waves are associated with a calm mental state, such as that produced by meditation or chanting. The rhythmic breathing that occurs during some forms of exercise also contributes to an increase in alpha-wave activity. Rhythmic activity performed to music may be stress relieving in other ways as well.

135

140

Finding Your Life Stress Score

To assess your life in terms of life changes, check all the events listed that have happened to you in the past year. Add up the points to derive your life stress score. (Based on data from Holmes & Masuda, 1974)

Rank	Life Event	Life Change Unit Value	Your Points
1.	Death of spouse	100	_____
2.	Divorce	73	_____
3.	Separation from living partner	65	_____
4.	Jail term or probation	63	_____
5.	Death of close family member	63	_____
6.	Serious personal injury or illness	53	_____
7.	Marriage or establishing life partnership	50	_____
8.	Getting fired at work	47	_____
9.	Marital or relationship reconciliation	45	_____
10.	Retirement	45	_____
11.	Change in health of immediate family member	44	_____
12.	Pregnancy or causing pregnancy	40	_____
13.	Sex difficulties	39	_____
14.	Gain of new family member	39	_____
15.	Business or work role change	39	_____
16.	Change in financial state	38	_____
17.	Death of a close friend (not a family member)	37	_____
18.	Change to different line of work	36	_____
19.	Change in number of arguments with spouse or life partner	35	_____
20.	Taking a mortgage or loan for a major purpose	31	_____

Rank	Life Event	Life Change Unit Value	Your Points
21.	Foreclosure of mortgage or loan	30	_____
22.	Change in responsibilities at work	29	_____
23.	Son or daughter leaving home	29	_____
24.	Trouble with in-laws or with children	29	_____
25.	Outstanding personal achievement	28	_____
26.	Spouse begins or stops work	26	_____
27.	Begin or end school	26	_____
28.	Change in living conditions (visitors, roommates, remodeling)	25	_____
29.	Change in personal habits (diet, exercise, smoking)	24	_____
30.	Trouble with boss	23	_____
31.	Change in work hours or conditions	20	_____
32.	Moving to new residence	20	_____
33.	Change in schools	20	_____
34.	Change in recreation	19	_____
35.	Change in religious activities	19	_____
36.	Change in social activities (more or less than before)	18	_____
37.	Taking out a loan for a lesser purchase (car or tv)	17	_____
38.	Change in sleeping habits	16	_____
39.	Change in frequency of family get-togethers	15	_____
40.	Change in eating habits	15	_____
41.	Vacation	13	_____
42.	Presently in winter holiday season	12	_____
43.	Minor violation of the law	11	_____

LIFE STRESS SCORE: _____

Samuel E. Wood, Ellen Green Wood, and Denise Boyd, Mastering the World of Psychology. *Adapted from the "Social Readjustment Rating Scale," by Thomas Holmes and Richard Rahe. The scale was first published in the* Journal of Psychosomatic Research, *vol. II, p. 214. Copyright 1967. Used by permission of Pergamon Press Ltd.*

Researchers Holmes and Rahe claim that there is a connection between the degree of life stress and major health problems. A person who scores 300 or more on the life stress test runs an 80 percent risk of suffering a major health problem within the next two years. Someone who scores 150 to 300 has a 50 percent chance of becoming ill.

Skill Development: Recall

Stop to self-test, relate, and react. Study your informal outline.

Your instructor may choose to give you a true-false comprehension review.

Write About the Selection

Explain how you can use the health and nutritional information in this selection to energize and stimulate your mental performance during exam week.
   Response Suggestion: List your energizing ideas with a purpose and examples for each.

Contemporary Link

During stressful times, some people eat more and some eat less. The "Freshman 15" refers not to an athletic team but to the 15 pounds that students often gain during the first year of college. Other students who are concerned with body image obsess about their weight and follow overly restrictive diets. How do you plan to use this information about nutrition, exercise, and stress to identify your needs and avoid unhealthy behaviors leading to excessive weight gain or loss?

Check Your Comprehension

After reading the selection, answer the following questions with *a, b, c,* or *d.* To help you analyze your strengths and weaknesses, the question types are indicated.

Main Idea

————— 1. Which is the best statement of the main idea of this selection?
   a. A balanced diet is the most effective way to decrease stress.
   b. Regular exercise and good eating habits contribute to stress reduction and both physical and emotional well-being.
   c. Stress negatively affects mental and physical performance.
   d. Avoiding sugar overload and including protein at every meal help regulate blood sugar.

Detail

————— 2. The pancreas is signaled to release insulin when
   a. protein is consumed.
   b. blood glucose levels rise.
   c. physical activity increases.
   d. blood sugar levels decrease.

Inference

————— 3. By using the term *fine cuisine,* the author suggests that
   a. "fine" meals include meat, potatoes, and vegetables.
   b. dessert is an important part of "fine dining."

    c. dining halls do not always serve good, nutritional
       meals.
    d. vegetables should be cooked without fats.

Detail   _____   4. People who experience symptoms of hypoglycemia should
    do all the following except
    a. eat three large meals per day and vary the times.
    b. combine proteins with carbohydrates.
    c. limit sugar intake.
    d. eat several small meals or snacks throughout the day.

Inference   _____   5. The implied similarity between drinking and eating problems
    is that
    a. many people who abuse alcohol are also prone to eating
       problems.
    b. compulsive eating is treated more easily than compulsive
       drinking.
    c. drinking alcohol and eating food sometimes are misguided
       responses to stress.
    d. the consumption of both food and alcohol releases endor-
       phins, which reduce stress.

Detail   _____   6. The production of norepinephrine is stimulated by eating
    a. proteins.
    b. fats.
    c. carbohydrates.
    d. caffeine.

Detail   _____   7. The beta-endorphins believed to be released by exercise have
    all the following benefits except
    a. inducing feelings of euphoria.
    b. inhibiting pain.
    c. regulating blood sugar.
    d. aiding memory.

Inference   _____   8. The activity most likely to increase alpha-wave activity in the
    brain would be
    a. playing a game of chess.
    b. jogging.
    c. lifting weights.
    d. playing baseball.

Inference   _____   9. For a midnight snack before bed, the author would most
    likely recommend
    a. a bagel.
    b. cappuccino.
    c. peanuts.
    d. a chicken leg.

Detail _____ 10. The author's attitude toward the use of caffeine by most
people is that
- a. caffeine can be used to decrease fear because it arouses
the fight-or-flight response.
- b. light amounts of caffeine appear harmless and can
increase alertness.
- c. caffeine should be avoided because it causes stomachaches, nausea, headaches, and irritability.
- d. when a person is truly fatigued, caffeine can increase
concentration.

Answer the following with *T* (true) or *F* (false).

Detail _____ 11. Glucose provides the primary fuel for the brain.

Detail _____ 12. Thirst is an adequate indicator of the body's optimal hydration level.

Inference _____ 13. The term *hungry heart* implies a need that food cannot satisfy.

Detail _____ 14. A glass of cola can be counted toward the number of cups of
fluid the body needs each day.

Inference _____ 15. The author suggests that serotonin is more important for
effective studying than dopamine and norepinephrine.

Build Your Vocabulary

According to the way the italicized word was used in the selection, select *a, b,
c,* or *d* for the word or phrase that gives the best definition. The number in
parentheses indicates the line of the passage in which the word is located.

_____ 1. "to *attribute* our moods" (14)
- a. to dissociate
- b. to credit
- c. to explain
- d. to reject

_____ 2. "can cause *crankiness*" (16)
- a. rage
- b. irritability
- c. drowsiness
- d. fatigue

_____ 3. "*optimal* levels" (48)
- a. medium
- b. low
- c. satisfactory
- d. regulatory

_____ 4. "its effects *mimic*" (56)
- a. distort
- b. imitate
- c. confuse
- d. falsify

_____ 5. "an already *aroused*"
(58)
- a. excited
- b. not stimulated
- c. settled
- d. relaxed

_____ 6. "beverages consumed
judiciously" (63)
- a. recklessly
- b. hastily

      c. cautiously
      d. carelessly

_____ 7. "we are *prone*" (78)
      a. damaged by
      b. inclined
      c. addicted
      d. connected

_____ 8. "the *precursor* molecules" (88)
      a. necessary
      b. final
      c. active
      d. forerunner

_____ 9. "*salient* discriminators" (110)
      a. noticeable
      b. instructive
      c. irrelevant
      d. damaging

_____ 10. "drug-induced *euphoria*" (122)
      a. insanity
      b. disorientation
      c. exhilaration
      d. serenity

Search the Net

Use a search engine such as Google, AltaVista, Excite, Infoseek, Dogpile, Yahoo, or Lycos to search for foods that can serve as remedies for specific ailments. Search for foods that help the body fight acne, cold sores, high blood pressure, and insomnia. For suggested Web sites and other research activities, go to http://www.ablongman.com/smith/.

Concept Prep

for Health

What is blood pressure?

Blood pressure is the measure of the pressure exerted by the blood as it flows through the arteries. Blood moves in waves and is thus measured in two phases. The **systolic pressure** is the pressure at the height of the blood wave when the left ventricle of the heart contracts to push the blood through the body. The **diastolic pressure** is the pressure when the ventricles are at rest and filling with blood. The figures are expressed as the systolic "over" the diastolic pressure. The average blood pressure of a healthy adult is **120 over 80.**

What can happen to arteries as we age?

Cholesterol—a white soapy substance that is found in the body and in foods such as animal fats—can accumulate on the inner walls of arteries—blood vessels that carry blood away from the heart—and narrow the channels through which blood flows. Nutritionists recommend eating **unsaturated fats** such as vegetable or olive oils as opposed to **saturated fats** (animal fats), which are solid at room temperature.

Another condition that lessens the flow of blood through the arteries is hardening of the arteries or **arteriosclerosis**. A surgical technique called an **angioplasty** is used to clear the arteries. A catheter with a small balloon is inserted into the arteries around the heart to compress fatty deposits and restore the flow of blood.

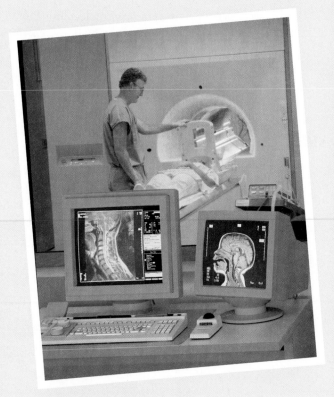

Radiologists are physicians who specialize in imaging technologies such as magnetic resonance imaging (MRI) for medical diagnosis.
Lester Lefkowitz/Taxi/Getty Images

What are some frequently discussed medical procedures?

- A **CAT scan** (computerized axial tomography) is a painless, noninvasive procedure that uses radiation to show a three-dimensional image of the body. The diagnostic procedure is used to detect tumors and other conditions. It shows differences in the density of soft tissue,

with high-density substances appearing white and low-density substances appearing dark.

- An **MRI** (magnetic resonance imaging) uses magnetic fields and radio waves to detect hidden tumors and other conditions by mapping the vibration of atoms. An MRI is painless and does not use radiation.

- **Chemotherapy** is a treatment for cancer in which the patient receives chemicals that destroy cancer cells. Currently, more than 50 anticancer drugs are available for use. Temporary hair loss is a common side effect of chemotherapy.

- **Radiation** is another treatment for destroying malignant cancer cells. Unfortunately, it also destroys some healthy cells.

- A **mammogram** is an X-ray of the breast to detect tumors that are too small to be detected by other means.

- A **Pap test** is a procedure in which cells are taken from the cervical region and tested for cancer.

- **PSA** (prostate-specific antigen) levels in the blood are measured to detect prostate cancer in men. A **prostatic ultrasound** can also be used.

- A **sonogram** or **ultrasound** test uses high-frequency sound waves to detect abnormalities. It is a noninvasive procedure that can be used to view the size, position, and sex of a fetus.

- **Amniocentesis** is a procedure for detecting abnormalities in the fetus. Fluid is drawn from the liquid surrounding the fetus by a needle through the mother's stomach. The fluid contains cells of the fetus that can be analyzed.

REVIEW QUESTIONS

After studying the material, answer the following questions:

1. What is the difference between systolic and diastolic pressure? _____

   _____

   _____

2. Which type of pressure should be higher? _____

   _____

3. How does cholesterol harm the body? _____

   _____

4. How can you distinguish saturated fats? _____

   _____

5. What does an angioplasty do? _____

   _____

6. What medical procedure uses drugs to cure cancer? _____

   _____

7. What procedure uses magnetic fields and radio waves to detect tumors and other conditions without radiation? _____

   _____

8. What test can indicate prostate cancer? _____

    _____

9. What procedure extracts fetal cells for diagnosis? _____

    _____

10. What type of X-ray is used to detect breast cancer? _____

    _____

Your instructor may choose to give a true-false review of these health concepts.

Vocabulary Booster

The Sun, the Moon, and the Stars

Roots
sol, helio: sun   *luna:* moon
aster, astro: star

Words with *sol, helio:* sun

A sundial is a primitive example of a *solar* chronometer, a device indicating the time by means of the sun.

■ **solar:** of or pertaining to the sun; proceeding from the sun; operating on energy from the sun

Solar panels on rooftops to heat water for homes have become a popular way to conserve energy.

■ **solarium:** a glass-enclosed room that is exposed to the sun's rays

A *solarium* in a home usually becomes the favorite spot in winter because it is naturally warmed by the sun.

■ **solstice:** either of two times a year when the sun is farthest from the equator

The summer *solstice*, the longest day in the Northern Hemisphere, occurs around June 21 or 22 when the sun is farthest north of the equator.

■ **heliotherapy:** treatment of disease by exposure to sunlight

Heliotherapy is prescribed sunbathing for certain illnesses such as tuberculosis or rickets.

■ **heliotropic:** turning or growing toward the light or sun

Without frequent turning, some *heliotropic* houseplants would grow only in one direction—toward the sunlight.

■ **helium:** an inert gaseous element present in the sun's atmosphere and in natural gas

Because *helium* is a chemically inactive gas, it is used as a substitute for flammable gases in dirigibles (blimps).

Words with *luna:* moon

The small *demilune* table was just the right size for the narrow foyer because its half-moon shape did not extend far into the room.

■ **lunar:** of or pertaining to the moon; round or crescent-shaped; measured by the moon's revolutions

A *lunar* month is equal to one revolution of the moon around the earth, approximately 29½ days.

■ *lunatic:* an insane or recklessly foolish person

The old gentleman was labeled a *lunatic* and unable to handle his legal affairs responsibly.

■ *lunatic fringe:* members on the edges of a group, such as a political or religious group, who hold extreme views

Members of the *lunatic fringe* of some environmentalist movements have destroyed property to protest further building in certain areas.

■ *lunar eclipse:* an obscuring of the light of the moon when the earth is positioned between the moon and the sun

During a *lunar eclipse*, the earth casts its shadow on the moon.

■ *lunar year:* a division of time equal to twelve lunar months

In a *lunar year* the moon orbits the earth 12 times.

Words with *aster, astro:* star

An *aster* is a daisylike flower with colored petals radiating around a yellow disk.

■ *asterisk:* a small, starlike symbol (*) used in writing and printing to refer to footnotes or omissions

An *asterisk* can be used to refer readers to an explanation of an item in the written material.

■ *asteroid:* a small, solid body orbiting the sun between Mars and Jupiter

Scientists believe that *asteroids* collided with earth in the past and predict they will do so again.

■ *astronomy:* the science that deals with the universe beyond the earth's atmosphere

Astronomy involves studying the motion, position, and size of celestial bodies.

■ *astronomical:* pertaining to astronomy; extremely large or enormous

Projected costs for the new hospital wing were so *astronomical* that the board decided to postpone the project.

■ *astrology:* the study that attempts to foretell the future by interpreting the influence of the stars on human lives

Most people don't believe in *astrology*; they believe they are responsible for what happens in their future.

astronauts: a person trained for space flight

The *astronauts* all went to bed early the night before their scheduled space shuttle mission.

Review

Part I

Choose the word from the boxed list that best completes each of the sentences below.

asterisks	asteroids	heliotherapy	helium
lunar	lunatic	fringe	solar	solstice

1. In *Stopping by Woods on a Snowy Evening,* Robert Frost refers to "The darkest evening of the year"—the winter _____, or the shortest day of the year.

2. When reading advertisements, you should look for _____ that might refer you to fine print that further explains pertinent conditions.

3. A _____ eclipse occurs when the moon comes between the sun and a point on the earth causing the sun to appear darkened from that point.

4. Ocean tides are affected by _____ attraction of the moon.

5. Another term for orbiting _____ is *space junk.*

6. Too much _____ can lead to sunstroke.

7. To accomplish their goal of saving lives, some of the _____ of the pro-life movement have taken extreme, contradictory measures such as bombing abortion clinics and killing doctors who perform abortions.

8. Besides enabling blimps to fly, _____ makes balloons float.

Part II

Indicate whether the italicized words are used correctly (C) or incorrectly (*I*) in the following sentences:

_____ 9. Kelly wants to study *astronomy* so that she knows the signs of the zodiac and can set up shop as a fortune-teller.

_____ 10. The *asters* blossomed across the backyard planting beds in colorful drifts of pink and white.

_____ 11. The *demilune* table that the Eriksons bought was too square and boxy for the round foyer.

_____ 12. The dermatologist told Angela that aging of the skin is attributed to exposure to *solar* rays.

_____ 13. Sue made sure to buy only *heliotropic* furniture so it would not be damaged if left in the sun.

_____ 14. Bill's friends all thought it was sheer *lunacy* for Bill to ski the expert slope on his first day of skiing.

_____ 15. One controversial theory about the extinction of the dinosaurs is that an *asteroid* hit the earth, destroying their food supply.

Your instructor may choose to give you a multiple-choice review.

Inference

- What is an inference; and what does it mean to read between the lines?
- What is the connotation of a word?
- Why do authors use figurative language; and how can understanding it enhance comprehension?
- Why is prior knowledge needed for implied meaning?
- How does a reader draw conclusions?

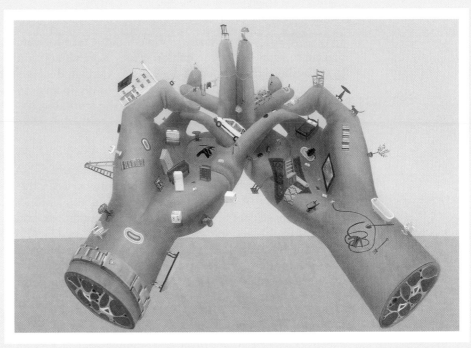

Everything I Own, by Frank Moore, 1992. Oil on canvas on wood with frame, canvas: 25 1/4 x 36 1/2 " (64 x 92.7 cm); frame: 28 5/8 x 40 1/4 x 2 1/4 " (72.7 x 102.27 x 5.7 cm). Courtesy Sperone Westwater, New York. Collection Janina Quint and David Leiber, New York, SW 92609.

What Is an Inference?

In the first and most basic level of reading, the *literal level*—the level that presents the facts—you can actually point to the words on the page that answer a literal question. However, for the second and more sophisticated level of reading—the *inferential level*—you no longer can point to the answer in the text but instead must form the answer from clues and suggestions within it.

EXAMPLE   In the following passage from Michael Ondaatje's novel *The English Patient*, the author implies an activity, and the reader infers what is happening. Mark the point at which you understand the activity.

> She moves backwards a few feet and with a piece of white chalk draws more rectangles, so there is a pyramid of them, single then double then single, her left hand braced flat on the floor, her head down, serious. . . .
>
> She drops the chalk into the pocket of her dress. She stands and pulls up the looseness of her skirt and ties it around her dress. She pulls from another pocket a piece of metal and flings it out in front of her so it falls just beyond the farthest square.
>
> She leaps forward, her legs smashing down, her shadow behind her curling into the depth of the hall. She is very quick, her tennis shoes skidding on the numbers she has drawn into each rectangle, one foot landing, then two feet, then one again until she reaches the last square.[1]

EXPLANATION   How many sentences did it take for you to infer that she is playing the game of hopscotch? You may have visualized the activity as early as the author's description of drawing "single then double then single"; or perhaps you caught on a bit later, when she jumps. In any case, you were able to make the inference when the clues from the text merged with your own prior knowledge.

In the vocabulary of inferential thought, the writer or speaker *implies* and the reader or listener *infers*. This merging of suggested thought for the reader or listener is also figuratively called **reading between the lines**. Throughout this text, many of the thought questions, or think-alouds, appearing in the margins alongside the longer reading selections ask you to read between the lines.

At the inferential level, authors not only entertain readers but also subtly manipulate them. When you read, always consider what is said as well as what is left unsaid. This is as true for the spoken word as it is for the written word. For example, when asked, "How do you like your new boss?" you might answer, "She is always well dressed" rather than saying, "I don't like her." By not volunteering information directly answering the question, you convey your lack of approval or, certainly, your lack of enthusiasm. In some

---

[1]Harvey, Stephanie, and Anne Goudvis. *Strategies That Work*. Portland, ME: Stenhouse Publishers, 2000, p. 37.

cases, this lack of information might be damaging. For example, when you graduate and look for that perfect position, you will need to ask professors and previous employers for job recommendations. Take care that the person you ask to recommend you is 100 percent on your team, as illustrated in the following exercise.

Exercise 7.1

Reading Between the Lines

Read the two recommendations and decide whom you would hire.

Carlos has been working as an assistant for one year and has been a valuable member of our team. He aggressively tackles new accounts, making calls after hours to track down customers and ship needed products. He excels in sales and follows through with the details in keeping customers satisfied. We want to keep Carlos but have no openings for advanced positions. I highly recommend him for the position at your company.

Roger has worked for our company for one year as an assistant. Our company sells chicken by-products, mostly thighs and legs that are not used in America, to Russia and third-world countries. Because of the international nature of our business, communication is extremely important. During his year with us, Roger has faithfully attended all meetings and has been friendly with our staff. We certainly wish him well.

Which one would you hire? Why? _I would hire Carlos because they talk about exactly how good his been with this company. For example They say he has been a valuable member of their team._

Similarly, inferential skills are important in persuasive reports and arguments because facts that are detrimental to the supported position might be omitted to manipulate a reader's opinion. Such omissions send a "Reader Beware" signal. One of the most effective tools that selectively uses words and photos to send persuasive messages is advertising.

Cigarette advertisements, for example, entice the public through suggestion, not facts, to spend millions of dollars on a product that is known to be unhealthy. Depending on the brand, smoking offers the refreshment of a mountain stream or the sophisticated elegance of the rich and famous. Never do the ads directly praise smoking or promise pleasure; instead, the ads *imply* smoking's positive aspects. The cigarette advertisers avoid lawsuits for false advertising by never putting anything tangible into print. The emotionalism of a full-page advertisement is so overwhelming that the consumer hardly notices the cautionary note in small print at the bottom of the page: "Warning: The Surgeon General Has Determined That Cigarette Smoking Is Dangerous to Your Health."

"We built a snowperson!"

Exercise 7.2

Implied Meaning in Advertisements

Advertisers can directly state that a detergent cleans, but the task of advertising other products can be more complicated. Look through magazines and newspapers to locate three advertisements: one each for cigarettes, alcoholic beverages, and fragrances. Answer the following questions about each:

1. What is directly stated about the product?
2. What does the advertisement suggest about the product?
3. Who seems to be the suggested audience or customer for the product? Why?

Authors and advertisers have not invented a new comprehension skill; they are merely capitalizing on an already highly developed skill of daily life. Think, for example, of the inferences you make every day by noticing what people say or don't say, by examining what they do or don't do, and by interpreting what others say or don't say about them. In fact, if you lacked these skills, you would miss out on a lot of the humor in jokes, cartoons, and sitcoms.

Implied Meaning in Humor

Jokes and cartoons require you to read between the lines and make connections. They are funny not so much because of what is said but because of what has been left unsaid. When you "catch on" to a joke, it simply means that you make the connection and recognize the **implied meaning**. To enjoy the joke, you link prior knowledge to what is being said. If you are telling a joke and your listener lacks the background knowledge to which the joke refers, your comic attempt will fall flat because the listener cannot understand the implied meaning. Listeners cannot connect with something they don't know, so be sure to choose the right joke for the right audience.

Biting humor has two levels of implied meaning. On the surface the joke makes us laugh. At a deeper level, however, the humor ridicules our beliefs, practices, or way of life.

EXAMPLE   What inference makes this joke funny?

> At an airline ticket counter, a small boy with his mother told the agent he was two years old. The man looked at him suspiciously and asked, "Do you know what happens to little boys who lie?"
> "Yes. They get to fly at half-price."
>
> Marleene Freedman in *Chevron USA, Laughter, the Best Medicine*

EXPLANATION   The inference is that the boy and his mother had lied about his age so he could fly for half the price. Children tend to speak the truth.

Exercise 7.3

Detecting Implied Humor in Jokes

Explain the inferences that make the following jokes funny.

Joke 1

"Take a pencil and paper," the teacher said, "and write an essay with the title 'If I Were a Millionaire.'"
Everyone but Philip, who leaned back with arms folded, began to write furiously. "What's the matter?" the teacher asked. "Why don't you begin?"
"I'm waiting for my secretary," he replied.

Bernadette Nagy, *Laughter, the Best Medicine*

Inference: _The inference is that Philip is the only millionaire in the class_

Joke 2

Mel's son rushed in the door. "Dad! Dad!" He announced. "I got a part in the school play!"
"That's terrific," Mel said proudly. "What part is it?"
"I play the part of the dad."
Mel thought this over. "Go back tomorrow," he instructed, "and tell them you want a speaking role."

Darleen Giannini, *Laughter, the Best Medicine*

Inference: _That Mel is as no write to speack at home_

Joke 3

A woman in Atlantic City was losing at the roulette wheel. When she was down to her last $10, she asked the fellow next to her for a good number. "Why don't you play your age?" he suggested.

The woman agreed, and then put her money on the table. The next thing the fellow with the advice knew, the woman had fainted and fallen to the floor. He rushed right over. "Did she win?" he asked.

"No," replied the attendant. "She put $10 on 29 and 41 came in."

Christine L. Castner, *Laughter, the Best Medicine*

Inference: *The women was really 41 so seen she lie thats why she fainted*

| Exercise 7.4 | **Finding Implied Meaning in Cartoons** |

Explain the inferences that make the following cartoons funny.

"Oh no, we're being spammed!"

© 2004 Arnie Levin from cartoonbank.com. All Rights Reserved.

Inference: _____

_____

_____

_____

THE FAR SIDE® BY GARY LARSON

© 1982 FarWorks, Inc. All Rights Reserved/Dist. by Creators Syndicate

The Far Side® by Gary Larson © 1982 FarWorks, Inc. All Rights Reserved. Used with permission.

"I've got it, too, Omar ... a strange feeling like we've just been going in circles."

Inference: _They have all the fat people on one side and all the skinee people on the other side_

In cartoons, the subtle expressions in the drawings, along with the words, imply meaning. In speech or writing, these expressions are suggested by carefully chosen words that imply attitude and manipulate the emotions of the reader.

Connotation of Words

Notice the power of suggested meaning in responding to the following questions:

1. If you read an author's description of classmates, which student would you assume is smartest?
    a. A student annotating items on a computer printout
    b. A student with earphones listening to a CD
    c. A student talking with classmates about *The Sopranos*

2. Which would you find described in a vintage small town of the 1960s?
   a. Movies
   b. Cinema
   c. Picture shows

3. Who probably earns the most money?
   a. A businessperson in a dark suit, white shirt, and tie
   b. A businessperson in slacks and a sport shirt
   c. A businessperson in a pale-blue uniform

Can you prove your answers? It's not the same as proving when the Declaration of Independence was signed, yet you still have a feeling for the way each question should be answered. Even though a right or wrong answer is difficult to explain in this type of question, certain answers can still be defended as most accurate; in the preceding questions, the answers are *a, c,* and *a.* The answers are based on feelings, attitudes, and knowledge commonly shared by members of society.

A seemingly innocent tool, word choice is the first key to implied meaning. For example, compare the following sentences:

Esmeralda is skinny.

Esmeralda is slender or slim.

If she is skinny, she is unattractive; but if she is slender or slim, she must be attractive. All three adjectives might refer to the same underweight person, but *skinny* communicates a negative feeling, whereas *slender* or *slim* communicates a positive one. This feeling or emotionalism surrounding a word is called **connotation. Denotation,** on the other hand, is the specific meaning of a word. The connotative meaning goes beyond the denotative meaning to reflect certain attitudes and prejudices of society. Even though it may not seem premeditated, writers select words, just as advertisers select symbols and models, to manipulate the reader's opinions.

Exercise 7.5	**Recognizing Connotation in Familiar Words**

In each of the following word pairs, write the letter of the word that connotes the more positive feeling:

_____	1. (a) guest	(b) boarder
_____	2. (a) surplus	(b) waste
_____	3. (a) conceited	(b) proud
_____	4. (a) buzzard	(b) robin
_____	5. (a) heavyset	(b) obese
_____	6. (a) explain	(b) brag
_____	7. (a) house	(b) mansion
_____	8. (a) song	(b) serenade
_____	9. (a) calculating	(b) clever

_____	10. (a) neglected	(b) deteriorated
_____	11. (a) colleague	(b) accomplice
_____	12. (a) ambition	(b) greed
_____	13. (a) kitten	(b) cat
_____	14. (a) courageous	(b) foolhardy
_____	15. (a) contrived	(b) designed
_____	16. (a) flower	(b) orchid
_____	17. (a) distinctive	(b) peculiar
_____	18. (a) baby	(b) kid
_____	19. (a) persuasion	(b) propaganda
_____	20. (a) well-groomed	(b) vain
_____	21. (a) slump	(b) decline
_____	22. (a) lie	(b) misrepresentation
_____	23. (a) janitor	(b) custodian
_____	24. (a) offering	(b) collection
_____	25. (a) soldiers	(b) mercenaries

© 2005 by Pearson Education, Inc.

Exercise 7.6

Choosing Connotative Words

For each word listed, write a word with a similar denotative meaning that has a positive (or neutral) connotation and one that has a negative connotation. Answers appear for all but creative answers will vary.

		Positive	Negative
Example:	chat	socialize	gossip
1.	dinner	_supper_	_breakfast_
2.	woman	_lady_	_baby_
3.	guy	_men_	_kid_
4.	apartment	_house_	_barn_
5.	speech	_narrative_	_talk_

Exercise 7.7

Connotation in Textbooks

For each of the underlined words in the following sentences, indicate the meaning of the word and reasons why the connotation is positive or negative.

EXAMPLE   While the unions fought mainly for better wages and hours, they also <u>championed</u> various social reforms.

Leonard Pitt, *We Americans*

<u>Championed:</u> Means "supported"; suggests heroes and thus a positive cause

1. The ad was part of the oil companies' program to sell their image rather than their product to the public. In the ad they <u>boasted</u> that they were reseeding all the disrupted areas with a newly developed grass that grows five times faster than the grass that normally occurs there.

   Robert Wallace, *Biology: The World of Life*

   boasted: *Increase*

2. At noon, a group of prominent bankers met. To stop the <u>hemorrhaging</u> of stock prices, the bankers' pool agreed to buy stocks well above the market.

   James Kirby Martin et al., *America and Its People*

   hemorrhaging: *Spread*

3. Tinbergen, like Lorenz and von Frisch, entered retirement by continuing to work. Tinbergen was a hyperactive child who, at school, was allowed to periodically dance on his desk to let off steam. So in "<u>retirement</u>" he entered a new arena, stimulating the use of ethological methods in autism.

   Robert Wallace, *Biology: The World of Life*

   "retirement": _____

4. The nation's capital is <u>crawling</u> with lawyers, lobbyists, registered foreign agents, public relations consultants, and others—more than 14,000 individuals representing nearly 12,000 organizations at last count—all seeking to influence Congress.

   Robert Lineberry et al., *Government in America, Brief Version*, 2nd ed.

   crawling: _____

5. Not since Wilson had tried to <u>ram</u> the League of Nations through the Senate had any president put more on the line.

   Leonard Pitt, *We Americans*

   ram: _____

Euphemisms and Politically Correct Language

A **euphemism** is a substitution of a mild, indirect, or vague term for one that is considered harsh, blunt, or offensive. It is a polite way of saying something that is embarrassing or indelicate. In the funeral business, for example, euphemisms abound. In fact, one Web site lists 213 terms for *death* or *dying* such as *pass to the great beyond* or *big sleep*.

When used to hide unpleasant ideas in politics or social interaction, euphemisms are sometimes called doublespeak or **politically correct language**. For example, *collateral damage* refers to civilian casualties. Other examples are the janitor being called the *sanitation engineer,* a handicapped person being called *differently abled*, or someone with a missing tooth being called *dentally disadvantaged*.

EXAMPLE

Euphemism: My stomach feels unsettled.

Politically correct: The troops were hit by friendly fire.

Figurative Language

What does it mean to say:

"She worked like a dog"?

To most readers it means that she worked hard, but since few dogs work, the comparison is not literally true or particularly logical. **Figurative language** is, in a sense, another language because it is a different way of using "regular" words so that they take on new meaning. For example, "It was raining buckets" and "raining cats and dogs" are lively, figurative ways of describing a heavy rain. New speakers of English, however, who comprehend on a literal level, might look up in the sky for the descending pails or animals. The two expressions create an exaggerated, humorous effect, but on a literal level, they do not make sense.

Consider an example from a Shakespearean play. When Hamlet prepares to confront his mother, he says, "I will speak daggers to her, but use none." With an economy of expression, he vividly suggests his feelings. Much more is implied than merely saying, "I will speak sternly to her." No one expects he will use a knife on his mother, but the connotation is that the words will be sharp, piercing, and wounding. Words can be hurtful or enriching; and an author uses figurative language, sometimes called **imagery**, to stimulate readers' minds to imagine beyond the printed page by adding color, attitude, or wit.

Idioms

When first used, the phrases "works like a dog" and "raining cats and dogs" were probably very clever. Now they have lost their freshness but still convey meaning for those who are "in the know." Such phrases are called **idioms,** or expressions that do not make literal sense but have taken on a new, generally accepted meaning over many years of use.

EXAMPLE

She tried to keep a stiff upper lip during the ordeal.

His eyes were bigger than his stomach.

EXPLANATION The first means to maintain control and the second means to ask for more food than you are able to eat.

Exercise 7.8	**Understanding Idioms**

What do the following idioms mean?

1. to lay an egg _____

2. a bone to pick _____

3. born with a silver spoon in her mouth _____

_____

4. chip on his shoulder _____

5. burn the midnight oil _____

Similes

A **simile** is a comparison of two unlike things using the words *like* or *as*.

EXAMPLE

The spring flower pushed up its bloom like a lighthouse beckoning on a gloomy night.
> And every soul, it passed me by,
> Like the whizz of my crossbow!

Samuel Taylor Coleridge, *The Rime of the Ancient Mariner*

Metaphors

A **metaphor** is a direct comparison of two unlike things (without using *like* or *as*).

EXAMPLE

The corporate accountant is a computer from nine to five.

Miss Rosie was a wet brown bag of a woman who used to be the best looking gal in Georgia.

Lucille Clifton, *Good Times*

Literary Analogies

A **literary analogy** is a comparison of two unlike things that can be a simile or a metaphor.

EXAMPLE

Workers are the clockwork in assembly line production. (metaphor)

Time is like a river. (simile)

Hyperbole

Hyperbole, sometimes called **overstatement**, is an exaggeration using figurative language to describe something as being more than it actually is. For example, *the lights of the village were brighter than a thousand stars*. An **understatement**, on the other hand, minimizes a point, such as saying, *"I covered expenses"* after winning $3 million in Las Vegas.

EXAMPLE

Hyperbole: I could sleep for 20 days and nights and still be tired.

Understatement: His clothes have seen better days.

Personification

Personification is the process of attributing human characteristics to nonhuman things.

EXAMPLE

The birds speak from the forest.

Time marches on.

Verbal Irony

Verbal irony is the use of words to express a meaning that is the opposite of what is literally said.[2] If the intent is to hurt, the irony is called **sarcasm.**

EXAMPLE

"What a great looking corporate outfit!" (Said to someone wearing torn jeans.)

"There is nothing like a sunny day for a picnic." (Said during a thunderstorm.)

Exercise 7.9

Discovering Figurative Language in Essays

Read the following essay titled "The Barrio" and enjoy the figurative language. Indicate *a* or *b* for the type of figurative language used, and write a response to the questions.

The train, its metal wheels squealing as they spin along the silvery tracks, rolls slower now. Through the gaps between the cars blinks a streetlamp and this pulsing light on a barrio streetlamp beats slower, like a weary heartbeat, until the train shudders to a halt, the light goes out, and the barrio is deep asleep.

Members of the barrio describe the entire area as their home. It is a home, but it is more than this. The barrio is a refuge from the harshness and the coldness of the Anglo world. It is a forced refuge. There is no want to escape, for the feeling of the barrio is known only to its inhabitants, and the material needs of life can also be found here.

The *tortilleria* [tortilla factory] fires up its machinery three times a day, producing steaming, round, flat slices of barrio bread. In the winter, the warmth of the tortilla factory is a wool *sarape* [blanket] in the chilly morning hours, but in the summer, it unbearably toasts every noontime customer.

---

[2]In situational irony, events occur contrary to what is expected, as if in a cruel twist of fate. For example, Juliet awakens and finds that Romeo has killed himself because he thought she was dead.

The *panaderia* [bakery] sends its sweet messenger aroma down the dimly lit street, announcing the arrival of fresh, hot sugary *pan dulce* [sweet rolls].

The pool hall is a junior level country club where *chucos* [young men], strangers in their own land, get together to shoot pool and rap, while veterans, unaware of the cracking, popping balls on the green felt, complacently play dominoes beneath rudely hung *Playboy* foldouts.

Richard Ramirez, in *Models for Writers*, 8th ed., by Alfred Rosa and Paul Escholz

_____ *b*   1. its metal wheels squealing: a. personification b. simile
_____ *b*   2. blinks a streetlamp: a. personification b. simile
_____ *a*   3. like a weary heartbeat: a. metaphor b. simile
_____ *b*   4. train shudders to a halt: a. personification b. simile
_____ *a*   5. the barrio is deep asleep: a. personification b. simile
_____ *a*   6. tortilla factory is a wool *sarape*: a. metaphor b. simile
_____ *b*   7. toasts every noontime customer: a. personification b. simile
_____ *a*   8. announcing the arrival: a. personification b. simile
_____   9. pool hall is a junior level country club: a. personification
             b. metaphor

10. How does the figurative language add to the pleasure of the essay? _____

_____

11. Why does the author use Spanish vocabulary words? _____

_____

12. What is the connotation of words like *home* and *refuge* in describing the

barrio? _____

Exercise 7.10

Identifying Figurative Language in Textbooks

The figurative expressions in the following sentences are underlined. Identify the figurative type, define each expression, and if possible, suggest the reason for its use.

EXAMPLE   As a trained nurse working in the immigrant slums of New York, she knew that <u>table-top abortions</u> were common among poor women, and she had seen some of the tragic results.

Leonard Pitt, *We Americans*

EXPLANATION   table-top abortions: It is a metaphor, which may now be an idiom, and means illegal. The connotation suggests the reality of where the operations probably occurred.

1. The War of 1812 was Tecumseh's final test. Although his alliance was incomplete, he recognized that the war was his last chance to prevail against the "Long

Knives," as the Americans were called. He <u>cast his lot</u> with the British, who at one point gave him command over a <u>red coat army</u>.

Leonard Pitt, *We Americans*

cast his lot: _Metaphor_

red coat army: _Metaphor_

2. Moist, lead-lemon Bangkok dawn: Miss Bi Chin's Chinese alarm clock goes off, a harsh metallic sound, <u>like tiny villagers beating pans</u> to frighten <u>the dragon of sleep</u>.

Kate Wheeler, *Under the Roof*

Like tiny villagers beating pans: _Simile_

The dragon of sleep: _____

3. Americans <u>"discovered"</u> the Spanish Southwest in the 1820s. Yankee settlers Moses and Stephen Austin took a party of settlers into Texas in 1821.

Leonard Pitt, *We Americans*

"discovered": _Simile_

4. I can still see myself, <u>like a wild bird set free of a cage</u>, running from one berry bush to another, filling <u>my little play bucket</u>, my heart beating with delight at the sight of beautiful mariposa lilies.

Maya Angelou, "Sister Monroe"

like a wild bird set free of a cage: _Simile_

5. The <u>Moving Finger</u> writes; and, having writ,
Moves on; nor all <u>your Piety nor Wit</u>
Shall lure it back <u>to cancel half a Line</u>,
Nor all your Tears <u>wash out a Word of it</u>.

Edward FitzGerald, trans., *The Rubáiyát of Omar Khayyám*

Moving Finger: _Metaphor_

your Piety nor Wit: _Metaphor_

to cancel half a Line: _____

Tears wash out a Word of it: _Metaphor_

Figurative Language and Implied Meaning in Poetry

Poets use connotations and imagery to appeal to the senses and convey striking pictures to us with great economy of words. Because much of the meaning in poetry is implied, this literary form can seem challenging. The highly condensed language of poetry makes every word valuable. Some poems are short rhymes or descriptions of love or emotion, whereas others have a plot and characters. To understand a poem, read it several times and at least once aloud. Know the meanings of words, and pay attention to sentence structure and line breaks. Visualize what you read, and use each part of the poem to help you understand the other parts.[3]

EXAMPLE   The *haiku* poetic form, adapted from Japanese tradition, expresses an insight or impression in 17 syllables and is usually arranged in three lines. What is the image and impression in the following by poet Raymond Roseliep?

> campfire extinguished
> the woman washing dishes
> in a pan of stars

EXPLANATION   When all light is extinguished outside, the stars are so bright that they illuminate the pan for washing.

Exercise 7.11

Understanding Poetry

Read the following poems, and answer the questions. The first poem builds on similes, and the second tells a story.

Poem 1

A Dream Deferred

By Langston Hughes

> What happens to a dream deferred?
> Does it dry up
> Like a raisin in the sun?
> Or fester like a sore—
> And then run?
> Does it stink like rotten meat?
> Or crust and sugar over—
> Like a syrupy sweet?
>
> Maybe it just sags
> Like a heavy load.
>
> Or *does it explode?*

1. What is the meaning of *deferred*? _____

2. List the five similes the author uses, and explain the meaning of each.
   Like a raisin in the sun, fester
   like a sore, Does it stink like a rotten
   meat, Like a syrupy sweet

[3]Heffernan, William, Mark Johnston, and Frank Hodgins. *Literature: Art and Artifact* (New York: Harcourt Brace Jovanovich, 1987), p. 555.

Like a heavy load

3. How many metaphors does the author use? Explain. _____ 1 _____

   What happened to a dream deferred

4. If compared to a luscious bunch of grapes rather than a raisin, how does the meaning change? _____ *It makes nice* _____

5. Why does the poet save *explode* to the end? _____

6. What is the meaning the poet is trying to convey? _____

Poem 2

Mid-Term Break

By Seamus Heaney

I sat all morning in the college sick bay
Counting bells knelling classes to a close.
At two o'clock our neighbors drove me home.
In the porch I met my father crying—
He had always taken funerals in his stride—
And Big Jim Evans saying it was a hard blow.
The baby cooed and laughed and rocked the pram
When I came in, and I was embarrassed
By old men standing up to shake my hand
And tell me they were "sorry for my trouble,"
Whispers informed strangers I was the eldest,
Away at school, as my mother held my hand
In hers and coughed out angry tearless sighs.
At ten o'clock the ambulance arrived
With the corpse, stanched and bandaged by the nurses.
Next morning I went up into the room. Snowdrops
And candles soothed the bedside; I saw him
For the first time in six weeks. Paler now,
Wearing a poppy bruise on his left temple,
He lay in the four foot box as in his cot.
No gaudy scars, the bumper knocked him clear.
A four foot box, a foot for every year.

1. What figure of speech is *bells knelling classes to a close,* and how does it fit the rest of the poem? _____

2. What are the images of grief that the narrator encounters upon entering the house? _____

_____

3. What form of figurative language is "sorry for my trouble"? What does it mean? _____

4. What happened to the brother? _____

5. How old was the brother? _____

6. How is this poem like a mystery? _____

_____

Inferences from Facts

Inferences can be suggested simply by juxtaposing facts. For example, an author selected the following facts from issues of *Time* magazine and presented them consecutively to suggest an inference. No direct connection is stated, so the reader must thoughtfully reflect on the suggested message. This pause for thought adds power to the message.

EXAMPLE

28%   Proportion of public libraries in the United States that offered Internet access in 1996

95%   Proportion of libraries that offer Internet access in 2002

17%   Increase in library attendance between 1996 and 2002

Inference: _____

EXPLANATION   The inference is that library attendance has improved because many more libraries have Internet access. Before libraries buy more computers, however, specific data on daily use should be collected.

Exercise 7.12

Inferring from Facts

400,000   Number of hot dogs ordered for the Winter Olympics

10   Number of days it took to go through the hot-dog supply

1. Inference: _____

_____

_____

1 billion	Number of birds killed by flying into glass windows in the United States each year.
121 million	Number of birds killed annually by U.S. hunters

2. Inference: _____

_____

408	Species that could be extinct by 2050 if global warming trends continue.
6.6 tons	Average amount of greenhouse gases emitted annually by each American, an increase of 3.4% since 1990.

3. Inference: _____

_____

42%	Percentage of adults who say the toothbrush is the one invention they could not live without
6%	Percentage who say the personal computer is the one invention they could not live without.

4. Inference: _____

_____

_____

1	Rank of Super Bowl Sunday, among all the days of the year, in pizza sales at the major U.S. pizza chains
20%	Increase in frozen-pizza sales on Super Bowl Sunday

5. Inference: _____

_____

_____

Appropriate and Inappropriate Inferences

Read the following excerpt about children and see if you can guess who is complaining.

> Children now love luxury. They have bad manners, contempt for authority. They show disrespect for elders. They contradict their parents, chatter before company, cross their legs and tyrannize their teachers.[4]

_____

[4]Platt, Suzy. *Respectfully Quoted* (Washington, DC: Library of Congress, 1989), p. 42.

Did you assume that this is a contemporary description of modern youth? Although it may sound that way, actually the Greek philosopher Plato attributed the quotation to his student and fellow philosopher Socrates, who lived more than 2,300 years ago. Perhaps the only phrase in the excerpt that does not fit a modern speaker is the "cross their legs." The rest of the clues sound deceptively modern, leading readers to make an inappropriate assumption.

How can you tell whether an inference is valid or invalid? If an inference is appropriate or valid, it is an assumption *supported by the clues within the passage.* The clues "add up," and the logic allows you to feel confidence in making certain assumptions. On the other hand, an inappropriate or invalid inference goes beyond the evidence and may be an "off the wall" stab at meaning that was never suggested or intended.

Readers and listeners alike are constantly making inferences; and as more information is revealed, self-corrections are necessary to make sure all the inferences are appropriately based on clues. As we listen to strangers talk, we make assumptions about their backgrounds, motives, and actions. Thus, dialogue is an especially fertile ground for the active mind to find hidden meaning.

| Exercise 7.13 | **Inferring Valid Assumptions from Dialogue** |

Considering the facts presented in the passage, mark the inferences as *V* (valid) or *I* (invalid).

Passage 1

I'm eight years old. But I have the mind of a nineteen-year-old. Mom says it's making up for all the wrong Dad did. Today there's going to be a whole camera crew here. They're going to film different angles of me beating myself at chess. Then they want me to walk around the neighborhood in my Eagle Scout uniform. Dad doesn't want to talk to them. So I guess they'll do an exterior of the penitentiary.

Matt Marinovich, *The Quarterly*

_____ 1. A film is being shot about the child because he is so smart for his age.
_____ 2. The child is a boy.
_____ 3. The father was abusive to the mother and child.
_____ 4. The child has been raised by his mother.
_____ 5. The father is in jail.

Passage 2

"Now how are we going to get across this monster?" Lisa asked.

"Easy," said John. "We take the rope over, get it around that big tree and use the winch to pull the Jeep across."

"But who swims the flood with the rope?"

Well, I can't swim," he said, "but you're supposed to be so good at it."

Anne Bernays and Pamela Painter, *What If?*

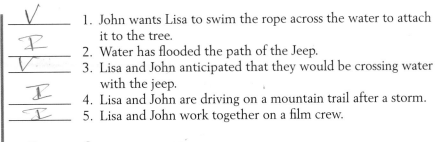

_____V_____ 1. John wants Lisa to swim the rope across the water to attach it to the tree.

_____I_____ 2. Water has flooded the path of the Jeep.

_____V_____ 3. Lisa and John anticipated that they would be crossing water with the jeep.

_____I_____ 4. Lisa and John are driving on a mountain trail after a storm.

_____I_____ 5. Lisa and John work together on a film crew.

Passage 3

So this ordinary patrolman drove me home. He kept his eye on the road, but his thoughts were all on me. He said that I would have to think about Mrs. Metzger, lying cold in the ground, for the rest of my life, and that if he were me, he would probably commit suicide. He said that he expected some relative of Mrs. Metzger would get me sooner or later, when I least expected it—maybe the very next day, or maybe when I was a man, full of hopes and good prospects, and with a family of my own. Whoever did it, he said, would probably want me to suffer some.

Kurt Vonnegut, Jr., *Deadeye Dick*

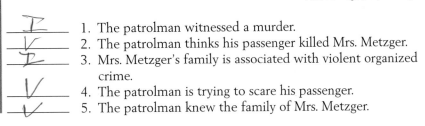

_____I_____ 1. The patrolman witnessed a murder.

_____V_____ 2. The patrolman thinks his passenger killed Mrs. Metzger.

_____I_____ 3. Mrs. Metzger's family is associated with violent organized crime.

_____V_____ 4. The patrolman is trying to scare his passenger.

_____V_____ 5. The patrolman knew the family of Mrs. Metzger.

Implied Meaning

Reading would be rather dull if authors stated every idea, never giving you a chance to figure things out for yourself. For example, in a mystery novel, you carefully weigh each word, each action, each conversation, each description, and each fact in an effort to identify the villain and solve the crime before it is revealed at the end. Although textbook material may not have the Sherlock Holmes spirit of high adventure, authors use the same techniques to imply meaning.

Note the inferences in the following example.

EXAMPLE

Johnson in Action

Lyndon Johnson suffered from the inevitable comparison with his young and stylish predecessor. LBJ was acutely aware of his own lack of polish; he sought to surround himself with Kennedy advisers and insiders, hoping that their learning and sophistication would rub off on him. Johnson's assets were very real—an intimate knowledge of Congress, an incredible energy and determination to succeed, and a fierce ego. When a young Marine officer tried to direct him to the proper helicopter, saying, "This one is yours," Johnson replied, "Son, they are all my helicopters."

LBJ's height and intensity gave him a powerful presence; he dominated any room he entered, and he delighted in using his physical power of persuasion.

> One Texas politician explained why he had given in to Johnson: "Lyndon got me by the lapels and put his face on top of mine and he talked and talked and talked. I figured it was either getting drowned or joining."
>
> Robert A. Divine et al., *America Past and Present*

Answer the following with *T* (true) or *F* (false).

_____ 1. Johnson was haunted by the style and sophistication of John F. Kennedy.

_____ 2. Johnson could be both egotistical and arrogant about his presidential power.

_____ 3. Even if he did not mentally persuade, Johnson could physically overwhelm people into agreement.

EXPLANATION   The answer to question 1 is *True*. He "suffered from the inevitable comparison" and he went so far as to retain the Kennedy advisers. Question 2 is *True*. The anecdote about the helicopters proves that. Question 3 is *True*. His delight in "using his physical powers of persuasion" and the anecdote about the Texas politician support that.

In the following exercises, you can see how authors use suggestions. From the clues given, you can deduce the facts.

Exercise 7.14

Inference from Description

> Looking back on the Revolutionary War, one cannot say enough about Washington's leadership. While his military skills proved less than brilliant and he and his generals lost many battles, George Washington was the single most important figure of the colonial war effort. His original appointment was partly political, for the rebellion that had started in Massachusetts needed a commander from the South to give geographic balance to the cause. The choice fell to Washington, a wealthy and respectable Virginia planter with military experience dating back to the French and Indian War. He had been denied a commission in the English army and had never forgiven the English for the insult. During the war he shared the physical suffering of his men, rarely wavered on important questions, and always used his officers to good advantage. His correspondence with Congress to ask for sorely needed supplies was tireless and forceful. He recruited several new armies in a row, as short-term enlistments gave out.
>
> Leonard Pitt, *We Americans*

Answer the following with *T* (true) or *F* (false):

___T___ 1. The author regards George Washington as the most brilliant military genius in American history.

___T___ 2. A prime factor in Washington's becoming president of the United States was a need for geographic balance.

___F___ 3. Washington resented the British for a past injustice.

_____ 4. The Revolutionary War started as a rebellion in the northeast.

_____ 5. The author believes that Washington's leadership was courageous and persistent even though not infallible.

**Exercise
7.15**

Inference from Action

> When he came to the surface he was conscious of little but the noisy water. After-
> ward he saw his companions in the sea. The oiler was ahead in the race. He was
> swimming strongly and rapidly. Off to the correspondent's left, the cook's great
> white and corked back bulged out of the water, and in the rear the captain was
> hanging with his one good hand to the keel of the overturned dinghy.
>
>   There is a certain immovable quality to a shore, and the correspondent won-
> dered at it amid the confusion of the sea.
>
> Stephen Crane, The Open Boat

Answer the following with *a, b, c,* or *d.* Draw a map indicating the shore and
the positions of the four people in the water to help you visualize the scene.

_____ 1. The reason that the people are in the water is because of
   a. a swimming race.
   b. an airplane crash.
   c. a capsized boat.
   d. a group decision.

_____ 2. In relation to his companions, the correspondent is
   a. closest to the shore.
   b. the second or third closest to the shore.
   c. farthest from the shore.
   d. in a position that is impossible to determine.

_____ 3. The member of the group that had probably suffered a previous injury is the
   a. oiler.
   b. correspondent.
   c. cook.
   d. captain.

_____ 4. The member of the group that the author seems to stereotype negatively as least physically fit is the
   a. oiler.
   b. correspondent.
   c. cook.
   d. captain.

_____ 5. The story is being told through the eyes of the
   a. oiler.
   b. correspondent.
   c. cook.
   d. captain.

<table>
<tr><td>**Exercise
7.16**</td><td>**Inference from Factual Material**</td></tr>
</table>

Mexico, by many indicators, should be among the most prosperous nations on earth. It is a large country, occupying some 72 percent of the land of Middle America and containing 57 percent of the population of that area. It has benefited throughout its history from some of the richest mineral deposits on earth—first its silver in the colonial period and now its petroleum and natural gas. Mexico's proximity to the technologically advanced and wealthy United States is also a potential economic advantage of significance as are its varied agricultural land-scapes, which range from irrigated deserts in the north to tropical rain forests in parts of the gulf coastal lowlands. To understand Mexico's limited economic achievement, we must evaluate the treatment of its people.

David Clawson and Merrill Johnson, World Regional Geography, 8th ed.

Answer the following with *T* (true) or *F* (false):

___T___ 1. The author implies that Mexico has fallen short of its economic potential.

___T___ 2. The author implies that Mexico's lag in economic achievement is due to its treatment of its people.

___F___ 3. The author implies that profits from Mexico's silver, oil, and gas were exploited or stolen by other countries.

___T___ 4. The author implies that Mexico does not have enough resources to compensate for its natural physical limitations.

___F___ 5. The author implies that economic trade advantages can be derived from bordering a wealthy country.

Prior Knowledge and Implied Meaning

Just as a joke is funny only if you have the right background knowledge, college reading is easier if you have **prior knowledge** needed to grasp the details that are frequently implied rather than directly spelled out. For example, if a sentence began, "Previously wealthy investors were leaping from buildings in the financial district," you would know that the author was referring to the stock market crash of 1929 on Wall Street in New York City. The details fall into an already existing schema. Although the specifics are not directly stated, you have used prior knowledge and have "added up" the details that are meaningful to you to infer time and place.

<table>
<tr><td>**Exercise
7.17**</td><td>**Inferring Time and Place**</td></tr>
</table>

Read the following passages and indicate *a, b,* or *c* for the suggested time and place. Use your prior knowledge of "anchor" dates in history to logically think about the possible responses. Underline the clues that helped you arrive at your answers.

Passage A

As women strove to maintain a semblance of home on the trail, they often experienced a profound sense of loss. The Sabbath, which had been ladies' day back home and an emblem of women's moral authority, was often spent working or traveling, especially once the going got rough. "Oh dear me I did not think we would have abused the Sabbath in such a manner," wrote one guilt-stricken female emigrant. Women also felt the lack of close companions, to whom they could turn for comfort. One woman, whose husband separated their wagon from the train after a dispute, sadly watched the other wagons pull away: "I felt that indeed I had left all my friends to journey over the dreaded plains without one female acquaintance even for a companion—of course I wept and grieved about it but to no purpose."

James Davidson et al., *Nation of Nations*

 1. The time when this takes place is probably in the
   a. 1710s.
   b. 1840s.
   c. 1920s.

 2. The section of the United States is most likely the
   a. west.
   b. south.
   c. north.

3. Underline the clues to your answers.

Passage B

There was an average of fifty storms a year. Cities kept their street lights on for twenty-four hours a day. Dust covered everything from food to bedspreads and piled up in dunes in city streets and barnyards. Thousands died of "dust pneumonia." One woman remembered what it was like at night: "A trip for water to rinse the grit from our lips, and then back to bed with washclothes over our noses, we try to lie still, because every turn stirs the dust on the blankets."

By the end of the decade three and a half million people had abandoned their farms and joined a massive migration to find a better life. Not all were forced out by the dust storms; some fell victim to large-scale agriculture, and many tenant farmers and hired hands were expendable during the depression. In most cases they not only lost their jobs, but they also were evicted from their houses.

Gary B. Nash et al., *The American People*

 4. The time is probably in the
   a. 1690s.
   b. 1770s.
   c. 1930s.

 5. The place is most likely
   a. New England.
   b. the Great Plains.
   c. the Deep South.

6. Underline the clues to your answers.

Passage C

On November 28 the first tea ship, the *Dartmouth,* docked. The local customs collectors fled to Fort Castle William, and the local committee of correspondence, headed by Samuel Adams and his associates, put guards on the *Dartmouth* and two other tea ships entering the port within the next few days. Repeatedly the popular rights faction insisted that the three tea ships be sent back to England. But Governor Hutchinson refused. Instead, he called upon Royal Naval vessels in the vicinity to block off the port's entrance.

James Martin et al., *America and Its People*

_____ 7. The time is probably in the
        a. 1770s.
        b. 1850s.
        c. 1920s.

_____ 8. The place is probably
        a. Washington, D.C.
        b. Boston.
        c. New Orleans.

           9. Underline the clues to your answers.

Expanding Prior Knowledge

Your response on the previous passages depends on your previous knowledge of history and your general knowledge. If you did not understand many of the inferences, you might ask, "How can I expand my prior knowledge?" The answer is not an easy formula or a quick fix. The answer is part of the reason that you are in college; it is a combination of broadening your horizons, reading more widely, and being an active participant in your own life. Expanding prior knowledge is a slow and steady daily process.

Drawing Conclusions

To arrive at a conclusion, you must make a logical deduction from both stated ideas and from unstated assumptions. Using the hints as well as the facts, you rely on prior knowledge and experience to interpret motives, actions, and outcomes. You draw conclusions on the basis of perceived evidence, but because perceptions differ, conclusions can vary from reader to reader. Generally, however, authors attempt to direct readers to preconceived conclusions. Read the following example and look for a basis for the stated conclusion.

EXAMPLE

Underground Conductor

Harriet Tubman was on a northbound train when she overheard her name spoken by a white passenger. He was reading aloud an ad which accused her of stealing $50,000 worth of property in slaves, and which offered a $5000 reward for her capture. She lowered her head so that the sunbonnet she was wearing hid her face. At the next station she slipped off the train and boarded another that was headed south, reasoning that no one would pay attention to a black woman traveling in that direction. She deserted the second train near her hometown in Maryland and bought two chickens as part of her disguise. With her back hunched over in imitation of an old woman, she drove the chickens down the dusty road, calling angrily and chasing them with her stick whenever she sensed danger. In this manner Harriet Tubman was passed by her former owner who did not even notice her. The reward continued to mount until it reached $40,000.

Leonard Pitt, *We Americans*

Conclusion: Harriet Tubman was a clever woman who became a severe irritant to white slave owners.

What is the basis for this conclusion?

_____

_____

EXPLANATION   Her disguise and subsequent escape from the train station provide evidence for her intelligence. The escalating amount of the reward, finally $40,000, proves the severity of the sentiment against her.

READER'S TIP

Making Inferences

◆ Consider attitude in the choice of words.

◆ Think about what might have been left out.

◆ Unravel actions.

◆ Interpret motives.

◆ Use suggested meaning and facts to make assumptions.

◆ Draw on prior knowledge to make connections.

◆ Base conclusions on stated ideas and unstated assumptions.

Exercise 7.18

Drawing Conclusions

Read the following passages. For the first passage indicate evidence for the conclusion that has been drawn. For the latter passages, write your own conclusion as well as indicate evidence. Use the suggestions in the Reader's Tip to help you.

Passage A

Parts of a dismembered corpse washed ashore in the Florida Keys. The body, which had been in the water no more than a few days, displayed clear evidence of shark bites, and local law enforcement officers concluded that the victim had fallen over-board from a passing ship and had been attacked by sharks. However, there had been no reports of missing persons in the area. A medical anthropologist, who became interested in the case and who was allowed to examine the body, identified fine scratches on the exposed surface to the top vertebra where the head seemed to have been bitten off. He positively identified the scratches as the result of a hacksaw.

William R. Maples, *Dead Men Do Tell Tales*

Conclusion: The victim had been murdered and partially dismembered before being dumped into the ocean.

What is the basis for this conclusion? _____

_____

Passage B

Beginning in the 1980s, Saudi Arabia initiated a policy of agricultural self-sufficiency. By 1991, for example, irrigated cereal production on 2 percent of the country's area had expanded to such an extent that the country was able to become a major exporter of wheat and other cereals. Production increases have been based on government subsidies and the introduction of modern groundwa-ter irrigation technology. These systems have consumed tremendous amounts of water. Agriculture consumes almost 90 percent of the water used in Saudi Arabia each year. Yet, agriculture generates only 7 percent of the national economic out-put and employs less than 10 percent of the Saudi labor force.

Adapted from David Clawson and Merrill Johnson, *World Regional Georgraphy*, 8th ed.

Conclusion: Agriculture is not a productive or sustainable use of a critically limited resources for Saudi Arabia

What is the basis for this conclusion? _____

_____

_____

Passage C

Writing is untidy and disconcerting. No successful ad company would want to mar-ket it. It's not fast, it's not predictable, it's not sweet. First we fantasize about that hushed moment when we'll be wonderfully alone with all our familiar, comforting writing implements at hand. I visualize a sunny room and my cup of tea. We savor the moment when, bulging with inspiration and wisdom, we at last lift our pen or start our computer and begin a new work. And work it is, though we forget that aspect in the amnesia necessary to bring us back to the blank page.

Pat Moro, "Universities," in *Nepantla*

Conclusion: _____

_____

What is the basis for this conclusion? _____

_____

Passage D

As social psychologist Sharon Brehm explains, "To meet people is not necessarily to love them, but to love them we must first meet them." In your classes, you are more likely to form relationships with classmates sitting on either side of you than with someone seated at the opposite end of the room. This is partly because physical **proximity** increases communication opportunities. We are more likely to talk, and therefore to feel attracted, to neighbors who live right next door than those who live down the block.

Steven Beebe et al., Communications

Conclusion: _____

_____

What is the basis for this conclusion? _____

_____

Exercise 7.19

Building a Story with Inferences

The following story unfolds as the reader uses the clues to predict and make inferences. To make sense out of the story, the reader is never told—but must figure out—who the main character is, what he is doing, and why he is doing it. Like a mystery, the story is fun to read because you are actively involved. Review the strategies for making inferences, and then use your inferential skills to figure it out.

Caged

Emphatically, Mr. Purcell did not believe in ghosts. Nevertheless, the man who bought the two doves, and his strange act immediately thereafter, left him with a distinct sense of the eerie.

Purcell was a small, fussy man; red cheeks and a tight, melon stomach. He owned a pet shop. He sold cats and dogs and monkeys; he dealt in fish food and bird seed, and prescribed remedies for ailing canaries. He considered himself something of a professional man.

There was a bell over the door that jangled whenever a customer entered. This morning, however, for the first time Mr. Purcell could recall, it failed to ring. Simply he glanced up, and there was the stranger, standing just inside the door, as if he had materialized out of thin air.

The storekeeper slid off his stool. From the first instant he knew instinctively, unreasonably, that the man hated him; but out of habit he rubbed his hands briskly together, smiled and nodded.

"Good morning," he beamed. "What can I do for you?"

The man's shiny shoes squeaked forward. His suit was cheap, ill-fitting, but obviously new. A gray pallor deadened his pinched features. He had a shuttling glance and close-cropped hair. He stared closely at Purcell and said, "I want something in a cage."

"Something in a cage?" Mr. Purcell was a bit confused. "You mean—some kind of pet?"

"I mean what I said!" snapped the man. "Something alive that's in a cage."

"I see," hastened the storekeeper, not at all certain that he did. "Now let me think. A white rat, perhaps."

"No!" said the man. "Not rats. Something with wings. Something that flies."

"A bird!" exclaimed Mr. Purcell.

"A bird's all right." The customer pointed suddenly to a suspended cage which contained two snowy birds. "Doves? How much for those?"

"Five-fifty. And a very reasonable price."

"Five-fifty?" The sallow man was obviously crestfallen. He hesitantly produced a five-dollar bill. "I'd like to have those birds. But this is all I got. Just five dollars."

Mentally, Mr. Purcell made a quick calculation, which told him that at a fifty-cent reduction he could still reap a tidy profit. He smiled magnanimously. "My dear man, if you want them that badly, you can certainly have them for five dollars."

"I'll take them." He laid his five dollars on the counter. Mr. Purcell teetered on tiptoe, unhooked the cage, and handed it to his customer. The man cocked his head to one side, listening to the constant chittering, the rushing scurry of the shop. "That noise?" he blurted. "Doesn't it get you? I mean all this caged stuff. Drives you crazy, doesn't it?"

Purcell drew back. Either the man was insane, or drunk.

"Listen." The staring eyes came closer. "How long d'you think it took me to make that five dollars?"

The merchant wanted to order him out of the shop. But he heard himself duti-fully asking, "Why—why, how long *did* it take you?"

The other laughed. "Ten years! At hard labor. Ten years to earn five dollars. Fifty cents a year."

It was best, Purcell decided, to humor him. "My, my! Ten years—"

"They give you five dollars," laughed the man, "and a cheap suit, and tell you not to get caught again."

Mr. Purcell mopped his sweating brow. "Now, about the care and feeding of—"

"Bah!" The sallow man swung around, and stalked abruptly from the store.

Purcell sighed with sudden relief. He waddled to the window and stared out. Just outside, his peculiar customer had halted. He was holding the cage shoulder-high, staring at his purchase. Then, opening the cage, he reached inside and drew out one of the doves. He tossed it into the air. He drew out the second and tossed it after the first. They rose like wind-blown balls of fluff and were lost in the smoky grey of the wintry city. For an instant the liberator's silent and lifted gaze watched after them. Then he dropped the cage. A futile, suddenly forlorn figure, he shoved both hands deep in his trouser pockets, hunched down his head and shuffled away. . . .

The merchant's brow was puckered with perplexity. "Now why," Mr. Purcell muttered, "did he do that?" He felt vaguely insulted.

Lloyd Eric Reeve, *Household Magazine*

1. Where had the man been? _____

2. How do you know for sure? Underline the clues. _____

_____

3. When did you figure it out? Circle the clincher. _____

_____

4. Why does he want to set the birds free? _____

_____

5. Why should the shopkeeper feel insulted? _____

_____

6. After freeing the birds, why is the stranger "a futile, suddenly forlorn figure," rather than happy and excited? _____

_____

Summary Points

● **What is an inference?**

The inferential level of reading deals with motives, feelings, and judgments. The reader must read between the lines and look for the implied meaning in words and actions. Understanding implied meaning can be the determining factor in a reader's comprehension of jokes, advertisements, poetry, and some prose.

● **What is the connotation of a word?**

The feeling or emotionalism surrounding a word is its connotation. The connotation reflects certain attitudes and prejudices of society that can be positive or negative. The author's choice of words can manipulate the reader.

● **What is figurative language?**

Figurative language creates images to suggest attitudes. It is a different way of using "regular" words so that the words take on new meaning. A simile is a comparison of two unlike things using the words *like* or *as*, whereas a metaphor is a directly stated comparison. A literary analogy includes both similes and metaphors. A euphemism is a more pleasant way of saying something that is embarrassing or indelicate. Hyperbole is a figurative exaggeration. Personification attributes human characteristics to nonhuman things. Verbal irony expresses a meaning the opposite of what is literally said.

● **Why is prior knowledge needed to grasp implied meaning?**

The reader must have background knowledge in a subject to understand the suggested or implied meaning.

● **How does a reader draw conclusions?**

The reader makes a logical deduction from hints, facts, and prior knowledge.

CONTEMPORARY FOCUS

No longer is Las Vegas the only glittering legal gambling town in the United States. More and more places are obtaining gaming rights and building large casinos. What drives people to gamble and to think they will beat the odds and win? What are the consequences of a big loss?

HIGH-STAKES PALACES OF GAMBLING

By Denis Horgan

Hartford Courant (Hartford, Connecticut), April 11, 2004

If The Donald's casinos are in trouble, don't blame me. I did my part, losing money there. In fact, I am an equal-opportunity loser. I lost money at all the casinos I visited. It's not hard to do. I lost at Harrah's. I lost at Bally's. I lost at two of the Trumps. I lost at Caesar's. I don't mean to brag but I could lose at tic-tac-toe. It's a gift.

The Atlantic City gambling hall gross take is $4.2 billion a year. (It takes us losing $4.2 billion for them to win $4.2 billion.)

Atlantic City on the outside may be bright and colorful and fresh and natural, but inside the casinos—new and old—it is the gambling business as usual. Largely mirthlessly, there is a sense of relentlessness about the gambling game, notably at the acres of slot machines where the distinction between the machine and the person operating it is hard to discern. Seemingly it is against the rules to demonstrate any emotion.

Diligently applying yourself, you can lose at the slots or at the table games. You can lose at blackjack, poker, Let It Ride, baccarat, carnival wheels, craps, roulette. If you lose all you have, there are cashiers' cages and ATMs and credit offices where you can get even more to lose. They are very polite and helpful, attending to your every opportunity to lose.

For all the money passing hands, fortunes being won and lost, it is a muted world with the edgy sense that fortune or calamity is in the next card, the next roll of the dice or spin of the wheel.

That said, if you set your limits and stick to them, there is the enduring, razory fascination that gambling generates. The spirit of greed and abandon and outlaw-playing is in the air. The human drama of winning and losing and watching others win or lose holds its own special fascination. It is never dull. Not ever.

Collaborate

Collaborate on responses to the following questions:

- Have you ever gambled?
- Why do people think they might win the lottery?
- If you wish to gamble, how should you control what you spend or lose?

Preview

Preview the next selection to predict its purpose and organization and to formulate your learning plan.

Activate Schema

When you were young, where did you hide your money?

Could you trust family members not to touch your hidden money?

Establish a Purpose for Reading

We all have "relationships" with our money. In this short story, Ah Bah loved money and was so careful with it that he kept it in several hiding places. Read to find out what happens to Ah Bah's money. Discover the writer's use of irony to establish the story's theme.

Increase Word Knowledge

doleful	defiance	conspicuous	feverishly	direful
vexation	portentous	reeking		ingenuity	assiduously

Your instructor may give a true-false vocabulary review before or after reading.

Integrate Knowledge While Reading

Inference questions have been inserted in the margin to stimulate your thinking and help you read between the lines. Remember to

Predict   Picture   Relate   Monitor   Correct

AH BAH'S MONEY

By Catherine Lim

Ah Bah's money, in two one-dollar notes and an assortment of coins, lay in a pile on the old handkerchief, but Ah Bah was reluctant to pull up the corners into a bundle to put inside the cigarette tin. Ah Bah was reluctant because the sight of his money gave him so much pleasure. He had already done the fol-
5   lowing things with his money: spread out the notes and arranged the coins in a row beside them, stacked up the coins according to their denominations, and stacked up the coins to make each stack come to a dollar. But still he wanted to go on touching his money. He could tell exactly which coin came from whom or where. The twenty-cent coin with the greenish stain on the edge was
10   given to him by Ah Lam Soh, who was opening her purse when the coin dropped out and he picked it up for her.

"You may keep it," she said, and thereafter Ah Bah watched closely every time Ah Lam Soh opened her purse or put her hand into her blouse pocket. The ten-cent coin, which had a better shine than all the rest, he

15 had actually found near a rubbish dump, almost hidden from sight by an old slipper. And the largest coin of all, the fifty-cent coin, he had earned. He was still rather puzzled about why Kim Heok Soh had given him so much money; he had been required merely to stand in the front portion of

20 the house and to say to any visitor, "Kim Heok Soh has gone to the dry goods shop and will not be back till an hour later. She has asked me to take care of her house for her." But all the time Kim Heok Soh was in the house; he knew because he could hear her in the room and there was somebody with her.

He counted his money—five dollars and eighty-five cents, and his heart
25 glowed. Very carefully, he pulled up the corners of the handkerchief at last into a tight bundle which he then put inside the cigarette tin. Then he put the cover on firmly, and his money, now safe and secure, was ready to go back into its hiding place in a corner of the cupboard behind the stacks of old clothes, newspapers and calendars.

30 And now Ah Bah became uneasy, and he watched to see if his father's eyes would rest on the old broken-down cupboard that held his treasure, for once his father had found his money—two dollars in twenty- and ten-cent coins—tied up in a piece of rag and hidden under his pillow, and had taken it away for another bottle of beer. His father drank beer almost every night.

35 Sometimes he was in a good mood after his beer and he would talk endlessly about this or that, smiling to himself. But generally he became sullen and bad-tempered, and he would begin shouting at anyone who came near. Once he threw an empty beer bottle at Ah Bah's mother; it missed her head and went crashing against the wall. Ah Bah was terrified of his father, but his

40 mother appeared indifferent. "The lunatic," she would say, but never in his hearing. Whenever he was not at home, she would slip out and play cards in Ah Lam Soh's house. One evening she returned, flushed with excitement, and gave him fifty cents; she said it had been her lucky day. At other times she came back with a dispirited look, and Ah Bah knew she had lost all her

45 money in Ah Lam Soh's house.

The New Year was coming and Ah Bah looked forward to it with an intensity that he could barely conceal. New Year meant *ang pows*; Ah Bah's thin little fingers closed round the red packets of money given him by the New Year visitors with such energy that his mother would scold him and shake her head

50 in doleful apology, as she remarked loudly to the visitors, "My Ah Bah, he feels no shame whatever!"

His forefinger and thumb feeling expertly through the red paper, Ah Bah could tell immediately how much was in the red packet; his heart would sink a little if the fingers felt the hard edges of coins, for that would be forty cents

55 or eighty cents at most. But if nothing was felt, then joy of joys! Here was at least a dollar inside.

This year Ah Bah had *eight* dollar notes. He could hardly believe it when he took stock of his wealth on the last day of the festive season. Eight new notes, crisp, still smelling new, and showing no creases except where they

60 had been folded to go into the red packets. Eight dollars! And a small pile

---

What was Kim Heok Soh's motivation for giving Ah Bah money and jobs?

Why does the author emphasize Ah Bah's love of money?

Colorful dragons decorate Singapore for Chinese New Year festivities.
Kevin R. Morris/CORBIS

of coins besides. Ah Bah experienced a thrill such as he had never felt before.

And then it was all anxiety and fear, for he realized that his father knew about his *ang pow* money; indeed his father had referred to it once or twice,
65 and would, Ah Bah was certain, be searching the bedding, cupboard and other places in the house for it.

Ah Bah's heart beat with the violence of angry defiance at the thought. The total amount in his cigarette tin was now seventeen dollars and twenty-five cents, and Ah Bah was determined to protect his money at all costs.
70 Nobody was going to take his money from him. Frantically, Ah Bah went to the cupboard, took out the bundle of money from the cigarette tin and stuffed it into his trouser pocket. It made a conspicuous bulge. Ah Bah didn't know what to do, and his little mind worked feverishly to find a way out of this very direful situation.

75 He was wandering about in the village the next day as usual, and when he

How old is Ah Bah?

returned home, he was crying bitterly. His pocket was empty. When his mother came to him and asked him what the matter was, he bawled. He told her, between sobs, that a rough-looking Indian had pushed him to the ground and taken away his money. His father, who was in the bedroom, rushed out
80 and made Ah Bah tell again what had happened. When Ah Bah had finished, sniffling miserably, his father hit him on the head, snarling," You idiot! Why were you so anxious to show off your *ang pow* money? Now you've lost it all!" And when he was told that the sum was seventeen dollars and twenty-five cents, his vexation was extreme, so that he would not be contented till he had
85 hit the boy again.

Ah Bah's mother cleaned the bruise on the side of his face where he had been pushed to the ground, and led him away from his father.

"You are a silly boy," she scolded. "Why did you carry so much money around with you? Someone was sure to rob you!" And feeling sorry for him,
90 she felt about in her blouse pocket and found she could spare fifty cents, so she gave it to him, saying, "Next time, don't be so silly, son."

He took the coin from her, and he was deeply moved. An then, upon impulse, he took her by the hand, and led her outside their house to the old hen-house, near the well, under the trees, and he whispered to her, his head
95 almost bursting with the excitement of a portentous secret successfully kept, "It's there! In the cigarette tin, behind that piece of wood!" To prove it, he squeezed into the hen house and soon emerged, reeking of hen house odors, triumphantly clutching the tin. He took off the lid and showed her the money inside.

100 She was all amazement. Then she began to laugh and to shake her head over the ingenuity of it all, while he stood looking up at her, his eyes bright and bold with victory.

"You're a clever boy," she said, "but take care that you don't go near the hen house often. Your father's pocket is empty again, and he's looking around to
105 see whose money he can get hold of, that devil."

Ah Bah earned twenty cents helping Ah Lau Sim to scrape coconut, and his mother allowed him to have the ten cents which he found on a shelf, under a comb. Clutching his money, he stole out of the house; he was just in time to back out of the hen house, straighten himself and pretend to be
110 looking for dried twigs for firewood, for his father stood at the doorway, looking at him. His father was in a restless mood again, pacing the floor with a dark look on his face, and this was the sign that he wanted his beer very badly but had no money to pay for it. Ah Bah bent low, assiduously looking for firewood, and then through the corner of his eye, he saw his
115 father go back into the house.

That night Ah Bah dreamt that his father had found out the hiding place in the hen house, and early next morning, his heart beating wildly, he stole out and went straight to the hen house. He felt about in the darkness for his cigarette tin; his hand touched the damp of the hen droppings and caught on a
120 nail, and still he searched—but the cigarette tin was not there.

He ran sniffling to his mother, and she began to scold him, "I told you not to go there too often, but you wouldn't listen to me. Didn't you know your father has been asking for money? The devil's found you out again!"

The boy continued to sniff, his little heart aching with the terrible pain of loss.
125 "Never mind," his mother said, "you be a good boy and don't say anything about it; otherwise your father's sure to rage like a mad man." She led him inside the house and gave him a slice of bread with some sugar.

She was glad when he quieted down at last, for she didn't want to keep Ah Lam Soh and the others waiting. The seventeen dollars and twenty-five
130 cents (she had hurriedly hidden the handkerchief and the cigarette tin) was secure in her blouse pocket, and she slipped away with eager steps for, as the fortune teller had told her, this was the beginning of a period of good luck for her.

Margin annotations:

Why does Ah Bah trust the mother?

How could you prove this theft in court?

Recall

Stop to self-test, relate, and react.

Your instructor may choose to give you a true-false comprehension review.

Write About the Selection

How was Ah Bah a victim of two addictions? Explain how his love of money could have been a reaction to their addictions.
   Response Suggestion: Define the father's and mother's addictions, and comment on Ah Bah's love of money.

Contemporary Link

What is it about gambling that makes people willing to risk money and family trust? If Ah Bah trusted his mother, why would she steal from her son? What was she thinking? Was her thinking the same as that of gamblers who go to casinos and play the slots and blackjack?

Skill Development: Implied Meaning

According to the implied meaning in the selection, answer the following with *T* (true) or *F* (false):

_____ 1. Ah Bah's parents did not serve as role models for his accumulating money.

_____ 2. The author suggests that Ah Bah stole some of his coins.

_____ 3. The reader can conclude that Kim Heok Soh probably overpaid Ah Bah because she wanted to silence him.

_____ 4. The author suggests that Ah Bah's parents also gave *ang pows*.

_____ 5. The author suggests that Ah Bah suspected his mother of taking his money.

Check Your Comprehension

Answer the following with *a, b, c,* or *d,* or fill in the blank. To help you analyze your strengths and weaknesses, the question types are indicated.

Main Idea   _____ 1. Which is the best statement of the main idea of this selection?
     a. Ah Bah worshiped his money and the money destroyed him.
     b. Ah Bah lied to safeguard his money and was punished.

c. Ah Bah cunningly guarded his money but lost it to the one person he trusted.

d. Ah Bah's parents ruined his life through dishonestly and corruption.

Detail _____ 2. Ah Bah does all the following with his money except

a. remember where he got each coin.

b. stack the coins to make dollars.

c. formulate a plan for spending his money.

d. arrange the coins in a row.

Inference _____ 3. As Ah Bah was paid to watch her house, the reader can most likely conclude that Kim Heok Soh was

a. gambling.

b. selling drugs.

c. seeing a lover.

d. at the dry goods shop.

Detail _____ 4. According to the passage, Ah Bah's father did all the following except

a. beat Ah Bah.

b. injure Ah Bah's mother through abuse.

c. steal Ah Bah's money.

d. drink too much to remain civil.

Detail _____ 5. According to the passage, the gambling of Ah Bah's mother was

a. known but ignored by his father.

b. known by Ah Bah.

c. fruitless because she never won.

d. an addiction she was trying to break.

Inference _____ 6. The reader can conclude that *ang pows* are

a. monetary good luck wishes for the family.

b. red gift packets to celebrate Christmas.

c. rewards for good behavior.

d. New Year's gifts for children.

Inference _____ 7. Ah Bah pretended a rough-looking Indian had taken his money because

a. his father would be afraid to chase the Indian.

b. his mother would sympathize and give him more money.

c. he wanted his father to believe the money was gone.

d. he wanted to share the money with his mother.

Inference _____ 8. Ah Bah divulged his most cherished secret only when faced with

a. punishment.

b. abuse.

c. trickery.

d. kindness.

Detail _____ 9. The mother passed the blame and ensured secrecy for her theft by
   a. returning the cigarette tin to the hen house.
   b. telling Ah Bah not to tell his father.
   c. purchasing liquor for the father.
   d. her willingness to replace the money with her gambling winnings.

Inference _____ 10. The irony in the story is
   a. Ah Bah's successful deception was unexpectedly over-turned by his mother's equally successful deception.
   b. love of money causes people to lie and steal.
   c. abuse and addiction hurt all members of a family.
   d. Ah Bah's love of money might help him escape the cycle of poverty.

Answer the following with *T* (true), *F* (false), or *CT* (can't tell).

Inference _____ 11. The fortune teller's advice to the mother did not accurately apply to Ah Bah.

Inference _____ 12. Ah Bah's mother craftily used past history and suspicious actions to implicate the father in the theft.

Inference _____ 13. The author suggests that Ah Bah's mother intended to replace the money after she won.

Inference _____ 14. The author suggests that Ah Bah's mother was surprised and pleased at Ah Bah's trickery in protecting his money.

Inference _____ 15. The author suggests that Ah Bah's mother comforted him and gave him fifty cents in hopes of finding out the truth about his money.

Build Your Vocabulary

According to the way the italicized word was used in the selection, select *a, b, c,* or *d* for the word or phrase that gives the best definition.. The number in parentheses indicates the line of the passage in which the word is located.

_____ 1. "*doleful* apology" (50)
   a. gracious
   b. quick
   c. shallow
   d. sad

_____ 2. "angry *defiance*" (67)
   a. rebelliousness
   b. horror
   c. wishes
   d. suffering

_____ 3. "*conspicuous* bulge" (72)
   a. ugly
   b. noticeable
   c. hidden
   d. irritating

_____ 4. "mind worked *feverishly*" (73)
   a. sickly
   b. openly
   c. slowly
   d. excitedly

_____ 5. "very *direful* situation" (74)
    a. exhausting
    b. confusing
    c. dreadful
    d. painful

_____ 6. "his *vexation* was extreme" (84)
    a. displeasure
    b. madness
    c. hopelessness
    d. security

_____ 7. "*portentous* secret" (95)
    a. blameless
    b. marvelous suspenseful
    c. dishonest
    d. abundant

_____ 8. "*reeking* of hen house" (97)
    a. welcoming
    b. escaping
    c. stinking
    d. stained

_____ 9. "over the *ingenuity* of it" (101)
    a. cleverness
    b. dishonesty
    c. trouble
    d. reaction

_____ 10. "*assiduously* looking for" (113)
    a. unknowingly
    b. tirelessly
    c. lazily
    d. carelessly

Search the Net

Use a search engine such as Google, AltaVista, Excite, Infoseek, Dogpile, Yahoo, or Lycos to find information on the impact of gambling addiction on families. Describe how this addiction can be treated. For suggested Web sites and other research activities, go to http://www.ablongman.com/smith/.

Concept Prep

for Philosophy and Literature

The ancient Greeks laid the foundations for Western traditions in science, philosophy, literature, and the arts. They set the standards for proportion and beauty in art and architecture, and we continue to ponder their questions about the good life, the duties of a citizen, and the nature of the universe.

Who were the most notable Greek philosophers?

- One of the most notable philosophers was **Socrates,** the teacher of Plato. Socrates sought an understanding of the world while other teachers of the time taught students how to get along in the world. Socrates proclaimed himself to be the wisest of all the thinkers because he knew how little he knew. He used a method of teaching that explored a subject from all sides with questions and answers, as opposed to the lecture method. Today this teaching technique is known as the **Socratic method.** Socrates took no pay for his teachings. As an old man, he was condemned to death by the citizens of Athens who claimed he denied the gods and corrupted the youth. More likely, however, Socrates was a natural target for enemies and was made the scapegoat for the city's military defeat. As ordered, Socrates drank poison hemlock and died. He left behind no written works, but his pupil Plato later immortalized his lively discussions in his own works.

- **Plato** is often considered the most important figure in Western philosophy. Without him, the thoughts of Socrates and previous philosophers might not be recorded. Plato used a dialogue format to explore many subjects such as ethics and politics. He founded a school in Athens called the Academy and became the teacher of Aristotle.

- **Aristotle** was a disciple of Plato and then broke away to develop his own philosophy and school, called the Lyceum. He wrote on virtually every subject and laid the foundation for analytical reasoning and logic. He was the tutor of Alexander the Great. In the political unrest following Alexander's death, Aristotle remembered the fate of Socrates and fled Athens to escape prosecution.

In Raphael's painting School of Athens, *Plato and Aristotle converse.*
School of Athens (detail) by Raphael. Vatican. Erich Lessing/Art Resource NY.

What are the literary genres?

Over hundreds of years, certain stories, essays, and poems have remained timeless in their appeal and relevance to human life. These works are considered **literature,** the art form of language. As you read a piece of literature, you are allowed inside the minds of characters, and you feel what they feel. You learn about life as the characters live it or as the poet entices you to feel it. After reading, you are enriched, as well as entertained. As defined in most college courses, literature includes four categories, or **genres:** poetry, drama, fiction, and essays.

Poetry

Poetry has its roots in the pleasure of rhythm, repetition, and sound. Before the written word, rhythm and repetition were used to help people organize and recall episodes in history. Poetry was danced, chanted, and performed with the whole body in tribal cultures as a way of keeping cultural truths alive. In the *Odyssey,* an ancient Greek epic by **Homer** that recounts the adventures of Odysseus during his return from the war in Troy to his home on a Greek island, the rhyme format made the epic easier to remember. Thus the poem became a vehicle for preserving the lore of the sea, warfare, and Greek mythology.

Poetry appeals to the senses, offering strong visual images and suggestive symbolism to enhance the pleasure. **Lyric** poems are brief and emotional, **narrative** poems tell a story with plot and characters, **dramatic** poems use dialogue to express emotional conflict, and **epic** poems tell a long narrative with a central hero of historical significance.

Drama

The origins of **drama** lie in religious ceremonies in ancient Greece, when masters of Greek drama competed for prizes by means of their plays. Without movies and television, the ancient Greeks created plays for religious instruction and for entertainment. These dramatic performances eventually evolved into comedy, tragedy, and romantic tragedy.

Plays are narratives and thus contain all the literary elements of short stories and novels. As in works of fiction, the main character in a play is sometimes called a **protagonist,** from the Greek word for "first actor." The character who is trying to move against or harm the main character is called the **antagonist** (from the prefix *anti*).

Plays are written to be performed rather than read. The actors interpret for the audience, and a single play can seem vastly different depending on which production company performs it. After hundreds of years, the plays of **William Shakespeare** are still relevant to the human condition; they entertained audiences in England in the late 1500s, on the American frontier in the mid-1800s, and both on stages and in movie theaters in the 2000s.

Fiction

Fiction creates an illusion of reality to share an experience and communicate universal truths about the human condition. Since each work of fiction is deliberate, each element has a meaning that is subject to interpretation on many different levels. Short stories and novels are written to entertain by engaging you in the life of another human being.

- A **short story** is a brief work of fiction ranging from 500 to 15,000 words. It is a narrative with a beginning, middle, and end that tells about a sequence of events. The **plot** of the story involves **characters** in one or more **conflicts.** As the conflict intensifies, the **suspense** rises to a **climax,** or turning point, which is followed by the **denouement,** or unraveling. Then the action falls for a **resolution.** Because the short story is brief and carefully crafted, some literary experts recommend reading a short story three times: first to enjoy the plot, second to recognize the elements, and third to appreciate how the elements work together to support the theme. Setting, point of view, tone, and symbolism all contribute to this appreciation.

- The **novel** is an extended fictional work that has all the elements of a short story. Because of its length, a novel usually has more characters and more conflicts than a short story.

The Essay

An **essay** is a short work of nonfiction that discusses a specific topic. Much of your own college writing will follow an essay format. The **title** of an essay suggests the contents, the **thesis** is usually stated in the **introduction,** the **body** provides evidence to prove the thesis, and the **conclusion** summarizes in a manner to provoke further thought.

REVIEW QUESTIONS

After studying the material, answer the following questions:

1. What is the Socratic method of teaching? _____

_____

2. What was the underlying reason Socrates was forced to drink poison? _____

_____

3. Why was Plato particularly important to the teaching of Socrates? _____

    _____

4. What acronym could you devise to remind you of the chronological order of the three famous

    philosophers? _____

    _____

5. What was a significant contribution of Aristotle? _____

    _____

6. What is a literary genre? _____

    _____

7. What was the original purpose of drama? _____

    _____

8. What was the purpose of the *Odyssey?* _____

    _____

9. Which genre is most frequently written by the majority of college students? _____

    _____

10. What is the typical relationship between the protagonist and the antagonist? _____

    _____

Your instructor may choose to give a true-false review of these philosophy and literature concepts.

CONTEMPORARY FOCUS

You have probably read "The Gift of the Magi," the popular Christmas classic of unselfish love and sacrifice. Written by William Sydney Porter, who wrote under the pen name of O. Henry, it tells of a young wife who sells her beautiful hair to buy a watch chain for her husband, Jim. Meanwhile, Jim sells his watch to buy expensive combs for his wife's long hair. With such twists of irony, O. Henry surprises and delights his readers in 256 short stories.

O. HENRY'S STORYTELLING

By Jim Schlosser

News & Record (Greensboro, N.C.), December 24, 1998

Many writers viewed...people collectively—the masses—but O. Henry saw them as individuals. He put them in stories that produced, as the *New York Times* interviewer wrote, "sobs, sniffles and smiles, with sniffles predominating."

O. Henry figured readers wanted something to brighten otherwise gloomy days at dull jobs. He was glad "to indulge his readers' weakminded craving for a little human enjoyment," O. Henry scholar Dale Kramer wrote in 1954. Porter could break up a cafe table with laughter when he veered from impeccable English into sentences filled with slang, broken grammar and pig-German. "I aint saw them since I saw them last," he wrote in a letter about missing papers.

He had a funny way of framing statements about himself. When asked if he went to college, he said, "No, that is one handicap that I went into this work of writing without."

Yet this man who has brought laughter, joy and warmth to readers all over the world was himself melancholy, insecure and terrified his criminal past would be discovered. Which is why he used a pen name. He was sure that someday, in a cafe or other public place, some ex-con would approach and say, "Hello, Bill. When did you get out of the Ohio Penitentiary?"

He would be amused at the statue of him at North Elm and Bellemeade streets in Greensboro, where he lived and jerked sodas until he was 18 and moved to Texas.

He's holding a pen and pencil.

Collaborate

Collaborate on responses to the following questions:

- What does O. Henry mean by his comment on not going to college?
- What is pig-German?
- Why would O. Henry be surprised by a statue of himself in Greensboro?

Preview

Preview the next selection to predict its purpose and organization and to formulate your learning plan.

Activate Schema

> When you see people repeatedly but do not know them, do you make up stories about their lives?
>
> Should you secretly try to help someone or announce your good deed?

Establish a Purpose for Reading

Sometimes we wonder about the people we meet in everyday life, and we make assumptions about their lives that are inappropriate. Read this short story to find out the consequences of doing this.

Increase Word Knowledge

garret	draughty	cunning	meager	affront
edibles	emblem	deception	viciously	ferociously

Your instructor may give a true-false vocabulary review before or after reading.

Integrate Knowledge While Reading

Inference questions have been inserted in the margin to stimulate your thinking and help you read between the lines. Remember to

Predict   Picture   Relate   Monitor   Correct

WITCHES' LOAVES
By O. Henry

Miss Martha Meacham kept the little bakery on the corner (the one where you go up three steps, and the bell tinkles when you open the door).

Was she attractive?

Miss Martha was forty, her bank-book showed a credit of two thousand dollars, and she possessed two false teeth and a sympathetic heart. Many people have married whose chances to do so were much inferior to Miss Martha's.

Two or three times a week a customer came in in whom she began to take an interest. He was a middle-aged man, wearing spectacles and a brown beard trimmed to a careful point.

He spoke English with a strong German accent. His clothes were worn and darned in places, and wrinkled and baggy in others. But he looked neat, and had very good manners.

He always bought two loaves of stale bread. Fresh bread was five cents a loaf. Stale ones were two for five. Never did he call for anything but stale bread.

Once Miss Martha saw a red and brown stain on his fingers. She was sure
then that he was an artist and very poor. No doubt he lived in a garret, where
he painted pictures and ate stale bread and thought of the good things to eat
in Miss Martha's bakery.

Often when Miss Martha sat down to her chops and light rolls and jam and
tea she would sigh, and wish that the gentle-mannered artist might share her
tasty meal instead of eating his dry crust in that draughty attic. Miss Martha's
heart, as you have been told, was a sympathetic one.

In order to test her theory as to his occupation, she brought from her room
one day a painting that she had bought at a sale, and set it against the shelves
behind the bread counter.

It was a Venetian scene. A splendid marble *palazzio* (so it said on the picture)
stood in the foreground—or rather forewater. For the rest there were gondolas
(with the lady trailing her hand in the water), clouds, sky, and *chiaro-oscuro* in
plenty. No artist could fail to notice it.

Two days afterward the customer came in.

"Two loafs of stale bread, if you blease.

"You haf here a fine bicture, madame," he said while she was wrapping up
the bread.

"Yes?" says Miss Martha, reveling in her own cunning. "I do so admire art
and" (no, it would not do to say "artists" thus early) "and paintings," she substi-
tuted. "You think it is a good picture?"

"Der balace," said the customer, "is not in good drawing. Der bairspective of
it is not true. Goot morning, madame."

He took his bread, bowed, and hurried out.

Yes, he must be an artist. Miss Martha took the picture back to her room.

How gently and kindly his eyes shone behind his spectacles! What a broad
brow he had! To be able to judge perspective at a glance—and to live on stale
bread! But genius often has a struggle before it is recognized.

What a thing it would be for art and perspective if genius were backed by
two thousand dollars in the bank, a bakery, and a sympathetic heart to—But
these were day-dreams, Miss Martha.

Often now when he came he would chat for a while across the showcase.
He seemed to crave Miss Martha's cheerful words.

He kept on buying stale bread. Never a cake, never a pie, never one of her
delicious Sally Lunns.

She thought he began to look thinner and discouraged. Her heart ached to
add something good to eat to his meager purchase, but her courage failed at
the act. She did not dare affront him. She knew the pride of artists.

Miss Martha took to wearing her blue-dotted silk waist behind the counter.
In the back room she cooked a mysterious compound of quince seeds and
borax. Ever so many people use it for the complexion.

One day the customer came in as usual, laid his nickel on the showcase,
and called for his stale loaves. While Miss Martha was reaching for them
there was a great tooting and clanging, and a fire engine came lumbering
past.

Margin annotations:

- Are these appropriate inferences? *(lines 15–16)*
- Why didn't she ask about his job? *(line 37)*
- What was she thinking? *(line 42)*
- Why was she changing? *(line 53)*

Line numbers shown in margin: 15, 20, 25, 30, 35, 40, 45, 50, 55

The author O. Henry might have visited this bakery in Austin, Texas.
Library of Congress

60   The customer hurried to the door to look, as any one will. Suddenly inspired, Miss Martha seized the opportunity.

On the bottom shelf behind the counter was a pound of fresh butter that the dairyman had left ten minutes before. With a bread knife Miss Martha made a deep slash in each of the stale loaves, inserted a generous quantity of
65   butter, and pressed the loaves tight again.

When the customer turned once more she was tying the paper around them.

When he had gone, after an unusually pleasant little chat, Miss Martha smiled to herself, but not without a slight fluttering of the heart.

Had she been too bold? Would he take offense? But surely not. There was
70   no language of edibles. Butter was no emblem of unmaidenly forwardness.

For a long time that day her mind dwelt on the subject. She imagined the scene when he should discover her little deception.

He would lay down his brushes and palette. There would stand his easel with the picture he was painting in which the perspective was beyond criticism.
75   He would prepare for his luncheon of dry bread and water. He would slice into a loaf—ah!

Miss Martha blushed. Would he think of the hand that placed it there as he ate? Would he—

The front door bell jangled viciously. Somebody was coming in, making a
80   great deal of noise.

Miss Martha hurried to the front. Two men were there. One was a young man smoking a pipe—a man she had never seen before. The other was her artist.

His face was very red, his hat was on the back of his head, his hair was wildly rumpled. He clinched his two fists and shook them ferociously at Miss
85   Martha. *At Miss Martha.*

"*Dummkopf!*" he shouted with extreme loudness; and then "*Tausendonfer!*" or something like it in German.

The young man tried to draw him away.

"I vill not go," he said angrily, "else I shall told her."

90   He made a bass drum of Miss Martha's counter.

"You haf shpoilt me," he cried, his blue eyes blazing behind his spectacles. "I vill tell you. You vas von *meddingsome old cat!*"

Miss Martha leaned weakly against the shelves and laid one hand on her blue-dotted silk waist. The younger man took the other by the collar.

95   "Come on," he said, "you've said enough." He dragged the angry one out at the door to the sidewalk, and then came back.

"Guess you ought to be told, ma'am," he said, "what the row is about. That's Blumberger. He's an architectural draftsman. I work in the same office with him.

100   "He's been working hard for three months drawing a plan for a new city hall. It was a prize competition. He finished inking the lines yesterday. You know, a draftsman always makes his drawing in pencil first. When it's done he rubs out the pencil lines with handfuls of stale bread crumbs. That's better than India rubber.

105   "Blumberger's been buying the bread here. Well, to-day—well, you know, ma'am, that butter isn't—well, Blumberger's plan isn't good for anything now except to cut up into railroad sandwiches."

Miss Martha went to the back room. She took off the blue-dotted silk waist and put on the old brown serge she used to wear. Then she poured

110   the quince seed and borax mixture out of the window into the ash can.

Recall

Stop to self-test, relate, and react.

Your instructor may choose to give you a true-false comprehension review.

Write About the Selection

What clues lead Miss Martha to her incorrect assumptions?

How did Miss Martha incorrectly stereotype?

Response suggestion: List Miss Martha's assumptions and the possible clues that led her to make them.

Contemporary Link

How does O. Henry achieve "sobs, sniffles and smiles, with sniffles predominating" in this story? How does he show the characters as individuals rather than simply blue-collar workers of the masses?

Skill Development: Implied Meaning

According to the implied meaning in the selection, answer the following with *T* (true) or *F* (false):

_____ 1. By describing Miss Martha's bakery as the one where "the bell tinkles when you open the door," the author implies that the store was always full of customers.

_____ 2. The Venetian scene in the painting depicted a palace with water and boats.

_____ 3. Miss Martha's fear of adding the butter was that it would be too flirtatious.

_____ 4. The compound of quince and borax were used to wash the pans from cooking.

_____ 5. The author suggests that Miss Martha did not ask Blumberger about adding a treat to the stale bread because she feared hurting his pride.

Check Your Comprehension

Answer the following with *a, b, c,* or *d,* or fill in the blank. To help you analyze your strengths and weaknesses, the question types are indicated.

Main Idea _____ 1. Which is the best statement of the main idea of this selection?
a. Miss Martha used her bread to further her own selfish interests and was not rewarded.
b. Based on false assumptions and without communication, well-meaning Miss Martha took action that led to unexpected negative results.
c. Miss Martha's actions showed that she was not worthy of being called Blumberger's friend
d. Miss Martha's goals were unrealistic because she wanted more than she could possibly have.

Detail _____ 2. The author describes Miss Martha as all the following except
a. 40 years old.
b. having two thousand dollars.
c. overweight because she baked delicious foods.
d. capable of day-dreaming.

Inference _____ 3. By saying that "Many people have married whose chances to do so were much inferior to Miss Martha's," the author implies
a. Miss Martha was a more acceptable mate than many who were already married.

    b. Miss Martha was inferior to most women who were already married.

    c. Miss Martha's eligibility for marriage was greater than most women who were already married.

    d. Miss Martha would have been among the last women a man would consider for marriage.

Detail   ————————   4. Blumberger was described as all the following except
    a. middle-aged.
    b. well dressed.
    c. German.
    d. mannerly.

Detail   ————————   5. All of Miss Martha's assumptions about Blumberger were incorrect except that
    a. he had paint on his fingers because he had been working.
    b. he was an artist.
    c. he was poor and without money to buy fresh bread.
    d. he ate the stale bread.

Detail   ————————   6. In speaking with his German accent, Blumberger mispronounced words by saying all the following except
    a. b for p.
    b. t for d.
    c. v for w.
    d. d for v.

Inference   ————————   7. The reader can assume that Blumberger commented on the palace in the Venetian painting because
    a. he was an artist.
    b. he drew buildings.
    c. he recognized the splendid marble palazzio.
    d. the perspective of the water in the foreground was confusing.

Inference   ————————   8. The reader can assume that
    a. the bread did not erase the pencil marks.
    b. the butter smeared the ink in the drawing.
    c. Blumberger had an additional copy of his drawing.
    d. Blumberger would still be able to enter the competition.

Inference   ————————   9. By calling Miss Martha a "medding some old cat," Blumberger indicated that he thought
    a. she put the butter in the bread by accident.
    b. she was trying cause him to lose the competition.
    c. she added the butter because she thought he was poor.
    d. she considered him to be an artist.

Inference _____ 10. The irony of this story is that
           a. good deeds should be announced rather than done in secret.
           b. asking questions reveals truth.
           c. a sympathetic act unintentionally turned into a destructive one.
           d. poor communication causes unfortunate errors.

Answer the following with *T* (true), *F* (false), or *CT* (can't tell):

Detail _____ 11. Blumberger purchased stale bread for half the price of fresh bread.

Inference _____ 12. In her thoughts of Bumberger, Miss Martha imagined herself married and sharing her finances with Blumberger to further his artist career.

Inference _____ 13. Miss Martha wore the blue-dotted shirt because she wanted to look more attractive to Blumberger.

Inference _____ 14. The reader can assume that prior to the butter incident, Blumberger had little interest in talking to Miss Martha.

Inference _____ 15. Without the fire engine, Blumberger might have entered his drawing in the prize competition.

Build Your Vocabulary

According to the way the italicized word was used in the selection, select *a, b, c,* or *d* for the word or phrase that gives the best definition. The number in parentheses indicates the line of the passage in which the word is located.

_____ 1. "lived in a *garret*" (15)
    a. house
    b. studio
    c. attic loft
    d. barn

_____ 2. "*draughty* attic" (20)
    a. ugly
    b. poorly insulated
    c. large
    d. cluttered

_____ 3. "her own *cunning*" (33)
    a. joy
    b. happiness
    c. curiosity
    d. craftiness

_____ 4. "his *meager* purchase" (51)
    a. skimpy
    b. unappetizing
    c. unhealthy
    d. unfortunate

_____ 5. "dare *affront* him" (52)
    a. scold
    b. scare
    c. offend
    d. fool

_____ 6. "language of *edibles*" (70)
    a. food
    b. traditions
    c. flirtations
    d. courting

_____ 7. "no *emblem* of" (70)
  a. lie
  b. fortune
  c. symbol
  d. misconception

_____ 8. "her little *deception*" (72)
  a. sorry
  b. wish
  c. trick
  d. favor

_____ 9. "bell jangled *viciously*" (79)
  a. knowingly
  b. suddenly
  c. surprisingly
  d. nastily

_____ 10. "shook them *ferociously*" (84)
  a. fiercely
  b. hesitantly
  c. continuingly
  d. righteously

CONTEMPORARY FOCUS

What are the contributions of Malcolm X to the civil rights movement? How did a hustler who spent years in prison rise to become a leader and spokesman for the cause?

REMEMBERING A CIVIL RIGHTS HERO

By Adil Ahmad

The Dartmouth via University Wire, Dartmouth College, April 12, 2004

Martin Luther King, Jr. Day is celebrated every year. Unfortunately, a different hero of the Civil Rights Movement of the 1950s and '60s remains forgotten. That man is El-Hajj Malik El-Shabazz, or Malcolm X, as he is more commonly known.

Malcolm X was born Malcolm Little into a poor Baptist family in Omaha, Neb., on May 19, 1925. The son of a Baptist preacher and "outspoken promoter of social and economic independence for blacks" who was brutally murdered by white supremacists, Malcolm had political activism in his blood.

After his house was burned down by the Ku Klux Klan, Little and his siblings were forced into foster homes and reform schools. Little moved to Boston to live with his half-sister in 1941 after he dropped out of school at age 15, then fell into the underworld of Harlem, New York, at the age of 17. There, he turned to a life of crime and drug-addiction, committing armed robberies for a living.

At the age of 21, he was sentenced to 10 years in prison for a minor robbery. In prison, Little began to read with enthusiasm. He started to read about Elijah Muhammad and his mis-named Nation of Islam, a Black Nationalist organization whose followers were called Black Muslims. After his release from prison in 1952, Little went to Detroit to become a full member of the Nation of Islam.

He changed his name to Malcolm X, dropping the "slave name" of Little. With his dazzling oratorical and people skills, Malcolm X soon rose up the ladder of the Nation of Islam. He soon surpassed Elijah as the foremost spokesman of the Nation.

However, Malcolm X's high-profile, radical agenda, and popularity among black Muslims and whites alike put him in direct conflict with Elijah Muhammad, and Malcolm X was consequently disbarred from the Nation in 1964.

Soon after, he started a new organization to promote his own beliefs. In 1964, he made a pilgrimage to Mecca, Saudi Arabia, and visited several other African and Muslim nations in which he was treated as a hero. On this trip he realized that his theories of black supremacy were false, and that whites were not necessarily evil after all. He then converted to Sunni Islam and changed his name to El-Hajj Malik El-Shabazz. After his return to the United States, he created the Organization of Afro-American Unity (OAAU), a nationalist organization that sought to unite all black organizations fighting racism against blacks. He renounced his racism against whites and began to encourage blacks to vote, to participate in the political system, and to work with each other and with sympathetic whites and Hispanics for an end to all forms of racial discrimination.

Malik El-Shabazz was assassinated on February 21, 1965, by members of the Nation of Islam, who, under orders from Elijah Muhammad, felt that El-Shabazz was a danger to their organization.

Collaborate

Collaborate on responses to the following questions:

- What factors contributed to Malcolm X ending up in jail?
- Why was Malcolm X assassinated?
- How did Malcolm X's philosophy change with each of his name changes?

Preview

Preview the next selection to predict its purpose and organization and to formulate your learning plan.

Activate Schema

Why do we hear more about Martin Luther King than Malcolm X?

Why was Malcolm X considered controversial?

Establish a Purpose for Reading

Malcolm X was a strong voice in the civil rights struggle of the 1960s. With his background, how did he become an educated spokesperson for a movement? Recall what you already know about Malcolm X, and read the following selection to find out how he learned to read.

Increase Word Knowledge

articulate	functional	emulate	riffling	aardvark
wedge	devour	engrossing	intervals	feigned

Your instructor may give a true-false vocabulary review before or after reading.

Skill Development: Integrate Knowledge While Reading

Inference questions have been inserted in the margin to stimulate your thinking and help you read between the lines. Remember to

Predict   Picture   Relate   Monitor   Correct

LEARNING TO READ: MALCOLM X

From *The Autobiography of Malcolm X* as told to Alex Haley

It was because of my letters that I happened to stumble upon starting to acquire some kind of a homemade education.

I became increasingly frustrated at not being able to express what I wanted to convey in letters that I wrote, especially those to Mr. Elijah Muhammad. In the street, I had been the most articulate hustler out there—I had commanded attention when I said something. But now, trying to write simple English, I not only wasn't articulate, I wasn't even functional. How would I sound writing in slang, the way I would *say* it, something such as, "Look, daddy, let me pull your coat about a cat, Elijah Muhammad—"

Many who today hear me somewhere in person, or on television, or those who read something I've said, will think I went to school far beyond the eighth grade. This impression is due entirely to my prison studies.

It had really begun back in Charlestown Prison, when Bimbi first made me feel envy of his stock of knowledge. Bimbi had always taken charge of any conversations he was in, and I had tried to emulate him. But every book I picked up had few sentences which didn't contain anywhere from one to nearly all of the words that might as well have been in Chinese. When I just skipped those words, of course, I really ended up with little idea of what

> How did he become so famous?

American Civil Rights leader Malcolm X speaks at an outdoor rally in 1963. *Bob Parent/Hulton | Archive/Getty Images*

the book said. So I had come to the Norfolk Prison Colony still going
20 through only book-reading motions. Pretty soon, I would have quit even
these motions, unless I had received the motivation that I did.

I saw that the best thing I could do was get hold of a dictionary—to study,
to learn some words. I was lucky enough to reason also that I should try to
improve my penmanship. It was sad. I couldn't even write in a straight line. It
25 was both ideas together that moved me to request a dictionary along with
some tablets and pencils from the Norfolk Prison Colony school.

I spent two days just riffling uncertainly through the dictionary's pages. I'd
never realized so many words existed! I didn't know *which* words I needed to
learn. Finally, just to start some kind of action, I began copying.

30 In my slow, painstaking, ragged handwriting, I copied into my tablet everything printed on that first page, down to the punctuation marks.

How did he read the defining words? → I believe it took me a day. Then, aloud, I read back, to myself, everything I'd
written on the tablet. Over and over, aloud, to myself, I read my own handwriting.

I woke up the next morning, thinking about those words—immensely
35 proud to realize that not only had I written so much at one time, but I'd written words that I never knew were in the world. Moreover, with a little effort, I
also could remember what many of these words meant. I reviewed the words
How was he a strategic learner? → whose meaning I didn't remember. Funny thing, from the dictionary's first
page right now, that "aardvark" springs to my mind. The dictionary had a pic-
40 ture of it, a long-tailed, long-eared, burrowing African mammal, which lives
off termites caught by sticking out its tongue as an anteater for ants.

I was so fascinated that I went on—I copied the dictionary's next page. And
the same experience came when I studied that. With every succeeding page, I
also learned of people and places and events from history. Actually the dictio-
45 nary is like a miniature encyclopedia. Finally the dictionary's A section had
filled a whole tablet—and I want on into the B's. That was the way I started
copying what eventually became the entire dictionary. It went a lot faster after
so much practice helped me to pick up handwriting speed. Between what I
wrote in my tablet, and writing letters, during the rest of my time in prison I
50 would guess I wrote a million words.

I suppose it was inevitable that as my word-base broadened, I could for the
first time pick up a book and read and now begin to understand what the
book was saying. Anyone who has read a great deal can imagine the new
world that opened. Let me tell you something: from then until I left that
55 prison, in every free moment I had, if I was not reading in the library, I was
reading on my bunk. You couldn't have gotten me out of books with a wedge.
Between Mr. Muhammad's teachings, my correspondence, my visitors, . . . and
my reading of books, months passed without my even thinking about being
imprisoned. In fact, up to then, I never had been so truly free in my life.

60 The Norfolk Prison Colony' library was in the school building. A variety of
classes was taught there by instructors who came from such places as Har-
In what state was the prison? → vard and Boston universities. The weekly debates between inmate teams
were also held in the school building. You would be astonished to know how
worked up convict debaters and audiences would get over subjects like
65 "Should Babies Be Fed Milk?"

Available on the prison library's shelves were books on just about every general subject. Much of the big private collection that Parkhurst had willed to the prison was still in crates and boxes in the back of the library—thousands of old books. Some of them looked ancient: covers faded, old-time parchment-looking binding. Parkhurst . . . seemed to have been principally interested in history and religion. He had the money and the special interest to have a lot of books that you wouldn't have in a general circulation. Any college library would have been lucky to get that collection.

As you can imagine, especially in a prison where there was heavy emphasis on rehabilitation, an inmate was smiled upon if he demonstrated an unusually intense interest in books. There was a sizable number of well-read inmates, especially the popular debaters. Some were said by many to be practically walking encyclopedias. They were almost celebrities. No university would ask any student to devour literature as I did when this new world opened to me, of being able to read and *understand*.

> How do values change in prison?

I read more in my room than in the library itself. An inmate who was known to read a lot could check out more than the permitted maximum number of books. I preferred reading in the total isolation of my own room.

When I had progressed to really serious reading, every night at about ten P.M. I would be outraged with the "lights out." It always seemed to catch me right in the middle of something engrossing.

Fortunately, right outside my door was a corridor light that cast a glow into my room. The glow was enough to read by, once my eyes adjusted to it. So when "lights out" came, I would sit on the floor where I could continue reading in that glow.

At one-hour intervals at night guards paced past every room. Each time I heard the approaching footsteps, I jumped into bed and feigned sleep. And as soon as the guard passed, I got back out of bed onto the floor area of that light-glow, where I would read for another fifty-eight minutes until the guard approached again. That went on until three or four every morning. Three or four hours of sleep a night was enough for me. Often in the years in the streets I had slept less than that.

Recall

Stop to self-test, relate, and react.

Your instructor may choose to give you a true-false comprehension review.

Write About the Selection

If you did not know how to read at 21 years of age, what methods would you use to teach yourself? Would you copy the dictionary? How did Malcolm X use some of the learning tips in this textbook to remember the words on the dictionary pages? How did he seize an unfortunate circumstance and make it into an opportunity? How are his efforts at self-improvement inspirational?

Response suggestion: Relate your own ideas to the path taken by Malcolm X.

Contemporary Link

Although Malcolm X changed, initially he opposed Martin Luther King, Jr.'s movement to promote racial change through nonviolence. He wanted a black revolution rather than compromise. How do you think the background experiences of Malcolm X might have shaped his beliefs and pulled him more toward violence than peaceful change?

   Response suggestion: List the different events and influences on his life and learning. Suggest how each experience shaped his philosophy.

Skill Development: Implied Meaning

According to the implied meaning in the selection, answer the following with *T* (true) or *F* (false).

_____ 1. The phrase "let me pull your coat about a cat" probably means that we need to put a coat around the cat to keep it warm.

_____ 2. The phrase "let me pull your coat about a cat" is a simile.

_____ 3. The phrase "gotten me out of books with a wedge" is an idiom.

_____ 4. It is ironic that Malcolm X felt truly free in prison.

_____ 5. The Norfolk Prison Colony was probably in the Northeast.

Check Your Comprehension

After reading the selection, answer the following questions with *a, b, c,* or *d.* To help you analyze your strengths and weaknesses, the question types are indicated.

Main Idea _____ 1. Which is the best statement of the main idea of this selection?
   a. Malcolm X was motivated by educated prisoners to change his life.
   b. While in prison, Malcolm X learned to read by coping and studying the dictionary.
   c. Malcolm X conquered prison with his positive attitude.
   d. Although mistreated in prison, Malcolm X was able to go to the library to read.

Detail _____ 2. Malcolm initially began his reading program because
   a. he wanted to read the Parkhurst books in the library.
   b. he wanted to write letters to Elijah Muhammad.
   c. he wanted to debate Bimbi.
   d. he wanted to entertain himself at night during the long hours of "lights out."

Inference   _____ 3. Malcolm X describes his learning as a "homemade education" because
    a. he started it at home.
    b. he made it up himself without professional help.
    c. it was designed by prison teachers.
    d. it was modeled after other efforts of prison education.

Detail   _____ 4. Malcolm X described his reading at Charlestown Prison as
    a. knowing most words in the sentences.
    b. knowing at least half the words in sentences.
    c. not knowing one to all words in most sentences.
    d. not knowing half the words in a few sentences.

Inference   _____ 5. Malcolm X would define book-reading motions as
    a. reading with understanding.
    b. reading aloud.
    c. reading without understanding.
    d. not bothering to try to read.

Detail   _____ 6. Malcolm X's decision to copy each page of the dictionary was motivated by all the following except
    a. a desire to learn words.
    b. a desire to improve his handwriting.
    c. a proven method.
    d. not knowing with which words to begin.

Inference   _____ 7. Malcolm X mentions *aardvark* because
    a. it is a funny word that he still remembers from the first page of the dictionary.
    b. he has used the word many times.
    c. he thinks that *aardvark* is an important word for all to know.
    d. the word shows how the dictionary is a miniature encyclopedia.

Inference   _____ 8. Malcolm X mentions the debate topic "Should Babies Be Fed Milk" to show that
    a. the inmate debaters would get excited over anything, even if it was irrelevant to them.
    b. the debaters were qualified on a wide range of subjects.
    c. the convicts took a special interest in family issues.
    d. it was a favorite topic with the inmate debaters and the audience.

Detail   _____ 9. Malcolm X implies that prison officials
    a. encouraged education.
    b. discouraged education.
    c. were not concerned with rehabilitation.
    d. gave favors for good behavior but not for educational efforts.

Inference   _____ 10. The reader can appropriately assume all the following except
                              a. after "lights out," no reading was allowed.
                              b. the glow of the corridor light after "lights out" was not
                                 strong enough to lie in his bunk and read by.
                              c. the night guards would object to Malcolm X reading after
                                 "lights out."
                              d. other prisoner would complain to the guards if Malcolm X
                                 read after "lights out."

              Answer the following with *T* (true) or *F* (false).

Detail   _____ 11. Malcolm X dropped out of school in the eighth grade.

Detail   _____ 12. Malcolm X began his attempts at reading at Charlestown
                              Prison before he went to Norfolk Prison Colony.

Inference   _____ 13. Bimbi suggested that Malcolm X use a dictionary to learn words.

Inference   _____ 14. Prisoners at Norfolk Prison Colony looked down on fellow
                              inmates who were well read.

Inference   _____ 15. Malcolm X suggests that university reading demands are
                              insufficient.

Build Your Vocabulary

According to the way the italicized word was used in the selection, select *a*, *b*,
c, or *d* for the word or phrase that gives the best definition. The number in
parentheses indicates the line of the passage in which the word is located.

_____ 1. "*articulate* hustler" (5)
   a. dangerous
   b. crafty
   c. unclear
   d. well-spoken

_____ 2. "wasn't even *functional*"
   (7)
   a. interested
   b. useful
   c. vocal
   d. determined

_____ 3. "tried to *emulate* him"
   (15)
   a. convince
   b. copy
   c. argue with
   d. advise

_____ 4. "*riffling* uncertainly
   through" (27)
   a. studying
   b. memorizing
   c. flipping
   d. reading

_____ 5. "'*aardvark*' springs to mind"
   (39)
   a. African burrow
   b. termite
   c. mammal
   d. anteater

_____ 6. "with a *wedge*" (56)
   a. bet
   b. tapered block
   c. hammer
   d. slap

_____ 7. "*devour* literature" (80)
    a. consume
    b. be assigned
    c. require
    d. discuss

_____ 8. "something *engrossing*" (87)
    a. absorbing
    b. confusing
    c. historical
    d. religious

_____ 9. "one-hour *intervals*" (92)
    a. watches
    b. reports
    c. walks
    d. periods

_____ 10. "*feigned* sleep" (93)
    a. begged for
    b. hoped for
    c. pretended
    d. accomplished

Search the Net

Use a search engine such as Google, AltaVista, Excite, Infoseek, Dogpile, Yahoo, or Lycos to find how Malcolm X's beliefs changed. Compare his initial beliefs with those he held when he died. For suggested Web sites and other research activities, go to http://www.ablongman.com/smith/.

for Political Science

"One of the difficult lessons we have learned," wrote Martin Luther King, Jr., "is that you cannot depend on American institutions to function without pressure. Any real change in the status quo depends on continued creative action to sharpen the conscience of the nation." Although the equal protection clause in the Fourteenth Amendment has been a part of the Constitution since 1868, social reformers such as Malcolm X and Martin Luther King, Jr. challenged and changed the interpretation of that amendment. Civil rights activists maintained that the Constitution was color-blind, and court decisions supported that policy.

What is the U.S. Constitution?

The **Constitution** is a document that defines the structure of our government and the roles, powers, and responsibilities of public officials. It was signed in Philadelphia in 1787. Before the Constitution, the **Declaration of Independence** in 1776 affirmed our independence from England. The **Articles of Confederation** were written to govern the resulting new union of states that joined to fight for freedom and forge a new democracy. The articles created a loose union and left most of the authority with the individual states. After the Revolution, as economic conflicts arose and more central control was needed, the Constitution was written to give more power to the federal government, replacing the Articles of Confederation. Our country is still governed by this same Constitution of 1787, which also guarantees our civil liberties and civil rights, including freedom of expression, due process, and equal protection.

Because no document is perfect, the writers of the Constitution allowed for amendments, and the Constitution has been amended 27 times.

What are the three branches of government?

The Constitution divides the federal government into the executive, legislative, and judicial branches.

- The **executive branch** consists of the president, whose powers include approving or vetoing (refusing to sign) laws passed by Congress, and the **president's cabinet,** an advisory group of 13 government department heads appointed by the president. For example, Madeline

Voters, using electronic voting machines, cast ballots in the 2004 Texas primary in Austin.
Bob Daemmrich/PhotoEdit Inc.

Albright was a member of former President Bill Clinton's cabinet.

- The **legislative branch** of the government consists of the two houses of Congress: the Senate and the House of Representatives. The **Senate** with 100 members (two from each state) and the **House of Representatives** with 435 members (apportioned to each state according to population) pass federal laws and serve on committees that investigate problems and oversee the executive branch.

- The **judicial branch** consists of a system of federal courts, the highest of which is the **Supreme Court.** It consists of a chief justice and eight associate justices who are appointed by sitting presidents. The Supreme

Court resolves conflicts among states and ensures uniformity in the interpretation of national laws.

Each of the three branches has checks and balances over the other branches so that errors can be addressed and power is shared.

What are political parties?

● Our president, senators, and representatives are nominated for office by a political party, an organization formed to support and elect candidates who uphold the views and beliefs of the group. Over the years, political parties have changed and some have disappeared. Today the two major parties are Republican and the Democrat.

● The **Republican Party,** also called the GOP, for "Grand Old Party," began in 1854. Its symbol is the elephant, and Abraham Lincoln was the first Republican president. The party tends to be against expanding the size and responsibilities of the federal government and to support private enterprise. The party image is **conservative,** an ideology or set of beliefs that prefers the existing order and opposes change.

● The **Democratic Party** was organized by Thomas Jefferson in the late eighteenth century, and its first elected president was Andrew Jackson. The party tends to support the expansion of federal programs and a tax system with a greater burden on the rich and corporations. Its symbol is the donkey. The party image is **liberal,** an ideology that supports the strong role of government in economic and social issues.

Before elections, both parties pay organizations such as **Gallup** to conduct **polls,** questioning voters about the most important issues and sampling public opinion on voting preferences.

What are capitalism, communism, and socialism?

● **Capitalism** is an economic system based on a free market for goods and services. Production centers such as factories seek profits and are owned by individuals as well as corporations and their stockholders, not the government. The United States has a capitalist economy, although it is not purely capitalistic since government does impose regulations on business.

● **Communism** is almost the opposite of capitalism. It is an economic, political, and social system in which there is no individual ownership. The government controls businesses, and goods and property are owned in common by all citizens. Goods are available to all people as they are needed. The communist system was envisioned by Karl Marx and is associated with the former Soviet Union and China.

● **Socialism** is an economic system advocating government or collective ownership of the goods, rather than private ownership. In Karl Marx's theory, it is the transition between capitalism and communism in which people are paid according to work done. Communists are socialists, but not all socialists are communists.

REVIEW QUESTIONS

After studying the material, answer the following questions:

1. Why were the Articles of Confederation replaced? _____
   _____

2. How does the Declaration of Independence differ from the Constitution? _____
   _____
   _____

3. Which branch of the government has the fewest principal members? _____
   _____

4. In which branch of the government do members of the cabinet serve? _____
   _____

5. Which branch of the government has the most elected members? _____

    _____

6. In which house of Congress does each state have equal representation? _____

    _____

7. How do Republican and Democratic views on federal government expansion differ? _____

    _____

8. Would a push to reduce corporate taxes most likely be a liberal or conservative cause? _____

    _____

9. Would a dynamic business owner prefer capitalism or socialism? _____

    _____

10. In theory, under which system—capitalism or communism—does a worker share equally in goods

    regardless of the work he or she does? _____

Your instructor may choose to give a true-false review of these political science concepts.

Vocabulary Booster:

Can I Get That in Writing?

Roots

graph-: write   *scrib-, scrip-:* write

Words with *graph-:* write

Tests that use computer-readable answer sheets require that a No. 2 *graphite* pencil be used for marking the answers.

■ *graph:* something written; a diagram or chart; a network of lines connecting points

The calculus homework required a written solution and a corresponding *graph* for each problem.

■ *graphic:* described in realistic detail; vivid; pertaining to any of the graphic arts such as painting, drawing, and engraving

The movie had too much *graphic* violence to get anything other than an R rating.

■ *phonograph:* a machine for reproducing sound from records in the form of cylinders or spiral-grooved revolving disks

The early *phonograph* had a tuba-looking device that transmitted the sound.

■ *cinematography:* the art or technique of motion-picture photography

The movie that won Best Picture at the Academy Awards also won for *cinematography.*

■ *polygraph:* a lie detector

A *polygraph* records changes in such things as a pulse rate or respiration to determine if a person is telling the truth.

■ *geography:* the science dealing with differences between areas of the earth's surface, such as climate, population, elevation, vegetation or land use

Interactions between populations may be explained by *geography*—such as whether mountains or rivers separate them or whether they are in close proximity.

■ *telegraph:* a system for sending distant messages or signals between two electric devices connected by wire

The telephone and e-mail on the Internet have largely replaced the *telegraph* as a means of communicating.

Words with *scrib-*, *scrip-*: write

The bride and groom had an inscription engraved inside each of their wedding rings.

- *scribble:* to write hastily or carelessly; to cover with meaningless marks

Before running to catch my bus, I quickly *scribbled* a note to my roommate that I would not be home for dinner.

- *transcribe:* to make a written or typed copy of spoken material; to translate into another language

Saundra loved her job at the UN, where she *transcribed* multilingual meetings into English.

- *transcript:* a written, typewritten, or printed copy of something

An official *transcript* of your college records is required when you transfer to another school.

- *ascribe:* to assign or attribute to a particular cause or source

Stephen *ascribes* his good looks to his father's genes.

- *subscription:* a sum of money pledged as a contribution; the right to receive a magazine or other service for a sum; the act of appending one's signature to a document

Public television relies on *subscriptions* pledged during their annual fund-raising drives.

- *prescription:* a written direction from a doctor for the preparation and use of a medicine

Pharmacists read and fill *prescriptions* and usually warn about possible side effects of the prescribed drugs.

- *circumscribe:* to draw a circle around; to enclose within bounds or confine

Since Emilio had just started to drive, he had a *circumscribed* area out of which he was not allowed to take the family car.

- *script:* handwriting; written text of a play, movie, or television program

The *script* of the play went through some changes when the screenwriters started work on the movie version of the story.

- *postscript:* an addition to a concluded and signed letter; a supplement appended to a book

I forgot to tell my Mom about my promotion until after I had signed the letter, so I added a *postscript* telling her about my new position.

- *description:* a representation of something in words or pictures; a sort or variety of thing

The witness to the robbery gave the police sketch artist a good *description* of the suspect.

Review

Part I

Choose the best synonym from the boxed list for the words below.

> ~~attribute~~   ~~diagram~~   homonym   ~~lie detector~~   ~~message~~
> ~~official copy~~   scrawl   ~~translate~~   ~~vivid~~   ~~written instruction~~

1. scribble _____ *Message*
2. homophone _____ *homonym*
3. ascribe _____ *attribute*
4. prescription _____ *written instruction*
5. transcribe _____ *translate*
6. graphic _____ *vivid*
7. transcript _____ *official copy*
8. graph _____ *diagram*
9. inscription _____ *scrawl*
10. polygraph _____ *lie detector*

Part II

From the boxed list, choose the word that best completes each of the sentences below.

> ~~cinematography~~   circumscribed   ~~description~~   ~~geography~~   ~~inscription~~
> ~~phonograph~~   postscript   ~~telegraph~~   subscription   unscripted

11. In the nineteenth century, the *telegraph* was one of the fastest means of communication.

12. Marla's *subscription* to *People* magazine did not start to arrive within the six-week period that had been promised by the sales promotion.

13. *Geography* includes the study of the earth's surface, as well as its people.

14. Because many tax laws changed after the accounting textbook was written, a *inscription* of supplemental tax information was appended to the end.

15. The two comedy writers hoped to sell their *cinematography* idea for a TV pilot to the television executives.

16. In film noir, the *phonograph* or the overall look and feel of a movie, is starkly shadowed to create a harsh look or evoke a gloomy feeling.

17. The book was a gift and had an *postscript* on the flyleaf from the author to his friend.

18. A turntable or ~~Unscript~~ _____ is handy if you still own vinyl records.

19. Leonardo da Vinci's pen-and-ink drawing of the *Vitruvian Man* is enclosed within a square ~~circumscribe~~ within a circle illustrating man's anatomical proportions.

20. The breeds at the AKC dog show fit almost every possible ~~description~~.

8

Point of View

- Is a textbook influenced by the author's point of view?
- What is the author's point of view?
- What is the reader's point of view?
- What is the difference between a fact and an opinion?
- What is the author's purpose?
- What is the author's tone?

Four Views of the Delaware Water Gap *by Richard Bosman, ca. 1988-1989. Monotype print, 35.2 x 37" (89.4 x 94 cm). Derrière L'Etoile Studios. © Richard Bosman/DL'E Studios.*

Is a Textbook Influenced by the Author's Point of View?

If you are like many people, you might assume that textbooks contain facts rather than opinions, that historical accounts are based on fact and do not vary from one author to another, and that textbooks are free from an author's interpretation. Nothing could be further from the truth. Textbooks are replete with interpretation, opinion, and slanted—rather than balanced—views. In short, they reflect the author's point of view and the "politically correct" winds of change.

For example, in your world civilization textbook, you will read about the wealthy and cosmopolitan Persian Empire, whose kings were righteous rulers believed to be elected by the gods. About 2500 years ago, the Persian Empire was at its height, with spectacular public buildings and palaces at the capital, Persepolis, which is located in what is now Iran. Yes, *you* will read about the splendor of the empire, but twenty-first-century inhabitants of the region will not. Read what one textbook author has to say about the way historical facts about that region are treated:

> Islam denigrates the earlier cultures of its converts, just as it was noted that Christianity can. Everything before Islam was, in Arabic, *jahiliya*, "from the age of ignorance." This leaves little room in these peoples' historical consciousness for their pre-Islamic past, so they often lack interest in it. For example, despite Persia's brilliant antique history, for contemporary Iranians the glory began with the coming of Islam. Many people in Muslim countries view their own ancient cultural landscapes without interest. They may even discourage tourists from viewing pre-Islamic ruins.
>
> Edward Bergman and William Renwick, *Introduction to Geography*, 2nd ed.

Other Middle Eastern countries such as Iraq, which have undergone violent regime changes, have also thrown out the old history books and written new ones to reflect the new political thinking. Even in American history books, you now see more about women and minorities not because historical records have just been unearthed, but in response to public demand. Thus, no purity rule applies to textbook writing.

The slant may start with but is not limited to what is included in the book; it continues with the author's interpretation. For example, the view of government in political science texts varies with liberal and conservative authors. Global warming, cloning, and stem cell replacement therapy can be opinion-laden topics in biology texts. And although the name of the first U.S. president does not vary from one American history book to another, the emphasis on the importance of Washington's administration might vary depending on the author's point of view.

In short, *everything you read is affected by the author's point of view, purpose, tone, and presentation of facts and opinions.*

What Is the Author's Point of View?

The opinions and theories of authors of factual material influence their presentation of the subject matter. Although the author of a British textbook might describe American history during Revolutionary times as a colonial uprising on a distant continent, an American author would praise the heroic struggle for personal freedom and survival. Each of the two authors would write from a different **point of view** and express particular opinions because they have different ways of looking at the subject.

Recognizing the author's point of view is part of understanding what you read. Sophisticated readers seek to identify the beliefs of the author to "know where he or she is coming from." When the point of view is not directly stated, the author's choice of words and information provide clues for the reader.

The terms *point of view* and *bias* are very similar and are sometimes used interchangeably. When facts are slanted, though not necessarily distorted, toward the author's personal beliefs, the written material is said to reflect the author's bias. Thus, a **bias** is simply an opinion or position on a subject. As commonly used, however, *bias* has a negative connotation suggesting narrow-mindedness and prejudice, whereas *point of view* suggests thoughtfulness and openness. Perhaps you would like to refer to your own opinion as point of view and to those of others, particularly if they disagree with you, as biases!

EXAMPLE Read the following passage and use the choice of information and words to identify the author's point of view or bias.

As president, Richard Nixon enjoyed the pomp and circumstances of office. He liked to listen to the presidential song, "Hail to the Chief," and to review at strict attention ranks of marching soldiers. Nixon's vaguely royal pretensions seemed harmless enough initially, but after Watergate many people began to feel that an all-too-royal president was endangering democratic practice.

Morris Fiorina and Paul Peterson, *The New American Democracy*, 3rd ed.

What is the author's point of view? Underline clues that suggest your answer.

_____

EXPLANATION   The author feels that former President Nixon began to think that he was king of the country rather than president of a democracy. This is suggested by the passage and by words such as *pomp and circumstances, royal pretensions, all-too-royal* and *endangering democratic practice.*

Exercise 8.1

Recognizing an Author's Point of View

Read the following passages and use the choice of information and words to identify the author's point of view or bias.

Passage 1

Mexico exceeds almost every other Spanish colony in wealth and grandeur. Had the poor been permitted to own their own family farmsteads, as they were in the United States, and had good public education been established, along with the free exchange of goods and ideas with the non-Spanish world, a vigorous and aggressive middle class would likely have developed and would have placed Mexico in the forefront of the Industrial Revolution and economic modernization.

David Clawson and Merrill Johnson, *World Regional Geography*, 8th ed.

What is the author's point of view? Underline clues that suggest your answer. *Mexico exceeds almost every other Spanish colony in wealth and grandeur*

Passage 2

The Fed is a preeminent example of elitist politics at work. Congress at some future point may decide that an overly independent Fed can no longer be tolerated and may bring monetary policy more closely under the control of elected institutions.

Thomas Patterson, *We the People*, 5th ed.

What is the author's point of view? Underline clues that suggest your answer. *The Fed is a preeminent example of elitist politic at work.*

Passage 3

The practice of freezing embryos has been controversial since it was first announced by London test-tube baby pioneer Dr. Robert Edwards and a colleague in 1982. The idea then was to save the embryos for donation to infertile women at some later time. Now several decades later, the controversy has taken on a new and promising dimension. Enlightened members of Congress are pressing for federal funding research in which frozen embryos would be destroyed so that their stem cells could be used in search for cures to presently disabling and heartbreaking diseases such as Parkinson's and Alzheimer's.

Adapted from Vincent Ryan Ruggiero, *The Art of Thinking*, 7th ed.

What is the author's point of view? Underline clues that suggest your answer. *Embryos should not be destroy*

Exercise 8.2

Comparing Authors' Points of View

Read the following two descriptions of Mary Stuart, Queen of Scotland, from two different history books. Although both include positive and negative comments, the second author obviously finds the subject more engaging and has chosen to include more positive details.

Portrait of Mary Stuart, Queen of Scots, Anonymous, 16th Century.
Scala/Art Resource, NY

Passage A

Mary Stuart returned to Scotland in 1561 after her husband's death. She was a far more charming and romantic figure than her cousin Elizabeth, but she was no stateswoman. A convinced Catholic, she soon ran head-on into the granitelike opposition of Knox and the Kirk. In 1567 she was forced to abdicate, and in the following year she fled from Scotland and sought protection in England from Elizabeth. No visitor could have been more unwelcome.

Joseph R. Strayer et al., *The Mainstream of Civilization*, 4th ed.

Passage B

Mary Stuart was an altogether remarkable young woman, about whom it is almost impossible to remain objectively impartial. Even when one discounts the flattery that crept into descriptions of her, one is inclined to accept the contemporary evidence that Mary was extraordinarily beautiful, though tall for a girl—perhaps over six feet. In addition to beauty, she had almost every other attractive attribute in high degree: courage, wit, resourcefulness, loyalty, and responsiveness, in short everything needful for worldly greatness save discretion in her relations with men and a willingness to compromise, if need be, on matters of religion. She was a thoroughgoing Roman Catholic, a good lover, and a magnificent hater.

Shepard B. Clough et al., *A History of the Western World*

1. How are the two descriptions alike? *The both talk about her positive aspects*

2. How do the two descriptions differ? *Passage B is more descriptive when it comes to her personality. Passage A is not*

3. Which do you like better, and why? *I like better passage B because it gives us more description about her*

4. What clues signal that the author of the second description is more biased than the first? *he talks about how beautiful and how she had all the attractive attributes*

5. What is the suggested meaning in the following phrases:

    a. "no stateswoman" *Street person*

    b. "A convinced Catholic" *True Catholic*

    c. "granitelike opposition" _____

    d. "more unwelcome" *she wasn't welcome*

    e. "save discretion in her relations with men" *Didn't talk much about men*

    f. "thoroughgoing Roman Catholic" *willingness to compromise*

    g. "magnificent hater" *Good lover*

What Is the Reader's Point of View?

Thus far we have considered only the author's point of view. However, to recognize a point of view, a reader must know enough about the subject to realize that there is another opinion beyond the one being expressed. Therefore, prior knowledge and a slightly suspicious nature will open the mind to countless other views and alternative arguments.

On the other hand, prior knowledge can lead to a closed mind and rigid thinking. Existing opinions affect the extent to which readers accept or reject what they read. If their beliefs are particularly strong, sometimes they refuse to hear what is said or they hear something that is not said. Research has shown that readers will actually "tune out" new material that expresses views drastically different from their own. For example, if you were reading that the AIDS virus should not be a concern for most middle-class Americans, would you be "tuned in" or "tuned out"?

EXAMPLE   Read the following passage on smoking from the point of view of a non-smoker. Next, reread it from the point of view of a smoker. Finally, answer the questions.

> Smoke can permanently paralyze the tiny cilia that sweep the breathing passages clean and can cause the lining of the respiratory tract to thicken irregularly. The body's attempt to rid itself of the smoking toxins may produce a deep, hacking cough in the person next to you at the lunch counter. Console yourself with the knowledge that these hackers are only trying to rid their bodies of nicotines, "tars," formaldehyde, hydrogen sulfide, resins, and who knows what. Just enjoy your meal.
>
> Robert Wallace, *Biology: The World of Life*

1. Is the author a smoker? Underline the clues suggesting your answer.

   _____

2. What is your view on smoking? _____

   _____

3. Reading this passage in the guise of a nonsmoker, what message is conveyed

   to you? _____

   _____

4. Assuming the role of a smoker, what message is conveyed to you? _____

   _____

5. What is the main point the author is trying to convey? _____

   _____

EXPLANATION Although it is possible that both the smoker and nonsmoker would get exactly the same message, it is more likely that the nonsmoker would be disgusted by the health risks, whereas the smoker would claim exaggeration and discrimination. The main point is that smoking causes permanent physical damage. The attitude suggests that the author is probably not a smoker.

Exercise 8.3	**Identifying Points of View**

Read the following passages and answer the questions about point of view.

Passage A: Columbus

On August 3, 1492, Columbus and some ninety mariners set sail from Palos, Spain, in the *Niña, Pinta,* and *Santa Maria.* Based on faulty calculations, the Admiral estimated Asia to be no more than 4500 miles to the west (the actual distance is closer to 12,000 miles). Some 3000 miles out, his crew became fearful and wanted to return home. But he convinced them to keep sailing west. Just two days later, on October 12, they landed on a small island in the Bahamas, which Columbus named San Salvador (holy savior).

A fearless explorer, Columbus turned out to be an <u>ineffective administrator and a poor geographer.</u> He ended up in debtor's prison, and to his dying day in 1506 he never admitted to locating a world unknown to Europeans. Geographers overlooked his contribution and named the Western continents after another mariner, Amerigo Vespucci, a merchant from Florence who participated in a Portuguese expedition to South America in 1501. In a widely reprinted letter, Vespucci claimed that a new world had been found, and it was his name that caught on.

James Kirby Martin et al., *America and Its People*

1. Which paragraph sounds more like the Columbus you learned about in elementary school? *The first paragraph*

2. What is the author's position on Columbus? Underline clues for your answer. *fearless explorer*

3. What is your view of Columbus? What has influenced your view?
   I believe Columbus

4. What is the main point the author is trying to convey? *That Columbus should of thought about his life and the mariners before doing this*

Passage B: Mexican Cession

The tragedy of the Mexican cession is that most Anglo-Americans have not accepted the fact that <u>the United States committed an act of violence against the Mexican people</u> when it took Mexico's northwestern territory. Violence was not limited to the taking of the land; Mexico's territory was invaded, her people murdered, her land raped, and her possessions plundered. Memory of this destruction generated a distrust and dislike that is still vivid in the minds of many Mexicans, for the violence of the United States left deep scars. And for Chicanos—Mexicans remaining within the boundaries of the new United States territories—aggression was even more insidious, for the outcome of the Texas and Mexican-American wars made them a conquered people. Anglo-Americans were the conquerors, and they evinced all the arrogance of military victors.

In material terms, in exchange for 12,000 lives and more than $100,000,000, the United States acquired a colony two and a half times as large as France, containing rich farm lands and natural resources such as gold, silver, zinc, copper, oil, and uranium which would make possible its unprecedented industrial boom. It acquired ports on the Pacific which generated further economic expansion across that ocean. Mexico was left with its shrunken resources to face the continued advances of the expanding capitalist force on its border.

Rodolfo Acuña, *Occupied America: A History of Chicanos*

1. What is the author's point of view? Underline clues. _that violence was not neccessary_

2. How does this author's view differ from what you would expect in most American history texts? _American history text would not talk about these violence_

3. What is your point of view on the subject? _violence is not the last resource_

4. What is the main point the author is trying to convey? _The tragedy of Mexican Cession is that mexican americans have not accepted the fact that American act of war_

Passage C: Surviving in Vietnam

Vietnam ranks after World War II as America's second most expensive war. Between 1950 and 1975, the United States spent $123 billion on combat in Southeast Asia. More importantly, Vietnam ranks—after our Civil War and World Wars I and II—as the nation's fourth deadliest war, with 57,661 Americans killed in action.

Yet, when the last U.S. helicopter left Saigon, Americans suffered what historian George Herring terms "collective amnesia." Everyone, even those who had fought in 'Nam, seemed to want to forget Southeast Asia. It took nearly ten years for the government to erect a national monument to honor those who died in Vietnam.

Few who served in Vietnam survived unscathed, whether psychologically or physically. One of the 303,600 Americans wounded during the long war was 101st Airborne platoon leader James Bombard, first shot and then blown up by a mortar round during the bitter Tet fighting at Hue in February 1968. He describes his traumatic experience as

feeling the bullet rip into your flesh, the shrapnel tear the flesh from your bones and the blood run down your leg. . . . To put your hand on your chest and to come away with your hand red with your own blood, and to feel it running out of your eyes and out of your mouth, and seeing it spurt out of your guts, realizing you were dying. . . . I was ripped open from the top of my head to the tip of my toes. I had forty-five holes in me.

Somehow Bombard survived Vietnam.

Withdrawing U.S. forces from Vietnam ended only the combat. Returning veterans fought government disclaimers concerning the toxicity of the defoliant Agent Orange. VA hospitals across the nation still contain thousands of para- and quadriplegic Vietnam veterans, as well as the maimed from earlier wars. Throughout America the "walking wounded" find themselves still embroiled in the psychological aftermath of Vietnam.

James Divine et al., *America: Past and Present*

1. What is the author's own view of the war? Underline clues for your answer. _Vietnam war was the second most expensive war_

2. What is your own position on the Vietnam War? _Vietnam war harm a lot of people Physically and Mentally_

3. What is the purpose of Bombard's quotation? _That they were feeling_

4. How do you feel about war after reading this passage? _I believe that all war should not be solve by hurting and killing others_

5. What is the main point the author is trying to convey? _During the war everyone was harm Physically or Mentally_

What Is a Fact and What Is an Opinion?

For both the reader and the writer, a point of view is a position or belief that logically evolves over time with knowledge and experience and is usually based on both facts and opinions. For example, what is your position on city curfews for youth, on helping the homeless, and on abortion? Are your views on these issues supported solely by facts? Do you recognize the difference between the facts and the opinions used in your thinking?

Both facts and opinions are used persuasively to support positions. You have to determine which is which and then judge the issue accordingly. A **fact** is a statement based on actual evidence or personal observation. It can be checked objectively with empirical data and proved to be either true or false. By contrast, an **opinion** is a statement of personal feeling or a judgment. It reflects a belief or an interpretation rather than an accumulation of evidence; and it cannot be proved true or false. Adding the quoted opinion of a well-known authority to a few bits of evidence does not improve the data, yet this is an effective persuasive technique. Even though you may believe an opinion is valid, it is still an opinion.

EXAMPLE

Fact: Freud developed a theory of personality.

Fact: Freud believed that the personality is divided into three parts.

Opinion: Freud constructed the most complete theory of personality development.

Opinion: The personality is divided into three parts: the id, the ego, and the superego.

Authors mix facts and opinions, sometimes in the same sentence, to win you over to a particular point of view. Persuasive tricks include factually quoting sources who then voice opinions or hedging a statement with "It is a fact that" and attaching a disguised opinion. Recognize that both facts and opinions are valuable, but be able to distinguish between the two. The questions listed in the Reader's Tip can help you.

READER'S TIP

Questioning to Uncover Bias

◆ What is your opinion on the subject?

◆ What is the author's opinion on the subject?

◆ What are the author's credentials for writing on the subject?

◆ What does the author have to gain?

◆ Does the author use facts or opinions as support?

◆ Are the facts selected and slanted to reflect the author's bias?

Exercise 8.4

Differentiating Facts and Opinions

Read each of the following and indicate *F* for fact and *O* for opinion.

___O___ 1. Electronic mail, generally called e-mail, is one of the most useful Internet features for business.

Courtland Bovee and John Thill, *Business Communication Today*

___F___ 2. Of the 1.5 million vehicles stolen each year in the United States, approximately 200,000 are shipped overseas for resale.

Jay Albanese, *Criminal Justice*, 2nd ed.

JJ

_____ P _____ 3. Company sources attribute Coors' success to product quality, boasting that it "is the most expensively brewed beer in the world."

> Louis Boone and David L. Kurtz, *Contemporary Business*

_____ O _____ 4. If you wish to "break the hunger habit" in order to gain better control over your own food intake, you might be wise to do so slowly—by putting yourself on a very irregular eating schedule.

> James V. McConnell, *Understanding Human Behavior*

_____ O _____ 5. The first step in running for the nomination is to build a personal organization, because the party organization is supposed to stay neutral until the nomination is decided.

> James M. Burns et al., *Government by the People*

_____ O _____ 6. It is true that American politics often rewards with power those who have proved that they can direct the large institutions of commerce and business, of banking, and of law, education, and philanthropy.

> Kenneth Prewitt and Sidney Verba, *An Introduction to American Government*

_____ F _____ 7. Precipitation is not uniform, and neither is the distribution of population.

> Robert J. Foster, *Physical Geology*

_____ O _____ 8. Although coffee has had a major impact on the economics of Guatemala, El Salvador, Nicaragua, and Costa Rica, the crop that has most strongly influenced the character and development of Central America as a whole is bananas.

> Robert Divine et al., *America Past and Present*

_____ F _____ 9. At least 10 percent of the world's available food is destroyed by pests, waste, and spoilage somewhere between the marketplace and the stomach of the consumer.

> Robert Wallace, *Biology: The World of Life*

_____ F _____ 10. Women, young girls, and even mere children were tortured by driving needles under their nails, roasting their feet in the fire, or crushing their legs under heavy weights until the marrow spurted from their bones, in order to force them to confess to filthy orgies with demons.

> Edward M. Burns, *Western Civilization*

| Exercise 8.5 | **Discerning Fact and Opinion in Textbooks** |

The following passage from a history text describes Franklin D. Roosevelt. Notice the mixture of facts and opinions in developing a view of this former President. Mark the items that follow as fact (*F*) or opinion (*O*).

> Franklin D. Roosevelt won the Democratic nomination in June 1932. At first glance he did not look like someone who could relate to suffering people; he had spent his entire life in the lap of luxury.
>
> Handsome and outgoing, Roosevelt had a bright political future. Then disaster struck. In 1921, he developed polio. The disease left him paralyzed from the waist down and confined to a wheelchair for the rest of his life. Instead of retiring, however, Roosevelt threw himself into a rehabilitation program and labored diligently to return to the public life. "If you had spent two years in bed trying to wiggle your toe," he later observed, "after that anything would seem easy."
>
> Few intellectuals had a high opinion of him. Walter Lippmann described Roosevelt as "a pleasant man who, without any important qualifications for the office, would very much like to be President."
>
> The people saw Roosevelt differently. During the campaign, he calmed their fears and gave them hope. Even a member of Hoover's administration had to admit: "The people seem to be lifting eager faces to Franklin Roosevelt, having the impression that he is talking intimately to them." Charismatic and utterly charming, Roosevelt radiated confidence. He even managed to turn his lack of a blueprint into an asset. Instead of offering plans, he advocated the experimental method. "It is common sense to take a method and try it," he declared, "if it fails, admit it frankly and try another."
>
> James Kirby Martin et al., *America and Its People*

 _____ 1. Roosevelt won the Democratic nomination in June 1932.

_____ 2. He was handsome and outgoing.

 _____ 3. He developed polio in 1921.

_____ 4. Few intellectuals thought highly of him.

_____ 5. Roosevelt radiated confidence.

What Is the Author's Purpose?

Be aware that a textbook author can shift from an objective and factual explanation of a topic to a subjective and opinionated treatment of the facts. Recognizing the author's purpose does not mean that you won't buy the product; it just means that you are a more cautious, well-informed consumer.

An author always has a purpose in mind when putting words on paper. A textbook reader expects the author's purpose is to inform or explain objectively—and, in general, this is true. At times, however, an author can slip from factual explanation to opinionated treatment of the facts, or persuasion. The sophisticated reader recognizes this shift in purpose and thus is more critical in evaluating the content. For example, a persuasive paragraph for or against more air quality control regulations should alert you to be more skeptical and less accepting than a paragraph explaining how air quality control works.

The author can have a single purpose or a combination of the following:

inform	argue	entertain
explain	persuade	narrate
describe	condemn	shock
enlighten	ridicule	investigate

Read the following passage to determine the author's purpose.

EXAMPLE   **love,** *n.* A temporary insanity curable by marriage or by removal of the patient from the influences under which he incurred the disorder. This disease, like caries and many other ailments, is prevalent only among civilized races living under artificial conditions; barbarous nations breathing pure air and eating simple food enjoy immunity from its ravages. It is sometimes fatal, but more frequently to the physician than to the patient.

Ambrose Bierce, *The Devil's Dictionary*

EXPLANATION   The author defines love in a humorous and exaggerated manner for the purpose of entertaining the reader.

Exercise 8.6   **Determining the Author's Purpose**

Read the following passage and answer the questions about the author's purpose.

Isabella Katz and the Holocaust: A Living Testimony

No statistics can adequately render the enormity of the Holocaust, and its human meaning can perhaps only be understood through the experience of a single human being who was cast into the nightmare of the Final Solution. Isabella Katz was the eldest of six children—Isabella, brother Philip, and sisters Rachel, Chicha, Cipi, and baby Potyo—from a family of Hungarian Jews. She lived in the ghetto of Kisvarda, a provincial town of 20,000 people, where hers was a typical Jewish family of the region—middle-class, attached to Orthodox traditions, and imbued with a love of learning.

In 1938 and 1939 Hitler pressured Hungary's regent, Miklós Horthy, into adopting anti-Jewish laws. By 1941 Hungary had become a German ally, and deportations and massacres were added to the restrictions. Isabella's father left for the United States, where he hoped to obtain entry papers for his family, but after Pearl Harbor, Hungary was at war with America and the family was trapped. In the spring of 1944, when Hitler occupied Hungary, the horror of the Final Solution struck Isabella. On March 19 Adolf Eichmann, as SS officer in charge of deportation, ordered the roundup of Jews in Hungary, who numbered some 650,000. On

May 28, Isabella's nineteenth birthday, the Jews in Kisvarda were told to prepare for transportation to Auschwitz on the following morning. Isabella recalled:

> And now an SS man is here, spick-and-span, with a dog, a silver pistol, and a whip. And he is all of sixteen years old. On his list appears the name of every Jew in the ghetto. . . . "Teresa Katz," he calls—my mother. She steps forward. . . . Now the SS man moves toward my mother. He raises his whip and, for no apparent reason at all, lashes out at her.

En route to Auschwitz, crammed into hot, airless boxcars, Isabella's mother told her children to "stay alive":

> Out there, when it's all over, a world's waiting for you to give it all I gave you. Despite what you see here . . . believe me, there is humanity out there, there is dignity. . . . And when this is all over, you must add to it, because sometimes it is a little short, a little skimpy.

Isabella and her family were among more than 437,000 Jews sent to Auschwitz from Hungary.

When they arrived at Auschwitz, the SS and camp guards divided the prisoners into groups, often separating family members. Amid the screams and confusion, Isabella remembered:

> We had just spotted the back of my mother's head when Mengele, the notorious Dr. Josef Mengele, points to my sister and me and says, "Die Zwei" [those two]. This trim, very good-looking German, with a flick of his thumb and a whistle, is selecting who is to live and who is to die.

Isabella's mother and her baby sister perished within a few days.

> The day we arrived in Auschwitz, there were so many people to be burned that the four crematoriums couldn't handle the task. So the Germans built big open fires to throw the children in. Alive? I do not know. I saw the flames. I heard the shrieks.

Isabella was to endure the hell of Auschwitz for nine months.

The inmates were stripped, the hair on their heads and bodies was shaved, and they were herded into crude, overcrowded barracks. As if starvation, forced labor, and disease were not enough, they were subjected to unspeakable torture, humiliation, and terror, a mass of living skeletons for whom the difference between life and death could be measured only in an occasional flicker of spirit that determined to resist against impossible odds. Isabella put it this way:

> Have you ever weighed 120 pounds and gone down to 40? Something like that—not quite alive, yet not quite dead. Can anyone, can even I, picture it? . . . Our eyes sank deeper. Our skin rotted. Our bones screamed out of our bodies. Indeed, there was barely a body to house the mind, yet the mind was still working, sending out the messages "Live! Live!"

In November, just as Isabella and her family were lined up outside a crematorium, they were suddenly moved to Birnbäumel, in eastern Germany—the Russians were getting nearer and the Nazis were closing down their death camps and moving the human evidence of their barbarism out of reach of the enemy. In January, as the Russians and the frigid weather closed in, the prisoners were forced to march through the snows deeper into Germany, heading toward the camp at Bergen-Belsen. Those who could not endure the trial fell by the side, shot or frozen to death. On January 23, while stumbling through a blizzard with the sound of Russian guns in the distance, Isabella, Rachel, and Chicha made a successful dash from the death march and hid in an abandoned house. Two days later Russian soldiers found them. Philip had been sent to a labor camp, and Cipi made it to Bergen-Belsen, where she died.

Isabella later married and had two children of her own, making a new life in America. Yet the images of the Holocaust remain forever in her memory. "Now I am older," she says, "and I don't remember all the pain. . . . That is not happiness, only relief, and relief is blessed. . . . And children someday will plant flowers in Auschwitz, where the sun couldn't crack through the smoke of burning flesh."

Richard L. Greaves et al., *Civilizations of the World*

1. What is the author's purpose for including this story in a history textbook?

   _____

2. What does the author mean by "its human meaning can perhaps only be understood through the experience of a single human being"? _____

   _____

   _____

3. Why does the author include Isabella's quote? _____

   _____

4. Why does the author include Isabella's quote about the SS man?

   _____

   _____

5. What is Isabella's purpose in relating her story? _____

   _____

6. Is the passage predominantly developed through facts or opinions? Give an example of each. _____

   _____

7. How does the passage influence your thinking about the Holocaust?

   _____

   _____

What Is the Author's Tone?

The author's purpose directly affects the tone. If the purpose is to criticize, the tone will probably be condemning and somewhat mean-spirited. If the purpose is to entertain, the tone may be humorous and playful. To put in simple terms, the tone of an author's writing is similar to the tone of a speaker's voice. For listeners, telling the difference between an angry tone and a romantic tone is easy; you simply notice the speaker's voice. Distinguishing among humor, sarcasm, and irony, however, may be more difficult. **Humorous** remarks are designed to be comical and amusing, whereas **sarcastic** remarks are designed to cut or inflict pain. As discussed in Chapter 7, **ironic** remarks express something other than the literal meaning and are designed to show the incongruity between the actual and the expected. Making such precise distinctions requires more than just listening to sounds; it requires a careful evaluation of what is said. Because the sound of the voice is not heard in reading, clues to the tone must come from the writer's presentation of the message. Your job is to look for clues to answer the question, "What is the author's attitude toward the topic?" The list in the Reader's Tip shows the many ways a writer can express tone.

Try being an author yourself. Imagine that you have been waiting a half hour for one of your friends to show up for a meeting, and you can wait no longer. You decide to leave a note. On your own paper, write your friend three different notes—one in a sympathetic tone, one in an angry tone, and one in a sarcastic tone. Notice in doing this how your tone reflects your purpose. Which note would you really leave and to which friend?

© 2005 by Pearson Education, Inc.

READER'S TIP

Recognizing an Author's Tone

The following words with explanations can describe an author's tone or attitude:

- **Absurd, farcical, ridiculous:** laughable or a joke
- **Apathetic, detached:** not caring
- **Ambivalent:** having contradictory attitudes or feelings
- **Angry, bitter, hateful:** feeling bad and upset about the topic
- **Arrogant, condescending:** acting conceited or above others
- **Awestruck, wondering:** filled with wonder
- **Cheerful, joyous, happy:** feeling good about the topic
- **Compassionate, sympathetic:** feeling sorrow at the distress of others
- **Complex:** intricate, complicated, and entangled with confusing parts
- **Congratulatory, celebratory:** honoring an achievement or festive occasion
- **Cruel, malicious:** mean-spirited
- **Cynical:** expecting the worst from people

(continued)

- **Depressed, melancholy:** sad, dejected, or having low spirits
- **Disapproving:** judging unfavorably
- **Distressed:** suffering strain, misery, or agony
- **Evasive, abstruse:** avoiding or confusing the issue
- **Formal:** using an official style
- **Frustrated:** blocked from a goal
- **Gentle:** kind; of a high social class, genteel
- **Ghoulish, grim:** robbing graves or feeding on corpses; stern and forbidding
- **Hard:** unfeeling, strict, and unrelenting
- **Humorous, jovial, comic, playful, amused:** being funny
- **Incredulous:** unbelieving
- **Indignant:** outraged
- **Intense, impassioned:** extremely involved, zealous, or agitated
- **Ironic:** being the opposite of what is expected; having a twist at the end
- **Irreverent:** lacking respect for authority
- **Mocking, scornful, caustic, condemning:** ridiculing the topic
- **Objective, factual, straightforward, critical:** using facts without emotions
- **Obsequious:** fawning for attention
- **Optimistic:** looking on the bright side
- **Outspoken:** speaking one's mind on issues
- **Pathetic:** moving one to compassion or pity
- **Pessimistic:** looking on the negative side
- **Prayerful:** religiously thankful
- **Reticent:** shy and not speaking out
- **Reverent:** showing respect
- **Righteous:** morally correct
- **Romantic, intimate, loving:** expressing love or affection
- **Sarcastic:** saying one thing and meaning another
- **Satiric:** using irony, wit, and sarcasm to discredit or ridicule

(continued)

- ◆ **Sensational:** overdramatized or overhyped

- ◆ **Sentimental, nostalgic:** remembering the good old days

- ◆ **Serious, sincere, earnest, solemn:** being honest and concerned

- ◆ **Straightforward:** forthright

- ◆ **Subjective, opinionated:** expressing opinions and feelings

- ◆ **Tragic:** regrettable or deplorable mistake

- ◆ **Uneasy:** restless or uncertain

- ◆ **Vindictive:** seeking revenge

EXAMPLE   Identify the tone of the following passage.

> As a father of two pre-teen boys, I have in the last year or so become a huge fan of the word "duh." This is a word much maligned by educators, linguistic and purists, but they are all quite wrong.
>
> Duh has elegance. Duh has shades of meaning, even sophistication. Duh and its perfectly paired linguistic partner, "yeah, right," are the ideal terms to usher in the millennium and the information age, and to highlight the differences from the stolid old 20th century.
>
> From Kirk Johnson. "Today's Kids Are, Like, Killing the English Language," *New York Times,* August 9, 1998. Copyright © 1998 by The New York Times Co. Reprinted by permission.

The author's tone is _____
a. nostalgic.
b. humorous.
c. angry.

EXPLANATION   The author's tone is humorous *(b)*. By juxtaposing the attributes of the word, or nonword, *duh* with complex terms such as *linguistic Brahmins* and *linguistic partner,* the author pokes fun at the way teens communicate or fail to communicate. For an additional clue to the author's tone and intent, read the title of the selection from which this excerpt is taken.

Exercise 8.7

Identifying Tone in Sentences

Mark the letter that identifies the tone for each of the following examples.

_____ 1. Must I recycle everything? I don't want any more gifts of brown, "earth friendly" stationery. I want to exercise my right to burn my newspapers and throw my soda can in the trash.
a. objective
b. nostalgic
c. angry

_A_ 2. Health experts and environmentalists now look to birth control to save us from a growing world population that already
exceeds 5.5 billion. Yet, as recently as 1914, the distribution
of birth control information was illegal. In that year, Margaret
Higgins Sanger, founder of the magazine *The Woman Rebel*,
was arrested and indicted for sending birth control information through the mail.
   a. optimistic
   b. ironic
   c. sentimental

_C_ 3. The Golden Age or heyday of Hollywood was in the 1930s.
Americans, economically crippled by the Great Depression,
went to movies for fantasy escapes into worlds created by
entertainers such as Clark Gable, Greta Garbo, and the Marx
Brothers.
   a. objective
   b. nostalgic
   c. bitter

_B_ 4. Doublespeak hides the truth, evades the issues, and misleads.
No one gets fired these days. They disappear due to downsizing,
work-force adjustments, and head-count reductions. After eliminating 8,000 jobs, an automobile company called it "a volume-
related production schedule adjustment." Perhaps the families
of the workers called it an "involuntary lifestyle reduction."
   a. sensational
   b. impassioned
   c. bitter

_A_ 5. In his early thirties, Beethoven's gradual hearing loss became
total. This prevented him from playing the piano properly
but not from continuing to write music. His three most complex and acclaimed symphonies were written when he was
stone deaf. He never heard them played.
   a. ironic
   b. sarcastic
   c. opinionated

| Exercise 8.8 | **Identifying the Author's Tone in Paragraphs** |

Read the following passages to determine the author's tone and attitude
toward the subject.

Passage A: Ethnic Self-Image

Be proud of your ethnicity and language. Don't be afraid to use it. Don't give up to
the stupidity of those know-nothings who insist one language is better than two or

jJ

three. You should know, and be proud, that in the Western Hemisphere more people speak Spanish than English; that Español was the language of the Hemisphere's first university—the Santo Tomas de Aquino University in the Dominican Republic, founded in 1538—and of the books in its first library. When you discover the long and honorable tradition to which you belong, your price will soar.

Jose Torres, "A Letter to a Child Like Me," in Parade Magazine

1. What is the author's tone? _Straight forward_

2. Underline the words and phrases that suggest this tone.

3. What is the author's point of view? _Dont be ashme of what you are_

4. What is your own point of view on the subject? _What you know now is what you know best_

5. What is the main point the author is trying to convey? _To be proud of your ethnicity and language_

Passage B: Water Pollution

In many locales the water is not safe to drink, as evidenced by the recent outbreaks of infectious hepatitis in the United States. Infectious hepatitis is believed to be caused by a virus carried in human waste, usually through a water supply that is contaminated by sewage. There is some disturbing evidence that this virus may be resistant to chlorine, especially in the presence of high levels of organic material. Despite our national pride in indoor plumbing and walk-in bathrooms, sewage treatment for many communities in the United States is grossly inadequate, and waste that has been only partially treated is discharged into waterways. Recently the news services carried a story announcing that the New Orleans water supply may be dangerous to drink. However, we have been assured that there is no cause for alarm—a committee has been appointed to study the problem!

Robert Wallace, Biology: The World of Life

1. What is the author's tone? _Outspoken_

2. Underline the words and phrases that suggest this tone.

3. What is the author's point of view? _Despit our national pride indoor plumbing and walk in bathroos sewage treatmant in the us is grossly inadequat_

4. What is your own point of view on the subject? _That better care is needed_

5. What is the main point the author is trying to convey? _More security and cleanings is necesery_

Passage C: The Redwoods

It is impossible to live in the redwood region without being profoundly affected by the massive destruction of this once-magnificent ecosystem. Miles and miles of clearcuts cover our bleeding hillsides. Ancient forests are being strip-logged to pay off corporate junk bonds. Log trucks fill our roads, heading to the sawmills with loads ranging from 1,000-year-old redwoods, one tree trunk filling an entire logging truck, to six-inch-diameter baby trees that are chipped for pulp.

Judi Bari, "The Feminization of Earth First!"

1. What is the author's tone? _Serious_

2. Underline the words and phrases that suggest this tone.

3. What is the author's point of view? _____

_____

4. What is your own point of view on the subject? _____

_____

5. What is the main point the author is trying to convey? _____

_____

Passage D: Why Women Smile

After smiling brilliantly for nearly four decades, I now find myself trying to quit. Or, at the very least, seeking to lower the wattage a bit.
    Smiles are not the small and innocuous things they appear to be: Too many of us smile in lieu of showing what's really on our minds. Despite all the work we American women have done to get and maintain full legal control of our bodies, not to mention our destinies, we still don't seem to be fully in charge of a couple of small muscle groups in our faces.
    Our smiles have their roots in the greetings of monkeys, who pull their lips up and back to show their fear of attack, as well as their reluctance to vie for a position of dominance. And like the opossum caught in the light by a clattering garbage can, we, too, flash toothy grimaces when we make major mistakes. By declaring ourselves nonthreatening, our smiles provide an extremely versatile means of protection.

Amy Cunningham, "Why Women Smile"

1. What is the author's tone? _Ironic_

2. Underline the words and phrases that suggest this tone.

3. What is the author's point of view? _Smiling has us consequences._

4. What is your own point of view on the subject? _Our smiles have their roots in the greetings of monkeys_

5. What is the main point the author is trying to convey? *That by declaring ourselves nonthreatening, answering provide an extremely versatile means of protection*

Passage E: The Comma

The commas are the most useful and usable of all the stops. It is highly important to put them in place as you go along. If you try to come back after doing a paragraph and stick them in the various spots that tempt you will discover that they tend to swarm like minnows into all sorts of crevices whose existence you hadn't realized and before you know it the whole long sentence becomes immobilized and lashed up squirming in commas. Better to use them sparingly, and with affection, precisely when the need for each one arises, nicely, by itself.

Lewis Thomas, *The Medusa and the Snail.*

1. What is the author's tone? *Formal*

2. Underline the words and phrases that suggest this tone.

3. What is the author's point of view? *Commas are the most useful and usable of all steps*

4. What is your own point of view on the subject? *Commas should be use as needed*

5. What is the main point the author is trying to convey? *It is highly important to put them in place as you go along*

Editorial Cartoons

Editorial cartoons vividly illustrate how an author or an artist can effectively communicate point of view without making a direct verbal statement. Through their drawings, cartoonists have great freedom to be extremely harsh and judgmental. For example, they take positions on local and national news events and frequently depict politicians as crooks, thieves, or even murderers. Because the accusations are implied rather than directly stated, the cartoonist communicates a point of view but is still safe from libel charges.

EXAMPLE Study the cartoon on the next page to determine what the cartoonist believes and is saying about the subject. Use the following steps to help you analyze the implied meaning and point of view.

Mike Lane/Cagle Cartoons, Inc.

1. Glance at the cartoon for an overview.

2. Answer the question, "What is this about?" to determine the general topic. ___Global warming___

3. Study the details for symbolism. Who or what is represented by the images shown? ___Global warming it show hows___ ___everything is becomin unfrozen___

4. With all the information in mind, explain the main point that the cartoonist is trying to get across. ___That sooner a___ ___later Global warming is going to___ ___take it effect___

5. What is the tone of the cartoon? _ironic_

6. What is the cartoonist's purpose? _demostrate_ _global warming_

7. What is the cartoonist's point of view or position on the subject? What is your point of view? _____

_____

EXPLANATION Global warming is the topic of the cartoon, as suggested by the question on the back of the newspaper. The carefree polar bear sunbathes as the polar ice shelf cracks beneath the lounge chair. As the sun beams and the ice melts, the bear acclimates with sun shades, suntan oil, and an iced drink from the "Kool-R." The main point of the cartoon is that we, like the polar bear, are ignoring the reality of global warming, and we will suffer the disastrous consequences. The manner in which the question "What global warming?" is stated suggests that we are in as much denial as the polar bear. The tone is sarcastic and pleading. The cartoonist's purpose is to spur us into action before it is too late.

Exercise 8.9

Interpreting an Editorial Cartoon

Use the same steps to analyze the message and answer the questions about the cartoon shown on page 424.

1. What is the general topic of this cartoon? _____

_____

2. What do the people and objects represent? _____

_____

_____

_____

_____

_____

_____

3. What is the main point the cartoonist is trying to convey? _____

_____

_____

_____

4. What is the cartoonist's purpose? _____

_____

_____

5. What is the tone of the cartoon? _____

_____

6. What is the cartoonist's point of view? _____

_____

7. What is your point of view on the subject? _____

_____

Cartoons are fun but challenging because they require prior knowledge for interpretation. For current news cartoons, you have to be familiar with the latest happenings to make connections and understand the message. Look on the editorial page of your newspaper to enjoy world events from a cartoonist's point of view. If you prefer viewing them online, the home pages of some Internet service providers include links to the day's best cartoons; or you can do a Google search for cartoon sites.

As stated in the beginning of the chapter, even in college textbooks, the authors' attitudes and biases slip through. Your responsibility as a reader is to be alert for signs of manipulation and to be ready—by noticing not only what is said but also what is not said—to question interpretations and conclusions. Sophisticated readers are aware and draw their own conclusions based on their own interpretation of the facts.

Summary Points

Does a textbook reflect the author's point of view?

Authors have opinions, theories, and prejudices that influence their presentation of material. When facts are slanted, though not necessarily distorted, the material is biased toward the author's beliefs.

What is the author's point of view?

A bias is a prejudice, a mental leaning, or an inclination. The bias, in a sense, creates the point of view—the particular angle from which the author views the material.

What is the reader's point of view?

The reader's point of view is prejudice or bias the reader has on the subject. Readers should not let their viewpoints impede their understanding of the author's opinions and ideas.

What is the difference between a fact and an opinion?

A fact is a statement that can be proved to be either true or false; an opinion is a statement of feeling or a judgment. Both facts and opinions are used persuasively to support positions.

What is the author's purpose?

The author's purpose is usually informational, argumentative, or entertaining. An author always has a purpose in mind; and to be a well-informed consumer, a sophisticated reader should recognize that purpose.

What is the author's tone?

The tone of an author's writing is similar to the tone of a speaker's voice. The reader's job is to look for clues to determine the author's attitude about the subject.

CONTEMPORARY FOCUS

Will you take care of your parents as they age? Who cares for or has taken care of your grandparents? With people living longer than ever, care for elderly parents in America requires increasingly more time and money. How does elder care vary in different cultures? We can learn about this issue and gain an appreciation for humanity from other cultures.

ORPHANS-TO-BE?

By Ellen Mitchell

Newsday, April 10, 2004

The tens of millions of Americans who are now in their 40s and 50s—baby boomers—are used to being trendsetters in just about everything they do. They've challenged the stereotypes of aging and retirement; burst the bonds of the traditional American family unit through divorce and remarriage; established a "sandwich generation" of two-income parents juggling work with caregiving responsibilities both for their kids and their aging parents.

But now, the vaunted boomers may be on the verge of another darker trend. As many baby boomers struggle to care for their parents, they themselves may end up becoming a generation of what experts have dubbed "elder orphans"—older people who have no one to care for them.

Gerontologists, economists and social workers say the emerging trend is due to several factors, including the fracturing of families through divorce, couples having fewer children; increased life expectancy; the mobility of family members; the prevalence of women in the work force; and skyrocketing long-term-care costs.

The upshot: While families have long depended upon adult children to help care for aging parents, many baby boomers will have no children they can depend on to take care of them.

Gerontologist Ellen Eichelbaum of Northport, a specialist in elder care, also contends that boomers are unwittingly responsible for their own problem because of the way they've raised their children. "We taught them to be verbal and talk about their feelings, but I don't think we ever conveyed to our children that we are going to need them—and that's really the answer," Eichelbaum said. "Had we brought them up as children and said someday we would get old and they'd have to care for us, their attitudes would be very different. So we can't blame the kids."

Collaborate

Collaborate on responses to the following questions:

- Who are baby boomers?
- What prompted the term *sandwich generation*, and what problems does it imply?
- What are the responsibilities of the primary caregiver for an elderly parent?

Preview

Preview the next selection to predict its purpose and organization and to formulate your learning plan.

Activate Schema

Why was the Vietnam War fought?

Why did many Vietnamese flee their country?

Establish a Purpose for Reading

How do different cultures vary in their feelings of responsibility toward their elderly citizens? Would you welcome an aging parent to live in your home? Analyze your feelings on this issue, and then read the selection to find out what we can learn about filial piety and the Vietnamese parent-child relationship.

Integrate Knowledge While Reading

Questions have been inserted in the margin to stimulate your thinking and help you read between the lines. Remember to

Predict   Picture   Relate   Monitor   Correct

ELDERLY PARENTS: A CULTURAL DUTY

From Ta Thuc Phu, *Orlando Sentinel*, May 2, 1998

A Vietnamese saying goes: "The father's creative work is as great as the Thai Son mountain; the mother's love is as large as the river flowing out to sea. Respect and love your parents from the bottom of your hearts. Achieve your duty of filial piety as a proper standard of well-behaved children."

5   I am pleased to answer the question, "How do you deal with your parents as they get older?" I want to relate some characteristics of the Vietnamese culture.

Living together with elderly parents under the same roof is one of our national traditions. In fact, I am honored to have my 92-year-old mother-in-law living with me and my wife.

10   The family is the basic institution with which to perpetuate society and provide protection to individuals. Generally speaking, the family structure in Southeastern Asia is more complex than the American family structure.

In Vietnamese society, the father is the head of the family. However, the father shares with his wife and children collective responsibilities—legally,

15   morally and spiritually—and these responsibilities continue, even after children

are grown up and married. Always, the mother has the same status as the father. In addition, she is the embodiment of love and the spirit of self-denial and sacrifice.

Vietnamese parents consider the parent-child relationship their most important responsibility, and they train their children for a lifetime. In effect, the family is the small school where children learn to follow rules of behavior and speaking. The cornerstone of the children's behavior in the family is filial piety. Filial piety consists of loving, respecting and obeying one's parents. As a result, the obligation to obey parents does not end with the coming of age or marriage. Filial piety means solicitude and support of one's parents, chiefly in their old age. Vietnamese elders never live by themselves or in nursing homes. Instead, they live with one of their children, usually the eldest son. This is a family custom practiced in all Vietnamese homes.

We do not want to live far apart from our parents, regardless of whether they are young or old, healthy or infirm, because we want to take care of them at any time until their deaths. That is our concept of gratitude to our parents for their hard work and sacrifice throughout the years.

I recall that, when I was growing up, my mother was severely crippled. When we walked together, she held on to my arm for balance. It was difficult to coordinate our steps. My wife and I took turns holding my mother when she cried, and we helped her to walk two hours a day to exercise her body.

By living with our aging parents under the same roof, we also have many occasions to demonstrate our respect for them in the solemn days of the lunar year, such as New Year's Day (Tet), and to celebrate their anniversaries. Our

Marginal notes:

How does the American culture differ?

Why might these beliefs promote longevity?

Vietnamese family honor: Ta Thuc Phu, MD, poses with his 92-year-old mother-in-law, Duong Thi Tri, and his wife, Hoang Thi Hanh.
© *Angela Peterson/The Orlando Sentinel*

40 children would present New Year's wishes and symbols of good luck, such as bright red ribbons, to their grandparents to represent prosperity and longevity.

Most important in the Vietnamese value system is undoubtedly our belief that children ought to be grateful to parents for the debt of birth, rearing and education. Children are taught to think of parents first, even at their own

45 expense, to make sacrifices for their parents' sake, to love and care for them in their old age. Unfortunately, that practice is denied now by the communist regime in Vietnam. Children have been taught to spy on their parents and report to the Communist Party any subversive talk or irregular behavior.

Above all, since April 30, 1975, after the collapse of Saigon with the

50 communist takeover of South Vietnam and the tragic exodus of more than 2 million refugees to all parts of the world in search of freedom and a better future, Vietnamese families still practice the custom of living with the parents under the same roof. Deep feelings for families and ties to elders are still strong. These feelings and ties will endure despite these times of change.

55 Even when our parents have been gone many years, we still think of them as living with us.

> How can American culture benefit from this Vietnamese view?

Recall

Stop to self-test, relate, and react.

Your instructor may choose to give you a true-false comprehension review.

Write About the Selection

Describe your family tradition and your philosophical view on the care of elderly parents. Also, describe your plan for the care of your own parents.

Contemporary Link

What has happened in America that the baby boomers are faced with being elderly orphans while the author of the selection is honored to have his elderly mother-in-law under the same roof? What contributes to the difference in attitude?

Skill Development: Explore Point of View

Form a collaborative group to discuss the following questions:

- What is your view on nursing homes?
- What do you feel is the government's responsibility in the care of the elderly?
- If financial assistance is needed, who should pay for the care of the elderly?
- Is the question of elder care only about money?

Check Your Comprehension

After reading the selection, answer the following with *T* (true) or *F* (false). To help you analyze your strengths and weaknesses, the question types are indicated.

Inference   _____ 1. The author's primary purpose is to argue that Americans should have elderly parents living with them under the same roof.

Inference   _____ 2. The author's tone is objective.

Inference   _____ 3. The author feels both honored and happy to have an elderly parent living in his home.

Inference   _____ 4. The author implies that the Communists in Vietnam are undermining the traditional parent-child relationship.

Detail   _____ 5. According to the author, there are no nursing homes in Vietnam.

Inference   _____ 6. The author's statement that a mother "is the embodiment of love and the spirit of self-denial and sacrifice" is a statement of fact.

Detail   _____ 7. The author suggests that in Vietnamese culture, the mother is the actual head of the family.

Inference   _____ 8. The author suggests that Vietnamese refugees in America have begun to abandon the custom of living with parents under the same roof.

Inference   _____ 9. The author probably supported the Communist takeover of South Vietnam.

Inference   _____ 10. The author implies that family comes before business in the Vietnamese culture.

Use your own words to define the following.

1. *filial* _____

2. *piety* _____

3. *filial piety* _____

Search the Net

Use a search engine such as Google, AltaVista, Excite, Infoseek, Dogpile, Yahoo, or Lycos to compare the prices of several retirement and assisted-living facilities in your area. For suggested Web sites and other research activities, go to http://www.ablongman.com/smith/.

CONTEMPORARY FOCUS

Islam is one of the fastest growing religions in the United States and Europe. How much do you know about Islam? Has Islam expanded past religion and become a political institution in some Middle Eastern countries? Do all Muslims share the same beliefs, or are there vast differences between conservative Muslims and fundamentalists?

BRIDGING THE GAP BETWEEN MUSLIMS AND THE WEST

By Amanda Quraishi

Austin American Statesman, May 1, 2004

As an American-born convert to Islam, I find myself in an increasingly frustrating position. I spend a lot of time trying to explain—to diverse parties—both my religion and my country.

Islam is the second-largest religion in the world. It is therefore shocking how very little is known about our religion here in the West. Muslims can share the blame for this lack of understanding, because we tend to keep to ourselves. The majority of Muslims in the United States are first-generation immigrants. America is a new world to them, and they have come here to make a life for themselves and their families. With the concerns of earning a living, family life, religion and orienting themselves to the language and culture, not much time is left for public relations.

The time has come, however, for Muslims to break out of our shells. We need to open ourselves up to our communities and take part in local charities, voting and social events. Muslims need to be a part of the American system, be proud of our culture and heritage and share it with fellow Americans rather than hide away in our suburban homes and let the corrupt leaders of Muslim countries, or the terrorism of the extreme fringe, speak for us.

Not all blame rests with the Muslim population, though. Most non-Muslim Americans would be hard-pressed if you asked them to name one positive aspect of Islam. The media rarely portrays the beautiful, extensive celebrations, the rich heritage of art and science, or the scenic beauty of these varied and distant lands.

Non-Muslims often lump Muslims into one category. Very few realize that the differences between Muslims from different parts of the world and in different sects are vast. The country with the largest Muslim population is Indonesia. The sixth-largest population of Muslims in the world resides in China—twice as many as those in Saudi Arabia. The great irony is that the word "Islam" means "peaceful submission" in Arabic. The great majority of Muslims are moderates working for peaceful and happy lives. Nevertheless, in the West, Muslims are often depicted as violent, misogynistic, and terroristic. The peaceful lives of the moderates are ignored.

Collaborate

Collaborate on responses to the following questions:

- How have Muslims become stereotyped in the United States?
- What are fundamentalists, and do they exist in other religions?
- What are the difficulties of being a Muslim in America today?

Preview

Preview the next selection to predict its purpose and organization and to formulate your learning plan.

Activate Schema

What countries are predominantly Muslim?

Who was the Shah of Iran, and what happened to him?

Establish a Purpose for Reading

The recent history of Iran has been turbulent and controversial. Recall what
you know about Iran, Islam, and Muslims. Read the selection to find out why
the author is discontent with the present Iranian government.

Skill Development: Integrate Knowledge While Reading

Questions have been inserted in the margin to stimulate your thinking and
help you read between the lines. Remember to

Predict   Picture   Relate   Monitor   Correct

LEAVING ISLAM AND LIVING ISLAM

By Azam Kamguian, in *Leaving Islam*, ed. Ibn Warraq

I left Islam long before I lived Islam. My being a Muslim, as with all other children who are accidentally born into Muslim families, was hereditary. My parents
were ordinary Muslims.

In my late teens, Iran was pregnant with revolution. The atmosphere was
5   for change, a profound demand for fundamental change in society. People
were marching and fighting for freedom and justice. Unfortunately, the
revolution was defeated by the Islamic tradition. The final decades of the
twentieth century witnessed another Holocaust, an Islamic one, because of
which thousands have been executed, decapitated, stoned to death, and tor-
10   tured by Islamic governments and Islamic movements. That was the beginning
of a dark era that has not ended. That was the beginning of the rise of political
Islam in the world, a period in history that most probably could be compared

> What happened in
> the 1930s?

to the 1930s. There have not been and there are no limits to murder and
repression: Young and old, women and men are all legitimate targets of Islam's
15   blind and bloody terror.

I have lived thousands of days in Iran when Islam has shed blood. A hundred
thousand have been executed in Iran since 1979. I have lived days when I,

along with thousands of men and women throughout the country, looked for the names of our lovers, husbands, wives, friends, daughters, sons, colleagues, and students in the papers that announced the names of executed on a daily basis. Days when the soldiers of Allah attacked bookstores and publishing houses and burned books. Days of armed attacks on universities and the killing of innocent students all over the country. Weeks and months of bloody attacks on workers' strikes and demonstrations.

Why do repressive regimes burn books?

I, along with thousands of political prisoners, was tortured. Thousands were shot by execution squads who recited Koranic verses while conducting the killings. Those who were in prisons and not yet executed were awakened every day at dawn only to hear more gunshots aimed at their friends and cell-mates. From the numbers of shotguns you could find out how many were murdered on that day. Fathers and mothers and husbands and wives who received the bloody clothes of their loved ones had to pay for the bullets. Islamic Auschwitz was created.

What was Auschwitz?

What is apartheid?

Why are beatings legal?

Women were and still are firsthand victims of Islamic regimes and Islamic forces. In Iran reigns a regime of enslavement of women and of the rule of sexual apartheid, where being a woman is itself a crime. In Iran women are legally the inferior sex and, according to Islamic doctrine, this inferiority is rooted in the nature of women. That is why wife beating is so prevalent in Muslim-inhabited countries. Life under Islamic law leaves women with battered bodies and shattered minds and souls.

20

25

30

35

An Iranian student holds gladioluses in Tehran to commemorate the first anniversary of a violent police assault on a university dormitory.
Scott Peterson/Liaison/Getty Images

40   Still, beatings are not the worst of female suffering. Each year hundreds of women die in "honor killings": murders by husbands or male relatives of women suspected of disobedience. Sexual anxiety lies at the heart of most Islamic strictures on women. In Iran:

- The legal age of marriage for girls is nine years.
45
- Women are stoned to death for engaging in voluntary sexual relations.
- Women do not have the right to choose their clothing.
- Women are barred from taking employment in a large number of occupations.
- Women are not free to choose their own academic or vocational field of
50   study.
- Women do not have equal rights to divorce.
- Women do not have the right to acquire passports and travel without the permission of their husbands/fathers.

During the years the Islamic government has been in power, thousands of
55   women have spent time in prison and been tortured for having ignored Islamic regulations. Disgust for the backward ruling culture is immense. Women and the youth are the champions of this battle. Any change in Iran will not only affect the lives of people living in Iran, but will have a significant impact on the region and worldwide.

Recall

Stop to self-test, relate, and react.

Your instructor may choose to give you a true-false comprehension review.

Write About the Selection

The author is adamant in her point of view and her criticism. What changes do you think the author would like to see in the Iranian government? How do you think those changes could be accomplished?

Contemporary Link

How are Muslims stereotyped in America? Is the violence and inequality described in Iran a true picture of most Muslims? What do you think Muslims can do to communicate a positive media image?

Skill Development: Explore Point of View

Form a collaborative group to discuss the following questions:

- What is your point of view, opinion, or bias on the government in Iran?
- What is the author's point of view on the government in Iran?
- What is the author's point of view of traditional Muslim men?
- What does the author mean by saying, "I left Islam long before I lived Islam"? What does the author mean by saying, "being a woman is itself a crime"?

Check Your Comprehension

After reading the selection, answer the following with *T* (true) or *F* (false). To help you analyze your strengths and weaknesses, the question types are indicated.

Inference   _____ 1. The author's primary purpose is to explain the violence and inhumanity of the present Iranian Islamic government.

Inference   _____ 2. The tone of the passage is one of anger and disgust.

Inference   _____ 3. The reader can conclude that the author is optimistic that the women of Iran will be liberated and laws with be changed to reflect equal rights.

Inference   _____ 4. The phrase "Iran was pregnant" is a simile.

Inference   _____ 5. The reader can conclude that the author is comparing the killings in the 1930s in Iran to the Jewish Holocaust.

Inference   _____ 6. The author implies that the initial revolution in Iran may have been positive except that it was taken over by the Muslim fundamentalists.

Inference   _____ 7. "The legal age of marriage for girls is nine years old" is a statement of opinion.

Inference   _____ 8. The reader can conclude that the families who received the clothing of executed relatives were also put in jail.

Inference   _____ 9. The author implies that Muslim men are actively involved in the battle against Islamic rule in Iran.

Inference   _____ 10. The term *sexual apartheid* suggests that the women are subject to a formal policy of segregation and discrimination.

Search the Net

Use a search engine such as Google, AltaVista, Excite, Infoseek, Dogpile, Yahoo, or Lycos to find information on the present government in Iran. Describe the leadership and the state of unrest that currently exists in Iran. For suggested Web sites and other research activities, go to http://www.ablongman.com/smith/.

Vocabulary Booster

Say, What?

Roots
dic-, dict-: say
lingu-: tongue

locu-, loqui-: speak

Words with *dic-, dict-:* say

Each morning Rose used a word processor to transcribe *dictation* from a recording machine on which her boss had recorded letters and memos the previous day.

- *dictate:* to say or read aloud for transcription; to command with authority

Sarena's parents *dictated* the nonnegotiable conditions of her upcoming slumber party: no boys, no alcohol.

- *dictator:* a ruler using absolute power without hereditary right or consent of the people

Fidel Castro, who staged a coup to oust former President Batista of Cuba, is a *dictator* who has remained in power for many years.

- *diction:* that aspect of speaking or writing dependent on the correct choice of words; the voice quality of a speaker or singer

Listening to public speakers with fine *diction* is much easier than trying to decipher the words of those whose speech is not clear and distinct.

- *contradict:* to state the opposite of or deny; to imply denial with actions

Mark's wild lifestyle seems to *contradict* his claim of being the quiet, studious type.

- *indict:* to charge with a crime; to seriously criticize or blame

The grand jury *indicted* the alleged computer hacker for breaking into banking system computers to illegally move funds electronically.

- *predict:* to declare in advance or foretell the future

Meteorologists *predict* the weather based on facts, experience, and complex meteorological instruments.

- *dictionary:* a reference book of alphabetically arranged words and their meanings

Word-processing computer programs usually contain a *dictionary* to run a spelling check on typed documents.

Words with *locu-, loqui-:* speak

The defendant's attorney was skilled in fluent, forceful, and persuasive speech, so it came as no surprise that his closing statement was *eloquent* enough to convince the jury of his client's innocence.

- *elocution:* the study and practice of public speaking; a style of speaking or reading aloud

Julianne was taking speech classes for all her electives, hoping that the *elocution* practice would help in the frequent presentations required in her chosen career of public relations.

- *locution:* a word or phrase as used by a particular person or group

In the late 1960s and early 1970s, the *locution* of hippies included words like "groovy" or "way out, man."

- *colloquial:* characteristic of informal speech or writing; conversational

Choosing the word "nope" instead of "no" is an example of using a *colloquial* expression.

- *soliloquy:* the act of speaking to oneself; a speech in a drama in which a character reveals innermost thoughts

Aspiring actors often use *soliloquies* from Shakespeare's plays as audition monologues.

- *loquacious:* tending to talk too much or too freely; garrulous

When meeting new people, Nadia often becomes nervous and *loquacious,* and tends to chatter on and on about unimportant things.

- *circumlocution:* a roundabout or indirect way of speaking; using more words than necessary

After all the *circumlocution* in Sydney's story, such as what she was wearing, what she had to eat, and what time they left, we finally got to hear whether or not she liked her blind date.

Words with *lingu-:* tongue

When you visit the doctor it is customary for the nurse to take your *sublingual* temperature and your blood pressure.

- *linguistics:* the study of language

Phonetics is a branch of *linguistics* involving the study of the production of and written symbols representing speech sounds.

- *multilingual:* able to speak several languages with some ease

Some public schools in the United States are experiencing a need for *multilingual* teachers due to the influx of immigrants who do not yet speak English.

Review

Part I

Choose the best antonym from the boxed list for each of the words below.

acquit or discharge	confirm	dialogue	directness	elected ruler
formal speech	obey	recall	silent	unconvincing

1. contradict _____

2. circumlocution _____

3. dictate _____

4. predict _____

5. loquacious _____

6. dictator _____

7. indict _____

8. eloquent _____

9. soliloquy _____

10. colloquial _____

Part II

From the boxed list, choose the word that best completes each of the sentences below.

contradiction	Dictaphone	dictatorship	diction	elocution
linguistics	multilingual	predict	soliloquy	sublingual

11. The _____ of Joseph Stalin in the Soviet Union was a government of harsh and oppressive tyranny.

12. The heavily accented sounds of Charo's Spanish singing voice and her comical destruction of the English language make it impossible to mistake her _____ for anyone else's.

13. Jose's continual _____ or denial of everything Juan said was getting on Juan's nerves.

14. _____ is a brand name for a type of dictating machine.

15. If you are taking a European tour of several countries, it might be helpful to take along a _____ pocket dictionary.

16. Political candidates need to have finely sharpened _____ skills to be able to make all the speeches required of anyone seeking public office.

17. Sean studied three languages and majored in _____.

18. Hamlet's famous _____ starting with the words "To be, or not to be" is one of the most well-known speeches from Shakespeare.

19. Digital thermometers read _____ temperatures in seconds.

20. It is difficult to _____ how someone will react when criticized.

Critical Thinking

- What is thinking?
- What is critical thinking?
- What are the characteristics of critical thinkers?
- What are the barriers to critical thinking?
- How do critical thinkers analyze an argument?
- What is the difference between inductive and deductive reasoning?
- What does creative thinking add to critical thinking?

Elusive Specificity of Random Compliments *by Rafal Olbinski, 2004. Lithograph, 24 x 24".* © *Rafal Olbinski. Image courtesy of S2Art Group.*

What Is Thinking?

Thinking is an organized and controlled mental activity that helps you solve problems, make decisions, and understand ideas. To think is not simply to ponder; it is demanding, challenging, and rewarding work requiring skill and confidence. All thinkers experience confusion, mental blocks, and failure at times. When faced with such adversity, poor thinkers get frustrated. They initially have trouble knowing where to begin and tend to jump haphazardly from one part of the problem to another. Lacking confidence, they eventually give up. Good thinkers, on the other hand, are strategic. They form a plan and systematically try different solutions. They work with confidence, persistently stick with the task, and find solutions.

**Exercise
9.1**

Problem Solving

Experience the thinking processes of good thinkers by solving the following problem. Warm up your thinking skills, formulate a plan, believe that you can do it (I did it, so can you!), be persistent, and solve this problem. Have fun with it!

Record your solution patterns as you "pour water" into empty glasses. If one approach fails, try another. This is not a trick but a problem that can be systematically solved—without throwing water away or estimating amounts. Use the illustration shown below to stimulate your thinking.

Rowena has three unmarked glasses of different sizes: 3 ounces, 5 ounces, and 8 ounces. The largest glass is full, and the other two glasses are empty. What can Rowena do to get 4 ounces of liquid into each of the two largest glasses?

Adapted from Vincent Ryan Ruggiero, *The Art of Thinking*

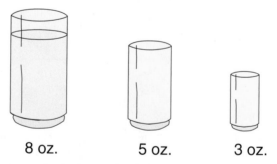

8 OZ.   5 OZ.   3 OZ.

There are several ways to solve this problem.

1. _____

   _____

   _____

2. _____

_____

3. _____

_____

If you worked on the exercise at length, you have now experienced the rigors of earnest thinking. Did you work strategically? What was your plan? What were the frustrations? Were you persistent? Did you believe in your ability to find a solution? Did you enjoy using thinking for problem solving?

Problems in real life are usually expressed as questions that need an action plan. For example, how would you respond if company executives decided that your job required you to solve the following problems?

■ How can workers be enticed to car pool?

■ How can awards be distributed to employees to mark each five years of service?

■ How can a dead elephant be removed from the parking lot after an unfortunate media event?

You would, of course, work systematically to find solutions to the stated problems.

What does all of this have to do with critical thinking? Assuming it was your managers who identified the bigger issues regarding the need for car pooling, five-year awards, and elephant removal, they were the ones who did the critical thinking, and you were the one who got to do the problem solving.

What Is Critical Thinking?

While problem solving is important in any job, **critical thinking**—deliberating in a purposeful, organized manner to assess the value of old and new information—precedes it and defines the problems to be solved. Critical thinkers search, compare, analyze, clarify, evaluate, and conclude. They build on previous knowledge, recognize both sides of an issue, and evaluate the reasons and evidence in support of each. And they often deal with issues that can be controversial and can be seen from several different viewpoints. "How can" usually begins a problem-solving question, whereas "Should" begins a critical thinking question.

For example, imagine the critical thinking needed to answer the controversial question "Should state legislators vote to take away the driver's licenses of students aged 16 to 18 who drop out of school?" Supporters would say that such a law would improve the educational system by reducing the number of high school dropouts; detractors would contend it would violate the rights of students; and others would dismiss the idea on the basis that government should not be in the parenting business. After forming a position, each side would line up evidence to build a persuasive argument for lobbying legislators. Both the

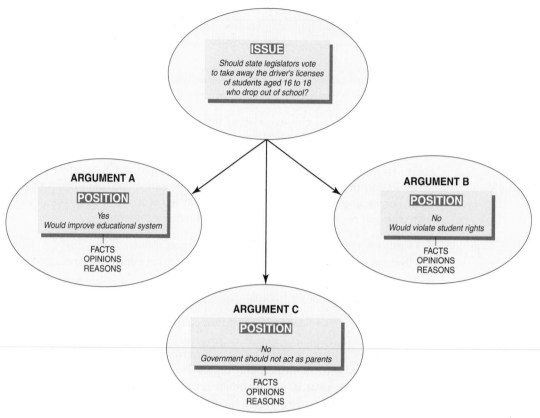

Depending on your position, many different arguments can be constructed for a single issue.

developers of the arguments and the legislators would be critical thinkers. For the 16- to 18-year-old dropouts, the stakes would be high for the winning argument. The diagram illustrates the parts and possibilities.

Some professors speak of critical thinking as if it were a special discipline rather than an application of many known skills. However, critical thinking actually uses the many skills covered in the preceding chapters of this textbook. Keep reading to discover how "old friends" like *topic, main idea, details*, and *point of view* can connect with new terminology to become powerful vehicles of persuasion. In this chapter, we discuss a few new techniques for identifying and evaluating the support in an argument.

Applying Critical Thinking Skills to Meet College Goals

Many colleges cite the ability to think critically as one of the essential academic outcomes of a college education. An educated person is expected to think systematically, to evaluate, and to draw conclusions based on logic. At your college, an emphasis on critical thinking probably crosses the curriculum and thus becomes a part of every college course. When an instructor returns a paper to you with notes like "Good logic" or "Not enough support" written on it, the comments are referring to critical thinking. The same is true if you make a class presentation and are told either that your thesis is very convincing or that you are missing vital support. See the Reader's Tip for four habits of effective critical thinkers.

READER'S TIP

Four Habits of Effective Critical Thinkers

◆ **Be willing to plan.** Think first and write later. Don't be impulsive. Develop a habit of planning.

◆ **Be flexible.** Be open to new ideas. Consider new solutions for old problems.

◆ **Be persistent.** Continue to work even when you are tired and discouraged. Good thinking is hard work.

◆ **Be willing to self-correct.** Don't be defensive about errors. Figure out what went wrong and learn from your mistakes.

Critical thinking instruction has its own specialized vocabulary, often using seemingly complex terms for simple ideas. As you work through this chapter, you will become familiar with the critical-thinking application of the following terminology:

analogy   argument   assertion   believability   conclusion   consistency

deduction   fallacy   induction   premise   relevance   reliability

Barriers to Critical Thinking

Some people are mired in their own belief systems and do not want to rethink, change, or be challenged. They may be gullible and thus easily persuaded by a slick presentation or an illogical argument. For many people, the following barriers interfere with critical thinking:[1]

1. *Frame of reference:* Each of us has an existing belief system that influences the way we deal with incoming information. We interpret new experiences according to what we already believe. We are culturally conditioned to resist change and feel that our own way is best. We refuse to look at the

---

[1]J. Rudinow and V. E. Barry, *Invitation to Critical Thinking* (New York: Harcourt Brace, 1994), pp. 11–19.

merits of something our belief system rejects, such as the advantages of legalizing drugs, for example.

2. *Wishful thinking:* We talk ourselves into believing things that we know are not true because we want them to be true. We irrationally deceive ourselves and engage in self-denial. For example, we might refuse to believe well-founded claims of moral corruption leveled at our favorite relative or a politician voted for.

3. *Hasty moral judgments:* We tend to evaluate someone or something as good or bad, right or wrong, and remain fixed in this thinking. Such judgments are often prejudiced, intolerant, emotional, and self-righteous. An example of this type of barrier to thinking critically would be the statement, "Abortion should never be legal."

4. *Reliance on authority:* An authority such as a clergy member, a doctor, or a teacher is an expert source of information. We give authorities and institutions such as churches or governments the power to think for us and thus block our own abilities to question and reason.

5. *Labels:* Labels ignore individual differences and lump people and things into categories. Labels oversimplify, distort the truth, and usually incite anger and rejection. To say, "People who love America and people who do not," forces others to take sides as a knee-jerk reaction.

Exercise 9.2	**Identifying Types of Barriers**

Read the numbered statements below and identify with *a, b, c,* or *d* the type of barrier the statement best represents:

a. Wishful thinking
b. Frame of reference or hasty moral judgment
c. Reliance on authority
d. Labels

EXAMPLE The new drug will not be helpful because the FDA has not yet approved it.

EXPLANATION The answer is c, reliance on authority, which in this case is a government agency. A critical thinker might argue that the FDA is slow to test and respond to new drugs, and that many drugs are used safely and successfully in other countries before the FDA grants approval for Americans.

1. Our country is divided into two groups of people: those who work and those who don't work.
2. In some countries, marriage of the children is arranged by the family, but this is wrong because a bride and groom should marry for love.

3. My son does not drive over the speed limit because he is a very careful driver and always mindful of the law.
4. To reduce the signs of aging, I am using a new vitamin cream on my skin that Dr. Juan Castillo of the New Life Clinic in Miami recommended as very effective.

Recognizing an Argument

Just as we may have barriers to critical thinking, we also need to recognize that not every statement is an argument. Assertions such as "I like soy milk" or "We had a huge overnight snowfall, and my car is covered" are nonargumentative statements that are intended to inform or explain. An argument, on the other hand, is an assertion that supports a conclusion and is intended to persuade. The difference is intent and purpose. For example, the statement "The grass is wet because it rained last night" is an explanation, not an argument. To say, however, "You should water the grass tonight because rain is not predicted for several days" constitutes an argument. In the latter case, the conclusion of watering the grass is based on a "fact," the forecast, and the intent is to persuade by appealing to reason. To identify arguments, use inferential skills and recognize the underlying purpose or intent of the author.

Exercise 9.3

Identifying Arguments

Practice recognizing arguments by identifying each of the following statements with *A* (argument) or *N* (nonargumentative statement of information).

EXAMPLE   The foods in salad bars sometimes contain preservatives to keep them looking fresh and appealing.

EXPLANATION   This is not an argument. It is not intended to move you to action. It is a statement of fact similar to "It sometimes snows at night."

1. Food preservatives can cause cancer, so you should avoid eating foods that contains them.
2. Because credit cards promote careless spending, anyone under 21 years of age should not be permitted to have one.
3. *The Lord of the Rings* was filmed in New Zealand.
4. The Internet should be censored because it is too easy for children to visit pornographic Web sites.
5. In the 1950s, students began the school day by pledging allegiance to the American flag.

© 2005 by Pearson Education, Inc.

Steps in Analyzing an Argument

Analyzing an argument through critical thinking and evaluation combines the use of most of the skills that have been taught in this text. The amount of analysis depends on the complexity of the argument. Some arguments are simple; others are lengthy and complicated. The following is a four-step procedure that you can use as a format to guide your critical thinking:

1. Identify the position on the issue.
2. Identify the support in the argument.
3. Evaluate the support.
4. Evaluate the argument.

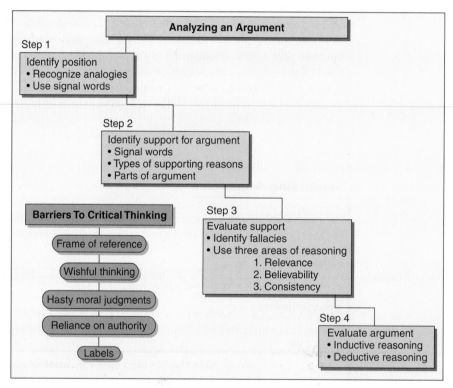

Use four sequential steps to analyze an argument. Be cautious of barriers that inhibit critical thinking.

Step 1: Identify the Position on the Issue

To identify the position on an issue or the conclusion in persuasive writing, use your main-idea reading skills. First, determine the topic that is the issue by asking yourself, "What is the passage primarily about?" Then ask, "What is the author trying to convey about the issue?" Your answer will be a statement of the position that is being argued—in other words, the main point, thesis, or conclusion. For example, on the topic or issue of searching school lockers for weapons, one position or main point might be that it can prevent violence and a contrasting position or main point might be that it is an invasion of privacy.

In a college course on critical thinking or logic, the parts of an argument that you would be asked to identify would probably be called the *conclusion* and the *premises*. The conclusion is the position on the issue or the main point, and the premises are the supporting points. For example, an argument now exists on the death of Alexander the Great more than 2,300 years ago. The conclusion that some epidemiologists have reached is that he died of West Nile virus rather than typhoid or malaria. One premise is that he became paralyzed before he died, and paralysis is a symptom of the brain infection that marks West Nile virus. Another premise is that Alexander saw ravens pecking each other, and some fell dead in front of him, and ravens are among the types of birds that are particularly susceptible to West Nile virus.

When reading an argument, be aware of the author's bias and your own biases. Do not allow your own beliefs to cloud your thinking. Guard against falling for the barriers to critical thinking that include limited frame of reference, wishful thinking, hasty moral judgments, reliance on authority, and labeling. Be sensitive to emotional language and the connotation of words. Cut through the rhetoric, and get to the heart of the matter.

EXAMPLE Read the following passage and identify the position on the issue that is being argued.

> The technology for television has far exceeded the programming. Viewers are recipients of crystal clear junk. Network programming appeals to the masses for ratings and advertising money and thus offers little creative or stimulating entertainment.

EXPLANATION Several debatable issues about television are suggested by this passage. They include the abundance of technological advancement, the power of ratings, and the importance of advertising money. The topic or issue, however, concerns the quality of network programming. Although it is not directly stated, the argument or central issue is "Network television programming offers little creative or stimulating entertainment."

Signal Words. We have said that the position on the issue may be stated as the thesis or main point. However, it does not necessarily appear at the beginning of an argument. Instead, it might be embedded within the passage or stated at the end as a conclusion. Look for the following key words that may be used to signal the central issue being argued:

as a result	finally	in summary	therefore
consequently	for these reasons	it follows that	thus, should

EXAMPLE   What is the position on the issue that is being argued in the following passage?

> Although a year in a U.S. prison costs more than a year at Harvard, almost no one leaves prison rehabilitated. Prisoners meet and share information with other hardened criminals to refine their "skills." It seems reasonable, therefore, to conclude that prisons in the United States are societal failures.

EXPLANATION The position on the issue of prison rehabilitation in this argument is directly stated in the last sentence. Note the inclusion of the signal word *therefore*.

Exercise 9.4

Identifying the Position on the Issue

Read the following sentence groups, and indicate the number of the sentence that states the position on the issue.

1. ¹ Soon baby boomers will be drawing Social Security checks. ² It is possible that more people will be receiving payments than will be paying into the system. ³ Thus, the Social Security system will be weakened and perhaps even threatened with bankruptcy.

   Position on issue: ___3___

2. ¹ The price of oil, gas, and electricity continues to rise for heating and cooling homes. ² Although still not perfected, solar heating could be a viable option. ³ If the price of installing solar heating panels declines, the result could be that more people would use solar energy as a source for home heating and cooling.

   Position on issue: ___3___

3. ¹ Shoplifting raises the price of what we purchase by more than 2 percent. ² Medicare fraud costs the average taxpayer several hundred dollars each year. ³ The cost of exaggerated insurance claims is passed along to all

policyholders in increased premiums.[4] For these reasons, no one should cheat corporations, because we are just cheating ourselves and our friends.

Position on issue: ____4____

4. The director chooses whether the film will be done in color or in black and white.[2] Colorizers should not be allowed to add color to an original black-and-white movie.[3] Perhaps the director doesn't want anyone to view the work in color.

Position on issue: ____2____

5. Reporting polling results before all national votes are cast allows the media too much influence on election results and should be stopped.[2] As soon as East Coast voting booths are closed, network reporters begin reporting private polling results and predicting a presidential front-runner.[3] Yet many West Coast voters have not cast their ballots.

Position on issue: ____1____

6. Gambling is legal in Nevada and a few other places, but it remains illegal in most states.[2] Perhaps this legal restriction on gambling is unfair and should be lifted.[3] After all, many state governments make millions on lotteries, which are a form of gambling.

Position on issue: ____2____

7. Fireworks can easily fly out of control, causing serious burns and blindness.[2] Thus, the law should prohibit the public from purchasing fireworks.[3] On the Fourth of July, people can enjoy municipal fireworks in a safe setting.

Position on issue: ____2____

8. The United States government should approve a new pipeline to drill for oil in Alaska.[2] The present pipeline has not harmed the wildlife.[3] New oil resources in Alaska could make our country less dependent on the Middle East.

Position on issue: ____1____

Step 2: Identify the Support in the Argument

In a college logic course, after identifying the position on the issue of an argument, you would be asked to identify and number the premises, or support statements. For example, in an argument about searching school lockers a proponent's first premise or support statement might be that *guns and knives are always found in searches*. Other premises, such as *the school owns the lockers* and *metal detectors at the school's entrance miss harmful, illegal drugs*, would have added further supporting evidence. In short, to identify the premises, simply identify significant supporting details for the main point.

Signal Words. Supporting reasons may be directly stated or may be signaled. The key words that signal support for an argument are in some cases the same as those that signal significant supporting details. They include the following:

because	if	assuming that
since	first, second, finally	given that

EXAMPLE What happens when the previous passage about U.S. prisons (see page 450) is rewritten so that signal words introduce supporting details? Read the following:

> One can conclude that prisons in the United States are societal failures. First, almost no one leaves prison rehabilitated. Second, prisoners meet and share information with other hardened criminals to refine their "skills." Taxpayers should also consider that a year in prison costs more than a year at Harvard.

EXPLANATION The argument is the same with or without the signal words. In a longer passage, the signal words usually make it easier to identify the significant supporting details or reasons.

Exercise 9.5

Identifying Support for the Argument

Read the following sentence groups, recording the number of the sentence that states the position on the issue that is being argued and the numbers of the support statements.

1. Some college sports involve more bodily contact than others.¹ With a surface injury, the chance of bleeding could be high.² Thus, college athletes on teams with high levels of bodily contact, such as wrestlers, should have mandatory testing for AIDS.³

   Position on issue: ___3___ Support: ___2___

2. Radar detectors on cars warn drivers of police surveillance.¹ With the beep,² drivers slow down to avoid tickets.³ Such devices should be banned because they promote driving beyond the legal limit.

   Position on issue: _____3_____ Support: _____1_____

3. Because of certain characteristics, shad and salmon are the best choices for sea ranching.¹ These fish use their own energies to swim upstream.² They grow in open waters and then swim back to be harvested.³

   Position on issue: _____1_____ Support _____3_____

4. Major game reserves in Africa such as the Ngorongoro Crater are in protected areas, but many lie adjacent to large tracts of land with no conservation status.¹ Animals that migrate off the reserves compete with humans for food and are endangered.² Thus, clear boundaries between areas for animals and people would minimize friction.³

   Position on issue: _____2_____ Support _____3_____

5. Some state laws prohibit the sale of obscene material to minors.¹ Consequently, in these states musicians who sell CDs with obscene lyrics should be prosecuted.² Such lyrics brutalize women and are audio pornographic.³

   Position on issue: _____2_____ Support _____3_____

6. Doctors should try to make a patient's visit to the office less humiliating.¹ First, you see a receptionist who tells you to fill out forms and wait your turn.² Next, the nurse takes your blood pressure and extracts blood while you look at the diplomas on the wall.³ Finally, you are led into a cold room to strip down and wait still longer for the doctor to appear for a few expensive minutes of consultation.⁴

   Position on issue: _____1_____ Support _____4_____

7. In most companies, college graduates get higher-paying jobs than those who do not attend college.¹ As the years go by in a company, promotions

and their accompanying raises tend to go primarily to the college graduates. [3]Thus, it can be concluded that a college degree is worth money.

Position on issue: ___1___ Support ___2___

8. [1]Some parents overreact at Little League games. [2]They scream for home runs. [3]Defeat is upsetting. [4]As a result, parents put intense pressure on their children to compete and win, which can be harmful.

Position on issue: ___2___ Support ___4___

Types of Supporting Reasons. Readers would probably prefer support for an argument to be in the simple form of a smoking gun with fingerprints on it, but such conclusive evidence is usually hard to find. Evidence comes in many different forms and may be tainted with opinion. The Reader's Tip contains some categories of "evidence" typically used as supporting reasons in an argument. Each type, however, has its pitfalls and should be immediately tested with an evaluative question.

READER'S TIP

Categories of Support for Arguments

◆ **Facts:** objective truths
Ask: How were the facts gathered? Are they true?

◆ **Examples:** anecdotes to demonstrate the truth
Ask: Are the examples true and relevant?

◆ **Analogies:** comparisons to similar cases
Ask: Are the analogies accurate and relevant?

◆ **Authority:** words from a recognized expert
Ask: What are the credentials and biases of the expert?

◆ **Causal relationship:** saying one thing caused another
Ask: Is it an actual cause or merely an association?

◆ **Common knowledge claim:** assertion of wide acceptance
Ask: Is it relevant? Does everyone really believe it?

◆ **Statistics:** numerical data
Ask: Do the numbers accurately describe the population?

◆ **Personal experiences:** personal anecdotes
Ask: Is the experience applicable to other situations?

Step 3: Evaluate the Support

As a reader, you will decide to accept or reject the author's conclusion based on the strength and acceptability of the reasons and evidence. Keep in mind that although strong arguments are logically supported by valid reasons and evidence, weak, invalid arguments also may be supported by the crafty use of reason and evidence. Your job is to assess the validity of the support.

In evaluating the support for an argument, teachers of logic warn students to beware of fallacies. A **fallacy** is an inference that appears to be reasonable at first glance, but closer inspection proves it to be unrelated, unreliable, or illogical. For example, to say that something is right because everybody is doing it is not a convincing reason for accepting an idea. Such "reasoning," however, can be compelling and is used so frequently that it is labeled a *bandwagon fallacy.*

Logicians have categorized, labeled, and defined more than 200 types of fallacies or tricks of persuasion. For critical thinkers, however, the emphasis should be less on memorizing a long list of fallacy types and more on understanding how such irrelevant reasoning techniques can manipulate logical thinking. Fallacies are tools employed in constructing a weak argument that critical thinkers should spot. In a court of law, the opposing attorney would shout "Irrelevant, Your Honor!" to alert the jury to the introduction of fallacious evidence.

Evaluate the support for an argument according to three areas of reasoning: (1) relevance, (2) believability, and (3) consistency. The following list of fallacies common to each area can sensitize you to the "tools" of constructing a weak argument.

1. Relevance fallacies: Is the support related to the conclusion?
- *Ad hominem:* an attack on the person rather than the issue, the hope being that the idea will be opposed if the person is opposed.
  Example: Do not listen to Mr. Hite's views on education because he is a banker.

- **Bandwagon:** the idea that everybody is doing it and you will be left out if you do not quickly join the crowd.
  Example: Everybody around the world is drinking Coke, so you should too.

- **Misleading analogy:** a comparison of two things suggesting that they are similar when they are in fact distinctly different.
  Example: College students are just like elementary school students; they need to be taught self-discipline.

- **Straw person:** a setup in which a distorted or exaggerated form of the opponent's argument is introduced and knocked down as if to represent a totally weak opposition.
  Example: When a teenaged daughter is told she cannot go out on the weeknight before a test, she replies, "It's unreasonable to say that I can never go out on a weeknight."

- **Testimonials:** opinions of agreement from respected celebrities who are not actually experts.
  Example: A famous actor endorses a headache pill.

■ **Transfer:** an association with a positively or negatively regarded person or thing to lend the same association to the argument (also guilt or virtue by association).
Example: A local politician quotes President Lincoln in a speech as if Lincoln would have agreed with and voted for the candidate.

2. Believability fallacies: Is the support believable or highly suspicious?

■ **Incomplete facts** or **card stacking:** omitting factual details to misrepresent reality.
Example: Buy stock in this particular restaurant chain because it is under new management and people eat out a lot.

■ **Misinterpreted statistics:** numerical data misapplied to unrelated populations that they were never intended to represent.
Example: More than 20 percent of people exercise daily and thus do not need fitness training.

■ **Overgeneralizations:** examples and anecdotes asserted to apply to all cases rather than a select few.
Example: High school students do little work during their senior year and thus are overwhelmed at college.

■ **Questionable authority:** testimonial suggesting authority from people who are not experts.
Example: Dr. Lee, a university sociology professor, testified that the DNA reports were 100 percent accurate.

3. Consistency fallacies: Does the support hold together or does it fall apart and contradict itself?

■ **Appeals to emotions:** highly charged language used for emotional manipulation.
Example: Give money to our organization to help the children who are starving orphans in desperate need of medical attention.

■ **Appeals to pity:** pleas to support the underdog, the person or issue that needs your help.
Example: Please give me an A for the course because I need it to get into law school.

■ **Begging the question** or **circular reasoning:** support for the conclusion that is merely a restatement of it.
Example: Drugs should not be legalized because it should be against the law to take illegal drugs.

■ **Oversimplification:** reduction of an issue to two simple choices, without consideration of other alternatives or "gray areas" in between.
Example: The choices are very simple in supporting our foreign-policy decision to send troops. You are either for America or against it.

■ **Slippery slope:** objecting to something because it will lead to greater evil and disastrous consequences.
Example: Support for assisting the suicide of a terminally ill patient will lead to the ultimate disposal of the marginally sick and elderly.

Signe Wilkerson/Cartoonists & Writers Syndicate/cartoonweb.com

**Exercise
9.6**

Identifying Fallacies

Identify the type of fallacy in each of the following statements by indicating *a*, *b*, or *c*.

_____ B _____ 1. Hollywood movie stars and rock musicians are not experts on the environment and should not be dictating our environmental policy.
   a. testimonial
   b. *ad hominem*
   c. bandwagon

_____ C _____ 2. Jennifer Lopez says, "I always wear evening gowns by this designer because the designer is the best."
   a. *ad hominem*
   b. misleading analogy
   c. testimonial

_____ C _____ 3. The fight for equal rights is designed to force men out of jobs and encourage women to leave their young children alone at home.
   a. bandwagon
   b. questionable authority
   c. straw person

JJ

_A_

_C_

_A_

_B_

_B_

_A_

_C_

_A_

_B_

4. People should give blood because it is important to give blood.
   a. begging the question
   b. appeal to pity
   c. appeal to emotions

5. Prayer in the schools is like cereal for breakfast. They both get the morning off to a good start.
   a. circular reasoning
   b. appeal to emotions
   c. misleading analogy

6. The advocate for rezoning of the property concluded by saying, "George Washington was also concerned about land and freedom."
   a. transfer
   b. *ad hominem*
   c. straw person

7. The explanation for the distribution of grades is simple. College students either study or they do not study.
   a. misinterpreted statistics
   b. oversimplification
   c. appeal to pity

8. Your written agreement with my position will enable me to keep my job.
   a. misinterpreted statistics
   b. appeal to pity
   c. card stacking

9. Everyone in the neighborhood has worked on the new park design and agreed to it. Now we need your signature of support.
   a. bandwagon
   b. appeal to emotions
   c. begging the question

10. Democrats go to Washington to spend money with no regard for the hardworking taxpayer.
    a. circular reasoning
    b. bandwagon
    c. overgeneralization

11. The suicide rate is highest over the Christmas holidays, which means that Thanksgiving is a safe and happy holiday.
    a. misinterpreted statistics
    b. card stacking
    c. questionable authority

12. The workers' fingers were swollen and infected, insects walked on their exposed skin, and their red eyes begged for mercy and relief. We all must join their effort.

a. oversimplification
b. appeal to emotions
c. overgeneralization

_____ C_ 13. Our minister, Dr. Johnson, assured the family that our cousin's cancer was a slow-growing one so that a brief delay in treatment would not be detrimental.
a. transfer
b. straw person
c. questionable authority

_____ B_ 14. Crime in this city has been successfully addressed by increasing the number of police officers, seeking neighborhood support against drug dealers, and keeping teenagers off the streets at night. The city is to be commended.
a. misleading analogy
b. incomplete facts
c. misinterpreted statistics

_____ A_ 15. A biology professor cannot possibly advise the swim coach on the placement of swimmers in the different races.
a. *ad hominem*
b. testimonial
c. transfer

Determine Missing Support. Arguments are written to persuade and thus include the proponent's version of the convincing reasons. Writers do not usually supply the reader with any more than one or two weak points that could be made by the other side. In analyzing an argument, remember to ask yourself, "What is left out?" Be an advocate for the opposing point of view, and guess at the evidence that would be presented. Decide if evidence was consciously omitted because of its adverse effect on the conclusion. For example, a businessperson arguing for an increased monthly service fee might neglect to mention how much of the cost is administrative overhead and profit.

Step 4: Evaluate the Argument

Important decisions are rarely made quickly or easily. A period of incubation is often needed for deliberating among alternatives. Allow yourself time to go over arguments, weighing the support and looking at the issues from different perspectives. Good critical thinkers are persistent in seeking solutions.

One researcher, Diane Halpern, expresses the difficulty of decision making by saying, "There is never just one war fought. Each side has its own version, and rarely do they agree."[2] As a reader, you are obligated to consider all factors

---

[2]Diane Halpern, *Thought and Knowledge*, 2nd ed. (Hillsdale, NJ: Lawrence Erlbaum, 1989), p. 191.

© 2005 by Pearson Education, Inc.

carefully in seeking the truth. Halpern uses a picture of a table that represents the position on an issue and compares the legs of the table to four different degrees of support.

1. Unrelated reasons give no support.

2. A few weak reasons do not adequately support.

3. Many weak reasons can support.

4. Strong related reasons provide support.

Remember, in critical thinking there is no "I'm right, and you're wrong." There are, however, strong and weak arguments. Strong relevant, believable, and consistent reasons build a good argument.

| Exercise 9.7 | **Evaluating Your Own Decision Making** |

Now that you are familiar with the critical thinking process, analyze your own thinking in making an important recent decision of where to attend college. No college is perfect; many factors must be considered. The issue or conclusion is that you have decided to attend the college where you are now enrolled. List relevant reasons and/or evidence that supported your decision. Evaluate the strength of your reasoning. Are any of your reasons fallacies?

Position: My decision to attend this college was based on the following:

1. _Closer to home_

2. _Good nursing programs_

3. _Great teachers_

4. _Community college_

5. _has everything I look for_

How would you evaluate your own critical thinking in making a choice of colleges? Perhaps you relied heavily on information from others. Were those sources credible?

Inductive and Deductive Reasoning

In choosing a college, did you follow an inductive or deductive reasoning process? Did you collect extensive information on several colleges and then weigh the advantages and disadvantages of each? Those who follow an

inductive reasoning process start by gathering data, and then, after considering all available material, they formulate a conclusion. Textbooks written in this manner give details first and lead you into the main idea or conclusion. They strive to put the parts into a logical whole and thus reason "up" from particular details to a broad generalization.

Deductive reasoning, on the other hand, follows the opposite pattern. With this type of reasoning, you start with the conclusion of a previous experience and apply it to a new situation. Perhaps your college choice is a family tradition; your parents are alumni, and you have always expected to attend. Perhaps you are attending the college closest to where you live. Although your thinking may have begun with the conclusion, you probably have since discovered many reasons why the college is right for you. When writers use a deductive pattern, they first give a general statement and then enumerate the reasons.

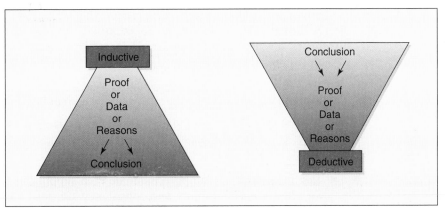

Helen R. Carr, San Antonio College.

Despite the formal distinction between inductive and deductive reasoning, in real life we switch back and forth as we think. Our everyday observations lead to conclusions that we then reuse and modify to form new conclusions.

Applying the Four-Step Format for Critical Thinking: An Example

The following is an example of how the four-step format can be used to evaluate an argument. Read the argument, analyze according to the directions for each step, and then read the explanation of how the critical thinking process was applied.

The Argument: Extraterrestrial Life

¹Surely life exists elsewhere in the universe. ²After all, most space scientists today admit the possibility that life has evolved on other planets. ³Besides, other planets in our solar system are strikingly like Earth. ⁴They revolve around the sun, they borrow light from the sun, and several are known to revolve on their axes, and to be subject to the same laws of gravitation as Earth. ⁵What's more, aren't those who make light of extraterrestrial life soft-headed fundamentalists clinging to the foolish notion that life is unique to their planet?

Joel Rudinow and Vincent Barry, *Invitation to Critical Thinking,* 3rd ed.

■ *Step 1:* Identify the position on the issue. What is the topic of this argument, and what is the main point the writer is trying to convey? Although many ideas may be included, what is the central concern being discussed and supported? Record the number for the sentence that states the position on the issue.

_____

■ *Step 2:* Identify the support in the argument. What are the significant supporting details that support the position that is being argued? Record the numbers for supporting statements.

_____

■ *Step 3:* Evaluate the support. Examine each supporting assertion separately for relevance, believability, and consistency. Can you identify any as fallacies that are intended to sell a weak argument? List each sentence that expresses a fallacy and identify the type of fallacy. Then identify the type of supporting information you feel is missing.

Fallacies: _____

_____

_____

Missing support: _____

_____

_____

■ *Step 4:* Evaluate the argument. What is your overall evaluation of the argument? Is the argument convincing? Does the argument provide good reasons and/or evidence for believing the thesis?

Explanation of the Steps

■ *Step 1:* Identify the position on the issue. The position, assertion, thesis, main point, or conclusion is directly stated in the first sentence. Good critical thinkers would note, however, that "life" is not clearly defined as plant, animal, or human.

■ *Step 2:* Identify the support in the argument. This argument contains three main premises or significant supporting details, in the following sentences:

Sentence 2: Space scientists admit the possibility that life has evolved from other planets.

Sentence 3: Other planets in our solar system are strikingly like Earth.

Sentence 5: Those who make light of extraterrestrial life are soft-headed fundamentalists clinging to the foolish notion that life is unique to this planet.

■ *Step 3:* Evaluate the support. The first supporting detail, sentence 2, is a vague appeal to authority that does not reveal who "most space scientists" are. Do the scientists work for NASA? The second premise, sentence 3, is also vague and presented as a misleading comparison. Other planets may be round, but they have different temperatures and different atmospheres. The third supporting statement, sentence 5, is an oversimplified, personal attack on those who may not agree with the argument. Scientific support for this argument seems to be missing.

■ *Step 4:* Evaluate the argument. This is not a good argument. There may be good reasons to believe that life exists on other planets, but this argument fails to provide them. The possibility of extraterrestrial life might be argued through statistics from astronomy and a specific definition of "life."

Exercise 9.8

Applying the Four Steps to Arguments

Read the following three arguments, and apply the four-step format for evaluation. Using the sentence numbers, identify the position on the issue and the support. Then evaluate the argument.

Argument 1: Child Criminal Offenders

1
Centuries ago, when there was little or no distinction between children and adults in daily life, children who committed crimes were treated exactly as adult offenders were treated. 2 More recently, they have been treated quite differently; they are

given special consideration for first offenses, receive lighter sentences for second and subsequent offenses, and are placed in special reform schools and rehabilitation centers rather than in prisons. But many people have begun to question
the wisdom of that special consideration. They reason that the crime in question,
and not the criminal's age, should dictate the punishment. Children who kill are
either guilty of murder or not guilty.

Adapted from Vincent Ryan Ruggiero, The Art of Thinking, 7th ed.

- *Step 1:* Identify the position on the issue. ————
- *Step 2:* Identify the support in the argument. ————
- *Step 3:* Evaluate the support. Examine each supporting assertion for relevance, believability, and consistency. List each sentence that expresses a fallacy and identify the type of fallacy. Then identify the type of supporting information you feel is missing.

Fallacies: _____

_____

Missing support: _____

- *Step 4:* Evaluate the argument. What is your overall evaluation and why?

_____

Argument 2: School Uniforms

A review of the evidence shows that a mandatory school uniform policy can be a solution to many high school learning and behavior problems. Studies show that in schools recently implementing a mandatory uniform policy, academic achievement has gone up and discipline problems have decreased. With the uniform policy, students are able to spend more time on their studies because they are not distracted by clothing choices. In addition, students who learn to respect and follow a dress code will also learn to respect other institutional rules. The principal of Taylor High School reported, "Our newly found success can be traced directly back to our uniform policy. The students enjoy and appreciate the opportunity to wear our school uniform." In light of this evidence, one can only conclude that denying our students the opportunity for uniforms is denying them academic success.

Joel Rudinow and Vincent E. Barry, Invitation to Critical Thinking, 3rd ed.

- *Step 1:* Identify the position on the issue ⟍⟋
- *Step 2:* Identify the support in the argument. ⎯⎯⎯⎯⎯
- *Step 3:* Evaluate the support. Examine each supporting assertion for relevance, believability, and consistency. List each sentence that expresses a fallacy and identify the type of fallacy. Then identify the type of supporting information you feel is missing.

Fallacies: ⎯⎯⎯⎯⎯⎯⎯⎯⎯⎯⎯⎯⎯⎯⎯⎯⎯⎯⎯⎯⎯⎯⎯⎯⎯

⎯⎯⎯⎯⎯⎯⎯⎯⎯⎯⎯⎯⎯⎯⎯⎯⎯⎯⎯⎯⎯⎯⎯⎯⎯⎯⎯⎯⎯⎯

⎯⎯⎯⎯⎯⎯⎯⎯⎯⎯⎯⎯⎯⎯⎯⎯⎯⎯⎯⎯⎯⎯⎯⎯⎯⎯⎯⎯⎯⎯

Missing support: ⎯⎯⎯⎯⎯⎯⎯⎯⎯⎯⎯⎯⎯⎯⎯⎯⎯⎯⎯⎯⎯⎯

⎯⎯⎯⎯⎯⎯⎯⎯⎯⎯⎯⎯⎯⎯⎯⎯⎯⎯⎯⎯⎯⎯⎯⎯⎯⎯⎯⎯⎯⎯

- *Step 4:* Evaluate the argument. What is your overall evaluation and why?

⎯⎯⎯⎯⎯⎯⎯⎯⎯⎯⎯⎯⎯⎯⎯⎯⎯⎯⎯⎯⎯⎯⎯⎯⎯⎯⎯⎯⎯⎯

⎯⎯⎯⎯⎯⎯⎯⎯⎯⎯⎯⎯⎯⎯⎯⎯⎯⎯⎯⎯⎯⎯⎯⎯⎯⎯⎯⎯⎯⎯

Argument 3: Invasion of Privacy

1
When you call 911 in an emergency, some police departments have a way of telling your telephone number and address without your saying a word. 2 The chief value of this, say the police, is that if the caller is unable to communicate for any reason, the dispatcher knows where to send help. 3 But don't be duped by such paternalistic explanations. 4 This technology is a despicable invasion of privacy, for callers may be unaware of the insidious device. 5 Even if they are, some persons who wish anonymity may be reluctant to call for emergency help. 6 Remember that the names of complainants and witnesses are recorded in many communities' criminal justice systems. 7 A fairer and more effective system seemingly would include an auxiliary number for 911 callers who wish anonymity.

Joel Rudinow and Vincent E. Barry, *Invitation to Critical Thinking*, 3rd ed.

- *Step 1:* Identify the position on the issue. ⎯⎯⎯⎯⎯
- *Step 2:* Identify the support in the argument. ⎯⎯⎯⎯⎯
- *Step 3:* Evaluate the support. Examine each supporting assertion for relevance, believability, and consistency. List each sentence that expresses a fallacy and identify the type of fallacy. Then identify the type of supporting information you feel is missing.

Fallacies: _____

_____

Missing support: _____

■ *Step 4:* Evaluate the argument. What is your overall evaluation and why?

_____

Argument 4: Ban Boxing

1
As a practicing physician, I am convinced that boxing should be banned. First,
2
boxing is a very visible example that violence is accepted behavior in our society—
3
outside the ring as well as inside. This sends the wrong message to America's
4
youth. Second, boxing is the only sport where the sole object is to injure the
5
opponent. Boxing, then, is morally offensive because its intent is to inflict brain
6
injuries on another person. Third, medical science can't take someone who has
suffered repeated blows to the head and restore that person to normal function.
7
This causes many physicians to conclude that our society should ban boxing.
8
Boxing is morally and medically offensive. So as a physician, I believe boxing
9
should be banned.

Adapted from Robert E. McAfee, USA Today, in Daniel McDonald and Larry W. Burton,
The Language of Argument, 9th ed.

■ *Step 1:* Identify the position on the issue. _____

■ *Step 2:* Identify the support in the argument. _____

■ *Step 3:* Evaluate the support. Examine each supporting assertion for relevance, believability, and consistency. List each sentence that expresses a fallacy and identify the type of fallacy. Then identify the type of supporting information you feel is missing.

Fallacies: _____

_____

_____

Missing support: _____

■ *Step 4:* Evaluate the argument. What is your overall evaluation and why?

_____

_____

Argument 5: Detect Online Romance

1
The following story is proof that surveillance software should be considered
2   3   4
ethically correct. The software is cheap. Its legality has not been questioned. It is
5
available from a host of companies. Computer spying woke me up to reality, as
the story explains.

6
"I'm not doing anything wrong, believe me," she'd said for weeks. But he didn't
buy it. He'd read her e-mail, listened in on her phone conversations. He watched
the chats, too. Fifty bucks bought him software to slip into the family computer and
secretly record his wife's every move.

So it's 5 A.M., she's sleeping upstairs, he ventures onto the computer. He
starts up the software and finds a series of black-and-white snapshots taken of
the screen while she was online. She calls herself "rita_neb" and her every
come-on, every flirtation, every misspelling, is saved. The correspondent is
some guy in Nebraska, and the talk is not just flirting but, you know, graphic—
and Greg Young begins to cry. His 22-year marriage is over.

Bill Hancock, "Spying at Home: A New Pastime to Detect Online Romance," in Joseph Williams
et al., *The Craft of Argument*

■ *Step 1:* Identify the position on the issue.
■ *Step 2:* Identify the support in the argument.
■ *Step 3:* Evaluate the support. Examine each supporting assertion for relevance, believability, and consistency. List each sentence that expresses a fallacy and identify the type of fallacy. Then identify the type of supporting information you feel is missing.

Fallacies: _____

_____

Missing support: _____

_____

■ *Step 4:* Evaluate the argument. What is your overall evaluation and why?

_____

_____

_____

Argument 6: Film Violence

¹I walked out of the movie after a half hour. ²It was either leave or throw up. ³In an early scene, a wolf attacks two young men, killing one and badly slashing the ⁴other. No gory detail is left to the imagination. ⁵Yet, somehow, many people around me in the theater found the visual assault enjoyable as they laughed and laughed. ⁶Chicago film critic Roger Ebert reports that in viewing another film on two separate occasions, he observed both audiences laughing in scenes showing a ⁷woman beaten, raped, and cut up. One respectable-looking man next to him ⁸kept murmuring, ⁹"That'll teach her." Ebert found that reaction frightening. Like any powerful experience, film viewing has the capacity to ¹⁰brutalize us. No one should ¹¹be permitted to poison the air the rest of us breathe. Neither should a filmmaker have the right to poison the social climate.

Adapted from Vincent Ryan Ruggiero, *The Art of Thinking*, 7th ed.

- *Step 1:* Identify the position on the issue. _____
- *Step 2:* Identify the support in the argument. _____
- *Step 3:* Evaluate the support. Examine each supporting assertion for relevance, believability, and consistency. List each sentence that expresses a fallacy and identify the type of fallacy. Then identify the type of supporting information you feel is missing.

Fallacies: _____

_____

_____

Missing support: _____
- *Step 4:* Evaluate the argument. What is your overall evaluation and why?

_____

_____

Creative and Critical Thinking

A chapter on critical thinking would not be complete without an appeal for creative thinking. You might wonder, "Are critical thinking and creative thinking different?" Creative thinking refers to the ability to generate many possible solutions to a problem, whereas critical thinking refers to the examination of those solutions for the selection of the best of all possibilities. Both ways of thinking are essential for good problem solving.

Diane Halpern uses the following story to illustrate creative thinking:

> Many years ago when a person who owed money could be thrown into jail, a merchant in London had the misfortune to owe a huge sum to a money-lender. The money-lender, who was old and ugly, fancied the merchant's beautiful teenage daughter. He proposed a bargain. He said he would cancel the merchant's debt if he could have the girl instead.
>
> Both the merchant and his daughter were horrified at the proposal. So the cunning money-lender proposed that they let Providence decide the matter. He told them that he would put a black pebble and a white pebble into an empty money-bag and then the girl would have to pick out one of the pebbles. If she chose the black pebble, she would become his wife and her father's debt would be canceled. If she chose the white pebble, she would stay with her father and the debt would still be canceled. But if she refused to pick out a pebble, her father would be thrown into jail and she would starve.
>
> Reluctantly the merchant agreed. They were standing on a pebble-strewn path in the merchant's garden as they talked, and the money-lender stooped down to pick up two pebbles. As he picked up the pebbles the girl, sharp-eyed with fright, noticed that he picked up two black pebbles and put them into the money-bag. He then asked the girl to pick out the pebble that was to decide her fate and that of her father.

Diane Halpern, Thought and Knowledge, 2nd ed.

If you were the girl, what would you do? Think creatively, and, without evaluating your thoughts, list at least five possible solutions. Next think critically to evaluate your list, and then circle your final choice.

1. _____

2. _____

3. _____

4. _____

5. _____

In discussing the possible solutions to the problem, Halpern talks about two kinds of creative thinking, vertical thinking and lateral thinking. **Vertical thinking** is a straightforward and logical way of thinking that would typically result in a solution like, "Call his hand and expose the money-lender as a crook." The disadvantage of this solution is that the merchant is still in debt, so the original problem has not been solved. **Lateral thinking,** on the other hand, is a way of thinking *around* a problem or even redefining the problem. DeBono suggests that a lateral thinker might redefine the problem from "What happens when I get the black pebble?"[3] to

_____

[3]E. DeBono, *New Think: The Use of Lateral Thinking in the Generation of New Ideas* (New York: Basic Books, 1968), p. 195.

"How can I avoid the black pebble?" Using this new definition of the problem and other seemingly irrelevant information, a lateral thinker could come up with a winning solution. When the girl reaches into the bag, she should fumble and drop one of the stones on the "pebble-strewn path." The color of the pebble she dropped could then be determined by looking at the one left in the bag. Since the remaining pebble is black, the dropped one that is now mingled in the path must have been white. Any other admission would expose the money-lender as a crook. Probably the heroine thought of many alternatives, but thanks to her ability ultimately to generate a novel solution and evaluate its effectiveness, the daughter and the merchant lived happily free of debt.

DeBono defines vertical thinking as "digging the same hole deeper" and lateral thinking as "digging the hole somewhere else."[4] For example, after many years of researching a cure for smallpox, Dr. Edward Jenner stopped focusing on patients who were sick with the disease and instead began studying groups of people who never seemed to get the smallpox. Shortly thereafter, using this different perspective, Dr. Jenner discovered the clues that led him to the smallpox vaccine.

Creative and critical thinking enable us to see new relationships. We blend knowledge and see new similarities and differences, a new sequence of events, or a new solution for an old problem. We create new knowledge by using old learning differently.

Summary Points

● What is thinking?

Thinking is an organized and controlled mental activity that helps you solve problems, make decisions, and understand ideas.

● What is critical thinking?

Thinking critically means deliberating in a purposeful, organized manner to assess the value of information, both old and new.

● What are the characteristics of critical thinkers?

Critical thinkers are flexible, persistent, and willing to plan and self-correct.

● What are the barriers to critical thinking?

Some people do not allow themselves to think critically because of their frame of reference or because of wishful thinking, hasty moral judgments, reliance on authority, and labels.

---

[4]E. DeBono, "Information Processing and New Ideas—Lateral and Vertical Thinking," in S. J. Parnes, R. B. Noller, and A. M. Biondi, eds., *Guide to Creative Action: Revised Edition of Creative Behavior Guidebook* (New York: Scribner's, 1977).

How do critical thinkers analyze an argument?

Critical thinkers can use a four-step plan for analyzing an argument: (1) identify the position on the issue, (2) identify the support in the argument, (3) evaluate the support, and (4) evaluate the argument.

What is the difference between inductive and deductive reasoning?

With inductive reasoning, the gathering of data precedes decision making; with deductive reasoning, the conclusion is arrived at first and is applied to a new situation.

What does creative thinking add to critical thinking?

Creative thinking involves both vertical and lateral thinking.

CONTEMPORARY FOCUS

Does personal appearance affect the way people are treated? If you like a person, does that affect your view of the person's attractiveness? Do attractive people have more advantages than their less attractive counterparts? If so, is this a form of discrimination that can be measured and proven?

PHYSICAL BEAUTY INVOLVES MORE THAN GOOD LOOKS

Ascribe Newswire (Madison, Wisconsin), April 15, 2004

There is more to beauty than meets the stranger's eye, according to results from three studies [by Kevin Kniffin and David Sloan Wilson of Binghamton University] examining the influence of non-physical traits on people's perception of physical attractiveness.

The results show that people perceive physical appeal differently when they look at those they know versus strangers. "In each case, non-physical traits known only to familiars, such as how much the person was liked, respected and contributed to shared goals, had a large effect on the perception of physical attractiveness that was invisible to the strangers," says Wilson.

According to evolutionary theory, many animals, including humans, are attracted to those who are likely to increase their own fitness—the likelihood of surviving and reproducing.

In the case of humans, "the fitness value of potential social partners depends at least as much on non-physical traits—whether they are cooperative, dependable, brave, hardworking, intelligent and so on—as physical factors, such as smooth skin and symmetrical features," says Wilson. "It follows that non-physical factors should be included in the subconscious assessment of beauty."

At the end of their paper, Kniffin and Wilson offer this beauty tip: "If you want to enhance your physical attractiveness, become a valuable social partner." Look at what that did for Abraham Lincoln.

"During his lifetime, he was regarded as so ugly that he once quipped, 'If I were two-faced, do you think I would be wearing this one?'" says Wilson. "Yet his physical features have become beloved, not because of their physical qualities per se, but because of what they stand for."

Collaborate

Collaborate on responses to the following questions:

- What is the biological theory that the researchers are using to explain their results?

- Why do we think friends look better than strangers might judge them to look?

- If we willingly engage in discrimination according to looks, is this an issue worth worrying about? Why or why not?

Preview

Preview the next selection to predict its purpose and organization and to formulate your learning plan.

Activate Schema

Why are most politicians good looking?

Did looks help Arnold Schwarzenegger become governor of California?

Establish a Purpose for Reading

Recall a time when you might have discriminated against a person or people on the basis of appearance. Then reflect on whether you have been discriminated against because you were not nicely dressed. Do well-groomed customers receive better service from sales people and restaurant staff? Read the selection to discover how we subconsciously favor good looks.

Integrate Knowledge While Reading

Questions have been inserted in the margin to stimulate your thinking while reading. Remember to

Predict   Picture   Relate   Monitor   Correct

THE IMPORTANCE OF BEING BEAUTIFUL

From Sidney Katz, in *Motives for Writing*, 3rd ed., ed. Robert Miller

Unlike many people, I was neither shocked nor surprised when the national Israeli TV network fired a competent female broadcaster because she was not beautiful. I received the news with aplomb because I had just finished extensive research into "person perception," an esoteric branch of psychology that
5 examines the many ways in which physical attractiveness—or lack of it—affects all aspects of your life.

Unless you're a 10—or close to it—most of you will respond to my findings with at least some feelings of frustration or perhaps disbelief. In a nutshell, you can't overestimate the importance of being beautiful. If you're beautiful,
10 without effort you attract hordes of friends and lovers. You are given higher school grades than your smarter—but less appealing—classmates. You compete successfully for jobs against men or women who are better qualified but less alluring. Promotions and pay raises come your way more easily. You are able to go into a bank or store and cash a check with far less hassle than

> Is this all true?
> Is it fair?

Models wearing Sue Wong creations walk the runway during the Mercedes Benz Fashion show in Culver City, California.
Carlo Allegri/Getty Images

15   a plain Jane or John. And these are only a few of the many advantages enjoyed by those with a ravishing face and body.

"We were surprised to find that beauty had such powerful effects," confessed Karen Dion, a University of Toronto social psychologist who does person perception research. "Our findings also go against the cultural grain. People like
20   to think that success depends on talent, intelligence, and hard work." But the scientific evidence is undeniable.

In large part, the beautiful person can attribute his or her idyllic life to a puzzling phenomenon that social scientists have dubbed the "halo effect." It defies human reason, but if you resemble Jane Fonda or Paul Newman it's
25   assumed that you're more generous, trustworthy, sociable, modest, sensitive, interesting, and sexually responsive than the rest of us. Conversely, if you're somewhat physically unattractive, because of the "horns effect" you're stigmatized as being mean, sneaky, dishonest, antisocial, and a poor sport to boot.

30   The existence of the halo/horns effect has been established by several studies. One, by Dion, looked at perceptions of misbehavior in children. Dion provided 243 female university students with identical detailed accounts of the misbehavior of a seven-year-old school child. She described how the youngster had pelted a sleeping dog with sharp stones until its leg bled. As the animal limped away,
35   yelping in pain, the child continued the barrage of stones. The 243 women were asked to assess the seriousness of the child's offense and to give their impression of the child's normal behavior. Clipped to half of the reports were photos of seven-year-old boys or girls who had been rated "high" in physical attractiveness; the other half contained photos of youngsters of "low" attractiveness. "We found,"

40 said Dion, "that the opinions of the adults were markedly influenced by the appearance of the children."

One evaluator described the stone thrower, who in her report happened to be an angelic-looking little girl, in these glowing terms: "She appears to be a perfectly charming little girl, well mannered and basically unselfish. She
45 plays well with everyone, but, like everyone else, a bad day may occur. . . . Her cruelty need not be taken too seriously." For the same offense, a homely girl evoked this comment from another evaluator: "I think this child would be quite bratty and would be a problem to teachers. She'd probably try to pick a fight with other children. . . . She would be a brat at home. All in all,
50 she would be a real problem." The tendency throughout the 243 adult responses was to judge beautiful children as ordinarily well behaved and unlikely to engage in wanton cruelty in the future; the unbeautiful were viewed as being chronically antisocial, untrustworthy, and likely to commit similar transgressions again.

> How might the halo or horn effect influence child development?

55 The same standards apply in judging adults. The beautiful are assumed innocent. John Jurens, a colorful private investigator, was once consulted by a small Toronto firm which employed 40 people. Ten thousand dollars' worth of merchandise had disappeared, and it was definitely an inside job. After an intensive investigation, which included the use of a lie detector, Jurens was
60 certain he had caught the thief. She was 24 years old and gorgeous—a lithe princess with high cheekbones, green eyes and shining, long black hair. The employer dismissed Juren's proof with the comment, "You've made a mistake. It just can't be her." Jurens commented sadly, "A lot of people refuse to believe that beautiful can be bad."

65 David Humphrey, a prominent Ontario criminal lawyer, observed, "If a beautiful woman is on trial, you practically have to show the judge and jury a movie of her committing the crime in order to get a conviction." The halo and horns effect often plays an important role in sentencing by courts. After spending 17 days observing cases heard in an Ontario traffic court, Joan Finegan, a
70 graduate psychology student at the University of Western Ontario, concluded that pleasant and neat-looking defendants were fined an average of $6.31 less than those who were "messy."

Careers

If you're a good-looking male over six feet tall, don't worry about succeeding at your career.

75 A study of university graduates by the *Wall Street Journal* revealed that well-proportioned wage earners who were six-foot-two or taller earned 12 percent more than men under six feet. "For some reason," explained Ronald Burke, a York University psychologist and industrial consultant, "tall men are assumed to be dynamic, decisive, and powerful. In other words, born
80 leaders." A Toronto consultant for Drake Personnel, one of the largest employment agencies in Canada, recalled trying to find a sales manager for an industrial firm. He sent four highly qualified candidates, only to have them all

turned down. "The fifth guy I sent over was different," said the consultant. "He stood six-foot-four. He was promptly hired."

85   The well-favored woman also has a distinct edge when it comes to getting a job she's after. "We send out three prospects to be interviewed, and it's almost always the most glamorous one that's hired," said Edith Geddes of the Personnel Centre, a Toronto agency that specializes in female placements. "We sometimes feel bad because the best qualified person is not chosen." Dr. Pam Ennis, a con-

90   sultant to several large corporations, observed. "Look at the photos announcing promotions in the *Globe and Mail* business section. It's no accident that so many of the women happen to be attractive and sexy-looking." Ennis, an elegant woman herself, attributes at least part of her career success to good looks. Her photograph appears on the brochures she mails out to companies soliciting new

95   clients. "About eight out of 10 company presidents give me an appointment," she said. "I'm sure that many of them are curious to see me in person. Beauty makes it easier to establish rapport."

> How can you capitalize on this observation?

Old Age

An elderly person's attractiveness influences the way in which he or she is treated in nursing homes and hospitals. Doctors and nurses give better care to

100   the beautiful ones.

Lena Nordholm, an Australian behavioral scientist, presented 289 doctors, nurses, social workers, speech therapists, and physiotherapists with photos of eight attractive and unattractive men and women. They were asked to speculate about what kind of patients they would be. The good-lookers were judged

105   to be more cooperative, better motivated, and more likely to improve than their less attractive counterparts. Pam Ennis, the consultant, commented, "Because the doctor feels that beautiful patients are more likely to respond to his treatment, he'll give them more time and attention."

We like to think we have moved beyond the era when the most desirable

110   woman was the beauty queen, but we haven't. Every day we make assumptions about the personality of the bank teller, the delivery man, or the waitress by their looks. The way in which we attribute good and bad characteristics still has very little to do with fact. People seldom look beyond a pleasing façade, a superficial attractiveness. But the professors of person perception are

115   not discouraged by this. They want to educate us. Perhaps by arming us with the knowledge and awareness of why we discriminate against the unattractive, we'll learn how to prevent this unwitting bigotry. Just maybe, we can change human nature.

> Should you fight this or use it?

Recall

Stop to self-test, relate, and react.

Your instructor may choose to give you a true-false comprehension review.

Skill Development: Think Critically

Apply the four-step format for evaluating the argument. Use the perforations to tear this page out for your instructor.

■ *Step 1:* Identify the position on the issue. State the main point the author is arguing.

_____

■ *Step 2:* Identify the support in the argument. Make a lettered list of the major assertions of support.

_____

_____

_____

_____

_____

_____

_____

_____

■ *Step 3:* Evaluate the support. Comment on weaknesses in relevance, believ-ability, and consistency for the assertions you listed in step 2. Label the fallacies. What support do you feel is missing?

_____

_____

_____

_____

■ *Step 4:* Evaluate the argument. What is your overall evaluation and why?

_____

What is your opinion on the issue? _____

_____

Write About the Selection

How do you plan to use the ideas from this selection to your benefit and apply the author's documented awareness of discrimination according to looks? Discuss this from two points of view: the way you manage yourself and the way you perceive and assess others.

Contemporary Link

Although different points are made, authors of both selections seek to prove their arguments by quantifying or measuring. Devise a research study of your own to prove or disprove the argument that attractive students get better grades than their smarter but less attractive counterparts. Design your study to account for different levels of ability. Also, consider the level of attractiveness and grades of a student who was previously known by the professor.

Check Your Comprehension

Answer the following questions about the selection:

1. Why do we like to believe that success depends on talent, intelligence, and hard work? _____

2. How does the study of the misbehaving seven-year-old prove the existence of the halo/horns effect? _____

   _____

   _____

3. What does the phrase, "you're a 10" mean? _____

   _____

4. What evidence shows that the beautiful are treated differently in legal matters? _____

   _____

   _____

5. Why do you think tall men are assumed to be born leaders?

   _____

   _____

6. What does the author mean by "Beauty makes it easier to establish rapport"?

    _____

    _____

7. For the elderly, why can looks be a life-and-death matter?

    _____

    _____

Search the Net

Use a search engine such as Google, AltaVista, Excite, Infoseek, Dogpile, Yahoo, or Lycos to find out how our perception of beauty in art has changed over the years. Select and describe several differences in other centuries. For suggested Web sites and other research activities, go to http://www.ablongman.com/smith/.

CONTEMPORARY FOCUS

What are the current health concerns about cell phones? Would cell phones be on the market if they caused cancer or brain damage? With so many people relying on cell phones, the research on long-term health hazards should be extensive and reliable. How can users feel confident about product safety?

CELL PHONES AND CANCER: NO CLEAR CONNECTION

By Tamar Nordenberg

U.S. Food and Drug Administration Consumer Magazine, November/December 2000, updated July 29, 2003

Current scientific evidence does not show any negative health effects from the low levels of electromagnetic energy emitted by mobile phones, says the Food and Drug Administration. But some recent studies suggest a possible link between mobile phones and cancer and warrant follow-up, the agency says, to determine with more certainty whether cell phones are safe.

"We don't see a risk looking at currently available data," says David Feigal, M.D., director of FDA's Center for Devices and Radiological Health. "But we need more definite answers about the biological effects of cell phone radiation, and about the more complicated question of whether mobile phones might cause even a small increase in the risk of developing cancer."

Like televisions, alarm systems, computers, and all other electrical devices, mobile phones emit electromagnetic radiation. FDA can regulate these devices to ensure that the radiation doesn't pose a health hazard to users, but only once the existence of a public health hazard has been established.

Many experts say that no matter how near the cell phone's antenna—even if it's right up against the skull—the six-tenths of a watt of power emitted couldn't possibly affect human health. They're probably right, says John E. Moulder, Ph.D., a cancer researcher and professor of radiation oncology at the Medical College of Wisconsin. It's true, he says, that from the physics standpoint, biological effects from mobile phones are "somewhere between impossible and implausible."

At the same time, Moulder supports further studies into the science of cell phone radiation. "Some people think the power emitted by the phones is so low, it's a silly thing to research. But I think it remains a legitimate area of study."

Collaborate

Collaborate on responses to the following questions:

- How often do you use a cell phone?
- What is the FDA's role in cell phone safety?
- Why are the credentials of the quoted doctors important?

Preview

Preview the next selection to predict its purpose and organization and to formulate your learning plan.

Activate Schema

Do you have any health concerns about using a cell phone?

Why should the government be involved in research on cell phone safety?

Establish a Purpose for Reading

What do you know about the safety and dangers of cell phone use? If you heard a negative report about cell phones, would you believe it? Would it affect your view or use of cell phones? Read this selection to discover the findings of one research study, and evaluate the argument for additional research.

Integrate Knowledge While Reading

© 2005 by Pearson Education, Inc.

Questions have been inserted in the margin to stimulate your thinking while reading. Remember to

Predict   Picture   Relate   Monitor   Correct

STUDY LINKS CELLPHONES TO BRAIN DAMAGE
From Elizabeth Svoboda, *Popular Science*, February 2004

The safety of cellphones has been called into question, again. This time the scientific community is paying very close attention.

Last summer neurosurgeon Leif Salford and colleagues at Lund University in Sweden published data showing for the first time an unambiguous link between microwave radiation emitted by GSM mobile phones (the most common type worldwide) and brain damage in rats. If Salford's results are
5   confirmed by follow-up studies in the works at research facilities worldwide, including one run by the U.S. Air Force, the data could have serious implications for the one billion-plus people glued to their cellphones.

What are the human effects?

The findings have re-ignited a long-standing debate among scientists and cellphone manufacturers over cellphone safety.
10   Many of the hundreds of studies performed during the past decade suggest cellphone use may cause a host of adverse effects, including headaches and memory loss. Other studies, however, have shown no such effects, and no scientific consensus exists about the effect of long-term, low-level radiation on the brain and other organs. A comprehensive $12 million federal investigation of cellphone
15   safety is currently under way but will take at least five years to complete.

Is the five-year study complete?

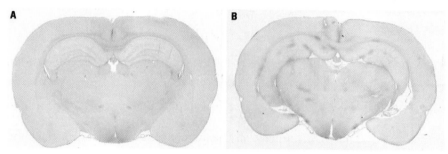

Researchers at Sweden's Lund University say these rat brain cross-sections show first-ever evidence of brain damage from cell phone radiation. According to their reseach: **A,** normal rat brain. **B,** rat brain after cell phone exposure. *(see p.593 for credit)*

Meanwhile, the research world is scrambling to replicate Salford's surprising results. His team exposed 32 rats to 2 hours of microwave radiation from GSM
20 cellphones. Researchers attached the phones to the sides of the rats' small cages using coaxial cables—allowing for intermittent direct exposure—and varied the intensity of radiation in each treatment group to reflect the range of exposures a human cellphone user might experience over the same time period. Fifty days after the 2-hour exposure, the rat brains showed significant blood vessel leakage,
25 as well as areas of shrunken, damaged neurons. The higher the radiation exposure level, the more damage was apparent. The controls, by contrast, showed little to no damage. If human brains are similarly affected, Salford says, the damage could produce measurable, long-term mental deficits.

How does this period compare with humans on phones?

The cellphone industry so far has been quick to dismiss the data, saying emis-
30 sions from current mobiles fall well within the range of radiation levels the FCC deems safe (body-tissue absorption rates of under 1.6 watts per kilogram). "Expert reviews of studies done over the past 30 years have found no reason to believe that there are any health hazards whatsoever," says Mays Swicord, scientific director of Motorola's Electromagnetic Energy Programs. Dr. Marvin
35 Ziskin, chair of the Institute of Electrical and Electronics Engineer's Committee on Man and Radiation, is similarly skeptical. "The levels of radiation they used seem way too low to be producing the kinds of effects they're claiming."

How is Motorola biased?

Salford is the first to admit that it's too early to draw any conclusions, but contends the unusual results deserve a closer look. "The cellphone is a mar-
40 velous invention; it has probably saved thousands of lives," he says. "But governments and suppliers should be supporting more autonomous research." Meanwhile, Salford advises users to invest in hands-free headsets to reduce radiation exposure to the brain.

Recall

Stop to self-test, relate, and react.

Your instructor may choose to give you a true-false comprehension review.

Skill Development: Think Critically

Apply the four-step format for evaluating the argument. Use the perforations to tear this page out for your instructor.

■ Identify the position on the issue.

_____

_____

■ Evaluate the following support for the argument:

1. Salford linked radiation emitted by cell phones to brain damage in rats.

_____

_____

2. No scientific consensus exists over dangers.

_____

3. Salford's 32 rats had 100 hours of radiation exposure causing damage.

_____

4. The cellphone industry dismisses the data.

_____

_____

5. Use a hands-free headset.

_____

6. What support do you feel is missing?

_____

_____

■ Evaluate the argument. What is your overall evaluation and why?

_____

What is your opinion? _____

_____

Write About the Selection

What factors operate against getting unbiased research on cell phone dangers? How does research on rats sometimes relate and sometimes not relate to humans?

Contemporary Link

What is your position on the health hazards of cell phones? What do you find lacking in the initial argument on cell phone safety? Describe the kind of report that you would like to see regarding cell phone safety. How would you like to see Selford's research answered by the FDA?

Check Your Comprehension

Answer the following questions about the selection.

1. What is meant by the phrase "unambiguous link" in Salford's research report? _____

   _____

2. Why would a replication of Salford's study by the U.S. Air Force be considered more valuable than a replication by another scientist? _____

   _____

   _____

3. What are your questions about the 100 hours of radiation the rats received in Salford's experiment? _____

4. What does the phrase "more autonomous research" mean? _____

   _____

   _____

   _____

5. Even if you wore a headset, if the cell phone were on your waist, do you think this would expose your body to radiation? _____

6. What would you need to hear to convince you to not use your cell phone?

   _____

Search the Net

Use a search engine such as Google, AltaVista, Excite, Infoseek, Dogpile, Yahoo, or Lycos to find the most recent research on the dangers of radiation from cell phone. Summarize your findings, and comment on the validity and relevance of the research. For suggested Web sites and other research activities, go to http://www.ablongman.com/smith/.

Vocabulary Booster

Lights, Camera, Action!

> **Roots**
> *luc-, lum-*: light   *photo-*: light
> *act-, ag-*: to do

Words with *luc-, lum-:* light

Mexican Christmas lanterns called *luminarias*—bags with sand and a lit candle inside—line streets and driveways, not only in the Southwest but all over America at Christmas.

- *lucid:* clear; glowing with light; easily understood; sane

 The patient's statements were not *lucid* when she was brought into the psychiatric treatment center.

- *luminescence:* the giving off of light without heat

 A fluorescent light bulb or tube is a *luminescent* fixture that gives off light but remains cool when the mercury vapor inside the tube is acted upon by electrons.

- *luminous:* radiating or reflecting light; well-lighted; shining; enlightened

 Due to neon lighting on most of the buildings, Las Vegas is one of the most *luminous* cities in the United States at night.

- *luminary:* a celestial body; a person who is a shining example in a profession

 Muhammad Ali is still a *luminary* in the boxing world.

- *illuminate:* to supply with light; light up; to make lucid or clarify

 Let me *illuminate* the facts for you before you take misinformed action.

- *elucidate:* to make lucid or clear; explain

 Mario had to successfully *elucidate* details about his new invention to investors in order to get funding.

- *translucent:* allowing light to pass through without being transparent

 The Martinez family chose a *translucent* frosted glass that would provide privacy for the renovated bathroom.

Words with *photo-:* light

The wrinkles and discolored skin on Brooke's face and hands were signs of *photoaging* from spending years in the sun without sunscreen protection.

- *photogenic:* having features that look attractive in a photograph

  The supermodel was extremely *photogenic*, and she could also act.

- *photography:* a process of producing images on sensitized surfaces by the chemical action of light or other forms of radiant energy

  Sensitized film in a camera receiving sunlight or flash lighting by opening the camera's aperture or eye is a form of *photography*.

- *photogrammetry:* the process of making surveys and maps through the use of aerial photographs

  The surveying firm had its own small airplane for taking aerial photos to use in the *photogrammetry* project for the National Park Service.

- *photosensitivity:* quality of being photosensitive; abnormal sensitivity of the skin to ultraviolet light

  Some prescription drugs can cause *photosensitivity*, requiring avoidance of the sun or use of a sunscreen.

- *telephoto lens:* a camera lens that produces a large image of distant or small objects

  George's *telephoto lens* made it possible to get close-up pictures of the inaccessible waterfall.

- *photocopy:* a duplicate of a document or print made on specialized copying equipment

  Xerox, the name of the first and most well-known *photocopy* machine manufacturer, is the word commonly used to mean "copy."

Words with *act-, ag-:* to do

The *actors* and *actresses* were waiting offstage for their cues to go onstage during Act Three of the play.

- *act:* anything done, being done, or to be done; a formal decision, law, or statute; a main division of a play

  A clown performing a magic *act* entertained the children at the six-year-old's birthday party.

- *activate:* to make active; to place a military unit on active status

  Before using her new credit card, Sheila *activated* it by calling a telephone number to notify the company that she received the card.

- *activism:* the practice of achieving political or other goals through actions of protest or demonstration

  During the 1960s, *activism* was used to protest the Vietnam War and civil rights injustices in the United States.

- *agent:* a representative working on behalf of another

  Toby's *agent* promised to get him a film role before the end of the year.

- *agency:* an organization that provides a particular service; the place of business of an agent

  The FBI is an *agency* of the U.S. government.

- *agenda:* a list or outline of things to be done or matters to be acted or voted upon

  A vote for a new accounting firm to represent the company was on the *agenda* for the annual stockholders' meeting.

- *acting:* serving as a temporary substitute during another's absence; the art of performing in plays, films, etc.

  While the city mayor was out on maternity leave, one of the council members served as *acting* mayor.

Review

Part I

Indicate whether the following statements are true (*T*) or false (*F*):

_False____ 1. The sun is the brightest luminary in our solar system.

_false____ 2. Photogrammetry makes use of pictures taken from above.

_true____ 3. An agent works for the benefit of someone else.

_false____ 4. Luminescence requires heat.

_false____ 5. Photography requires the use of an airplane.

_True____ 6. People with photosensitivity do not like to have their pictures taken.

_false____ 7. Activists are usually politically passive.

_True____ 8. The speaker who elucidates the details of a project will be the most effective.

_true____ 9. In times of civil emergency, the state or federal government can activate the National Guard.

_True____ 10. The agenda of a meeting lists items to be addressed.

Part II

Choose an antonym from the boxed list for each of the words below.

blocking light   confuse   darken   demobilize   glowing with heat
insane   not pretending   original   dull   unattractive

11. photogenic _unattractive_

12. translucent _blocking light_

13. illuminate _Darken_

14. luminous _Confuse_

15. photocopy _Original_

16. lucid _Insane_

17. acting _not pretending_

18. activate _demobilize_

19. elucidate _Dull_

20. luminescent _glowing with heat_

10

Graphic Illustrations

- What do graphics do?
- What is a diagram?
- What does a table do?
- What is most helpful on a typical map?
- What does a pie graph represent?
- How do you read a bar graph?
- What is a line graph?
- What information does a flowchart convey?

Derby Hat 2 by Paul Giovanopoulos, 1998-99. Acrylic on canvas, 36 x 48". Derby Hat 2 © 1998-99 Paul Giovanopoulos. Image courtesy of ispot.com.

What Graphics Do

If a picture is worth a thousand words, a graphic illustration is worth at least several pages of facts and figures. Graphics express complex interrelationships in simplified form. Instead of plodding through repetitious data, you can glance at a chart, a map, or a graph and immediately see how everything fits together as well as how one part compares with another. Instead of reading several lengthy paragraphs and trying to visualize comparisons, you can study an organized design. The graphic illustration is a logically constructed aid for understanding many small bits of information.

Graphic illustrations are generally used for the following reasons:

1. **To condense.** Pages of repetitious, detailed information can be organized into one explanatory design.
2. **To clarify.** Processes and interrelationships can be more clearly defined through visual representations.
3. **To convince.** Developing trends and gross inequities can be forcefully dramatized.

READER'S TIP

How to Read Graphic Material

◆ **Read the title to get an overview.** What is it about?

◆ **Look for footnotes and read introductory material.**
Identify the who, where, and how.
How and when were the data collected?
Who collected the data?
How many persons were included in the survey?
Do the researchers seem to have been objective or biased?
Taking all this information into account, does the study seem valid?

◆ **Read the labels.**
What do the vertical columns and the horizontal rows represent?
Are the numbers in thousands or millions?
What does the legend represent?

◆ **Notice the trends and find the extremes.**
What are the highest and lowest rates?
What is the average rate?
How do the extremes compare with the total?
What is the percentage of increase or decrease?

◆ **Draw conclusions and formulate future exam questions.**
What does the information mean?
What purpose does the information serve?
What wasn't included?
What else is there to know about the subject?

There are five kinds of graphic illustrations: (1) diagrams, (2) tables, (3) maps, (4) graphs, and (5) flowcharts. All are used in textbooks, and the choice of which is best to use depends on the type of material presented. This chapter contains explanations and exercises for the five types of graphic illustrations. Read the explanations, study the illustrations, and respond to the questions as instructed. The Reader's Tip opposite gets you started by summarizing how to read graphics to get the most information from them.

Diagrams

A *diagram* is an outline drawing or picture of an object or a process. It shows the labeled parts of a complicated form, such as the muscles of the human body, the organizational makeup of a company's management and production teams, or the flow of nutrients in a natural ecological system.

Exercise 10.1

Diagrams

The diagrams display the major structures of the human ear. Refer to the diagram to respond to the following statements with *T* (true), *F* (false), or *CT* (can't tell).

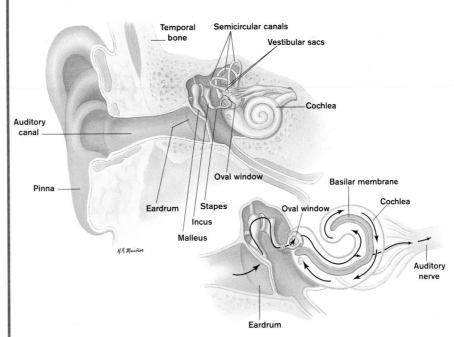

Major Structures of the Human Ear

Illustration on page 90, Psychology: An Introduction *by Josh R. Gerow. © 1997 Addison-Wesley Educational Publishers Inc.*

_____ T _____ 1. Sound enters the ear through the auditory canal.
_____ T _____ 2. The cochlea can be seen by looking through the auditory canal.
_____ F _____ 3. Sound travels through the cochlea to the auditory nerve.
_____ F _____ 4. Most hearing problems result from damage to the eardrum.
_____ F _____ 5. The nerves in the pinna conduct sound directly to the oval window.
_____ T _____ 6. The basilar membrane is a part of the cochlea.
_____ F _____ 7. The malleus, incus, and stapes are positioned to transmit sound from the eardrum to the oval window.
_____ T _____ 8. According to the diagram, the semicircular canals contain the basilar membrane.
_____ F _____ 9. If punctured, the eardrum cannot be adequately repaired.
_____ T _____ 10. The cochlea could be described as snail-like in appearance.

11. The purpose of each diagram is _To show us each part of the ear_

Tables

A *table* is a listing of facts and figures in columns and rows for quick and easy reference. The information in the columns and rows is usually labeled in two different directions. First read the title for the topic and then read the footnotes to judge the source. Determine what each column represents and how they interact.

Exercise 10.2

Tables

Refer to the table shown on page 493 to respond to the following statements with *T* (true), *F* (false), or *CT* (can't tell). Note the average numbers for the three different body weights.

_____ T _____ 1. Bicycling at 13 mph burns more than twice the average number of calories for the three weight groups as bicycling at 5.5 mph.
_____ F _____ 2. Of the activities listed in this table, the two with the highest expenditure of calories in all three weight groups are running at 9 mph and walking upstairs.
_____ T _____ 3. Waterskiing and snow skiing expend approximately the same number of calories per hour.
_____ T _____ 4. On average, a baseball or softball pitcher expends about 80 more calories an hour than does an outfielder.
_____ F _____ 5. On average, a 154-pound golfer expends more calories per hour playing in a foursome than would a golfer of the same weight playing in a twosome.
_____ F _____ 6. On average, a 110-pound person must swim the backstroke at the rate of 20 yards per minute to burn 165 calories in an hour.

Burning Calories: The Average Caloric Expenditure by Activity (per hour)

	Body Weight				Body Weight		
	110 lbs	**154 lbs**	**198 lb**		**110 lb**	**154 lb**	**198 lb**
Baseball/softball				Running			
Infield/outfield	220	280	340	5.5 mph	515	655	795
Pitching	305	390	475	7 mph	550	700	850
Basketball				9 mph	720	920	1120
Moderate	435	555	675	Sailing (calm water)	120	155	190
Vigorous	585	750	910	Sawing wood	180	230	280
Bicycling				Shoveling snow	475	610	745
On level 5.5 mph	190	245	295	Skating (ice)			
13 mph	515	655	790	Moderate	275	350	425
Bowling (nonstop)	210	270	325	Vigorous	485	620	755
Bricklaying	160	205	250	Skiing			
Calisthenics	235	300	365	Downhill	465	595	720
Canoeing (4 mph)	490	625	765	Cross-country (5 mph)	550	700	950
Chopping wood	355	450	550	Soccer	470	600	730
Gardening	155	215	280	Swimming			
Gardening and weeding	250	315	380	Backstroke 20 yds/min	165	235	305
Golf				Breaststroke	210	295	380
Twosome	295	380	460	10 yds/min			
Foursome	210	270	325	Butterfly (per hour)	490	630	760
Handball/racquetball	610	775	945	Crawl 20 yds/min	235	300	365
Hill climbing	470	600	730	Sidestroke (per hr)	230	320	420
Hoeing, raking, and	205	285	370	Tennis			
planting				Moderate	335	425	520
Housework	175	245	320	Vigorous	470	600	730
House painting	165	210	255	Volleyball (moderate)	275	350	425
Motorcycling	165	205	250	Walking			
Mountain climbing	470	600	730	2 mph	145	185	225
Mowing grass				4.5 mph	325	450	550
Power, self-propelled	195	250	305	Downstairs	355	450	550
Not self-propelled	210	270	325	Upstairs	720	920	1120
				Waterskiing	335	475	610
				Yardwork	155	215	

Source: B. E. Pruitt and Jane J. Stein, Decisions for Healthy Living.

_____ T 7. Of the activities listed, yardwork typically burns more calories per hour than vigorous sports.

_____ T 8. Canoeing with a partner burns fewer calories per hour than canoeing alone.

_____ F 9. Of the listed activities, the two with the highest caloric expenditure per hour require a team, a coach, and expensive equipment.

_____ F 10. For vigorous tennis in the two groups over 110 pounds, add an average of 130 calories for each additional 44 pounds.

11. The purpose of the table is _To show us_
The Average caloric expenditure
by Activity per hour

Maps

Traditional *maps*, such as road maps and atlas maps, show the location of cities, waterways, sites, and roads, as well as the differences in the physical terrain of specified areas. A modern use of the map as a visual aid is to highlight special characteristics or population distributions of a particular area. For example, a map of the United States might highlight all states with gun control laws in red and all states without gun control laws in blue.

Begin reading a map by noting the title and source. The legend of a map, which usually appears in a corner box, explains the meanings of symbols and shading.

**Exercise
10.3**

Maps

Read the following passage about national exports and state economies. Then use the legend on the map shown on page 495 to help you respond to the subsequent statements with *T* (true), *F* (false), or *CT* (can't tell).

All states are affected by the global economy, but some states are more dependent on it. Exports are a larger fraction of their economies. For example, the state of Washington, with its aerospace, fishing, and logging industries, depends most heavily on trade with other countries. Exports account for nearly 20 percent of Washington State's economy.

Most of the top exporting states are located on the nation's borders, which gives them easier access to other countries. For example, the state of Washington abuts Canada, and its seaports are a departure point for goods destined for Asia.

Thomas E. Patterson, *We the People*

_____F_____ 1. The western states bordering the Pacific Ocean are all among the highest exporters in the nation.

_____T_____ 2. Each island state exports more than 5 percent of its total economy.

_____T_____ 3. Each state bordering the Atlantic Ocean exports 3 percent or more of its total economy.

_____F_____ 4. Nevada does not export more than 5 percent of its total economy because gambling is legal in Nevada.

_____F_____ 5. Each state bordering Canada exports 3 percent or more of its total economy.

_____F_____ 6. Each state bordering Mexico exports 3 percent or more of its total economy.

_____T_____ 7. Florida and Maine export the same dollar amount of goods.

_____T_____ 8. Only 18 states export more than 5 percent of their total economies.

_____T_____ 9. Although the map shows they export the same percentage, California and Arizona could differ on the actual dollar

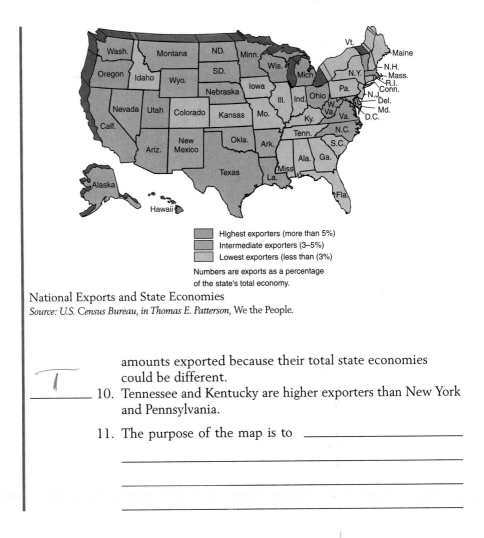

Highest exporters (more than 5%)
Intermediate exporters (3–5%)
Lowest exporters (less than (3%)
Numbers are exports as a percentage
of the state's total economy.

National Exports and State Economies
Source: U.S. Census Bureau, in Thomas E. Patterson, We the People.

amounts exported because their total state economies
could be different.

_____ 10. Tennessee and Kentucky are higher exporters than New York
and Pennsylvania.

11. The purpose of the map is to _____

_____

_____

_____

**Exercise
10.4**

Geographic Review

Use the map on page 496 to test your knowledge of world geography.

Citizens of the World Show Little Knowledge of Geography

In the spring of 1988, twelve thousand people in ten nations were asked to identify sixteen places on the following world map. The average citizen in the United States could identify barely more than half. Believe it or not, 14 percent of Americans tested could not even find their own country on the map. Despite years of fighting in Vietnam, 68 percent could not locate this Southeast Asian country. Such lack of basic geographic knowledge is quite common throughout the world. Here is the average score for each of the ten countries in which the test was administered.

Country	Average Score
Sweden	11.6
West Germany	11.2
Japan	9.7
France	9.3
Canada	9.2
United States	8.6
Britain	8.5
Italy	7.6
Mexico	7.4
Former Soviet Union	7.4

How would you do? To take the test, match the numbers on the map to the places listed.

Robert L. Lineberry et al., *Government in America*

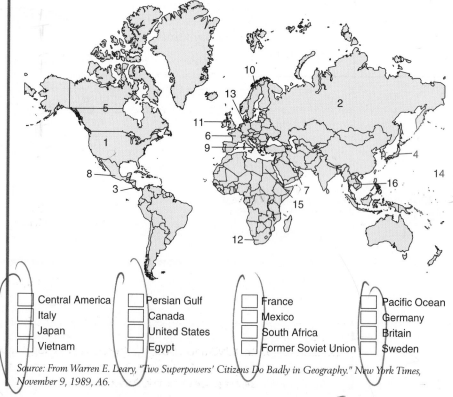

Central America
Italy
Japan
Vietnam

Persian Gulf
Canada
United States
Egypt

France
Mexico
South Africa
Former Soviet Union

Pacific Ocean
Germany
Britain
Sweden

Source: From Warren E. Leary, "Two Superpowers' Citizens Do Badly in Geography." New York Times, November 9, 1989, A6.

Pie Graphs

A *pie graph* is a circle divided into wedge-shaped slices. The complete pie or circle represents a total, or 100 percent. Each slice is a percentage or fraction of that whole. Budgets, such as the annual expenditure of the federal or state governments, are frequently illustrated by pie graphs.

Exercise 10.5

Pie Graphs

Refer to the pie graphs shown here to respond to the following statements with *T* (true), *F* (false), or *CT* (can't tell). Note that the figures are percentages rather than actual numbers.

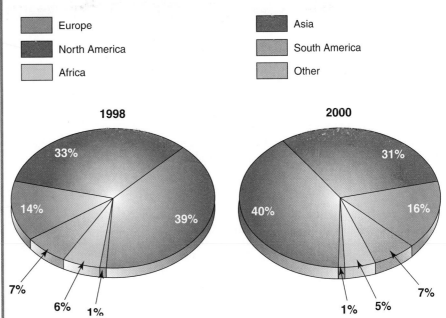

National Origins of Legal Immigrants to the United States, 1998 and 2000
Source: U.S. Census Bureau, 1999 Statistical Abstract, Table 8, in Linda L. Lindsey and Stephen Beach, Sociology, 3rd ed.

____ 1. In 1998 and 2000, the majority of legal immigrants to the United States were from Mexico and Canada.

____ 2. The percentage of legal European immigrants to the United States decreased from 1998 to 2000.

____ 3. In 1998 and 2000, the percentage of legal immigrants to the United States from Asia is more than three times the percentage from South America.

_____ T _____ 4. The actual number of legal immigrants coming to the United States from South America was the same for 1998 and 2000.

_____ T _____ 5. In 2000, only 1 percent of legal immigrants to the United States came from Australia.

_____ F _____ 6. In 2000, more than half the legal immigrants to the United States came from Europe and Asia.

7. The purpose of the pie graph is to _____

_____

_____

Bar Graphs

A *bar graph* is a series of horizontal or vertical bars in which the length of each bar represents a particular amount or number of what is being discussed. A series of different items can be quickly compared by noting the different bar lengths.

Exercise 10.6

Bar Graphs

Refer to the bar graph shown on page 499 to respond to the following statements with *T* (true), *F* (false), or *CT* (can't tell)

_____ T _____ 1. The biggest reason Americans gave for not voting was "too busy."

_____ T _____ 2. Despite what analysts predict, bad weather kept less than 1 percent of people from voting in 2000.

_____ F _____ 3. A higher percentage of people forgot to vote than refused to vote.

_____ F _____ 4. A combined 19.7 percent of Americans were either not interested or refused to vote in 2000.

_____ F _____ 5. A greater percentage of people not voting in 2000 had transportation problems than had registration problems.

_____ T _____ 6. The people who were not interested in voting in 2000 probably did not like the candidates.

_____ T _____ 7. The 18- to 24-year-olds formed the largest group of non-registered voters.

_____ T _____ 8. The majority of the 18- to 24-year-olds who did not vote in 2000 were unregistered.

_____ T _____ 9. The percentage of unregistered 45- to 64-year-olds was larger than the percentage of unregistered voters 65 years old and over.

_____ T _____ 10. Of the 6.9 percent of voters who did not vote in 2000 because of registration problems, 40 percent were 25 to 44 years of age.

11. The purpose of the bar graphs is _To Show_ _us the reasons for_ _people not voting_

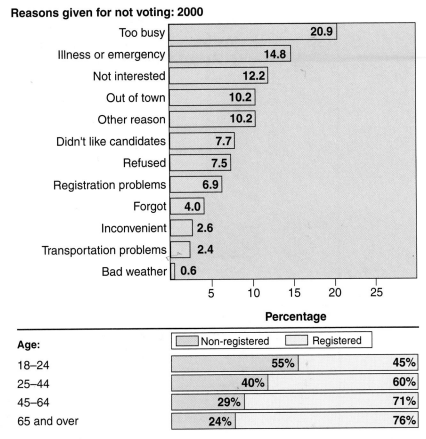

Reasons given for not voting: 2000

Reason	Percentage
Too busy	20.9
Illness or emergency	14.8
Not interested	12.2
Out of town	10.2
Other reason	10.2
Didn't like candidates	7.7
Refused	7.5
Registration problems	6.9
Forgot	4.0
Inconvenient	2.6
Transportation problems	2.4
Bad weather	0.6

Percentage

Age:	Non-registered	Registered
18–24	55%	45%
25–44	40%	60%
45–64	29%	71%
65 and over	24%	76%

Why People Don't Vote

Source: U. S. Census Bureau, Current Population Survey, November 2000, in Karen O'Conner et al., American Government.

Cumulative Bar Graphs

Both bar graphs and line graphs can be designed to show cumulative effects in which all the lines or segments add up to the top line or total amount. Rather than having multiple bars or lines, the groups are stacked on top of each other to dramatically show differences. The bar graph shown here illustrates a cumulative effect.

Exercise 10.7

Cumulative Bar Graphs

Refer to the cumulative bar graph on page 500 to respond to the following statements with *T* (true), *F* (false), or *CT* (can't tell).

_____ 1. From 1999 to 2070, the percentage of the population of American Indians is expected to shrink.

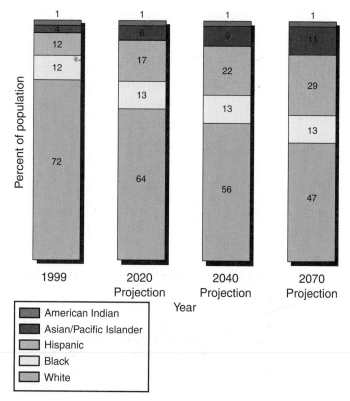

Projected U.S. Ethnic Composition, 1999 to 2070
*Source: Modified from the U.S. Census Bureau, National Projections, 2020–2070,
in Les Rowntree et al.,* Diversity and Globalization.

F ___ 2. In each projected year, the percentage of the population that is white decreases.

T ___ 3. From 1999 to 2070, the percentage of Hispanics in the population more than triples.

T ___ 4. The black percentage of the population decreases between 2020 and 2070.

F ___ 5. Asian/Pacific Islanders as a percentage of the total population increase at a higher rate than blacks from 1999 to 2070.

F ___ 6. The number of African Americans in the population is not projected to increase from 2020 to 2070.

T ___ 7. In 2070, whites and Asian/Pacific Islanders are projected to comprise more than half the population.

8. The purpose of the bar graph is __to illustrate a cummulative effect__

Line Graphs

A *line graph* is a continuous curve or frequency distribution in which numbers are plotted in an unbroken line. The horizontal scale measures one aspect of the data and the vertical line measures another aspect. As the data fluctuate, the line will change direction and, with extreme differences, will become very jagged.

Exercise 10.8

Line Graphs

Read the following passage from a sociology text and then examine the line graph to respond to the subsequent questions with *T* (true), *F* (false), or *CT* (can't tell). Notice that the graph's horizontal axis indicates the year, and the vertical axis measures the numbers of people in billions

Why Do the Least Industrialized Nations Have So Many Children?

First is the status of parenthood. In the least industrialized nations, motherhood is the most prized status. Similarly, a man proves his manhood by fathering children. Second, the community supports this view. By producing children, people reflect the values of their community and achieve status.

Third, for poor people in the least industrialized nations, children are economic assets. These people have no social security or medical and unemployment insurance. They rely on their children to take care of them. The more children they have, the broader their base of support.

James Henslin, *Essentials of Sociology*, 5th ed.

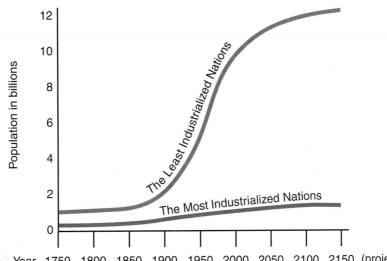

World Population Growth, 1750–2150
Source: James Henslin, Essentials of Sociology, *5th ed., p. 391.*

_F_   1. In 2000, the populations of the least industrialized nations totaled more than 8 billion.

_T_   2. In 2050, the total population of the most industrialized nations is projected at less than 2 billion, while the least industrialized nations have a total population of almost 10 billion.

_T_   3. By 2150, the least industrialized nations are projected to have a total population more than five times that of the most industrialized nations.

_T_   4. In 1800, the total population of the least industrialized nations was only about twice as much as that of the most industrialized nations.

_F_   5. According to the line graph, the least industrialized nations will be able to grow more food to support higher populations in future years.

_F_   6. Since 1750, the population of the most industrialized nations has more than tripled.

_F_   7. Since 1750, the population of the least industrialized nations has increased 25 times.

8. The purpose of the line graph is _to show the number of people in billions_

Flowcharts

A _flowchart_ shows the sequence of a set of elements and the relationships among them. Flowcharts were first used in computer programming. Key ideas are stated in boxes, and supporting ideas are linked by arrows. In the flowchart shown on page 503, arrows point toward a progression of steps required for a bill to become a law in the United States.

Exercise 10.9

Flowcharts

Bills introduced in the U.S. House of Representatives or Senate follow a specific path before being passed into laws. Refer to the flowchart on page 503 to respond to the following statements with _T_ (true), _F_ (false), or _CT_ (can't tell).

_T_   1. If a bill is introduced in the Senate, the chart indicates that it can be debated in the House before it is passed in the Senate.

_F_   2. After both the House and Senate vote on a bill, it goes to the Conference Committee.

3. The House has a Rules Committee action stage that the Senate does not have.

_T_   4. The president can veto and override a bill that has been passed and approved by both the House and Senate.

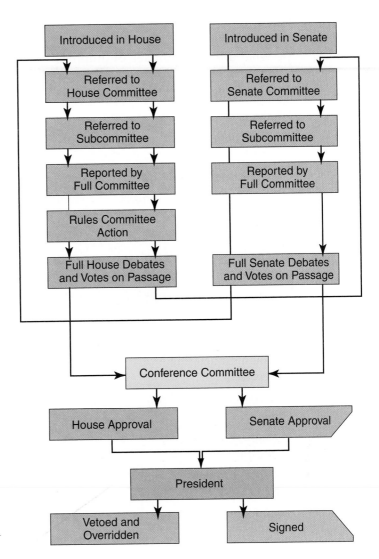

How a Bill Becomes Law
Source: Morris Fiorina, Paul Peterson, and Bertram Johnson, The New American
Democracy, *3rd ed.*

_____ T _____ 5. Full Senate debate on a bill occurs before the full committee
report.

_____ F _____ 6. If a bill has solid support from both the House and Senate,
the president usually signs the bill into law.

7. The purpose of the flowchart is _It shows_
the sequence of a set
of elements and relation
ships among them.

Summary Points

● What are the purposes of graphics?

Graphic illustrations condense, clarify, and convince. They express complex interrelationships in simplified form.

● What is a diagram?

A diagram is an outline drawing or picture of an object or a process with labeled parts.

● What does a table do?

A table lists facts and figures in columns for quick and easy reference. You must determine what the columns represent and how they interact.

● What is most helpful on a typical map?

The legend on a map of a geographic area explains the symbols and shading used to convey information.

● What does a pie graph represent?

A pie graph depicts a total, or 100 percent, divided into wedge-shaped slices.

● How do you read a bar graph?

You must determine what the length of each horizontal or vertical bar represents.

● What is a line graph?

A line graph represents a frequency distribution. To read a point on the continuous line, you must identify what the horizontal and vertical scales measure.

● What information does a flowchart convey?

A flowchart provides a diagram of the relationship and sequence of events of a group of elements. Key ideas usually appear in boxes, and arrows are used to connect the elements.

CONTEMPORARY FOCUS

Student alcohol consumption is a concern on most college campuses, not only in the United States but in other countries such as Australia. To avert the problem, most colleges offer programs to educate students about drinking, hoping that knowledge about how alcohol is processed by the body will influence student alcohol consumption decisions. What kinds of educational programs do you think can make a difference? Do you think abstinence is a realistic and achievable goal? Do you think campus activities should be cancelled for fear of student alcohol abuse?

MESSAGE IN A BOTTLE

Alice Russell

The Age, Melbourne, Australia, June 7, 2004, pg. 6 in Education

Alcohol is an ambiguous substance. It's drunk unceremoniously at family meals. It's an integral part of any sophisticated dinner or celebration. It's considered, in some forms and quantities, to be beneficial to health. It's also a large contributing factor to road deaths, sex assaults and violence, and the drug most likely to harm young Australians.

"Of all the drug issues, alcohol is the biggest one for students," says Richard Midford, associate professor at the National Drug Research Institute. "It often gets a bit lost when people get hysterical about other drug use, but if you look at the statistics, the drug that causes the most immediate harm to students is alcohol."

"The issue for students is drinking large quantities in a short period of time, and being inexperienced, and being in dangerous settings," Professor Midford says.

The consequences, particularly when they involve rowdy celebrations, increasingly draw attention. Schoolies week annually generates media coverage of teenagers who have fuelled the heady mix of post-exam relief and nascent adulthood with generous quantities of alcohol. Recently, two Melbourne schools cancelled end-of-year formal dinners because of the risks associated with the inevitable "after parties".

Over the past few decades, the philosophical approach to drug education has shifted. In the 1970s, abstinence was the usual aim. That's still popular in America but here is mostly considered unrealistic and unachievable. The current "harm minimisation" approach acknowledges that most young people will at least experiment and works to help them reduce the associated dangers.

With alcohol, this means focusing on strategies to avoid the risks that can come with being drunk: risks of violence, of road accidents, of being vulnerable to sexual assault.

Collaborate

Collaborate on responses to the following questions:

- How does college drinking adversely affect you?
- Why do some college organization promote excessive drinking?
- What can realistically be done to limit college drinking?

Skill Development: Preview

Preview the next selection to predict its purpose and organization and to formulate your learning plan.

Activate Schema

What is the legal limit on a breathalyzer test for driving a car?

How much alcohol is considered to constitute one drink?

Can an intoxicated person sober up by drinking coffee or water?

Establish a Purpose for Reading

Most people are aware of alcohol's intoxicating effects, but did you know that the brain shrinks in people who drink even moderately? In what other ways does alcohol affect the brain and internal organs? What are the long-term toxic effects of alcohol on the metabolic, digestive, and immune systems? After recalling what you already know about the effects of alcohol on the body, read the selection to discover the serious consequences of alcohol abuse.

Increase Word Knowledge

What do you know about these words?

counterparts	diffuse	sedating	lethal	toxic
enhanced	prudent	ruefully	abstinence	devastates

Your instructor may give a true-false vocabulary review before or after reading.

Skill Development: Integrate Knowledge While Reading

Questions have been inserted in the margin to stimulate your thinking while reading. Remember to

Predict	Picture	Relate	Monitor	Correct

ALCOHOL AND NUTRITION
From Eva May Nunnelley Hamilton et al., *Nutrition*

People naturally congregate to enjoy conversation and companionship, and it is natural, too, to offer beverages to companions. All beverages ease conversation whether or not they contain alcohol. Still, some people choose alcohol over cola, milk, or coffee, and they should know a few things about alcohol's
5 short-term and long-term effects on health. One consideration is energy—alcohol yields energy to the body, and many alcoholic drinks are much more fattening than their nonalcoholic counterparts. Additionally, alcohol has a tremendous impact on the overall well-being of the body.

People consume alcohol in servings they call "a drink." However, the serving
10 that some people consider one drink may not be the same as the standard drink that delivers ½ ounce pure ethanol:

> 3 to 4 ounces wine
> 10 ounces wine cooler
> 12 ounces beer
> 1 ounce hard liquor (whiskey, gin, brandy, rum, vodka)

The percentage of alcohol in distilled liquor is stated as *proof:* 100-proof liquor is 50 percent alcohol; 90-proof is 45 percent, and so forth. Compared with hard liquor, beer and wine have a relatively low percentage of alcohol.

Alcohol Enters the Body

15 From the moment an alcoholic beverage is swallowed, the body confers special status on it. Unlike foods, which require digestion, the tiny alcohol molecules are all ready to be absorbed; they can diffuse right through the walls of an empty stomach and reach the brain within a minute. A person can become intoxicated almost immediately when drinking, especially if the person's
20 stomach is empty. When the stomach is full of food, molecules of alcohol have less chance of touching the walls and diffusing through, so alcohol affects the brain a little less immediately. (By the time the stomach contents are emptied into the small intestine, it doesn't matter that food is mixed with the alcohol. The alcohol is absorbed rapidly anyway.)

25 A practical pointer derives from this information. If a person wants to drink socially and not become intoxicated, the person should eat the snacks provided by the host (avoid the salty ones; they make you thirstier). Carbohydrate snacks are best suited for slowing alcohol absorption. High-fat snacks help too because they slow peristalsis, keeping the alcohol in the stomach longer.

30 If one drinks slowly enough, the alcohol, after absorption, will be collected into the liver and processed without much affecting other parts of the body. If one drinks more rapidly, however, some of the alcohol bypasses the liver and flows for a while through the rest of the body and the brain.

What is "slowly enough"?

Alcohol Arrives in the Brain

People use alcohol today as a kind of social anesthetic to help them relax or to
relieve anxiety. One drink relieves inhibitions, and this gives people the
impression that alcohol is a stimulant. Actually the way it does this is by
sedating *inhibitory* nerves, allowing excitatory nerves to take over. This is temporary. Ultimately alcohol acts as a depressant and sedates all the nerve cells.
Figure R1 describes alcohol's effects on the brain.

It is lucky that the brain centers respond to elevating blood alcohol in the
order described in Figure R1 because a person usually passes out before managing to drink a lethal dose. It is possible, though, for a person to drink fast
enough so that the effects of alcohol continue to accelerate after the person
has gone to sleep. The occasional death that takes place during a drinking con-
test is attributed to this effect. The drinker drinks fast enough, before passing
out, to receive a lethal dose. Table R1 shows the blood alcohol levels that cor-
respond with progressively greater intoxication, and Table R2 shows the brain
responses that occur at these blood levels.

Brain cells are particularly sensitive to excessive exposure to alcohol. The
brain shrinks, even in people who drink only moderately. The extent of the
shrinkage is proportional to the amount drunk. Abstinence, together with
good nutrition, reverses some of the brain damage—possibly all of it if heavy

Is this how students die?

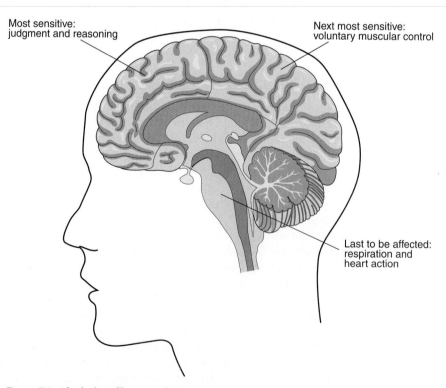

Figure R1. Alcohol's Effects on the Brain

Table R1   **Alcohol Doses and Blood Levels**

	Percent Blood Alcohol by Body Weight				
Number of Drinks[a]	**100 lb**	**120 lb**	**150 lb**	**180 lb**	**200 lb**
2	0.08	0.06	0.05	0.04	0.04
4	0.15	0.13	0.10	0.08	0.08
6	0.23	0.19	0.15	0.13	0.11
8	0.30	0.25	0.20	0.17	0.15
12	0.45	0.36	0.30	0.25	0.23
14	0.52	0.42	0.35	0.34	0.27

[a]*Taken within an hour or so.*

Table R2   **Alcohol Blood Levels and Brain Responses**

Blood Level (%)	**Brain Response**
0.05	Judgment impaired
0.10	Emotional control impaired
0.15	Muscle coordination and reflexes impaired
0.20	Vision impaired
0.30	Drunk, totally out of control
0.35	Stupor
0.50–0.60	Total loss of consciousness, finally death

14

drinking has not continued for more than a few years—but prolonged drinking beyond an individual's capacity to recover can cause severe and irreversible effects on vision, memory, learning ability, and other functions.

55   Anyone who has had an alcoholic drink knows that alcohol increases urine output. This is because alcohol depresses the brain's production of **antidiuretic hormone.** Loss of body water leads to thirst. The only fluid that will relieve dehydration is water, but if alcohol is the only drink available, the thirsty person may choose another alcoholic beverage and worsen the problem. The

60   smart drinker, then, alternates alcoholic beverages with nonalcoholic choices and when thirsty chooses the latter.

The water loss caused by hormone depression involves loss of more than just water. The water takes with it important minerals, such as magnesium, potassium, calcium, and zinc, depleting the body's reserves. These minerals are vital to the maintenance of fluid balance and to nerve and muscle action and coordination.

Alcohol Arrives in the Liver

The capillaries that surround the digestive tract merge into veins that carry the alcohol-laden blood to the liver. Here the veins branch and rebranch into capillaries that touch every liver cell. The liver cells make nearly all of the body's alcohol-processing machinery, and the routing of blood through the liver allows the cells to go right to work on the alcohol. The liver's location at this point along the circulatory system guarantees that it gets the chance to remove toxic substances before they reach other body organs such as the heart and brain.

The liver makes and maintains two sets of equipment for metabolizing alcohol. One is an enzyme that removes hydrogen from alcohol to break it down; the name almost says what it does—**alcohol dehydrogenase (ADH)**.[1] This handles about 80 percent or more of body alcohol. The other alcohol-metabolizing equipment is a chain of enzymes (known as the **MEOS**) thought to handle about 10 to 20 percent of body alcohol. With high blood alcohol concentrations, the MEOS activity is enhanced, as will be shown later. But let us look at the ADH system first.

The amount of alcohol a person's body can process in a given time is limited by the number of ADH enzymes that reside in the liver.[2] If more molecules of alcohol arrive at the liver cells than the enzymes can handle, the extra alcohol must wait. It enters the general circulation and is carried to all parts of the body, circulating again and again through the liver until enzymes are available to degrade it.

The number of ADH enzymes present is affected by whether or not a person eats. Fasting for as little as a day causes degradation of body proteins, including the ADH enzymes in the liver, and this can reduce the rate of alcohol metabolism by half. Prudent drinkers drink slowly, with food in their stomachs, to allow the alcohol molecules to move to the liver cells gradually enough for the enzymes to handle the load. It takes about an hour and a half to metabolize one drink, depending on a person's body size, on previous drinking experience, on how recently the person has eaten, and on general

---

[1] There are actually two ADH enzymes, each for a specific task in alcohol breakdown. Enzyme 1, alcohol dehydrogenase, converts alcohol to acetaldehyde. Enzyme 2, acetaldehyde dehydrogenase, converts acetaldehyde to a common body compound, acetyl CoA, identical to that derived from carbohydrate and fat during their breakdown.

[2] Some ADH enzymes reside in the stomach, offering a protective barrier against alcohol entering the blood. Research shows that alcoholics make less stomach ADH, and so do women. Women may absorb about one-third more alcohol than men, even when they are the same size and drink the same amount of alcoholic beverage.

health at the time. The liver is the only organ that can dispose of significant
quantities of alcohol, and its maximum rate of alcohol clearance is fixed.
100   This explains why only time will restore sobriety. Walking will not; muscles
cannot metabolize alcohol. Nor will it help to drink a cup of coffee. Caffeine
is a stimulant, but it won't speed up the metabolism of alcohol. The police
say ruefully that a cup of coffee will only make a sleepy drunk into a wide-
awake drunk.

105   As the ADH enzymes break alcohol down, they produce hydrogen ions

Chart this
complex process
to understand.

(acid), which must be picked up by a compound that contains the B vitamin
niacin as part of its structure. Normally this acid is disposed of through a
metabolic pathway, but when alcohol is present in the system, this pathway
shuts down. The niacin-containing compound remains loaded with hydrogens
110   that it cannot get rid of and so becomes unavailable for a multitude of other
vital body processes for which it is required.

The synthesis of fatty acids also accelerates as a result of the liver's exposure to alcohol. Fat accumulation can be seen in the liver after a single night of
heavy drinking. **Fatty liver,** the first stage of liver deterioration seen in heavy
115   drinkers, interferes with the distribution of nutrients and oxygen to the liver
cells. If the condition lasts long enough, the liver cells die, and fibrous scar tissue invades the area—the second stage of liver deterioration called **fibrosis.**
Fibrosis is reversible with good nutrition and abstinence from alcohol, but the
next (last) stage—**cirrhosis**—is not. All of this points to the importance of
120   moderation in the use of alcohol.

The presence of alcohol alters amino acid metabolism in the liver cells.
Synthesis of some proteins important in the immune system slows down,
weakening the body's defenses against infection. Synthesis of lipoproteins
speeds up, increasing blood triglyceride levels. In addition, excessive alcohol
125   increases the body's acid burden and interferes with normal uric acid metabolism, causing symptoms like those of **gout.**

Liver metabolism clears most of the alcohol from the blood. However,
about 10 percent is excreted through the breath and in the urine. This fact is
the basis for the breathalyzer test that law enforcement officers administer
130   when they suspect someone of driving under the influence of alcohol.

Alcohol's Long-Term Effects

By far the longest-term effects of alcohol are those felt by the child of a
woman who drinks during pregnancy. Pregnant women should not drink at
all. For nonpregnant adults, however, what are the effects of alcohol over the
long term?

135   A couple of drinks set in motion many destructive processes in the body,
but the next day's abstinence reverses them. As long as the doses taken are
moderate, time between them is ample, and nutrition is adequate meanwhile,
recovery is probably complete.

If the doses of alcohol are heavy and the time between them is short,
140   complete recovery cannot take place, and repeated onslaughts of alcohol

gradually take a toll on the body. For example, alcohol is directly toxic to skeletal and cardiac muscle, causing weakness and deterioration in a dose-related manner. Alcoholism makes heart disease more likely probably because alcohol in high doses raises the blood pressure. Cirrhosis can
145 develop after 10 to 20 years from the additive effects of frequent heavy drinking episodes. Alcohol abuse also increases a person's risk of cancer of the mouth, throat, esophagus, rectum, and lungs. Women who drink even moderately may run an increased risk of developing breast cancer. Although some dispute these findings, a reliable source tentatively ranks daily human
150 exposure to ethanol as high in relation to other possible carcinogenic hazards. Other long-term effects of alcohol abuse include:

Ulcers of the stomach and intestines
Psychological depression
Kidney damage, bladder damage, prostate gland damage, pancreas damage
Skin rashes and sores
Impaired immune response
Deterioration in the testicles and adrenal glands, leading to feminization and sexual impotence in men
Central nervous system damage
Malnutrition
Increased risk of violent death

This list is by no means all inclusive. Alcohol has direct toxic effects, independent of the effect of malnutrition, on all body organs.
The more alcohol a person drinks, the less likely that he or she will eat
155 enough food to obtain adequate nutrients. Alcohol is empty calories, like pure sugar and pure fat; it displaces nutrients. In a sense, each time you drink 150 calories of alcohol, you are spending those calories on a luxury item and getting no nutritional value in return. The more calories you spend this way, the fewer you have left to spend on nutritious foods. Table R3 shows the calorie
160 amounts of typical alcoholic beverages.

Make a list of effects.

Alcohol abuse not only displaces nutrients from the diet but also affects every tissue's metabolism of nutrients. Alcohol causes stomach cells to oversecrete both acid and an agent of the immune system, histamine, that produces inflammation. These changes make the stomach and esophagus linings vulnerable to
165 ulcer formation. Intestinal cells fail to absorb thiamin, folate, and vitamin B_{12}. Liver cells lose efficiency in activating vitamin D and alter their production and excretion of bile. Rod cells in the retina, which normally process vitamin A alcohol (retinol) to the form needed in vision, find themselves processing drinking alcohol instead. The kidneys excrete magnesium, calcium, potassium, and zinc.
170 Alcohol's intermediate products interfere with metabolism too. They dislodge vitamin B_6 from its protective binding protein so that it is destroyed, causing a vitamin B_6 deficiency and thereby lowered production of red blood cells.
Most dramatic is alcohol's effect on folate. When alcohol is present, it is as though the body were actively trying to expel folate from all its sites of action

Table R3 **Calories in Alcoholic Beverages and Mixers**		
Beverage	**Amount (ounces)**	**Energy (calories)**
Beer	12	150
Light beer	12	100
Gin, rum, vodka, whiskey (86 proof)	$1\frac{1}{2}$	105
Dessert wine	$3\frac{1}{2}$	140
Table wine	$3\frac{1}{2}$	85
Tonic, ginger ale, other sweetened carbonated waters	8	80
Cola, root beer	8	100
Fruit-flavored soda, Tom Collins mix	8	115
Club soda, plain seltzer, diet drinks	8	1

175 and storage. The liver, which normally contains enough folate to meet all needs, leaks folate into the blood. As the blood folate concentration rises, the kidneys are deceived into excreting it, as though it were in excess. The intestine normally releases and retrieves folate continuously, but it becomes damaged by folate deficiency and alcohol toxicity; so it fails to retrieve its own folate and misses out on
180 any that may trickle in from food as well. Alcohol also interferes with the action of what little folate is left, and this inhibits the production of new cells, especially the rapidly dividing cells of the intestine and the blood. Alcohol abuse causes a folate deficiency that devastates digestive system function.

Nutrient deficiencies are thus a virtually inevitable consequence of alcohol
185 abuse, not only because alcohol displaces food but also because alcohol directly interferes with the body's use of nutrients, making them ineffective even if they are present. Over a lifetime, excessive drinking, whether or not accompanied by attention to nutrition, brings about deficits of all the nutrients mentioned in this discussion and many more besides.

Alcohol and Drugs

190 The liver's reaction to alcohol affects its handling of drugs as well as nutrients. In addition to the ADH enzymes, the liver possesses an enzyme system that metabolizes *both* alcohol and drugs—any compounds that have certain chemical features in common. As mentioned earlier, at low blood alcohol concentrations, the MEOS handles about 10 to 20 percent of the alcohol consumed.
195 However, at high blood alcohol concentrations, or if repeatedly exposed to alcohol, the MEOS is enhanced.

As a person's blood alcohol concentration rises, the alcohol competes with—and wins out over—other drugs whose metabolism relies on the MEOS. If a person drinks and uses another drug at the same time, the drug
200   will be metabolized more slowly and so will be much more potent. The MEOS is busy disposing of alcohol, so the drug cannot be handled until later; the dose may build up to where its effects are greatly amplified—sometimes to the point of killing the user.

In contrast, once a heavy drinker stops drinking and alcohol is not present to
205   compete with other drugs, the enhanced MEOS metabolizes those drugs much faster than before. This can make it confusing and tricky to work out the correct dosages of medications. The doctor who prescribes sedatives every four hours, for example, unaware that the person has recently gone from being a heavy drinker to an abstainer, expects the MEOS to dispose of the drug at a certain predicted
210   rate. The MEOS is adapted to metabolizing large quantities of alcohol, however. It therefore metabolizes the drug extra fast. The drug's effects wear off unex-

> Be careful with medicine. ⟶ pectedly fast, leaving the client undersedated. Imagine the doctor's alarm should a patient wake up on the table during an operation! A skilled anesthesiologist always asks the patient about his drinking pattern before putting him to sleep.

215   This discussion has touched on some of the ways alcohol affects health and nutrition. Despite some possible benefits of moderate alcohol consumption, the potential for harm is great, especially with excessive alcohol consumption. Consider that over 50 percent of all fatal auto accidents are alcohol related. Translated to human lives, more than 25,000 people die each year in alcohol-related
220   traffic accidents. The best way to avoid the harmful effects of alcohol is, of course, to avoid alcohol altogether. If you do drink, do so with care—for yourself and for others—and in moderation.

Skill Development: Recall

Stop to self-test, relate, and react.

Your instructor may choose to give you a true-false comprehension review.

Write About the Selection

Use the information in this selection to write a letter to a friend who drinks and drives. In a scientific manner, explain to your friend why driving after having a few drinks is dangerous.

Contemporary Link

How should your college organize an educational program on alcohol abuse? What should be the goals of the program, what content should be covered, and how should it be presented to students? Explain how you would design a program to engage students rather than turn them off.

Skill Development: Graphics

Refer to the designated graphic and answer the following items with T (true) or F (false).

_____ 1. According to Figure R1, alcohol first affects muscular control.

_____ 2. According to Table R1, a person who has two drinks and weighs 120 pounds would have 13 percent blood alcohol level.

_____ 3. According to Table R2, a blood alcohol level of 0.35 will cause a stupor.

_____ 4. According to Tables R1 and R2, a person weighing 150 pounds who has eight drinks would have impaired vision.

_____ 5. According to Table R3, vodka has more calories than rum.

Check Your Comprehension

After reading the selection, answer the following questions with a, b, c, or d. To help you analyze your strengths and weaknesses, the question types are indicated.

Main Idea _____ 1. What is the best statement of the main idea of this selection?
   a. Alcohol is involved in more than half the fatal auto accidents each year.
   b. Alcohol is processed by the liver.
   c. Alcohol is a drug rather than a food.
   d. Alcohol is a drug that has complex and interrelated effects on the body.

Detail _____ 2. When the stomach is full of food, alcohol
   a. goes directly to the liver.
   b. bypasses the liver for the bloodstream.
   c. affects the brain less immediately.
   d. rapidly diffuses through the walls of the stomach.

Detail _____ 3. The brain responds to elevated blood alcohol in all the following ways except
   a. loss of consciousness.
   b. shrinking.
   c. sedating nerve cells.
   d. increasing production of antidiuretic hormones.

Detail _____ 4. Most of the body's processing of alcohol is done by the
   a. liver.
   b. brain.

c. stomach.
d. blood.

Detail   _____ 5. Alcohol reaches the liver through
a. direct absorption.
b. veins and capillaries.
c. the intestines.
d. loss of body water.

Detail   _____ 6. When enzymes are not available to degrade the total amount of alcohol consumed, this extra alcohol that cannot be immediately processed by the liver
a. waits in the liver for enzymes to become available.
b. circulates to all parts of the body.
c. is metabolized by the MEOS.
d. is sent to the stomach for storage.

Detail   _____ 7. All the following are true about ADH except
a. its production can be accelerated to meet increased demand.
b. it removes hydrogen from the alcohol.
c. the number of ADH enzymes is affected by the presence of food in the stomach.
d. ADH enzymes can reside in the stomach.

Detail   _____ 8. The destruction of vitamin B6 by alcohol results in
a. the excretion of bile.
b. a reduction in the number of red blood cells.
c. the oversecretion of acid and histamine.
d. loss of retinol by the rod cells in the eye.

Detail   _____ 9. The negative influence of alcohol on production of new cells is due to
a. folate excretion.
b. ulcer formation.
c. esophagus inflammation.
d. carcinogenic hazards.

Detail   _____ 10. If a doctor knows that a patient has recently progressed from being a heavy drinker to an abstainer, the doctor should expect that prescribed drugs will be metabolized
a. at a normal rate.
b. slower than normal.
c. faster than normal.
d. only when the MEOS has returned to normal.

Answer the following with *T* (true) or *F* (false):

Inference   _____ 11. The sentence in the first paragraph, "All beverages ease conversation whether or not they contain alcohol," is a statement of fact.

Detail   _____ 12. Carbohydrate snacks slow alcohol absorption.

Detail   _____ 13. Alcohol can bypass the liver and flow directly to the brain.

Detail   _____ 14. High doses of alcohol can raise blood pressure.

Detail   _____ 15. Men absorb alcohol faster than women.

Build Your Vocabulary

According to the way the italicized word was used in the selection, indicate *a, b, c,* or *d* for the word or phrase that gives the best definition. The number in parentheses indicates the line of the passage in which the word is located.

_____ 1. "their nonalcoholic *counterparts*" (7)
a. duplicates
b. sugars
c. energy sources
d. stimulants

_____ 2. "*diffuse* right through the walls" (17)
a. disappear
b. weaken
c. stick together
d. spread widely

_____ 3. "*sedating* inhibitory nerves" (37)
a. soothing
b. connecting
c. closing
d. exciting

_____ 4. "drink a *lethal* dose" (42)
a. complete
b. large
c. legal
d. deadly

_____ 5. "remove *toxic* substances" (74)
a. inhibiting
b. foreign
c. poisonous
d. digestive

_____ 6. "MEOS activity is *enhanced*" (82)
a. increased
b. condensed
c. redirected
d. consolidated

_____ 7. "*Prudent* drinkers" (93)
a. older
b. wise
c. experienced
d. addicted

_____ 8. "police say *ruefully*" (102)
a. happily
b. angrily
c. mournfully
d. humorously

_____ 9. "next day's *abstinence*" (136)
a. headache
b. sickness
c. repentance
d. giving up drinking

_____ 10. "*devastates* digestive system" (183)
a. destroys
b. divides
c. follows
d. loosens

Search the Net

Use a search engine such as Google, AltaVista, Excite, Infoseek, Dogpile, Yahoo, or Lycos to find information on several treatment programs for alcoholism. Explain how they differ. For suggested Web sites and other research activities, go to http://www.ablongman.com/smith/.

Concept Prep

for Life Science

How are living things organized?

The **life sciences,** sometimes called biology, encompass the study and classification of the millions of living things on earth, from the tiniest microorganisms to the largest ecosystems. Biologists organize life into a hierarchy of structural levels, with each level building on the level below it. The basic unit of life is the **cell,** which has reproductive powers and contains **genes,** the units of inheritance, which are made of DNA.

A recent system of classification divides all organisms into two major groups: **prokaryotes** and **eukaryotes.** Prokaryotes, which are bacteria and blue-green algae, have very simple cells with no distinct subcellular structures. Comprising all other forms of life, eukaryotes are more complex cells with structures called **organelles** and a **nucleus** containing DNA.

Eukaryotes are divided into four groups: (1) **protists,** which have only a single cell; (2) **animals,** which are multicellular and obtain energy by eating other organisms; (3) **fungi,** which are multicellular and obtain energy by absorbing food directly through their cell membranes; and (4) **plants,** which are multicellular and use light energy to make food. The five major groups of living things (prokaryotes and the four eukaryote groups) are referred to as the **five kingdoms** of living things.

The five kingdoms are subdivided into **phyla** (plural for **phylum**) for animals and **divisions** for plants and plantlike protists. These groups are then further divided into classes, orders, families, genera, and finally into single **species,** particular groups of organisms with shared characteristics that can mate and produce fertile offspring. The scientists who study animals are **zoologists,** and those who study plants are **botanists**.

What is natural selection?

One of the great contributions to biology was made by the British naturalist **Charles Darwin** (1809–1882). As a young man in 1831, Darwin set sail on **HMS Beagle** to help chart the South American coastline. He observed nature, kept records, and collected specimens. By the mid-1800s, Charles Darwin presented a logical argument for evolution in his book, **On the Origin of Species.** He used his observations on the coast and the **Galapagos Islands** to explain **natural selection,** a process in which organisms adapt to their envi-

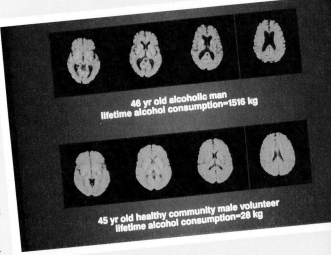

An MRI of the brain of an alcoholic male (top) *shows damage compared with an MRI of the brain of a healthy male* (bottom).
Illustration courtesy of Dr. Adolf Pfefferbaum of SRI International and Stanford University, with support from the National Institute on Alcohol Abuse and Alcoholism (NIAAA).

ronment with varying degrees of success. The organisms that are best adapted are those that survive, reproduce, and pass their characteristics to the next generation. Over time, natural selection thus works as a natural editing process that favors traits best suited to the environment.

What is genetic engineering?

Another important contribution to the life sciences was made by **Gregor Mendel** (1822–1884), an Austrian monk born in what is today the Czech Republic. Mendel discovered the basic **laws of genetics** by experimenting with the size, seed appearance, and flower color of pea plants. He was the first person to experiment and reason that genetic traits are inherited as separate particles from each parent. Today those separate particles are known as genes. Genes are made of **DNA,** the molecule that carries genetic information in all living things, and are studied by **geneticists.**

DNA can be manipulated by **genetic engineering** to produce modified organisms, such as disease-resistant crops, by inserting or deleting genes. Through **cloning,** scientists now have the capability to reproduce identical organisms.

The most recent controversy in genetics involves **stem cell research,** the extraction of stem cells from the inner core of a newly fertilized human embryo for medical experimentation. Scientists say they can trigger these stem cells to grow tissues to treat spinal cord injuries and diseases such as heart failure, Alzheimer's, Parkinson's, diabetes, and cancer.

REVIEW QUESTIONS

After studying the material, answer the following questions:

1. What is the basic unit of life? _____

2. How do prokaryotes differ from eukaryotes? _____

   _____

3. Are plants and animals eukaryotes or prokaryotes? _____

4. In the classification system, how does a phylum relate to a species? _____

   _____

5. What was the contribution of Charles Darwin? _____

   _____

6. Why do the characteristics of a species change over time through natural selection? _____

   _____

7. What area of life science did Mendel research? _____

8. What is DNA? _____

9. What is genetic engineering? _____

10. What is a clone? _____

Your instructor may choose to give a true-false review of these life science concepts.

Vocabulary Booster

Play It Again, Sam

Prefix Root
re-: back, again   *lud-, lus-:* to play

Words with *re-:* back, again

Although Humphrey Bogart never said the line "Play it again, Sam" in the movie *Casablanca*, it has been *repeatedly* attributed to his character, Rick.

- *reconcile:* to cause to become friendly or peaceable again; to cause one to accept something not desired

  The purpose of the peace conference was to get the opposing sides to *reconcile* their differences and find a way to coexist in the region.

- *reconstruct:* to build again; to create again in the mind from available information

  The witness to the auto accident was asked by the police officer to *reconstruct* from memory the events leading up to the crash.

- *recriminate:* to bring a countercharge against an accuser

  Melissa feared that legally accusing her ex-husband of being an unfit father would cause him to *recriminate* against her as an unfit mother.

- *refrain:* to keep oneself from doing something

  I had to *refrain* from laughing when the professor walked into class wearing bedroom slippers.

- *regress:* to revert to an earlier or less advanced state

  The paralyzed patient had been making progress in physical therapy, but suddenly she *regressed* to being unable to walk a single step.

- *reiterate:* to say or do repeatedly

  The infomercial *reiterated* the cleaning product's claims until I became annoyed at hearing over and over how white my shirts could be.

- *rejuvenate:* to make young again; to make new again

  The facial product line was promoted as being able to *rejuvenate* a user's skin by reducing wrinkles and uneven skin tones within two weeks with a money back guarantee.

- *renege:* to go back on one's word

  Daniel had to *renege* on his promise to drive his friends to the football game after his father refused to lend him the car.

- *repel:* to push away by force; to fail to mix with; to resist absorption; to cause distaste in

  Oil and water do not mix; rather, they *repel* each other.

- *repercussion:* an effect of some previous action; recoil after impact; reverberation

  Excessive running on pavement can have serious *repercussions* on your health, such as wearing out the knee joints from the constant impact.

- *retract:* to withdraw a statement or opinion as inaccurate; to withdraw a promise

  Celebrities often sue magazines or newspapers asking for *retractions* of inaccurate statements printed about them.

- *revenge*: to inflict pain or harm in return for a wrong received; to get even or get satisfaction

  Cindy's *revenge* for Sonia's lies was not inviting Sonia to the best party of the year.

Words with *lud-, lus-:* to play

The *prelude* or introductory piece of music to an opera is called an overture.

- *ludicrous:* causing laughter because of absurdity; ridiculous

  Durwood looked *ludicrous* in the extremely short haircut that made his ears stick out.

- *allude:* to refer casually or indirectly to

  He will *allude* to his days as a football star whenever the guys start discussing sports.

- *allusion:* a casual or passing reference to something, either direct or implied

  A casual *allusion* to Shakespeare would be to call him the Bard.

- *interlude:* any intermediate performance or entertainment, such as between the acts of a play

  The instrumental *interlude* between the verses of the song had a melancholy sound.

- *delude:* to mislead the mind or judgment of

  Jonathan felt silly when he realized the two con artists who tricked him out of his money had *deluded* him.

- *elude:* to avoid capture; to escape perception or comprehension of

  The reason for her popularity *eludes* me; I just don't get it.

- *illusion*: an unreal or misleading appearance or image

  Faux finishes like marbleizing a column with paint create an inexpensive *illusion* in home decorating.

Review

Part I

Indicate whether the italicized words are used correctly (C) or incorrectly (I) in the following sentences:

_____C_____ 1. It is best to *reconcile* oneself to the fact that college requires a certain amount of studying.

_____C_____ 2. Trying to *refrain* from smoking is difficult for many people who have become addicted to nicotine.

_____I_____ 3. Trompe l'oeil, literally meaning "fool the eye" in French, is a form of painting that creates an *allusion* that appears to be real.

_____C_____ 4. Martin is extremely naive and easy to *delude* by playing upon his trusting nature.

_____C_____ 5. The twins knew that missing their curfew again would cause serious *repercussions* from their parents.

_____C_____ 6. Denise *regressed* on her promise to lend her new dress to her sister for an important date.

_____I_____ 7. The newspaper issued a formal *retraction* of the previous day's incorrect story about the mayor accepting a bribe in exchange for awarding a contract for services.

_____I_____ 8. The escaped convict managed to *allude* capture until after dark.

_____C_____ 9. The organist performed a *prelude* as the church filled before the christening ceremony.

_____C_____ 10. The witness was able to *recriminate* the robbery suspect from a police lineup.

Part II

Indicate whether the following statements are true (T) or false (F):

_____T_____ 11. To reconstruct is to rebuild.

_____F_____ 12. *Reiterate* is another word for repeat.

_____T_____ 13. A neighbor who feels mistreated might possibly seek revenge.

_____F_____ 14. If sensitive people engage in ludicrous behavior, they risk having their feelings hurt when others laugh at them.

_T_ _____ 15. An interlude comes at the beginning of a song.

_T_ _____ 16. A soaking wet raincoat is one that has failed to repel the rain.

_T_ _____ 17. To rejuvenate a piece of furniture is to antique it to make it look old.

_F_ _____ 18. A message that is completely understood is a message that has eluded everyone.

_F_ _____ 19. You can be easily trusted if you can be relied on to renege on your word.

_T_ _____ 20. Having an illusion about a friend's true character is not seeing him for what he really is.

11

Rate Flexibility

- What is your reading rate?
- How fast should you read?
- How do faster readers maintain a better reading rate?
- What are some techniques for faster reading?
- What happens during regression?
- Why skim?
- What is scanning?

Red Cross Train Passing a Village (Train de la Croix Rouge traversant un village by Gino Severini, Summer 1915. Oil on canvas, 35 x 45 3/4" (88.9 x 16.2 cm). Solomon R. Guggenheim Museum, New York, 44.944. © 2006 Artist Rights Society (ARS), New York/ADAGP, Paris.

Why Is Rate Important?

Professors of college reading are far more concerned with comprehension than with a student's rate of reading. They would say that students should not attempt to "speed read" textbooks, and they would be right.

However, when students are asked what they would like to change about their reading, most will say, "I read too slowly. I would like to improve my reading speed." Whether or not this perception is accurate, rate is definitely a concern of college students. Whether you are reading a magazine or a textbook, reading 150 words per minute takes twice as long as reading 300 words per minute. Understanding the factors that contribute to rate can both quell anxiety and help increase reading efficiency.

What Is Your Reading Rate?

How many words do you read on the average each minute? To find out, read the following selection at your usual reading rate, just as you would have read it before you started thinking about speed. Time your reading of the selection so that you can calculate your rate. Read carefully enough to answer the ten comprehension questions that follow the selection.

Exercise 11.1

Assessing Rate

Time your reading of this selection so that you can compute your words-per-minute rate. To make the calculations easier, try to begin reading on the exact minute, with zero seconds. Record your starting and finishing times in minutes and seconds, and then determine your rate from the rate chart at the end of the passage. Answer the ten questions that follow, and determine your comprehension rate by calculating the percentage of correct answers. Remember, read the selection at your normal rate.

Starting time: _____ minutes _____ seconds

Sea Lions

"Hey, you guys, hurry up? They're gonna feed the seals!" No visit to the zoo or the circus would be complete without the playful antics of the trained "seal." However, the noisy animal that barks enthusiastically while balancing a ball on its nose is not really a seal at all. In reality, it is a small species of sea lion.

Like all mammals, sea lions are air breathers. Nevertheless, they spend most of their lives in the ocean and are skilled and graceful swimmers. Two species live off the Pacific coast of North America. The California sea lion is the smaller and more southerly. This is the circus "seal." An adult male may measure over seven feet in length and weigh more than 500 pounds. Females are considerably smaller, with a length of six feet and a weight of 200 pounds.

The larger northern, or Steller, sea lion lives off the Alaskan shore in summer and off the California coast in winter. Bulls may weigh over a ton and reach a length of more than eleven feet. Cows weigh some 750 pounds and are about nine feet long. The northern sea lion is generally not as noisy as the California sea lion, but it can bellow loudly when it wants to make its presence known.

At one time, sea lions were hunted almost to extinction for their hides, meat, and oil. Eskimos even stored the valuable oil in pouches made from the sea lion's stomach. Today, sea lions are protected by law, but many fall prey to their natural enemies, the shark and the killer whale. Sea lions are often disliked and sometimes killed by fishermen who accuse them of eating valuable fish and damaging nets. For the most part, the accusations are untrue. The northern sea lion eats mostly "trash fish," which are of little commercial value. The California sea lion prefers squid. Although sea lions do eat salmon, they also eat lampreys, a snakelike parasitic fish that devours salmon in great numbers. By controlling the lamprey population, the sea lion probably saves more salmon than it eats.

Sea lions come ashore in early summer to give birth and to mate. First to arrive are the bulls, which immediately stake out individual territories along the beach. The cows follow and soon give birth to the single pup that each has been carrying since the previous summer. The newborn pup has about a dozen teeth. Its big blue eyes are open from birth and will turn brown after a few weeks.

The pup is born into a tumultuous world of huge, bellowing adults, and it must mature quickly to avoid being trampled by the teeming mob around it. It can move about within an hour, and can be seen scrambling nimbly among its elders within a few days. It doubles its weight in the first month or two. The quick weight gain is largely attributable to the extremely rich milk of the sea lion mother. Low in water and high in protein, the milk is almost 50 percent fat, whereas cow's milk is about 4 percent fat. Zookeepers have found it difficult to provide sea lion pups with adequate nourishment in the absence of the mother. At Marineland of the Pacific, an orphaned pup was successfully raised on a diet of whipping cream, liquefied mackerel muscle, calcium caseinate, and a multivitamin syrup. Not a very delectable-sounding menu, perhaps, but the pup loved it.

Throw a human infant into the ocean and it would drown. So would a sea lion baby. The only mammals that are known to swim from birth are whales and manatees. Although it will spend most of its twenty-year life in the ocean, the sea lion pup is at first terrified of water. The mother must spend about two months teaching it to swim.

Mating is no quiet affair among the sea lions. Almost immediately after the birth of the pups the huge bulls begin to wage bloody battles, trying to keep control of their harems of about a dozen cows. Using their long canine teeth as weapons, they fight with great ferocity for possession of the females. Fighting and mating consume so much of the bulls' time and energy during this period that little time is left for sleeping or eating.

At the end of the summer, the sea lions return to the ocean. The bulls, thin and scarred after a busy breeding season, regain their lost weight with several months of active feeding. As the weather grows colder, the huge northern sea lions begin their southward migration, leaving deserted the northern beaches which in warm weather were covered with their massive dark bodies.

The sea lion has to adapt to a considerable range of climate conditions. Its thick blubber and rapid metabolism are assets in the cold northern waters. But the California sea lion ranges as far south as the Galapagos Islands off the coast of South America. How does it adapt to a hot and dry environment?

The most important thing that the sea lion does to stay cool is to sleep in the daytime and take care of business during the cooler night hours. Sea lions in warm climates spend a great deal of time sleeping on the wet sand. Their bodies are designed in such a way that a large surface of the torso comes in contact with the cool ground when the animal lies down. About 10 percent of body heat can be lost in this way. Furthermore, the animal produces nearly 25 percent less heat while it sleeps than it does when awake and active.

Unfortunately, none of the sea lion's cooling mechanisms are highly effective. Ultimately, the animal relies on immersion in the ocean to keep itself cool.

Victor A. Greulach and Vincent J. Chiappetta, *Biology*

958 words

Finishing time: _____ minutes _____ seconds

Reading time in seconds: _____

Words per minute: _____

Time (Min.)	Words per Minute	Time (Min.)	Words per Minute
3:00	319	5:10	185
3:10	303	5:20	180
3:20	287	5:30	174
3:30	274	5:40	169
3:40	261	5:50	164
3:50	250	6:00	160
4:00	240	6:10	155
4:10	230	6:20	151
4:20	221	6:30	147
4:30	213	6:40	144
4:40	205	6:50	140
4:50	198	7:00	137
5:00	190		

Mark each statement with *T* (true) or *F* (false).

_____ 1. The author focuses mainly on the sea lion's insatiable appetite for high-protein food.

_____ 2. The larger northern sea lion is the circus "seal."

_____ 3. Sea lions eat lampreys, which eat salmon.

_____ 4. Sea lions both give birth and get pregnant in the summer.

_____ 5. Sea lion milk contains a higher percentage of fat than cow's milk.

_____ 6. Baby sea lions, like whales and manatees, are natural swimmers.

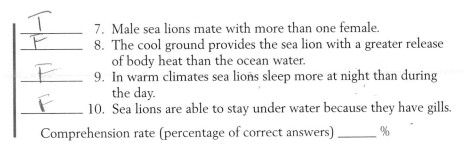

_____T_____ 7. Male sea lions mate with more than one female.

_____F_____ 8. The cool ground provides the sea lion with a greater release of body heat than the ocean water.

_____F_____ 9. In warm climates sea lions sleep more at night than during the day.

_____F_____ 10. Sea lions are able to stay under water because they have gills.

Comprehension rate (percentage of correct answers) _____ %

How Fast Should You Read?

Reading specialists say that the average adult reading speed on relatively easy material is approximately 250 words per minute at 70 percent comprehension. The rate for college students tends to be a little higher, averaging about 300 words per minute on the same type of material with 70 percent comprehension. However, these figures are misleading for a number of reasons.

Anyone who says to you, "My reading rate is 500 words per minute" is not telling the whole story. The question that immediately comes to mind is, "Is that the rate for reading the newspaper or for a physics textbook?" For an efficient reader, no one reading rate serves for all purposes or for all materials. Efficient readers demonstrate their flexibility by varying their rate according to their own purpose for reading or according to their prior knowledge of the material being read.

Rate Variations and Prior Knowledge

One reason textbooks usually require slower reading than newspapers is that the sentences are longer, the language is more formal, the vocabulary and ideas are new, and prior knowledge may be limited. If you already have a lot of knowledge on a topic, you can usually read about it at a faster rate than if you are exploring a totally new subject. For example, a student who has some experience in the field of advertising will probably be able to work through the advertising chapter in a business textbook at a faster rate compared with a chapter on a less familiar topic, like supply-side economics. The student might need to slow to a crawl at the beginning of the economics chapter to understand the new concepts, but as the new ideas become more familiar, he or she might be able to read at a faster rate toward the end of the chapter.

The "difficulty level" of a textbook is primarily measured according to a student's schemata of the subject. Another measure combines the length of the sentences and the number of syllables in the words. The longer sentences and words indicate a more difficult level of reading. Freshman textbooks vary greatly in difficulty from field to field and from book to book. Some are written at levels as high as the sixteenth-grade level (senior in college), whereas others may be at the eleventh- or twelfth-grade level. Even within a single textbook, the levels vary from one section or paragraph to another. Unfamiliar technical vocabulary can bring a reader to a complete stop. Complex sentences are more difficult to read than simple, concise statements. Sometimes the difficulty is caused by the complexity of the ideas expressed and sometimes, perhaps unnecessarily, by the formality of the author's writing style.

Before starting on the first word and moving automatically on to the second, third, and fourth at the same pace, take a minute to ask yourself, "Why am I reading this material?" and, based on your answer, vary your speed according to your purpose. Do you want 100 percent, 70 percent, or 50 percent comprehension? In other words, figure out what you want to know when you finish and read accordingly. If you are studying for an examination, you probably need to read slowly and carefully, taking time to monitor your comprehension as you progress. Because 100 percent comprehension is not always your goal, be willing to switch gears and move faster over low-priority material even though you may sacrifice a few details. If you are reading only to get an overview or to verify a particular detail, read as rapidly as possible to achieve your specific purpose.

Techniques for Faster Reading

Concentrate

Fast readers, like fast race-car drivers, concentrate on what they are doing; they try to think quickly while they take in the important aspects of the course before them. Although we use our eyes, we actually read with our minds. If our attention is veering off course, we lose some of that cutting-edge quickness necessary for success. Slow readers tend to become bored because ideas are coming too slowly to keep their minds alert. Fast readers are curious to learn, mentally alert, and motivated to achieve.

Distractions that interfere with concentration, as mentioned in Chapter 1, fall into two categories: external and internal. External distractions, the physical happenings around you, are fairly easy to control with a little assertiveness. You can turn the television off or get up and go to another room. You can ask people not to interrupt or choose a place to read where interruptions will be minimal. Through prior planning, you can set yourself up for success and create a physical environment over which you have control.

Internal distractions, the irrelevant ideas that pop into your head while reading, are more difficult to control. As mentioned in Chapter 1, a to-do list will help. Write down your nagging concerns as a reminder for action. Spend less time worrying and more time doing, and you will clear your head for success. Visualize as you read so that you will become wrapped up in the material.

Stop Regressing

During your initial reading of material, have you ever realized halfway down the page that you have no idea what you have read? Your eyes were engaged, but your mind was wandering. Do you ever go back and reread sentences or paragraphs? Were you rereading because the material was difficult to understand, because you were tired and not concentrating, or because you were daydreaming? This type of rereading is called **regression.**

Regression can be a crutch that allows you to make up for wasted time. If this is a problem for you, analyze when and why you are regressing. If you discern that your regression is due to distracting thoughts, start denying yourself the privilege in order to break the habit. Admit, "OK, I missed that paragraph because I was thinking of something else. I shouldn't do that now, because I've got to keep studying and start paying close attention." One effective strategy is to schedule a special time with yourself to deal with those internal distractions. Tell yourself, for example, "I'll give myself a chance to think about that stuff for 15 minutes after lunch—I'll take a 15-minute 'me break.'"

Rereading because you did not understand is a legitimate correction strategy used by good readers who monitor their own comprehension. Rereading because your mind was asleep is a waste of time and a habit of many slow readers.

Daydreaming is a habit caused by lack of involvement with the material. Be demanding on yourself and expect 100 percent attention to the task. Visualize the incoming ideas, and relate the new material to what you already know. Don't just read the words; think the ideas.

Expand Fixations

Your eyes must stop in order to read. These stops, called **fixations,** last a fraction of a second. On the average, 5 to 10 percent of reading time is spent on fixations. Thus, reading more than one word per fixation will reduce your total reading time.

Research on vision shows that the eye is able to see about one-half inch on either side of a fixation point. This means that a reader can see two or possibly three words per fixation. To illustrate, read the following phrase:

in the car

Did you make three fixations, two, or one? Now read the following word:

entertainment

You can read this word automatically with one fixation. As a beginning reader, however, you probably stopped for each syllable for a total of four fixations. If you can read *entertainment*, which has 13 letters, with one fixation, you can certainly read the 8-letter phrase *in the car* with only one fixation.

Use your peripheral vision on either side of the fixation point to help you read two or three words per fixation. In expanding your fixations, take in phrases or thought units that seem to go together automatically. To illustrate, the following sentence has been grouped into thought units with fixation points:

After lunch,   I studied   in the library   at a table.

By expanding your fixations, the sentence can easily be read with four fixations rather than ten and thus reduce your total reading time.

Monitor Subvocalization

Subvocalization is the little voice in your head that reads for you. Some experts say that subvocalization is necessary for difficult material, and others say that fast readers are totally visual and do not need to hear the words. Good college readers will probably experience some of both. With easy reading tasks you may find yourself speeding up to the point that you are not hearing every word, particularly the unimportant "filler" phrases. However, with more difficult textbook readings, your inner voice may speak every word. The voice seems to add another sensory dimension to help you comprehend. Because experts say that the inner voice can read up to about 400 words per minute, many college students can make a considerable improvement in speed while still experiencing the inner voice.

Vocalizers, on the other hand, move their lips while reading to pronounce each word. This is an immature habit that should be stopped. Putting a slip of paper or a pencil in your mouth while reading will alert you to lip movement and inspire you to stop.

Preview

Size up your reading assignment before you get started. If it is a chapter, glance through the pages and read the subheadings. Look at the pictures and notice the italicized words and boldface print. Make predictions about what you think the chapter will cover. Activate your schema or prior knowledge on the subject. Pull out your mental computer chip and prepare to bring something to the printed page.

Use Your Pen as a Pacer

The technique of using your pen or fingers as a pacer means pointing under the words in a smooth, flowing motion, moving back and forth from line to line. Although as a child you were probably told never to point to words, it is a very effective technique for improving reading speed. The technique seems to have several benefits. After you overcome the initial distraction, the physical act of pointing tends to improve concentration by drawing your attention directly to the words. The forward motion of your pen tends to keep you from regressing because rereading would interrupt your established rhythm. By pulling your eyes down the page, the pen movement helps set a rapid, steady pace for reading and tends to shift you out of word-by-word reading and move you automatically into phrase reading. Obviously, you cannot read a whole book using your pen as a pacer, but you can start out with this technique. Later, if you feel yourself slowing down, use your pen again to get back on track.

The technique is demonstrated in the following passage. Your pen moves in a *Z* pattern from one side of the column to the other. Because you are trying to read several words at each fixation, your pen does not have to go to the extreme end of either side of the column.

Rapid ~~reading requires quick thinking~~ and intense concentration. ~~The~~ reader must be alert and ~~aggressive. Being interested in the subject helps improve~~ speed.

As you begin to read faster and become more proficient with the Z pattern, you will notice the corners starting to round into an S. The Z pattern is turning into a more relaxed S swirl. When you get to the point of using the S swirl, you will be reading for ideas and not reading every word. You are reading actively and aggressively, with good concentration. Use the Z pattern until you find your pen or hand movement has automatically turned into an S. The following illustration compares the two patterns.

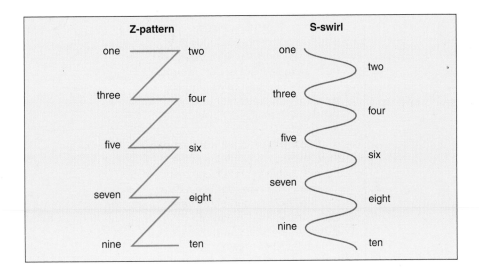

Push and Pace

Be alert and aggressive, and try to read faster. Sit up straight and attack the text. Get uncomfortable and force yourself to hurry. Changing old habits is difficult. You will never read faster unless you try to read faster.

Set goals and pace yourself. Count the number of pages in your homework assignments, and estimate according to your reading rate how many pages you can read in 30 minutes. Use a paper clip or a sticky note to mark the page you are trying to reach. Push yourself to achieve your goal.

**Exercise
11.2**

Pacing

The following passages are written in columns with approximately six words on each line. Using your pen as a pacer, read each passage, and try to make only two fixations per line. A dashed line has been placed down the middle of the column to help you with the fixations. Record your time for reading each passage, and determine your rate from the rate chart at the end of the passage. Then answer the comprehension questions.

Before reading the following passage, use the title and any clues in the passage to predict organization: Is it definition or description? _description_

Skunks

Skunks are small, omnivorous animals found throughout most of the United States. Striped skunks are at home in practically every habitat in every state, living in dens and often beneath abandoned buildings. They can be seen wandering around on cloudy days and at sunset. They eat a variety of fruits, berries, insects, earthworms, other small invertebrates, and some rodents. They sport many color variations, from almost black to almost white.

Spotted skunks are also found throughout a good portion of the country, but they are not common in some of the more northerly states and the northern part of the East Coast. They eat a variety of invertebrates, eggs, and sometimes small birds. The hognose skunk and the hooded skunk are found in the Pacific Southwest and extend down into Mexico and parts of Central America.

In a country where millions of dollars are spent every year on human deodorants, it is not to be wondered that the skunk is not favored. Then, too, the animal can carry rabies. Thus removal procedures are the order of the day when skunks invade suburban areas or campgrounds in large numbers. They can be kept away from buildings by repellents—moth balls (paradichlorobenzene) are effective. Screens can prevent them from getting under buildings. Proper fencing will keep them from chicken coops or apiaries (skunks like honeybees). Removal of insects from golf-course grasses is useful.

Despite their bad reputation, skunks do help keep small rodent and insect populations in check.

Stanley Anderson, *Managing Our Wildlife Resources*

245 words

Time: _____120_____

Words per minute: _____210_____

Time (Min.)	Words per Minute	Time (Min.)	Words per Minute
0:30	490	1:10	210
0:40	368	1:20	184
0:50	294	1:30	163
1:00	245	1:40	147

Mark each statement with *T* (true) or *F* (false).

_____ 1. Skunks eat rats and insects.

_____ 2. Skunks are repelled by mothballs.

Exercise 11.3

Pacing

Predict organization: Is the following passage organized in a time order or definition with examples? _____Time order_____

African American Music

African music arrived in Virginia with the slave ships even before the *Mayflower* landed in New England, and it appeared in print form during the Civil War. It evolved into black spirituals, work songs, blues, and jazz. During the 1700s and 1800s early African Americans blended these songs with European religious music to create spirituals. The first black spiritual appeared in print in 1862, and the first collection of black sheet music was published five years later. African Americans sang work songs on the docks and in the cotton fields of the South.

These songs had no instrumental accompaniment, and workers used them both to help bear harsh working conditions and as clandestine protest songs, which created the base of the blues tradition.

Blues songs were personal music about an individual's troubles. After the Civil War, wandering musicians helped to spread the spontaneous music with impromptu lyrics, and at the turn of the twentieth century, W. C. Handy immortalized the genre with his song "The St. Louis Blues." The song was so popular that it earned Handy $25,000 a year in royalties forty years after it was written.

Early jazz music developed from the ragtime and blues played in New Orleans and was spread northward by musicians such as Louis Armstrong, whose career paralleled the growing popularity of jazz. Elements of jazz and blues ultimately became a critical element in rock 'n' roll.

Jean Folkerts and Stephen Long, *The Media in Your Life,* 3rd ed.

233 words

Time: _____

Words per minute: _____

Mark each statement with *T* (true) or *F* (false).

Time (Min.)	Words per Minute	Time (Min.)	Words per Minute
0:30	458	1:10	196
0:40	344	1:20	171
0:50	275	1:30	153
1:00	229	1:40	137

_____ 1. African American spirituals were not in print until after the turn of the twentieth century

_____ 2. Handy earned royalties on his popular blues song for at least 40 years after it was written.

**Exercise
11.4**

Pacing

Predict organization: Is the following passage organized by definition with examples or a simple listing? *examples*

The Impact of the Automobile

If we try to pick the single item that has had the greatest impact on social life in the past 100 years, the automobile stands out. Let's look at some of the ways in which it has changed U.S. society.

The decline in the use of streetcars changed the shape of U.S. cities. U.S. cities had been web-shaped, for residences and businesses had located along the streetcar lines. When automobiles freed people from having to live so close to the tracks, they filled in the areas between the "webs."

The automobile had a profound impact on farm life and villages. Before the 1920s, most farmers were isolated from the city. Because using horses for a trip to town was slow and cumbersome, they made such trips infrequently. By the 1920s, however, the popularity and low price of the Model T made the "Saturday trip to town" a standard event. There, farmers would market products, shop, and visit with friends. This changed farm life. Mail-order catalogs stopped being the primary source of shopping, and access to better medical care and education improved. Farmers also began to travel to bigger towns, where they found more variety of goods. As farmers began to use the nearby villages only for immediate needs, these flourishing centers of social and commercial dried up.

James M. Henslin, *Sociology*, 5th ed.

222 words

Time: ___1:20___

Words per minute: ___167___

Time (Min.)	Words per Minute	Time (Min.)	Words per Minute
0:30	444	1:10	190
0:40	333	1:20	167
0:50	266	1:30	148
1:00	222	1:40	133

Mark each statement with *T* (true) or *F* (false).

___T___ 1. The popularity of the automobile led to a decline in the mail-order catalog business.

___F___ 2. With the rise of the automobile, small villages grew because farmers were able to drive to them quickly.

**Exercise
11.5**

Pacing

Predict organization: Is it simple listing or description? _description_

Spam

Anybody with an e-mail address gets it—spam, or unsolicited e-mail. Several spam items invite you to apply for very inexpensive life insurance. "John" offers you an opportunity to earn $50,000 with only a $20 investment. How about getting a university diploma without studying or going to class? Though most of us would prefer not to be spammed, it's as difficult to rid the public Internet of spam as it is to rid our mail boxes of junk mail. Just like at home, we must sort through the spam to find our legitimate e-mail. Also, people are concerned that spam is taking up valuable bandwidth on the Internet, stressing the information capacity of the Net.

Let's dispel the myth that the term, *spam*, was derived from the SPAM luncheon meat made by Hormel Foods. Actually, the derivation of spam can be traced back to an old Monty Python comedy routine where Vikings howled "spam spam spam spam" to drown out other conversations. Similarly, spam tends to overwhelm people's e-mail boxes, making important messages difficult to find.

Spammers get your e-mail address through a variety of sources. It is difficult to track how you turn up on somebody's spam list. One thing is for sure, spam costs you more to receive than it does for it to be sent. Consider the fact that millions of spam messages are sent each day to AOL users. The result is that these users must spend up to 10 cumulative person-years simply deleting these unwanted messages.

Larry Long and Nancy Long, *Computers,* 11th ed.

251 words

Time: _1:00_

Words per minute: _272_

Time (Min.)	Words per Minute	Time (Min.)	Words per Minute
0:30	544	1:10	233
0:40	408	1:20	204
0:50	326	1:30	181
1:00	272	1:40	163

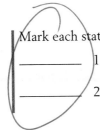

Mark each statement with *T* (true) or *F* (false).

_____ 1. According to the authors, spam does not stress the information capacity of the Internet.

_____ 2. According to the authors, spam received its name from the Hormel Foods product.

Skimming

Skimming is a technique of selectively reading for the main idea. Because it involves processing material at rates of around 900 words per minute, it is not defined by some experts as reading. Skimming involves skipping words, sentences, paragraphs, and even pages. It is a method of quickly overviewing material to answer the question, "What is this about?"

Skimming and previewing are very similar in that both involve getting an overview. Previewing sets the stage for later careful reading, whereas skimming is a substitute for a complete reading. Skimming is useful for material that you want to know about but don't have the time to read. For example, you might want to skim some supplemental articles that have been placed on reserve in the library because your professor expects you only to understand the main idea of each article and a complete reading would be unnecessary. Or you may want to pick up a book and just "get the idea" but not read it completely. Skimming is a useful tool. The technique is presented in the Reader's Tip.

READER'S TIP

Techniques for Skimming

◆ Read the title and subheadings as well as words in italics and boldface print to get an idea of what the material is about.

◆ Try to get an insight into the organization of the material, as discussed in Chapter 5, to help you anticipate where the important points will be located. Look for certain organizational patterns and understand their functions:

Simple listing: explains items of equal value.

Definition: defines a term and gives examples to help the reader understand the term.

Time order or sequence: presents items in chronological order.

Comparison-contrast: compares similarities and differences of items.

(continued)

Description: explains characteristics of an item.

Cause and effect: shows how one item has produced another.

Addition: provides more information.

Classification: divides items into groups or categories.

Generalization and example: explains with examples to illustrate.

Location or spatial order: identifies the whereabouts of objects.

Summary: condenses major points.

◆ If the first paragraph is introductory, read it. If not, skip to a paragraph that seems to introduce the topic.

◆ Move rapidly, letting your eyes float over the words. Try to grasp the main ideas and the significant supporting details.

◆ Notice first sentences in paragraphs, and read them if they seem to be summary statements.

◆ Skip words that seem to have little meaning, like *a, an,* and *the.*

◆ Skip sentences or sections that seem to contain the following:

Familiar ideas

Unnecessary details

Superfluous examples

Restatements or unneeded summaries

Material irrelevant to your purpose

◆ If the last paragraph of a section is a summary, read it if you need to check your understanding.

Scanning

Because **scanning** is a process of searching for a single bit of information, it is more of a locating skill than a reading skill (see the following Reader's Tip). A common use of scanning is looking up a number in a telephone book. When scanning for information, you are not trying to understand the meaning of the material; instead you are merely trying to pinpoint a specific detail. For example, you might find that after reading a chapter on pricing in your marketing textbook, you cannot recall the definition of *price lining.* To locate the information, you would not reread the entire chapter but scan it to find the term *price lining* and then review the definition. This same scanning technique works well when you use a glossary or an index or when you do research on the Internet.

> ### READER'S TIP
>
> ## Techniques for Scanning
>
> ◆ Figure out the organization of the material. Get an overview of which section will probably contain the information you are looking for.
>
> ◆ Know specifically what you are looking for. Decide on a key expression that will signal your information, but be ready to switch to a related idea if that doesn't work.
>
> ◆ Repeat the phrase and hold the image in your mind. Concentrate on the image so that you will recognize it when it comes into view.
>
> ◆ Move quickly and aggressively. Remember, you are scanning, not reading.
>
> ◆ Verify through careful reading. After locating your information, read carefully to make sure you have really found it.

Researchers use a combination of skimming and scanning. If you are working on a research paper on paranoia, you might have a list of 30 books and articles to read. A complete reading of each reference is probably unnecessary. Instead, you can scan to locate the information relevant to your topic and skim to get the main idea.

Summary Points

● What is your reading rate?

Your individual reading rate can be calculated if you know your total reading time and the total number of words read during that time.

● How fast should you read?

The average adult reading speed on relatively easy material is approximately 250 words per minute at 70 percent comprehension.

● How do faster readers maintain a better reading rate?

Faster readers concentrate, are curious to learn, stay mentally alert, and are motivated to achieve.

● What are some techniques for faster reading?

Before reading, make predictions, anticipate organization, and activate schemata. Using the pen as a pacer is an important technique that can improve both concentration and rate.

● **What happens during regression?**

With regression, you must go back and reread material because of inattention. Regression thus wastes time.

● **Why skim?**

Skimming is a technique that allows you to get a quick overview of the material.

● **What is scanning?**

Scanning is the process of searching for a single bit of information.

Skill Development: Skimming

Skim to find the definition of asthma: _____

_____

_____

Skill Development: Scanning

Scan to find the likely number of passive smoke lung cancer deaths each year as reported by the 1993 EPA report: _____ deaths per year

Skill Development: Rate

Now read the selection to answer five true-false items. Use your pen as a pacer, and time your reading.

Starting time: _____ minutes _____ seconds

PASSIVE SMOKING

From Curtis Byer and Louis Shainberg, *Living Well*

The right of nonsmokers to a smoke-free environment has become an emotional issue. The controversy centers around how seriously the nonsmoker is threatened by **passive smoke,** also called "second-hand" or "side-stream" smoke.

Studies have shown that the danger from passive smoking is very real.
5 The smoke rising from a burning cigarette resting in an ashtray or in a smoker's hand is *not* the same as the smoker is inhaling. The smoker is inhaling smoke that has been filtered through the tobacco along the length of the cigarette (and usually by its filter) while the nonsmoker is inhaling smoke that is totally unfiltered. Of course, the smoker also inhales this unfiltered
10 smoke. Unfiltered "side-stream" smoke contains 50 times the amounts of carcinogens, is twice as high in tar and nicotine, has 5 times the carbon monoxide, and has 50 times as much ammonia as smoke inhaled through the cigarette. Although the nonsmoker does not usually inhale side-stream smoke in the concentration that the smoker inhales the **mainstream smoke,**
15 the concentration inhaled still amounts to, for the average person in the United States, the equivalent of smoking one cigarette per day. For people working in very smoky places, such as a bar or office, passive smoking can reach the equivalent of 14 cigarettes per day.

A New York Greenwich Village restaurant provides wool cloaks for guests who must stand outside to smoke.
Monika Graff/The Image Works

Cancer Affecting Passive Smokers

In January 1993, a long-awaited Environmental Protection Agency (EPA)
20 report classified passive cigarette smoke as a human carcinogen that causes
lung cancer in nonsmokers. According to the report, passive smoking causes
somewhere between 700 and 7000 lung cancer deaths a year in the United
States. The agency said that the most likely number is about 3000 deaths a
year. This report is expected to result in additional limits on smoking in public
25 places and federal regulations on smoking in the workplace. Predictably, the
tobacco industry said that the report was based on inadequate scientific data.

Other Effects

Passive tobacco smoke is a major lung irritant. At the very least, breathing
second-hand smoke causes discomfort and coughing. Research has demonstrated
that children raised in homes of smokers show early signs of conditions known to
30 lead to heart disease in adulthood. For example, they show increased stiffness of
the arteries, thickened walls of the heart chambers, and an unfavorable change in
the blood's ratio of high-density lipoprotein to low-density lipoprotein.

For people susceptible to **asthma** (attacks of difficult breathing
caused by narrowing of the bronchioles), passive smoking can bring on

35 a full-blown asthma attack. This is especially true for children. The incidence of asthma is higher among children who live in homes where someone smokes than among those from homes in which no one smokes. One estimate is that passive smoking may cause up to 100,000 new cases of childhood asthma in the United States each year. Further, asthmatic chil-
40 dren from homes in which someone smokes are likely to be in poorer health than asthmatic children from homes where no one smokes. Infants living in homes with smokers also experience twice as many respiratory infections as other infants.

Societal Issues

Many people do not enjoy the smell of burning tobacco, do not want to have
45 the taste of their dinner spoiled by the smell of smoke, do not want their clothing or hair contaminated with the smell of stale smoke, and consider it very rude to be subjected to these intrusions.

Conversely, many smokers are addicted to nicotine and are thus uncomfortable if required to forgo smoking for extended periods. Many have tried to
50 quit smoking without success. To be denied the right to smoke in public places makes it difficult or impossible for them to enjoy restaurant dining and other activities. As long as there are both smokers and nonsmokers we can expect to see conflicts regarding the rights of each group.

629 words

Finishing time: _____ minutes _____ seconds

Calculate Your Reading Rate

Subtract your starting time from your finishing time and then use the time chart to find your rate in words per minute.

Words per minute: _____

Time (Min.)	Words per Minute	Time (Min.)	Words per Minute	Time (Min.)	Words per Minute
1:00	629	2:10	290	3:20	189
1:10	539	2:20	270	3:30	180
1:20	471	2:30	252	3:40	175
1:30	419	2:40	236	3:50	164
1:40	377	2:50	222	4:00	157
1:50	343	3:00	210	4:10	151
2:00	314	3:10	199	4:20	145

Check Your Comprehension

Mark each statement with T (true) or F (false). To help you analyze your strengths and weaknesses, the statement types are indicated.

Detail 1. Side-stream smoke contains 50 times the carcinogens as smoke inhaled through a cigarette.

Detail 2. The smoker inhales passive smoke and the observer inhales mainstream smoke.

Detail 3. A nonsmoker in an environment with smokers can inhale the equivalent of 14 cigarettes per day.

Inference _____ 4. The author suggests that the rate of lung cancer deaths and the incidence of asthma are higher among nonsmokers than among smokers.

Inference 5. The author suggests that government regulations eventually will solve most of the problems between smokers and non-smokers.

Comprehension (% correct) _____ %

Writing About the Selection

Why are nonsmokers sometimes reluctant to ask others not to smoke? Why should they not be reluctant?

Skill Development: Skimming

Skim the two paragraphs to find the names of the identical twins: _____

_____

Skill Development: Scanning

Scan to find which twin was reared in Czechoslovakia: _____

Skill Development: Rate

Now read the selection to answer five true-false items. Use your pen as a pacer, and time your reading.

Starting time: _____ minutes _____ seconds

HEREDITY OR ENVIRONMENT?
THE CASE OF IDENTICAL TWINS
From James M. Henslin, *Sociology*, 5th ed.

Identical twins share exact genetic heredity. One fertilized egg divides to produce two embryos. If heredity determines personality—or attitudes, temperament, skills, and intelligence—then identical twins should be identical not only in their looks but also in these characteristics.

5 The fascinating case of Jack and Oskar helps us unravel this mystery. From their experience, we can see the far-reaching effects of the environment—how social experiences override biology.

Jack Yufe and Oskar Stohr are identical twins born in 1932 to a Jewish father and a Catholic mother. They were separated as babies after their par-
10 ents divorced. Oskar was reared in Czechoslovakia by his mother's mother, who was a strict Catholic. When Oskar was a toddler, Hitler annexed this area of Czechoslovakia, and Oskar learned to love Hitler and to hate Jews. He became involved with the Hitler Youth (a sort of Boy Scout organization, except that this one was designed to instill the "virtues" of patriotism, loyalty,
15 obedience—and hatred).

Like these two, most identical twins are reared together and thus reveal less than separated twins to researchers studying the influences of heredity and environment on human development and behavior. *George Shelley/CORBIS*

Jack's upbringing was in almost total contrast to Oskar's. Reared in Trinidad by his father, he learned loyalty to Jews and hatred of Hitler and the Nazis. After the war, Jack emigrated to Israel, where at the age of 17, he joined a kibbutz. Later, Jack served in the Israeli army.

In 1954, the two brothers met. It was a short meeting, and Jack had been warned not to tell Oskar that they were Jews. Twenty-five years later, in 1979, when they were 47 years old, social scientists at the University of Minnesota brought them together again. These researchers figured that because Jack and Oskar had the same genes, whatever differences they showed would have to be due to the environment—to their different social experiences.

Not only did Oskar and Jack have different attitudes toward the war, Hitler, and Jews, but also their basic orientations to life were different. In their politics, Oskar was conservative, while Jack was more liberal. Oskar enjoyed leisure, while Jack was a workaholic. And, as you can predict, Jack was very proud of being a Jew. Oskar, who by this time knew that he was a Jew, wouldn't even mention it.

That would seem to settle the matter. But there was another side to the findings. The researchers also found that Oskar and Jack both liked sweet liqueur and spicy foods, excelled at sports as children but had difficulty with math, and had the same rate of speech. Both flushed the toilet both before and after using it and enjoyed startling people by sneezing in crowded elevators.

425 words

Finishing time: _____ minutes _____ seconds

Calculate Your Reading Rate

Subtract your starting time from your finishing time and then use the time chart to find your rate in words per minute.

Words per minute: _____

Time (Min.)	Words per Minute	Time (Min.)	Words per Minute	Time (Min.)	Words per Minute	Time (Min.)	Words per Minute
1:00	727	2:00	363	3:00	242	4:00	182
1:10	623	2:10	336	3:10	230	4:10	174
1:20	545	2:20	312	3:20	218	4:20	168
1:30	485	2:30	291	3:30	208	4:30	162
1:40	436	2:40	273	3:40	198	4:40	156
1:50	397	2:50	257	3:50	190	4:50	150
						5:00	145

Check Your Comprehension

Mark each statement with *T* (true) or *F* (false). To help you analyze your strengths and weaknesses, the statement types are indicated.

Detail   ___F___   1. Jack and Oskar were separated at birth because of World War II.

Inference   ___F___   2. The author implies that the Hitler Youth was a propaganda machine to mold the minds of the young.

Detail   ___F___   3. Oskar spent his childhood years growing up in Israel with his father.

Inference   ___T___   4. The research with Jack and Oskar suggests that values and beliefs are determined by environment rather than heredity.

Inference   ___T___   5. The researchers would most likely conclude that the taste buds and sports ability are determined by heredity rather than environment.

Comprehension (% correct) _____%

Write About the Selection

Why are identical twins the best subjects for studying the influence of heredity and environment on abilities and attitudes? Why are identical twins who have been raised separately rare to find but particularly desirable to study?

Vocabulary Booster

Foreign Terms

- *bon vivant:* a lover of good living; a gourmet

  While living in Paris with plenty of money, he enjoyed the lifestyle of a *bon vivant.*

- *avant-garde:* advance guard, pioneers, offbeat

  The radical ideas of the sociology professor may be too *avant-garde* for the conservative freshmen.

- *carte blanche:* "white paper," unlimited authority, blanket permission

  The new company gave her *carte blanche* to entertain the top three customers at the convention.

- *magnum opus:* great work

  After seven years of work, the novel was recognized as the author's *magnum opus.*

- *de rigueur:* strict etiquette, very formal, in good taste at the moment

  A jacket and necktie are *de rigueur* for the occasion.

- *déjà vu:* already seen

  The feeling of *déjà vu* became more intense as the same people seemed to be saying the same things as in 1997.

- *double entendre:* allowing two interpretations with one usually being off color

  As soon as the sentence was uttered, the speaker realized the *double entendre* and laughed knowingly.

- *faux pas:* "false step," or mistake

  I realized the *faux pas* when I saw my friends giggling in the background.

- *joie de vivre:* "joy for living"

  The guide's *joie de vivre* was contagious, making the trip enjoyable for us all.

- *esprit de corps:* group spirit of pride

  Through shared experiences, the marines build a strong *esprit de corps.*

- *coup d'état:* sudden stroke that overturns the government

  The foreign diplomats sought to leave before the predicted *coup d'état.*

- *raison d'être:* "reason for being," justification

  For the last three years, raising my child has been my *raison d'être.*

- *potpourri:* mixture

  A *potpourri* ideas was presented for the group to consider.

- *nouveau riche:* newly rich, suggesting poor taste

  Have you seen the pillow that says, "Better to be *nouveau riche* than not rich at all"?

- *nom de plume:* pen name, pseudonym

  Samuel Clemens used Mark Twain as his *nom de plume.*

- *junta:* group of political plotters

  By gaining control of the military, the *junta* overthrew the existing government.

- *sotto voce:* "under the voice," whisper

  The criticism was overheard even though it was said *sotto voce.*

- *vendetta:* blood feud

  Because of the assault, the gang continued the *vendetta.*

- *alfresco:* "in the fresh air," outdoors

  During the summer months, the restaurant offered *alfresco* dining.

- *fait accompli:* finished action

  Submit your comments to the dean before the decision becomes a *fait accompli.*

Review

Part I

Indicate whether the following sentences are true (*T*) or false (*F*):

_____F_____ 1. A *vendetta* is an agreement between two countries.

_____F_____ 2. A *double entendre* often includes a sexual twist.

_____T_____ 3. An artist's *magnum opus* could be a painting or a sculpture.

_____T_____ 4. A *junta* will plot against the existing government but seldom try to seize power.

_____T_____ 5. A *potpourri* of guests can be a mixture of friends, relatives, and coworkers.

_____T_____ 6. A *nom de plume* can also be the real name of the writer.

_____F_____ 7. A *bon vivant* usually does not like wine and food.

_____T_____ 8. As a client, you would usually welcome *carte blanche* treatment.

_____T_____ 9. *Déjà vu* is like a replay from the past.

_____F_____ 10. In a *coup d'état* the existing government remains the same.

F _____ 11. A *raison d'être* is a central driving force.

_____ T 12. Winning sports teams usually lack *esprit de corps*.

Part II

Choose the word from the boxed list that means the opposite of the words below.

> joie de vivre   faux pas   de rigueur   nouveau riche
> sotto voce   fait accompli   avant-garde   alfresco

13. incomplete ___*Fait accompli*___

14. informal, without rules ___*de rigueur*___

15. indoors ___*alfresco*___

16. loud ___*sotto voce*___

17. behind the times ___*avant-garde*___

18. unhappy outlook ___*Joie de vivre*___

19. poor ___*Nouveau Riche*___

20. correct action ___*Faux Pas*___

12

Test Taking

- Can being testwise improve your score?
- How should you prepare before a test?
- What should you notice during a test?
- What strategies should you use to read a comprehension passage?
- What are the major question types?
- What hints help with multiple-choice items?
- How do you answer an essay question?

The Glacier de Tacconay sfrom "Scenes from the Snowfields" engraved by Vincent Brooks, 1859. Color lithograph by Edward Thomas Coleman (fl.1839-77) (after). Royal Geographical Society, London, UK. The Bridgeman Art Library International

Can Being Testwise Improve Your Score?

Are you preparing for a midterm or another important exam? Is it a multiple-choice or essay test? Can test-taking tricks help you get a higher score?

Research shows that gimmicks, such as schemes involving length of responses or the likelihood of *b* or *c* being the right answer, don't work.[1]

However, insight into the testing experience can help. High scores depend on preparation, both mental and physical.

The purpose of this chapter is to help you gain points by being aware. You can improve your score by understanding how tests are constructed and what is needed for maximum performance. Study the following and do everything you can both mentally and physically to gain an edge.

Strategies for Mental and Physical Awareness

Before Taking a Test

Get Plenty of Sleep the Night Before. How alert can you be with inadequate sleep? Would you want a surgeon operating on you if he had slept only a few hours the night before? The mental alertness you derive from a good night's sleep can add as much as six points to your score and mean the difference between passing or failing. Why gamble by staying up late? Prioritize tasks and budget your time during the day so you can go to bed on time.

Arrive Five or Ten Minutes Early and Get Settled. If you run in to class flustered at the last second, you will spend the first five minutes of the test calming yourself rather than getting immediately to work. Avoid unnecessary stress by arriving for the test early. Find a seat, get settled with pen or pencil and paper, and relax with a classmate by making small talk.

Know What to Expect on the Test. Ask beforehand if the test will be essay or multiple choice so that you can anticipate the format when you study. Both stress main ideas, and research shows that one is not easier than the other.[2]

Have Confidence in Your Abilities. Achieve self-confidence by being well prepared. Be optimistic, and approach the test with a positive mental attitude. Lack of preparation breeds anxiety, but positive testing experiences tend to

---

[1]W. G. Brozo, R. V. Schmelzer, and H. A. Spires, "A Study of Test-Wiseness Clues in College and University Teacher-Made Tests with Implications for Academic Assistance Centers," *College Reading and Learning Assistance*, Technical Report 84–01 (ERIC 1984), ED 240928.

[2]P. M. Clark, "Examination Performance and Examination Set," in D. M. Wark, ed., *Fifth Yearbook of the North Central Reading Association* (Minneapolis: Central Reading Association, 1968), pp. 114–122.

breed confidence. Don't miss quizzes; research shows that students who have frequent quizzes during a course tend to do better on the final exam.[3]

Know How the Test Will Be Scored. If the test has several sections, be very clear on how many points can be earned from each section so you can prioritize your time and effort. Determine if some items are worth more points than others. Find out if there is a penalty for guessing and, if so, what it is. Because most test scores are based on answering all the questions, you are usually better off guessing than leaving items unanswered. Research shows that educated guessing can add points to your score.[4]

Plan Your Attack. At least a week before the test, take an inventory of what you need to do and make plans to achieve your goals. Preparation can make a difference for both standardized tests and with content area exams. The Reader's Tip lists the elements of a sound test preparation strategy.

READER'S TIP

Preparing for a Test

Professors report that students gain awareness before content area exams by writing truthful answers to questions like the following:

◆ **How will the test look?** How many parts will the test have? What kinds of questions will be asked? How will points be counted?

◆ **What material will be covered?** What textbook pages will the test cover? What lecture notes will be included? Will outside reading be significant?

◆ **How will you study?** Have you made a checklist or study guide? Have your read all the material? Will you study notes or annotations from your textbook? Will you write down answers to potantial essay questions? Will you include time to study with a classmate?

◆ **When will you study?** What is your schedule the week before the test? How long will you need to study? How much of the material do you plan to cover each day? What are your projected study hours?

◆ **What grade are you honestly working to achieve?** Are you willing to work for an A, or are you actually trying to earn a B or C?

---

[3]M. L. Fitch, A. J. Drucker, and J. A. Norton, "Frequent Testing as a Motivating Factor in Large Lecture Classes," *Journal of Educational Psychology* 42 (1951): 1–20.
[4]R. C. Preston, "Ability of Students to Identify Correct Responses Before Reading," *Journal of Educational Research* 58 (1964): 181–183.

During the Test

Concentrate. Tune out internal and external distractions and focus your attention on the test. Visualize and integrate old and new knowledge as you work. Read with curiosity and an eagerness to learn something new. Predict, picture, relate, monitor, and use correction strategies. If you become anxious or distracted, close your eyes and take a few deep breaths to relax and get yourself back on track.

On a teacher-made test, you may have a few thoughts that you want to jot down immediately on the back of the test so you don't forget them. Do so, and proceed with confidence.

Read and Follow Directions. Find out what to do and then do it. On a multiple-choice test, perhaps more than one answer is needed. Perhaps on an essay exam you are to respond to only three of five questions.

Schedule Your Time. Wear a watch and use it. When you receive your copy of the test, look it over, size up the task, and allocate your time. Determine the number of sections to be covered, and organize your time accordingly. As you work through the test, periodically check to see if you are meeting your time goals.

On teacher-made tests, the number of points for each item may vary. Do the easy items first, but spend the most time on the items that will yield the most points.

Work Rapidly. Every minute counts. Do not waste the time that you may need later by pondering at length over an especially difficult item. Mark the item with a check or a dot and move on to the rest of the test. If you have a few minutes at the end of the test, return to the marked items for further study.

Think. Use knowledge, logic, and common sense in responding to the items. Be aggressive and alert in moving through the test.

If you are unsure, use a process of elimination to narrow down the options. Double-check your paper to make sure you have answered every item.

Ignore Students Who Finish Early. Early departures draw attention and can create anxiety for those still working, but reassure yourself with the knowledge that students who finish early do not necessarily make the highest scores. Rapid workers do not necessarily work more accurately. If you have time, carefully review test items that you found yourself answering with less confidence. If your reassessment leads you to another response, change your answer to agree with your new thoughts. Research shows that scores can be improved by making such changes.[5]

---

[5]F. K. Berrien, "Are Scores Increased on Objective Tests by Changing the Initial Decision?" *Journal of Educational Psychology* 31 (1940): 64–67.

After the Test

Analyze Your Preparation. Question yourself after the test, and learn from the experience. Did you study the right material? Do you wish you had spent more time studying any particular topic? Were you mentally and physically alert enough to function at your full capacity?

Analyze the Test. Decide if the test was what you expected. If not, what was unexpected? Did the professor describe the test accurately or were there a few surprises? Why were you surprised? Use your memory of the test to predict the patterns of future tests.

Analyze Your Performance. Most standardized tests are not returned, but you do receive scores and subscores. What do these scores tell you about your strengths and weaknesses? What can you do to improve?

Content area exams are usually returned and reviewed in class. Ask questions about your errors. Find out why any weak responses did not receive full credit. Look for patterns of strengths and weaknesses in planning for the next test.

Meet with your professor if you are confused or disappointed and ask for suggestions for improvement. Find out if tutorial sessions or study groups are available for you to join. Ask to see an "A" paper. Formulate a plan with your professor for improved performance on the next test.

Strategies for Standardized Reading Tests

Read to Comprehend the Passage as a Whole

Students often ask, "Should I read the questions first and then read the passage?" Although the answer to this is subject to some debate, most reading experts would not recommend this practice.

The reasoning behind reading the passage first and then answering the questions is convincingly logical. Examining the questions first burdens the reader with a confusing collection of key words and phrases. Rather than reading to comprehend the author's message, you must instead search for many bits of information. Reading becomes fragmented and lacks focus; and few people are capable of reading with five or six purposes in mind. Not only is the reading-of-questions-first method confusing, but because it is detail oriented, it does not prepare you for more general questions concerning the main idea and implied meanings.

Read to understand the passage as a whole. If you understand the central theme or main idea, the rest of the ideas fall into place. The central theme may have several divisions that are developed in the different paragraphs. Attempt to understand what each paragraph contributes to the central theme. Don't fret over details, other than understanding how they contribute to the central theme. If you find later that a minor detail is needed to answer a question, you can quickly use a key word to locate and reread for accuracy the sentence in which it appears.

Anticipate What Is Coming Next

Most test passages are untitled and thus offer no initial clue for content. Before reading, glance at the passage for a repeated word, name, or date. In other words, look for any quick clue to let you know whether the passage is about Queen Victoria, pit bulls, or chromosome reproduction.

Do not rush through the first sentence. The first sentence further activates your schema and sets the stage for what is to come. In some cases, the first sentence might give an overview or even state the central theme. In other cases, it might simply pique your curiosity or stimulate your imagination. You might begin to guess what will come next and how it will be stated.

Read Rapidly, but Don't Allow Yourself to Feel Rushed

Use your pen as a pacer to direct your attention both mentally and physically to the printed page. Using your pen will help you focus your attention, particularly at the times during the test when you feel more rushed.

Be aware of the times when you might feel rushed and uneasy. Such feelings tend to be with you at the beginning of a test when you have not yet begun to concentrate—during those unsettled moments just before you become mentally involved with the work. In the middle of the test, you might feel anxious again if you look at your watch and discover you are only half finished and half your time is gone (which is where you should be). Toward the end of the test, when the first person finishes, you will again feel rushed if you have not finished. Check your time, keep your cool, and use your pen as a pacer. Continue working with control and confidence.

Read with Involvement to Learn and Enjoy

Reading a passage to answer five or six questions is reading with an artificial purpose. Usually you read to learn and enjoy, not for the sole purpose of quickly answering questions. However, most test passages can be fairly interesting to a receptive reader. Use the thinking strategies of a good reader to become involved in the material. Picture what you read, and relate the ideas to what you already know.

Self-Test for the Main Idea

Pull it together before pulling it apart. At the end of a passage, self-test for the main idea. This is a final monitoring step that should be seen as part of the reading process. Take perhaps 10 or 15 seconds to pinpoint the focus of the passage and to review the point that the author is trying to make. Again, if you understand the main point, the rest of the passage will fall into place.

Read the following passage, and pretend it is part of a reading comprehension test. Read it using the suggestions just discussed. Note the handwritten reminders to make you aware of a few aspects of your thinking.

Certainly your reading of the passage contained many more thoughts than those indicated on the page. The gossip at the beginning of the passage

Practice Passage A

No title, so glance for key words. Dates? Names?

Great image In January 1744 a coach from Berlin bumped its way eastward over ditches and mud toward Russia. It carried Sophia, a young German princess, on a bridal journey. At the Russian border she was met with pomp, appropriate for one chosen to be married to Peter, heir to the Russian throne. The wedding was celebrated in August 1745 with gaiety and ceremony. *Why wait 1½ years?*

Surprise! For Sophia the marriage was anything but happy because the seventeen-year-old heir was "physically less than a man and mentally little more than a child." The "moronic booby" played with dolls and toy soldiers in his leisure time. He neglected his wife and was constantly in a drunken stupor. Moreover, *Will he be tsar?* Peter was strongly pro-German and made no secret of his contempt for the Russian people, intensifying the unhappiness of his ambitious young wife. This *What is she planning?* dreary period lasted for seventeen years, but Sophia used the time wisely. She set about "russifying" herself. She mastered the Russian language and avidly embraced the Russian faith; on joining the Orthodox church, she was renamed Catherine. She devoted herself to study, reading widely the works of Montesquieu, Voltaire, and other Western intellectuals. *What is that? How?*

Did she kill him? When Peter became tsar in January 1762, Catherine immediately began plotting his downfall. Supported by the army, she seized power in July 1762 and tacitly consented to Peter's murder. It was announced that he died of "hemorrhoidal colic." Quickly taking over the conduct of governmental affairs, *Ironic, since she's not Russian* Catherine reveled in her new power. For the next thirty-four years the Russian people were dazzled by their ruler's political skill and cunning and her superb conduct of tortuous diplomacy. Perhaps even more, they were intrigued by gossip concerning her private life. *What gossip? Lovers?*

Unusual term Long before she became empress, Catherine was involved with a number of male favorites referred to as her house pets. At first her affairs were clandestine, but soon she displayed her lovers as French kings paraded their mistresses. *Did she kill them?* Once a young man was chosen, he was showered with lavish gifts; when the empress tired of him, he was given a lavish going-away present.

Now moving from personal info to accomplishments Catherine is usually regarded as an enlightened despot. She formed the Imperial Academy of Art, began the first college of pharmacy, and imported foreign physicians. Her interest in architecture led to the construction of a number of fine palaces, villas, and public buildings and the first part of the Hermitage in Saint Petersburg. Attracted to Western culture, she carried on correspondence with the French *philosophes* and sought their flattery by seeming to champion liberal causes. The empress played especially on Voltaire's vanity, sending him copious praise about his literary endeavors. In turn this *philosophe* became her most ardent admirer. Yet while Catherine discussed liberty and equality before the law, her liberalism and dalliance with the *Double check years—not long* Enlightenment was largely a pose—eloquent in theory, lacking in practice. The lot of serfs actually worsened, leading to a bloody uprising in 1773. This revolt brought an end to all talk of reform. And after the French Revolution, strict censorship was imposed. *Changes to foreign policy accomplishments*

So, she did little toward human progress In her conduct of foreign policy, the empress was ruthless and successful. She annexed a large part of Poland and, realizing that Turkey was in decline, waged two wars against this ailing power. As a result of force and diplomacy, Russian frontiers reached the Black Sea, the Caspian, and the Baltic. Well could this shrewd practitioner of power tell her adopted people, "I came to Russia a poor girl. Russia has dowered me richly, but I have paid her back with Azov, the Crimea, and Poland." *What was the point?*

T. Walter Wallbank et al., *Civilization Past and Present*

humanizes the empress and makes it easier for the reader to relate emotionally to the historic figure. Did you anticipate Peter's downfall and Catherine's subsequent relationships? Did you note the shift from gossip to accomplishments, both national and international? The shift signals the alert reader to a change in style, purpose, and structure.

Before proceeding to the questions that follow a passage, take a few seconds to regroup and think about what you have read. Self-test by pulling the material together before you tear it apart. Think about the focus of the passage, and then proceed to the questions.

Recognizing the Major Question Types

Learn to recognize the types of questions asked on reading comprehension tests. Although the phraseology might vary slightly, most tests will include one or more questions on main idea, details, inference, purpose, and vocabulary.

Main Idea

Main-idea questions test your ability to find the central theme, central focus, gist, controlling idea, main point, or thesis. These terms are largely interchangeable in asking the reader to identify the main point of the passage. Main-idea items are stated in any of the following forms:

> The best statement of the main idea is . . .
>
> The best title for this passage is . . .
>
> The author is primarily concerned with . . .
>
> The central theme of the passage is . . .

Incorrect responses to main-idea items tend to fall into two categories. Some responses will be too general and express more ideas than are actually included in the passage. Other incorrect items will be details within the passage that support the main idea. The details might be interesting and grab your attention, but they do not describe the central focus of the passage. If you are having difficulty with the main idea, reread the first and last sentences of the passage. Sometimes, though not always, one of the two sentences will give you an overview or focus.

The following main-idea items apply to Practice Passage A on Catherine the Great.

EXAMPLE   Read the following main-idea items. The italicized parenthetical remarks reflect the thinking involved in judging a correct or incorrect response.

_____ The best statement of the main idea of this passage is
a. Peter lost his country through ignorance and drink.
(Important detail, but focus is on her.)

b. Gossip of Catherine's affairs intrigued the Russian people. (*Very interesting, but a detail.*)
c. Progress for the Russian people was slow to come. (*Too broad and general, or not really covered.*)
d. Catherine came to Russia as a poor girl but emerged as a powerful empress and a shrewd politician. (*Yes, sounds great.*)

_____ The best title for this passage is
a. Catherine Changes Her Name. (*Detail.*)
b. Peter Against Catherine. (*Only part of the story, so detail.*)
c. Catherine the Great, Empress of Russia. (*Sounds best.*)
d. Success of Women in Russia. (*Too broad—this is only about one woman.*)

Details

Detail questions check your ability to locate and understand explicitly stated material. Frequently, such items can be answered correctly without a thorough understanding of the passage. To find the answer to such an item, note a key word in the question and then scan the passage for the word or a synonym. When you locate the term, reread the sentence to double-check your answer. Lead-ins for detail questions fall into the following patterns:

The author states that . . .

According to the author . . .

According to the passage . . .

All of the following are true except . . .

A person, term, or place is . . .

Incorrect answers to detail questions tend to be false statements. Sometimes the test maker will trick the unsophisticated reader by using a pompous or catchy phrase from the passage as a **distractor**—a word that is meant to divert your attention away from the correct response. The phrase might indeed appear in the passage and sound authoritative, but on close inspection, it means nothing.

EXAMPLE Read the following detail question on Catherine the Great, and note the remarks in parentheses:

_____ Catherine changed all the following except (*look for the only false item as the answer*)
a. her religion. (*True, she joined the Orthodox church.*)
b. her name. (*True, from Sophia to Catherine.*)
c. Russia's borders. (*True, she gained seaports.*)
d. the poverty of the serfs. (*The serfs were worse off but still in poverty, so this is the best answer.*)

Implied Meaning

Questions concerning implied meaning test your ability to look beyond what is directly stated and your understanding of the suggested meaning.

Items testing implied meaning deal with the writer's attitudes, feelings, or the motivation of characters. They may come in the form of sarcastic comments, snide remarks, favorable and unfavorable descriptions, and a host of other hints and clues. Lead-ins for such items include the following:

> The author believes (or feels or implies) . . .
>
> It can be inferred from the passage . . .
>
> The passage or author suggests . . .
>
> It can be concluded from the passage that . . .

To answer inference items correctly, look for clues to help you develop logical assumptions. Base your conclusions on what is known and what is suggested. Incorrect inference items tend to be false statements.

EXAMPLE   Study the following inference question. The parenthetical italicized remarks reflect the thought process involved in selecting the correct answer.

_____   The author implies that Catherine
   a. did not practice the enlightenment she professed. (*Yes, "eloquent in theory but lacking practice."*)
   b. preferred French over Russian architecture. (*Not suggested.*)
   c. took Voltaire as her lover. (*Not suggested.*)
   d. came to Russia knowing her marriage would be unhappy. (*Not suggested.*)

Purpose

The purpose of a reading passage is not usually stated; it is implied. In a sense, the purpose is part of the main idea; you probably need to understand the main idea to understand the purpose. Generally, however, reading comprehension tests include three basic types of passages, and each type tends to dictate its own purpose. Study the following three types.

1. Factual
   Identification: gives the facts about science, history, or other subjects.
   Strategy: if complex, do not try to understand each detail before going to the questions. Remember, you can look back.
   Example: textbook.
   Purposes: to inform, to explain, to describe, or to enlighten.

2. Opinion
   Identification: puts forth a particular point of view.
   Strategy: the author states opinions and then refutes them. Sort out the opinions of the author and the opinions of the opposition.
   Example: newspaper editorial.
   Purposes: to argue, to persuade, to condemn, or to ridicule.

3. Fiction
   Identification: tells a story.
   Strategy: read slowly to understand the motivation and interrelationships of characters.
   Example: novel or short story
   Purposes: to entertain, narrate, describe, or shock.

EXAMPLE   Read the following test item, and identify the purpose:

_____   The purpose of the passage on Catherine is
  a. to argue. (*No side is taken.*)
  b. to explain. (*Yes, because it is factual material.*)
  c. to condemn. (*Not judgmental.*)
  d. to persuade. (*No opinion is pushed.*)

Vocabulary

Vocabulary items test your general word knowledge as well as your ability to use context to figure out word meaning. The typical form for vocabulary items on reading comprehension tests is as follows:

As used in the passage, the best definition of _____ is _____.

Note that both word knowledge and context are necessary for a correct response. The item is qualified by "As used in the passage," so you must go back and reread the sentence (context) in which the word appears to be sure you are not misled by multiple meanings. To illustrate, the word *pool* means *a body of water* as well as *a group of people* as in *the shrinking pool of job applicants.* As a test taker, you would need to double-check the context to see which meaning appears in your test passage. In addition, if you knew only one definition of the word *pool,* rereading the sentence would perhaps suggest the alternate meaning to you and help you answer the item correctly.

EXAMPLE   Read the following vocabulary test item, and note the reader's thought process in the parenthetical statements:

_____   As used in the passage, the best definition of *dreary* (see the second paragraph) is
  a. sad. (*Yes, unhappiness is used in the previous sentence.*)
  b. commonplace. (*Possible, but not right in the sentence.*)
  c. stupid. (*Not right in the sentence.*)
  d. neglected. (*True, but not the definition of the word.*)

Strategies for Multiple-Choice Items

Consider All Alternatives Before Choosing an Answer

Read all the options. Do not rush to record an answer without considering all the alternatives. Be careful, not careless, in considering each option. Multiple-choice test items usually ask for the best choice for an answer, rather than any choice that is reasonable.

EXAMPLE   Choose the best answer.

_____   Peter was most likely called a "moronic booby" because
a. he neglected Catherine.
b. he drank too much.
c. he disliked German customs.
d. he played with dolls and toys.

EXPLANATION Although the first three answers are true and reasonable, the last answer seems to be most directly related to that particular name.

Anticipate the Answer and Look for Something Close to It

As you read the beginning of a multiple-choice item, anticipate what you would write for a correct response. Develop an answer in your mind before you read the options, and then look for a response that corroborates your thinking.

EXAMPLE   Before choosing from among *a*, *b*, *c*, and *d*, try to anticipate the correct response. Note the reader's thought process in italics.

_____   The author suggests that Catherine probably converted to the Russian Orthodox church because . . . *she wanted to rule the country and wanted the people to think of her as Russian, rather than German.*
a. she was a very religious person.
b. Peter wanted her to convert.
c. she was no longer in Germany.
d. she wanted to appear thoroughly Russian to the Russian people.

EXPLANATION The last answer most closely matches the kind of answer you were anticipating.

Avoid Answers with 100 Percent Words

All and *never* mean 100 percent, without exceptions. A response containing either word is seldom correct. Rarely can a statement be so definitely inclusive or exclusive. Here are some other 100 percent words to avoid:

no	none	only
every	always	must

EXAMPLE Answer the following with *true* or *false:*

_____ Catherine the Great was beloved by all the Russian people.

EXPLANATION *All* means 100 percent and thus is too inclusive. Surely one or two Russians did not like Catherine, so the answer must be *false.*

Consider Answers with Qualifying Words

Words like *sometimes* and *seldom* suggest frequency but do not go so far as to say *all* or *none*. Such qualifying words can mean more than *none* and less than *all*. By being so indefinite, the words are difficult to dispute. Therefore, qualifiers are more likely to be included in a correct response. Here are some other qualifiers:

few	much	often	may
many	some	perhaps	generally

EXAMPLE Answer the following with *true* or *false:*

_____ Catherine was beloved by many of the Russian people.

EXPLANATION The statement is difficult to dispute, given Catherine's popularity. An uprising against her occurred, but it was put down, and she maintained the support of many of the Russian people. Thus, the answer would be *true.*

Choose the Intended Answer Without Overanalyzing

Try to follow logically the thinking of the test writer rather than overanalyzing minute points. Don't make the question harder than it is. Use your common sense and answer what you think was intended.

EXAMPLE Answer the following with *true* or *false:*

_____ Catherine was responsible for Peter's murder.

EXPLANATION This is false in that Catherine did not personally murder Peter. On the other hand, she did "tacitly consent" to his murder, which suggests responsibility. After seizing power, it was certainly in her best interest to

© 2005 by Pearson Education, Inc.

get rid of Peter permanently. Perhaps without Catherine, Peter would still be playing with his toys, so the intended answer is true.

True Statements Must Be True Without Exception

A statement is either totally true or it is incorrect. Adding an incorrect *and*, *but*, or *because* phrase to a true statement makes the statement false and thus an unacceptable answer. If a statement is half true and half false, mark it *false*.

EXAMPLE   Answer the following with *true* or *false:*

_____   Catherine was an enlightened despot who did her best to improve the lot of all her people.

EXPLANATION It is true that Catherine was considered an enlightened despot, but she did very little to improve the lot of the serfs. In fact, conditions for the serfs worsened. The statement is half true and half false, so it must be answered *false*.

If Two Options Are Synonymous, Eliminate Both

If *both* is not a possible answer and two possible answers say basically the same thing, then neither can be correct. Eliminate the two and spend your time on the others.

EXAMPLE   Choose the correct answer, watching for synonyms.

_____   The purpose of this passage is
a. to argue.
b. to persuade.
c. to inform.
d. to entertain.

EXPLANATION Because *argue* and *persuade* are basically synonymous, you can eliminate both and move to the other options.

Study Similar Options to Determine the Differences

If two similar options appear, frequently one of them will be correct. Study the options to see the subtle difference intended by the test maker.

EXAMPLE   Choose the correct answer, noticing options that are similar.

_____   Catherine was
a. unpopular during her reign.
b. beloved by all of the Russian people.

c. beloved by many of the Russian people.

d. considered selfish and arrogant by the Russians.

> **EXPLANATION** The first and last answers are untrue. Close inspection shows that the 100 percent *all* is the difference between the second and third answers that makes the second answer untrue. Thus, the third answer with the qualifying word is the correct response.

Use Logical Reasoning If Two Answers Are Correct

Some tests include the options *all of the above* and *none of the above*. If you see that two of the options are correct and you are unsure about a third choice, then *all of the above* would be a logical response.

EXAMPLE   Choose the best answer. Be alert to the possibility that two options are actually correct.

_____   Catherine started

a. the Imperial Academy of Art.

b. the first college of pharmacy.

c. the Hermitage.

d. all of the above.

> **EXPLANATION** If you remembered that Catherine started the first two but were not sure about the Hermitage, *all of the above* would be your logical option because you know that two of the above *are* correct.

Look Suspiciously at Directly Quoted Pompous Phrases

In searching for distractors, test makers sometimes quote a pompous phrase from the passage that doesn't make much sense. Students read the phrase and think, "Oh, yes, I saw that in the passage. It sounds good, so it must be right." Beware of such repetitions and make sure they make sense before choosing them.

EXAMPLE   Choose the answer that makes the most sense.

_____   In her country, Catherine enacted

a. few of the progressive ideas she championed.

b. the liberalism of the Enlightenment.

c. laws for liberty and equality.

d. the liberal areas of the philosophers.

> **EXPLANATION** The first response is correct because Catherine talked about progress but did little about it. The other three answers sound impressive and are quoted from the text but are totally incorrect.

Simplify Double Negatives by Canceling Out Both

Double negatives are confusing to unravel and time consuming to think through. Simplify a double negative statement by first canceling out both negatives. Then reread the statement without the confusion of the two negatives, and decide on the accuracy of the statement.

EXAMPLE   Answer the following with *true* or *false*, being alert for double negatives:

_____   Catherine's view of herself was not that of an unenlightened ruler.

EXPLANATION   Cancel out the two negatives, the *not* and the *un* in the word *unenlightened*. Reread the sentence without the negatives and decide on its accuracy: Catherine's view of herself was that of an enlightened ruler. The statement is correct, so the answer is *true*.

Use Can't-Tell Responses If Clues Are Insufficient

Mark an item *can't tell* only if you are not given clues on which to base an assumption. In other words, there is no evidence to indicate the statement is either true or false.

EXAMPLE   Use *true, false,* or *can't tell* to describe the following item:

_____   Catherine the Great had no children.

EXPLANATION   From the information in this passage, which is the information on which your reading test is based, you do not have any clues to indicate whether she did or did not have children. Thus, the answer must be *can't tell*.

Validate True Responses on "All the Following Except"

In this type of question, you must recognize several responses as correct and find the one that is incorrect. Corroborate each response and, by the process of elimination, find the one that does not fit.

Note Oversights on Hastily Constructed Tests

Reading tests developed by professional test writers are usually well constructed and do not contain obvious clues to the correct answers. However, some teacher-made tests are hastily constructed and contain errors in test making that can help a student find the correct answer. Do not, however, rely on these flaws to make a big difference in your score because they should not occur in a well-constructed test.

Grammar. Eliminate responses that do not have subject-verb agreement. The tense of the verb as well as modifiers such as *a* or *an* can also give clues to the correct response.

EXAMPLE Choose the correct answer to the following, paying attention to grammar:

_____ Because of his described habits, it is possible that Peter was an
a. hemophiliac.
b. alcoholic.
c. Catholic.
d. barbarian.

EXPLANATION The *an* suggests an answer that starts with a vowel. Thus *alcoholic* is the only possibility.

Clues from Other Parts of the Test. If a test has been hastily constructed, information in one part of the test might help you with an uncertain answer.

EXAMPLE Select the word that completes the following sentence correctly. Keep in mind the question you answered in the previous example.

_____ Not only was Peter childlike and neglectful, but he was also frequently
a. abusive.
b. drunk.
c. dangerous.
d. out of the country.

EXPLANATION The previous question gives this answer away by stating that he was possibly an alcoholic.

Length. On poorly constructed tests, longer answers are correct more frequently.

EXAMPLE Identify the option that completes the following sentence correctly:

_____ The word *cunning* used in describing Catherine suggests that she was
a. evil
b. dishonest.
c. untrustworthy.
d. crafty and sly in managing affairs.

EXPLANATION In an effort to be totally correct without question, the test maker has made the last answer so complete that its length gives it away.

Absurd Ideas and Emotional Words. Avoid distractors with absurd ideas or emotional words. The test maker probably got tired of thinking of distractors and in a moment of weakness included nonsense.

EXAMPLE   Choose the answer that makes the most sense.

————————   As used in the passage, the term *house pets* refers to
a. Peter's toys.
b. Catherine's favorite lovers.
c. the dogs and cats in the palace.
d. trained seals that performed for the empress.

EXPLANATION   Yes, the test maker has, indeed, become weary. The question itself has very little depth, and the last two answers are particularly flippant.

Exercise 12.1

Reading with Understanding

Pretend that the following selection is a passage on a reading comprehension test. Use what you have learned to read with understanding and answer the questions.

It seems odd that one of the most famous figures of antiquity—the founder of a philosophical movement—was a vagrant with a criminal record. Diogenes the Cynic began life as the son of a rich banker. This fact may not seem so strange when one remembers the rebellious young people of the late 1960s in America, many of whom also came from affluent families.

The turning point in Diogenes' life came when his father, Hikesios, treasurer of the flourishing Greek commercial city of Sinope in Asia Minor, was found guilty of "altering the currency." Since Hikesios was a sound money man concerned about maintaining the high quality of the Sinopean coinage, this was obviously a miscarriage of justice. The Persian governor of nearby Cappadocia had issued inferior imitations of the Sinopean currency, and Hikesios, who realized that this currency was undermining the credit of Sinope, ordered the false coins to be defaced in order to put them out of circulation. But a faction of Sinopean citizens—it is not clear whether for economic or political reasons—successfully prosecuted Hikesios. Hikesios was imprisoned, and Diogenes, who was his father's assistant, was exiled. He eventually settled in Athens.

The shock of this experience caused Diogenes to become a rebel against society—to continue "altering the currency," but in a different way. He decided to stop the circulation of all false values, customs, and conventions. To achieve this goal, he adopted the tactics that made him notorious—complete freedom in speaking out on any subject and a type of outrageous behavior that he called "shamelessness."

Diogenes called free speech "the most beautiful thing in the world" because it was so effective a weapon. He shocked his contemporaries with such statements as "Most men are so nearly mad that a finger's breadth would make the difference." He advocated free love, "recognizing no other union than that of the man who persuades with the woman who consents." He insisted that "the love of money is the mother of all evils"; when some temple officials caught someone stealing a bowl from a temple, he said, "The great thieves are leading away the little thief." He liked to point out that truly valuable things cost little, and vice versa. "A statue sells for three thousand drachmas, while a quart of flour is sold for two copper coins." And when he was asked what was the right time to marry, he replied, "For a young man not yet; for an old man never at all."

Diogenes' "shamelessness"—his eccentric behavior—was his second weapon against the artificiality of conventional behavior as well as his means of promoting what he called "life in accordance with nature," or self-sufficiency. He believed that gods are truly self-sufficient and that people should emulate them: "It is the privilege of the gods to want nothing, and of men who are most like gods to want but little." It was said that he "discovered the means of adapting himself to circumstances through watching a mouse running about, not looking for a place to lie down, not afraid of the dark, not seeking any of the things that are considered dainties." And he got the idea for living in a large pottery jar—his most famous exploit—from seeing a snail carrying its own shell. Above all, Diogenes admired and emulated the life-style of dogs because of their habit of "doing everything in public." For this reason he was called *Kynos,* "the Dog," and his disciples were called Cynics.

"We live in perfect peace," one Cynic wrote, "having been made free from every evil by the Sinopean Diogenes." Eventually the citizens of Sinope also came to honor their eccentric exile with an inscription in bronze:

Even bronze grows old with time, but your fame, Diogenes, not all eternity shall take away. For you alone did point out to mortals the lesson of self-sufficiency, and the easiest path of life.

T. Walter Wallbank et al., *Civilization Past and Present*

Identify each question type and answer with *a, b, c,* or *d*. In the right-hand column, explain what is wrong with the incorrect distractors.

_____ 1. What is the best statement of the main idea of this passage?
(Question type _____) (Explain errors)
   a. The turning point in the life of Diogenes was the imprisonment of his father.
   b. The eccentric Diogenes founded a philosophy and promoted self-sufficiency. _____
   c. Diogenes became famous for living the life of a dog. _____
   d. The Greek way of life and thought changed under the influence of Diogenes. _____

_____ 2. The best title for this passage is
(Question type _____) (Explain errors)
   a. "Diogenes Shocks Athens." _____
   b. "Great Greek Philosophers." _____
   c. "The Eccentric Behavior of a Philosopher." _____
   d. "Diogenes, the Self-Sufficient Cynic." _____

_____   3. Diogenes' father
(Question type _____)   (Explain errors)
a. was exiled from Athens.   _____
b. destroyed counterfeit money.   _____
c. stole from the treasury.   _____
d. was treasurer of Sinope and Cappadocia.   _____

_____   4. The author believes that Diogenes was all the following except
(Question type _____)   (Explain errors)
a. uninhibited by tradition.   _____
b. insincere in not practicing what he
   preached.   _____
c. angered by his father's persecution.   _____
d. vocal in advocating free speech.   _____

_____   5. The author's purpose is to
(Question type _____)   (Explain errors)
a. argue.   _____
b. inform.   _____
c. ridicule.   _____
d. persuade.   _____

_____   6. As used in the passage, the best definition of *affluent* is
(Question type _____)   (Explain errors)
a. wealthy.   _____
b. close-knit.   _____
c. loving.   _____
d. politically prominent.   _____

Strategies for Content Area Exams

Almost all professors would say that the number one strategy for scoring high on content area exams is to study the material. Although this advice is certainly on target, there are other suggestions that can help you gain an edge.

Multiple-Choice Items

Multiple-choice, true-false, or matching items on content area exams are written to evaluate factual knowledge, conceptual comprehension, and application skill. *Factual questions* tap your knowledge of names, definitions, dates, events, and theories. *Conceptual comprehension* questions evaluate your ability to see relationships, notice similarities and differences, and combine information from different parts of a chapter. *Application questions* provide the opportunity to generalize from a theory to a real-life illustration; these are particularly popular in psychology and sociology.

To study for a multiple-choice test, make lists of key terms, facts, and concepts. Quiz yourself on recognition and general knowledge. Make connections and be sure you know similarities and differences. Finally, invent scenarios that depict principles and concepts.

EXAMPLE The following is an example of an application question from psychology:

_____ An illustration of obsessive-compulsive behavior is
a. Maria goes to the movies most Friday nights.
b. Leon washes his hands more than a hundred times a day.
c. Pepe wants to buy a car.
d. Sue eats more fish than red meat.

EXPLANATION The second response is obviously correct, but such questions can be tricky if you have not prepared for them. Use your own knowledge, plus the previous suggestions for multiple-choice tests, to separate answers from distractors.

Short-Answer Items

Professors ask short-answer questions because they want you to use your own words to describe or identify. For such questions, be sure that you understand exactly what the professor is asking you to say. You do not want to waste time writing more than is needed, but on the other hand, you do not want to lose points for not writing enough. Study for short-answer items by making lists and self-testing, just as you do when studying for multiple-choice items. For history exams, especially, be prepared to identify who, what, when, where, and why.

Essay Questions

Essay answers demand more effort and energy from the test taker than multiple-choice items. On a multiple-choice test, all the correct answers are before you. On an essay exam, however, the only thing in front of you is a question and a blank sheet of paper. This blank sheet can be intimidating to many students. Your job is to recall appropriate ideas, organize them under the central theme designated in the question, and create a response in your own words. The following suggestions can help you respond effectively.

Translate the Question. Frequently, an essay "question" is not a question at all but a statement that you are asked to support. When you see this type of question on a test, your first step is to read it and then reread it to be sure you understand it. Next, reword it into a question. Even if you begin with a question, translate it into your own words. Simplify the question into terms you can understand. Break the question into its parts.

Convert the translated parts of the question into the approach that you will need to use to answer each part. Will you define, describe, explain, or compare? State what you will do to answer. In a sense, this is a behavioral statement.

EXAMPLE   The following example demonstrates the translation process.

- **Statement to support:** It is both appropriate and ironic to refer to Catherine as one of the great rulers of Russia.

- **Question:** Why is it both appropriate and ironic to refer to Catherine as one of the great rulers of Russia?

- **Translation:** The question has two parts:
  1. What did Catherine do that was great?
  2. What did she do that was the opposite of what you would expect (irony) of a great Russian ruler?

- **Response approach:** List what Catherine did that was great and then list what she did that was the opposite of what you would expect of a great Russian ruler. Relate her actions to the question. (See page 561.)

Answer the Question. Make sure your answer is in response to the question that is asked, rather than a summary of everything you know about a particular subject. Write with purpose so that the reader can understand your views and relate your points to the subject. Padding your answer by repeating the same idea or including irrelevant information is obvious to graders and seldom appreciated.

EXAMPLE   The following is an inappropriate answer to the question "Why is it both appropriate and ironic to refer to Catherine as one of the great rulers of Russia?"

> Catherine was born in Germany and came to Russia as a young girl to marry Peter. It was an unhappy marriage that lasted seventeen years. She . . .

EXPLANATION   This response does not answer the question; rather, it is a summary.

Organize Your Response. Do not write the first thing to pop into your head. Take a few minutes to brainstorm and jot down ideas. Number the ideas in the order that you wish to present them, and use the plan shown on the opposite page as your outline for writing.

In your first sentence, establish the purpose and direction of your response. Then list specific details that support, explain, prove, and develop your point. Reemphasize the points in a concluding sentence, and restate your purpose. Whenever possible, use numbers or subheadings to simplify your message for the reader. If time runs short, use an outline or a diagram to express your remaining ideas.

> I. Appropriate
> 1. Acquired land
> 2. Art, medicine, buildings
> 3. 34 years
> 4. Political skill & foreign diplomacy
>
> II. Ironic (opposite)
> 1. Not Russian
> 2. Killed Peter
> 3. Serfs very poor
> 4. Revolt against her

EXAMPLE To answer the previous question, think about the selection on Catherine and jot down the ideas that you would include in a response.

Use an Appropriate Style. Your audience for this response is not your best friend but your learned professor who is giving you a grade. Be respectful. Do not use slang. Do not use phrases like "as you know," "like," or "well." They may be appropriate in conversation, but they are not appropriate in formal writing.

Avoid empty words and thoughts. Words like *good*, *interesting*, and *nice* say very little. Be more direct and descriptive in your writing.

State your thesis, supply proof, and use transitional phrases to tie your ideas together. Words like *first*, *second*, and *finally* help to organize enumerations. Terms like *however* and *on the other hand* show a shift in thought. Remember, you are pulling ideas together, so use phrases and words to help the reader see relationships.

EXAMPLE Study the following response to the question for organization, transition, and style.

> Catherine was a very good ruler of Russia. She tried to be Russian but she was from Germany. Catherine was a good politician and got Russia seaports on the Baltic, Caspian, and Black Sea. She had many boyfriends and there was gossip about her. She did very little for the Serfs because they remained very poor for a long time. She built nice buildings and got doctors to help people. She was not as awesome as she pretended to be.

EXPLANATION Notice the response's lack of organization, weak language, inappropriate phrases, and failure to use transitional words.

Be Aware of Appearance. Research has shown that, on the average, an essay written in a clear, legible hand receives a score that is one grade level higher than does the essay written somewhat illegibly.[6] Be particular about appearance and considerate of the reader. Proofread for correct grammar, punctuation, and spelling.

Predict and Practice. Predict possible essay items by using the table of contents and subheadings of your text to form questions. Practice brainstorming to answer these questions. Review old exams for an insight both into the questions and the kinds of answers that received good marks. Outline answers to possible exam questions. Do as much thinking as possible to prepare yourself to take the test before you sit down to begin writing. The Reader's Tip shows the range of demands you might encounter in essay exams for your courses.

READER'S TIP

Key Words in Essay Questions

The following key words of instruction appear in essay questions.

◆ **Compare:** List the similarities between things.

◆ **Contrast:** Note the differences between things.

◆ **Criticize:** State your opinion and stress the weaknesses.

◆ **Define:** State the meaning so that the term is understood, and use examples.

◆ **Describe:** State the characteristics so that the image is vivid.

◆ **Diagram:** Make a drawing that demonstrates relationships.

◆ **Discuss:** Define the issue and elaborate on the advantages and disadvantages.

◆ **Evaluate:** State positive and negative views and make a judgment.

◆ **Explain:** Show cause and effect and give reasons.

◆ **Illustrate:** Provide examples.

◆ **Interpret:** Explain your own understanding of a topic that includes your opinions.

(continued)

---

[6]H. W. James, "The Effect of Handwriting upon Grading," *English Journal* 16 (1927): 180–185.

- ◆ **Justify:** Give proof or reasons to support an opinion.
- ◆ **List:** Record a series of numbered items.
- ◆ **Outline:** Sketch out the main points with their significant supporting details.
- ◆ **Prove:** Use facts as evidence in support of an opinion.
- ◆ **Relate:** Connect items and show how one influences another.
- ◆ **Review:** Write an overview with a summary.
- ◆ **Summarize:** Retell the main points.
- ◆ **Trace:** Move sequentially from one event to another.

View Your Response Objectively for Evaluation Points. Respond to get points. Some students feel that filling up the page deserves a passing grade. They do not understand how a whole page written on the subject of Catherine could receive no points.

Although essay exams seem totally subjective, they cannot be. Students need to know that a professor who gives an essay exam grades answers according to an objective scoring system. The professor examines the paper for certain relevant points that should be made. The student's grade reflects the quantity, quality, and clarity of these relevant points.

Unfortunately, essay exams are shrouded in mystery. Sometimes the hardest part of answering an item is to figure out what the professor wants. Ask yourself, "What do I need to say to get enough points to pass or to make an A?"

Do not add personal experiences or extraneous examples unless they are requested. You may be wasting your time by including information that will give you no points. Stick to the subject and the material. Demonstrate to the professor that you know the material by selectively using it in your response.

The professor scoring the response to the question about Catherine used the following checklist for evaluation:

Appropriate	Ironic
1. Acquired land	1. Not Russian
2. Art, medicine, buildings	2. Killed Peter
3. 34 years	3. Serfs very poor
4. Political skill and foreign diplomacy	4. Revolt against her

The professor determined that an "A" paper should contain all the items. To pass, a student should include five of the eight categories covered. Listing and explaining fewer than five would not produce enough points to pass. Naturally, the professor would expect clarity and elaboration in each category.

After the Test, Read an "A" Paper. Maybe the "A" paper will be yours. If so, share it with others. If not, ask to read an "A" paper so that you will have a model from which to learn. Ask your classmates or ask the professor. You can learn a lot from reading a good paper; you can see what you could have done.

When your professor returns a multiple-choice exam, you can reread items and analyze your mistakes to figure out what you did wrong. However, you cannot review essay exams so easily. You may get back a "C" paper with only a word or two of comment and never know what you should have done. Ideally, essay exams should be returned with an example of what would have been a perfect "A" response so that students can study and learn from a perfect model and not make the same mistakes on the next test, but this is seldom, if ever, done. Your best bet is to ask to see an "A" paper.

EXAMPLE   Study the following response to the previous question. The paper received an A.

> To call Catherine one of the great rulers of Russia is both appropriate and ironic. It is appropriate because she expanded the borders of Russia. Through her cunning, Russia annexed part of Poland and expanded the frontier to the Black, Caspian, and Baltic seas. Catherine professed to be enlightened and formed an art academy and a college of pharmacy, and she imported foreign physicians. She built many architecturally significant buildings, including the Hermitage. For thirty-four years she amazed the Russian people with her political skill and diplomacy.
>
> On the other hand, Catherine was not a great Russian, nor was she an enlightened leader of all the people. First, she was not Russian; she was German, but she had worked hard to "russify" herself during the early years of her unhappy marriage. Second, and ironically, she murdered the legitimate ruler of Russia. When she seized power, she made sure the tsar quickly died of "hemorrhoidal colic." Third, she did nothing to improve the lot of the poor serfs and after a bloody uprising in 1773, she became even more despotic. Yet, Catherine was an engaging character who, through her cunning and intellect, has become known to the world in history books as "Catherine the Great."

EXPLANATION   Note the organization, logical thinking, and effective use of transitions in this response.

Locus of Control

Have you ever heard students say, "I do better when I don't study," or "No matter how much I study, I still get a C"? According to Julian Rotter, a learning theory psychologist who believes that people develop attitudes about control of their lives, such comments reflect an *external locus of control* regarding test taking.[7] People with an external locus of control, called "externalizers," feel that fate, luck, or other people control what happens to them. Because they feel they can do little to avoid what befalls them, they do not face matters directly and thus do not take responsibility for failure or credit for success.

On the other hand, people who have an *internal locus of control* feel that they, not "fate," have control over what happens to them. Such students might evaluate test performance by saying, "I didn't study enough" or "I should have spent more time organizing my essay response." "Internalizers" feel their rewards are due to their own actions, and they take steps to be sure they receive those rewards. When it comes to test taking, be an internalizer: Take responsibility, take control, and accept credit for your success.

Summary Points

● Can being testwise improve your score?

Test taking is a serious part of the business of being a college student. Preparation and practice—being testwise—can lead to improved scores on both standardized reading tests and content area exams.

● How should you prepare before a test?

Study according to the type of test you are taking. Plan your study times to avoid having to cram. Arrive rested and alert.

● What should you notice during a test?

Read the directions, and keep up with the time.

● What strategies should you use to read a comprehension passage?

Items on standardized reading tests tend to follow a predictable pattern and include five major question types. Learn to recognize these types and the skills needed for answering each.

● What are the major question types?

They are (1) main idea, (2) details, (3) inference, (4) purpose, and (5) vocabulary.

● What hints help with multiple-choice items?

Be careful, not careless; consider all options; notice key words; and use logical reasoning.

● How do you answer an essay question?

Be sure you understand the question, brainstorm your response, organize your thoughts, and write in paragraphs with specific examples.

[7]Julian Rotter, "External Control and Internal Control," *Psychology Today* 5, no. 1 (1971): 37–42.

ESL: Making Sense of Figurative Language and Idioms

What Is ESL?

How many languages can you speak? Are you a native English speaker who has learned Spanish, or are you a native Farsi speaker who has learned English? If you have acquired skill in a second or third language, you know that it takes many years and plenty of patience to master the intricacies of a language. Not only must you learn new words, but you must also learn new grammatical constructions. For example, the articles that are habitually used in English such as *a, an,* or *the* do not appear in Russian, Chinese, Japanese, Thai, or Farsi. In Spanish and Arabic, personal pronouns restate the subject, as in *My sister she goes to college.* In Spanish, Greek, French, Vietnamese, and Portuguese, "to words" are used rather than "-ing words," as in *I enjoy to play soccer.* These complexities, which are innately understood by native speakers, make direct translation from one language to another difficult. The English language, especially, has many unusual phrases and grammatical constructions that defy direct translation.

To assist students with these complexities, most colleges offer courses in ESL, which stands for English as a Second Language. These courses are designed to teach language skills to nonnative speakers of English. If you are an ESL student, you may have been recruited through an international exchange program with another college, you may be a newly arrived immigrant, or you may be a citizen with a bilingual background. You bring a multicultural perspective to classroom discussions and campus life that will broaden the insights of others. Not only are some obvious things like holidays different from those of others, but your sense of family life, work, and responsibility may also be different. Share your thoughts and ideas with native English speakers as they share the irregularities of the language with you.

What Is Figurative Language?

One aspect of the English language that defies direct translation and confuses nonnative speakers, and sometimes even native speakers, is figurative language. This is the manipulation of the language to create images, add interest, and draw comparisons by using figures of speech (see Chapter 7 on inference). The two most commonly used figures of speech are *similes* and *metaphors.*

Simile: a stated comparison using *like* or *as*

The baby swims like a duck.

© 2005 by Pearson Education, Inc.

Metaphor: an implied comparison

The baby is a duck in water.

Many figurative expressions are common in English. As in the previous metaphor, the *baby* is not actually a *baby duck*, but the implication is that *the baby swims very well*. However, neither direct translation nor a dictionary will unlock that meaning. When you encounter a figure of speech, look for clues within the sentence to help you guess the meaning.

Directions

The following practice exercises contain figurative language. Read each dialogue passage for meaning and then use the context clues to match the number of the boldfaced figure of speech with the letter of the appropriate definition. To narrow your choices, the answers to questions 1 through 5 can be found in choices a through e, and the answers to questions 6 through 10 can be found in choices f through j.

Exercise 1

Angelina: You're (1) **as busy as a bee**. What are you working on?

Ginger: I'm working (2) **like gangbusters** on plans for Tony's twenty-first birthday party. Of the new associates hired last summer, Tony is (3) the **cream of the crop**. We are only inviting people from our office and Tony's old friends, but I know that (4) **every Tom, Dick, and Harry** will want to come.

Angelina: Can I (5) **give you a hand** so the party (6) **gets off the ground** smoothly?

Ginger: Sure. You can help me (7) **dig up** some of Tony's old pals who have been living (8) **like nomads** since high school.

Angelina: I've been (9) **down in the dumps,** so this is a good project for me.

Ginger: Terrific! Just remember, it's a surprise, so (10) **keep it under your hat**.

_____	1. as busy as a bee	a. best
_____	2. like gangbusters	b. average person
_____	3. cream of the crop	c. buzzing with activity
_____	4. every Tom, Dick, and Harry	d. help you
_____	5. give you a hand	e. with energetic speed
_____	6. gets off the ground	f. wandering from place to place
_____	7. dig up	g. go into action; gets started
_____	8. like nomads	h. keep it secret
_____	9. down in the dumps	i. find; locate
_____	10. keep it under your hat	j. depressed

Exercise 2

Julio: I wish everyone would (1) **get off my case**.

Renae: Did you (2) **get up on the wrong side of the bed?** What's wrong?

Julio: My professor (3) **caught me off guard** yesterday when she wanted a quick answer to a difficult question, and I couldn't (4) **pull it out of a hat**. I got upset, and the situation (5) **went from bad to worse**. Next, I (6) **got behind the eight ball** with my boss when I arrived late for work. (7) **The final straw** came when my folks got (8) **up in arms** last night because I'm behind in my schoolwork.

Renae: I'm glad I could listen while you (9) **let off some steam**.

Julio: Thanks for listening. Now I need to (10) **get my act together**.

_____	1. get off my case	a.	produce as if by magic
_____	2. get up on the wrong side of the bed	b.	deteriorated
		c.	stop nagging or criticizing
_____	3. caught me off guard	d.	be in a bad mood
_____	4. pull it out of a hat	e.	surprised me
_____	5. went from bad to worse	f.	release tension by talking
_____	6. got behind the eight ball		unrestrainedly
_____	7. the final straw	g.	got in an unfavorable position
_____	8. up in arms	h.	to behave responsibly and efficiently
_____	9. let off some steam	i.	the last insult one can endure
_____	10. get my act together	j.	angered; feeling displeasure

Exercise 3

Rodney: This car I bought is (1) **a lemon**. The gas gauge and speedometer seem to have (2) **given up the ghost**. Next time I buy a used car, I'm going to have a mechanic (3) **go over** it (4) **with a fine-tooth comb**.

Jamal: My brother is a mechanic. He is busy, but if you need (5) an **ace in the hole**, I'll ask him to help you. He is certainly (6) **on the up and up**.

Rodney: Great! I'm going to (7) **bite the bullet** and (8) **dump** this car. Imagine if I run out of gas on the highway or get a speeding ticket on a date. That wouldn't (9) **go over big** with the girl.

Jamal: Maybe you should (10) **have it out with** the guy who sold it to you.

_____	1. a lemon	a.	resource in reserve
_____	2. given up the ghost	b.	very carefully
_____	3. go over	c.	merchandise that is defective
_____	4. with a fine-tooth comb	d.	examine
_____	5. ace in the hole	e.	not be working
_____	6. on the up and up	f.	accept the unpleasant reality
_____	7. bite the bullet	g.	discuss the conflict
_____	8. dump	h.	get rid of
_____	9. go over big	i.	trustworthy
_____	10. have it out with	j.	impress

What Are Common English Idioms?

An **idiom** is an expression with a special meaning that cannot be understood by directly translating each individual word. Because of years of exposure to the language, native speakers usually understand idioms. However, they are confusing if you are learning English as a second language.

Idioms are more common in spoken and informal language than in formal writing. In fact, most idiomatic expressions can usually be replaced by a single formal word. To add to the confusion, some idioms have more than one meaning, and many idioms are grammatically irregular.

EXAMPLE   What does the idiomatic expression *go over* mean in the following sentences?

(a) How did my speech *go over?*

(b) I want to *go over* the exam paper with the professor.

EXPLANATION   In both sentences, the use of the idiom is informal. A more formal version of each would be the following:

(a) How was my speech *received* by the audience?

(b) I want to *review* the exam paper with the professor.

Notice the grammatical irregularity in the first sentence. *Over* is not followed by a noun (the name of a person, place, or thing) as a preposition (a connecting word, like *in*, *out*, and *at*) normally would be according to the rules of grammar. Instead, *over* becomes part of the verb phrase (words showing action). Thus, the translation requires a change in wording, whereas the second use of the idiom is grammatically correct and can be directly translated by the single word *review*.

READER'S TIP

Categorizing Idioms

Idioms are sometimes categorized into the following groups:

◆ Word families: grouping around a similar individual word

Down as in *step down, take down, pipe down, narrow down, nail down, run down, tear down, knock down, let down, die down, cut down*, etc.

◆ Verb + preposition: action word plus a connecting word

Hammer away means persist, *stand for* means represent, and *roll back* means reduce.

◆ Preposition + noun: connecting word plus the name of a person, place, or thing

On foot means walking, *by heart* means memorized, and *off guard* means surprised.

◆ Verb + adjective: action word plus a descriptive word

Think twice means consider carefully, *hang loose* means be calm, and *play fair* means deal equally.

◆ Pairs of nouns: two words naming a person, place, or thing

Flesh and blood means kin, *part and parcel* means total, and *pins and needles* means nervous.

◆ Pairs of adjectives: two descriptive words

Cut and dried means obvious, *fair and square* means honest, *short and sweet* means brief.

No one will argue that understanding idioms is easy. If you go to a bookstore, you will see that entire books have been written about categorizing, recognizing, and translating thousands of them. To help clear up the confusion, some books group idioms according to families like root words, and others categorize them according to grammatical constructions. Either way, understanding idiomatic expressions depends more on using context clues to figure out meaning and familiarity with the informal, spoken language than with learning rules.

In the following practice exercises, use the context clues within each sentence to write the meaning of the boldfaced idiom in the blank provided.

Exercise 4

1. If you call Esmeralda at work, **cut to the chase** quickly because she is very busy creating the new product advertisements. _____

2. When Marcy stopped him in the hall, Jim was **in a rush** because his math class had already begun. _____

3. Tom hadn't been notified that the party was formal and he looked **out of place** in his jeans. _____

4. Juanita had a **heart-to-heart** talk about boys and dating with her younger sister. _____

5. His channel surfing and the constant clicking of the TV remote control are getting **on my nerves**. _____

6. Miguel is going to backpack through Europe after he graduates, but it will have to be **on a shoestring** because he hasn't been able to save much money. _____

7. Denise didn't study for the exam she is taking; she decided to **wing it** and hope for the best. _____

8. I can't **get over** how much my blind date last night looked like Brad Pitt. _____

9. Rather than being timid about the new job, just **give it your best shot**. _____

10. Being assigned to the new project at work will finally give me a chance to **pull out all the stops** and show them what I'm really worth. _____

Exercise 5

1. I try to do my homework every night because I feel anxious if it starts to **pile up** and I get behind schedule. _____

2. I'm feeling **on top of the world** with my new laptop computer. _____

3. Sergio and I are **on the same wavelength** about how the club money should be spent. _____

4. Let's **put our heads together** and see if we can grill hamburgers without buying more charcoal. _____

5. When you go on the job interview, don't **sell yourself short** by being too modest about your skills. _____

6. After her husband's lung cancer, my aunt quit smoking *cold turkey*. _____

7. Melinda seemed to be **having a bad hair day,** so Tonya delayed mentioning that the concert tickets were twice the amount anticipated. _____

8. Mandy's little brother is too much of a **live wire** for me to baby-sit. _____

9. We might as well go in and **face the music** for breaking Dad's tool that we weren't supposed to be using. _____

10. I don't know how Eduardo can afford to buy every electronic gadget that comes on the market and still **make ends meet**. _____

Exercise 6

1. The city official gave an **in your face** answer to a taxpayer with a very legitimate question about an excessive water bill. _____

2. Her mother must have **nerves of steel** to be able to stay in a house full of screaming children and still remain sane. _____

3. Wanda has been walking around in a daze with her **head in the clouds** ever since she started dating Jose. _____

4. I've **had it** with Bill borrowing money and never paying it back. No more! _____

5. My little brother is **a pain in the neck** when he'd rather annoy my friends than stay in his room. _____

6. Tina is **playing with fire** by accepting rides from total strangers. _____

7. I just got paid, and I'm finally going to **shell out** for the new DVD player I've wanted to buy. _____

8. Without **a nest egg** for major expenses, senior citizens face financial difficulties trying to live solely on Social Security. _____

9. Roberto was **flying high** after he got accepted at the college of his first choice. _____

10. The senator was in a **catch-22** situation on the environmental issue because half of the voters in her constituency were for the new dam and half were against it. _____

Glossary

acronym An abbreviation pronounced as a word and contrived to simplify a lengthy name and gain quick recognition for an organization or agency. For example, *UNICEF* is the acronym for the United Nations International Children's Emergency Fund.

addition A pattern of organization that provides more information about something that has already been explained.

ad hominem An argument in which the person is attacked rather than the issue.

analogy A comparison showing connections with and similarities to previous experiences.

annotating A method of using symbols and notations to highlight textbook material for future study.

antonym A word that means the opposite of another word.

appeals to emotions A critical thinking fallacy that uses highly charged language used for emotional manipulation.

appeals to pity A critical thinking fallacy that pleas to support the underdog, the person or issue that needs your help.

argument Assertions that support a conclusion with the intention of persuading.

assertion A declarative statement.

attention Uninterrupted mental focus.

bandwagon A critical thinking fallacy that gives the idea that everybody is doing it and you will be left out if you do not quickly join the crowd.

bar graph An arrangement of horizontal or vertical bars in which the length of each represents an amount or number.

begging the question A critical thinking fallacy that gives support for the conclusion that is merely a restatement of it.

believability Support that is not suspicious but is believable.

bias An opinion or position on a subject recognized through facts slanted toward an author's personal beliefs.

bookmarking On the Internet, a save-the-site technique that lets you automatically return to the designated Web site with just one or two mouse clicks.

browser The software that searches to find information on the Internet.

cause and effect A pattern of organization in which one item is shown as having produced another.

chronological order A pattern of organization in which items are listed in time order or sequence.

circular reasoning A critical thinking fallacy that gives support for the conclusion that is merely a restatement of it.

classification A pattern of organization dividing information into a certain number of groups or categories. The divisions are then named and the parts are explained.

cognitive psychology A body of knowledge that describes how the mind works or is believed to work.

comparison A pattern of organization that presents items according to similarities between or among them.

comparison-contrast A pattern of organization in which similarities and differences are presented.

concentration The focusing of full attention on a task.

conclusion Interpretation based on evidence and suggested meaning.

connotation The feeling associated with the definition of a word.

consistency Support that holds together and does not contradict itself.

context clues Hints within a sentence that help unlock the meaning of an unknown word.

contrast A pattern of organization that presents items according to differences between or among them.

Cornell Method A system of notetaking that involves writing sentence summaries on the right side of the page with key words and topics indicated on the left.

creative thinking Generating many possible solutions to a problem.

critical thinking Deliberating in a purposeful, organized manner to assess the value of information or argument.

cumulative bar graph A bar graph that shows a cumulative effect in which all the bar's segments add up to a total. Rather than having multiple bars or lines, the groups are stacked on top of each other to dramatically show differences.

databases Computer-based indexes to assist research. A single article may be listed under several topics and may appear in several different indexes.

deductive reasoning Thinking that starts with a previously learned conclusion and applies it to a new situation.

definition A pattern of organization devoted to defining an idea and further explaining it with examples.

denotation The dictionary definition of a word.

description A pattern of organization listing characteristics of a person, place, or thing, as in a simple listing.

details Information that supports, describes, and explains the main idea.

diagram A drawing of an object showing labeled parts.

distractor A response on a multiple-choice test that detracts the reader from the correct response.

domain name A name registered by a Web site owner.

domain type The category to which a Web site owner belongs; for example, *edu* is the domain type for colleges and universities.

download A method of transferring a file from the Internet to a particular computer.

emoticons In e-mail communication, symbols such as smiley faces :) used to represent emotions in a lighthearted way. They are not appropriate for formal correspondence but are frequently used in informal contexts.

etymology The study of word origins involving the tracing of words back to their earliest recorded appearance.

euphemism A substitution of a mild, indirect, or vague term for one that is considered harsh, blunt, or offensive.

external distractors Temptations of the physical world that divert the attention from a task.

fact A statement that can be proved true.

fallacy An inference that first appears reasonable but closer inspection proves it to be unrelated, unreliable, or illogical.

figurative language Words used to create images that take on a new meaning.

fixation A stop the eyes make while reading.

flaming Offensive e-mails that make personal attacks.

flowchart A diagram showing how ideas are related, with boxes and arrows indicating levels of importance and movement.

generalization A pattern of organization in which a general statement or conclusion is supported with specific examples

habit A repetitious act almost unconsciously performed.

home page The entry point to a Web site through which other pages on the site can be reached.

homonyms Words with different meanings that are spelled and sound alike such as *bear* in "bear the burden" or "kill the bear."

humorous Comical, funny, or amusing.

hyperbole Exaggeration using figurative language to describe something as being more than it actually is.

hypertext links In Web technology, phrases that appear as bold blue or underlined text. Clicking on them will not only move you from one page to another within the Web site, but can also send you to other related Web sites. The words chosen and underlined as the link describe the information you are likely to find at that destination.

idiom A figurative expression that does not make literal sense but communicates a generally accepted meaning.

imagery Mental pictures created by figurative language.

implied meaning Suggested rather than directly stated meaning.

incomplete facts or **card stacking** A critical thinking fallacy that gives or leaves out factual details in order to misrepresent reality.

inductive reasoning Thinking based on the collection of data and the formulation of a conclusion based on it.

inference Subtle suggestions expressed without direct statement.

intent A reason or purpose for writing, which is usually to inform, persuade, or entertain.

internal distractions Concerns that come repeatedly to mind and disturb concentration.

Internet An electronic system of more than 25,000 computer networks using a common language that connects millions of users around the world. The Internet is the networked system that allows the World Wide Web to function.

irony A twist in meaning or a surprise ending that is the opposite of what is expected and may involve a humorous undertone.

knowledge network A cluster of knowledge about a subject; a schema.

lateral thinking A way of creatively thinking around a problem or redefining it to seek new solutions.

learning style A preference for a particular manner of presenting material to be learned.

line graph A frequency distribution in which the horizontal scale measures time and the vertical scale measures amount.

main idea A statement of the primary focus of the topic in a passage.

map A graphic designation or distribution.

mapping A method of graphically displaying material to show relationships and importance for later study.

metacognition Knowledge of how to read as well as the ability to regulate and direct the process.

metaphor A figure of speech that directly compares two unlike things (without using the words *like* or *as*).

misinterpreted statistics A critical thinking fallacy that improperly applies numerical data to unrelated populations that they were never intended to represent.

misleading analogy A critical thinking fallacy that gives a comparison of two things suggesting that they are similar when they are in fact distinctly different.

mnemonic A technique using images, numbers, rhymes, or letters to improve memory.

multiple intelligences The theory explained by Howard Gardner that there are eight different ways of being smart and some people develop certain intelligences to a greater extent than others.

multiple meanings The defining of a word in several ways. For example, the dictionary lists over thirty meanings for the word *run*.

notetaking A method of writing down short phrases and summaries to record textbook material for future study.

opinion A statement of a personal view or judgment.

outlining A method of using indentations, Roman numerals, numbers, and letters to organize a topic for future study.

overgeneralizations Examples and anecdotes asserted to apply to all cases rather than a select few. *Example:* High school students do little work during their senior year and thus are overwhelmed at college.

oversimplification A critical thinking fallacy that reduces an issue to two simple choices, without consideration of other alternatives or "gray areas" in between.

overstatement Exaggeration using figurative language to describe something as being more than it actually is.

pattern of organization The structure or framework for presenting the details in a passage.

personification Attributing human characteristics to nonhuman things.

pie graph A circular graph divided into wedge-shaped segments to show portions totaling 100 percent.

point of view A position or opinion on a subject.

politically correct language Doublespeak that is used to hide unpleasant ideas in politics or social interaction.

prefix A group of letters added to the beginning of a word and causing a change of meaning.

premise The thesis or main point of an argument.

previewing A method of glancing over a reading passage to predict what the passage is about and thus assess your prior knowledge and needed skills.

prior knowledge Previous learning about a subject.

propaganda A systematic and deliberate attempt to persuade others to a particular doctrine or point of view and to undermine any opposition.

purpose A writer's underlying reason or intent for writing.

questionable authority A critical thinking fallacy that gives a testimonial suggesting authority from people who are not experts.

rate Reading pace calculated according to the number of words read in one minute.

reading between the lines The figurative phrase for suggested thought for the reader or listener.

recall Reviewing what was included and learned after reading a passage.

regression Rereading material because of a lack of understanding or concentration.

relevance The degree to which related material supports a topic or conclusion.

root The stem or basic part of a word; in English, roots are derived primarily from Latin and Greek.

sarcasm A tone or language that expresses biting humor, usually meaning the opposite of what is said, with the purpose of undermining or ridiculing someone.

scanning Searching reading material quickly to locate specific points of information.

schema A skeleton or network of knowledge about a subject.

simile A comparison of two things using the words *like* or *as*.

simple listing A pattern of organization that lists items in a series.

skimming A technique for selectively reading for the gist or main idea.

slippery slope A critical thinking fallacy that objects to something because it will lead to greater evil and disastrous consequences.

spatial order A pattern of organization that identifies the whereabouts of a place or object.

straw person A critical thinking fallacy that gives a setup in which a distorted or exaggerated form of the opponent's argument is introduced and knocked down as if to represent a totally weak opposition.

study system A plan for working through stages to read and learn textbook material.

subvocalization The inaudible inner voice that is part of the reading process.

suffix A group of letters added to the end of a word and causing a change in meaning as well as the way the word can be used in the sentence.

summary A concise statement of the main idea and significant supporting details.

synonym A word with the same meaning of another word.

table A listing of facts and figures in columns for quick reference.

testimonials A critical thinking fallacy that gives opinions of agreement from respected celebrities who are not actually experts.

thesis statement A sentence that states the author's main point.

thinking An organized and controlled mental activity that helps you solve problems, make decisions, and understand ideas.

time order A pattern of organization that presents items in the chronological order in which they occurred.

to-do list A reminder list of activities that you need to accomplish.

tone A writer's attitude toward a subject.

topic sentence A sentence that condenses the thoughts and details of a passage into a general, all-inclusive statement of the author's message.

topic A word or phrase that labels the subject of a paragraph.

topic sentence A sentence that condenses the thoughts and details of a passage into a general, all-inclusive statement of the author's message.

transfer A critical thinking fallacy that gives an association with a positively or negatively regarded person or thing in order to lend the same association to the argument (also guilt or virtue by association).

transition A signal word that connects the parts of a sentence and leads readers to anticipate a continuation or a change in the writer's thoughts.

transitional words Connecting words that signal the direction of the writer's thought or the pattern of organization.

understatement Figurative language that minimizes a point.

Uniform Resource Locator (URL) The address for finding a specific site on the World Wide Web, just as an address and zip code are required to mail a letter. A URL is similar to an e-mail address, except that it routes you to a source of information called a *Web page* or *Web site* rather than to the mailbox of an individual person.

vertical thinking A straightforward and logical way of thinking that searches for a solution to the stated problem.

Web directory A type of search engine that organizes hypertext links into categories similar to the way in which libraries organize books into categories.

Web pages The formal presentation of information provided by individual people, businesses, educational institutions, or other organizations on the Internet.

World Wide Web (WWW) An electronic information network that is similar to an enormous library, with Web sites being like books and Web pages being like the pages in the books.

Credits

Joe Bauman, "Lions, Tigers, Wild Animals; Not Pets" from Deseret Morning News, November 3, 2003. Reprinted by permission.

Ramola Talwar Badam, "Police in India to Monitor Cyber Cafes" from AP, International Newswire, January 18, 2004. Reprinted with permission of The Associated Press.

Neil A. Campbell, Jane B. Reece, Eric J. Simon, *Essential Biology*, 2nd Edition © 2004. Reprinted by permission of Pearson Education, Inc., Upper Saddle River, NJ.

Daniel G. Bates, Elliot M. Fratkin, *Cultural Anthropology* 3e Published by Allyn and Bacon, Boston MA, © 2004 by Pearson Education. Reprinted by permission of publisher.

Sam, Max and Brian Burchers, *Vocabulary Cartoons* © 1997 New Monic Books, Inc. Reprinted by permission of the authors.

Michael H. Mescon, Courtland L. Bovee, John V. Thill, *Business Today*, 10th Edition, © 2002. Adapted by permission of Pearson Education, Inc., Upper Saddle River, NJ.

E. B. Harris, "He's Been Sleeping In My Bed" from the North Carolina Cattle Connection © June, 2003. Reprinted by permission of the author.

Suzanne C. Ryan, "Remembering the Alamo From a Tejano Perspective" from The Boston Globe, © 2004 by Globe Newspaper Co. (MA). Reprinted with permission of Globe Newspaper Co. (MA) in the format Textbook via Copyright Clearance Center.

David Atkinson, "Mixed Signals: Research Your Destination's Cultural Etiquette" from Business Traveler, January 1, 2004. Reprinted by permission of the author.

James K. Martin, Randy Roberts, Steven Mintz, Linda O. McMurry, James H. Jones, "Tejanos at The Alamo", from *America and It's Peoples: A Mosaic in the Making* (Vol. 1, 5th Edition) © 2004. Reprinted by permission of Pearson Education, Inc.

Randall Roberts, "U.S. Coast Guard's Efforts to Protect Ports" from AP, International Newswire, February 8, 2004. Reprinted with permission of The Associated Press.

Lee Arnold, "Centers Strive to Break Cycle of Violence" from The Herald Dispatch, November 1, 2003. Reprinted by permission of The Herald Dispatch.

Yashekia Small, "Former LA Gang Member to Recite Poetry" from The Daily News: Ball State University, February 18, 2004. Reprinted by permission of The Daily News.

Steven E. Barkin, George J. Bryjak, *Fundamentals of Criminal Justice*, published by Allyn and Bacon, Boston MA, © 2004 by Pearson Education. Reprinted by permission of publisher.

B. E. Pruitt, Jane J. Stein, *Decisions For Healthy Living*, © 2004 Reprinted by permission of Pearson Education, Inc.

John Vivian, *The Media of Mass Communication*, 6th Edition. Published by Allyn and Bacon, Boston MA, © 2003 by Pearson Education. Reprinted by permission of the publisher.

Alex, Thio, *Sociology* 5th Edition. Published by Allyn and Bacon, Boston MA, © 1998 by Pearson Education. Reprinted by permission of the publisher.

Stephen M. Kosslyn, Robin S. Rosenberg, *Psychology: The Brain, the Person, The World*, 2nd Edition. Published by Allyn and Bacon, Boston MA, © 2004 by Pearson Education. Reprinted by permission of publisher.

Michael H. Mescon, Courtland L. Bovee, John V. Thill, *Business Today*, 10th Edition. © 2002. Adapted by permission of Pearson Education, Inc., Upper Saddle River, NJ.

David L. Clawson, James Fisher, Samuel Aryeetey-Attoh, Roger Theide, *World Regional Geography: A Developmental Approach*, 8th Edition, © 2004. Reprinted by permission of Pearson Education, Inc., Upper Saddle River, NJ.

James MacGregor Burns, J. W. Peltason, Thomas E. Cronin, David E. Magleby, David M. O'Brien, Paul C. Light, *Government By The People*, 20th Edition, © 2004. Reprinted by permission of Pearson Education, Inc., Upper Saddle River, NJ.

Charles R. Swanson, Neil C. Chamelin, Leonard Territo, Criminal Investigation, 8th Edition © 2003 by McGraw-Hill Company. Reprinted by permission of McGraw-Hill Company.

John W. Santrock, Psychology, 7th Edition © 2003 by McGraw-Hill Company. Reprinted by permission of McGraw-Hill Company.

James K. Martin, Randy Roberts, Steven Mintz, Linda O. McMurry, James H. Jones, "The New Immigration", from *America and It's Peoples: A Mosaic in the Making* (Vol. 2, 5th Edition) © 2004. Reprinted by permission of Pearson Education, Inc.

Rebecca Donatelle, Access To Health, 8th Edition, © 2004. Reprinted by permission of Pearson Education, Inc.

John Keenan, "Low Carb Pizza Options" from The Omaha World-Herald, February 23, 2004. Reprinted with permission from the Omaha World-Herald.

James K. Martin, Randy Roberts, Steven Mintz, Linda O. McMurry, James H. Jones, *America and It's Peoples: A Mosaic in the Making* (Vol. 2, 5th Edition) © 2004. Reprinted by permission of Pearson Education, Inc.

Ricky W. Griffin, Ronald J. Ebert, Business, 7th Edition © 2004. Reprinted by permission of Pearson Education, Inc., Upper Saddle River, NJ.

Saul Kassin, Psychology, 4th Edition © 2004. Reprinted by permission of Pearson Education, Inc., Upper Saddle River, NJ.

Barbara D. Miller, Cultural Anthropology, 2nd Edition. Published by Allyn and Bacon, Boston MA, © 2004 by Pearson Education. Reprinted by permission of publisher.

Jessica Smith, "Lack of Moral Judgment Leads People To Do Things They Regret", from The Sentry (Crowder College, MO), February 3, 2004. Reprinted by permission of The Sentry via U-Wire.

John Pavlik, Shawn McIntosh, Converging Media: An Introduction to Mass Communication. Published by Allyn and Bacon, Boston MA, © 2004 by Pearson Education. Reprinted by permission of publisher.

John Vivian, The Media of Mass Communication, 6th Edition. Published by Allyn and Bacon, Boston MA, © 2003 by Pearson Education. Reprinted by permission of the publisher.

Samuel E. Wood, Ellen Green Wood, Denise Boyd, Mastering the World of Psychology. Published by Allyn and Bacon, Boston MA, © 2004 by Pearson Education. Reprinted by permission of publisher.

Time Magazine Pics.

Anne Bernays, Pamela Painter, What If? Writing Exercises for Fiction Writers, 2nd Edition. An Excerpt by Robie Macauly, "Handling the Problems of Time and Pace". © 2004. Reprinted by permission of Pearson Education, Inc.

Matt Marinovich, "Intelligence" published in The Quarterly. Reprinted by permission of the author.

Langston Hughes, "A Dream Deferred" from *The Panther and The Lash*. © 1951 by Langston Hughes. Reprinted by permission of Alfred A. Knopf, Inc.

Seamus Heaney, "Mid-Term Break" from *Opened Ground: Selected Poems 1966–1996*. Copyright © 1998 by Seamus Heaney. Reprinted by permission of Farrar, Straus and Giroux, LLC.

Kurt Vonnegut, Jr., *Deadeye Dick* © 1982 Dell Publishing. Reprinted by permission of publisher.

Kate Wheeler, *Not Where I Started From*, © 1993 by Kate Wheeler. Reprinted by permission of Houghton Mifflin Company. All rights reserved.

Michael Ondaatje, The English Patient, © 1992 by Harper & Row. Reprinted by permission of Random House, Inc.

Catherine L. Castner, Marlene Freedman, Bernadette Nagy, Darleen Giannini, excerpt jokes from the "Laughter, the Best Medicine" © 1997 by Reader's Digest.

O. Henry, Selected Stories. Edited by Guy Davenport © 1993 Penguin Group (USA) Inc. Public Domain.

Adil Ahmad, "Remembering A Civil Rights Hero" from The Dartmouth via U-Wire, April 12, 2004. Reprinted by permission of The Dartmouth via U-Wire.

William Maples, Dead Men Do Tell Lies, © 1994

Gary Larson, The Far Side, © 1982 Andrews and McMeel. Reprinted by permission of Creator's Syndicate.

Denis Horgan, "How I Lost It At The Glittery, High-Stakes Palaces of Gambling", from The Hartford Courant, April 11, 2004. Reprinted by permission of The Hartford Courant.

Catherine Lim, "Ah Bah's Money" © 1980. Reprinted by permission of the author.

Alex Haley and Malcolm X, "A Homemade Education" copyright © 1964. Copyright © 1965 by Alex Haley and Betty Shabazz, from The Autobiography of Malcolm X by Malcolm X and Alex Haley. Used by permission of Random House, Inc.

Evan Hunter, "Happy New Year Herbie and Other Stories" from On the Sidewalk Bleeding © 1963. Reprinted by permission of the author.

Robert Ramirez, "The Woolen Sarape". Reprinted by permission of the author.

Raymond Roseliep, "Campfire Extinguished" from Listen to Light: Haiku, © 1980 Alembic Press, Mayaquez, PR. Reprinted by permission.

Jim Schlosser, "O. Henry's Tender Story of Love and Sacrifice has Become a Christmas Classic," from The News & Record, NC, December 12, 1998. Reprinted by permission of the News & Record.

David L. Clawson and Merrill L. Johnson, World Regional Geography: A Development Approach, 8th Edition, © 2004. Reprinted by permission of Pearson Education, Inc.

Ellen Mitchell, "Orphans-to-be?", from Newsday (NY), April 10, 2004. Reprinted by permission of the author.

Ibn Warraq, Leaving Islam, © 2003 by Ibn Warraq (Amherst, NY: Prometheus Books). Reprinted with permission.

Amanda Quraishi, "Bridging the Gap between Muslims and the West", from The Austin American-Statesman, May 1, 2004. Reprinted by permission of the author.

Patrick Osio, Jr., "English, Spanish: The Must-Know Languages in the Western Hemisphere," from the Charleston Gazette, April 25, 2004. Reprinted by permission of the author.

David L. Clawson and Merrill L. Johnson, World Regional Geography: A Development Approach, 8th Edition, © 2004. Reprinted by permission of Pearson Education, Inc.

Edward F. Bergman and William H. Renwick, Introduction to Geography: People, Places and Environment, 2nd Edition, © 2003 Pearson Education. Inc. Reprinted with permission of Pearson Education, inc.

Jose Torres, "A Letter To A Child Like Me", from Parade Magazine, February 24, 1991. Reprinted by permission of the author and reprinted with permission from Parade, © 1991.

Thomas E. Patterson, We The People, A Concise Introduction to American Politics, 5th Edition, © 2004, The McGraw-Hill Company. Reprinted by permission of The McGraw-Hill Company.

Jay S. Albanese, Criminal Justice, 2nd Edition. Published by Allyn and Bacon, Boston MA, © 2002 by Pearson Education. Reprinted by permission of publisher.

Vincent Ryan Ruggiero, The Art of Thinking, 7th Edition, © 2004 Pearson Education, Inc. Reprinted by permission of Pearson Education, Inc.

Morris P. Fiorina, Paul E. Peterson, Bertram Johnson, The New American Democracy, 3rd Edition, © 2003. Reprinted by permission of Pearson Education, Inc.

B. E. Pruitt, Jane J. Stein, Decisions For Healthy Living, © 2004. Reprinted by permission of Pearson Education, Inc.

Linda L. Lindsey and Stephen Beach, Sociology, 3rd Edition, © 2004. Also: Source: Bouvier, Leon F., and Robert W. Gardner, 1986. "Immigration to the U.S.: An Unfinished Story." Population Bulletin 41 (November). 1999 U.S. Statistical Abstract, Table 8. Reprinted by permission of Pearson Education, Inc.

Karen O'Connor, Larry J. Sabato, Stefan D. Haag, Gary A. Keith, American Government: Continuity and Change, 2004 Texas Edition, © 2004. Reprinted by permission of Pearson Education, Inc.

Morris P. Fiorina, Paul E. Peterson, The New American Democracy, 3rd Edition, © 2003. Reprinted by permission of Pearson Education, Inc.

Thomas E. Patterson, We The People, A Concise Introduction to American Politics, 5th Edition, © 2004, The McGraw-Hill Company. Reprinted by permission of The McGraw-Hill Company.

Vincent Ryan Ruggiero, The Art of Thinking, 7th Edition, © 2004 Pearson Education, Inc. Reprinted by permission of Pearson Education, Inc.

Elizabeth Svoboda, "Neuroscience: A Swedish Study links Mobile Phones To Brain Damage," from Popular Science Online, February, 2004. Reprinted by permission.

Tamar Nordenberg, "Cell Phones and Cancer: No Clear Connection," from FDA Consumer Magazine, November–December, 2000. Reprinted by permission.

James M. Henslin, Essentials of Sociology, 5th Edition. Published by Allyn and Bacon, Boston MA, © 2004 by Pearson Education. Reprinted by permission of publisher.

James M. Henslin, Essentials of Sociology, 5th Edition. Published by Allyn and Bacon, Boston MA, © 2004 by Pearson Education. Reprinted by permission of publisher.

Les Rowntree, Martin Lewis, Marie Price, William Wyckoff, Diversity Amid Globalization: World Regions, Environment, Development, 2nd Edition, © 2003 Pearson Education, Inc. Reprinted by permission of Pearson Education, Inc.

James K. Martin, Randy Roberts, Steven Mintz, Linda O. McMurry, James H. Jones, America and It's Peoples: A Mosaic in the Making (Vol. 2, 5th Edition) © 2004. Reprinted by permission of Pearson Education, Inc.

Jean Folkerts and Stephen Lacy, The Media in Your Life: An Introduction to Mass Communication, 3rd Edition. Published by Allyn and Bacon, Boston MA, © 2004 by Pearson Education. Reprinted by permission of publisher.

Larry Long, Nancy Long, Computers: Information Technology in Perspective, 11th Edition, © 2004. Reprinted by permission of Pearson Education, Inc., Upper Saddle River, NJ.

The Economist Newspaper Ltd. "Modern Slavery," February 21, 2004. © 2004 The Economist Newspaper Ltd. All rights reserved. Reprinted with permission. Further reproduction prohibited.

Thomas Sowell, "Playing That Media Game" from the Contra Costa Times (Walnut Creek, CA), April 30, 2004. Reprinted by permission of the author.

Barbara Brehm, Stress Management: Increasing Your Stress Resistance. Published by Allyn and Bacon, Boston MA, © 2004 by Pearson Education. Reprinted by permission of author.

Alice Russell, "Message In A Bottle," from The Age (Melbourne, Australia), June 7, 2004. Reprinted by permission of the author.

Tom Muha, "Achieving Happiness: Worrying Makes Matters Worse" from The Capital Gazette, August 1, 2004. Reprinted by permission of the author.

Carl E. Rischer and Thomas A. Easton, Focus on Human Biology 2e, Longman © 1995 Pearson Education. Inc. Reprinted with permission of Pearson Education, Inc.

Photo credit:
Illustration from research article "Nerve Cell Damage in Mammalian Brain after Exposure to Microwaves from GSM Mobile Phones" by Leif G. Salford, Dept. of Neurosurgery; Arne E. Brun, Dept. of Neuropathology; Jacob L. Eberhardt, Dept. of Medical Radiation Physics; Lars Malmgren, Dept. of Applied Electronics and Bertil R.R. Persson, Dept. of Medical Radiation Physics. Lund University, The Rausing Laboratory and Lund University Hospital, Lund, Sweden.

Index of Concept Prep Terms